a

The law changes, but Nolo is on top of it! We offer several
ways to make sure you and your Nolo products are up to date:

1 Nolo's Legal Updater
We'll send you an email whenever a new edition of this book is
published! Sign up at **www.nolo.com/legalupdater**.

2 Updates @ Nolo.com
Check **www.nolo.com/update** to find recent changes
in the law that affect the current edition of your book.

3 Nolo Customer Service
To make sure that this edition of the book is the most
recent one, call us at **800-728-3555** and ask one of
our friendly customer service representatives.
Or find out at **www.nolo.com**.

please note

We believe accurate, plain-English legal information should help you solve many of your own legal problems. But this text is not a substitute for personalized advice from a knowledgeable lawyer. If you want the help of a trained professional—and we'll always point out situations in which we think that's a good idea—consult an attorney licensed to practice in your state.

11th edition

Solve Your Money Troubles

Get Debt Collectors off Your Back

& Regain Financial Freedom

by Robin Leonard and
Attorney John Lamb

ELEVENTH EDITION   MAY 2007

Editor   LISA GUERIN

Production   TERRI HEARSH

Proofreading   ROBERT WELLS

Index   THÉRÈSE SHERE

Cover Photography   TONYA PERME (www.tonyaperme.com)

Printing   DELTA PRINTING SOLUTIONS, INC.

Leonard, Robin.
  Solve your money troubles : get debt collectors off your back & regain
financial freedom / by Robin Leonard and John C. Lamb. -- 11th ed.
      p. cm.
  Includes index.
  ISBN-13: 978-1-4133-0631-6 (pbk.)
  ISBN-10: 1-4133-0631-4 (pbk.)
  1. Debtor and creditor--United States--Popular works. 2. Credit--Law and
legislation--United States--Popular works. I. Lamb, John C. II. Title.
KF1501.Z9L46 2007
346.7307'7—dc22

                                                      2006039221

For information on bulk purchases or corporate premium sales, please contact the Special
Sales department. For academic sales or textbook adoptions, ask for Academic Sales. Call
800-955-4775 or write to Nolo at 950 Parker St., Berkeley, CA 94710.

Table of Contents

Glossary

Appendixes

B **State and Federal Exemption Tables**

C **Worksheets and Forms**

Index

I

Being in Debt Is Not as Bad as You Think

The so-called debtor class ... are not dishonest because they are in debt.

— Grover Cleveland
22nd & 24th President of the United States,
1837-1908

If you have debt problems, you probably feel very alone. But you shouldn't. Millions of honest, hard-working people are having problems paying their debts. Take a look at these statistics describing American consumers:

- More than 1.5 million people each year seek assistance from debt counseling agencies such as Consumer Credit Counseling Service.
- More than two million personal bankruptcy cases were filed in 2005.
- In 2005, outstanding consumer installment debt totaled over $2 trillion, and it continues to grow.
- Most Americans carry six or seven payment cards (credit, debit, and retail cards combined). In late 2006, the average family owed approximately $9,000 on their credit cards.
- College freshmen are offered numerous credit cards in their first semester. Credit card companies set up tables on campuses and offer college students

free T-shirts, pizza, and other goodies if they sign up. Card issuers target college students, knowing that more than 70% hold on to their first card. Seventy-five percent of college students have credit cards, and more than 40% have at least four. College seniors have an average credit card debt of nearly $2,900; freshmen have an average of nearly $1,600. The average graduate student has six credit cards, and one in seven owes more than $15,000.

Even though your situation is far from unique, being in debt may seem like the end of the world. You may be afraid to answer your phone or open your mail. Your self-esteem may be shot. Your stomach, back, and head may ache. You may feel guilty, angry, depressed, or all three. You may consider yourself a failure.

But there is good news. By knowing your legal rights and asserting them, you can get the bill collectors off your back and give yourself a fresh financial start. And, often, it's easier than you think to fight back and affirmatively deal with your debt problems. One reason is that many creditors and bill collectors have modified their expectations and collections practices in response to mushrooming consumer debt. Debtors who assert themselves are getting more time to pay, late fees dropped, debts settled for less than the full amount, and even reestablished credit.

Solve Your Money Troubles can help you take charge. This book:

Shows you how to protect your legal rights. For example, *Solve Your Money Troubles* explains in detail how to respond to a lawsuit, wage attachment, car repossession, foreclosure proceeding, or property lien.

Helps you understand your debts. If you know how the law categorizes different kinds of debts, you'll know what kinds of collection efforts you can expect from different creditors and which negotiating strategies you can try with them.

Shows you effective alternatives to bankruptcy. Bankruptcy is the right tool for many people to deal with their debt problems, but it's not for everyone. *Solve Your Money Troubles* shows you the steps you can take to avoid bankruptcy when appropriate.

Gives you practical tips and information. *Solve Your Money Troubles* contains over 20 sample letters and statements that you can use to:

- get the bill collectors off your back
- ask a creditor for more time to pay, or
- ask a creditor to lower the amount of a bill.

Solve Your Money Troubles also refers you to places to lodge a complaint or ask for information, and contains charts of state laws summarizing consumer laws, debt collection laws, credit bureau regulations, and more.

Helps you evaluate your individual debt situation. *Solve Your Money Troubles*

includes several worksheets to help you figure out how much you earn, how much you owe, how much you spend, and what you own. With these worksheets, you can prioritize your debts, determine whether you are judgment-proof, and decide what approach to take: do nothing, negotiate with your creditors, get outside help negotiating, or possibly file for bankruptcy.

Icons Used in This Book

WARNING
A caution to slow down and consider potential problems.

TIP
This icon alerts you to a practical tip or good idea.

FAST TRACK
"Fast track" lets you know that you may be able to skip some material that doesn't apply to your situation.

RESOURCES
Suggested references for additional information.

CROSS-REFERENCE
This icon points you to additional information within this book.

■

Secured and Unsecured Debts

Dreading that climax of all human ills,
The inflammation of one's weekly bills.

—George Gordon, Lord Byron,
English poet, 1788-1824

A debt is an obligation to pay someone money. It may be a large obligation, such as a home mortgage or monthly rent, or a small obligation, like a newspaper or magazine bill. If you don't pay, you often suffer some consequences. At the serious end of the scale, if you don't pay your mortgage or rent, your house may be foreclosed on or you may be evicted. At the minor inconvenience end, if you overlook paying a subscription, it will be canceled and you will be sent letters demanding that you pay for copies you've already received.

The purpose of this chapter is to help you figure out the kinds of debts you have. You may think of your debts in several different ways, such as:

- Debts to people you know, such as a loan from your Aunt Muriel or a bill you owe Angelo, the owner of the local grocery store—versus debts you owe to impersonal creditors, for example, a credit card company.
- Your regular monthly obligations, for instance, rent, phone bill, or gas bill—versus debts you pay only when you buy something on credit.
- Debts for goods or services you are currently receiving, for example, a newspaper subscription or credit card bill—versus debts to repay money borrowed many years ago, such as a student loan.

- Debts you'd rather not pay and wonder if you really owe, such as back taxes—versus debts you don't have any reasonable grounds to object to paying, for example, your utility bill.

Groupings such as these may help you decide how and in what order you will pay your bills. Legally, however, these categories are irrelevant. Instead, the law puts debts into two primary groups: secured and unsecured. To understand your debts and to intelligently decide what to do about each one, you must understand the difference. You must also understand that the consequences of not paying a secured debt differ tremendously from not paying an unsecured debt. (These consequences are explained in Chapter 8.)

The importance of correctly distinguishing between secured and unsecured debts can't be overemphasized. If, after reading this chapter, you are still not sure you can tell a secured debt from an unsecured debt, reread the material.

Secured Debts

A secured debt means that a specific item of property (called "collateral") guarantees payment of the debt. If you don't pay, the creditor is entitled to take the collateral. If you've ever had property, such as a car, repossessed when you failed to make a loan payment, you already know how secured debts work.

These debts should be your highest priority. If you don't pay them, you will lose the collateral backing them up. Even if you don't hear from these creditors, don't assume they won't collect the debt. Because secured collectors have such a powerful weapon (they can seize the collateral if you stop making payments), they don't need to hound you the way that collectors with lower-priority debts do.

There are two types of secured debts: those you agree to and those created without your consent.

Security Interests: Liens You Agree To

A security interest is an agreement in which you specify precisely what collateral the creditor can take if you default. A security interest also creates a "lien": the creditor's legal right to take the collateral if you don't pay. There are two kinds of security interests:

Purchase money. With a purchase money security interest, you pledge as collateral the property you buy using the loan proceeds. This is usually a home, motor vehicle, piece of furniture, large appliance, or electronic equipment.

Nonpurchase money. With a nonpurchase money security interest, you simply borrow a sum of money and pledge some property you already own as collateral. Personal loans from a bank and home equity loans are typical nonpurchase money agreements.

Some common examples of security interests—both purchase money and non-purchase money—include the following:

- Mortgages (sometimes called deeds of trust), which are loans to buy or refinance a house or other real estate. The house or other real estate is collateral for the loan. If you fail to pay, the lender can foreclose on the house or property.
- Home equity lines of credit or loans (sometimes called HELOCs or second mortgages) from banks or finance companies, such as loans to do work on your house. The house or other real estate is collateral for the loan. If you fail to pay, the lender can foreclose on the house or property.
- Loans for cars, vans, trucks, boats, tractors, motorcycles, RVs, for which the vehicle is the collateral. If you fail to pay, the lender can repossess the vehicle.
- Store charges with a security agreement—for example, when you buy furniture or a major appliance using a store credit card. If you don't pay back the loan, the seller can take the property. Only a few department stores use security agreements. Most store purchases are unsecured (discussed below).
- Personal loans from finance companies. Often your personal property, such as your furniture or electronics equipment, is pledged as collateral.

Mortgages, vehicle loans, and store charges with a security agreement are purchase money security interests. Home equity loans and personal loans from finance companies are nonpurchase money security interests.

Federal law limits the ability of certain creditors to take security interests in household goods (for example, appliances, a television, kitchenware, or personal effects).

These creditors cannot take a security interest in household goods unless it is a purchase money security interest, or unless they take possession of the goods when they make the loan.

Nonconsensual Liens: Liens Created Without Your Consent

In some circumstances, a creditor can get a lien on your property without your consent. These secured debts are called nonconsensual liens. A creditor with a nonconsensual lien claims you owe money and, to secure payment, places a lien on your property. To get paid, the creditor may be able to force the sale of the property. This is called a foreclosure. In practice, however, few creditors holding nonconsensual liens foreclose on property because of the time and expense involved. Instead, creditors generally wait until you sell the property to get paid.

There are three major types of nonconsensual liens:

- **Judicial liens.** A judicial lien can be placed on your real property only after somebody sues you and wins a money judgment against you. In most states, the judgment creditor then must record (file) the judgment with the local land records office. The recorded judgment creates a lien on your real property. In a few states, a judgment entered against you by a court automatically creates a lien on the real property you own in that county—that is, the judgment creditor doesn't have to record the judgment to get the lien. In some states, judicial liens apply to personal property as well.

- **Statutory liens.** Some liens are created automatically by law. For example, if you hire someone to work on your house, and you don't pay the contractor or supplier of materials (or you pay the contractor, who fails to pay the supplier), whoever doesn't get paid can place a lien on your home, without going to court. This is called a mechanic's lien or a materialman's lien. In some states, a homeowners' association can do this as well, if you don't pay your association dues.

- **Tax liens.** Federal, state, and local governments have the authority to place liens on your property if you owe delinquent taxes.

Unsecured Debts

An unsecured debt is one for which no specific item of property guarantees payment of the debt. In other words, an unsecured debt is not secured by collateral. For example, when you charge clothing on your bank credit card, you don't sign a security agreement specifying that the clothing is collateral for your repayment. With no collateral, the bank has nothing to take if you don't pay. This leaves the bank that issued the credit card only one option if you don't pay voluntarily: to sue you, get a judgment for the money you owe, and try to collect on it. To try to collect on the judgment, the bank can go after a portion of your wages, your deposit accounts, and other property that can be taken under your state's laws to satisfy money judgments. (See Chapter 14.)

Most debts that people incur are unsecured. Common ones include:

- credit card cash advances
- credit card purchases
- gasoline and department store charges, unless you sign a security agreement
- loans from friends and relatives
- student loans
- alimony and child support
- medical and dental bills
- accountants' and lawyers' bills
- rent
- utility bills
- church or synagogue dues
- health club dues, and
- union dues.

Not all unsecured debts are created equal. Collectors of some unsecured debts such as student loans and unpaid child support are allowed to use more aggressive collection tactics than the typical unsecured creditor. (See Chapters 14 and 15 for information on these types of debts.)

■

Figuring Out How Much You Owe

*There can be no freedom or beauty about
a home life that depends on borrowing and
debt.*

— Henrik Ibsen, Norwegian poet
and dramatist, 1828-1906

To successfully plan your strategies with your creditors, you need to spend time coming to terms with your total amount of debt. This may make you shudder. Some people with debt problems believe that the less they know, the less it hurts. They think, "I'm having trouble paying a lot of my bills. I can't stand the thought of knowing just how much I can't pay."

Happily, most credit counselors will tell you that people tend to overestimate their debt burdens. This may bring little comfort if you find out that you owe more than you thought, but knowing the total amount of your debts will make a crucial difference in how you proceed.

To figure out your financial situation, you need to compare what you bring in each month with what you spend each month on your monthly expenses (such as food, housing, and utilities) and your other debts (for example, student loan payments).

To figure out how much you earn and how much you owe (both in monthly payments and overall), use the worksheets provided below. If you are married or have jointly incurred most of your debts with someone other than a spouse, fill out the worksheets together.

Warning Signs of Debt Trouble

If you have panic attacks when you try to figure out your total debt burden, you'll feel better if you skip this chapter and come back to it when you are better able to confront the information. Before doing that, however, ask yourself the following questions. If you answer "yes" to any one of them, you are probably in or headed for serious debt trouble:

- Are your credit cards charged to the maximum?
- Do you use one credit card to pay another?
- Are you making only minimum payments on your credit cards while continuing to incur charges?
- Do you skip paying certain bills each month?
- Have creditors closed any accounts on you?
- Have you taken out a debt consolidation loan? Are you considering doing so?
- Have you borrowed money or used your credit cards to pay for groceries, utilities, or other necessities (for reasons other than to get perks on a credit card)?
- Have you bounced any checks?
- Are collection agencies calling and writing you?

How Much Do You Earn?

Start by figuring out how much you earn each month. Complete Worksheet 1, by entering your monthly income from each listed source. If you have income that doesn't fit into one of these categories list it as "other."

Worksheet 1: Monthly Income

(Combine for you and your spouse, partner, or other joint debtor)

You need to compute your monthly net income. Net income is your gross income less deductions, such as federal, state, and local taxes; FICA; union dues; and money your employer takes out of your paycheck for your retirement plan, health insurance, child support, or loan repayment.

To figure out your monthly net income, do the following calculations (unless you are paid once a month):

- If you're paid weekly, multiply your net income by 52 and divide by 12.
- If you're paid every two weeks, multiply your net income by 26 and divide by 12.
- If you're paid twice a month, multiply your net income by 2.
- If you're paid irregularly, divide your annual net income by 12.

Net Wages or Salary	You		Spouse, Partner, or Joint Debtor		Total Monthly Income
Job 1	$	+	$	=	$
Job 2		+		=	
Other Monthly Income					
Bonuses		+		=	
Commissions		+		=	
Tips		+		=	
Dividends or interest		+		=	
Rent, lease, or license payments		+		=	
Royalties		+		=	
Note or trust payments		+		=	
Alimony or child support		+		=	
Pension or retirement pay		+		=	
Social Security		+		=	
Disability pay		+		=	
Unemployment insurance		+		=	
Public assistance		+		=	
Help from relatives or friends		+		=	
Other		+		=	
Total Income	$	+	$	=	$

How Much Do You Owe?

In Worksheet 2, you figure out your debts. Be as thorough and complete as possible. The completed Worksheet 2 will tell you exactly how much you should be paying each month (to be current on your debts) and how far behind you are. Here's how to fill it out.

Column 1: Debts. In Column 1, enter the type of debt. Don't enter a debt more than once.

If you are married, you may not be certain which debts are yours and which belong to your spouse. If your marriage is intact and you're having mutual financial problems, approach your debt problems as a team. That is, enter all your debts in Column 1. If, however, you are separated or recently divorced, or are married but having financial problems of your own, see Chapter 3 for help on figuring out the debts for which you are obligated. If you live with someone else, determine whether you have any joint debts (debts that you both owe). If you generally share expenses and maintain a household with someone else, consider combining your income and paying all of your debts with joint funds, regardless of who actually incurred the debt. Enter both partners' debts in Column 1.

Column 2: Outstanding balance. In Column 2, enter the entire outstanding balance on the debt. For example, if you borrowed $150,000 for a mortgage and still owe $125,000, enter $125,000. If you don't know how much you owe, consider contacting the creditor. If you'd prefer that the creditor not hear from you, make your best guess. Many creditors today have automated systems that

you can use to find out your account status and the amount you owe without speaking to a live person.

Columns 3 and 4: Monthly payment and total you are behind. In Columns 3 and 4, enter the amount you currently owe on the debt. If the lender has not established set monthly payments—for example, for a doctor's bill—enter the entire amount of the debt in Column 4 and leave Column 3 blank. If the debt is one for which you make regular monthly payments—such as your car loan or mortgage—enter the amount of the monthly payment in Column 3 and the full amount you are behind (monthly payment multiplied by the number of missed months) in Column 4.

For credit card, department store, and similar debts, enter the monthly minimum payment in Column 3 and your entire balance in Column 4. But keep in mind that eventually you should make more than the minimum payment on your credit cards. (See Chapter 10 for information on the danger of making only minimum payments each month.)

Column 5: Is the debt secured? In Column 5, indicate whether the debt is secured or unsecured. Remember, a secured debt is one for which a specific item of property (called "collateral") guarantees payment. If you signed a security agreement pledging property as security for your payment or the creditor has filed a lien against your property, the debt is secured. Specify the collateral the creditor is entitled to grab if you default. (For more on determining whether a debt is secured or unsecured, see Chapter 1.)

Worksheet 2: Your Debts

(Combine for you and your spouse, partner, or other joint debtor)

1	2	3	4	5
Debts and other monthly living expenses	Outstanding balance	Monthly payment	Total you are behind	Is the debt secured? (If yes, list collateral)
Home loans—mortgages, home equity loans				
Homeowners' Association Dues				
Motor vehicle loans/leases				
Personal and other secured loans				
Department store charges with security agreements				
Judgment liens recorded against you				
Statutory liens recorded against you				
Total this page	$	$	$	

Debts and other monthly living expenses	Outstanding balance	Monthly payment	Total you are behind	Is the debt secured? (If yes, list collateral)
Tax debts (lien recorded)				
Student loans				
Unsecured personal loans				
Medical bills				
Lawyers' and accountants' bills				
Credit card bills				
Total this page	$	$	$	

Debts and other monthly living expenses	Outstanding balance	Monthly payment	Total you are behind	Is the debt secured? (If yes, list collateral)
Department store (unsecured) and gasoline company bills				
Alimony and child support				
Back rent				
Tax debts (no lien recorded)				
Unpaid utility bills				
Other				
Total this page	$	$	$	
Total page 1				
Total page 2				
Total all pages				
Total Monthly Income (from Worksheet 1)				

Add it up. When you've entered all your debts in the Worksheet, total up Columns 2, 3, and 4. Column 2 represents the total balance of all your debts, even though some of it may not be due now; Column 3 represents the amount you are obligated to pay each month; and Column 4 shows the amount you would have to come up with to get current on all your debts.

CROSS-REFERENCE

Don't forget your other expenses. None of us have monthly expenses consisting entirely of loan or credit payments. We also have to pay rent and buy groceries, pay to go out to the movies and have dinner out, buy clothing and household goods, and so on. These other expenses are covered in Chapter 17, which also offers a worksheet for figuring out what you spend.

■

If You're Married, Divorced, or Separated

*It will be the duty of some, to prepare
definitely for a separation.*

— Josiah Quincy, American lawyer,
1772-1864

Single people who have never been
legally married owe their debts and
own their property as individuals.
No fuss, no muss. Legal marriage, however,
complicates both of these situations both
during the marriage and after it ends. The
same is true of domestic partnerships and
civil unions, in a handful of states. If one
of these relationships has been part of your
life, this chapter helps you understand:

- what debts you owe individually
- what debts you owe jointly with your
  current or ex-spouse or partner
- what property you own individually
- what property you own jointly with
  your current or ex-spouse or partner,
  and
- when your property may be taken for
  each type of debt.

Although each state has its own rules
on marital property ownership, there are
several broad principles that provide a
general idea of how your property is owned
and debts are owed. Which principles
govern your situation depend on whether
you live in a community property state or a
common law property state. This distinction
is by far the most important in determining
who owes and owns what in the course of
a marriage.

Domestic Partnerships and Civil Unions

In recent years, some states have extended
many of the rights and obligations of
marriage—including those that apply to
debts and ownership of property—to
couples who register as domestic partners
or have a civil union. These laws are often
intended to give same-sex couples the
option of being treated as a married couple
for purposes of state law; opposite-sex
couples may also qualify to register, in
certain circumstances.

The states that currently offer a registration procedure for unmarried couples are
California (domestic partnership), Connecticut (civil union), New Jersey (civil union), and
Vermont (civil union). If you have registered
in one of these states, you and your partner
are subject to your state's rules for married couples, including the community or
common law property rules discussed in this
chapter. Same-sex couples are allowed to
marry in Massachusetts, and those who do
will be treated like all other married couples
when it comes to property and debts.

Who Owes What Debts in a Community Property State?

If you live in a community property state
(see "The Community Property States,"
below), which spouse owes which debts
depends on when the debts were incurred
and whether you are still married, separated,
or divorced.

The Community Property States

The following states are community property states: Alaska (if the spouses agree in writing), Arizona, California, Idaho, Louisiana, Nevada, New Mexico, Texas, Washington, and Wisconsin.

If your state is not listed above, it is a common law property state. Similarly, if you live in Alaska and have not agreed in writing to treat your property as community property, then common law property rules apply.

Debts Incurred Before Marriage or After Divorce

All debts someone incurs before the marriage or after the marriage is dissolved are owed only by that person.

> **EXAMPLE:** Ted owes $3,000 to a computer company for a complete system he bought before he married Jill. Only Ted is responsible for that debt.

Debts Incurred During Marriage and Before Permanent Separation

Most debts incurred during the course of the marriage and before permanent separation are joint debts for which both spouses are liable, even if only one spouse is a party to the debt (for example, because only that spouse signed the paperwork). There is an exception to this rule: If the creditor had no knowledge of the marriage and was looking only to the spouse who incurred the debt for payment, only the spouse who incurred the debt is liable for the debt.

> **EXAMPLE:** On a credit application for a kayak purchase, Roger claims to be unmarried and does not include his spouse's income or job. Roger's spouse, Catherine, would not be liable to pay for the kayak if Roger defaults.

Typically, the couple's community property is liable only for debts incurred for the benefit of the community (the couple, not either one of them individually), but this is not always true. For example, if a spouse owes a separate income tax debt or has a child or spousal support obligation from a prior relationship, community property can be taken to pay these debts. The other spouse may be entitled to reimbursement of the community assets used to pay these kinds of debts.

Debts Incurred During Marriage but After Permanent Separation

For debts incurred during the marriage but after the spouses have permanently separated, the following rules apply: If the debt was incurred for necessities of life for both husband and wife or their children, then both spouses are liable for paying it. If both parties agree to a purchase, or the purchase is necessary to maintain a jointly owned asset (for example, to repair a leaky roof in the home they own together), then both are liable. If one spouse incurs a debt for that spouse's benefit only (a vacation, for example), only that spouse owes the debt.

> **EXAMPLE:** After permanently separating from her husband, Paula uses her credit line at Home Depot to fix the roof of the family home that they own together. Because everyone in the family benefits from the repaired roof, Paula's husband would also be liable for repayment of the debt.

> **EXAMPLE:** Justine, a married woman, uses her separate credit card to charge a trip to the Bahamas that she is taking with her lover. Ira, the spouse who stayed at home, would not be liable for the debt since it does not benefit him and the creditor was not looking to his assets for repayment.

Who Owns What Property in a Community Property State?

If you live in a community property state, property is owned jointly or separately, depending on:

- when you got the property
- whether you were married, separated, or divorced at the time you got it
- how you got the property—for example, whether it was a gift or inheritance, purchased with other separate property, or purchased with joint property
- how you hold title to the property— for example, if title to your house is in both your and your spouse's names,

it is community property (if separate property is used to pay down the mortgage or make repairs, however, a mixture of community and separate property results)

- whether you and your spouse entered into a written premarital agreement that changes the property law rules that would otherwise apply
- whether you or your spouse "transmuted" (changed) the character of the property in a written agreement; and,
- whether community or separate funds were used to acquire the property and whether the two funds were "commingled" (mixed together). When the form of ownership is not stated in writing and the asset was purchased with commingled funds, then the asset is considered to be entirely community property unless a spouse can clearly trace and identify his or her separate contribution.

Property Acquired Before Marriage or After Divorce

All property owned by a spouse prior to marriage or acquired after the marriage is dissolved by a final court judgment is that spouse's separate property.

> **EXAMPLE:** Gillian, a single woman, owns $10,000 worth of a stock. She marries Otis in 2003. They remain married until 2007, when they separate and later divorce. At that time the stock has appreciated in value to $25,000.

Because Gillian came into the marriage with the stock and held it in her name alone, it is all her separate property.

Property Acquired During Marriage and Before Permanent Separation

All property acquired by one or both spouses during the marriage but before a permanent separation is community property, unless either of the following is true:

- The spouse acquired the property as a gift or inheritance.
- The property was paid for with funds from other separate money, and both spouses' names do *not* appear on the account, deed, title, or ownership papers.

EXAMPLE: Andy and Portia get married while they are still in school. Andy graduates and starts a business that generates a large income. Both the business and the income are community property, because they were acquired during the marriage.

EXAMPLE: Joan and David marry in a community property state. Shortly afterward, Joan learns that she has inherited $50,000 from her grandmother. This is Joan's separate property.

EXAMPLE: After marriage, David's brother gives him an expensive bass fishing boat. This is a gift, so it is David's separate property.

EXAMPLE: When he gets married, Rudy already owns a valuable coin collection. A couple years later, Rudy sells the collection and buys the equipment necessary to start a radio station. The equipment is Rudy's separate property because it was purchased with money from the sale of his separate property assets.

Property Acquired After Permanent Separation

All property acquired by a spouse during the marriage but after a permanent separation is separate property.

EXAMPLE: Gillian buys a summer cabin in Idaho after she and Otis permanently separate. This is Gillian's separate property. If Otis and Gillian divorce and then get back together, the cabin would still be Gillian's separate property.

What Property Is Liable for Payment of Debts in a Community Property State?

If you live in a community property state, which property is liable for payment of which debts depends on two factors: whether the property is separate or community property, and whether the debt is an individual debt of one spouse or a joint debt of both spouses.

Separate Property

The separate property of a spouse is liable for that spouse's individual debts (debts incurred solely for her benefit). The separate property of one spouse is also liable for all joint debts. However, it is not liable for the other spouse's individual debts (debts incurred solely for his benefit).

> **EXAMPLE:** Bill and Hillary are married and live in a community property state. Each came into the marriage with a sizable trust estate inherited from their respective grandfathers. These trust estates are the separate property of each spouse, because they were acquired prior to the marriage. Bill's trust estate is liable for his premarital debts, and Hillary's trust estate is liable for her premarital debts. But neither estate is liable for the other spouse's premarital debts.

> **EXAMPLE:** Shortly after they are married, Bill and Hillary buy a business. The business fails and they become delinquent on the note. The holder of the note can go after both trust estates, even though they are separate property, because the debt was jointly incurred.

Community Property

Community property is liable for all joint debts (debts incurred for the benefit of the community). In addition, a spouse's share of the community property is liable for that spouse's separate debts.

> **EXAMPLE:** Gus and Susie marry in a community property state and buy a home. Because the home was bought during the marriage, it is community property. Without telling Susie, and using his separate credit history, Gus signs a promissory note for $100,000 to purchase a new Maserati, which he parks at his office. Several months later, Gus is unable to make the payments, and the holder of the note comes calling. The creditor can go after Gus's separate property and can also assert a claim against one-half the home's value: Gus's share of the community property.

> **EXAMPLE:** Assume now that Gus and Susie had permanently separated when Gus bought the Maserati. This would make no difference, because Gus's share of the community property home is still liable for Gus's separate debts.

Who Owes What Debts in a Common Law State?

If you live in a common law property state (see "The Community Property States," above), who owes what debts depends on when the debt was incurred and, in some instances, what the debt was for.

Debts Incurred Before Marriage or After Divorce

All debts incurred by a spouse prior to the marriage or after the marriage has ended are that spouse's individual debts.

EXAMPLE: Ted owes $8,000 on a professional video system he purchased before he married Jill. The $8,000 is Ted's separate debt, and only he is responsible for it.

Debts Incurred During Marriage

All debts incurred by the spouses jointly during the marriage are joint debts. All debts incurred by an individual spouse during the marriage but before permanent separation are separately owed by that spouse unless any of the following is true:

- The creditor looked to both spouses for repayment or considered both spouses' credit information.
- The debt was incurred for family necessities such as food, clothing, and shelter.
- The debt was incurred for medical purposes (in about half the common law states).

EXAMPLE: On a credit application for the purchase of a kayak, Tammy claims to be unmarried and does not include her spouse's income or job. Tammy's spouse Chris would not be liable to pay for the kayak if Tammy defaults.

EXAMPLE: Paula uses her personal credit card to pay for her husband Ray's emergency room visit. In about half the states, this would be a joint debt; in the other half, only Paula would be held liable for the debt.

Debts Incurred After Permanent Separation

An individual is liable for his or her own debts incurred during the marriage but after permanent separation, unless the debt was incurred for family necessities.

EXAMPLE: After Dewevai and Angie permanently separate, Angie borrows $1,000 to pay their child's school tuition. Because this is a family necessity, both Dewevai and Angie are liable for the debt.

Who Owns What Property in a Common Law State?

If you live in a common law state, how property is owned before, during, and after marriage is governed by when the property was acquired, whether the property was paid for with joint or separate funds, and how title is held.

Property Acquired Before Marriage or After Divorce

All property one spouse owned before marriage, acquired during marriage by gift or inheritance, or acquired after divorce is that spouse's separate property.

EXAMPLE: When Joan and Fred got married, Joan owned five valuable paintings, and Fred owned an expensive bass fishing boat. The paintings are

Joan's separate property, and the boat is Fred's separate property.

A spouse's separate property remains separate unless it's "commingled" (mixed together) with marital property or the other spouse's separate property. If this happens, that separate property might become marital property or the other spouse's separate property unless the spouse who originally owned it can trace back his or her contribution and show how it become commingled.

Property Acquired During Marriage

Because state laws differ, you will need to consult an attorney or do some legal research to get information on the marital property laws of your state (see Chapter 19). Generally speaking, in the District of Columbia and a large majority of states, property and earnings accumulated during marriage are marital (joint) property and are subject to division and equitable distribution in a divorce proceeding.

In some common law states, the rules for property ownership during marriage, whether or not the spouses are permanently separated, are as follows:

- All property acquired by a spouse during marriage that has a title document in that spouse's name only (such as a deed or investment account) is that spouse's individual property.

  EXAMPLE: After Maria and Russ marry, they buy a house and put the house in Russ's name only. The house is Russ's separate property.

- All nontitled property acquired by a spouse during marriage with that spouse's separate funds is that spouse's separate property.

  EXAMPLE: Cherish, who is married to Scott, uses her personal savings account to buy a computer. Cherish owns the computer as her separate property.

- All property acquired by the spouses jointly, or acquired by an individual spouse from joint funds, is joint property (unless title is taken in the name of one spouse only).

  EXAMPLE: Cherish and Scott, a married couple, use their joint savings account to buy matching kitchen appliances. Appliances don't come with title documents, so Cherish and Scott own them jointly.

What Property Is Liable for Debts in a Common Law State?

If you live in a common law state, which spousal property is liable for which debts depends on whether the property is separately or jointly owned; whether separately owned property was used to pay for necessities; and, in some states, whether joint property is held by "tenancy in the entirety."

Separate Property

A spouse's separate property is liable for that spouse's separate debts and for the couple's joint debts. It is also liable for the other spouse's separate debts if they were incurred for necessities.

> **EXAMPLE:** Ralph and Toni, a married couple, live in a home that Ralph owns in his name only. A bank sues Toni for payment of a $5,000 loan that she used to pay for a vacation to Italy. Because this is Toni's separate debt and the house is Ralph's separate property, the bank may not take the house to pay for Toni's separate debt.

> **EXAMPLE:** Instead of a vacation, Toni uses the loan to repair the roof on the home. Because the debt is for a necessity benefiting Ralph as well as Toni, Ralph's separate property, including the house, is liable for the debt.

Joint Property

With one major exception, a couple's jointly owned property is liable for the separate debts of each spouse as well as for their joint debts. The exception is this: In a number of common law states, a married couple can hold property jointly in the form of "tenancy by the entirety." In many of these states, the creditor of either spouse cannot reach property held as "tenancy by the entirety" unless the debt is a joint debt.

> **EXAMPLE:** Kai and Irina, a married couple, own a home in Wyoming in both their names as "tenants by the entirety." Kai runs up a large balance on his personal credit card. Even though the home is jointly owned, the credit card company has no recourse against it because of the way title is held.

> **EXAMPLE:** Same case, but the home is held in both names as joint tenants. Here, Kai's creditor could proceed against the home as jointly owned property.

■

Debts You May Not Owe

The buyer needs a hundred eyes, the seller not one.

— George Herbert, English poet, 1593-1633

This book is primarily about being in over your head with debts you know you owe. Less space is spent explaining your rights when you've been cheated by dishonest creditors, or when the merchandise you've just purchased stops working. Those subjects are for a book on consumer rights.

Nevertheless, it's important to focus some attention on debts you feel you shouldn't have to pay. Consumers' rights and debtors' rights are closely linked. If you bring something home and it stops working right away, do you have to pay for it if the seller refuses to refund your money or replace the item? If you want to cancel a door-to-door contract shortly after you signed it, can you? If you're sent unordered merchandise and a week later you get a bill, do you owe it?

 FAST TRACK

Skip this chapter if you don't dispute any of your debts. Not everyone has bills they legitimately dispute. And, while some people will fight tooth and nail against any perceived injustice, others would rather try to work out a compromise with their creditors. If you really don't have anything to fight about—or if you aren't in a fighting mood—skip ahead to Chapter 5.

The Seller Breaches a Warranty

A warranty is a guarantee or promise about something you buy. There are two basic types of warranties:

- An *express warranty* is a seller's promise or factual statement about an item that the buyer relies on when deciding to purchase it. The seller's statement creates an express warranty that the item will live up to the promise or affirmation of fact. The seller's statement can be written, oral, or in an ad. A seller doesn't have to use the words "warranty" or "guarantee" to create an express warranty, but if one of those words is used, an express warranty is created. Express warranties can be made in retail and private sales of new and used consumer goods.

- An *implied warranty* is provided automatically by law. The implied warranty usually means that an item is fit for its ordinary purposes (for example, a refrigerator is fit for cooling food). Less commonly, it means that an item is fit for the buyer's specific purpose that the buyer has explained to the seller. Implied warranties exist automatically in retail sales of new and used consumer goods, unless there's a proper "as is" disclaimer.

Implied Warranties on Consumer Goods

There are two types of implied warranties: the "implied warranty of merchantability" and the "implied warranty of fitness."

- **Implied warranty of merchantability** is an automatic guarantee by a retail seller implied by law that the item is fit for its ordinary purpose. For example, if you buy a new refrigerator and your food spoils because the refrigerator won't go below 55 degrees—a refrigerator should be 45 degrees or less—you can safely assume there's a violation of the implied warranty of merchantability. (There also may be a violation of the express warranty; see below.)

  If you buy a used item from a retail seller, the warranty of merchantability is a guarantee that the product will work as expected, given its age and condition. If a used refrigerator cools down to 45 degrees without any problem, but the door sticks or the light flashes every so often, this isn't a breach of the warranty of merchantability.

  Virtually every item you buy at retail comes with an implied warranty of merchantability, unless it's properly disclaimed.

- **Implied warranty of fitness** applies when you buy a new or used item with a specific—even unusual—purpose in mind. If you relate your specific needs to the retail seller and rely on the seller to select a suitable item, the implied warranty of fitness assures you that the item will fill your need. For example, if you buy new tires for your bicycle after telling the store clerk you plan to do mostly off-road, mountain cycling, and the tires puncture every time you pass over a small rock, the tires don't

conform to the implied warranty of fitness.

Many sellers try to avoid these implied warranties by informing you that the product is sold "as is" or that they are "disclaiming" the warranty. In many cases, these tactics violate federal or state laws that prohibit or limit "as is" sales. For example, "as is" sales are not allowed in any of the following cases:

- There is an express written warranty.
- You buy a service contract from the seller within 90 days after purchasing the product.
- There is a state law explicitly prohibiting or limiting "as is" sales.
- The seller doesn't comply with state law requirements for selling a product "as is."
- The seller does not provide a conspicuous notice that the sale is "as is."

An "as is" disclaimer, when effective, disclaims only implied warranties. It does not disclaim an express warranty, if one is present.

Express Warranties on Consumer Goods

Most express warranties state something like "the product is warranted against defects in materials or workmanship" for some specified time period. Here are some examples of more specific express warranties:

- furniture—"We guarantee all furniture against defects in construction for one year. When a structural defect is brought to our attention, we will repair or replace it at our option."

- fabric shield—"We warrant that if this fabric becomes stained during its lifetime as a result of ordinary water or oil-based spills, we will service the stained area of the fabric at no cost to you."
- trash can—"If your new trash can cracks during normal usage within five years of the date of purchase, we will arrange for a replacement of the broken part."
- stereo speakers—"We warrant that these speakers will perform within two decibels of their advertised specifications for five years from the date of purchase."
- wrist watch—"We promise to repair or replace, at our option, your watch if it fails to function within its original tolerances of timing, that is, within 1–5 minutes per day, fast or slow, within one year of the date of purchase."

Most express warranties either come directly from the manufacturer or are included in your sales contract. But an express warranty may also be created by a statement in an advertisement or on a sign in the store ("all dresses 100% silk").

An express warranty may also be oral. Oral express warranties are hard to prove, because they pit your word against the seller's. If the seller describes a product you are considering buying, but the description isn't in writing anywhere, ask the seller to jot it down on a business card, letterhead, or the sales receipt.

If you purchase an item that comes with a written express warranty, the seller or manufacturer—depending on who issued

the warranty—must stand behind the writing. Again, the writing may consist of a sign in the store, an advertisement, the contract you sign, or a separate warranty statement. But don't be ready to call absolutely everything written about an item an express warranty; retailers are allowed to exaggerate a little when they advertise, as long as a reasonable person would know it's an exaggeration. For example, everyone knows that a retailer is exaggerating when it claims that "our product is the best in the world." If the product isn't actually the best in the world, you can't sue the retailer for breach of warranty.

Most manufacturers and sellers provide express warranties, but you don't have an automatic right to receive one. If you are given an express warranty, however, it must be clear and easy to understand. In addition, if you ask the seller if the item comes with a warranty, and it does, the seller must make it available for your inspection before you buy the item.

Enforcing Warranties

If an express warranty is breached, you may be entitled to have the item repaired, or to get a replacement, a refund, or damages. Most states require that you sue the seller or manufacturer within four years of when you discovered the defect, if the seller or manufacturer won't or can't repair a defect covered by the warranty. In most situations, you are required to notify the seller of the problem before you sue and give the manufacturer or seller a reasonable opportunity to fix the defect. Remember, however, that damaging or abusing the item relieves the warrantor of its obligations.

In some situations, the period of time you have to make a claim under the warranty may be extended. For example, in most states, the period of time you have to make a claim under the warranty is extended by the amount of time the product is with the manufacturer or seller for repair.

 RESOURCES

Want more information on suing for breach of warranty? You'll find a thorough discussion in *Everybody's Guide to Small Claims Court,* by Ralph Warner (Nolo).

Most of the time, if an item you buy is defective, the defect will show up immediately. If the defect is covered by the warranty, you can ask the seller or manufacturer to repair the defect or replace the item. If they won't, or they try only once but the item is still defective, you have to decide on your next step.

You have three options. You can sue the manufacturer or seller (as explained above), you can try to resolve the dispute through arbitration or mediation (in some cases, you must do this before suing), or you can stop making payments on the item.

If you decide to stop making payments, be careful. If you took out a loan to purchase the product, the lender may not care whether it works properly. Even though technically you may be "in the right," the lender may sue you if you stop making payments. Also, not all problems or defects are serious enough to allow you to stop

making payments. In order to have a good reason to stop payments, the problem must be substantial, you must not have known about the problem when you bought the product, you must have given the warrantor a reasonable chance to repair the warranty problem, and you must not have damaged or abused the product. Even if you meet these criteria, withholding payments can be a risky strategy. If you are making payments to the manufacturer or seller, they may not agree with your version of events and may sue you for not making payments. If you aren't sure what to do, consider consulting an attorney.

There may be other reasons why withholding payment is not a good option for you. For example, if maintaining a good relationship with the seller is important (perhaps the seller provides you with medical devices you can't live without), you might be better off working out a compromise or payment arrangement. If you can't reach an agreement, ask if the seller would agree to mediate the dispute through a community or Better Business Bureau mediation program.

If you decide to withhold payment and you are paying the seller directly (for example, you charged an item on a department store account), send the seller a letter explaining the problem and why you intend to stop making payments, then stop paying. (Keep a copy of the letter and any enclosures, such as repair receipts.) If you charged the item on a credit or charge card, you can normally withhold payment by following a specific procedure. (See Chapter 10 for the details.)

If Your Product Breaks After the Warranty Expires

One common consumer story starts out, "I bought this great _____ (fill in the blank) several years ago. It hardly gave me any trouble. But wouldn't you know it—the day after the warranty expired, it died."

Most of us figure we're out of luck—but that's not necessarily the case. In most states, if your product gave you some trouble while it was under the warranty and you had it repaired by someone authorized by the manufacturer to make repairs, the manufacturer must extend your original warranty for the amount of time the item was out of service. Call the manufacturer and ask to speak to the department that handles warranties. Any agreement you reach should be followed up by a letter from you confirming your understanding—and asking that the manufacturer contact you if it disagrees.

If your product was trouble-free during the warranty period, the manufacturer may offer a free repair for a problem that arose after the warranty expired if the problem is a widespread one. Many manufacturers have secret "fix it" lists—items with defects that don't affect safety and therefore don't require a recall, but that the manufacturer will repair for free. It can't hurt to call and ask. A few states have specific laws covering automobile "secret warranties." See "Your Car Is a Lemon," below.

Do You Have an Extended Warranty?

Merchants often encourage consumers to buy extended warranties or so-called "service contracts" when buying autos, appliances, or electronic items. Service contracts are a source of big profits for stores, which may pocket up to 50% of the amount you pay. In addition, the salesperson may collect 15% to 20% of the amount of the contract.

Rarely will you have the chance to exercise your rights under your extended warranty. Name-brand electronic equipment and appliances usually don't break down during the first few years, and, if they do, they're covered by the original warranty. Furthermore, most new items have a life span well beyond the length of the extended warranty. (If, however, the item has a short warranty and would cost quite a bit to repair or replace, it might make sense to purchase a service contract that isn't too expensive.)

If you try to get something repaired under a service contract or an extended warranty, you may be told that the problem isn't covered, or that the company that sold the contract or extended warranty went out of business, leaving you out in the cold. To avoid these kinds of problems, some states require the seller to make the service contract available for you to look at before you purchase it and to allow you to cancel the contract for a certain time after you buy it, if you decide that the coverage isn't adequate. Some states require that companies selling contracts and extended warranties post a bond. You might be able to locate a service company by contacting your state department of consumer affairs (see Appendix A) and asking how to locate bonded warranty companies.

Your Car Is a Lemon

The average new car costs over $30,000. For that amount of money, you expect a safe and reliable product. Unfortunately, many vehicles sold each year are lemons. Buyers find themselves in and out of the shop month after month, with problems ranging from annoying engine "pings," to frequent stalls, to safety hazards, such as poor acceleration or carbon monoxide leaks.

Every state has enacted some sort of "lemon law" to help consumers who get stuck with lemons. In most states, you can get help under the lemon law if you meet the following criteria:

- Your new car must have a "substantial warranty defect" within one year or a certain mileage period, whichever comes first. About a dozen states extend this period to two years. A substantial defect is one that impairs the car's use, value, or safety, such as brakes or turn signals that don't work. Minor defects, such as a loose radio knob or door handle—even several minor defects or one that remains unfixed after many attempts—don't qualify.

  As with most legal definitions, the line between a "minor" and a "substantial" defect is not always clear. Some problems that might seem minor,

such as defective paint jobs or horrible smells in the car, have been found to be substantial defects.

- The defect must be covered by the express warranty and must remain unfixed after three or four repair attempts or after the car has been in the shop a cumulative total of 30 days during the time or mileage period.

If your car meets the lemon law requirements in your state, you have the right to obtain a refund or replacement car from the manufacturer. The steps you must take to get this relief vary from state to state. In all states, you must first notify the manufacturer of the warranty defect. If the manufacturer does not offer a satisfactory settlement, in most states, you must then submit the dispute to an "informal dispute mechanism" (IDM). IDM is similar to arbitration. For the most part, the arbitration is free and designed to take place without a lawyer. Automakers usually use one of the following arbitration programs:

- in-house programs run by the auto-makers
- programs set up by the Better Business Bureau's Auto Line
- programs run by the American Automobile Association (AAA) or the National Automobile Dealer's Association (NADA), or
- programs run through a state consumer protection agency.

Unfortunately, few consumers get to choose which program to use. If you have a choice, keep in mind that consumers who appear before a state consumer protection agency usually fare better than those who use a manufacturer's in-house program or a private program run by the BBB, AAA, or NADA.

Most IDM programs allow you to request an in-person hearing. You should do this if you can. Telling your story in person usually works in your favor. At the hearing, the hearing officer listens to both sides of the dispute. The officer then has approximately 40–60 days (sometimes less) to decide whether the car is a lemon and you are entitled to a refund or a replacement. Consumers who bring substantial documentation to the hearing tend to do better than those with little evidence to back up their claims. The types of documentation that can help include:

- brochures and ads about the vehicle— an arbitration panel is likely to make the manufacturer live up to its claims
- service records showing how often you took the vehicle into the shop—if the mechanics take your complaint orally, make sure they write up a repair order that describes your complaint accurately, and
- any other documentation you can find, including calendars and phone records that show your various attempts to talk to the dealer or otherwise get the dealer to repair the car.

Manufacturers are typically bound by the hearing officer's decision, though consumers can usually go to court if they don't like the ruling. The hearing officer may not be able to award "consequential" damages, such as the cost of renting a car while the lemon was in the shop.

This whole process can take a long time. Most lemon laws allow you to keep using your car while pursuing a claim. But be careful. Never use your car if doing so would be unsafe. Even if you can drive your car safely, some courts may view your case less favorably if they know that you were able to use your car while you awaited resolution of the problem. Continued use that is "reasonable" typically is allowed.

Motor Vehicle "Secret Warranties"

Virtually all automobile manufacturers have secret warranty or warranty adjustment programs. Under these programs, a manufacturer makes free repairs on vehicles with persistent problems after a warranty expires, in order to avoid a recall and bad press.

Unfortunately, consumers often aren't told of these secret warranties unless they come forward after the warranty has expired, complain about a problem, and demand that the manufacturer repair it. A few states require manufacturers to tell eligible consumers when they adopt a secret warranty program, but the vast majority do not.

You can find out about many of these programs from the Center for Auto Safety (www.autosafety.org).

RESOURCES

If you think your new car is a lemon, you can learn more about your options at www. autopedia.com. Autopedia also maintains a state-by-state summary of lemon laws. The nonprofit Center for Auto Safety (at www.autosafety.org) has detailed information about specific defects in various car makes and models. The National Highway Traffic and Safety Administration investigates and researches consumer complaints about car defects. Visit its website at www.nhtsa.dot.gov or call the NHTSA Auto Safety Hotline at 888-327-4236 (TTY 800-424-9153). Finally, *Return to Sender: Getting a Refund or Replacement for Your Lemon Car,* by Nancy Barron (NCLC), is a comprehensive guide to your rights and remedies under state lemon laws. It is available from the National Consumer Law Center (www.nclc.org or 617-542-9595).

Although lemon laws typically apply only to the purchases of defective new cars, you might have some recourse if your used car turns out to have a substantial warranty defect. Here are some ways you might get relief:

- Read the written sales documents or car stickers you received when you purchased the vehicle. They may create an express warranty that cannot be disclaimed by the seller. (See "The Seller Breaches a Warranty," above.)
- Some states have lemon laws covering used cars. Check your state's rules at www.autopedia.com.
- In many states, used cars must meet certain minimum safety and equipment standards. A seller can't avoid these requirements by selling a vehicle "as is."
- Several other states prohibit or limit the sale of a used car "as is" or require special disclosures when any used

product, including a motor vehicle, is sold "as is." Check your state statutes for used product sales (Chapter 20 explains how).
- In many states, the new car lemon law applies to demonstrator cars.

You Are the Victim of Fraud

Each state and the federal government prohibit businesses from deceiving, misleading, or cheating consumers or engaging in other unfair business practices. Laws banning this behavior are called unfair and deceptive acts and practices (UDAP) laws. They apply to most, but not all, private sellers. In addition to UDAP laws, there are many other state and federal laws that protect consumers. Often those laws apply to a particular type of business, such as health clubs, or a particular type of business practice.

Examples of practices that UDAP laws prohibit include:

- using form contracts that hide unfair terms in pages of complicated legal jargon
- using high-pressure sales tactics, and
- taking advantage of vulnerable groups such as children, people with physical or mental disabilities, or seniors.

In some cases, you can use state UDAP and other laws to cancel a contract or get your money back. Raising these claims, however, can be tricky. If you've already been sued by a creditor or collection agency, you can raise UDAP violations (or violations of other consumer protection laws) as a defense to the lawsuit.

Another way to get relief under these laws is to bring your own lawsuit against the seller. If you plan to sue, you should first send a demand letter to the seller explaining the problem and asking the seller to fix the problem or give your money back. Be sure to keep a copy of the letter, and don't send originals of any supporting documents, such as a contract, receipt, or canceled checks. Many states require that you send the seller a demand letter before you sue. Even if it's not a requirement in your state, it's a good idea. If the seller doesn't respond or give you what you want, you can sue in small claims court if the amount is relatively small. If you can't, or don't want to, sue in small claims court, you may need to hire a lawyer to help you bring a lawsuit in civil court. If you decide to go it alone, you'll need to find out more about the requirements of the UDAP law in your state. A good resource is *Unfair and Deceptive Acts and Practices* (NCLC). To order this book, contact the National Consumer Law Center at 617-542-9595 or visit its website at www.nclc.org. Chapter 19 also provides basic information on how to find state laws.

Whether you decide to sue the seller or not, it's always a good idea to report the problem to the appropriate government consumer agency. If agencies receive enough complaints about a particular business or problem, they are more likely to take action. That could mean preventing the company from ripping off other people. In counties with active and well-funded consumer protection agencies, investigators may even try to provide help in your particular situation.

But don't get your hopes up. Government investigations can take a long time and rarely result in the return of your money.

Of course, if a government agent places even a single telephone call to the seller (which is more likely than a full-blown investigation), this may prompt the seller to return your money. And, be sure to send copies of all complaint letters to the seller. Often, if a seller knows you are complaining to authorities, it will be more willing to negotiate with you or may even return your money.

Some agencies to complain to include:

- **Federal Trade Commission.** You will almost always want to contact the FTC, which oversees the federal consumer product warranty law, as well as advertisers, door-to-door sellers, mail-order companies, credit bureaus, and most retailers. Contact information is in Appendix A.

- **Consumer Product Safety Commission.** Let them know about hazardous consumer products. Contact CPSC at 800-638-2772 (800-638-8270 (TTY)); www.cpsc.gov.

- **Federal Communications Commission.** If you were defrauded by a telephone solicitor, or sucked in when a merchant aired a fraudulent advertisement on radio or television, tell the FCC. Contact the FCC at 888-225-5322; 888-835-5322 (TTY); www.fcc.gov.

- **Department of Transportation.** If you were cheated by an airline, contact the Aviation Consumer Protection Division, U.S. Department of Transportation, at

202-366-2220; 202-366-0511 (TTY); http://airconsumer.ost.dot.gov.

- **U.S. Postal Service.** If you were cheated by a mail-order company or any other seller who used the U.S. mail—including a magazine advertiser—contact a postal inspector. Look in the government listings of your telephone white pages for the local address. The USPS website also has a locator service that displays the appropriate inspector for your zip code, www.usps.gov/postalinspectors. If you can't find one, write to the Criminal Investigation Service Center, Attn: Mail Fraud, Suite 1250, 222 S. Riverside Plaza, Chicago, IL 60606-6100.

One-Stop Fraud Complaining

The National Fraud Information Center, a project of the National Consumers League, can also help you if you feel you've been defrauded. NFIC provides the following services:

- assistance in filing complaints with all appropriate federal agencies by filling out a single form
- recorded information on current fraud schemes
- tips on how to avoid becoming a fraud victim
- direct ordering of consumer publications in English or Spanish.

Here's how to reach the NFIC:

Telephone   800-876-7060
Web   www.fraud.org

You should also complain to state and local agencies. You can find contact info for consumer protection agencies at www.consumeraction.gov/caw_state_resources.shtml You may also want to complain to:

Local prosecutor (such as the District Attorney or State's Attorney) in the county where you live. Call and ask if there is a consumer fraud division.

State licensing boards for licensed professionals, such as contractors, lawyers, doctors, mechanics, and funeral directors. Never hesitate to file a complaint about a licensed professional. If, for example, you ordered a $500 pine coffin, and when you arrived for the funeral your mother was laid out in a $3,000 walnut coffin and the funeral director refused to make a change, report the director to your state's funeral home licensing board. To find the address and phone number, call directory assistance for your state capital, or ask the local prosecutor's office.

In addition, you'll want to contact the customer service department or even the chief executive officer for the main office of any major company you complain about. Most of these corporate addresses are available on the Internet. Also, public libraries should have directories containing addresses and phone numbers of large companies.

When you send a letter to a government agency, be sure to attach copies (never the originals) of all receipts, contracts, warranties, service contracts, advertisements, and other documents relating to your purchase. Keep a copy of your letter for your records.

Finally, contact your local newspaper, radio station, or television station "action line." Especially in metropolitan areas, these folks often have an army of volunteers ready to try to right consumer complaints.

You Want to Cancel a Contract

For the most part, you cannot cancel a contract after you sign it simply because you change your mind. However, there is an exception to this general rule for certain types of contracts: You can cancel those types of contracts (discussed below) if you act quickly—most laws require that you cancel a contract within three business days of signing. *Saturdays are considered a business day; Sundays and federal holidays are not.* If you weren't told of your right, you may have longer than the standard three business days to cancel.

Canceling Door-to-Door Sales Contracts

The Federal Trade Commission has a three-day cooling-off rule that lets you cancel certain consumer contracts, in person or by mail, until midnight of the third business day after the contract was signed. You can cancel the contract without any penalty or obligation. (16 C.F.R. § 429.1.) Every state has enacted a similar law. You must be told of your right to cancel and be given a cancellation form when you sign the contract. The form must be in the same language as the oral presentation. Although the issue has not been settled in every state, in most cases if the seller did

not give you a cancellation form or if there was a problem with the form that kept you from understanding your right to cancel the contract, you have a continuing right to cancel. If you are given proper notice at a later date, you have three business days from that date to cancel the contract.

The FTC rule covers contracts for the sale, lease, or rental of consumer goods or services. The contracts you can cancel are:

- door-to-door sales contracts for $25 or more, and
- a contract for $25 or more made anywhere other than the seller's normal place of business, if the seller personally solicited the sale—for instance, at a sales presentation at a friend's house, hotel or restaurant, outdoor exhibit, computer show, or trade show. Public car auctions and crafts fairs are exempted from coverage, as are most sales made by mail or telephone, even if you called from home. But other laws may allow you to cancel mail or phone sales contracts. (See below for an explanation of these other laws.)

After canceling, the seller must refund your money within ten business days. Then, the seller must either pick up the items purchased or reimburse you within 20 days (40 days in some states) for your expense of mailing the goods back to the seller. If the seller doesn't come for the goods or make an arrangement for you to mail them back, you can keep them. If you send them back but aren't refunded for your mailing costs, you can sue the seller in small claims court.

Canceling Home Equity Loans

Whenever you pledge your personal residence as security for any consumer loan, the federal Truth in Lending Act requires the lender to tell you, "clearly and conspicuously," that you have three business days to cancel the contract. The lender must give you all required cancellation forms. Your right to cancel lasts until midnight of the third business day (as mentioned above, this includes Saturdays) after you sign the contract or receive the notice and cancellation forms, whichever is later.

This cancellation right applies to home improvement loans, second mortgages, consolidation loans, and any loan for which a security interest is taken in your home. The cancellation right does not apply to:

- A mortgage to purchase the house where you live.
- A refinancing or consolidation, by the same creditor, of a loan already secured by the house where you live. (The right to cancel does apply if the refinancing involves a new extension of credit, but applies only to the new credit.)
- Advances under a home equity line of credit where the security interest already exists.

The right to cancel can last up to *three years* if the creditor doesn't give you all the material disclosures of the loan terms or the notice of cancellation form before you sign the loan papers. If you're past the three business days but think you have grounds for canceling, consult a lawyer right away.

If you cancel, you don't have to pay any finance charges, and the lender's security interest in your property is nullified. After the lender gets your notice of cancellation, it has 20 days to give back any property you provided (such as a down payment or earnest money). You must then return any property the lender gave you or pay its reasonable value. (15 U.S.C. § 1635; 12 C.F.R. § 276.13.)

Contracts You Can Cancel Under State Laws

Most states have their own laws that allow consumers to cancel certain written contracts not covered by the FTC or state three-day cooling-off rule or the Truth in Lending Act. These contracts are usually for services purchased at the service provider's location, not necessarily at your home. Typical contracts you may be allowed to cancel include the following:

- timeshares
- health club memberships
- dating services
- credit repair services (federal law also provides for cancellation of these services) ·
- dance lessons, and
- camping memberships.

A few states allow you to cancel a contract if you negotiate in a language other than English and are not given a translation of the contract in that other language.

You usually have between three and ten days to cancel, depending on the state and the kind of contract. For specific information on canceling a contract in your state, contact your state department of consumer affairs. (See Appendix A.)

 WARNING

No right to cancel auto contract. You don't have a right to cancel a contract to buy or lease a car. However, a new California law requires car dealers to offer those who buy certain new vehicles the opportunity to buy a two-day contract cancellation option. (Cal. Civ. Code § 2982; Cal. Veh. Code § 11713.21.)

How to Cancel a Contract

To cancel a contract under the FTC's cooling-off rule, the Truth in Lending Act, or your state law, call the seller or lender and say that you want to cancel the contract. If you call, the seller can't claim not to have known that you wanted to cancel in the event your cancellation form is lost. *But calling isn't enough.* You must sign and date one copy of the cancellation form you were given. Send it by certified mail, return receipt requested, so you have proof of the date you mailed it. Or, you can write the seller a letter identifying the transaction and stating "I hereby cancel this transaction," and sign and date the letter. Send the notice or letter to the seller's address specified in the contract.

In this electronic age, can you fax or email a notice to cancel the transaction? Common sense says yes, particularly because faxes and emails are automatically time- and date-stamped. However, the law does not specifically authorize these delivery methods (the law authorizes only delivery by mail, telegram, or in person). If you have no option but to give notice by fax or email, we suggest that you follow up immediately by personally delivering a hard copy, or by mailing or telegraphing it using the fastest delivery method possible.

Contract Defenses

Even if there is no cooling-off period, you still might be able to cancel a contract due to certain circumstances that existed at the time you signed it. These "contract defenses" can be complicated. If you think one might apply to your situation, you will probably need to consult with an attorney. Contract defenses include:

- **Incapacity.** You must have the mental capacity to make a contract in order for it to be valid. If you were not able to comprehend the contract when you signed it, you might be able to cancel it.
- **Minors.** If you were a minor when you signed the contract, normally you will not be bound by it. Although the age of minors varies by state law, in most states, minors are under the age of eighteen.
- **Duress.** You may be able to cancel a contract if you signed it under extreme duress or coercion.
- **Fraudulent misrepresentation.** A contract may be cancelled if the seller intentionally misrepresented critical terms of the contract and you relied on the seller's claims when you decided to sign the contract.

- **Unconscionability.** Courts sometimes allow you to cancel a contract because the terms are so horrible that they "shock the conscience" or because the bargaining process was extremely unfair.

Canceling Goods Ordered by Mail, Phone, Computer, or Fax

If you order goods by mail, phone, computer, or fax—other than photo development, magazine subscriptions, goods ordered COD, or seeds or plants—you have rights under the Federal Trade Commission's Mail or Telephone Order Rule. (16 C.F.R. 435.) First, the seller must ship to you within the time promised ("allow 4–6 weeks for delivery") or, if no time was stated, within 30 days. This time is extended to 50 days if you are applying to the seller for credit to pay for your purchase.

If the seller cannot ship within those times, the seller must send you a notice with a new shipping date and offer you the option of canceling your order and getting a refund or accepting the new date. If your financial picture has worsened since you ordered the goods, here is your opportunity to save your money.

If you've already opted for the second deadline, but the seller can't meet it, the seller must send you a notice requesting your signature to agree to yet a third date. If you don't return the second notice, your order must be automatically canceled and your money refunded. But don't rely on the seller automatically canceling. Let the seller know you want your money back.

The seller must issue the refund promptly —within seven days if you paid by check or money order and within one billing cycle if you charged your purchase. If your credit or charge card was never billed, but the time promised for sending has passed and you no longer want the goods, immediately telephone the company to cancel your order. (See Chapter 10 for information on your rights to cancel goods ordered and paid for by credit card.)

Complaining About Mail-Order Companies

The Direct Marketing Association is a membership organization made up of mail-order companies and other direct marketers. If you have a complaint about a particular company, contact the DMA, 212-790-1500; www. the-dma.org. If you want to be removed from direct marketing lists, you can send in a form online (www.dmaconsumers.org) or download the form and mail it to: Mail Preference Service, Attn: Dept. 16645574, Directing Marketing Association, P.O. Box 282, Carmel, NY 10512. There's a $1 fee either way.

Although many fraudulent operators will not respect your request to be removed from their mailing list, at least you will stop receiving junk mail from DMA members. Your name stays on file with DMA for five years after you register.

Canceling Goods Ordered From a Phone Solicitor

Telephone soliciting is a big business. Sales through telemarketing exceed $400 billion a year. Telephone solicitation fraud is also a big business. The Department of Justice has estimated that one out of six consumers is cheated by a telemarketing business every year.

Although most telemarketing calls are from legitimate companies, according to the AARP, approximately 14,000 fraudulent telemarketing operations call hundreds of thousands of callers each day. Telemarketing scams come in all shapes and sizes. A few of the common ones include:

- "Recovery room" scams where telemarketers prey on people who have already been victimized at least once before by other telemarketers. They promise, for a fee paid in advance, to get refunds for the victims or secure the prizes that were promised by previous scammers.
- 900 numbers where consumers are lured into paying for phone calls in order to receive information that they could otherwise get for free, such as how to save money on groceries or how to receive free credit cards.
- Sweepstakes and prize offers where telemarketers promise cash or other prizes that are never delivered.
- Groups that present themselves as nonprofit charities but operate only to steal your money. (See "Beware of Scam Charities," below.)

If a telephone solicitor calls you and you like what's being offered, ask for the name of the caller, the company, the address, and the phone number. Also ask the solicitor to send you written materials. If the seller refuses or seems reluctant to do this, consider it a warning sign: Don't order from the company. If the company is willing to send written materials, you should end the call and check up on the company with your state consumer protection agency and the Better Business Bureau in the city where the telemarketer is located. If all is clean and you still want to make the purchase, call the telemarketer back.

If you change your mind after making your purchase, you may have the right to cancel your contract. You can cancel your purchase if the goods don't arrive within the time promised or 30 days. (See "Canceling Goods Ordered by Mail, Phone, Computer, or Fax," above.) In addition, if you use a credit card, you can withhold payment if there's a problem with the purchase. (See Chapter 10.)

You may also have the right to cancel a non-credit-card purchase under one of the conditions listed below. To find out if any of these laws have been adopted in your state, do some legal research. (See Chapter 19 to learn how.) Also, try calling the state agency that regulates telephones, such as the Public Utilities Commission. Someone in the public information office should be able to help you.

Stop Telemarketing Calls

A single toll-free call or a visit to the Federal Trade Commission (FTC) website will put your name off limits to every professional telemarketing company nationwide. The federal "Do Not Call" law applies to calls that cross state lines.

To sign up with the national Do Not Call registry, call 888-382-1222 (TDD 888-290-4236), or go to the website www.donotcall. gov. Telemarketers must update their Do Not Call lists with names from the national registry at least once every 31 days. A telemarketer who calls a number that has been on the federal list for more than 31 days faces a fine of up to $11,000 per violation. Your name stays on the list for five years, and then you can renew your listing. For more information, see the FTC's website, www.ftc.gov/donotcall or www.donotcall.gov.

Who can still call you. Registering with the federal "do not call" registry will stop many calls by people who want to sell you something. However, you may still be legitimately contacted by research surveys, charities, political parties, long-distance phone companies, airlines, some insurance companies, companies that sold you something within the last 18 months, or companies to which you made an inquiry or submitted an application in the last three months.

If you tell a company you have an established business relationship with not to call again, it must honor your request.

Beware of Scam Charities

Many telemarketing and direct mail scammers claim to be a charity. If you've never heard of the charity before or are otherwise suspicious, ask how much of your donation goes to the actual charity and how much goes to administrative costs. You should also contact your state consumer protection office (see Appendix A for a list of state consumer protection offices) and ask if the charity is registered. To find out if an organization claiming to be a national charity is a scam, contact the Better Business Bureau's Wise Giving Alliance, 703-276-0100; www.give.org.

To report a scam charity, contact the Federal Trade Commission's Consumer Response Center, Federal Trade Commission, CRC-240, Washington, DC 20580; 877-FTC-HELP (voice); 866-653-4261 (TTY). Or, fill out a complaint form online at www.ftc.gov.

Cooling-off rules. Telephone solicitors in many states are covered by state cooling-off rules, as explained above. After you agree to purchase the goods, these rules typically require the phone solicitor to send you a written contract confirming your order. This contract must state that you are not obligated to purchase the item you ordered unless you sign the contract and return it to the seller.

In addition, separate phone solicitation laws in a number of states provide that you have until midnight of the third business day following the day you signed the contract to cancel it.

Prohibited computer-generated calls. Computer-generated sales calls, sometimes referred to as calls generated by automatic dialing devices, are prohibited in several states. If you live in a state that prohibits computer-generated sales calls and you order something in response to such a call, you can cancel the order because it was obtained in violation of the law. Report the company to your state Attorney General's office, the Federal Communications Commission, and the Federal Trade Commission. But realize that in the meantime, the seller may refuse to consider your order canceled and may initiate collection efforts. Then, you'll have to decide whether you want to take the time and trouble to fight or pay the bill.

Regulated computer-generated calls. The federal Telephone Consumer Protection Act of 1991 prohibits telemarketing phone calls using automatic dialing devices or artificial or prerecorded voices if the seller doesn't have your prior consent or doesn't have a personal or an established business relationship with you. (47 U.S.C. § 227; 47 C.F.R. § 64.1200.) If the caller has your consent or an established business relationship with you, the message, at the outset, must identify the caller. At some point in the call, the message must give the caller's phone number. You can eliminate most computer-generated calls by listing your home telephone number with the National Do Not Call Registry described in "Stop Telemarketing Calls," above.

Miscellaneous Remedies

If you are billed for merchandise you didn't order, you need not pay. In addition, you may not owe the bill for:

- goods you put on layaway
- items you returned or tried to return, or
- a service paid for through an automatic deduction after you stopped the deduction.

You Receive Unordered Merchandise

You certainly don't owe any money if you receive an item you never ordered—it's considered a gift. If you get bills or collection letters from a seller who sent you something you never ordered, write to the seller stating your intention to treat the item as a gift. If the bills continue, insist that the seller send you proof of your order. If this doesn't stop the bills, notify the state consumer protection agency in the state where the merchant is located. (See Appendix A for contact information.)

If you receive unordered merchandise as the result of an honest shipping error (for example, you were sent ten blankets instead of one), you may have a legal right to keep the goods, but ethically you probably shouldn't. Write the seller (or call, especially if the seller has an 800 phone number) and offer to return the items if the seller pays for the shipping.

Give the seller a specific length of time—ten days is about right—to pick up the merchandise or arrange for you to send it back at no cost. Ask the business for its UPS or other delivery service shipping number.

Let the seller know that if it doesn't retrieve the goods by the end of the ten days, you plan to keep the items or dispose of them as you see fit.

If you sent away for something in response to an advertisement claiming a "free" gift or "trial" period and are now being billed, be sure to read the fine print of the ad. It may say something about charging shipping and handling; even worse, you may have inadvertently joined a club or subscribed to a magazine. Write the seller, offer to return the merchandise and say if you believe the ad was misleading. Send copies of the letter to the agencies listed in "You Are the Victim of Fraud," above.

Subscriptions to Magazines You Didn't Order

Your mailbox contains a promotion for a new magazine—"Free trial issue. No obligation." You send for the trial issue and don't like the publication. A month later you get a bill.

Send the bill back, enclosing a note that you requested a free trial issue and you don't want a subscription, even if it is months after you requested the free trial issue. If that doesn't work, contact the FTC, at www.ftc.gov, or 877-FTC-HELP, and ask them to help you get the magazine company to stop billing you.

If you have been victimized by any fraudulent promotion offer by mail, you can also contact the United States Postal Inspection Service (USPIS). Call your local post office or go to at www.usps.gov/postalinspectors.

Canceling Goods Paid on Layaway

If you're purchasing an item on a layaway plan—where the seller keeps the merchandise until you pay for it in full—and you decide before you've finished paying that you no longer want it, read your written layaway agreement. Find out if you have the right to stop paying and get a refund of what you've paid. If you do, the seller may be able to keep a portion of your payments as a service fee. But this should be a small fee—the cost of storing your goods—and you should get the rest back.

If the contract is silent about your right to a refund, stop paying and ask for your money back. If the seller refuses and there's no law giving you a right to a refund, you're probably out of luck.

Your Right to a Cash Refund

Unfortunately, no law requires a merchant to give you a refund. In fact, many merchants don't offer refunds and instead offer to exchange goods. And some sellers have neither a refund nor an exchange policy.

Some states do have refund laws. However, if you want to return an item you purchased in one of those states, be sure you understand your rights fully. Not all products are covered.

Gift certificates and gift cards normally cannot be redeemed for cash. Check the terms of your gift certificates or cards to make sure that their value isn't getting eaten up by usage or dormancy fees.

Canceling Automatic Deduction Payments

Automatic deductions from bank accounts can be a convenient way to pay some regular bills, saving you time, checks, and postage. Nowadays, people preauthorize monthly debits for everything from mortgages, student loans, and utilities to car payments, life insurance premiums, and health club memberships.

But you can find yourself dealing with some unusual problems when you let your bank pay your bills for you. If your bank doesn't make automatic payments on time, for example, it will be you who suffers the consequences: late fees and a blemish on your credit report.

In addition, you might find yourself with the reverse problem: You want the bank to stop deducting a payment from your account, but every time you open your bank statement, there it is again. What started out as a convenience has become a costly nuisance.

Stopping payments. You have the right to halt unauthorized and most preauthorized deductions at any time. If you're having trouble stopping an automatic debit, the fastest way to get results is to contact your bank, not the business that's receiving payments.

Under federal law, you must call or write your financial institution requesting a stop at least three business days before the scheduled debit. If you make an oral request, the bank may require you to confirm it in writing within 14 business days of your call.

If you revoked authorization for a deduction but the bank deducted your money anyway, file a complaint with the bank. The bank must receive your complaint within 60 days after sending you the first statement that shows the unauthorized transfer. Your complaint should include your name, account number, and an explanation why the transfer was not authorized. In general, once you report an error, the bank must investigate within ten business days and report the results to you within three business days after that. If the bank finds an error, it has one additional business day to correct it. If the bank needs more time to investigate, it can have 45 days but must provisionally credit your account in the meantime. (See 12 C.F.R. 205.11(c).)

Late payments. If you've been hit with late fees because the bank was tardy, don't just pay up. Check your deposit agreement to see if the bank is liable for the late payment fee.

Canceling Long Distance Phone Charges When You've Been "Slammed"

Sometimes a telephone company will switch your local or long distance phone service carrier without your knowledge or consent. This is called "phone slamming," and it is prohibited by federal law. According to the federal law, you do not have to pay a slammer or your preferred carrier for any calls you've made within the first 30 days after you've been slammed. After the first 30 days, you are required to pay only the amount that your preferred carrier would have charged for the calls. (47 C.F.R. § 64.1140.)

What if you discover that you've been slammed only after you pay the slammer? The slammer is supposed to pay your preferred carrier 150% of the charges that you paid, and your preferred carrier then is supposed to reimburse you 50% of what you paid. For example, if you paid the slammer $100, it is supposed to pay your preferred carrier $150, and your preferred carrier is supposed to reimburse you $50.

Slamming sometimes happens by mistake, but, in many cases, the slammer deliberately tricks you into switching carriers. If you've been slammed, you should:

- Call your preferred phone company and ask to be reconnected to your preferred local or long distance carrier. Explain that you did not order the service from the new company and that any "change charge" should be taken off of your bill.

- If you have paid the slammer, ask your preferred carrier to seek the 150% penalty from the slammer and to reimburse you 50% of what you paid.

- Call the carrier that slammed you and ask it to remove all charges incurred within 30 days of the slamming. Calls after that time should be recalculated according to your preferred provider's rate. If you have paid the slammer, remind it that it must pay the 150% penalty to your preferred carrier.

- If the company that slammed you refuses to cooperate, complain to the Federal Communications Commission by calling 888-225-5322 or filling out a complaint form online at www.fcc.gov/slamming.

■

Prioritizing Your Debts

I'm living so far beyond my income that we may almost be said to be living apart.

— e.e. cummings, American poet, 1894-1962

By this time, you should have a good grasp on how much you make, how much you are obligated to pay on your debts each month, and how much you would have to pay to get current on all of your debts (see Chapter 2). This chapter helps you to prioritize your debts so that you can decide which debts are essential to pay and which you might ignore for a while. Chapter 6 gives tips on working with your creditors to negotiate reduced payments or payments over time. Chapter 8 explores the consequences of doing nothing.

Whether or not a particular debt is essential will ultimately be dictated by your situation. Nevertheless, some debts are more important than others. Return to Chapter 2 and look at Worksheet 2: Your Debts. Then read the lists of common essential and nonessential debts, below. Use these lists as guides to help you figure out which of your debts are critical and which are not. Consider the consequences of not paying each debt. If they are severe, paying the debt is essential. If they aren't, payment is less essential. Also, review Chapter 1; repayment of secured debts is almost always a top priority.

When you prioritize your debts, you will need to decide whether you can pay all of your debts or whether you should stop paying some of your less-essential debts, either temporarily or permanently.

If You're Considering Bankruptcy

If you think that filing for bankruptcy may be a viable option for you (because someone has suggested it or you have researched the option), read Chapter 15 before you make any payments on your debts. It makes no sense to pay debts you will eventually erase (discharge) in bankruptcy. Also, some payments made during the 90 days before filing for bankruptcy—or one year for payments to, or for the benefit of, a relative or business associate—may be canceled by the bankruptcy court.

If, after reading Chapter 15, you decide that Chapter 7 bankruptcy might work for you, put this book down and get a copy of *How to File for Chapter 7 Bankruptcy*, by Stephen Elias, Albin Renauer, and Robin Leonard (Nolo), a detailed bankruptcy guide with all the forms and instructions necessary for filing your own Chapter 7 bankruptcy. If a Chapter 13 bankruptcy seems like the right approach, get a copy of *Chapter 13 Bankruptcy: Repay Your Debts*, by Stephen Elias and Robin Leonard (Nolo). If you're unsure and need more information, see *The New Bankruptcy: Will It Work for You?* by Stephen Elias (Nolo).

If you decide to put some debts on hold, don't deviate from your plan just because creditors are breathing down your neck. If you give in to creditors that are trying to collect less-essential debts, you may not have enough money to pay your essential debts. For example, if you pay a few dollars on an old hardware store bill just because its collector is the loudest or most persistent, you may face eviction or have your heat turned off because you don't have enough money left to pay the rent or your utility bill.

Essential Debts

An essential debt is one that you should make a top—or near top—priority to pay. If you let an essential debt slide, you could face serious, even life-threatening, consequences. Usually the most important debts are those secured by collateral that you want to keep, such as your house. (See Chapter 1 for a review of secured and unsecured debt.) However, an unsecured debt may also be essential.

> **EXAMPLE:** Josh is taking an experimental heart medication for which his health insurance only pays 50%. His outstanding bill to his pharmacist is currently $350. Although this is an unsecured debt, if he doesn't pay it, he won't be able to get the prescription refilled at that store. Because he has a poor credit history, he probably can't get credit elsewhere. Unless Josh can find other assistance, such as subsidized prescription benefits, this is an essential debt that he should pay.

Other essential debts include the following.

Rent. Payments for a place to live are obviously essential. Many people get into serious debt problems—and find themselves on the streets—because they fail to stay current on their rent. Unless you know you are going to move and have a new place to live, you'll probably want to make paying your rent a top priority. If necessary, ask your landlord for a temporary rent reduction. Explain your financial problems and when you'll be able to resume making full payments. Other alternatives include moving into a less-expensive unit owned by the landlord or doing repairs or providing services in return for reduced rent. In any of these cases, be sure you get written confirmation of your agreement from your landlord.

 WARNING

Don't leave yourself homeless. Make sure you can replace the roof over your head before you give up your home. If your credit history is so bad that a landlord isn't likely to rent to you on your own, be sure to line up a cosigner or even a roommate before you give up your apartment or sell your house. If neither of those are possibilities, find someone you can stay with until you can find your own place.

Mortgage. House payments are a little different than rent. If you're a homeowner in financial trouble, look for a roommate to help with the mortgage, or work with the lender to temporarily reduce the mortgage payments. (See Chapter 6 for information about negotiating with your mortgage lender.) As a last resort, you can sell the house and use the proceeds to pay your creditors and rent a place to live.

Essential or Nonessential?

Some debts may straddle the line between essential and nonessential. That is, not paying won't cause dire consequences in your personal life but could prove painful nonetheless. In deciding whether to pay these debts, consider your relationship with the creditor—is this a friend, valued family member, someone you depend on? You'll naturally want to honor those debts if you can. Also, consider whether the creditor has begun collection efforts. You may be tempted to ignore a creditor who has contacted you for the first time but will want to deal with the one who is about to get a judgment against you. On the other hand, it's easier to negotiate terms of payment earlier in the process.

Some important debts to review are:

- **Auto insurance.** In some states, you can lose your driver's license if you drive without insurance. Also, lenders usually consider failing to maintain insurance to be a default, which can lead to repossession of your vehicle. To lower the cost, look for insurance with the minimum required coverage and a high deductible.

- **Medical insurance.** Especially if you are currently under a physician's care, you'll want to continue making payments on your medical insurance. Sometimes, you can lower your monthly premium payment by agreeing to a higher deductible. If you have medical insurance through work and you lose your job, you'll probably be able to keep your insurance coverage for at least 18 months and, in some cases, 36 months, but you will have to pay the whole premium.

- **Car payments for a car that is not essential for your job.** If not having a car is extremely inconvenient, making car payments may make sense.

- **Items your children need.** Paying for a tutor for your child may not seem essential, but if the alternative is to have your child grow up unable to read, you probably want to keep paying for the help. Or, look for a free tutor through your child's school or local community center.

- **Court judgments.** Once a creditor has a judgment, the creditor can collect it by taking a portion of your wages or other property. If a particular judgment creditor is about to grab some of your pay, payment to this creditor may be essential, even if the original debt wasn't.

- **Federal student loans.** Although student loans are unsecured, those debts may merit higher priority in certain circumstances. For example, a defaulted student loan can keep you from getting a new student loan or grant to go back to school. Also, student loan collectors have special rights that are not available to the average unsecured creditor. For example, the IRS can intercept your income tax refund to collect a defaulted student loan. Agencies that guarantee student loans and the Department of Education can garnish up to 15% of your disposable income (see Chapter 12). Finally, student loans are very difficult to discharge in bankruptcy.

WARNING

Carefully consider all the pros and cons before you sell your house. In today's housing market, your house may be worth more in six months or a year than it is today. Selling it will deprive you of an asset that can make you money over time and may result in your being locked out of the housing market once you are back on your feet. At the very least, consider that you may get more for your house if you sell it later on, giving you more money to pay your creditors. On the other hand, if you bought your house with little or nothing down, you have no equity in it, and your mortgage payment is growing astronomically every few months, it may not be as important to try to keep the house.

If you decide to stay put, making payments on a home equity line of credit or second mortgage is also essential, because you can lose your house if you don't pay.

Utility bills. Being without gas, electricity, heating oil, water, or a telephone is dangerous.

Child support. Not paying can land you in jail. Also, your children may be depending on this money to meet their basic needs. If you really cannot pay the required child support, and your income has dropped sharply, you may be eligible for a reduction of your obligation. See Chapter 13.

Car payments. If you need your car to keep your job, make the payments. If you don't, consider selling it to avoid repossession, which will inevitably occur if you fall behind on the payments. You may be able to use the money to buy a cheaper car. If you sell the vehicle, but the sales amount falls short of what you owe your lender, you

will have to make up any difference. If you don't sell the vehicle and it's repossessed, the lender will sell it at a fraction of its value, and you'll usually owe the difference. (See Chapter 8 for more information.)

If you lease your car, you can't just sell it. Instead, you must call the leasing company and arrange to terminate (end) the lease early. You will have to pay any past-due payments and an early termination penalty (which can be large), but at least you will be out from under the monthly lease payments.

Don't even consider transferring the car to someone who promises to make the monthly payments for you. Such a transfer almost certainly will violate your purchase contract or lease and probably is illegal. Of more practical concern, the business or person who takes the car probably won't make the payments. You'll be responsible for the resulting default on the loan, which will become part of your credit record.

In deciding whether to hold onto the car, consider the amount of your monthly insurance payment. You will have to keep your insurance current if you decide to keep the car. Lenders usually consider failure to maintain insurance to be an event of default, which can lead to repossession. Also, the lender can obtain insurance to protect its interest in the car, which usually is very expensive, and hold you responsible for the premiums.

Other secured loans. Secured debts, you'll recall, are linked to specific items of property. (See Chapter 1.) You've already considered money owed on your house and car—both of these are secured debts. In addition, debts on boats, RVs, and expensive electronic gear are likely to be secured. This means that the property (called collateral) guarantees payment of the debt. If you don't repay the debt, most states let the creditor take the property without first suing you and getting a court judgment. If you don't care if the property is taken, don't worry too much about missing a payment or two. If the property is something you cannot live without, however, and you think the creditor will take it, you'll need to keep that debt current. Or, try to work out a compromise with the creditor. (See Chapter 6.) Remember: If you bought the boat, RV, or home theater system using your equity line or a second mortgage, missing a payment is just like missing a mortgage payment—you could wind up losing your house.

Unpaid taxes. If the IRS is about to take your paycheck, bank account, house, or other property, you'll want to negotiate to set up a repayment plan immediately. You have the right to an installment agreement if all of the following are true:

- The amount you owe is $10,000 or less.
- You've paid your income taxes and filed your returns on time for the past five years.
- You haven't entered into an installment agreement with the IRS during that period.
- The IRS determines that you can't pay the full amount of taxes you owe when they are due.
- You agree to pay the full amount within three years. (See IRS Form 9465, *Installment Agreement Request*, for additional information (available at www.irs.gov).)

Even if the amount you owe exceeds $10,000, or you've defaulted on an agreement with the IRS in the past, the taxman might still be willing to negotiate a payment plan if you can convince the agency that you'll stick with it.

RESOURCES

Want more information on tax negotiation? The best resource available to help you deal with the IRS is *Stand Up to the IRS*, by Frederick W. Daily (Nolo).

Nonessential Debts

A nonessential debt is one with no immediate or devastating effects if you fail to pay. Paying these debts is a desirable goal, but not a top priority.

Credit cards. In most cases, credit card debt fits into the nonessential category. True, the consequences of not paying credit card debt have increased significantly in recent years, and for people on the edge financially, the effects of not paying could be "immediate and devastating." But in general, if you don't pay your credit card bill, the worst that will happen before the creditor sues you is that you will lose your credit privileges. If you need a credit card, for example, to charge an upcoming medical operation or to rent a car on a business trip, keep—and pay the minimum on—one card, and put that card on your priority list.

You should be aware that many credit card companies today will charge you a higher interest rate if you default on an obligation to *another* creditor. Many creditors review their customers' credit reports regularly to identify "risky" cardholders. If the creditor thinks that lending to you has become riskier, it may raise your interest rate even though you have never made a late payment to it.

If, after prioritizing your debts, you decide that paying off your entire credit card bill is a realistic goal, making minimum payments should be a short-term remedy only. You'll have to pay more than the minimum if you want to make a dent in the debt. See Chapter 10 for more on the dangers of making only minimum payments.

Department store and gasoline charges. As with credit cards, if you fail to pay these bills, you'll probably lose your credit privileges and, if the debt is large enough, you may be sued. If you miss a payment, your other creditors may raise the interest rate they charge you. If the creditor took a security interest in personal property you bought using the credit card, the creditor may try to repossess the property. If you must keep the property (your refrigerator, for example), you may need to make minimum payments. Keep in mind, however, that personal property other than a motor vehicle is rarely repossessed.

Loans from friends and relatives. You may feel a moral obligation to pay, but these creditors—who probably seem the least like creditors of anyone—should be the most understanding with you.

Newspaper and magazine subscriptions. These debts are never essential.

Legal, medical, and accounting bills. These debts are rarely essential. A medical bill may be, however, if you are still receiving necessary treatment from the provider to whom you owe money.

Other unsecured loans. Remember, an unsecured loan is not tied to any item of property. (See Chapter 1.) The creditor cannot take your property. If you refuse to pay, the creditor can collect from you only by suing you and obtaining a court judgment. These unsecured debts are rarely, if ever, essential to pay first. Keep in mind, however, that a court judgment turns an otherwise nonessential, unsecured debt into an essential one. Creditors can collect on a court judgment by taking a portion of your wages or other property. (See Chapter 14.)

Review Your Lists

Take a look at your essential and non-essential lists. At the end of each month, do you have enough to pay everything on the essential list? If you don't, read it over. Move the least-essential debts on this list to the nonessential list, and keep moving debts until you can pay each month what is on the essential list. Remember: Some things must go. You can't afford to pay for everything you'd like to. This doesn't mean you're a bad person. It just means you need to buckle down and tighten up your finances for a while.

Another option is to negotiate with creditors of essential debts so that you pay only a portion of those debts. This will leave you with more money to pay less-essential debts. How to negotiate with creditors is discussed in the next chapter.

■

Negotiating With Your Creditors

Let us never negotiate out of fear, but let us never fear to negotiate.

— John F. Kennedy
35th President of the United States,
1917-1963

By now you have prioritized your debts and decided which are essential and which are less essential. You also have an idea as to whether you may not owe some debts.

This chapter will help you negotiate with your creditors regarding debts that you owe but can't pay. You should definitely consider this strategy for essential debts such as your house and utilities. And, once you've stabilized your financial situation, you may also want to try to work out a deal with creditors for nonessential debts that you believe you can afford to keep up.

By negotiating with creditors, you may be able to get lower payments or other more favorable terms to help you get through rough times. Often, creditors are willing to work with you, especially if your financial woes will be temporary.

FAST TRACK

Skip this chapter if you'd prefer not to contact your creditors. Staying in touch with your creditors is often a good idea, even if you can't pay anything. It doesn't always make sense, however. For example, if you just moved to get a new start and to get away from hounding creditors, and you will probably file for bankruptcy before long, then contacting your creditors is the last thing you should do. Also, you may not want to contact creditors about nonessential debts that you don't plan to pay.

Communicate With Your Creditors

The first step to working out a deal with creditors is to keep the lines of communication open. It may surprise you, but creditors often will reduce payments, extend time to pay, drop late fees, and make similar adjustments if they believe you are making an honest effort to deal with your debt problems.

As soon as it becomes clear to you that you're going to have trouble paying your bills, write to your creditors. Explain the problem: accident, job layoff, emergency expense for your child or aged family member, or unexpected tax bill, for example. Be sure to mention any development that points to an encouraging financial condition: disability benefits beginning soon, job prospects improving, child finishing school, and the like. Also, let the creditor know that you've taken many steps to cut your expenses.

Your success with getting creditors to give you time to pay will depend on the types of debts you have, how far behind you are, and the creditors' policies toward delinquencies.

If you are not yet behind on your bills, be aware that a number of creditors have a ridiculous policy that requires you to default—and, in some cases, become at least 90 days past due—before they will negotiate with you. If any creditor makes this a condition of negotiating, find out from the creditor how you can keep the default out of your credit report.

In addition, increasing numbers of creditors simply will not negotiate with debtors. Despite the fact that creditors get at least something when they negotiate settlements with debtors, many ignore debtors' pleas for help, continue to call demanding payment, and leave debtors with few options other than filing for bankruptcy. In fact, nearly one-third of the people who filed for bankruptcy during the 1990s said that the final straw that sent them into bankruptcy was the unreasonableness of their creditors or the collection agencies hired by their creditors.

Even though some creditors may refuse to negotiate with you, it is still in your best interest to try. The following sections give you a general idea of what you can expect when you negotiate with your creditors about certain types of debts.

Rent Payments

Few landlords will reduce your monthly rent. But it never hurts to ask. If the landlord knows it will be difficult to rerent your place, the landlord may agree to accept a partial payment now and the rest later or temporarily lower your rent, rather than have to evict you. The landlord might agree to let you pay a little bit each month to make up any back rent you owe.

If your landlord agrees to a rent reduction or lets you make up past-due payments, send the landlord a letter confirming the arrangement by certified mail, return receipt requested. (See sample letter, below.) Be sure to keep a copy for yourself. Once the

understanding is written down, the landlord will have a hard time evicting you for not paying the rent, as long as you make the payments under your new agreement.

Sample Letter to Landlord

Frank O'Neill
1556 North Lakefront
Minneapolis, MN 67890

September 22, 2007

Dear Frank:

Thanks for being so understanding about my being laid off. This letter is to confirm the telephone conversation we had yesterday.

My lease requires that I pay rent of $750 per month. You agreed to reduce my rent to $600 per month, beginning October 1, 2007, and lasting until I find another job, but not to exceed three months. That is, even if I haven't found a new job, my rent will go back to $750 per month on January 1, 2008. If this is not your understanding, please contact me at once.

Thank you again for your understanding and help. As I mentioned on the phone, I hope to have another job shortly, and I am following all leads in order to secure employment.

Sincerely,

Abigail Landsberg
Abigail Landsberg

If you decide to move but have months remaining on a lease, your landlord might try to sue you for the remaining months' rent. Legally, however, in most states the landlord has a duty to use reasonable efforts to rerent the place to minimize the loss. This is called mitigating damages. (If the landlord can't rerent it despite making reasonable efforts, you will be on the hook for the balance of the rent.) If you advanced one or two months' rent or paid a security deposit when you moved in, the landlord should put that money toward any rent you owe.

Mortgage Payments

Over the years, lenders have learned that high foreclosure rates can cost them lots of money. As a result, they are often willing to work with you to avoid foreclosure. Depending on your financial situation, this can mean agreeing to an informal payment plan to make up missed payments, giving you a short-term break on interest or payments, or refinancing your loan so you can afford the payments.

Mortgage lenders and consumer credit counselors agree: When you know you're going to fall behind on your mortgage payments, you should call the lender. The sooner you get in contact with the lender, the more options you will have to cure the delinquency and save your house.

Informal Payment Plans

If you want to keep your home and you've only missed a payment or two, most mortgage companies will let you make up the delinquency through a repayment plan. For example, if you missed two payments of $1,000 each, your lender may allow you to pay the $2,000 over six months. Other short-term fixes that your lender may agree to include deferring or waiving late charges, temporarily reducing your interest rate, or temporarily reducing or suspending payments.

Mortgage Workouts

If your problem looks like it will be long term, most lenders will require more than an informal payment plan or short-term break on interest or payments. Usually, they will insist on a more formal process called a "mortgage workout." Many lenders require this formal process even for short-term fixes. A workout is any agreement you make with the lender that changes how you pay the delinquency on your mortgage or otherwise keeps you out of foreclosure.

Here are some workout options your lender might agree to:

- Spread repayment of missed payments over a few months. For example, if your monthly payment is $1,000 and you missed two payments ($2,000), the lender might let you pay $1,500 for four months.
- Reduce or suspend your regular payments for a specified time, and then add a portion of your overdue amount to your regular payments later on.
- Extend the length of your loan and add the missed payments at the end.
- For a period of time, suspend the amount of your monthly payment that

Tips on Negotiating

Here are some basic guidelines for negotiating:

- **Identify your bottom line.** If you owe a doctor $1,100 and are unwilling to pay more than $600 on the debt over six months' time, don't agree to pay more.

- **Try to identify the creditor's bottom line.** If a bank offers to waive two months' interest as long as you pay the principal on your car loan, that may mean that the bank will waive three or four months of interest. Push it.

- **Bill collectors lie a lot.** If they think you can pay $100, they will vow that $100 is the lowest amount they can accept. Don't believe them.

- **Make concessions to pay less rather than more.** If a creditor will settle for 50% of the total debt if you pay in a lump sum, but will insist on 100% if you pay over time, try to get the money to pay the half and settle the matter. If you settle the debt, or are put on a new payment schedule, insist that associated negative information in your credit bureau file be removed and that your account be re-aged (that is, reported as current as long as you make the payments on the new schedule). See Chapters 9 and 17.

- **Don't split the difference.** If you offer a low amount to settle a debt and the creditor proposes that you split the difference between the creditor's higher demand and your offer, don't agree to it. Treat the split-the-difference number as a new top and propose an amount between that and your original offer.

- **Mention bankruptcy.** If you mention that you may have no option but to file for bankruptcy if the creditor refuses to make concessions, you might find that an unreasonable creditor is willing to compromise. But think carefully before doing this. In most cases, a "mentioned bankruptcy" notation will immediately be added to your account file with that creditor. If you incur any additional debt after that date—even with a different creditor—you will have a very difficult time eliminating that debt in bankruptcy if you do eventually file. The creditor will argue that once you mentioned bankruptcy, you had no intention of repaying your bills and that all debts you incurred after that date should not be wiped out. And a bankruptcy judge is likely to agree.

If you don't feel comfortable negotiating—for example, you hate bargaining at flea markets and would rather sell your used car to a dealer than find a buyer yourself—ask a friend or relative to negotiate on your behalf. This can often work well for you. As long as your negotiator knows and will keep to your bottom line, it will be hard for the creditor to shame or guilt the negotiator into agreeing that you will pay more. Some creditors are reluctant to negotiate with anyone other than you or your lawyer. If need be, prepare a power of attorney for your negotiator, giving that person the right to handle your debts on your behalf.

goes towards the principal and only require payment of interest, taxes, and insurance.

- Let you sell the property for less than you owe the lender and waive the rest. This is called a "short sale."

Before you contact the lender about a workout, you should prepare information about your situation, including:

- A reasonable budget for the future and an assessment of your current financial situation.
- A plan to deal with other essential debts, such as utility payments and a car loan if you need it for work.
- A hardship letter explaining why you fell behind on your mortgage. Emphasize the most sympathetic aspects of your situation.
- Information about the property and its value.
- Information about your loan and the amount of the default.

You should also find out if your mortgage is insured by the Federal Housing Administration (FHA) or the U.S. Department of Housing and Urban Development (HUD). Borrowers with these types of mortgages have some special rights that those with "conventional" mortgages don't have.

It's a good idea to look for a nonprofit debt counselor or lawyer who has experience with mortgage workouts to help you. For information on HUD-approved counseling agencies in your area, call 800-569-4287. It's best to start the workout negotiations as early as possible.

Be advised that workouts are not for everyone, nor will the lender always agree

---

When Your Loan Is Owned by the Federal Government

Millions of American homeowners' loans are owned by Fannie Mae or Freddie Mac, private corporations created by the federal government. Both Fannie Mae and Freddie Mac's default programs emphasize foreclosure prevention whenever feasible. Both mortgage holders offer rate reductions, term extensions, and other changes for people in financial distress, especially for people experiencing involuntary money problems such as an illness, death of a spouse, or job loss. One possible option would allow you to make partially reduced payments for up to 18 months.

If you can't get help from your loan servicer, contact Fannie Mae or Freddie Mac directly at:

- Fannie Mae, 800-732-6643 (the Consumer Resource Center), www. fanniemae.com.
- Freddie Mac, www.freddiemac.com.

---

to a workout. Be realistic about your situation before you approach the lender. If it is likely that you will lose your house anyway because of your dire financial situation or because you have other pressing financial problems, it doesn't make sense to keep paying your mortgage through a workout.

Refinancing

If you can't afford your current mortgage payments, your lender may let you refinance the loan to reduce the amount of the monthly payments, assuming you can convince the lender that you have enough income to make the reduced payments. Typically, a lender looks at the ratio of your total monthly debt burden to your monthly net income. If the ratio is between 25% and 33%, you'll probably qualify for the refinancing. If your ratio is higher the lender may balk, unless the lender thinks it will be hard to resell your house at a profit if it foreclosed. Be realistic when refinancing. If you can't afford your new payments, the process is likely to hurt more than it helps.

RESOURCES

Online mortgage calculator. If you need help figuring out how much mortgage payment you can afford—and what terms you'd need to qualify—visit Nolo's website, www.nolo. com. Under the tab "property & money," click on "real estate." There, in "tools & resources," click on "Calculator: Mortgage Qualification Estimate." (You can search the website for other helpful calculators, as well.)

If you are considering refinancing your home loan, try to avoid or minimize the following:

- **Rapidly increasing interest.** For example, the interest begins low (such as 3%), so that you qualify for the loan, but after six months or a year, the interest rises to the prime rate. Every six months or year after that, the interest rate rises a point or two above the prime rate.

- **Points.** Real estate loans usually come with points, an amount of money equal to a percentage of your loan, that you pay to your lender simply for the privilege of borrowing money. If you refinance with the same lender from whom you originally borrowed, the lender may waive the points. Loans with very high points and other charges are subject to the requirements of a federal law called HOEPA. (See Chapter 11 for more information.)

- **Insurance and other extras.** Consumer loans, including refinanced loans, are often loaded with extra products that most consumers don't need. You should especially look out for credit insurance charges. (See Chapter 11.)

- **Prepayment penalties.** Expensive prepayment penalties almost always go hand in hand with refinancing. Even if the new loan does not contain prepayment penalties, some states allow creditors to calculate payoff figures for the old loan that are to the creditor's, not the borrower's, advantage.

If you are considering a high-cost (often called predatory) loan, take extra care. These are loans with very high interest rates that are usually, but not always, sold to consumers who have had credit problems in the past. Such loans often contain terms unfavorable to borrowers, such as large balloon payments (jumbo payments due at the end of the loan term) and negative amortization (loans where your monthly payment does not cover the interest due that period). (See Chapter 11 for more on consumer loans.)

If you don't like what your lender offers, shop around. If you've already applied for a loan and decide you don't like the terms, you may be able to cancel the transaction within three business days after the terms are properly disclosed to you or three business days after you sign the loan documents, whichever is later (see Chapter 4 for more information). You may find another lender who will lend you money to pay off all or some of your first loan. If you've missed only a few payments, you can prevent foreclosure by paying what you missed and then obtaining the new loan. If the original lender has accelerated the loan—declared the entire balance due because you've missed several payments —you'll have to refinance the entire loan to prevent foreclosure.

> **EXAMPLE:** Jessica owes $213,000 on her mortgage, which has monthly payments of $1,400. She has missed four payments and received a letter from the lender stating that it has "accelerated" the mortgage as permitted under the loan agreement. All $213,000—not merely the $5,600 in missed payments—is due immediately. For Jessica to save her house, she will need to get a loan from a second lender to cover the full $213,000, unless the original lender agrees to reinstate her loan.

In this situation, it may be difficult for you to get a new loan. The new lender will do a credit check. If your original lender has reported your mortgage delinquency, it will show up on the credit check. You'll have to convince the new lender that you won't default on the new loan.

Be wary when shopping for a new loan. Many unscrupulous creditors make a lot of money by taking advantage of people facing foreclosure. These rip-off artists know that homeowners are often desperate to save their homes. If a deal seems too good to be true, it's probably a scam. In particular, avoid:

- sale/leaseback schemes (where someone offers to buy your house and rent or lease it back to you)
- high-rate loans to get you out of foreclosure
- "easy credit," low-cost loans regardless of credit history (they often have hidden costs)
- "equity skimmers" (who try to buy houses for a small fraction of their market value, often through misrepresentation, deceit, or intimidation), and
- "foreclosure consultants" (who promise to help homeowners in foreclosure, charge high fees for little or no service, and then purchase the home at a fraction of its value).

If you've been victimized by one of these companies, seek legal help right away.

Selling Your House

If you don't want to keep your house, or you've come to the conclusion that you can't afford it, your best option may be to sell it.

If you decide to do this, you can probably stop making mortgage payments.

Even at this late date, consumer credit counselors suggest that you contact the lender and ask for time to list the house with a real estate agent and sell it. If your payments aren't too far behind and you've kept in contact with the lender, it may agree.

> ⚠ **WARNING**
>
> **The long-term consequences of default, foreclosure, or repossession may be severe.** Not only will your credit suffer, but losing your home will deprive you of an asset that will usually make you money over time. Selling the house later will at least provide more money to pay your creditors than giving it up now.

If the lender chooses to foreclose, it may take anywhere from six months to a year and a half. If you're willing to take any reasonable offer, you can probably sell your house much sooner.

The lender may also agree to a "short sale." This happens when the money you get from selling your house is less than the amount you owe to your lender. In a "short sale," the lender agrees to accept the proceeds from the sale and forgo the remainder of the loan balance. Some lenders require documentation of any financial or medical hardship you are experiencing before agreeing to a short sale.

By accepting a short sale, the lender can avoid a lengthy and costly foreclosure, and you're able to pay off the loan for less than you owe. These sales are common when the real estate market is depressed.

Deed in Lieu of Foreclosure

If you get no offers for your house or the lender won't approve a short sale, your other option is to walk away from your house. To do this, you transfer your ownership interest in your home to the lender—called a deed in lieu of foreclosure, or "deed in lieu," for short. Lenders don't have to accept your deed in lieu, but many will. Keep in mind that you won't get any cash back, even if you have lots of equity in your home. And it may have negative tax consequences. The deed in lieu will appear on your credit report as a negative mark for several years.

If you opt for a deed in lieu, try to get concessions from the lender—after all, you are saving it the expense and hassle of foreclosing on your home. For example, ask the lender to eliminate negative references on your credit report or give you more time to stay in the house.

Utility and Telephone Bills

If you miss one month's utility bill—including a bill for heating oil or gas deliveries—you probably won't hear from the company, unless you have a poor payment history. If you ignore a few past-due notices, however, the company will threaten to cut off your service. Call the company before the threats become dire. Most utility companies will let you get two or three months behind as long as you tell them when you'll be able to make up what you owe. If your service has been shut off, the company will most likely require you to make a security deposit—usually for about three times the average of your monthly bill—before it reconnects you. The deposit rates following disconnects are regulated in some states. You may want to call a Legal Aid or Legal Services office (see Chapter 19) to learn about your state's law.

Many utility companies offer reduced rates and payment plans to elderly and low-income people. In addition, the federal Low Income Home Energy Assistance Program (LIHEAP), which is state-run, helps low-income customers pay their utility bills. To find out if you qualify, call the utility company and ask, or go to www.acf.hhs. gov/programs/liheap. If you do, you'll be able to get future bills reduced—and may be able to spread out payments on past bills.

Some consumers fall behind on energy bills during periods when they use a lot of energy and incur high bills (winter in the north, for example). Many energy utilities offer programs that average your periods of high and low usage and allow you to pay a uniform monthly payment all year long.

Most northern states prohibit termination of heat-related utilities during the winter. Other states protect households with elderly or disabled residents, and occasionally households with infants. Usually, you must show financial hardship to qualify. But, even if you qualify for a prohibition against utility shutoff, you'll still owe the bill.

Finally, don't overlook the cost savings that come with conserving energy. Local utility companies offer utility conservation assistance programs, often at no cost. These measures can often cut your bill by as much as one-third to one-half.

Can't Understand Your Phone Bill?

Of all utility bills, the phone bill is often the most difficult to understand. Charges may be posted by at least three separate companies: your local carrier, long distance carrier, and Internet service provider. You might also have special features billed to you, such as call waiting or voice mail. On top of that, unscrupulous carriers sometimes try to switch ("slam") customers' carriers without the customers' knowledge and consent. (See Chapter 4 for more on slamming.)

If you can't understand your phone bill, ask for clarification. The Federal Communications Commission's "Truth-in-billing" guidelines (available at www.fcc. gov) are meant to counter the confusion, anxiety, and concern expressed by the more than 60,000 consumers who call the FCC each year. Under the guidelines, consumers must be told who is asking them to pay for service, what services they are being asked to pay for, and where they can call to get more information about the charges appearing on their bill. For example, new service providers must be highlighted on the bill, and all bills must contain full and nonmisleading descriptions and a clear identification of the service provider responsible for each charge on their bill.

Carriers also must clarify when consumers may withhold payment for service, for example, to dispute a charge, without risking the loss of their basic local service. Finally, the guidelines require a label next to charges appearing on bills that relate to federal regulatory action

To reduce your telephone bill, it often pays to change some of the terms of your telephone plan. For example, you might cancel voice mail, call forwarding, call waiting, or high-speed Internet service. If you rarely make long distance calls, it might be cost-effective to cancel your long distance plan and make your rare long distance calls using a prepaid calling card or dial-around (10-10) service. If you decide to use a prepaid card, be sure to shop around. Some of these cards are rip-offs.

Car Payments

Your options for handling car payments depends on whether you are buying or leasing your vehicle.

Purchase Payments

If you expect you'll have trouble making your car payments for several months, your best bet is to sell the car, pay off the lender, and use whatever is left to either pay your other debts or buy a reliable used car.

If you want to hold onto your car and you miss a payment, immediately call the lender and speak to someone in the customer service or collections department. Don't delay. Cars are more quickly repossessed than any other type of property. One reason for this is that the creditor doesn't have to get a court judgment before seizing the car. (See Chapter 8.) Another reason is that cars lose value fast—if the creditor has to auction it off, it wants the largest possible return. Also, cars have been known to disappear before they can be repossessed.

If you present a convincing argument that your situation is temporary, the lender will sometimes grant you an extension, meaning the delinquent payment can be paid at the end of your loan period. The lender probably won't grant an extension unless you've made at least six payments. Also, most lenders charge a fee for granting an extension and don't grant more than one a year. Fees for extending car loans vary tremendously. Some lenders charge a flat fee, such as $25. Others charge a percentage (usually 1%) of the outstanding balance. Others charge one month's worth of interest. Be sure to call your lender and ask.

Instead of granting an extension, the lender may offer to rewrite the loan to reduce the monthly payments. This means, however, that you'll have to pay for a longer time period and you'll have to pay more total interest. Make sure that getting a lower monthly payment doesn't require you to take out a larger total loan. Try to avoid loans that have a prepayment penalty or that include interest calculated in any way other than the simple interest method.

Lease Payments

Many consumers decide to lease, rather than purchase, automobiles. The reasons are many, with the lower monthly payments that usually accompany vehicle lease contracts topping the list.

If you can't afford your lease payments, your first step is to review your lease agreement. If your total obligation under the lease is less than $25,000 and the lease term exceeds four months (many car leases meet these two requirements), the federal Consumer Leasing Act (15 U.S.C. §§ 1667-1677f, 12 C.F.R. Part 213) requires that consumer vehicle leases disclose the following information about the lease:

- the amount due (including an itemization) at the time the lease is signed
- payment schedule and total payments
- payment calculation
- notice that the charge for early termination of the lease may be substantial
- the conditions under which the lease may be terminated early
- the early termination fee or a description of how the fee is calculated
- the mileage limitation and the charge for excess miles, if any, and
- vehicle wear and tear standards.

The Act requires other disclosures as well. In addition, many states impose extra requirements.

If you want to cancel your lease, look carefully at the provisions in your contract describing what happens if you default and how you can terminate the lease early. Many of these provisions include claims that you'll owe a very large sum of money or complex formulas that are difficult to understand. Ending a lease early is expensive—you can expect the early termination fee to be hefty. But if the fee seems way out of line, you may be able to get the lessor to agree to some kind of reduction. Look in your lease agreement for the explanation of how the early termination fee is calculated. Under the federal Consumer Leasing Act, the explanation must be "clear and conspicuous" and the amount must be "reasonable." (15

U.S.C. § 1667a(5), 12 C.F.R. § 213.4(g).) Mention these requirements if you attempt to negotiate a lower early termination fee.

If you want to pursue this further, you'll probably need a lawyer. Consumers have brought successful court challenges to their leases' explanations of early termination fees, but the results have been mixed. (See Chapter 19 for information on how to find a lawyer.)

Secured Loan Payments

If a personal loan or store agreement is secured—for example, you borrowed money to purchase a refrigerator or couch and you pledged it as security for your repayment—the lender probably won't reduce what you owe. Instead, the lender may threaten to send a truck to pick up the property if you don't make reasonable payments. Some states require that the lender have a court judgment before taking your personal property other than a car. (See Chapter 8 for more information.)

But few lenders take personal property other than vehicles. The resale value of used property is low. Most items bought through security agreements are furniture, appliances, and electronic equipment, which depreciate fast. The lender is not in the used furniture business and doesn't want your dining room table or stereo. Almost always, the lender values the debt—even if it is hard to collect—more than the property. Also, the lender can't get into your house to get the property without a court order or your permission. Few lenders ever go to the expense of getting a court order. This means you have the upper hand in the negotiation.

The lender may extend your loan or rewrite it to reduce the monthly payments. Be prepared to discuss your financial situation.

Insurance Payments

You may consider your medical, homeowners', or auto insurance payments to be fairly essential debts. At the same time, your life or disability insurance payments probably aren't, unless you or other members of your family are very, very ill.

Most policies have 30-day grace periods—that is, if your payment is due on the tenth of the month and you don't pay until the ninth of the following month, you won't lose your coverage. A few companies may let you get away with 60 days, but don't count on it. After 60 days, your policy is sure to lapse.

If you want to keep your insurance coverage, contact your insurance company. Your insurance agent probably can't let you reduce your premium payments or spread out back payments over a few months. But you can reduce the amount of your coverage and increase your deductibles, thereby reducing the overall amount you pay, including the premium payments. This can usually be done easily for auto, medical, dental, renters', life, and disability insurance.

It will be harder to reduce coverage for homeowners' insurance, because the lender won't want your house to be underinsured. But you can choose a higher deductible

If you have a life insurance policy with a cash value that you really want to keep, you usually can apply that money toward your premium payments. And if the cash value is large enough, consider using the money for your debts. You can ask the company to use the cash reserves as a loan. Your policy's cash value won't decrease, but you are theoretically required to repay the money. If you don't repay it, when you die the proceeds your beneficiaries receive will be reduced by what you borrowed. Or, you can simply ask that the cash reserves be used to pay the premiums. This will reduce your cash value, but you won't have to repay it.

Another way to keep life insurance coverage but reduce the payments is to convert a whole or universal policy (relatively high premiums and a cash value buildup) into a term policy (low premiums and no cash value). You may lose a little of the existing cash value as a conversion fee, but if you believe life insurance coverage is essential, losing a few dollars may be worth it in exchange for getting a policy that will cost far less to maintain.

If your insurance policy—life or otherwise—has lapsed, and your financial picture is improving, many insurance companies will let you reinstate your policy if you pay up what you owe within 60 days of when the premium payment first became due. You may also have to pay interest on your back premiums, usually between 5% and 10%. After 60 days, the company will probably make you reapply for coverage. If your risk factors have increased since you originally took out the insurance—for example, you took out auto insurance two years ago and have since had a car accident and a moving violation, and your insurance just lapsed—

you may be denied coverage or offered coverage only at a higher rate.

Medical, Legal, and Other Service Bills

Before assuming that your bill is correct, review it carefully and be sure that you understand and agree with every charge. With hospital bills and lawyers' bills in particular, ask for specific itemization if the bill gives only broad categories. And if the bill is filled with indecipherable codes, ask someone in the billing office to explain what every code means.

Once you understand what each charge is, look for mistakes. The federal General Accounting Office estimates that 99% of all hospital bills contain overcharges, and one insurance company stated that the average hospital bill contains almost $1,400 of inflated charges (such as a $5 aspirin tablet), charges for items never received by the patient, and double billing for the same item. Overbilling is also common in lawyers' bills.

Assuming you do owe the full amount of the bill or can't afford the corrected bill, many doctors, dentists, lawyers, and accountants will accept partial payments, reduce the total bill, drop interest or late fees, and delay sending bills to collection agencies if you clearly communicate how difficult your financial problems are and try to get their sympathy. Some doctors, especially, won't spend too much effort in collecting the outstanding bills of long-time patients who suddenly find themselves unable to pay.

If your insurance will eventually cover all or most of your medical bill, but the medical provider is pursuing you because the insurer hasn't paid yet, gather together evidence of:

- your submission of the bill to your insurance company, and
- your insurance company's coverage for the specific medical care you (or your other family member) received.

Armed with this information, call the doctor or hospital's collections department and ask for an appointment. At the meeting, provide the collector with copies of your documentation and plead with the person to cease collection efforts against you. Let the collections representative know that your medical condition may worsen if the stress of the collection calls and letters doesn't stop (if this is in the fact true). If you get nowhere with the collections representative, make an appointment to see the department supervisor. Also, if the bill is from a hospital, see if the facility has an ombudsman or patient's advocate. Such a person works to help resolve disputes between patients and the hospital. But remember: If you haven't yet paid the amount of any deductible, you still owe it. The insurance company won't pay it, and the doctor or hospital will continue to come after you.

Child Support and Alimony Payments

No matter what your hardship, your duty to pay court-ordered child support or alimony won't go away unless you take affirmative steps to legally reduce your payment obligation. Because a court ordered you to pay, only a court can reduce the amount. Thus, when your income drops, immediately file a paper (usually called a motion, petition, or order to show cause) with the court asking that your future child support or alimony payments be reduced, at least temporarily.

The court cannot retroactively reduce child support or alimony. The court can set up a payment schedule for you to get current, but if you miss payments before you ask for a reduction, the court can't erase your debt. See Chapter 13 for information on reducing child support or alimony.

Income Taxes

If you cannot pay the IRS taxes you owe, the IRS will encourage you to charge the extra amount on your credit card. This may be a bad idea, because the interest on your credit card will probably be a lot higher than the interest and penalties the IRS will charge if you reach an agreement with them.

If you owe the IRS up to $10,000 and you have not been in tax trouble recently, you are entitled to an installment agreement to pay your taxes. (If you owe the IRS more than $10,000, you may still request an installment agreement, but the IRS gets to decide whether to give you one.) Interest and a penalty are added to your tax debt each month. You can have up to three years to pay what you owe.

If you cannot afford an installment agreement, you can make an "offer in compromise." This means that you make a lump sum offer to the IRS to settle what you owe. The IRS will accept an offer in compromise only if all of the following are true:

- Doubt exists that the assessed tax is correct.
- Doubt exists that you have the ability to pay the full amount owed.
- Collection of the full liability would cause you economic hardship.
- You have filed all required federal tax returns.
- You are not in bankruptcy.
- You submit with your offer an application fee (currently $150), and a payment equal to either your first proposed payment (if you propose periodic payments) or 20% of your offer amount (if you propose a cash or lump sum offer). (See IRS Form 656, *Offer in Compromise*, for additional information (available at www.irs.gov).)

Finally, you may be able to eliminate, reduce, or spread out your IRS debt by filing for bankruptcy. (Bankruptcy is covered in Chapter 15.)

RESOURCES

For a complete discussion of your options with the IRS, see *Stand Up to the IRS*, by Frederick W. Daily (Nolo).

Student Loan Payments

We cover student loan debts in Chapter 12. For now, we'll just mention your basic options. If you are current on your payments on government student loans, you can probably get those payments postponed if you are out of work, disabled, suffering from an economic hardship, or, in certain circumstances, serving in the military. If you are current on your payments and you can afford to pay something, but not the amount you are obligated to pay, you can probably negotiate a new repayment plan for lower payments over a longer period of time. If you are in default and want to avoid the harsh collection tactics of the government, you should be able to negotiate a repayment plan that's both reasonable and affordable, based on your financial situation.

Credit Card Payments

If you can't pay anything on your credit card, and have decided that keeping the card isn't essential, don't pay. You will lose your credit privileges. You may also be sued, but that will take some time. You should also be aware, though, that many credit card companies today will charge you a higher interest rate if you default on an obligation to *another* creditor. If your credit report makes you look like a riskier borrower, creditors may raise your interest rate, even though you have never made a late payment to them. And, missed payments will bring down your credit score (see Chapter 11).

If you want to keep the card, most card companies insist that you make the monthly minimum payment, which is usually as low as 2%–2.5% of the outstanding balance. But if you can convince the company that your immediate financial situation is truly difficult, your payments may be cut in half and you won't be charged late fees while you're paying what you owe. In some cases,

the creditor may waive payments altogether for a few months. This courtesy is usually extended only to people who have never been late with a payment.

You should also call your credit card company and ask for a lower interest rate. A study conducted by the United States Public Interest Research Group in 2002 found that more than half of the consumers who complained to their credit card company were able to reduce their interest rate, usually by as much as one-third. The study found a number of connections between the cardholder's credit history and the likelihood of success. Not surprisingly, the deeper in debt you are, the less likely it is that the credit company will work with you. The most important factors affecting the success rate were:

- length of time with a particular card (longer is better)
- credit limit on that card (a higher limit is better)
- unpaid balance-to-limit ratio on that card—how "maxed out" the cardholder is (a lower balance is better)
- unpaid balance-to-limit ratio on all cards (a lower balance is better), and
- number of times the customer missed or paid late on a loan or a credit card other than the one in question (fewer is better).

If you are unsuccessful in negotiating lower interest payments on your own or feel that you could use some help, try contacting a nonprofit debt counseling agency such as Consumer Credit Counseling Services. (See Chapter 19 for information on debt counseling agencies.)

Protections Available to Those in the Military

The Servicemembers Civil Relief Act or SCRA (50 U.S.C. App. § 501 and following) gives servicemembers and their spouses a number of special rights, including:

- A servicemember may terminate (end) a lease on a vehicle if he or she leased it before entering military service and then went on active duty. A servicemember who is reassigned outside the continental U.S., or who is sent on temporary duty for 180 days or longer, also can terminate a vehicle lease. The lessor cannot charge an early termination penalty, but can charge for excess mileage and wear and tear.

- A servicemember may terminate a lease on a home or office if he or she signed the lease before entering military service and then went on active duty. A servicemember also can terminate a lease signed when he or she was on active duty if the servicemember is reassigned or deployed for 90 days or more.

- The interest rate on credit cards, mortgages, bank loans, vehicle financing, and the like is reduced to 6% annually for the entire time the servicemember is on active duty. This reduction applies only to obligations incurred by the servicemember, or the member and spouse jointly, before the member went on active duty. The creditor must forgive any interest that exceeds 6% for the entire time of active duty.

- A creditor's right to rescind or terminate an installment contract for real or personal property due to a breach of the contract's terms are limited if the breach happened prior to or while the servicemember is on active duty.

- Service members have protections against default judgments being entered against them in civil actions.

There are steps and procedures you have to follow to use these rights, and there are exceptions and limitations. For more information, contact your military legal assistance lawyer. You can find helpful resources on the SCRA at www.military.com (select the "Benefits" tab) and at www.jag.navy.mil/documents/SSCRA.htm.

WARNING

Keep it short. Paying nothing or very little on your credit card should be a temporary solution. The longer you pay only a small amount, the quicker your balance will increase due to interest charges.

Call or Write Your Creditors

Below is a sample letter you can modify and send to your creditors to request a reduction, extension, or other repayment program. It may help to send a copy to the company president. The information you gather to modify this letter will also help you prepare to call your creditor's customer service department. Work your way up the chain until you find someone who can make a decision on your proposal. Follow up a phone conversation with a confirming letter, stating whom you talked to and what agreement you reached. Keep a copy of your letter.

CROSS-REFERENCE

See Appendix C for a sample letter. Once you've had an initial discussion with a creditor, you should write to confirm the agreement you reached. In Appendix C, you'll find a blank letter you can use for this purpose; it also asks the creditor to agree to either remove negative information about the debt from your credit report or to "re-age" the debt—to start it over, so your initial repayment is shown as your first payment on the debt (this way, your account won't show any past late payments, although you may owe for a longer period of time).

Negotiating When the Creditor Has a Judgment Against You

If you don't pay your debts, your creditors may sue you. Once they have a judgment against you, they also have an expanded arsenal of collection techniques. For example, a creditor can put a lien on your house, empty your bank accounts, or attach a portion of your wages. An otherwise nonessential debt can quickly become essential when it's turned into a judgment, so ideally, you'll avoid getting a judgment against you. But even if there is a judgment against you, you can still negotiate, using the tools discussed in this chapter. Consider making an offer to the creditor, pointing out that it would save the creditor the trouble and expense of enforcing the judgment. Chapter 14 discusses what to do if you are sued.

Try to Pay Off a Debt for Less Than the Full Amount

If you owe a creditor $750, you may be tempted to send a check for $450 and write on the check that "cashing this check constitutes payment in full." Almost all states have adopted laws that allow you to send a partial payment as "payment in full," but only if you meet these requirements: The amount of the claim must be uncertain, or you must have a good faith dispute over the amount of the claim and you must offer the check in good faith as full satisfaction of the claim. This is a way to resolve a disputed bill informally. It is not meant as a way to

Sample Letter to Creditors

Collections Department
Big Bank of Bismarck
37 Charles Street
Bismarck, ND 77777

August 19, 2007

Re: Amy and Robert Grange Account 411-900-LOAN

To Whom It May Concern:

On June 5, 2005, your bank granted us a three-year $3,300 personal loan. Our agreement requires us to pay you $125 per month, and we have diligently made those payments since July 1, 2005.

We now, however, face several emergencies. Robert had a heart attack last April and has been out of work ever since. His doctors do not believe that he'll be able to work again until this November. On top of that, Amy's company filed for bankruptcy and laid her off last week. She will receive unemployment and is looking for work. Unfortunately, though, many industries in our town have closed down, and the prospects for a 46-year-old semiskilled worker are few. Amy may be able to work in her uncle's office, but it's a 90-minute drive each way and she can't afford the time while Robert is recovering.

We cannot pay you more than $20 a month right now. We expect to resume the full $125-per-month payments this November. We ask that you please accept our $20 a month until then, and just add the balance we miss to the end of our loan and extend it the few months necessary.

Thank you for your understanding and help. If we do not hear from you within 20 days, we will assume that this arrangement is acceptable.

Sincerely,

Amy Grange
Robert Grange
Amy and Robert Grange 701-555-8388

cc: Leonard O'Brien, President, Big Bank of Bismarck

"pay pennies on the dollar" for a debt you know you owe.

Here are some practical applications. Suppose you are dealing with an agent of the creditor who has direct responsibility for the disputed claim—for example, the manager of the store where you purchased defective goods, or a collection agency working for the creditor to collect the claim. In this situation, a week or two before sending the check, send the agent a letter saying that you dispute the amount of the debt in good faith and that you will send a check for a lesser amount in full satisfaction of the claim. When you send the check, write on it and in your cover letter that the check is offered as full satisfaction of the claim. (See Sample Letter 1, below.) If the creditor cashes the check and all of the other conditions have been met, your debt is fully satisfied and the claim is discharged.

If you are dealing generally with the creditor's billing or collection department, rather than one person having direct responsibility for the disputed claim, refer to Sample Letter 2, below. In this situation, state on the check and in a cover letter that the check is offered as full satisfaction of the claim, and send the check and letter to the person, office, or place specified by the creditor for this purpose (typically in a billing statement).

If the creditor cashes the check and all of the other conditions have been met, your debt is fully satisfied and the claim is discharged. However, if the creditor establishes either of the following, the claim will *not* be discharged:

- You didn't send the check and letter to the person or address specified by the creditor
- The creditor repays the amount of the check within 90 days after cashing it. (However, if the creditor specified a person or place to send communications about disputed claims, it cannot avoid the discharge by repaying the amount of the check.)

This system for resolving disputed debts has been adopted in some form by almost all states. The important things are that you dispute the amount you owe in good faith, you're clear that you're offering a lesser amount in full satisfaction of the claim, you send the check to the person with direct responsibility for the claim or to the address the creditor specifies, and the creditor keeps the money. It doesn't matter if the creditor strikes out "payment in full" or writes "I don't agree" before cashing the check.

After sending the letter, wait a reasonable time, before sending the check and a second letter. Two weeks probably is reasonable, but a longer or shorter time may be reasonable in your particular situation. When you send the check, don't forget to write on it and in your cover letter that the check is offered as full satisfaction of the claim.

Don't Write a Bad Check

People who are broke and desperate are often tempted to write bad checks. If you're faced with the prospect of no food or the electricity being cut off, writing a bad check

Sample Letter #1 Regarding Full Payment Check

Hermann's Hardware World, Inc.
1145 North Francisco Blvd.
Chico, CA 90000

Attn: Jose Smith, Manager

July 17, 2007

Re: Philip Van Bugle Account Number: PVB-92-4545

Dear Mr. Smith:

This letter concerns the money that you claim I owe you. For the past three months, I have received bills from you stating that I owe $300 for a three-day rental of your New-Finish-Now hardwood floor finisher. You will recall that I have spoken to you about this bill several times during the last three months.

As you will recall, I rented the finisher on a Friday evening intending to return it on Sunday, for a total of two days' rental. When I came to your store on Sunday, it was closed and I could not return the finisher until Monday. None of Hermann's employees told me that the store would be closed on Sunday. I believe that I owe you no more than $200, and it is obvious that there is a good-faith dispute over the amount of this bill.

In a good-faith effort to satisfy this debt, I will send you a check for $200 in full satisfaction of your claim against me. If you cash the check, it will fully satisfy my debt to you and will discharge your claim against me.

Sincerely,

Philip Van Bugle
Philip Van Bugle

Sample Letter #2 Regarding Full Payment Check

Hermann's Hardware World, Inc.
1145 North Francisco Blvd.
Mail Stop 1630
Chico, CA 90000

Attn: Billing Dispute Dept.

August 3, 2007

Re: Philip Van Bugle Account Number: PVB-92-4545

Dear Sir or Madam:

I enclose a check for $200 in full satisfaction of the balance due on account PVB-92-4545. Please note that I have written on the check "this check is tendered in full satisfaction of your claim against me." If you cash the check it will fully satisfy my debt to you and will discharge your claim against me.

As specified in your billing statement, I am sending this check to the attention of the Billing Dispute Department at Mail Stop 1630.

Sincerely,

Philip Van Bugle
Philip Van Bugle

can seem like a reasonable solution. It isn't. You may face all of the following: criminal prosecution, hefty bad check processing fees (from the bank), and a lawsuit from the creditor to whom you wrote the bad check.

In every state, writing a bad check when you know you don't have the money to cover it is a crime. Aggressive district attorneys don't hesitate to prosecute, especially given that an estimated 450 million rubber checks are written each year. It is not a crime, however, if you stopped payment because of a good-faith dispute you are having with a merchant.

If you are prosecuted, you may be able to avoid the ordeal of a trial if your county has a diversion program. Instead of being tried, you are given the option of attending classes for bad check writers. If you choose to go, you must pay the tuition, which usually ranges from $40 to $125 per session. In addition, you must make restitution (that is, make good on the bad checks you wrote).

Some check diversion programs are able to use collection tactics that other debt collectors can't use. Because of recent amendments to the federal Fair Debt Collection Practices Act (FDCPA), private check diversion programs that are under contract with a district attorney and meet certain other requirements are not covered by the FDCPA or its restrictions. (See Chapter 9 for information on the FDCPA.) So, for example, you might receive letters

from the diversion program on the district attorney's letterhead.

If you escape criminal prosecution, you'll still be charged a bad check processing fee by your bank. Many banks charge more than $30.

In addition, the person to whom you write a bad check—or one where a stop payment was later ordered—can sue for damages unless you stopped payment because of a good-faith dispute. Before you can be sued for damages for writing a bad check, the payee must have made a written demand that you make good on the bad check. If you don't pay within the time limits of the demand (usually 30 days), the payee can sue you.

If you lose the lawsuit, you are likely to be ordered to pay the following:
- the face value of check
- collection and mailing costs
- interest from the date of the check, and
- court and attorney fees.

In most states additional damages can be awarded against you for writing a bad check. The maximum amount of damages allowed varies from state to state. In many states, you must pay three times the amount of the check, with a cap of $500 or $1,000. In a few states, the additional damages are limited to a small amount ($50 or $100). If you plead financial hardship, the court may reduce the additional damages.

Stale Checks: How Long Will a Check Be Honored?

If you wrote a payee a check several months ago, but the payee has not yet cashed it, can you add the balance back into your checkbook?

Perhaps, but not necessarily. A bank, savings and loan, or credit union is not required to honor a check presented for cashing more than six months after the check was written. Most banks do, however, unless the check has an express notation on it "not valid after six months."

What does this mean for you? If you wrote a check more than six months ago and the payee still hasn't cashed it, you can call your bank and put a stop payment on it. The debt, however, does not go away. Be prepared for the payee to try to collect, arguing that your stop payment was not in good faith. You should respond that you waited six months, and if a bank isn't obligated to honor a check that old, you shouldn't be, either.

A federal law called "Check 21" may make stale checks a thing of the past. This law allows banks to process electronic images of checks instead of the paper originals. One result is that checks can be processed much faster than before.

Writing a Postdated Check Is a Bad Idea

Many aggressive bill collectors will try to pressure you into sending them a postdated check: a check that bears a future date. Sending a postdated check is always a bad idea. When you write a postdated check, you are committing yourself to having the money in your checking account when the date on the check arrives. If you are already having debt problems, this is a commitment you might not be able to keep.

Although it's usually legal for creditors themselves to accept postdated checks, they don't always wait to deposit them until the date on the check. Instead of writing a postdated check, you might tell the creditor that you will personally deliver the check on the day you write it (assuming the creditor is local).

By contrast, it is illegal for professional debt collectors to accept a check postdated by more than five days, unless they notify you between three and ten days in advance of when they will deposit it. It's also illegal for debt collectors to deposit the check before the date stated on the check or to solicit a postdated check for the purpose of threatening or instituting criminal prosecution. (15 U.S.C. § 1692f.)

Beware of the IRS If You Settle a Debt

If you settle a debt with a creditor, or the creditor writes off a debt you owe, you could wind up owing income tax on that money. Here's how: Creditors often write off debts after a set period of time—such as one, two, or three years after default. That means they cease collection efforts, declare the debt uncollectible, and report it to the IRS as lost income, so they can reduce their taxes. The same is true for negotiated reduction of a debt. The flip side of that is that the IRS thinks that you've gained income, because you don't have to pay the debt anymore. Debts subject to this law include money owed after a house foreclosure, after a property repossession, or on a credit card bill you don't pay.

Any bank, credit union, savings and loan, finance company, financial institution, credit card company, or federal government agency that forgives or writes off $600 or more of the principal amount of a debt (the amount not attributable to interest or fees) must send you and the IRS a Form 1099-C at the end of the tax year. You must report the amount on this form as income when you file your tax return for the tax year in which your debt was settled or written off.

Even if you don't get a Form 1099-C from a creditor, the creditor may very well have submitted one to the IRS. If you don't list the income on your tax return and the IRS has the information, it will send you a tax bill (or worse, an audit notice), which could end up costing you more in IRS interest and penalties in the long run.

Don't panic: There are important exceptions to this rule. Even if you and the IRS got a Form 1099-C, you do not have to report the income on your tax return if any of the following is true:

- A nonbusiness debt was canceled as a result of Hurricane Katrina (see IRS Publication 525, *Taxable and Nontaxable Income,* for details).
- A student loan was canceled because you worked in a profession and for an employer as promised when you took out the loan (see IRS Publication 525,

Taxable and Nontaxable Income, for details).
- The canceled debt would have been deductible if you had paid it.
- You discharged the debt in a Chapter 11 bankruptcy (financial reorganization of an individual or business).
- The cancellation or write-off of the debt is intended as a gift (but this would be unusual).
- You were insolvent before the creditor agreed to settle or wrote off the debt.

Insolvency means that your debts exceed the value of your assets. Therefore, to figure out whether or not you are insolvent, you will have to total up your assets and your debts, including the debt that was settled or written off.

EXAMPLE: Your assets are worth $35,000, and your debts total $45,000. That means you are insolvent to the tune of $10,000. You settle a debt with a creditor who agrees to forgive $8,500. You do not have to report any of that money as income on your tax return.

EXAMPLE: This time your assets are still worth $35,000 and your debts still total $45,000, but the creditor writes off a $14,000 debt. You don't have to report $10,000 of the income, but you will have to report $4,000 on your tax return.

If you calculate that your debts exceed the value of your assets (that is, you're insolvent), you'll have to include IRS Form 982 with your tax return. You can download the form from the IRS website at www.irs.gov.

Finding Money to Pay Your Debts

How pleasant it is to have money.

—Arthur Hugh Clough, English poet, 1819-1861

You may be considering several methods of raising cash to pay your debts. Before doing so, ask yourself if bankruptcy is a realistic option for you. (Chapter 15 can help you make this decision.) If it is, raising cash to pay debts you will ultimately erase in bankruptcy is a waste of your time and already-stretched resources. On the other hand, if you can raise the cash to pay off your debts with a reasonable amount of effort, avoiding bankruptcy is preferable.

Below are several different methods of raising cash. Many have costs associated with them—such as penalties, interest, and fees. A few may cost you more money than the cash raised is worth. So read on and make sure you'll get some net benefit before taking any action.

Increase Your Income

The first and most obvious way to raise more money is to earn more money. We're willing to bet that this has already occurred to you, if you're working now. There are a number of ways to earn more money:

- increase the hours you work (for many people this means getting a second job or starting a business on the side)
- increase the amount you earn in the time you work (this may mean switching jobs)

- have every person in your family work who is capable of working, even students, and
- make sure your investments are giving you the best possible return.

Consider these options, but be sensible. Any of these strategies could backfire on you. Taking a second job or having your spouse go back to work could mean you're suddenly paying a lot for babysitters, fast food, transportation, dry cleaning, and additional income taxes, with precious little net benefit to your overall situation. Nor will it help to work yourself into a nervous breakdown or invest in speculative schemes.

Keep in mind that you need cash on hand to pay your living expenses and essential debts (such as housing and transportation). This is a good time to prioritize your needs and to be conservative about expenses.

Sell Some Stuff

One way you can raise money is to convert something you already own into cash. While this can take some work, and should be done carefully, it can also be financially worthwhile.

Sell a Major Asset

You can raise cash and keep associated costs to a minimum by selling a major asset, such as a car or, as a last resort, your house. This may be a good idea if you can no longer afford your house or car payments— or if you happen to have a second house or car you can do without.

Don't sell your home or car unless you have affordable alternative housing or transportation. Otherwise, you could end up in worse shape than before—without a roof over your head or a car to get to work.

Don't automatically decide to sell property. Try to be realistic about how much you can get for it and whether it's worthwhile to sell. For example, you may be better off keeping a useful car that's now worth less than its remaining loan balance. And remember, if you lease your car, you must return it to the lessor; you can't just sell it. If you decide to sell, you will net the most money if you own the property free and clear, although you should plan to pay taxes and other expenses from the proceeds of the sale.

It is almost always possible to sell property that you haven't finished paying off. You will almost always do better selling the property yourself rather than waiting to get cash back from a foreclosure or repossession sale. (You may also get a better price if you don't have to sell in a hurry.) With the proceeds of the sale, you'll have to pay off the lender(s) and any secured creditor to whom you pledged the asset as collateral. Then you'll have to pay off any liens placed on the property by your creditors. You can use what's left to help pay your other debts. Even if nothing is left, getting rid of large monthly payments may help you afford your other bills.

 WARNING

Don't forget possible tax conse-quences. If you are selling stocks, real estate, or anything else that is valuable that has appreciated (or depreciated) or on which you might owe capital gains or some other transaction tax, consult a tax professional *before* the sale. Sometimes a sale can be legally structured to obtain a favorable tax result. Other times, you may find out that the tax consequences of selling are so unpleasant that you would be better off doing something different, such as using the asset as collateral for a loan or choosing another asset to sell.

Sell Smaller Items

Even if you're not a packrat, you probably own things you never use or don't need any more. Thanks to the Internet, it has never been easier to get rid of property you have no use for. All kinds of property can be sold on eBay (www.ebay.com) and similar auction websites. These sites are proof of the old maxim, "One man's trash is another man's treasure." They provide an instant audience of millions of potential buyers of practically anything.

With any luck, you'll connect with a collector of obscure items in your clutter. Baseball cards and comic books have been collected for years, but there are also collectors of dolls, ashtrays, electronic equipment, musical instruments, "retro" furniture, old dishes, china, and antiques of any kind. A good way to figure out what an item is worth is to search eBay for similar items and see what buyers are bidding for them.

In addition to auction sites, some retailers (including Amazon.com) let you sell used books and CDs to other customers. You may not get much money for each individual book or CD, but if you have a several dozen or some hundreds to sell, it can provide some badly needed cash.

WARNING

It can cost money to sell things. When you sell online, it's up to you to pack up the sold item and pay for shipping. Make sure you're getting enough for the item to make a profit after the costs of shipping. Also, *beware of scams.* Reputable websites like Amazon and eBay are careful to collect the money from the buyer, but if you sell directly to an online buyer, you could ship off your stuff and never get any money back. Check out "Internet Auctions: A Guide for Buyers and Sellers" at www.ftc.gov/bcp/conline/pubs/online/auctions.pdf, particularly the sections on arranging for payment and fake checks and money orders.

You don't have to know how to use a computer to get rid of your belongings. There are always the traditional low-tech ways to sell:

- Advertise in the newspaper.
- Have a yard sale (be sure to ask about a local permit).
- Take a load to the flea market (you may need to rent a space).
- Take vintage or expensive clothing to a resale shop.
- Take books (and perhaps musical recordings, depending on the reseller) to a used book store.
- Take good jewelry to a jeweler who sells "estate jewelry."

Before you go to a reseller, have a ballpark idea of what your things are worth and a realistic idea of what condition they're in. That way, you'll be a better negotiator, you won't get cheated, and you won't insist on an unrealistically high price that results in no sale.

A consignment shop is another option, but make sure that it's reputable and well-established in your community. Check with your local Better Business Bureau to see if there are complaints (go to www.bbb.org and click on the "Locate a Bureau" button). Consignment shops usually keep 35%–50% of what they can sell an item for, and give you the rest.

TIP

You may collect more money if you sell it yourself. The reason? At a shop, resale items in good condition are often priced at about 70% of what they would bring if they were new. (We're not talking about collectors' items here.) A shop has overhead, and it needs to make a profit on the items it sells—typically, by charging almost double what it pays for an item. At most the shop will offer you about a third of what the item would sell for, new. If you invest some time in a yard sale or flea market, you could likely sell it for more.

Cut Your Expenses

Another excellent way to raise cash is to cut your expenses. It will also help you negotiate with your creditors, who will want to know why you can't pay your bills and what efforts you've taken to live more frugally.

Where and how you cut expenses will depend on your income, your debt level, and your standard of living. If you have a large income but also high expenses and enormous debt, you need to review your priorities. It's up to you to decide what is a necessity and what is a luxury. You may be in a position to cut expenses significantly if you:

- take the children out of private schools
- move to a smaller house
- reduce the number of vehicles you own
- switch to less costly cars
- put off expensive vacations
- stop buying clothes or lavish gifts, or
- eat at home instead of going out.

If your savings from the steps above are not enough to deal with your debt, or you never spent money on private schools and fancy cars to begin with, here are some more modest suggestions for cutting expenses and making your income go further:

- Shrink food costs by clipping coupons, buying sale items, purchasing generic brands, buying in bulk, and shopping at discount outlets.
- Improve your gas mileage by tuning up your car, checking the air in the tires, and driving less: carpool, work at home (telecommute), ride your bicycle, take the bus or train, and combine trips.
- Conserve gas, water, and electricity by turning off lights, televisions, and stereos when they are not in use. Run the dishwasher and washing machine with full loads and less frequently.
- Discontinue cable, or at least the premium channels. Most cable companies offer a very low rate basic service that they don't advertise. Ask about rates for basic service, and also whether you'll be charged a penalty if you switch plans.
- Instead of buying books and CDs or renting videos, borrow them from the public library. Read magazines and newspapers there, too, instead of subscribing to them.
- Look for new ways to spend time socializing. Take walks with friends instead of meeting for lunch. Get together to devote time to charity work—cleaning up a park or delivering meals to the elderly.
- Make long distance calls only when necessary and at off-peak hours. Also, compare programs offered by the various long distance carriers to make sure you are getting the best deal. If you're considering switching plans or carriers, call your current carrier to find out if you'll have to pay a fee.
- Carry your lunch to work; eat breakfast and dinner at home, not at restaurants.
- Buy secondhand clothing, furniture, and appliances.
- Stop spending on gifts and vacations.
- Cancel your private mortgage insurance (PMI), if you're eligible to do so. Lenders typically require home buyers who put less than 20% down to pay for insurance to protect the lenders in case the buyer defaults before building up equity. A lender rarely offers to cancel the policy after the buyer reaches 20% equity, however, and buyers often unnecessarily pay for PMI for years. A federal law

applying to most mortgages obtained after July 29, 1999 requires lenders to automatically cancel PMI once the equity reaches 22% and allows buyers with good payment histories to request cancellation of the PMI once the equity reaches 20%. (12 U.S.C. §§ 4901 and following.) If the law doesn't apply to you (for example, you took out your mortgage earlier than July 1999), you can still contact your lender and request cancellation. Most will do so once the equity reaches 20%. Some states also have laws regulating PMI.

- Stop charging small purchases. People today charge everything on their credit cards—dry cleaning, sandwiches, frappuccinos, groceries, movies, cocktails, postage, gum, and so on—and feel that their finances are under control because they have cash in their wallets or purses. These little expenses are hard to keep track of and add up quickly by the end of the month, often becoming budget busters. Try leaving the credit cards at home and paying cash for these things or forgoing them. If you really don't want to go without a $5 coffee drink, pay cash for it (so that you'll appreciate how much it costs); better yet, enjoy it as a reward when your finances are back on track.

Withdraw Money From a Tax-Deferred Account

If you have an IRA, 401(k), or other tax-deferred retirement account, you can get cash to pay off debts by withdrawing money before retirement. But if you do so, you'll probably have to pay a penalty and taxes. Another option is to borrow money from your 401(k) plan instead of withdrawing it. There are serious disadvantages to both options. You should only consider these if you have other substantial retirement funds or you are truly desperate. Also, consult your tax adviser before you do anything. Always look to raise money from nonretirement resources first.

RESOURCES

Need more information on retirement accounts? If you are considering withdrawing or borrowing money from your retirement account to pay off debts, get a copy of *IRAs, 401(k)s and Other Retirement Plans: Taking Your Money Out*, by Twila Slesnick and John C. Suttle (Nolo).

Apply for Government and Agency Help

When you find yourself having money troubles, don't overlook official help. Despite a steady contraction in social services in recent years, the government still provides something of a "social safety net" to help people with temporary money problems.

Unemployment Insurance Benefits

You may be eligible to apply for unemployment benefits if any of the following occurs:

- You are fired for any reason, other than for gross misconduct.
- You quit your job for an extremely good job-related reason.
- You are laid off.

Your telephone book should have the phone number for the closest unemployment office, so check the state government listing sections. For a link to the unemployment insurance website in your state, see the Department of Labor's Education & Training Administration website at http://workforcesecurity.doleta.gov/map.asp. And there's a handy online calculator—sponsored by the Economic Policy Institute—that estimates what your unemployment benefits might be, based on your answers to a series of questions: www.epinet.org (select "Online Calculators"). Be sure to ask your state agency these questions:

- How much is my benefit amount? (It will depend on how much you earned at work.)
- How long can I collect benefits? (You can typically collect for up to 26 weeks.)
- If I start working again before then, will my benefits be reduced? (You may be able to increase your income, up to a point, without losing all of your benefits.)

WARNING

Unemployment programs typically require a fair amount of paperwork. You are expected to look for work while you are collecting benefits, and you may have to report in writing on your search.

Human Service Agencies

Contact other agencies to find out if you qualify for Food Stamps, Medicaid, general assistance, veterans' benefits, workers' compensation, Social Security, or disability benefits.

- Supplemental Security Income (SSI) provides cash assistance to persons who are at least 65 years old, or people of any age who are blind or disabled, who have limited incomes and few resources. In most states, people eligible for SSI are automatically enrolled in Medicaid.
- Medicaid is a government program that provides health and medical coverage to low-income people. Medicaid covers things that Medicare does not, such as prescription drugs and long-term care.
- The Medicare Savings Programs are government programs that provide financial help with Medicare expenses for senior citizens with limited incomes and resources.
- The Food Stamp Program provides monthly assistance to low-income persons to purchase food at grocery stores.

Human service agencies in each state administer several federal benefit programs for persons with low incomes, including Medicaid, Medicare Savings Programs, and Food Stamps. These agencies go by various names depending on the state, such as Department of Social Services, Human Services, or Public Aid. Older people can also apply for Food Stamps at their local Social Security Administration (SSA) office.

You can find the nearest Social Security Office by using the SSA's Social Security Office Locator at www.ssa.gov or by calling 800-772-1213.

Your state website may provide Medicaid information online at www.state.*.us. (*Substitute the two-letter postal abbreviation for your state. For instance, California is www.state.ca.us.)

RESOURCES

More information on benefits.
BenefitsCheckup, sponsored by the National Council on the Aging, is a free online service (www.benefitscheckup.org). You anonymously fill out a questionnaire, and the website finds public benefits programs for which you may be eligible and tells you how to apply. These programs may pay for some of the costs of prescription drugs, health care, utilities, and other essential items or services. Nolo also publishes a variety of products that deal specifically with applying for several kinds of benefits:

Nolo's Guide to Social Security Disability: Getting & Keeping Your Benefits, by David A. Morton III, M.D.

Social Security, Medicare, & Government Pensions: Get the Most Out of Your Retirement & Medical Benefits, by Joseph L. Matthews with Dorothy Matthews Berman.

Long-Term Care: How to Plan & Pay For It, by Joseph L. Matthews.

Private Agencies

There may be a host of nonprofit associations available to help you out. In some cases it helps if you are a member of a fraternal organization or an ethnic or religious group, a native son or daughter, and so on. You can get to the right organizations by using your phone book, surfing the Internet, or calling friends, your local senior center, or local churches.

Consider a Home Equity Loan

Many banks, savings and loans, credit unions, and other lenders offer home equity loans, also called second mortgages, and home equity lines of credit also called HELOCs. Traditionally, lenders who make home equity loans establish how much you can borrow by starting with a percentage of the market value of your house—usually between 50% and 80%—and deducting what you still owe on it. The lender will also consider your credit history, income, and other expenses in deciding whether—and how much—to lend you.

> **EXAMPLE:** Winnie's house is worth $200,000, and she owes $120,000 on her first mortgage. A bank has offered her a home equity loan at 75%, that is, for $30,000. The lender figures it like this: 75% of $200,000 is $150,000; $150,000 less $120,000 is $30,000.

Until the late 1990s, home equity lenders rarely would lend a borrower more than 80% of the equity in the house. But as the consumer lending market became more competitive, rising numbers of consumers found themselves in debt, and lenders' desire for profits skyrocketed, home equity lenders began offering loans well in excess of the 80%—125% was not uncommon. Loans for more than 100% of a house's value are less common today because lenders now heed their risk, but they still are available.

> WARNING
>
> **Many people who borrow on their house lose their houses to the home equity lenders.** As a general rule of thumb, if your debts are mostly unsecured and your house is exempt from collection, you are better off keeping current on your house payments or trying to negotiate a mortgage workout with the lender. (See Chapter 6 for information on mortgage workouts.) If you do opt for a home equity loan, be sure you understand all the terms before you sign on the dotted line.

Think long and hard if you're tempted by a 100% (or more) home equity loan, especially if your goal is to save your house. First, in taking out such a loan, you're gambling that the value of your home will increase enough to cover what you owe on the equity line plus the mortgage. The recent peaks and valleys in the housing market show that prices don't always go up. Second, be careful that you don't simply max out your credit cards again after you use your home equity to pay down your debts. Many borrowers wind up deeper in debt—this time with a large equity line to repay as well.

Advantages of Home Equity Loans

Home equity loans have a number of advantages, including:

- You can obtain a closed-end loan. You borrow a fixed amount of money and repay it in equal monthly installments for a set period (a home equity loan). Or you can obtain a line of credit— you borrow as you need the money, drawing against the amount granted when you opened the account (a home equity line of credit). Be sure you understand the difference.
- The interest you pay may be fully deductible on your income tax return.

Disadvantages of Home Equity Loans

Home equity loans also have several disadvantages, including:

- Some home equity loans are sold by predatory lenders at very high rates. Predatory lenders target people in financial trouble or with past credit problems. Often, predatory lenders count on the borrower not being able to make the loan payments and expect to foreclose on the house when the borrower fails to make payments. The Federal Trade Commission (FTC) recommends avoiding any lender who tells you to falsify information on a loan application, pressures you into applying for more money than you need, or pressures you into accepting monthly payments you cannot afford.

- You are obligating yourself to make another monthly or periodic payment. If you are unable to pay, you may have to sell your house or, even worse, face the possibility of the lender foreclosing. *Before you take out a home equity loan, be sure you can make the monthly payment.*

- Some home equity loans are "interest only" loans—your monthly payments pay only the interest on the loan and do not reduce the principal amount that you borrowed. You could make payments for years and still owe the full amount you borrowed.

- While interest may be deductible (it isn't always), it may be high. Check Bankrate.com for current rates (www. bankrate.com).

- You'll have to pay an assortment of up-front fees for such costs as an appraisal, credit report, title insurance, and points. These fees can be as much as $1,000 or more. In addition, for giving you an open line of credit, many lenders charge a yearly fee of $25 to $50.

- You must pay what you still owe on the equity loan, plus what you owe on the mortgage, when you sell your house

Before obtaining a home equity loan, carefully evaluate your situation. You're trying to take steps to help you pay your debts; you don't want to make your debt burden worse.

Canceling a Home Equity Loan

Under the federal Truth in Lending Act, you have the right to cancel a home equity loan or second mortgage until midnight of the third business day (excluding Sundays and federal holidays *but including Saturdays*) after you sign the contract or are given the loan disclosures, whichever is later. You must be given notice of your right to cancel and a cancellation form when you sign the contract. (See Chapter 4 for more information.)

Use the Equity in Your Home If You Are 62 or Older

A variety of plans are designed to help older homeowners make use of the accumulated value (equity) in their homes without requiring them to move, give up title to the property, or make payments on a loan. The most common types of plans are called reverse mortgages and deferral loans for property tax and home repair.

These plans can raise a senior citizen's standard of living and help an older person maintain independence by providing cash for everyday living expenses, home maintenance, or in-home care. But they're not for everybody.

Reverse Mortgages

Reverse mortgages are loans that senior homeowners (age 62 or older) take out against the equity in their home. A reverse mortgage provides cash advances to the owner and requires no repayment until the end of the loan term or when the home is sold. The borrower can receive the cash in several ways, and usually does so in a combination of the following:

- a lump sum (often used to pay off any existing mortgages, and perhaps to take out some extra cash to pay off other bills or do home repairs)
- a line of credit or "creditline" (you use the money only if you need it, while unused funds earn interest and grow)
- regular monthly payments (because these are less flexible, they are not recommended if a line of credit will do).

What a reverse mortgage is called will vary, as shown in the chart below, depending on how you will receive money and when you have to pay the loan back. Any of the *mortgages* listed below can combine one or more of the *payment methods* listed above.

To determine the amount it will lend to you, a reverse mortgage lender will usually look at your age, the amount of equity you have in your home, and current interest rates. All reverse mortgages cost money: closing costs (title insurance, escrow fees, and appraisal fees), loan origination fees, accrued interest, and, in most cases, an additional charge to offset the lender's risk that you may default (not pay). Reverse mortgages through a private, for-profit company are often very expensive and come with high interest rates.

The most widely available reverse mortgages are the FHA's Home Equity Conversion Mortgage (HECM) Program and Fannie Mae's Home Keeper Mortgage

Reverse Mortgage Types		
Name of Mortgage	What You Get	When It's Due
Fixed Term Reverse Mortgage	If you receive monthly advances, they stop after a specified period of time.	At the end of the period, the advances stop and you must repay the loan.
Tenure Reverse Mortgage	If you receive monthly advances, they keep coming as long as you stay in your home.	Once you leave (for example, you sell your house or go into a nursing home), you must repay the loan.
Portable Reverse Mortgage	You receive a lump sum advance in order to purchase an annuity that will pay you a fixed amount as long as you are alive, no matter where you live.	Once you leave the house, you must repay the loan. **Note:** This kind of mortgage is complicated. You will probably need a lawyer.
Lump Sum	You receive the entire loan amount in one lump sum.	Once you leave the house, you must repay the loan.

Program. The HECM includes the attractive credit line option that allows your unused balance to earn interest over time. (Fannie Mae, which was formerly an FHA program, is a private financial services corporation that assists lenders.) These are federally insured loans available through private lenders. Federally insured reverse mortgages limit loan costs that lenders can charge and guarantee that lenders will meet their obligations. Even so, reverse mortgages are not inexpensive.

Some states also offer very low cost government-sponsored reverse mortgages that are available only for specific purposes. (See "Deferral Payment Loans," below.)

There are pros and cons to reverse mortgages. In general, a reverse mortgage works best for older people with a lot of equity in their homes.

The lender or a third party may suggest that you purchase an annuity in conjunction with a reverse mortgage. An annuity is an insurance product financed out of the

---

Disadvantages of Reverse Mortgages

- Once you borrow against your equity with a reverse mortgage, there's no turning back. This equity will not be available to you unless you pay off the loan.

- The costs of a reverse mortgage can be very high, and some mortgages have unfair terms.

- Some unscrupulous lenders offer products that sound like reverse mortgages, but are really conventional loans. Others sell reverse mortgages that lend more money than you need, are very high cost, or have unfair terms. Some unscrupulous individuals offer to refer senior homeowners to lenders that provide reverse mortgages, in exchange for a percentage of the loan. Information on reverse mortgages is free from the U.S. Department of Housing and Urban Development. (See "Additional Resources," below).

- A reverse mortgage makes it difficult to give your home to your heirs after you die, because your estate has to pay the loan back—and, usually, the house is sold to cover the debt.

- Because you don't make payments, the amount of money owed increases over the life of the loan. While you retain title to your home, you must pay the property taxes, insurance, and the costs of keeping up the property.

- A reverse mortgage (or annuity payments funded by a lump sum reverse mortgage) may affect your ability to receive need-based government benefits such as Supplemental Security Income (SSI). Although loan advances from a reverse mortgage are not considered "income," they may increase your amount of "liquid assets" above limits set by government benefit programs.

home's equity, which provides monthly payments to the borrower beginning immediately or some years later.

Think carefully about whether an annuity is right for you. Many consumer experts recommend against purchasing an annuity because it ties up the money from the reverse mortgage for an extended period, imposes additional transaction costs, imposes substantial penalties for early withdrawal, and may not benefit elderly homeowners (who may not live to see their first annuity payment, if there is a delay of several years). Indeed, California now prohibits lenders from requiring homeowners to purchase an annuity as a condition of obtaining a reverse mortgage.

Deferral Payment Loans

Deferral payment loans are need-based loans used for a special purpose: to make property tax payments or to pay for home repairs. The cost of these loans is very low, and repayment is deferred as long as you live in your home. Deferral payment loans are generally available through state or local government agencies.

There are two types of deferral payment loans:

- **Property tax deferral loans.** Many states provide vouchers to approved applicants to pay their property taxes. Contact your tax assessor to see if such a program is available in your county.
- **Home repair deferral loans.** These are loans for home repairs at no or very low interest.

Additional Resources

The following organizations and agencies offer free or low-cost information about reverse mortgages, deferred payment loans, and other options to tap into your home equity:

- U.S. Department of Housing and Urban Development, 800-569-4287 or www.hud.gov.
- AARP, 800-687-2277. AARP has a good informational booklet about reverse mortgages available at its website, www.aarp.org.
- Fannie Mae, 800-732-6643, www. fanniemae.com.
- The National Center for Home Equity Conversion, www.reverse.org.
- Your local senior center or the county office of your state's Department of Aging should also have more information about ways to tap your house's equity.

Be very wary of anyone who would charge you—often as much as 10% of the loan amount—for information about how you can use your house's equity.

Borrow the Money

If you have good credit and have hit a temporary rough patch, you might be able to get an unsecured personal loan from a bank or credit union. (This means that you sign loan papers and make regular payments but give them no collateral.) Another potential source for a loan is a community development bank or loan fund that makes loans to businesses and in distressed communities not served by other lenders. (Your local bank may have a program like this or know who offers them locally.) But before you borrow money from an institution, ask yourself:

- Can you pay back the money?
- Can you find a loan on better terms?

Some people are lucky enough to have friends or relatives who can and will help out. Before asking your college roommate, Uncle Paul, or someone similar for help, consider the following:

- Can the lender really afford to help you? If the person is on a fixed income and needs the money to get by, you should probably look elsewhere for a loan.

- Do you want to owe this person money? If the loan comes with emotional strings attached, be sure you can handle the situation before taking the money.

- Will the loan help you out, or will it just delay the inevitable (most likely, filing for bankruptcy)? Don't borrow money to make payments on debts you will eventually discharge in bankruptcy.

- Will you have to repay the loan now, or will the lender let you wait until you're back on your feet? If you have to make payments now, you're just adding another monthly payment to your already unmanageable pile of debts.

- If the loan is from your parents, can you treat it as part of your eventual inheritance? If so, you won't ever

have to repay it. If your siblings get angry that you are getting some of your parents' money, be sure they understand that your inheritance will be reduced accordingly.

RESOURCES

Resources for personal loans. *101 Law Forms for Personal Use,* by Robin Leonard and Ralph Warner (Nolo), includes customizable promissory notes for lending money between family members. Nolo's website at www.nolo.com also sells interactive "webforms" that you can use to create and print your own promissory note on your home computer.

WARNING

One word of warning: If a friend or relative lends you money at a below-market interest rate or gives you cash as a gift, that person may have to pay gift taxes. As of 2006, gifts of more than $12,000 per person per year are subject to gift taxes. And the definition of "gift" includes a break on interest (although because the amount of the "gift" is the break on interest per year, not the amount loaned, most loans won't incur gift taxes on the principal amount borrowed).

Get Your Tax Refund Fast

Sometimes, getting a tax refund quickly will help you through a crisis, especially if the IRS owes you a lot.

If you're getting a refund, file your tax return early. You can file your return electronically or by fax and have your refund deposited directly into your account. But don't get a tax refund anticipation loan in the meantime; see "Tax Refund Anticipation Loans," below, to find out why this is a bad idea.

WARNING

Student loan debtors: don't count your dollars before they're hatched. If you are expecting a large tax refund—and you've defaulted on a student loan—don't count on seeing the money. Intercepting tax refunds is the method most frequently used by the government to collect outstanding student loan dollars. Yearly, the federal government pockets more than $900 million by grabbing tax refunds and other federal offsets from defaulted student loan borrowers. And if you legitimately owe the money, stopping a tax refund intercept is very difficult. For more information on student loan collections, see Chapter 12.

What to Avoid When You Need Money

Making wise financial decisions when the bills are piling up is not easy. But, even if you feel desperate, don't jump at every opportunity to get cash fast. If you make a bad choice, you'll just get yourself deeper into debt. This section discusses some of the options that you should avoid. It's not a complete list. Unfortunately, new scams and bad deals crop up every day. So, proceed cautiously, whatever you are considering.

Finance Companies

Some consumer finance companies lend money to consumers in the form of consolidation loans. Finance companies make secured consolidation loans, usually requiring that you pledge your house or car as collateral. These loans are just like second mortgages or secured vehicle loans, and you'll usually be charged interest between 10% and 15%. If you default on the loan, the finance company can foreclose on your home or take your car or other property.

TIP

You might be able to cancel the loan. If the consolidation loan is secured by your principal residence, you can cancel it for up to three business days after you sign the loan papers. See Chapter 4 for more information.

Finance companies and similar lenders also make unsecured consolidation loans— that is, they lend you some money without requiring that you pledge any property as a guarantee that you'll pay. But the interest on these loans often reaches 25% or more. They also charge all kinds of fees or require you to purchase insurance, often bringing the effective interest rate closer to 50%.

If you still want to take out a consolidation loan, you are better off borrowing from a bank or credit union than a finance company. Many finance companies engage in illegal or borderline collection practices if you default and are not as willing as banks and credit unions to negotiate if you have trouble paying. Furthermore, loans from finance companies may be viewed negatively by potential creditors who see them in your credit file.

 WARNING

Be careful when pledging your home. Think carefully about whether you want to convert unsecured debts (for example, credit card debt) into debt that's secured by your home. If you can't make the payments on the secured debt, you could lose your home.

Tax Refund Anticipation Loans

Although getting a tax refund fast is often a good way to get quick cash (see above), you should avoid a tax refund anticipation loan (RAL). A tax refund anticipation loan is a loan, offered by a private company for the short period between when the taxpayer receives the RAL and when the IRS repays the RAL by depositing the taxpayer's refund into the lender's account (usually only a week or two). The amount of the loan is the amount of your anticipated refund, less fees for the loan, electronic filing, and tax preparation. For example, if your refund is $2,500 (the recent average), the loan fee would be about $100 and the application fee would be about $40. That's an effective annual percentage rate (APR) of about *200%*! If you also paid the average tax preparation fee of $150, your total loan costs could be as much as $290. "Instant" RALs charge an additional $20-$55 in fees. The effective APR for some RALs can be as high as 500%.

This is a very expensive way to borrow money, especially when you can get the full amount of your refund just by being patient. In addition, RALs also pose some risks. You must repay the loan even if your refund is denied, is less than expected, or is frozen. If you can't repay the loan, the lender may assign the debt to a collection agency, and the unpaid debt will appear on your credit report. If you apply for an RAL next year, the lender may take that refund to pay for this year's unpaid RAL debt. Information from your tax form can be shared with the lending bank when you apply for an RAL if you unwittingly agree when signing forms in your tax return package.

Alternatives to RALs for low-income taxpayers include the Volunteer Income Tax Assistance (VITA) program and the AARP's TaxAide. To locate a VITA office, go to www.irs.com, or call 800-829-1040; to locate a TaxAide office, go to www.aarp.org or call 888-227-7669. The IRS Free File program is available for taxpayers who earn less than $52,000 (this program no longer markets RALs). Some free tax preparation programs can also help you open a bank account into which your refund can be directly deposited.

It is usually better to be patient and wait for your refund, rather than pay the high fee for a tax refund anticipation loan. In most cases, you can file your return electronically and get the money quickly (by having the refund deposited directly into your account, for example). For more information on how to get a refund sooner and for answers to other tax questions, contact the IRS at 800-829-1040 (voice) or 800-829-4059 (TDD), or visit its website at www.irs.gov.

Pawnshops

Visiting a pawnshop should be one of the last ways you consider raising cash. At a pawnshop, you leave your property—the most commonly pawned items are jewelry, electronic and photography equipment, musical instruments, and firearms. In return, the pawnbroker lends you approximately 50% to 60% of the item's resale value. The average amount of a pawnshop loan is only $50 or so.

You are given a few months to repay the loan and are charged interest, often at an exorbitant rate. Although you borrow money for only a few months, paying an average of 10% a month interest means that you are paying an annual interest rate of 120%. You might also be charged storage costs and insurance fees.

If you default on your loan to a pawnshop, the property you left at the shop to obtain the loan becomes the property of the pawnbroker. You are usually given some time to pay your debt and get your property back; if you don't, the pawnbroker can sell it. In about a dozen states, if the sale brings in money in excess of what you owe on the loan, storage fees, and sales costs, you're entitled to the surplus. But don't count on getting anything.

Car Title Loans

A bank or other financial institution may agree to make a secured loan against the value of your car, called a "car title loan," "auto title pawn," or "car equity loan." You keep and drive the car, but the lender keeps the title as security for repayment of the loan, as well as a copy of your keys. These loans are dangerous, because missing even one payment can mean losing your car, even if the car is worth far more than the amount you owe. Lenders may also ask you to use your home, as well as your car, as collateral. This means that if you miss any payments, you risk losing your house as well as the car. These loans can come with a steep interest rate, because your car is considered a used car and its value rapidly decreases. For example, you might pay $63 to $181 for a one-month $500 title loan. Monthly finance charges of 25% (300% annual interest) are common. Online title lenders quote annual percentage rates (APRs) of up to 651%.

Auto title loan businesses often target members of the military. Under a new federal law, creditors cannot take a vehicle's title as security in any extension of consumer credit to active duty servicemembers or their dependents (other than purchase loans).

Payday Loans

Payday loans, deferred deposit loans, cash for checks—no matter what they're called, they're a very expensive way to borrow money. Here's how they work: You give the lender a check and get back less cash than the face value of the check. For example, if you give the lender a check for $300, it might give you $250 in cash and keep the remaining $50 as its fee. The lender will hold your check for a specified time, often two or three weeks until your payday. Then the loan is due, and you have three choices:

- Allow the lender to cash your $300 check, and you're done with the loan.

Based on the original $50 fee, you've paid 20% interest for a few weeks, which would be more than a 300% annual interest.

- Pay the lender $300 from some other source and take the check back. Again, you've paid 20% interest for several weeks.
- Extend the loan, usually by writing another postdated check or paying another fee ($50 in our example). At this point, you owe the lender $300 (the $250 borrowed plus the first $50 fee), plus a new fee of $50. So now you owe $350 on a $250 loan.

Many people who can't make the original check good describe a "treadmill of debt," because they must keep writing new checks to cover the fees that have accumulated, in addition to paying off the amount borrowed.

The same scenarios play out if the lender asks you to authorize automatic debits from your account. Payday loans have been a particular problem for members of the military in recent years. A new federal law limits to 36% the annual percentage rate (APR) that lenders can charge active duty service members or their dependents in extensions of consumer credit, including payday loans. This means, for example, that a payday lender cannot charge a servicemember more than $1.38 in interest on a $100 loan for two weeks.

To find out more about payday loans, visit the website of the National Consumer Law Center, www.nclc.org (select "Action Agenda," then "Payday Loans" for more information and details about each state's laws).

Scams That Target Military Personnel

Companies that offer payday loans, refund anticipation loans, auto title (auto pawn) loans, and rent-to-own, as well as used car dealers that emphasize in-house financing, cluster around military bases and advertise inside bases in official-looking military newspapers. These businesses target military personnel because servicemembers:

- have regular government paychecks
- are not subject to being laid off
- may be relatively young and economically unsophisticated
- are easy to track down, and
- are subject to military conduct codes that call for order in every part of their lives, including their finances.

Scams include excessive interest rates on purchases and excessive interest rates on loans (such as auto title and payday loans). Victims tend not to complain for fear of hurting their careers.

As explained above, a new federal law limits interest rates on payday loans to active duty personnel. It also limits the use of vehicle titles as security in credit extensions to active duty personnel (see "Car Title Loans," above). The Servicemembers Civil Relief Act provides additional protections, as explained in Chapter 6. Hopefully, these laws will reduce, perhaps substantially, the incentive to prey on active duty military personnel. As with all consumer scams, however, the best defense is to understand how the scams work and how to avoid them.

Debt-Consolidating and Debt Negotiating Companies

You have probably seen ads or billboards for companies that promise to "cut your debt in half" and combine all your debts into one easy, affordable payment. Be *very* careful about entering into any contract with these groups. Debt-consolidating companies—also called debt-pooling, budget-planning, debt-adjusting, or debt-prorating companies—often produce poor results. Although they may pay a few of your creditors, they may also siphon off your limited resources in debt consolidation charges and jeopardize much of your property. Some charge outrageously high interest; others charge ridiculously high fees. Some promise a "quick fix" to your financial problems, by which they mean filing for bankruptcy. Some are outright crooks that hide their high fees in the footnotes and misrepresent the loan terms (such as turning a 10% loan into a 20% loan at the time of closing).

Debt negotiation companies claim that they can negotiate with creditors on behalf of consumers, promising substantially reduced payments and an end to collection calls from creditors. Most consumers can do this on their own, without paying the debt negotiators' hefty fees. Instead of obtaining relief and working their way out of debt, consumers who rely on debt negotiation companies often wind up with even more negative information in their credit reports, and facing lawsuits by collectors. In extreme cases, companies reportedly have used consumers' money to pay operating expenses instead of the consumers' creditors. Even if the company provides the services promised, you're better off using the money you would have spent on negotiator fees to make payments to your creditors.

Some debt-consolidating companies may counsel you to refinance your house to pay off medical bills or credit cards. Doing so turns unsecured debt into secured debt—which is a very bad idea because it risks your home, which would otherwise be safe from those creditors. You'll also be socked with major up-front costs and fees.

Debt consolidators often claim that you'll save money with a home loan, but be sure to weigh the risks. They'll tell you that mortgage interest is tax-deductible. In fact, you would save money from a home loan only if you itemize deductions on your tax return, the costs of refinancing don't eat up the savings, and you meet all of the requirements for tax deductibility. (And don't forget the most significant risk: You'll be turning unsecured debt into secured debt, for which you could lose your home.)

If you're considering refinancing your home, first ask a tax professional on deductibility if any one of the following statements is true:

- The loans on your house will total more than your house is worth.
- You want to use $100,000 or more of the loan money on something other than your house.
- You are subject to the alternative minimum tax.

TIP

A good alternative to debt consolidators. Debt consolidation businesses are regulated in most states, but there are loopholes in the laws and not a lot of enforcement. A safer and less-expensive alternative is to find a reputable credit counseling agency. See Chapter 19 for more information.

■

The Consequences of Ignoring Your Debts

The payment of debts is necessary for social order. The nonpayment is quite equally necessary for social order. For centuries, humanity has oscillated, serenely unaware, between these two contradictory necessities.

—Simone Weil
Jewish labor organizer and mystic
1909-1943

This chapter discusses the consequences of ignoring your creditors completely. This is not usually a recommended strategy, but it's one many people follow—at least for a while. It also may be your only option for nonessential debts that you can't pay.

If you ignore your creditors long enough, they will probably take legal action to try and get either the money you owe or the secured property you pledged to guarantee repayment. You may lose some property, including your bank accounts, your car, a portion of your wages—and possibly your house.

But it's not always as bad as you might think. Exemption laws may protect essential property such as your clothing, public benefits, household goods, and most of your wages. (See Chapter 16 for more information.) And most important, for all debts (except possibly child support), no matter how much you owe, you won't lose your liberty unless you do something foolish that infuriates a judge, such as deliberately disobeying an order or lying in court or in a court document.

Eviction

If you don't have a legal reason for not paying your rent, your landlord can evict you. In many states, an eviction can take as long as a month or two. In other states, where the courts are not so busy or the laws favor landlords, the process can be as short as a couple of weeks. In every state, however, the landlord must begin by giving you a notice to pay or get out. If you do neither, the landlord can file a lawsuit. You then have a set number of days to respond (five is common), and then a week or two later the court holds a hearing.

Even if you ignore the lawsuit and the landlord gets a default judgment against you, the landlord must take that judgment to the local sheriff. Many states require that the sheriff give you a week's advance notice of when the eviction is scheduled. If you're not out by the selected day, the sheriff comes and gives you the boot.

Evictions don't always take a month, however. In states—or communities—with few protections for tenants, an eviction can take place even faster. The landlord gives you just a few days' notice to pay what you owe or defend in court, or you'll be on the street. And no matter where you live, a landlord can sue you for the back rent you owe.

To make matters worse, once you've been evicted, it will be harder for you to rent a new place once you're back on your feet. Specialized credit bureaus, often called tenant screening agencies, collect information from court records on eviction actions and report it to landlords when they check on prospective tenants. Most landlords consider being evicted, or even having an eviction action filed against you, a significant blot on your tenant history.

WARNING

Landlord-tenant rules vary throughout the country. Landlord-tenant rules vary tremendously from state to state, or even city to city. If paying your rent becomes a problem, seriously consider getting some help from a tenants' advocacy or other consumer group. Also, see *Every Tenants' Legal Guide* or *Renters' Rights*, both by Janet Portman and Marcia Stewart (Nolo), which suggest ways to deal with late rent and what happens in an eviction. If you think you have a defense to not paying your rent—for example, your living conditions are substandard—you can find out whether your state allows you to move out, withhold the rent, or repair the problem yourself and deduct the cost from the rent.

Foreclosure

If you get behind on your mortgage or home equity loan payments, the lender has the right to foreclose—force a sale of your house—to recover what you owe. But mortgage lenders don't always foreclose, even if they have the right. Foreclosing can be expensive and time-consuming, and the house often sells for only a part of what is owed.

There are two types of foreclosure: judicial and nonjudicial. They are vastly different. A judicial foreclosure requires the creditor to file an action in court, which typically gives you a year or more before you have to part with your property. Nonjudicial foreclosures do not go through a court and often can be carried out within a three- to four-month period.

Why do some foreclosures go through court while others don't? It depends on how the foreclosure came about. If the reason was a default in payments on a real estate loan that is secured by a deed of trust, the foreclosure process often occurs outside of court—that is, nonjudicially. (Most real estate loans involve deeds of trust.) On the other hand, if the foreclosure stems from a true mortgage or creditor's judgment against you in a lawsuit, the foreclosure probably will end up in court. (For a discussion of the difference between mortgages and deeds of trust, see "Mortgages and Deeds of Trust," below.)

Mortgages and Deeds of Trust

Some home loans are called mortgages. Others are secured by a deed of trust. Here's the difference:

Mortgage. A loan in which you put up the title to real estate as security for the loan. If you don't pay back the debt on time, the lender can foreclose on the real estate and have it sold through a court proceeding to pay off the loan.

Deed of trust. An alternative method of financing a real estate purchase. The deed of trust transfers the title to the property to a trustee, often a title company, who holds it as security for a loan. If you default on the loan, the trustee can sell the property at auction and pay the lender from the proceeds without going to court. Deeds of trust are often used in the West.

The judicial foreclosure process varies enormously from state to state, while the process for nonjudicial foreclosures tends to be more standardized.

Notice of Missed Payments

The foreclosure process starts after you stop paying your loan on time. After you miss a payment or two, the lender will send you a letter reminding you that your payment is late and imposing a late fee—often 5% or 6% of the payment. If you still don't pay up, the lender will typically send more letters and often call, demanding payment.

Notice of Default

If you don't pay or contact the lender to discuss your situation, after about 60–90 days the lender will typically send you a formal notice telling you that it has declared your loan in default. This notice, often called a Notice of Default, states that foreclosure proceedings will begin unless payment is received. These notices are required by state law.

Time to Cure Default

After the lender sends you the Notice of Default, you usually have approximately 90 days to "cure" the default and reinstate the loan; that is, to pay all your missed payments, late fees, and other charges. If you don't cure the default, you will typically have to refinance the entire loan to hold on to the home, although some lenders will reinstate the loan any time before the sale, if you make all payments to bring the loan current.

Notice of Sale

Once the period for curing the default has passed, you usually receive a Notice of Sale that sets a sale date 15 to 30 days in the future. Lenders usually are required to advertise the home for sale (after giving you the notice of default and other required notices). The sale must be conducted in public and usually involves an auction procedure. See "The Sale," below.

In order to challenge a nonjudicial foreclosure, you must file a lawsuit asking the court to stop the sale of your house. In most cases, you will need an attorney's assistance to do this.

Alternatives to Foreclosure

You may be able to avoid the actual foreclosure and often minimize the damage to your credit rating by selling the house before it is sold through the foreclosure process. Many buyer-investors purchase houses about to go into foreclosure, but they are not willing to pay—and you shouldn't expect to get—top dollar.

Some will pay enough to cover what you owe your lender, but you are likely to lose whatever equity you have in your house. And others will offer you less than what you owe. If you can convince your lender to take a "short sale"—that is, to let you sell the property for less than what you owe and

Beware of Foreclosure Scams

Once the foreclosure process starts, you are likely to be contacted by all sorts of people and companies offering help. Some will be legitimate; others won't. Many unscrupulous people make money by taking advantage of people facing foreclosure.

Don't get taken by "equity skimmers" or "foreclosure consultants," who often prey on people facing foreclosure. Equity skimmers try to buy houses for a small fraction of their market value, often through misrepresentation, deceit, or intimidation. Foreclosure consultants promise to help homeowners in foreclosure, charge high fees for little or no service, and then purchase the home for a fraction of its value.

Foreclosure scams flourish in times such as these, when foreclosures are on the rise. Don't be so desperate that you unwittingly sign away your home to one of these vultures. If you need help, seek counseling through the federal Department of Housing and Urban Development program (www.hud.gov) or a reputable nonprofit organization such as Consumer Credit Counseling Service (see Chapter 19).

A recent national study found that foreclosure scams fall into three general categories. These scams rely on the homeowner's desperation and ignorance for their success. They also often rely on the homeowner's faith in humanity ("No one would kick me when I'm down") or shared heritage or national origin ("Someone of my culture wouldn't trick me"). The more you know about these scams, the less likely you are to fall victim to one of them, so here are brief summaries of the three types:

- **Phantom rescue:** The scammer charges excessive fees for a few phone calls or a little paperwork that the homeowner could have done and for a promise of representation that never happens. The scammer abandons the homeowner when the time for reinstatement—which should have been used to get current on the loan, negotiate with the lender, or find effective assistance—runs out. The foreclosure then proceeds.

- **Bailout:** The scammer tells the homeowner to surrender title to the house, with the promise that he or she can rent it and buy it back from the scammer later. The homeowner may be told that surrender of the title is necessary so that someone with better credit can get new financing to save the house. The terms of the buyback are so onerous that the homeowner can't buy the house back, and the rescuer pockets the equity.

- **Bait and switch:** Here, the homeowner doesn't realize that he or she is surrendering title to the house in exchange for the promised rescue. The scammer may trick the homeowner into surrendering title (perhaps when signing new loan documents), or may simply forge the homeowner's signature on the deed. The scammer then keeps the house or sells it and keeps the profit.

write off the rest—you'll probably be able to avoid foreclosure.

Loan Acceleration

In most states, if you don't cure the default or sell the house during the time allowed, the lender "accelerates" the loan. When a lender accelerates a loan, the total amount of the loan becomes due. At this point, the only way you can keep your home in most states is to pay off the entire outstanding loan balance. This is called "redeeming" the loan. Usually, if you are in financial trouble, the only way to pay off the entire loan balance is to refinance the loan. Think carefully before doing so. You don't want to end up with another loan you can't afford. (See Chapter 6 for more information on refinancing home loans.)

In many (but not all) states, in order to accelerate the loan, the lender must send you a notice of acceleration. If you get a notice of acceleration, be warned: The lender is serious about foreclosing and will probably move quickly to do so.

WARNING

A short sale could increase your tax bill. Any time a lender writes off $600 or more of the principal you owe, the lender must report it to the IRS on a Form 1099-C or 1099-A, a report of miscellaneous income. This means you generally must include the written-off portion of the debt as income on your tax return the following tax year,

unless you are insolvent or eliminate the debt in bankruptcy. See "Beware of the IRS If You Settle a Debt" in Chapter 6 for more information.

Overview of Judicial Foreclosures

As mentioned, the process for judicial foreclosures varies from state to state. If your state requires a lender to get a court order in order to foreclose (see "Mortgages and Deeds of Trust," above), you will receive a summons or other notice. The notice will explain your rights, including how much time you have to respond to the attached court papers. You have the right to challenge the legality of the foreclosure in court. See "Defenses to Foreclosure," below, and consult an attorney if you might have a reason to stop or delay foreclosure. If you don't respond to the papers or you lose in court, the court will issue a judgment to the lender, permitting it to hold a foreclosure sale.

The Sale

Once the lender has a court order permitting it to sell the house (if required), it publishes a notice of the sale in a newspaper in the county where your house is located. The notice includes information about the loan and the time and location of the sale—in most states, the sale must take place at least three to five weeks after the notice is published.

At the foreclosure sale, anyone with a financial interest in your house will probably attend. This includes the first, second, and even third mortgage (or deed of trust) holders and any creditor (such as the IRS or a contractor) that has placed a lien on your house. Investors who like to purchase distressed property (real estate lingo for property that's been through foreclosure) will also be present.

The lender who foreclosed makes the first bid, usually for the amount owed but often for less. It may seem like the lender is bidding to buy the house from itself. Both you and the lender have ownership interest in the house, however, and by bidding, the lender is essentially buying you out. If the house sells for more than you owe creditors who have a security interest in your house, you're entitled to the excess. But the foreclosing lender first gets to deduct the costs of foreclosing and selling, usually several thousand dollars. Don't expect to leave a foreclosure sale with money in your pocket.

Any other lender or lienholder will get worried if the foreclosing lender's bid is the only one, because that bid covers only what that lender is owed. If the sale goes through at that price, the other lenders and lienholders will get nothing from the sale. So if your property is worth more than the amount the foreclosing lender bid, another lender or lienholder may bid to protect her interest. So might a potential buyer who sees that the property's value exceeds the amount owed the lenders and lienholders. The house is sold to the highest bidder.

EXAMPLE: Steve's house is worth $210,000, though he paid only $120,000 for it ten years ago. He has now hit hard times. He owes the original lender $74,000. A few years back he took out a home equity loan and owes that lender $35,000. He also owes the IRS $43,000 in back taxes, interest, and penalties. Thus, Steve's creditors are owed a total of $152,000.

The foreclosing lender starts the bidding at $74,000. The holder of the home equity loan then bids $109,000 (the amount of the original loan plus the home equity loan). The successful bid is by an investor for $165,000, $45,000 less than the house is worth, but enough to pay off the $152,000 due to Steve's creditors who have a security interest in his house. Most of the $13,000 balance is used to cover the costs of the foreclosure sale. Because the house is worth $210,000, the investor enjoys a tidy "profit" of $45,000, assuming it can later sell the house at full value.

If no one bids more than the foreclosing lender at the sale, the house reverts to the lender for the amount of its bid. In many states, the successful bidder doesn't actually get title to the house for a period of time, from several days to several months, known as the redemption period. During that period, you can "redeem" the property, by paying the foreclosing lender the entire balance you owe it, plus the lender's costs. A one-bid foreclosure is more likely in very depressed markets. In stronger markets, however, investors or other buyers will probably bid.

Defenses to Foreclosure

You may be able to delay or stop the foreclosure if you have defenses to paying the mortgage or the lender has not properly followed state foreclosure procedures. If you think you might have a defense to foreclosure, contact a lawyer immediately. Some possible defenses are:

- **Violations of the federal Truth in Lending law.** The federal Truth in Lending law requires the lender to provide certain information about your loan before you sign the papers. If the lender failed to provide this information, you may be able to cancel the mortgage. This right to cancel applies only to loans *not* used to purchase your home. (See Chapter 4 for more on this law.)

- **Home improvement fraud.** If you took out a mortgage to finance improvements to your home, and the contractor ripped you off (for example, the work was shoddy or incomplete), you may be able to cancel the loan.

- **Interest rates or loan terms that violate state or federal law.** Some states limit how much interest can be charged on a loan. Federal law prohibits lenders from making deceptive or false representations about the loan and from charging high closing costs and fees. And for certain very expensive loans, federal law requires extra disclosures and prohibits some terms, like balloon payments. (See Chapter 11 for more on these expensive loans.) If your interest is very high or your lender didn't tell you the truth about the terms of your loan, consult a lawyer.

- **Failure to follow foreclosure procedures.** Each state requires lenders to follow specific procedures when foreclosing on a home. If the lender doesn't follow these rules (for example, by not giving proper notice of the foreclosure or failing to inform you of certain rights), you may be able to delay the foreclosure.

- **Automatic stay in bankruptcy.** The filing of a bankruptcy petition automatically stays or stops foreclosure proceedings, at least temporarily. See Chapter 15 for more information.

Finding defenses to foreclosure is not easy. Nor is raising these defenses in court. If you think you might have a defense to foreclosure, consult an attorney. (See Chapter 19 for information on how to find a lawyer.)

Watch Out for Deficiency Balances

A deficiency balance is the difference between what you owe the foreclosing lender and what the lender received at the sale. In many states, if the sale doesn't cover what you owe, the lender is entitled to a "deficiency" for the difference. The lender usually must schedule a court hearing and present evidence of the value of the property to obtain the deficiency.

Any balance owed to "junior" lienholders—creditors whose liens were filed after the foreclosing lender's lien was filed—are extinguished by the sale. Therefore, there is no deficiency owed to those creditors.

A lender with a deficiency can use the collection techniques covered in Chapter 9 and will often accept less than the full amount if you can offer a lump sum settlement. If you owe a lot of money, or there's an easy target for collection (such as a large bank account or monthly wages), the lender is likely to pass your debt to a collection agency or a lawyer (to sue you).

One possible way to avoid a deficiency balance is to deed the property back to the lender in lieu of foreclosure. (This strategy is discussed in Chapter 6.) If the lender agrees to accept the deed, the lender is essentially agreeing that the amount you owe equals the current value of the property, eliminating any deficiency balance. One catch, however, is that the IRS will probably consider the amount of the deficiency forgiven by the lender taxable income to you and require you to report it on your tax return. Also, the "deed in lieu" will be a black mark on your credit report for seven years.

Finally, if you plan to file for bankruptcy, you probably don't need to worry about a deficiency balance, because you will probably be able to discharge it in the bankruptcy.

Repossession

As explained in Chapter 1, a secured debt is one for which a specific item of property—called collateral—guarantees payment of the debt. If you don't pay a debt secured by personal property, the creditor has the right to take the property pledged as collateral for the loan. The creditor can't just walk into your house and take your couch, however; the creditor must have a court order or permission from someone in your household to enter your home.

There are two basic kinds of secured debts: voluntary security interests and liens. They are described in detail in Chapter 1, which also describes limits on creditors taking security interests in household goods. Creditors who don't have a security interest in an item of property can't take it without approval of a judge or court clerk. (See below.)

What Constitutes a Default?

Unless your contract says otherwise, if you miss even one payment, you have defaulted on your loan and, under most security agreements, the creditor is entitled to take the goods. If you make your payments but otherwise fail to comply with an important term of the security agreement, the creditor can declare you in default and take the property. Be sure to read the security agreement's fine print carefully. Sometimes lenders have the right to declare a secured debt in default, even if you're all paid up. This may happen in any of the following cases:

- You sell the collateral.
- The collateral is destroyed or stolen, or its value substantially depreciates.
- You let required insurance lapse— some lenders require that you have collision and comprehensive insurance on motor vehicles, or that you buy credit life or credit disability insurance.
- You become insolvent (as defined by your lender).
- You refuse to let the creditor examine the collateral at its request.
- The creditor feels that the prospect of your paying is uncertain.

When You Have Defaulted

Whether a creditor has to notify you before it takes your property depends on what state you live in and on the terms of your original agreement with the creditor. Unless the contract specifically says otherwise, the creditor must notify you that it has accelerated the debt and that the full contract amount is due. This advance warning can give you time to figure out a plan. However, in many contracts, you waive the right to receive advance notice. In some cases you can challenge these waiver clauses, but you will likely need the assistance of an attorney to do so.

Fortunately for consumers, many states require creditors to notify you of a "right to cure" the default. If you want to take advantage of the "right to cure," you must do so before the debt is accelerated and the property is repossessed. You get a certain period of time (usually a few weeks) to pay all missed payments and any late charges, get required insurance, or otherwise rectify the situation that caused the default. You will need to research your state law to see if you have a right to cure where you live. (See Chapter 19 for information on how to research your state law.)

A few states prohibit creditors from repossessing property without first getting a court order. Some Native American tribes have also passed tribal laws prohibiting repossessions without court orders.

But even outside of these states, a creditor is unlikely to go ahead and take your property unless you have defaulted in the past, have missed several payments, or are uncooperative, or the creditor has learned something worrisome about your finances.

You can voluntarily return the collateral, but the creditor doesn't have to take it. And he or she probably won't if it's worth far less than you owe. If you want to give the property back, first call the creditor—ask to speak to someone in the collections department—and find out whether your entire debt will be canceled when the collateral is returned. If the creditor agrees to cancel the entire debt, get written confirmation. Also find out whether the creditor will refrain from reporting the default on your credit report. If the entire

States That Limit Deficiency Balances After Foreclosure

State	Code Section	Limits on Deficiency Balances After Foreclosure
Alaska	Alaska Stat. §§ 34-20-100, 09-45-180	If foreclosure is under deed of trust, debtor is not liable for deficiency. If foreclosure is made under mortgage, debtor is liable for deficiency.
Arizona	Ariz. Rev. Stat. §§ 33-729, 33-814	If foreclosure is by original lender on property of 2½ acres or less with a single one- or two-family residence, debtor is not liable for deficiency unless decrease in value is due to debtor's neglect. If foreclosure is under deed of trust on property of 2½ acres or less with a single one- or two-family residence, debtor is not liable for deficiency; on all other deed of trust foreclosures, lender has 90 days to begin proceedings to recover deficiency.
Arkansas	Ark. Code Ann. §§ 18-49-105, 18-50-112	If foreclosure is under deed of trust, lender has 12 months to begin proceedings to recover deficiency.
California	Cal. Civ. Proc. Code §§ 580a, 580b, 580d, 725a, 726	In nonjudicial foreclosures on a mortgage or deed of trust, debtors are not liable for a deficiency. For other liens, the newly unsecured creditor could sue to try to collect on the underlying debt. In some circumstances, judicial foreclosures permit deficiency judgments.
	Cal. Health & Safety Code § 18038.7	If foreclosure is made by original lender under mortgage or deed of trust on a floating home that serves as a residence for no more than four families (including debtor), debtor is not liable for deficiency.
Connecticut	Conn. Gen. Stat. Ann. § 49-14	If foreclosure is under mortgage, lender has 30 days to begin proceedings to recover deficiency.
Florida	Fla. Stat. Ann. §§ 702.06 to 702.065	If original lender buys foreclosed property at sale, lender is entitled only to deficiency set by court and may not sue debtor. If foreclosure is uncontested, debtor not liable for deficiency.
Georgia	Ga. Code Ann. § 44-14-161	If foreclosure is under mortgage or deed of trust, lender must obtain order of approval from superior court within 30 days of sale and must give debtor at least five days' notice of court hearing, or debtor is not liable for deficiency.

States That Limit Deficiency Balances After Foreclosure (continued)		
State	**Code Section**	**Limits on Deficiency Balances After Foreclosure**
Hawaii	Haw. Rev. Stat. § 667-38	In alternate foreclosure by sale (lender must be a bank, credit union, or institutional investor and must hold two open houses), debtor not liable for deficiency (applies to mortgages and loans created after 7/1/1999).
Idaho	Idaho Code § 45-1512	If foreclosure is under deed of trust, lender has three months to begin proceedings to recover deficiency.
Illinois	735 Ill. Comp. Stat. §§ 5/15-1401 to -1402	If debtor and lender agree to voluntary foreclosure, debtor is not liable for deficiency. If foreclosure is under deed of trust, debtor is not liable for deficiency.
Indiana	Ind. Code Ann. § 32-30-10-4	If foreclosure is under mortgage, there must be an agreement either in the mortgage or in a separate contract for the exact payment due, or lender may not collect deficiency.
Iowa	Iowa Code Ann. §§ 628.26, .27; 654.20, .26	Debtor is not liable for deficiency: 1) if property is less than ten acres, and 2a) both parties agree to a redemption period of six months, or 2b) property is abandoned and the redemption period is reduced to 60 days. If property is a one- or two-family personal residence and lender chooses to foreclose without a redemption period, debtor is not liable for deficiency.
Kansas	Kan. Stat. Ann. § 40-3511	If debtor has mortgage insurance for a single-family owner-occupied residence, debtor is not liable to insurance company for any deficiency after foreclosure sale.
Maine	Me. Rev. Stat. Ann. tit. 14, §§ 6203-D to 6203-E	Debtor is not liable for deficiency unless: 1) at least 21 days before the foreclosure sale lender sends debtor a notice of the sale which includes a statement that debtor is liable for deficiency; 2) within 30 days of sale lender submits affidavit that notice was sent. Lender has two years to begin proceedings to recover deficiency.
Massachusetts	Mass. Gen. Laws Ann. Ch. 244, §§ 17A to 17B	Debtor is not liable for deficiency unless: 1) at least 21 days before the foreclosure sale lender sends debtor a notice of the sale which includes a statement that debtor is liable for deficiency; 2) within 30 days of sale lender submits affidavit that notice was sent. Lender has two years to begin proceedings to recover deficiency.

States That Limit Deficiency Balances After Foreclosure (continued)

State	Code Section	Limits on Deficiency Balances After Foreclosure
Minnesota	Minn. Stat. Ann. §§ 582.30 to 582.32, 582.032, 580.23	Debtor not liable for deficiency in the following situations: 1) redemption period is six months; 2) redemption period is five weeks on property that is less than 10 acres, not used for agriculture, and abandoned; 3) debtor and lender have agreed to voluntary foreclosure. If property is used for agriculture, lender has 90 days to begin proceedings to recover deficiency and three years to collect.
Mississippi	Miss. Code Ann. § 15-1-23	Lender has one year to begin proceedings to recover deficiency.
Montana	Mont. Code Ann. §§ 71-1-232, 71-1-317	If foreclosure is made by original lender under mortgage, debtor is not liable for deficiency. If foreclosure is under deed of trust, debtor is not liable for deficiency.
Nebraska	Neb. Rev. Stat. § 76-1013	If foreclosure is under deed of trust, lender has three months to begin proceedings to recover deficiency.
Nevada	Nev. Rev. Stat. §§ 40.455, 40.457	If lender foreclosed on single piece of property, lender has six months to begin proceedings to recover deficiency. If lender foreclosed on more than one piece of property, lender has two years to begin proceedings to recover deficiency.
New Jersey	N.J. Stat. Ann. §§ 2A:50-2, 2A:50-2.1	Lender has three months to begin proceedings to recover deficiency.
New Mexico	N.M. Rev. Stat. Ann. § 48-10-17	If foreclosure is under deed of trust, lender has 12 months to begin proceedings to recover deficiency. Low-income households are not liable for deficiency.
New York	N.Y. Real Prop. Acts. Law §§ 1371, 1419	Lender has 90 days to begin proceedings to recover deficiency. (This 1998 law was repealed effective July 1, 2005. You can do some legal research to learn whether state legislature extended the law.)
North Carolina	N.C. Gen. Stat. § 45-21.38	If foreclosure is under deed of trust or mortgage, debtor is not liable for deficiency.
North Dakota	N.D. Cent. Code § 32-19-06	Lender has 90 days to begin proceedings to recover deficiency and three years to collect. Fair value of the property must be determined by jury.

States That Limit Deficiency Balances After Foreclosure (continued)		
State	**Code Section**	**Limits on Deficiency Balances After Foreclosure**
Ohio	Ohio Rev. Code Ann. § 2329.08	If foreclosure is on residence property for one or two families, lender has two years to collect deficiency.
Oklahoma	Okla. Stat. Ann. tit. 12, § 686; tit. 46, § 43(c)	If debtor notifies lender that property is a homestead 10 days before foreclosure sale, debtor is not liable for deficiency. If debtor does not send notice or if lender contests homestead status of property, lender has 90 days to begin proceedings to collect deficiency.
Oregon	Or. Rev. Stat. §§ 86.770, 88.070	If foreclosure is on a first mortgage on a primary or secondary personal residence, debtor is not liable for deficiency. If foreclosure is under deed of trust, debtor is not liable for deficiency.
Pennsylvania	42 Pa. Cons. Stat. Ann. §§ 5522(b)(2), 8103	Lender has six months to begin proceedings to recover deficiency.
South Carolina	S.C. Code Ann. §§ 15-39-760, 29-3-660	If foreclosure is under mortgage, bidding must remain open for 30 days after sale, unless lender agrees not to claim deficiency.
South Dakota	S.D. Codified Laws Ann. §§ 44-8-20, 21-48A-1, 21-47-16, 21-49-27	If foreclosure is by original lender, debtor is not liable for deficiency. If debtor and lender agree to voluntary foreclosure, debtor is not liable for deficiency. In other mortgage foreclosures where lender is bidding on the foreclosed property, lender must bid the amount of debt remaining or get a court appraisal of fair market value and bid that in order to get deficiency.
Texas	Tex. Prop. Code Ann. §§ 51.003 to .004	If foreclosure is under mortgage, lender has two years to begin proceedings to recover deficiency; if foreclosure is under deed of trust, lender has 90 days to begin proceedings to recover deficiency.
Utah	Utah Code Ann. § 57-1-32	If foreclosure is under deed of trust, lender has three months to begin proceedings to recover deficiency.
Washington	Wash. Rev. Code Ann. §§ 61.12.093 to .095, 61.24.100	If foreclosure is on property that is not used primarily for agriculture and has been abandoned for six months, debtor is not liable for deficiency. If foreclosure is under deed of trust, debtor is not liable for deficiency.

Current as of February 2007

debt isn't canceled, there probably isn't much point in returning the item, as you'll be liable for the difference between what the collateral sells for and what you owe.

How Motor Vehicles Are Repossessed

The first property most lenders go after is a motor vehicle, especially if the loan agreement was to finance the purchase of a new car or truck. In a number of states, however, the lender must first send you notice of the default and give you the right to make up the payments, called a right to "cure," before repossessing your car.

In addition, a repossession company can't use force to get to your vehicle—repossessions must occur without any breach of the peace. Unfortunately, "breach of the peace" is defined very broadly. It's legal for a repossessor to hotwire a car. It's legal to use a duplicate key and take a car. Most courts have said it's legal to remove a car from a carport or an open garage (meaning the door is up). In most states, it's legal to take a car from a garage if the door is closed but unlocked, but a few cautious repossessors won't do this. It's illegal to break into a locked garage, even by using a duplicate key. But a repossessor might anyway, especially in parts of the country where the repossession won't be nullified and all the lender will be required to do is fix the lock.

To take your car, the repossession company will have to find it. The lender will supply the repossessor with your home and work addresses, and any other useful information (such as where you attend school). Many

vehicle purchase and lease agreements today authorize the lessor to use the vehicle's electronic locating device to locate the vehicle. If the repossessor finds the car in your driveway or on the street in front of your house, the repossessor will wait until you're asleep or out, use a master key or hotwire it, and then drive away.

If the car isn't near your house, the repossessor will search the neighborhood. Many debtors, fearful of having their car repossessed, park it about three blocks from their home. This is the distance they figure is far enough away to be hard to find, but close enough to still be convenient to use. Repossessors know this trick, however, and often find a car within ten minutes after starting to search. Knowing this, some people leave their car in a neighbor's locked garage, an approach that will frustrate the repossessor at least for a little while. If, however, a court finds that you acted in bad faith, you may lose your right to get the car back if and when it's finally found.

Although it might seem otherwise, the repossession company does not have unlimited power to take your car. If you or someone else (like a relative) objects at the time the repossessor tries to take your car, he or she must stop. However, this doesn't mean you get to keep your car. The repossessor can try again another day or get a court order to take the car.

How Other Property Is Taken or Repossessed

Few creditors use their collections personnel or hire repossessors to take back personal property other than motor vehicles, for these reasons:

- The loan is often for only a few thousand dollars or less.
- The property may be worth far less than you owe.
- The repossessor will have a hard time getting into your house.

A few major department stores encourage debtors to return property. If the property is less than a year old, ask if they'll credit your account for 100% of what you owe if you return the property voluntarily. (This means that your entire balance is wiped out, even if the property is worth less than the amount you owe.)

If the lender hires repossessors to take back the property, you don't have to give it back or let them into your house unless a sheriff shows up with a court order telling you to do so. If, however, the property is sitting in the backyard—for example, a new gas barbecue and lawn furniture—it's generally fair game. But the repossessor can't use force to get into your house or to take your backyard furniture—for example, you can't be thrown out of a lawn chair. Some repossessors will jump a fence or even pick a lock, but most won't enter the premises unless they are invited or have a court order. Entering your house when you are away with a duplicate key to take your refrigerator or living room sofa is seldom done by repossessors, because it is illegal. As stated above, repossessions must occur without any breach of the peace.

As with car repossessions, if you or a member of your family ask the repossessor to leave your property, and the repossessor doesn't, this is a breach of the peace. So is using abusive language or violence or showing up with a gun-carrying sheriff in an effort to intimidate you. But lying or tricking you usually isn't a breach of the peace.

Can You Get Your Property Back?

If your car or other property is taken, some states give you a short time during which you can get it back by reinstating the contract. Reinstatement means getting the property back and resuming the payments under the terms of the original agreement. In order to reinstate, you must fix the problem that caused the creditor to declare the default—for example, by paying all past-due payments and late fees, getting required insurance coverage, or paying unpaid fines or taxes—and pay the costs the lender has incurred in taking and storing the property, often a few hundred dollars. The right to reinstate is limited, however, and, depending on your state law, you probably can't get the property back if you:

- had the contract reinstated in the past
- lied on your credit application
- hid the property to avoid repossession, or
- didn't take care of the property and its value has substantially diminished.

The lender must give you notice of your right to reinstate the contract after repossession, even if the lender thinks you have given up the right. If the lender doesn't give you this notice, you may have the right to get the property back for nothing—but you will have to resume making payments on your loan. If you have been given notice and want to try to reinstate the contract, contact the lender as soon as possible to work out an agreement.

If you don't reinstate the contract within the time permitted by the agreement, the lender will send you a formal notice of its intent to sell the property.

Although only some states allow you to reinstate the contract, every state allows you to redeem the property. There are important differences between reinstatement and redeeming. Reinstatement allows you to get the property back by paying past-due amounts or otherwise fixing the problem that caused the default, and paying repossession costs. In addition, you can reinstate only within a specific period of time after the repossession. To redeem property, you must pay the entire balance of the contract (instead of just the past amounts due) plus repossession and storage costs. You can redeem property any time before it is sold.

Despite its seeming advantages, redemption is rarely feasible. If you couldn't make payments in the first place, you probably can't come up with the entire balance due under the contract. Some people take out a home equity loan to get the money. This is dangerous: If you default on the home equity loan, you might end up losing your house instead of the personal property. Redemption might make sense if the property, such as your car, is essential to your livelihood and you can get someone to help you come up with the money to redeem it.

Personal Property in Repossessed Motor Vehicles

If the repossessor takes your motor vehicle, you're entitled to get back all your personal belongings inside of, but not attached to, the vehicle when it was repossessed. This means that you can get back your gym shorts, but not the $500 stereo system you installed. (You are entitled to a removable radio, however.) Also, make sure you look at your loan agreement. Some say that you must make that request within 24 hours of the repossession. Although such time limits may not hold up in court, it's safest to act quickly. Promptly contact the lender after your vehicle is repossessed and ask that your property be returned. Put the request in writing and list everything you left in the car. If the lender is uncooperative—which is unlikely—consider suing in small claims court.

Beware of Deficiency Balances

If you don't reinstate or redeem the property within the time provided in the lender's notice of its intent to sell the property, the property will be sold. If the proceeds don't cover the total of what you owe—and they never do—you may be liable for the balance, called a deficiency.

FAST TRACK

If you're planning to file for bankruptcy. If you're planning to file for bankruptcy, you probably don't have to worry about any deficiency—it will likely be wiped out in your bankruptcy case.

The lender must send you a notice that the property will be sold and must give the date, time, and location of the sale. The notice must also tell you whether you are liable for any deficiency and must provide a phone number where you can find out how much you still owe. You are entitled to attend the sale and bid. There are two kinds of sales: a public sale, which is open to anyone; or a private sale, to which the lender invites only certain people who it feels might be interested. A private sale can only be held if the item "is of a type customarily sold in a recognized market" or "is the subject of widely distributed standard price quotations." Cars are frequently sold at private sales to which used car dealers and others who regularly buy repossessed cars are invited. If the notice doesn't give you the date and location of the sale, call the lender and find out.

The law requires that the lender conduct every aspect of the disposition of the vehicle in a "commercially reasonable" manner, but no one knows quite what that means. In fact, repossession sales are often attended only by used car dealers, who have a motive to keep the bids very low. This is one reason why most property sold at repossession sales brings in far less than the lender is owed.

For instance, a car valued at $12,000 might sell for $5,000, and a refrigerator worth $800 might sell for $250. And even though you could have sold the item for twice as much, the sale usually will be considered "commercially reasonable." If you attend, you can bid (if you have the cash), but the dealers are apt to outbid you.

After the item is sold, the sale price is subtracted from what you owe the lender. Then, the cost of repossessing, storing, and selling the property is added to the difference. Very often, you are liable for that balance: the deficiency balance.

Here's one suggestion for avoiding a deficiency balance: If your property, especially a motor vehicle, is about to be repossessed, ask for a contract reinstatement just to get the vehicle back so you can sell it yourself. Even if you get $7,000 for a $9,000 car, it's better than the lender repossessing it and selling it for $3,000. You can use the $7,000 to pay off your lender and will owe only $2,000 more, far less than the $6,000 you'd owe if the lender sold it through repossession.

Some lenders will forgive or write off the deficiency balance if you clearly have no assets. Where the amount forgiven is $600 or more, the lender will issue you a Form 1099-C or 1099-A, and the IRS will expect you to report the forgiven balance as income on your tax return.

If the lender doesn't forgive or write off the balance, expect dunning letters and phone calls, probably from a collection agency.

States That Don't Impose Deficiency Balances on Personal Property

State	Code Section	When Deficiency Balance Prohibited
Alabama	Ala. Code § 5-19-13	If you paid $1,000 or less for the collateral.
Arizona	Ariz. Rev. Stat. § 44-5501	If you paid $1,000 or less for the collateral.
California	Cal. Civil Code § 1812.5	If you bought goods on installment.
	Cal. Health & Safety Code § 18038.7	On a mobile home, manufactured home, commercial coach, truck camper, or floating home.
Colorado	Colo. Rev. Stat. § 5-5-103	If you paid $3,000 or less for the collateral.
Connecticut	Conn. Gen. Stat. § 36a-785(f),(g)	All repossession sales except for cars or boats with a cash price over $2,000.
Dist. of Col.	D.C. Code Ann. § 28-3812(e)	If you paid $2,000 or less for the collateral.
Florida	Fla. Stat. Ann. § 516.31(3)	If you paid $2,000 or less for the collateral.
Idaho	Idaho Code § 28-45-103(3)	If you paid $1,000 or less for the collateral.
Indiana	Ind. Code Ann. § 24-4.5-5-103; 750 Ind. Admin. Code § 1-1-1	If you paid $3,300 or less for the collateral.
Kansas	Kan. Stat. Ann. § 16a-5-103	If you paid $1,000 or less for the collateral.
Louisiana	La. Rev. Stat. Ann. § 13:4108.2	If the seller does not get an appraisal before the sale, unless you have agreed in writing to a sale without an appraisal.
Maine	Me. Rev. Stat. Ann. tit. 9-A § 5-103	If you paid $2,800 or less for the collateral.
Maryland	Md. Com. Law § 12-626	If you paid $2,000 or less for the collateral.
Massachusetts	Mass. Gen. Laws ch. 255, § 13J(e)	If unpaid balance is under $2,000.
Minnesota	Minn. Stat. Ann. § 325G.22	If amount financed was $5,700 or less.
Missouri	Mo. Rev. Stat. § 408.556	If amount financed was $500 or less.
Nebraska	Neb. Rev. Stat. § 45-1054	If unpaid balance is $3,000 or less.
Oklahoma	14A Okla. Stat. Ann. § 5-103	If you paid $3,800 or less for the collateral.
South Carolina	S.C. Code Ann. § 37-5-103	If you paid $4,200 or less for the collateral.
Utah	Utah Code Ann. § 70C-7-101	If you paid $3,000 or less for the collateral.
West Virginia	W.Va. Code Ann. § 46A-2-119	If unpaid balance is $1,000 or less.
Wisconsin	Wis. Stat. § 425.209	If unpaid balance is $1,000 or less.
Wyoming	Wyo. Stat. Ann. § 40-14-503	If you paid $1,000 or less for the collateral.

Current as of February 2007

In half the states (see "States That Don't
Impose Deficiency Balances on Personal
Property," above), you won't be liable for
a deficiency balance if the amount you
originally paid is less than a few thousand
dollars. (If your state is not on the chart
above, it means the state does not place
additional limits on deficiency balances after
repossession.) Given the price of cars, you will
almost always be liable for a deficiency if a
motor vehicle is taken.

If a lender sues you instead of repossessing
the property, you are not likely to be liable
for any deficiency.

It is common for creditors to make mistakes in the repossession process. Most
states bar creditors from collecting a
deficiency balance if they fail to comply with
notice requirements (such as notifying you of
the right to cure or of the sale) or didn't sell
the property in a commercially reasonable
manner. If you think the creditor made a
mistake, you must raise this defense at the
time you are sued for the deficiency balance.
Because these cases can be complex, it's a
good idea to consult a lawyer.

If the creditor sues you, you should file
an answer with the court. Your first line of
defense is to review how your repossession
was handled. You can argue that the creditor
isn't entitled to a deficiency if it didn't inform
you about your right to cure the default or
redeem the property (if you live in a state

where you have these rights), didn't sell the
item in a commercially reasonable manner,
or didn't give you the date and location of
the sale.

If you'd rather take the offensive, you can
sue the lender for wrongful repossession.
For large items, such as cars, you'll probably
need a lawyer. But for smaller items, you
can probably represent yourself in small
claims court. (See Chapter 14 for more
information.)

Prejudgment Attachment of Unsecured Property

Prejudgment attachment is a legal procedure
that lets a creditor tie up property before
obtaining a court judgment. It is the *unsecured
creditor's* way of telling the world that the
property covered by the attachment can be
used to pay the creditor if it wins in court.
(*Secured creditors* don't need to attach your
property, because they can just repossess it
if you don't pay. See "Repossession," above.)

Creditors may especially try to attach
your property if you live out of state or have
fled the state, or if the creditor believes you
are about to spend, sell, or conceal your
property.

In most states, a prejudgment attachment
works like this: When the creditor is about
to sue you, it prepares a document called
a "writ of attachment," listing the property
you own that it believes you are hiding
or about to sell, or that someone else is
keeping for you. In some states, the creditor
must file a bond in order to get a writ of
attachment. The writ of attachment must be

approved by a judge or court clerk. Writs are usually approved as long as there is no dispute that the property to be attached is yours. Then the creditor serves it on you and on everyone it thinks has some of your property. (Serving means providing a copy.) Usually, you must be hand-delivered a copy, but in some cases the creditor can just mail it to you. The most common property to attach is deposit accounts: savings, checking, money markets, certificates of deposit, and the like.

Serving the writ freezes your property—the holder of your property can't let you sell it, give it away, or, in the case of deposit accounts, make withdrawals. You must be given the opportunity to have a prompt court hearing. This isn't the trial where you argue whether or not you owe the debt. This hearing pertains only to the attachment, and you'll want to argue that the attached property is exempt (see Chapter 16), you need the property to support yourself and your family, or the value of the property attached exceeds what you owe.

If you don't attend the hearing or you lose the hearing, the court will order that the attachment remain on your property pending the outcome of the lawsuit. You won't be able to withdraw or otherwise dispose of any of the attached property. You can get the attachment released by filing a bond for the amount of money you owe. But if you don't file a bond, and the creditor wins the lawsuit, the judgment is almost certain to be paid out of the attached property. Prejudgment attachment is not available in some states (California, for example), if the claim is based on a consumer debt.

Lawsuit

If you don't pay a debt, the most likely consequence is that you will be sued, unless the creditor thinks you are judgment proof or decides not to sue for other reasons. Being judgment proof means that you don't have any money or property that can legally be taken to pay the debt and aren't likely to get any soon. But because most court judgments last many years (up to 20 years in some states), and can often be renewed indefinitely, people who are broke may nevertheless be sued on the creditor's assumption that someday they'll come into money or property (and then will no longer be judgment proof). Similarly, very old people or people with terminal illness who are judgment proof may get sued by their creditors simply because the creditors know that it's easier to collect the debt at death (through the probate process) if they have a judgment than if they don't.

Being judgment proof doesn't mean that you have no money or property at all, although many people who are judgment proof have virtually nothing. Being judgment proof means that if a creditor obtains a court judgment, you are allowed to keep all of your property because it is "exempt." Each state has declared certain items of property beyond the reach of creditors—these items are called exempt property. (Exempt property is covered in detail in Chapter 16.) Suffice it to say that if you receive no income except government benefits, such as Social Security or unemployment, and have limited personal property and no real property, you are almost always judgment proof, at least right now. There are a few exceptions to this general rule. For example, most government agencies are permitted to collect debts owed to them by taking a percentage of certain federal benefits, such as Social Security.

If a creditor sues you in regular court (as opposed to small claims court) and you fight it, the lawsuit can take time—often several years—to run through the court system. If you don't oppose the lawsuit, or you let the court automatically enter a judgment against you (called a default judgment), the case could be over in 30 to 60 days.

If the creditor gets a judgment, it has a number of ways to enforce it. If you are working, the most common method is to attach your wages, meaning that up to 25% of your take-home pay is removed from your paycheck and sent to the creditor before you ever see it. The next most common method to collect a judgment is to seize your deposit accounts. Chapter 14 contains details on getting sued and defending against judgment collections.

Lien on Your Property

A lien is a notice attached to your property telling the world that a creditor claims you owe it some money. Liens on real property are a common way for creditors to collect what they are owed. Liens on personal property, such as motor vehicles, are less frequently used but can be an effective way for someone to collect. To sell or refinance property, you must have clear title. A lien on your house, mobile home, car, or other property makes your title unclear. To clear

up the title, you must pay off the lien. Thus, creditors know that putting a lien on property is a cheap and almost guaranteed way of collecting what they are owed—sooner or later.

A creditor usually can place a lien on your real property—and occasionally on personal property—after it sues you and wins a court judgment. But many creditors need not wait that long. Here are examples of other property liens:

- **Property tax liens.** If you don't pay your property taxes, the county can place a lien on your real property. When you sell or refinance your place, or a lender forecloses on it, the government will stand in line to get paid out of the proceeds.

- **IRS liens.** If you fail to pay back taxes after receiving notices from the IRS, it may place a lien on all of your property, especially if you're unemployed, self-employed, or sporadically employed and the IRS would have trouble attaching your wages. Many creditors with property liens simply wait until the house is sold or refinanced to get paid. The IRS, however, doesn't like to wait and may force a sale if the amount you owe is substantial. For more information on dealing with IRS liens, see *Stand Up to the IRS*, by Frederick W. Daily (Nolo).

- **Child support liens.** If you owe a lot in child support or alimony, the recipient may put a lien on your real property. The lien will stay until you pay the support you owe or until you sell or refinance your property, whichever happens first. (See Chapter 13.)

- **Mechanic's liens.** If a contractor works on your property or furnishes construction materials to be used on your property, and you don't pay up, the contractor can record a lien on your property called a mechanic's lien. In most states, the contractor must record the lien within one to six months of when the contractor wasn't paid. The contractor then must sue you to enforce the lien within about one year (the range is one month to six years, depending on the state) of when the contractor recorded it. If the contractor wins the lawsuit, the contractor may be able to force the sale of your home.

- **Lis pendens.** A spouse in a marital action who asserts a claim against real property held solely in the other spouse's name may record a lis pendens against the property. A lis pendens is notice to purchasers and creditors that the property is subject to the marital action. It prevents the owner spouse from conveying or encumbering the recording spouse's interest until the court rules on the claim.

- **Family Law Real Property Lien.** In California, a spouse may file a lien against his or her interest in community real property to secure payment of attorney fees in a marital action. The lien affects only the filing spouse's interest in the property.

Jail

Jailing someone for not paying a debt is prohibited in most instances. In a few situations, however, you could land behind bars:

- You willfully violate a court order. This comes up most frequently when you fail to make court-ordered child support payments, the recipient requests a hearing before a judge, and the judge concludes that you could have paid, but didn't. (See Chapter 13.) But imprisonment for willful violation of a court order is not limited to child support situations. In a few states, a court can order you to make periodic payments on a debt. If you don't, the court can hold you in contempt and theoretically put you in jail. That rarely happens, however.

- You are convicted of willfully refusing to pay income taxes.

- You fail to show up for a debtor's examination. A debtor's examination is a procedure where a judgment creditor, with court approval, orders you to come to court and answer questions about your property and finances. (See Chapter 14.)

- You live in a state that allows imprisonment for certain types of debts. Even so, the state law may allow debtors to avoid imprisonment if they can show that they really don't have the money or other assets to pay the debt. (To find out how to research your state's laws, see Chapter 19.)

Debtors' Prisons—A Little History

The mere thought of debtors' prison probably sends shivers up your spine. It should. As unusual and cruel as it seems today, debtors' prison was a major collection method in the 18th and mid-19th centuries of our republic. The legal system of the American colonies included debtors' prisons, which the English Parliament created under the Statute of Merchants in 1285. Creditors who were owed money could simply ask the sheriff to arrest the debtor and throw him (literally him—women were not allowed to own property and therefore couldn't get into debt trouble) in jail. If he couldn't raise the bail, and most couldn't as they had no money, he sat in his cell until someone paid his bill or bailed him out.

Many creditors felt the humiliation of jail was too much to impose on debtors without first giving them a chance to pay what they owed. Those creditors, rather than having the debtor arrested, sued to obtain a judgment entitling them to payment. If the debtor didn't pay after a judge ordered it, the creditor then asked the sheriff to arrest the debtor and toss him in jail.

Local businesses, preachers, butchers, and market keepers often felt sorry for these prisoners and would try to help them out, but most sat in their cells until someone paid their debts. Even royalty felt compassion for many imprisoned debtors. Just outside of the Palace at Holyrood in Edinburgh, Scotland, there was (and still is) a small triangular-shaped area in which debtors could stay free from their creditors.

In 1830, an American Indian prisoner lamented on the absurdity of his being imprisoned as punishment for not delivering the payment of beaver skins. "If I was put there to compel me to perform my agreement, my prosecutors have selected a poor place for me to catch beavers."

Public indignation with debtors' prisons found a voice in Silas M. Stillwill, a New York lawyer. In 1831 he introduced the Act to Abolish Imprisonment for Debt. In the federal judicial system, debtors' prisons were gone by 1833. Most American states quickly followed suit, abolishing them in the 1830s and 1840s. And by 1870, nearly 600 years after they were created, England said "no more" to debtors' prisons.

Bank Setoff

A bank setoff happens when a financial institution such as a bank, savings and loan, or credit union removes money from a deposit account—checking, savings, certificate of deposit, or money market account—to cover a payment you missed on the loan owed that institution.

There are a few limitations on bank setoffs. For instance, most courts have said that banks cannot use setoffs to take income that is otherwise exempt under state or federal law (such as Social Security benefits, unemployment compensation, public assistance or disability benefits). (See Chapter 16 for information on exempt property.) In addition, financial institutions cannot take money out of your account to cover missed credit card payments, unless you previously authorized the bank to pay your credit card bill by automatic withdrawals from your account. (15 U.S.C. § 1666h; Regulation Z of the Truth in Lending Act, 12 C.F.R. § 226.12(d).)

Some states impose limits on bank setoffs as well. For example, with limited exceptions, California prohibits state-chartered savings and loan setoffs if the aggregate balance of all your accounts with the financial institution is under $1,000. (California Financial Code § 6660.) And in Maryland, all bank setoffs are prohibited unless you have explicitly authorized the setoff or a court has ordered one. (Maryland Commercial Law § 15-702.)

Collection of Unsecured Debts From Third Parties

If a third party holds property for you or owes you money, most states give creditors the right to sue those third parties to get your property or money. Sometimes that third party is a financial institution, such as a bank, savings and loan, or credit union, where you have a deposit account. Or, it may be a landlord or utility company to whom you've made a security deposit. Or, it could be a financial adviser, such as a stock broker, with whom you've deposited funds to invest on your behalf.

In a few states, a creditor can't pursue a third party until it has obtained a court judgment against you and tried to collect. In most states, however, the creditor can sue the third party even before getting a judgment against you. If that happens, you will have to be notified of the suit and allowed the opportunity to contest the debt.

Interception of Your Tax Refund

If you are in default on your student loan payments, or are behind in your income taxes or child support, the agency trying to collect can request that the IRS intercept your federal income tax refund and apply the money to your debt.

Before the IRS takes your money, it must notify you of the proposed interception. You are given the opportunity to present written evidence or to have a hearing to show that any of the following is true:

• Your debt has been paid.

- The amount of the proposed intercept is more than you owe.
- The intercept is not legally enforceable.

If you are married and the intercept is for child support from a previous relationship, your spouse can file a claim for her share of the refund.

Tax refund intercepts are most common in the case of a defaulted student loan. Each year, for example, the federal government pockets over $500,000,000 by grabbing tax refunds from more than 500,000 former students. For more information on student loan collections—including stopping or avoiding future tax refund intercepts—see Chapter 12.

Loss of Insurance Coverage

If you miss payments on any insurance policy, your coverage will end. Most insurance companies give you a 30-day grace period—that is, if your payment is due on the tenth of the month and you don't pay until the ninth of the following month, you won't lose your coverage. A few companies may let you get away with 60 days, but don't count on it. After 60 days, your policy is sure to lapse.

If your policy has lapsed, and your lender required you to obtain the insurance as a condition of your loan, you could face more than a canceled insurance policy. Because lenders who make secured loans are usually the ones who require insurance coverage, the lender could declare you in default of your loan and either repossess your personal property or foreclose on your house.

However, it is more likely that the lender will get an insurance policy for you and bill you for the premiums. This is called "force placed insurance." Often, lenders will require consumers to pay for coverage that is not actually required by the credit agreement, which can end up being very expensive. The lender may also fail to notify you before it gets this insurance and bills you for it. These types of practices may violate your state Unfair and Deceptive Acts and Practices statute (see Chapter 4 for an explanation of these laws) and other laws.

Loss of Utility Service

If you miss payments on your utility or telephone bill, the utility company will attempt to cut off your service. If the utility company is publicly owned, it must give you notice of the disconnect and the opportunity to discuss it with a representative of the utility company. This is because a publicly owned utility company cannot deprive you of due process of the law, according to the U.S. Supreme Court. (*Memphis Light, Gas & Water Div. v. Craft*, 436 U.S. 1 (1978).) In most states, a private utility company doesn't need to give you any notice. (California is one of a handful of exceptions to this rule.)

In some states, private utilities are also required to give notice or follow other rules before cutting off service. For example, in most northern states, utility companies are not allowed to shut off heat-related utility services to residential customers between November 1 and March 31. In many other states, there are limits to when a utility company can shut off utilities for elderly or disabled residents and, occasionally, for households with infants.

Take a Deep Breath

This chapter has just described many worst-case scenarios. If you ignore all your creditors and you have some property and a job, then some of these things will happen to you. This is why you should not stick your head in the sand. Instead, review your list of essential and nonessential debts. After reading this chapter, you should know where you are most vulnerable—that is, where you are most likely to lose some property. If not paying a debt you considered nonessential means you'll probably lose something you really need, move that debt to the essential list and rethink your strategy to your debt situation.

Most important, focus on finding a solution.

■

When the Debt Collector Calls

The most trifling actions that affect a man's credit are to be regarded. The sound of your hammer at five in the morning, or nine at night, heard by a creditor, makes him easier six months longer; but if he sees you at a billiard table, or hears your voice at a tavern when you should be at work, he sends for his money the next day.

—Benjamin Franklin, American statesman, philosopher, and inventor, 1706-1790

Not many years ago, bill collectors regularly threatened, scared, lied to, harassed, intimidated, and otherwise abused debtors. Debtors were told they'd go to jail for not paying their bills; friends and relatives were often interrogated and threatened with financial and bodily harm if they didn't tell where runaway debtors were living; and bill collectors published lists of people who didn't pay their debts.

The federal Fair Debt Collection Practices Act (FDCPA), passed in 1977, outlaws unfair collection practices including debtor harassment. This law has greatly improved conditions for debtors, although an unfortunate number of collectors still resort to abusive practices.

There is one important rule to remember when dealing with a bill collector: Adopt a plan and stick with it. One choice—if you have no money, plan to file for bankruptcy, or choose not pay right now—is to refuse to talk with the collector. As explained in "Debt Collection Practices," below, you can request that a debt collector from a collection agency

stop contacting you. However, many debt counselors feel that, unless you're judgment proof or truly plan to file for bankruptcy, the best overall advice is to not ignore the debt or try to hide from the collector. Usually, the longer you put off resolving the issue, the worse the situation and consequences will become. Whether you negotiate directly with the collector or obtain a lawyer's assistance, many counselors feel the best strategy almost always is to engage the collector.

If you really need more time to pay, another option is to contact the bill collector to negotiate a payment schedule. If you do contact a bill collector, realize that as nice as a bill collector may appear, he or she is not your friend and does not have your best interest at heart. The collector wants your money. To get it, he or she may ask you about your personal problems, or may claim to be interested in saving you from ruining your credit. Don't believe it: The collector doesn't really care about your problems or your credit rating. The collector's only goal is to get your money. Stick to your plan. If you want extra time to pay or to lower your payments, insist on it. If you want the bill collector to go away, tell him or her not to contact you.

 WARNING

This chapter assumes you have not been sued. This chapter focuses on prejudgment collection efforts. If the creditor or a collection agency has sued you and obtained a court judgment, the collection options are different. See Chapter 14 for more information.

Original Creditor or Collection Agency?

To understand your rights when dealing with a bill collector, you must keep in mind the difference between the original creditor and a collection agency (or a "third party collector"). As you read further in this chapter, this distinction will be important, primarily because the federal law regulating collection agencies generally doesn't apply to original creditors, unless they take steps to act like third party collectors.

Original creditor. An original creditor is a business or person who first extended you credit or loaned you money. Sometimes original creditors are called credit grantors.

Collection agency. A collection agency or third party collector is someone an original creditor uses to collect the original creditor's debt. Under the FDCPA, a collection agency or third party collector also includes:

- an original creditor that collects its debts under a different name or by sending letters signed by lawyers
- a lawyer who regularly collects debts owed to others (see *Heintz v. Jenkins*, 115 S.Ct. 1489 (1995)), and
- any company that purchases debts for the purpose of collecting them.

Bill collector or debt collector. The term bill collector or debt collector can refer to either an original creditor or a collection agency. Be sure you know who you are dealing with.

As mentioned above, the difference between an original creditor and a collection agency is important. Original creditors generally are not governed by the FDCPA.

Several states, however, have debt collection laws that apply to both original creditors and collection agencies. Also, many states have laws regulating collection agencies more strictly than the FDCPA. (See "State or Local Laws Prohibiting Unfair Debt Collections," below.)

Efforts to collect past-due bills usually follow a standard pattern. Original creditors first try to collect their own debts. When you initially owe money, you'll receive a series of letters or phone calls from the original creditor's collections or customer service department. Although most creditors make first contact a few weeks after you miss a payment, some more aggressive companies begin hard-core collection efforts within 24 to 36 hours after your payment is due. If you don't respond to the letters or calls within a few months, most original creditors will charge off your account—that is, either send it to a collection agency or write it off as a bad debt.

> **WARNING**
> **Written-off debts could increase your tax bill.** if a creditor writes off a debt, it means that collection efforts will end. That's the good news. The bad news is that the creditor may be obligated to report your windfall to the IRS—and you may have to report it as income and pay taxes on it. See Chapter 6 for more information.

Some original creditors, concerned about their reputations, hire collection agencies known for less aggressive tactics. They realize that you may be a customer again in the future, and they don't want to alienate you. Some creditors, however, couldn't care less about what you think of them. They are fed up with you for not paying and will find the most aggressive collection agency around.

Original Creditors' Collection Efforts

How an original creditor goes about collecting an outstanding bill will depend on the type of creditor it is. Small local creditors, like a corner store or accountant's office, may have a person on staff who handles delinquent accounts. More often than not, however, the responsibility of collecting overdue money rests with the business owner or manager. Department stores, banks, and other creditors with several branches usually begin their collection efforts with the store or office that handled your transaction. National creditors—for example, banks that issue credit cards—have centrally located, in-house collection departments.

If you've moved since you incurred the debt, many original creditors will still try to find you. Many have access to computer databases compiled (usually by credit bureaus) to help creditors find debtors. You may unknowingly supply information about your new location to these databases when you rent a new place, send your credit card company a change of address, or apply for a credit card at your new address.

If the original creditor can't find you, it will probably send your account to a collection agency.

Collection Letters

Original creditors usually begin their collection efforts with collection ("dunning") letters.

One day, several weeks after a bill is past due, you open your mail box and find a polite letter from a creditor reminding you that you seem to have overlooked the company's most recent bill. "Perhaps it is already in the mail. If so, please accept our thanks. If not, we would appreciate prompt payment," the letter states.

This "past due" form letter is the kind that almost every creditor sends to a customer with an overdue account. If you ignore it, you'll get a second one, also automatically sent. In this letter, most creditors remain friendly but want to know what the problem is: "If you have some special reason for withholding payment, please let us know. We are here to help." Some creditors also suspend your credit at this point; the only way to get it back is to send a payment.

If you don't answer the second letter, you'll probably receive three to five more form letters. Each will get slightly firmer. The next-to-last letter will likely contain a veiled threat: "Paying now will protect your credit rating." By the last letter, however, the threat won't be so subtle: "If we do not receive payment within ten days, your credit privileges will be canceled (if they haven't already been), your account sent to a collection agency, and your delinquency reported to the national credit reporting agencies. You could face a lawsuit, wage attachment, or lien on your property."

An original creditor cannot threaten to take action that it cannot or does not intend

Form Letters From an Attorney

If you get what appears to be a form collection letter with a lawyer's mechanically reproduced signature at the bottom (and perhaps letterhead at the top), the sender of the letter (not necessarily the lawyer) and the lawyer may be violating the FDCPA—and you may have grounds to sue.

Under the FDCPA, lawyers must be involved in each individual collection case before their names appear on any collection letters. They can't authorize a form letter and then let the bill collector mail out letters bearing their signature without reviewing each particular debtor's file. (See *Avila v. Rubin*, 84 F.3d 222 (7th Cir. 1996); *Clomon v. Jackson*, 988 F.2d 1314 (2d Cir. 1993); *Nielsen v. Dickerson*, 307 F.3d 623 (7th Cir. 2002).)

If you suspect this is happening, call the law firm on the letterhead and ask to speak with the attorney. If the attorney doesn't exist or has no recollection of you or your debt, send a letter to the collections manager, president, and CEO of the original creditor. Point out the blatant violation of the FDCPA and your right to sue.

If you get no satisfaction from them and you feel litigious, you may want to find an experienced consumer lawyer who will file a lawsuit for you against the collection lawyer and the collection agency. Some consumer lawyers will file this lawsuit for you in exchange for a percentage of the money you might win, without asking you to pay fees. (This is called a contingency arrangement.) One place to find a consumer lawyer is the National Association of Consumer Advocates website, www.naca.net. Or, look in your telephone book for a legal referral hotline.

You can also file complaints about the collection lawyer with the Federal Trade Commission (www.ftc.gov) and with the state bar or other lawyer discipline agency. Attorneys who let someone else use their name to practice law violate both the FDCPA and the attorney code of ethics.

to take. For example, one creditor recently got in trouble for threatening to refer an overdue account to an attorney and file a lawsuit when it apparently never intended to do either. The creditor sent a collection letter to a debtor stating that she must make payment arrangements in five days or the matter *could* result in referral to an attorney and a lawsuit being filed. The U.S. Court of Appeals found that it would be deceptive for the creditor to claim that it could take actions it had no intention of taking and had rarely taken before. (*Brown v. Card Service Center*, 464 F.3d 450 (3d Cir. 2006).)

Original creditors hate it when collection efforts reach this stage. They want you to pay your bill, but they also want to be nice so that you'll remain a customer. If the original creditor's letter-writing campaign fails or the person assigned to your account prefers direct contact, you'll probably receive a phone call.

EXAMPLES:

"We are not here to beat you up or yell at you. Tell us your problems so we can help you and your family. We want you to remain our customer."

"Oh-no; don't tell me you're considering bankruptcy! It's a big mistake. I'll bet you didn't know that a bankruptcy will stay on your credit record for ten years."

"Is the payment schedule convenient for you? Would it help if we moved your due date up a few days so that your payment is due just a day or two after you get paid?"

"Do you need help planning a budget or paying your bills? Let me suggest that you contact your local Consumer Credit Counseling Service office." [Consumer Credit Counseling Service (CCCS) is a national, nonprofit organization, sponsored and paid for by major creditors. CCCS helps debtors plan budgets and pay their bills. CCCS can be very helpful, but you, not the creditor, should make that decision. See Chapter 19 for a full discussion of CCCS.]

"How would you, if you were a creditor, handle overdue accounts?"

"Do you have $100 a month to pay your debts? I'm sure you realize that our debt is your most important one. We would have to insist that you pay us $75 a month and distribute the rest to your other creditors."

"Did you know that our store's 75th anniversary sale is next month? Everything will be on sale at 50% off. We'll be happy to let you have your $1,000 line of credit back as soon as you clear up this debt."

"Please, why don't you just send the minimum—$20—to prove to me that you are a sincere person."

"I know people who make much less than you do and who pay their bills on time."

An increasing number of collectors working for original creditors are abandoning the standard letter/phone call tactic if it is obvious early on that it won't work. Instead, these collectors contact debtors and encourage them to call a toll-free number to set up a repayment plan.

How to Respond

When the first overdue notice arrives, your first response may be to throw it away. And if the letter is from a creditor whose debt is on your "nonessential" debt list (see Chapter 5), throwing it away may be your best alternative. Remember, however, that the original creditor won't end its collection efforts with that first letter. Assuming the debt is one you want to pay but you need a little more time, you're better off writing or calling the creditor and asking for an extension. And if you got a message to call a toll-free number and work out a repayment plan, by all means call back if you can squeeze out a small amount each month and still pay your essential debts.

WARNING

Don't write a letter if the statute of limitations has run out. If your debt is so old that the creditor or collection agency is time-barred from collecting it—six years old, in many states—then you shouldn't say anything in a letter or on the phone that acknowledges the debt. If you admit that you owe the money now or ever owed it in the past, this could turn your debt into a brand new debt, which gives the creditor or agency another six years to collect. Collection agencies often try to keep you on the phone until you say something that "revives" the statute of limitations. Don't fall for it—the best practice is simply not to talk to collection agencies about very old debts. See "Time-Barred or 'Zombie' Debts," below, for more information.

When you get in touch with the creditor, you will need to explain your problem and, if possible, suggest an approximate date when you expect to be able to make full payments. Don't give a work phone number unless the creditor already knows where you work and you don't mind calls at your job.

Sending a partial, even token, payment will show that you are earnestly trying to pay. It is not essential, however, especially if it will keep you from paying priority debts. A sample letter asking for more time is below.

Sample Letter Asking for More Time

Collections Department
Rease's Department Store
5151 South Keetchum Place
Chicago, IL 60600

April 18, 2007

Re: Amy Jones Account No. 1294-444-38RD

To Whom It May Concern:

I've received your notice indicating that my account is overdue.

I would like to pay, but a family emergency has prevented me from doing so. My daughter was in a severe automobile accident. She is unable to go to school and I have had to take time off to care for her.

My financial situation will improve in the near future. I will be returning to work in a few weeks and I expect to be able to pay you on July 1, 2007.

Thank you for your consideration in this matter. If you wish to speak to me, please feel free to call me at my home at 312-555-9333.

Sincerely,

Amy Jones

Amy Jones

If the creditor rejects your proposal or wants more evidence that you are genuinely unable to pay, consider asking a debt counselor to intervene on your behalf. (See Chapter 19.) Or, if the debt is quite large or one of many debts, consider hiring a lawyer to write a second letter asking for additional time. (This is also covered in Chapter 19.) The lawyer won't say anything different than you would, but a lawyer's stationery carries clout. This will cost some money, but it may be worth it. When a creditor learns that a lawyer is in the picture, the creditor often suspects that you'll file for bankruptcy if it isn't accommodating. So you can often save more in payments than the lawyer costs.

When Your Debt Is Sent to a Collection Agency

If you ignore the original creditor's letters and phone calls, or you set up a repayment schedule but fail to make the payments, your bill will most likely be turned over to a collection agency and your delinquency reported to a credit bureau. This will probably take place about four to six months after you default. By taking some time to understand how collection agencies operate, you'll know how to respond when they contact you so that you can negotiate a payment plan or get the agency off your back.

First, if a collection agency has been hired by an original creditor, it generally must take its cues from the creditor. It can't sue you without the original creditor's authorization. If the original creditor insists that the agency collect 100% of the debt, the agency cannot accept less from you. Before accepting a reduced amount, the collection agency must get the original creditor's okay, or you'll have to contact the original creditor yourself. In recent years, however, original creditors have been giving collection agencies more discretion. Some are authorized to settle a debt for less than 100%.

Second, you can expect to hear from a collection agency as soon as the original creditor passes on your debt. Professional debt collectors know that the earlier they strike, the higher their chance of collecting.

Third, bill collecting is a serious—and lucrative—business. Collection agents are good at what they do. Some earn high salaries. Other companies pay their collectors meager wages plus commissions. But paying low wages generally leads to high turnover, low morale, and general burnout. For you, it often means you'll be called by a stressed-out, rude collector who doesn't much care what the law allows.

Fourth, a collection agency usually keeps between 10% and 60% of what it collects. The older the account, the higher the agency's fee. Sometimes, the agency charges per letter it writes or phone call it places—usually about 50¢ per letter or $1 per call. In that situation, the collection agencies will be quite aggressive in collecting.

Fifth, before a collection agency tries to collect, it evaluates its likelihood of success. It may carry thousands—or even tens of thousands—of delinquent accounts and must prioritize which ones to go after. If success looks likely, the agency will move full speed ahead. If the chances of finding you are low, the odds of collecting money from you are somewhere between slim and nil, or your credit file shows that you've defaulted on 20 other accounts, the agency may give your debt low priority.

How Collection Agencies Find People

Collection agencies hunt people down using several possible resources. Even agencies that search diligently make mistakes. Most hire fairly low-paid clerks to collect and sift through mountains of data. These clerks can put information about other people into your file and information about you into other files, effectively losing you.

Just because a collection agency calls or writes to you, don't assume that it knows where you live, especially if you've moved since you transacted business with the original creditor. All the bill collector knows is that it mailed a letter or left a phone message that wasn't returned.

Here are the primary resources a collection agency uses to find people.

Information on your credit application. The original creditor provides the collection agency with the information on your credit application: address, phone number, employer, bank, credit references, nearest living relative, and the like. If you've moved, someone listed on a credit application may know where you are.

Relatives, friends, employers, and neighbors. Collection agents often call relatives, friends, employers, or neighbors, posing as a friend or relative. However, the federal fair debt collection law limits these types of calls. For more information on what is legal and what isn't, see "Debt Collection Practices," below.

Phone books. White and Yellow Pages of phone books and their online counterparts are good sources of names, addresses, and phone numbers. If a collection agency has your phone number, it may be able to find your location information using a reverse directory.

Post office. The agency may check the post office for a forwarding address and is likely to examine several regional phone books. Also, major credit bureaus with their own collection agencies receive change-of-address information for two million people each month from the U.S. Postal Service.

State motor vehicle department. It used to be that anyone could get your current address by paying a small fee to your state's motor vehicle department to check your car registration and driver's license records. The federal Driver Privacy Protection Act of 1994 now prevents these casual searches. However, some people are still allowed to use that database for some purposes. A legitimate creditor or its agent or contractor (the collection agency) can use the motor vehicle department's database to verify your address in order to collect a debt and pursue its legal remedies against you. (Some states do not permit this use of their motor vehicle department records.)

Voter registration records. Some collection agents check voter registration records in the county of your last residence. If you've reregistered in the same county, the registrar will have your new address. If you've moved out of county and reregistered, your new county would have forwarded cancellation information to your old county, and the registrar may make that information available.

Utility companies. Although this process is difficult, an agency collector may be able to find you through the electric or phone company, especially if you are still in the same service area. Even if you move farther, the company may have your new address as a place to send your final bill.

Banks. If you move but leave your old bank account open—even if you don't still do business with the bank—the bank will probably have your new address and may provide it to a collection agency.

Credit bureaus. If a collection agency is associated with a credit bureau (see Chapter 17), the collection agency will have access to all kinds of information, such as your address, phone number, employer, and credit history. Even if the collection agency isn't part of a credit bureau, for a small fee the collector can place your name on a credit bureau locate list. In theory at least, if you apply for credit—even if you've moved hundreds or thousands of miles from where you previously lived—your name will be forwarded to the collection agency.

Data aggregators and Internet search engines. Data aggregators gather information on millions of people from public records, surveys, purchase data, and demographic data. Internet search engines list everything from aircraft owners to high school classmates. Chances are that contact information for you will show up in these kinds of databases, which are available to debt collectors.

Skip tracers. Creditors and collectors use skip tracers to locate people. Skip tracers locate people using traditional and high-tech techniques, such as telephone books, email address finders, Social Security number searches, telephone company call records, public records, domain name lookups, military and Selective Service lookups, prison inmate lookups, professional license lookups, apartment locators, hotel/motel locators, business and corporate records, hunting and fishing licenses, and even eBay seller searches.

Pretexters. Pretexters get people's personal information using false pretenses. A pretexter might call you and say he's from a survey firm. He might ask you some questions to elicit basic personal information. When the pretexter has enough information, he calls your financial institution and pretends to be you or someone who is authorized to access your account. He gets more personal information from the bank. He then uses this information to investigate or sue you, or sells it to someone who may use it to get credit in your name or steal your assets. Pretexting is illegal, but occurs anyway.

Government Records Are Off Limits

Social Security, unemployment, disability, census, and other government records are not public documents, so bill collectors can't get them.

In most cases, collectors that try hard will be successful in finding you. Often, your energy is better spent getting your finances in order rather than hiding from a collection agency. Even so, there may be instances when you really don't want to be found. Here are a few tips to avoid detection by collection agencies:

- Don't reveal your new address, city, or state (if you have moved) to anyone except a few trusted people.
- Keep your new phone number unlisted.
- Close your old bank accounts; open new ones at different banks.
- Don't apply for new credit.
- Screen your phone calls using caller ID. Be aware that some collection agencies block their own numbers from being displayed, knowing that curious people tend to pick up the phone when no number is displayed.
- Invest in a "TeleZapper," a device that detects calls coming from an autodialer system. When the device detects an autodialer call, it sends back a signal that your telephone has been disconnected. This signal triggers the debt collector's autodialer to take your phone number off its call list. You can buy a TeleZapper for $35 to $50 at an electronics store or on the Internet. (Remember, it will discourage *all* automated calls, including calls from your doctor confirming an appointment, or from your library saying that your books have arrived).
- Go to the Internet and search for your own name, using Google, Altavista, Yahoo!, Internet Explorer, and so on.

Most search programs with a "people locator" have a way for you to opt out and get your address unlisted.

- Keep a low profile locally. Of course, newspapers are on the Web, but even clubs, churches, and PTAs put their newsletters online now, so your affiliations could show up in an Internet search. Then the organization might innocently help the collection agency find you.

If You're the Cosigner of a Loan

When you cosign for a loan, you assume full responsibility for paying back the loan if the primary borrower defaults. In almost every state, the creditor can go after a cosigner without first trying to collect from the primary borrower. But most creditors try to collect first from the primary borrower. So, if you've been contacted by a collection agency, you can assume that the primary debtor defaulted.

Your best bet is to pay the debt if you can (and save your credit rating) and then try to collect from the primary debtor. For more information on cosigned debts, see Chapter 11.

Asking That the Creditor Take Back the Debt

If you are ready to negotiate on a debt, you will probably be better off if the debt is with the creditor, not a collection agency. This is because the creditor has more discretion and

Time-Barred or "Zombie" Debts

A creditor or collector has a limited number of years to sue you if you fail to pay a debt. This time period is set by a law called the statute of limitations, and varies by state. (See Chapter 14 for more information.) In most states, the statute of limitations on debts is between three and ten years.

In recent years, aggressive debt collectors have begun trying to enforce debts that are barred by the statute of limitations. They buy these debts from original creditors for pennies on the dollar, so they make a tidy profit when they collect anything. In 2004, debt buyers bought some $72 billion worth of aged consumer debt.

These debt buyers use aggressive tactics when they try to collect on their time-barred debts. According to media reports, they abuse and harass debtors, "re-age" accounts on debtors' credit reports, and try to trick debtors into reaffirming debts so that the statute of limitations begins anew.

What can you do if a debt collector tries to collect a time-barred debt from you? The most important thing is not to say or do anything that in any way acknowledges that you owe the debt. Acknowledging the debt or making even a token payment can restart the statute of limitations in some states.

If you're absolutely certain that the statute of limitations has expired on the debt, you can tell the collector to stop contacting you, and the collector must abide by your wishes. The only downside is that the debt will appear on your credit report until the seven-year reporting period ends, which may hinder your efforts to get a mortgage or car loan.

The collector should not be able to re-age your account so that the debt appears on your credit report for more than seven years. The federal Fair Credit Reporting Act sets strict rules for the reporting of delinquencies and the start of the seven-year reporting period. At least in theory, the original creditor should have reported that date and the collector should not be able to change it. (See Chapter 17 to learn about disputing inaccurate information in your credit report.)

Courts say that debt collectors can legally try to collect time-barred debts. After all, you still owe the debt; the collector is just prevented from using the courts to try to collect it. The collector can seek voluntary payment of the debt, but can't sue you or threaten to sue you, *unless* the statute of limitations has started anew. A collector cannot try to collect a debt that you discharged in bankruptcy.

flexibility in negotiating with you, and the creditor sees you as a former and possibly future customer. So ask the collector from the collection agency for the phone number of the collections department of the original creditor. Then call the creditor and ask if you can negotiate on the debt.

Here are the possible responses:

- The creditor immediately begins negotiations with you, takes the debt back from the collection agency, and keeps it as long as you make the agreed-on payments. Only a few creditors will do this.

- The creditor rejects your proposal but lets you know that if you negotiate with the collection agency, establish a repayment plan, and make two or three payments under the plan, the creditor will take your debt back and eventually give you a new line of credit. This helps you take care of your debt problems and begin to rebuild your credit. Many creditors will do this.

- The creditor rejects your proposal but negotiates a payment plan with you and requires that its collection agency abide by the plan. A few creditors will do this.

- The creditor rejects your proposal and tells you that your only option is to negotiate with the collection agency. Some creditors will do this.

Any agreement you reach with the creditor should be put in writing—preferably, in a letter from the creditor to you, although a letter from you to the creditor confirming the agreement and asking the creditor to correct any errors is better than nothing. A copy of the letter should be sent to the collector. The danger in working with the creditor rather than the collector is that the collector may have bought the debt, and may refuse to give you credit for payments made directly to the creditor.

Negotiating With a Collection Agency

Although collection agencies must follow original creditors' instructions, few original creditors put significant restrictions on collection agencies. The original creditor has all but given up on you and will be thrilled if the collection agency can use legal means to collect anything. The collection agency knows you are having debt problems and have been evading your creditors.

Your options and how you approach the negotiation will depend on whether the debt is secured or unsecured. (See Chapter 1 for an explanation of secured and unsecured debts.)

Unsecured Debts

Most debts that go to collection agencies are unsecured debts, such as credit card debt and medical bills. If the original creditor is flexible, it may be happy to accept a settlement below the full amount to avoid spending months futilely trying to collect the whole thing. As you negotiate, remember two key points:

- The collection agency didn't lend you the money or extend you credit initially. It doesn't care if you owe $250 or $2,500. It just wants to maximize its return, which is usually a percentage of what it collects.

- Time is money. Every time the collection agency writes or calls you, it spends money. The agency has a strong interest in getting you to pay as much as you can as fast as possible. It has less interest in collecting 100% over five years.

Before you contact a collection agency, review your debt priority plan. (See Chapter 5.) If you don't have the cash to make a realistic lump sum offer or to propose a payment plan, don't call—you may make promises you can't keep or give the agency more information than it already has. Or, worse, you may say something that turns an old time-barred debt into a brand-new debt.

Offer a Lump Sum Settlement

If you decide to offer a lump sum, understand that no general rule applies to all collection agencies. Some want 75%–80% of what you owe. Others will take 50%. Those that have given up on you may settle for one-third. Before you make an offer, however, decide your top amount and stick to it. Once the collector sees you will pay something, it will try to talk you into paying more. Don't agree to pay more than you can afford.

A collection agency will have more incentive to settle with you if you can pay all at once. If you owe $500 and offer $300 on the spot to settle the matter, the agency can take its fee, pay the balance to the original creditor (who treats the amount you don't pay as a business loss), and close its books.

If the collection agency agrees to settle a debt with you, ask—as a condition of your paying—to have any negative information about the debt removed from your credit files. The collection agency may tell you that this is not its decision—that only the original creditor can remove the information. Ask for the name and phone number of the person with the original creditor who has authority to make this decision. Call that person and plead. Explain that you are taking steps to repay your debts, clean up your credit, and be more responsible. Emphasize that a clean credit report will help you achieve your goals.

If you do reach an agreement, be sure to get written confirmation from the creditor or collector. The confirmation should say that it will acknowledge the debt as paid in full when you pay the agreed amount, and that it will submit a Universal Data Form to the three major credit bureaus deleting the account/trade line (there's a sample letter in Appendix C you can use for this purpose).

Offer to Make Payments

If you offer to pay the debt in monthly installments, the agency has little incentive to compromise for less than the full amount. It still must chase you for payment, and it knows from experience that there's a good chance you'll stop paying after a month or two.

Before a collection agency considers accepting monthly installments, it may have you fill out asset, income, and expense statements. Two points to keep in mind:

- You could be giving the collection agency more information about you than it previously had, and that might not be to your advantage.

- Don't lie. You'll be signing these forms under penalty of perjury. It's unlikely that you would ever be prosecuted for lying on the forms, but if the creditor later sues over the debt, lies on the forms can only hurt your case.

WARNING

Beware of "urgency-payment" suggestions. If your bill is seriously past due (90 days or more) and you've just agreed to a send a bill collector some money, don't be surprised if the creditor urges you to:

- Send the check by express or overnight mail.
- Wire the money, using Western Union's Quick Collect or American Express's Moneygram.
- Put the payment on a credit or charge card. (If you're having debt problems, the last thing you need to do is incur more debt.)
- Have a bank wire the money.
- Visit the creditor directly and bring the payment.
- Let the collector come to your home to pick up the check.

Your best bet is to resist all urgency suggestions. Many will cost you money (using express or overnight mail or wiring the money) or time (visiting the collector in person) or are unnecessary incursions into your private life (the collector visiting you in person).

If you reach an agreement with the collector, get a written confirmation. You can use the letter in Appendix C for this purpose as well.

Secured Debts

As explained in Chapter 1, a secured debt guarantees repayment, because the creditor has the right to take a specific item of property (the collateral) to pay the debt. Secured creditors rarely hound you to pay back debts. They don't have to. As long as they comply with state or federal laws that require them to notify you that you are behind on your payments and then follow the proper repossession procedures, they can simply come and take your property.

Can you just give back the collateral and call it even? If you don't need or want the collateral, you can offer to give it back to the creditor or collection agency. They don't have to take it, however, and probably won't if the item has substantially decreased in value or is hard to sell.

Even if the creditor or collection agency takes the property back, in most states you'll be liable for the difference between what you owe and what the creditor is able to sell the property for. This difference is called a deficiency and, as explained in Chapter 8, is often reason enough to avoid having property repossessed.

If you can no longer afford to keep the property, your best strategy in many cases is to offer to give it back in exchange for a written agreement waiving any deficiency. If the creditor refuses, you may be better off trying to sell the item yourself and using the proceeds to pay your debts.

Negotiating Tips

- Be honest, but paint the bleakest possible picture of your finances. Explain illnesses and accidents, job layoffs, car repossessions, major back taxes that you owe, and the like.
- If you are considering bankruptcy, say so. But be sure you don't incur any more debt after mentioning bankruptcy. If you do, you may not be able to discharge that new debt in your bankruptcy case.
- Never disclose where you work or bank. If you are asked, simply say "no comment"—this isn't the time to worry about being polite. If the collection agency or original creditor later sues you and gets a judgment, knowing where you bank or work will make it easy to collect the judgment.
- If you do make a payment, don't send a check from your bank—get a money order or cashier's check from a different bank or the post office.
- If you're thinking of hiring a lawyer, remember that while a lawyer can carry clout, is probably experienced at negotiating, and can convincingly mention bankruptcy, a lawyer costs money. Don't hire one unless you owe a lot and the lawyer has a realistic chance of negotiating a favorable settlement, such as getting a debt reduced to $5,000 from $10,000. After all, if the amount you pay the collection agency and the lawyer totals what you originally owed, you should have just paid the full amount to the collection agency. Also, make sure the lawyer quotes you the fee and doesn't charge more, or you could have one more creditor at your door.
- If you're contacted by more than one collection agency for the same debt, it means the creditor has hired a secondary collection agency. The original creditor and at least one collection agency have given up on you. A collection agency that agrees to take your debt at this time will insist that the original creditor pay a generous fee (usually 50%–60% of what's recovered) and give the agency substantial freedom in negotiating with you. At this point, you can probably settle the bill for far less than you owe. Many secondary agencies will take 33¢–50¢ on the dollar. If the agency hasn't been able to reach you by phone but knows that you are receiving its letters, it may settle for even less.
- If the collection agency agrees to settle for less than you owe, be sure it also agrees to report the debt as "satisfied in full" to the credit bureaus.
- If a debt collector agrees to settle with you for far less than you owe, be sure the deal makes financial sense. Depending on the type of creditor and amount of the debt, you may owe income taxes on the amount waived. See Chapter 6 for more information.

Exemptions won't help you. Chapter 16 covers exempt property—the property your creditors, including collection agencies, can't take even if you file for bankruptcy or get sued. There's one major exception to exempt property: collateral for a secured debt. You can't keep a creditor from repossessing the collateral just because it's exempt.

When the Collection Agency Gives Up

If all efforts by the collection agency fail, the agency is likely to send the bill back to the original creditor. The creditor and the collection agency will decide whether or not to pass your debt on to an attorney. No matter how much you owe, the creditor will consider the following before filing a lawsuit:

- **The chances of winning.** Lawyers do not like to lose cases. Most debt collection lawsuits are filed only if winning is a sure thing.
- **The chances of collecting.** If you are judgment proof and likely to stay that way (see Chapter 8), the creditor many not bother suing you.
- **The lawyer's fees.** The older or more difficult your debt will be to collect, the larger the lawyer's fee is likely to be. The creditor doesn't want to have to pay a lot to collect.
- **If you recently received a Chapter 7 bankruptcy discharge.** You can't file more than once every eight years. If you filed recently, you won't be able to discharge the debt in another Chapter

7 bankruptcy and are a good lawsuit target.

- **The relationship of the lawyer and the creditor.** Sometimes, a lawyer will take small debts along with several large ones to stay in good standing with the creditor.

If you are sued, the original creditor, the collection agency, or both will be named as plaintiff in the court papers. If only the collection agency is named, you may have difficulty figuring out who the original creditor is. For this reason, many collection lawsuits are filed in the name of the original creditor or both the original creditor and the collection agency.

WARNING

If you are sued, go to Chapter 14 of this book. If you ignore any lawsuit, the creditor will quickly get a judgment against you and possibly garnish up to 25% of your wages each pay period. If you're not working, you risk having your bank accounts emptied and a lien recorded against your real property. This isn't the time to bury your head in the sand.

Debt Collection Practices

The federal Fair Debt Collections Practices Act (FDCPA) requires that a collection agency make certain disclosures, and also prohibits the collector from engaging in many kinds of abusive or deceptive behavior. (15 U.S.C. §§ 1692 to 1692p.) Most important, the FDCPA gives you the right to tell a collection agency to cease communicating with you, if you are convinced that this is the best course in your situation.

What Is a Debt?

The Fair Debt Collection Practices Act applies when a collection agency is seeking to collect a debt, which is defined as an obligation of a consumer to pay money arising out of a transaction which is primarily for personal, family, or household purposes. Nothing in the FDCPA requires that the creditor have originally extended credit to the debtor. The FDCPA also applies to debts that are not the result of an extension of credit, including:

- bounced checks
- payment of condominium and homeowner association fees
- medical bills, and
- utility bills.

Required Disclosures by a Collection Agency

Normally, the collection agency's first letter gives you the following information (if it doesn't, by law it has five days from the initial letter to tell you):

- the amount of the debt
- the name of the original creditor
- that you have 30 days to dispute the validity of the debt
- that if you don't dispute the debt's validity, the collector will assume it is valid, and

- that if you do dispute the debt's validity within the 30 days, the agency will send you verification of it.

It's wise to send a written request for verification of the name and address of the original creditor. A collection agency cannot resume collection efforts before double-checking the debt information with the original creditor and mailing you the verification, including the original creditor's name and address. The results of this check may help you decide whether you have grounds to dispute the debt. Collection agencies and original creditors are busy. While verification may seem as if it should take only a simple phone call, it often takes several weeks or months.

If you don't dispute the validity of the debt (or part of it) or don't request the original creditor's name and address within 30 days of receiving the first collection letter, the agency can assume the debt is valid and can pursue collection during the 30 days. The surest way to shut down collection efforts during the 30-day period is to dispute the debt or request the original creditor's name and address. You can still challenge collection of the debt after the 30 days, but you no longer have the rights described in this and the preceding paragraph.

In the first communication, the collection agency must state that it is trying to collect a debt and that any information collected will be used for that purpose. In all subsequent communications, the collector need only state that the communication is coming from a collection agency.

Collection agencies usually provide the required communications but often violate the FDCPA anyway through other statements. Often, the first letter states that it is an effort to collect a debt and that you have 30 days to dispute the debt's validity. Then the text of the letter demands payment, usually immediately, or threatens that if payment is not received immediately, the debt will be reported as delinquent to credit bureaus, and you may be sued. Many courts have held that this kind of statement effectively overshadows or contradicts the debtor's right to dispute the debt for 30 days and therefore violates the FDCPA. (See, for example, *Swanson v. Southern Oregon Credit Services, Inc.*, 869 F.2d 1222 (9th Cir. 1988); *Veillard v. Mednick*, 24 F. Supp. 2d 863 (N.D. Ill. 1998).) In such a situation, you are entitled to damages from the agency if you sue and win. Many cases settle, with the debt erased or greatly reduced in exchange for the debtor dropping the FDCPA violation claim.

What if the collector sues you, and the first communication you receive is a formal pleading in a civil action? In this circumstance, the collector isn't required to provide any of the validation information described above, and the lawsuit can proceed during the 30-day period.

Actions Debtors Can Take

Your most powerful weapon against a collection agency is your right to demand to be left alone, whether you owe the debt or not. In writing, simply tell the collection agency to cease all communications with you. It must do this, except to tell you either of the following:

- Collection efforts against you have ended, or
- The collection agency or the original creditor may invoke a specific remedy against you, such as suing you.

Furthermore, if the collection agency does contact you to tell you that it intends to pursue a specific remedy, the agency must truly intend to do so. It cannot simply write to you four times saying, "We're going to sue you."

Below is a sample letter you can use to get a collection agency off your back. Although it is not required, you might also want to tell the collector why you are in financial trouble. Be brief. If you are judgment proof, which means you don't have anything that the agency can legally take from you (see Chapter 16 for more on this), you should let the collector know that. If the collection agency knows it can't get anything from you, it is less likely to sue.

While this powerful weapon is available to you, it is not always the best approach. Many debt counselors feel that, unless you're judgment proof or truly plan to file for bankruptcy, the best overall advice is to not ignore the debt or try to hide from the collector. Usually, the longer you put off resolving the issue, the worse the situation and consequences will become. For example, if you don't negotiate with the collector, you run the risk that the collector will file a lawsuit that ultimately may require you to pay more than the amount of the original claim, and much more than a negotiated settlement. Plus, the judgment will stay on your credit record for seven years and will lower your credit score. Whether you negotiate directly with the collector or obtain a lawyer's assistance, many counselors feel the best strategy almost always is to engage the collector.

Sample Letter to Collection Agency to Tell It to Cease Contacting You

Sasnak Collection Service

49 Pirate Place

Topeka, Kansas 69000

November 11, 2007

Attn: Marc Mist

Re: Lee Anne Ito
    Account No. 88-90-92

Dear Mr. Mist:

For the past three months, I have received several phone calls and letters from you concerning an overdue Rich's Department Store account.

This is my formal notice to you under 15 U.S.C. § 1692c to cease all further communications with me except for the reasons specifically set forth in the federal law.

This letter is not meant in any way to be an acknowledgment that I owe this money.

Very truly yours,

Lee Anne Ito
Lee Anne Ito

Prohibited Collection Agency Actions

Below are some collection actions prohibited by the FDCPA.

Communications with third parties. For the most part, a collection agency cannot contact third parties about your debt. There are a few exceptions to this general rule. Collectors are allowed to contact:

- Your attorney. If the collector knows you are represented by an attorney, it must talk only to the attorney, not you, unless you give it permission to contact you or your attorney doesn't respond to the agency's communications.
- A credit reporting agency.
- The original creditor.

Collectors are also allowed to contact your spouse, your parents (only if you are a minor), and your codebtors. But they cannot make these contacts if you have sent a letter asking them to stop contacting you.

There is one other exception. Debt collectors are allowed to contact third parties for the limited purpose of finding information about your whereabouts. In these contacts, the collector:

- must state his name and that he is confirming location information about you
- cannot state his employer's name unless asked
- cannot state that you owe a debt
- cannot contact a third party more than once unless required to do so by the third party, or unless he believes the third party's earlier response was wrong or incomplete and that the

third party has correct or complete information

- cannot communicate by postcard
- cannot use any words or symbols on the outside of an envelope that indicate he's trying to collect a debt (including a business logo or letterhead) if either would give away the purpose of the letter, and
- cannot call third parties for location information once he knows an attorney represents you.

Communications with a debtor. As mentioned, a debt collector's first communication with you must tell you that he or she is attempting to collect a debt and that any information obtained from you will be used for that purpose. In subsequent communications, the collector must tell you his or her and the collection agency's name.

A collector cannot contact you:

- at an unusual or inconvenient time or place—calls before 8 a.m. and after 9 p.m. are presumed to be inconvenient (but, if you work nights and sleep during the day, a call at 1 p.m. may also be inconvenient)
- directly, if it knows or should have known that you have an attorney, or
- at work if it knows that your employer prohibits you from receiving collections calls at work. (If you are contacted at work, tell the collector that your boss prohibits such calls.)

WARNING

If your debt is so old that it is "time-barred," you should never talk to the collection

agency about it at all. Just hang up the phone, or put the receiver down and walk away. Otherwise, you might get tricked into explaining why you can't pay. If you ever acknowledge in any way that you still owe the debt, that can turn it into *a brand-new debt,* with more legal remedies for the collection agency.

Harassment or abuse. In general, a collection agency cannot engage in conduct meant to harass, oppress, or abuse. Specifically, it cannot:

- use or threaten to use violence
- harm or threaten to harm you, another person, or your or another person's reputation or property
- use obscene or profane language
- publish your name as a person who doesn't pay bills (child support collection agencies are exempt from this—see Chapter 14)
- list your debt for sale to the public
- call you repeatedly, or
- place telephone calls to you without identifying the caller as a bill collector.

You never have to put up with harassment. Just hang up the phone, or put the receiver down (without hanging up) and walk away.

False or misleading representations. A collection agency can't lie. For example, it can't:

- claim to be a law enforcement agency or suggest that it is connected with the federal, state, or local government (a collector making this kind of claim is probably lying, unless it's trying to collect unpaid child support, or it's a private check diversion program under contract with a district attorney)

• falsely represent the amount you owe or the amount of compensation the collection agency will receive

• claim to be an attorney or that a communication is from an attorney

• claim that you'll be imprisoned or your property will be seized, unless the collection agency or original creditor intends to take action that could result in your going to jail or your property being taken (you can go to jail only for extremely limited reasons—see Chapter 8)

• threaten to take action that isn't intended or can't be taken—for example, if a letter from a collection agency states that it is a "final notice," it cannot write you again demanding payment

• falsely claim you've committed a crime

• threaten to sell a debt to a third party, and claim that, as a result, you will lose defenses to payment you had against the creditor (such as a breach of warranty)

• communicate false credit information, such as failing to state that you dispute a debt

• send you a document that looks like it's from a court or attorney or part of a legal process

• use a false business name, or

• claim to be employed by a credit bureau, unless the collection agency and the credit bureau are the same company.

Unfair practices. A collection agency cannot engage in any unfair or outrageous method to collect a debt. Specifically, it can't:

• add interest, fees, or charges not authorized in the original agreement or by state law

• accept a check postdated by more than five days unless it notifies you between three and ten days in advance of when it will deposit the check

• deposit a postdated check prior to the date on the check

• solicit a postdated check for the purpose of then threatening you with criminal prosecution

• call you collect or otherwise cause you to incur communications charges

• threaten to seize or repossess your property if it has no right to do so or no intention of doing so

• communicate with you by postcard, or

• put any words or symbols on the outside of an envelope sent to you that indicates it's trying to collect a debt.

If a Collection Agency Violates the Law

Some collection agencies engage in illegal practices when attempting to collect debts. Here are some of the more atrocious acts collection agencies have committed:

• Sending debtors fake legal papers and then pretending to be sheriffs. They tell debtors to pay immediately or threaten that the debtors will lose their personal possessions.

Interest Rate a Collection Agency Can Charge Before Getting a Judgment

This chart gives the interest rates set by state law for situations where the contract or agreement does not set an interest rate. If a contract or agreement does set an interest rate, then that is the one the collection agency can charge, even if it is different from the state rate. For a discussion of state usury limits on interest rates, see "Why Are Credit Card Interest Rates So High?" in Chapter 10.

State	Code Section	Rate
Alabama	Ala. Code. § 8-8-1	6%
Alaska	Alaska Stat. § 45.45.010	10.50%
Arizona	Ariz. Rev. Stat. Ann. § 44-1201(A)	10%
Arkansas	Ark. Const. Art. 19, § 13(d)(i)	6%
California	Calif. Civ. Code § 3289(b)	10%
Colorado	Colo. Rev. Stat. § 5-12-101	8%
Connecticut	Conn. Gen. Stat. Ann. § 37-1	8%
Delaware	Del. Code Ann. tit. 6, § 2301(a)	5% above the Federal Reserve discount window rate at the time interest is due (www.federalreserve.gov/releases/h15)
District of Columbia	D.C. Code Ann. § 28-3302	6%
Florida	Fla. Stat. Ann. §§ 687.01, 55.03	5% above average Federal Reserve Bank of N.Y. discount window rate for preceding year
Georgia	Ga. Code Ann. §§ 7-4-2, 7-4-18	7%
Hawaii	Haw. Rev. Stat. § 478-2	10%
Idaho	Idaho Code § 28-22-104(1)	12%
Illinois	815 Ill. Comp. Stat. §§ 205/1, 2	5%
Indiana	Ind. Code Ann. § 24-4.6-1-102	8%
Iowa	Iowa Code § 535.2	5%
Kansas	Kan. Stat. Ann. § 16-201	10%
Kentucky	Ky. Rev. Stat. Ann. § 360.010	8%
Louisiana	La. Rev. Stat. 9:3500	12% maximum; must be in writing

Interest Rate a Collection Agency Can Charge Before Getting a Judgment (cont'd)

State	Code Section	Rate
Maine	Me. Rev. Stat. Ann. tit. 9A, §2-401(7)	$5 on loans up to $75; $15 on loans over $75 and under $250; and $25 on loans of $250 or more
Maryland	Md. Const. Art. 3, § 57; Md. Code Ann. [Com. Law.] § 12-102	6%
Massachusetts	Mass. Gen. Laws ch. 107, § 3	6%
Michigan	Mich. Comp. Laws § 438.31	5%
Minnesota	Minn. Stat. Ann. § 334.01(Subd. 1)	6%
Mississippi	Miss. Code Ann. § 75-17-1(1)	8%
Missouri	Mo. Rev. Stat. § 408.020	9%
Montana	Mont. Code Ann. § 31-1-106	10%
Nebraska	Neb. Rev. Stat. § 45-102	6%
Nevada	Nev. Rev. Stat. Ann § 99.040	2% above the prime rate at Nevada's largest bank on January 1 or July 1 (posted at www.fid.state.nv.us; click on "Prime Interest Rate")
New Hampshire	N.H. Rev. Stat. Ann. § 336:1(I)	10%
New Jersey	N.J. Stat. Ann. § 31:1-1(a)	6%
New Mexico	N.M. Stat. Ann. § 56-8-3	15%
New York	N.Y. Gen. Oblig. Law § 5-501(1)	6%
North Carolina	N.C. Gen. Stat. § 24-1	8%
North Dakota	N.D. Cent. Code § 47-14-05	6%
Ohio	Ohio Rev. Code Ann. §§ 1343.03(A), 5703.47	Federal short-term rate to nearest whole percent plus 3%. (Calculated each October, effective for one year based on July federal rate.)
Oklahoma	Okla. Const. Art. 14, § 2; Okla. Stat. Ann. tit. 15, § 266	6%
Oregon	Or. Rev. Stat. § 82.010(1)	9%
Pennsylvania	41 Pa. Cons. Stat. Ann. § 202	6%

Interest Rate a Collection Agency Can Charge Before Getting a Judgment (cont'd)

State	Code Section	Rate
Rhode Island	R.I. Gen. Laws § 6-26-1	12%
South Carolina	S.C. Code Ann. § 34-31-20(A)	8.75%
South Dakota	S.D. Codified Laws Ann. §§ 54-3-4, 54-3-16(3)	12%
Tennessee	Tenn. Code Ann. § 47-14-103(3)	10%
Texas	Tex. Fin. Code Ann. § 302.002	6%
Utah	Utah Code Ann. § 15-1-1	10%
Vermont	Vt. Stat. Ann. tit. 9, § 41a(a)	12%
Virginia	Va. Code Ann. § 6.1-330.53	6%
Washington	Wash. Rev. Code Ann. § 19.52.010(1)	12%
West Virginia	W.Va. Code Ann. § 47-6-5(a)	6%
Wisconsin	Wis. Stat. Ann. § 138.04	5%
Wyoming	Wyo. Stat. § 40-14-106(e)	7%

Current as of February 2007

- Using vulgarity and profanity to threaten debtors.
- Harassing a debtor's parents—in particular, impersonating a government prosecutor and requesting that the parent ask the debtor to contact the collector.
- Soliciting a postdated check, depositing it early, and threatening the debtor with prosecution for writing a bad check.
- Suggesting that a debtor take up prostitution to increase income.
- Threatening to report Latino and Asian debtors to the U.S. Citizenship and Immigration Services (formerly the INS) and posing as immigration officers.
- Engaging in repeated violations of the law—such as verbal harassment, late night calls, and calls to neighbors and friends—especially at the end of each month when collectors are trying to reach their monthly collection quotas.

If a collection agency violates the law—whether it's a large or small violation—try to collect proof of the violation. Written threats are the best proof, but collectors usually know better than to threaten you in writing. Another effective way to collect evidence is to keep a written log of all calls you get from the agency. Write down the agent's name, date and time of call, and any information you remember about what the collection agent told you.

In some states, you can tape the conversation without the collector's knowledge. Only do this if you are sure it's legal. Many states allow it—but in California it's a crime, and the tape cannot be used as evidence, except to prosecute you. (Cal. Penal Code § 632.) To find out if it's legal in your state, you'll have to do some legal research on your own. (See Chapter 19 to learn more about legal research.) If it's not legal to do this in your state (or you aren't sure), try to have a witness present during your conversations. If you're loud enough about the abuse you suffered—and you've got proof backing you up—you have a chance to get the whole debt canceled in exchange for agreeing not to file a complaint

Suppose the collector is foolish enough to leave a message with illegal content (profanity, for example) on your answering machine. Even in a state with a law like California's, the recording probably can be used as evidence, provided that it can be properly authenticated.

To complain, contact the Federal Trade Commission. (See Appendix A for the address.) Also complain to the state agency that regulates collection agencies for the state where the agency is located. (See Appendix A for contact information.)

The Federal Trade Commission or the state agency may send you a form to help it process your complaint. Be thorough. Include dates, times, and the names of any witnesses to unlawful conversations, and attach copies (keep the originals for yourself) of all offending materials you received. The FTC normally cannot help individual consumers. However, it may take enforcement action against a collector if it receives numerous complaints.

Also, write to the original creditor and send a copy of this letter to the collection agency, the Federal Trade Commission, and the state agency. The original creditor may be concerned about its own liability and offer to cancel the debt at once.

You also have the right to sue a collection agency for harassment. You can represent yourself in small claims court or hire an attorney. Attorney fees and court costs are recoverable if you win. You're entitled to any actual damages, including pain and suffering. And, even if you did not suffer any actual damages, you can still recover up to $1,000 for any violation of the FDCPA. You might also be able to get punitive damages if the collector's conduct was particularly horrible. But, if you can't document repeated abusive behavior, you'll probably have a tough time winning. For example, if the collector calls five times in one day and then you never hear from him or her again, you'll probably lose in court.

In truly outrageous cases, consider hiring a lawyer to represent you in regular court. Some private lawyers specialize in debt collection abuse cases. Call your state or local bar association or lawyer referral service, or look in the phone book. You may be able to find a referral through the National Association of Consumer Advocates' website, www.naca.net.

Sample Letter to Original Creditor

Stonecutter Furniture Factory
4500 Wilson Boulevard
Bloomington, IN 47400

April 19, 2008

Dear Stonecutter:

On May 10, 2007, I purchased a bedroom set from you for $2,000 ($500 down and the rest at $100 per month). I paid $900 and then lost my job, became ill, and was unable to pay you.

In early 2007, I was contacted by R. Greene at the Drone Collection Agency. R. Greene called me twice a day for nearly three weeks and used profanity at me, my husband, and my 11-year-old son. In addition, he called my father and threatened him with a lawsuit, even though he is a 76-year-old diabetic with a heart condition and has had no connection with this transaction.

I have contacted the Federal Trade Commission and I am considering seeing an attorney. I am fully prepared to take the steps necessary to protect my family and me from further harassment. I am writing you in the hope that you have not condoned Drone's practices and will instruct Drone to stop harassing and abusing my family and me. I also would appreciate any other assistance or consideration you may be able to provide.

Very truly yours,

Karen Wood
Karen Wood

cc: Indiana Secretary of State; Drone Collection Agency; Federal Trade Commission

You might especially choose this route if the mental abuse inflicted on you is substantial and you have reports from therapists and doctors documenting your suffering. In 1995, a Texas jury awarded $11 million (this amount was later reduced by an appellate court) to a debtor and her spouse against both a collection agency and a creditor after the collection agency called the debtor repeatedly at home and work and made death threats and bomb threats. The debtor, fearing for her and her husband's safety, moved out of town. (*Driscol v. Allied Adjustment Bureau*, Docket #92-7267 (El Paso, Texas, 1995).)

In addition to bringing a lawsuit against a collector, you can also raise FDCPA violations in a collection lawsuit brought against you by a creditor or collection agency. These are called "counterclaims." See Chapter 14 for more on counterclaims.

State or Local Laws Prohibiting Unfair Debt Collections

Several states have enacted laws prohibiting unfair debt collection practices. A few laws are similar to the federal legislation. Some, however, go further. The most valuable state laws prohibit unethical and abusive collection practices by collection agencies and original creditors. (Remember, the federal law applies only to collection agencies.) Some key provisions of each state's laws, and where to find them, appear below.

State Debt Collection Laws Providing Additional Protections

State	Code Section	Summary
Alaska	Alaska Admin. Code tit. 3 § 01.210	Creditor cannot contact debtor at work unless employer allows employees to receive those communications during work hours, and creditor has debtor's prior written consent.
Arizona	Ariz. Admin. Code § R20-4-1512	Collection agency cannot contact debtor at work unless agency has made reasonable attempt to contact debtor at home and such attempt has failed. Cannot contact relatives, friends, or any other third parties to ask them to pressure the debtor to pay the debt or pay it themselves.
	§ R20-4-1514	In the first contact, collection agency must disclose name of original creditor, time and place debt was incurred, merchandise or service purchased, and date account was turned over to agency. Debtor has right to see agency's books and records concerning debt and right to copies of all relevant documents in agency's possession.
Arkansas	Ark. Code Ann. § 17-24-307(12)	Collection agency cannot send mail or telephone debtor at work unless agency has made good-faith attempt to contact debtor at home and such attempt has failed.
California	Calif. Civil Code §§ 1788.10 to .17	Creditor collecting own debt must comply with all provisions of the Fair Debt Collection Practices Act (FDCPA), except disclosures outlined in "Required Disclosures by a Collection Agency," above.
Colorado	Colo. Rev. Stat. § 12-14-106(1)(f)	Collection agency collector must identify self within first 60 seconds after the party answering the telephone is identified as debtor.
	§ 12-14-105(3)	Collection agency must, in its initial written communication to the debtor, state that information about the Colorado Fair Debt Collections Act is available at www.ago.state.co.us/cadc/cadcmain.cfm.
	Colo. Collection Agency Board Rule 2.05	Collection agency must provide debtor with receipt for payments made in cash or by any other means which does not provide evidence of payment. (Check drawn on debtor's bank account would not require receipt.) Receipt must be provided within five days after payment is received (Sundays and holidays excluded).
	Rule 2.06	If debtor requests in writing, collection agency must provide, within ten days of request, at no cost, once per year, statement of debtor's payments since collection agency has had assignment of the debt. Statement must include debtor's name; creditor's name; amounts paid; dates payments were received; allocation of money to principal, interest, court costs, attorneys' fees; and other costs. Collection agency may charge no more than $5 for subsequent statements.

State Debt Collection Laws Providing Additional Protections (cont'd)		
State	**Code Section**	**Summary**
Connecticut	Conn. Gen. Stat. § 36a-646	Creditor collecting own debt cannot use abusive, harassing, fraudulent, deceptive, or misleading practices to collect debt.
District of Columbia	D.C. Code Ann. § 28-3814	Actions prohibited under the FDCPA, outlined in "Prohibited Collection Agency Actions," above, apply to creditor collecting own debt.
	§ 22-3401	Collection agency may not use "D.C." or "District of Columbia" in any way that would imply that it is an agency of the government.
Florida	Fla. Stat. Ann. § 559.72	Creditor collecting own debt cannot use collection practices prohibited by the FDCPA, as outlined in "Prohibited Collection Agency Actions," above. In addition, creditor collecting own debt and debt collector cannot: • communicate with debtor's employer before a judgment is obtained unless debtor consents • include the debtor in a "deadbeat" list.
Georgia	Ga. Code Ann. § 7-3-25(5)	Collection agency cannot contact debtor by phone or in person after 10 p.m. or before 5 a.m.
	Ga. Rules of Comptroller General R. 120-1-14.23(c)	Collection agency cannot attempt to lure debtor into giving information by claiming it has something of value to offer debtor.
	R. 120-1-14.24	Collection agency cannot seek or obtain statement in which debtor agrees: • to pay debt discharged in bankruptcy without clearly disclosing nature and consequence of agreement and fact that debtor is not legally obligated to pay debt • that debt was incurred to pay for necessaries of life when debt was not for that purpose.
Hawaii	Haw. Rev. Stat. Ann. § 443B-19	Collection agency cannot seek or obtain statement in which debtor agrees: • that debt was incurred to pay for necessaries of life when debt was not for that purpose • to pay debt discharged in bankruptcy without clearly disclosing nature and consequence of agreement and fact that debtor is not legally obligated to pay debt • to pay collection agency's fee.
	§ 480D-3	Creditor collecting own debt cannot use collection practices prohibited by the FDCPA, as outlined in "Prohibited Collection Agency Actions," above.

State	Code Section	Summary
State Debt Collection Laws Providing Additional Protections (cont'd)		
Hawaii (continued)	§ 480D-3 (continued)	In addition, creditor collecting own debt and debt collector cannot: • threaten to hire collector who will violate the law • threaten to sell debt to third party, and claim that as a result, debtor will lose defenses to payment debtor had against creditor (such as breach of warranty) • seek or obtain statement in which debtor agrees that the debt was incurred to pay for necessaries of life when debt was not incurred for that purpose • collect or attempt to collect interest or other charges unless authorized by contract or by law.
Idaho	Idaho Code § 26-2229A(2)	If collection agency and creditor have a financial or a managerial interest in the other, that information must be disclosed to the debtor in every communication.
	§ 28-45-109	Creditor collecting own debt cannot use or threaten to use violence or other criminal means to cause harm to the debtor's person, reputation, or property.
Illinois	225 Ill. Comp. Stat. § 425/9(14), (19)	Collection agency cannot contact or threaten to contact debtor's employer unless debt is more than 30 days past due; at least five days before contacting employer, agency must notify debtor in writing that it intends to do so. Collection agency cannot engage in conduct which is intended to cause and does cause mental or physical illness to debtor or debtor's family.
Indiana	Ind. Code Ann. § 24-4.5-5-107(1)	Creditor collecting own debt cannot use or threaten to use violence or other criminal means to cause harm to the debtor's person, reputation, or property.
Iowa	Iowa Code § 537.7103	Creditor collecting own debt cannot use collection practices prohibited by the FDCPA, as outlined in "Prohibited Collection Agency Actions," above. In addition, creditor collecting own debt and debt collector cannot: • disseminate information relating to debt to third persons (other than credit bureaus, attorneys, and others who may have location information; also, may contact debtor's employer once a month to verify debtor's employment; once every three months may contact debtor's employer or credit union to pass on debt counseling information to debtor; once every three months may contact parents of minor debtor or trustee, conservator, or guardian of debtor)

State Debt Collection Laws Providing Additional Protections (cont'd)		
State	**Code Section**	**Summary**
Iowa (continued)	Iowa Code § 537.7103 (continued)	• include debtor in "deadbeat" list • fail to state name and address of business originally owed money • obtain statement that both husband and wife are liable on debt when only one is • seek or obtain statement in which debtor agrees to pay debt discharged in bankruptcy without clearly disclosing nature and consequence of agreement and fact that debtor is not legally obligated to pay the debt • attempt to collect collection agency's fee unless authorized by law • collect or attempt to collect interest or other charges unless authorized by contract or by law.
Kansas	Kan. Stat. Ann. § 16a-5-107(1)	Creditor collecting own debt cannot use or threaten to use violence or other criminal means to cause harm to the debtor's person, reputation, or property.
Louisiana	La. Rev. Stat. Ann. § 9:3562	Creditor collecting own debt cannot contact any person not residing in debtor's household other than another creditor or credit bureau, except: • to ascertain location information if creditor believes debtor has moved or changed jobs • to discover property owned by debtor which may be seized to satisfy a judgment. If debtor has told creditor to cease communicating with debtor, creditor may mail notices to debtor once a month as long as they are not designed to threaten action. Creditor may make four personal contacts with debtor in attempt to settle debt. Creditor may resume contacts if creditor has obtained a judgment against debtor.
Maine	Me. Rev. Stat. Ann. tit. 9-A, § 5-116	Creditor collecting own debt cannot: • threaten or use violence or force • threaten criminal prosecution • disclose information about debt to third persons other than debtor's spouse or person who has a business need for information • fail to state to third persons that debtor disputes debt • simulate legal process or government agency • communicate or threaten to communicate with debtor's employer more than twice concerning existence of debt • attempt to collect debt that is legally uncollectable.

State Debt Collection Laws Providing Additional Protections (cont'd)		
State	**Code Section**	**Summary**
Maine (continued)	Me. Rev. Stat. Ann. tit. 32, § 11013	Maine has been granted an exemption from the FDCPA. Most of the state law is the same as the FDCPA. Additional laws provide that collection agency cannot: • use shame cards, shame automobiles, or similar devices to bring public notice that debtor has not paid debt • falsely state that account was sold to third persons • use notary public, constable, sheriff, or other person authorized to serve legal papers to collect debt • hire attorney to collect debt unless authorized to do so by creditor.
Maryland	Md. Code Ann. [Com. Law] § 14-202	Creditor collecting own debt cannot use collection practices prohibited by the FDCPA, as outlined in "Prohibited Collection Agency Actions," above. In addition, creditor collecting own debt and debt collector cannot contact debtor's employer before obtaining a court judgment.
Massachusetts	Mass. Gen. Laws ch. 93, § 49	Creditor collecting own debt cannot use collection practices prohibited by the FDCPA, as outlined in "Prohibited Collection Agency Actions," above.
	Mass. Regs. Code tit. 209, Ch. 18 § 18.13	• Collector may not communicate with a third party except to seek consumer's location • Collector may not contact third party more than once unless requested by the person or because the collector reasonably believes information given was erroneous or incomplete, and that the person now has complete location information • Collector may not refer to debts when communicating with third party.
	Mass. Regs. Code tit. 209, Ch. 18 § 18.14	• No communication at unusual or inconvenient time or place • No direct communication with a debtor known to be represented by counsel, unless attorney consents or fails to respond • No communication at workplace if employer prohibits or if consumer made oral or written request • Must provide specific notice of consumer's right to prevent calls to the workplace • No more than two calls a week to the home and no more than 2 calls in 30 days to places other than home, per debt • No unauthorized communications with third parties about the debt • Only specified communication permitted if consumer notifies collector in writing to cease further communication.

State Debt Collection Laws Providing Additional Protections (cont'd)		
State	**Code Section**	**Summary**
Massachusetts (continued)	Mass. Regs. Code tit. 209, Ch. 18 § 18.15	• No more than one home visit in 30 days without consent, no entry without invitation • No office visit without consent • No confrontations in public places .
	Mass. Regs. Code tit. 209, Ch. 18 § 18.17	• No attempt to get consumer to reaffirm debt discharged in bankruptcy, without conspicuous disclosure of the consequences • No reports to credit bureau in the name of the debt collector, without consent of the creditor • Cannot purport to practice law or give legal advice • Must disclose office phone number and office hours on all written communications with debtor.

	Mass. Regs. Code tit. 209, Ch. 18 § 18.18	• Within five days, must provide consumer or counsel with:
		  • all papers in the collector's possession bearing the consumer's signature and concerning the debt being collected
		  • ledgers, account cards, or similar records in the collector's possession showing the date and amount of payments, credits, and charges on the debt.

	Mass. Regs. Code tit. 209, Ch. 18 §18.19	If there are multiple debts, consumer's payment cannot be applied to a disputed debt and must be applied according to consumer's instructions, if any.
Michigan	Mich. Comp. Laws §§ 339.915(m), (q)	Collection agency cannot: • use shame cards, shame automobiles, or similar devices to bring public notice that debtor has not paid debt • fail to implement procedures designed to prevent law violations by agency employees.
	§§ 339.915a(d) and (l)	Collection agency cannot: • hire an attorney to collect debt unless authorized by creditor • fail to provide debtor with receipt for cash payments and other payments when specifically requested.
	§ 445.252	Actions prohibited under the FDCPA, outlined in "Prohibited Collection Agency Actions," above, apply to creditor collecting own debt.
Minnesota	Minn. Stat. Ann. § 332.37	Collection agency cannot: • communicate in such a way to imply or suggest that health care services will be withheld from the debtor in an emergency • contact a neighbor or other third party (other than a person with whom the debtor lives) to request that the debtor contact the collector when a debtor has a listed telephone number

State	Code Section	Summary
State Debt Collection Laws Providing Additional Protections (cont'd)		
Minnesota (continued)	Minn. Stat. Ann. § 332.37 (continued)	• use shame cards or shame automobiles, advertise or threaten to advertise for sale any claim in order to force payment • transact business or hold itself out as a debt prorater or debt adjuster or someone who will pool, settle, or pay the debtor's debts, unless there is no charge to the debtor, or the pooling or liquidation is done pursuant to court order • use an automatic recorded message unless, prior to the message, a live operator tells the debtor that the message is from the collection agency and is intended to solicit payment and gets the debtor's consent to hear the message • fail to provide the debtor with the full name of the collection agency • accept cash without providing a receipt to the debtor • during first mail contact, fail to include a disclosure stating, "This collection agency is licensed by the Minnesota Department of Commerce."
Nebraska	Neb. Rev. Stat. Ann. § 45-1043	Bank lender cannot contact person who does not live in debtor's home regarding the debt except for debtor's spouse or attorney, another creditor, or a credit bureau.
Nevada	Nev. Admin. Code § 649.050	Collection agency may not use machine-derived form letter unless it has received prior approval from the state.
	Nev. Rev. Stat. Ann. § 649.375(8)	Collection agency cannot operate consumer debt counseling service where debtor turns over earnings or money for payment or adjustment of debt.
New Hampshire	N.H. Rev. Stat. Ann § 358-C:3	Creditor collecting own debt cannot use collection practices prohibited by the FDCPA, as outlined in "Prohibited Collection Agency Actions," above. In addition, creditor collecting own debt and debt collector cannot: • communicate with third persons about debt except with others who live in debtor's household, an attorney, a financial counseling organization, another person claiming to represent debtor, or a credit bureau • communicate with debtor's spouse, or parent or guardian if debtor is a minor, except to ascertain location information. However, collector must have been unable to locate debtor by any other means for at least 30 days, and collector must not attempt to contact spouse, parent, or guardian again. • call debtor at work more than once a month unless debtor agrees in writing to more frequent calls.

State Debt Collection Laws Providing Additional Protections (cont'd)		
State	**Code Section**	**Summary**
New York	N.Y. Gen. Bus. Law § 601	Creditor collecting own debt cannot use collection practices prohibited by the FDCPA, as outlined in "Prohibited Collection Agency Actions," above. In addition, creditor collecting own debt and debt collector cannot: • contact debtor's employer unless creditor has court judgment or is seeking wage attachment, which debtor has consented to • attempt to enforce right collector knows does not exist.
New York City	Rules of the City of N.Y. Tit. 6, § 5-77	Creditor collecting own debt cannot use collection practices prohibited by the FDCPA, as outlined in "Prohibited Collection Agency Actions," above. In addition, creditor collecting own debt and debt collector cannot: • contact a third party more than once when trying to locate the debtor unless requested by the person or because the collector reasonably believes information given was erroneous or incomplete, and that the person now has complete location information • fail to send written notice within five days of initial communication with debtor that states the amount of debt, to whom debt is owed, when debt is due, and that the debtor has the right to dispute the validity of the debt • fail to respond in writing if the debtor disputes the validity of the debt • fail to end contact with debtor upon debtor's request (except that creditor can contact debtor one last time to advise debtor that it will invoke a specific remedy, such as bring a lawsuit).
North Carolina	N.C. Gen. Stat. § 58-70-70	Collection agency must provide debtor with receipt for all payments made in cash. Receipt must include name, address, and permit number of collection agency, name of creditor, amount and date paid, and name of person accepting payment.
	§ 58-70-110(3)	Collection agency cannot claim it has something of value in its possession to lure debtor.
	§ 58-70-115	Collection agency cannot: • seek or obtain statement in which debtor agrees to pay debt discharged in bankruptcy or barred by statute of limitations, without disclosing the consequences and that the debtor is not legally obligated to do so • collect or attempt to collect the agency's fee, unless legally entitled to do so.

State Debt Collection Laws Providing Additional Protections (cont'd)		
State	**Code Section**	**Summary**
North Carolina (continued)	§§ 75-51 to 55	Creditor collecting own debt cannot use collection practices prohibited by the FDCPA, as outlined in "Prohibited Collection Agency Actions," above. In addition, creditor collecting own debt and debt collector cannot: • contact debtor's employer, against debtor's express desire, unless collector does not have phone number to reach debtor during nonworking hours • communicate with third persons other than debtor's attorney unless debtor consents, for the sole purpose of locating the debtor and without discussing the debt, or third person is credit bureau, debt collector or collection agency, spouse of debtor, or parent or guardian of minor debtor • claim it has something of value in its possession to lure debtor • seek or obtain statement in which debtor agrees to pay debt discharged in bankruptcy, barred by the statute of limitations, or not legally collectible without disclosing nature and consequence of agreement and fact that debtor is not legally obligated to pay debt • sue debtor in county other than that where debt was incurred or debtor lives if distance makes it impractical for debtor to defend claim.
Oklahoma	Okla. Stat. Ann. tit. 14A, § 5-107(1)	Creditor collecting own debt cannot use or threaten to use violence or other criminal means to cause harm to the debtor's person, reputation, or property.
Oregon	Or. Rev. Stat. § 646.639	Creditor collecting own debt cannot use collection practices prohibited by the FDCPA, as outlined in "Prohibited Collection Agency Actions," above.
Pennsylvania	73 Pa. Cons. Stat. Ann. §§ 2270.3, 2270.4	Actions prohibited under the FDCPA, outlined in "Prohibited Collection Agency Actions," above, apply to creditor collecting own debt.
	18 Pa. Cons. Stat. Ann. § 7311(d)	Collection agency cannot offer debt adjustment or debt settlement services.
South Carolina	S.C. Code Ann. § 37-5-107	Creditor collecting own debt cannot use or threaten to use violence or other criminal means to cause harm to the debtor's person, reputation, or property.

State Debt Collection Laws Providing Additional Protections (cont'd)		
State	**Code Section**	**Summary**
South Carolina (continued)	§ 37-5-108	Creditor collecting own debt cannot use collection practices prohibited by the FDCPA, as outlined in "Prohibited Collection Agency Actions," above. In addition, creditor collecting own debt and debt collector cannot communicate with the debtor or a family member at frequent intervals during a 24-hour period or under other circumstances that make it reasonable to infer that the primary purpose of the communication was to harass the debtor.
Tennessee	Tenn. Code Ann. § 62-20-111(b)	In all written communications collection agency must state that it is licensed by the state collection services board of the Department of Commerce.
Texas	Tex. Fin. Code Ann. §§ 392.303, 392.304(3)	Actions prohibited under the FDCPA, outlined in "Prohibited Collection Agency Actions," above, apply to creditor collecting own debt. In addition, collection agency and creditor collecting own debt cannot: • seek or obtain statement in which debtor agrees that debt was incurred to pay for necessaries of life when debt was not for that purpose • claim it has something of value in its possession to lure debtor.
Utah	Utah Code Ann. § 70C-7-105	Creditor collecting own debt cannot use or threaten to use violence or other criminal means to cause harm to the debtor's person, reputation, or property.
Vermont	Vt. Consumer Fraud Rules CF 104.01 to 104.07	Creditor collecting own debt cannot use collection practices prohibited by the FDCPA, as outlined in "Prohibited Collection Agency Actions," above. In addition, debt collector and creditor collecting own debt cannot: • lure the debtor by claiming it has information or something of value in its possession • in the first demand for money, fail to disclose the name and address of the person to whom the claim has been assigned • seek or obtain an affirmation of a debt by a debtor who has received a discharge in bankruptcy, whose debt is barred by the statute of limitations, or whose debt is otherwise not collectible, without clearly disclosing to debtor that he is not legally obligated to pay the debt and the consequences of the affirmation.

State Debt Collection Laws Providing Additional Protections (cont'd)		
State	**Code Section**	**Summary**
Washington	Wash. Rev. Code Ann. § 19.16.250, §§ 308-29-070 to -080	In all written communications, collection agency must include name and address of agency and name of creditor. In first communication, collection agency must include an itemization showing: • amount owed on original obligation • interest (including rate charged), service charges, collection costs, and late fees assessed by creditor • attorneys' fees • any other charges. Collection agency cannot: • threaten debtor with impairment of credit rating if claim is not paid • communicate with debtor more than three times in one week or communicate with debtor at work more than once per week. Collection agency cannot make more than one contact with debtor concerning debts that arise from dishonored checks or ATM transactions if debtor's checkbook was stolen or account information was obtained by fraud; within 180 days debtor must notify collection agency in writing and send certified copy of police report and copy of photo I.D. containing debtor's signature.
West Virginia	W. Va. Code Ann. §§ 46a-2-124 to 128	Actions prohibited under the FDCPA, outlined in "Prohibited Collection Agency Actions," above, apply to creditor collecting own debt. In addition, collection agency and creditor collecting own debt cannot: • communicate with debtor's employer before obtaining court judgment except through court process • communicate with relative of debtor other than those in debtor's household except through court process • claim it has something of value in its possession to lure debtor • seek or obtain statement in which debtor agrees that debt was incurred to pay for necessaries of life when debt was not incurred for that purpose • seek or obtain statement in which debtor agrees to pay debt discharged in bankruptcy without clearly disclosing nature and consequence of agreement and fact that debtor is not legally obligated to pay debt • attempt to collect collection agency's fee.

State Debt Collection Laws Providing Additional Protections (cont'd)		
State	**Code Section**	**Summary**
Wisconsin	Wis. Admin. Code Ch. DFI-Bkg 74.11	Within 10 days of written request from debtor, collection agency must provide a written statement of the debtor's payments for as long as the collection agency has had the account. Must be provided without cost and upon request once in every 12-month period. When debt has been paid in full and upon request by the debtor, must provide written statement that the debt was paid in full.
	Wis. Stat. Ann. § 427.104	Creditor collecting own debt cannot use collection practices prohibited by the FDCPA, as outlined in "Prohibited Collection Agency Actions," above.
	§ 425.108(1)	Creditor collecting own debt cannot use or threaten to use violence or other criminal means to cause harm to the debtor's person, reputation, or property.
Wyoming	Wyo. Stat. § 40-14-507(a)	Creditor collecting own debt cannot use or threaten to use violence or other criminal means to cause harm to the debtor's person, reputation, or property.

Current as of February 2007

■

Credit and Debit Cards

Getting along with women, Knocking around with men, Having more credit than money, Thus one goes through the world.

—Johann Wolfgang von Goethe
German poet and dramatist
1749-1832

I n 1927, Farrington Manufacturing Company in Boston issued the first merchant charge card (it reportedly looked like a dog tag) to be used by American consumers. Following World War II, many more merchants offered charge cards to their customers. In 1950, 22 New York restaurants and one hotel agreed to honor a card to let their customers dine (or sleep) now and pay later. Little did they know that the industry started by their "Diners Club" card would quickly become an indispensable part of our economy. By 1960, the Diners Club card had about 1.1 million card holders and was accepted in all kinds of retail establishments—not just New York restaurants.

Seeing the success of the Diners Club card, a small number of banks offered credit cards during the 1950s. Few merchants accepted these cards, however, and it wasn't until Bank of America in San Francisco came out with the BankAmericard (now Visa) in 1966 that the idea caught on. East Coast banks quickly followed suit with a credit card that became known as the MasterCard.

Throughout the 1970s, '80s, and '90s, the credit card industry grew beyond everyone's wildest expectations. Today, most Americans have six or seven credit cards. The average American holds about four

retail, three bank, one phone, one gas, and one travel and entertainment card (such as Diners Club). Over half of these consumers carry a balance on at least one of these cards. In 2006, the average family owed approximately $9,000 on their credit cards.

As consumers are bombarded with more and more solicitations (credit card issuers send out more than six billion solicitations each year), it has become increasingly difficult to understand the offers, choose the best deals, and use the cards wisely. This chapter explains the key credit card agreement terms, provides tips on how to save money when using credit cards, and summarizes laws that apply to credit card use.

Credit Cards

Credit cards can amount to nothing other than very expensive loans made by banks, gasoline companies, and department stores. Today, credit cards are by far more common than charge cards. Even gas companies have converted their charge cards to credit cards, and American Express offers credit cards.

The Credit Card Industry

The way credit cards work is fairly straightforward: The credit card issuer gives you a card. You use the card to pay for items and services up to a certain total amount—your credit limit. The store merchant or service provider collects what you owe from the card issuer, whom you repay. You're allowed to pay off what you owe little by little each month, as long as you pay a minimum amount each time. You're charged interest on the balance you owe (sometimes as high as 29% a year) at the end of each period unless you pay the full balance when your bill arrives.

Credit cards yield high profits to their issuers for several reasons. The most important is the high rate of interest— interest on credit cards alone accounts for about 65% of the profits earned by banks that issue credit cards. Credit card companies often charge interest at rates of 20% or higher. The justification for these rates is hard to find. Consider this: Banks that offer credit cards often borrow money at an interest rate of 1% to 2%, then turn around and charge interest rates of 20% or more to credit card customers. Some say the big credit card companies charge such high rates because they lack competition. Credit card companies say they must charge high rates in order to compensate for the many people who default on their accounts. Yet despite this claim, defaulted credit card accounts have decreased, while profits have dramatically increased for most credit card companies. In addition, credit card companies continue to send out billions of solicitations each year, often to people with marginal credit histories.

In order to profit from high interest rates, the credit card industry is dependent on users who don't pay off their credit card balance each month. More than 60% of credit card holders revolved (carried) a balance and 45% made only minimum payments in recent years. As a result, credit

card issuers earned more than $71 billion in interest revenue in 2005.

Interest is not the only source of profit. Many companies charge an annual fee for issuing a credit card, and most companies charge late fees, over-the-limit fees, and other miscellaneous charges. In fact, revenue from annual fees, cash advance fees, and penalties was more than $16 billion in 2005. Finally, the companies profit by charging merchants and service providers a fee each time a customer uses the company's credit card in the merchant's establishment.

 RESOURCES

More on the industry and credit card dependency. For an excellent analysis of consumer dependence on credit cards and the consequences, take a look at *Credit Card Nation*, by Robert D. Manning (Basic Books 2000).

How to Choose a Credit Card

You may be shopping for a new credit card, or perhaps you want to close all your existing accounts except one. Which card should you choose? Use these guidelines.

If you have more than one credit card account and plan to close all accounts but one, here's how to decide which one to keep: If you're delinquent on any account, close it—otherwise, the credit card issuer may close it for you. If you're delinquent on all your accounts, keep open the account you are least behind on. To close your account, send a letter to the customer service department of the card issuer stating that you wish to close your account and further stating that your credit report should state "closed by consumer." It's also a good idea to cut up your card. You can close the account even if you haven't paid off the balance—the card issuer will close your account, cancel your privileges, and send you monthly statements until you pay off your balance.

WARNING

Closing accounts can lower your credit score. When you cancel a credit card, especially one you've had for a long time, it might bring down your credit score. Check out "What a FICO Score Considers" and "Understanding Your FICO Score," both available at www.myfico.com, for more information. Chapter 11 covers credit scores in detail.

If you still don't know which card to keep (or which to sign up for, if you're looking for a new one), consider how much it will cost you to have a particular card. If you don't carry a monthly balance or only occasionally do, keep (or get) a card with no annual fee, but make sure it has a grace period. If the card issuer later tacks on an annual fee, call and say you'll cancel your card if it doesn't waive the fee. Many will. If you carry a balance each month or most of the time, get rid of (or don't sign up for) the cards that come with the worst of the following features:

- **High interest rates.** If possible, keep the card with the lowest rate. If the only card you plan to hang on to has a

Soft and Hard Closes

When you ask your credit card issuer to close your account and cancel your card, you probably assume that the issuer closes your account and cancels your card. Not necessarily. Credit card issuers often have two kinds of closes: soft closes and hard closes. If your card received only a soft close, it means that the issuer will reactivate the account and allow new charges to go through, even though you requested that the account be closed. Asked why they do this, issuers answer: "So that if you're in a store and accidentally try to pay with a card for which you closed the account, you won't be embarrassed by having the merchant reject your card."

Of course, this policy leaves you vulnerable to fraud. If you want to make sure your account is hard closed, call the issuer and request that the account be hard closed. Follow up with a confirming letter that also instructs the issuer to report "closed by consumer" to the credit bureaus. Keep a copy of the letter. If the issuer refuses, ask how long the soft close will remain and then diligently watch your mail for new charges. If you move, be sure to let the issuer know your new address so you'll get a statement if someone else reactivates your account. Don't let statements go to your old address. Someone may steal your statement and use your identifying information to access your account or get credit in your name.

high interest rate and you're up to date on your payments, call and ask for an interest rate reduction. Some card issuers will do this over the phone, but you must be current on your account. According to a 2002 Public Interest Research Group study, 56% of those who called their credit card issuer and requested a lower interest rate were successful.

- **Early interest posting dates.** Card issuers used to charge interest from the date a charge was posted. Now, most charge from the date of the purchase, which will be a few days earlier.

- **Unfavorable interest calculations.** Some card issuers charge interest on the balance owed. A growing number, however, charge interest based on the average daily balance. For example, say you charge $1,500 on your credit card and pay $1,200 on the due date. When your next bill arrives, a card issuer using the average daily balance will charge interest on the $1,500 average daily balance from the previous month, not on the $300 you still owe. (See "Understanding Finance Charges," below, for more information.)

- **No grace period.** Some card issuers have done away with the grace period—a 24- or 30-day period during which you can pay your bill in full without incurring interest charges. Even if your card does have a grace period, however, it won't apply if you carry a balance, even as to new purchases. This means that not only does interest accrue on the balance

carried from the previous month, but it also accrues on new charges from the date of purchase.

- **Nuisance fees.** Card issuers are looking for new ways to make money. Most now assess late payment fees (as high as $40) and over-the-limit fees (as high as $25). Many issuers charge a fee if your account is inactive. A few charge fees for not carrying a balance—that is, for paying off your bill—or for carrying a balance under a certain amount. Some charge a monthly fee that's a percentage of your credit limit—the higher your limit, the higher your fee. Others charge fees if you are late on one or two payments during the year. You might also face balance transfer fees, credit limit increase fees, set-up fees, return item fees, and fees for paying by telephone.

- **Teaser rates.** Many credit card companies offer a "teaser" rate. This is a temporary low interest rate that lasts for a few months only. Once that period is over, a higher interest rate kicks in. Often, consumers fail to read the fine print and don't realize that the teaser rate is temporary. Others are aware of the rate but forget to switch cards when the new high rate starts. If you want to take advantage of teaser rate offers, keep careful track of the time. Many people forget to switch cards. Juggling cards can end up costing more in the long run.

- **Higher interest rates for cash advances.** Virtually all credit card companies charge higher interest rates and transaction fees for cash advances. Be sure to check the fine print.

- **Rebates, free miles, and other perks that aren't worth the extra cost.** Many credit cards now allow you to earn rebates, free airline miles, discounts on goods and services, funds for charity, or other bonuses by using the card. Don't sign up for a card based on these perks alone—be sure to consider the card's other terms as well. If you will pay high interest and high annual fees, you are better off without the perks.

WARNING

Your credit card terms can and do change. In most states, credit card issuers can change the terms of your cardholder agreement with as little as 15 days' notice. Read the inserts that come with each credit card statement for notice of these changes. If you don't like the changed terms, it's time to shop around again or call the credit card issuer.

Finally, if you can't qualify for a regular credit card because of your poor credit history, you may want to consider a secured credit card. For information on secured credit cards, see Chapter 17.

As a general rule of thumb, avoid having too many credit cards. Usually, two is plenty.

RESOURCES

To search for a card that matches your needs, visit www.consumer-action.org, www.cardtrack.com, www.bankrate.com, or www.federalreserve.gov/pubs/shop.

Why Are Credit Card Interest Rates So High?

Some states have laws that limit the amount of interest a creditor can charge. These are called "usury" laws, and charging over the legal limit is called "usury." Many states prohibit charging more than 6% to 12% interest. (For a chart of maximum interest rates by state, see the Resource Center at the Caine & Weiner website, www.caine-weiner.com.)

If there's a low limit on interest rates in your state, why can the credit card companies charge you nearly 30% on an unpaid balance? Because the U.S. Supreme Court told the credit card companies they can charge as much interest as their *home* state allows, even if their customers live in other states. (*Marquette v. First Omaha Service Corp.*, 439 U.S. 299 (1978).) After that decision, many large credit card companies moved their headquarters to a state with no usury law and no limits on credit card interest and fees.

Charge Cards

Charge cards, also called travel and entertainment cards, are different from credit cards. Charge cards, such as American Express and Diners Club, have no credit limit. You can usually charge as much as you'd like, but you are expected to pay off your entire balance when your bill arrives.

Diners Club gives you one billing cycle (up to 32 days) to pay off your charges.

Diners Club normally charges a late fee of 2.5% *per month* on unpaid balances, plus a $30 flat fee. (It's important to understand that this is the equivalent of 30% *per year*, *not* 2.5% per year.)

American Express now offers many different kinds of cards, including rewards cards, cash-back cards, and air mileage cards. Many of these act like regular credit cards: You get a grace period for purchases, then you pay about 15% annually on the unpaid balance. Seriously overdue accounts may be charged up to 35% annually.

The charge card issuer makes its profit by charging very high annual fees—around $90—and by charging merchants fairly high fees each time a customer pays using the issuer's charge card.

Required Disclosures by Credit Card Issuers

When a credit card issuer sends you an application form or preapproved solicitation letter, it must, under the federal Truth in Lending Act, fully disclose the terms of your agreement. (15 U.S.C. § 1637.) (See the sample disclosure form, below.)

For credit cards, such as Visa and MasterCard, where the card issuer charges you interest and lets you pay off your charges by taking as long as you'd like, if you pay the minimum required each billing period, the application or solicitation must give you certain information about the card, including:

- the yearly interest rate (called the annual percentage rate or APR)
- if there is a teaser or introductory rate, the regular rate that will go into effect once the introductory period is over
- how a variable rate is determined (if there is a variable rate)
- penalties for late payments and other circumstances
- any annual, periodic, or membership fee
- the method for computing the balance for purchases (for example, the average daily balance method)
- the minimum charge, and
- the period of days you have to pay off the entire balance without incurring any interest charge (called the grace period) or that no grace period is available.

For charge cards such as American Express and Diners Club, where you are not charged interest but must pay off the entire balance when you get the bill, the application or solicitation must include all the items listed above that apply, and any fee imposed or interest charged for granting an extension to pay.

If a card issuer fails to disclose information or discloses wrong information, you can complain to the appropriate federal agency that regulates the credit card issuer. (See Appendix A for more information.)

Here is a sample disclosure form:

Sample Disclosure Form

Annual percentage rate (APR) for purchases	2.9% until 11/1/06; after that, 14.9%
Other APRs	Cash-advance APR: 15.9% Balance-Transfer APR: 15.9% Penalty rate: 23.9% See explanation below.*
Variable-rate information	Your APR for purchase transactions may vary. The rate is determined monthly by adding 5.9% to the Prime Rate.**
Grace period for repayment of balances for purchases	25 days on average
Method of computing the balance for purchases	Average daily balance (excluding new purchases)
Annual fees	None
Minimum finance charge	$.50

Transaction fee for cash advances: 3% of the amount advanced
Balance-transfer fee: 3% of the amount transferred
Late-payment fee: $25
Over-the-credit-limit fee: $25

* Explanation of penalty. If your payment arrives more than ten days late two times withing a six-month period, the penalty rate will apply.
** The Prime Rate used to determine your APR is the rate published in the *Wall Street Journal* on the 10th day of the prior month.

WARNING

Banks can change existing credit card terms without warning. Interest rates may be raised, fees added, and grace periods eliminated, even if you have a history of perfect payment. The issuers often disclose these changes in a small brochure, hidden by advertising materials in your credit card statement. Your only choices are to accept the changes or shop around for a new credit card.

Unrequested Credit and Charge Cards

A company that issues credit or charge cards cannot legally send you one except in response to your request or application. If a card issuer sends you an unrequested card (except to replace an expiring one), the company assumes full responsibility for its use unless you "accept" the card—use it, sign it, or notify the card issuer in writing that you plan to keep it. (15 U.S.C. § 1642.)

Understanding Finance Charges

You can shop for better credit card terms and save some money by understanding how issuers use the annual percentage rate (APR) and the account balance to come up with the finance charge each month. The finance charge is the dollar amount you pay to use the credit.

Each month, the credit card issuer applies the APR to the account balance to compute the finance charge for that month. The account balance may include purchases, previous months' unpaid balances, transaction charges, and other fees (see below). The APR is the best single indicator of the actual interest you will pay.

> **EXAMPLE:** Suppose that you have a credit card with a whopping 28.6% APR and that your balance last month was $1,203.38. To calculate this month's finance charge, the credit card issuer multiplies the outstanding balance by one-twelfth of the annual rate ($1,202.38 x 2.422% = $29.15). If you make the minimum payment of $40, $29.15 pays off this month's finance charge and only $10.85 goes to reducing your outstanding balance.

A credit card may have several APRs. For example, one may apply to purchases, one to cash advances, and another to balance transfers. APRs also may be fixed or adjustable. As a general rule, look for the lowest and most stable APR that will apply to the way you plan to use the credit card. If you carry a balance from month to month, even a small difference in the APR can make a big difference in how much you'll pay over a year.

Credit card issuers calculate the account balance over one billing cycle or two (a one-cycle billing period will usually result in lower charges), and may include or exclude new purchases in the balance (excluding new purchases is usually better for consumers). The balance may be calculated in one of these three ways:

- **Adjusted balance method.** The credit card issuer computes the finance charge by taking the amount you owed at the start of the billing cycle and subtracting any payments made during the cycle. New purchases are not included.
- **Previous balance method.** The issuer uses the amount you owed at the beginning of the billing cycle to compute the finance charge.
- **Adjusted daily balance method.** The issuer adds your balances for each day in the billing cycle and then divides that total by the number of days in the cycle. Payments made during the period are subtracted to get the daily amounts you owe. New purchases may or may not be included, depending on the plan. If the issuer uses the two-cycle average daily balance method, it uses the average daily balance for two billing cycles. New purchases may or may not be included in the total.

Once you accept the card, you become liable for all charges made after your acceptance.

If a company wants to issue you a credit card without a detailed application, it can legally send you a letter of congratulations (or something similar) telling you that you have prequalified for a certain amount of credit, accompanied by a very simple application form, which usually requires little more than your signature. This is called a preapproved solicitation or preapproval letter.

The law requires that a preapproval letter be a "firm" offer of credit. Originally, this meant that the credit card issuer had to grant you credit, without further checking. But, a number of loopholes allow companies that send out preapproval offers to require further information before granting credit. (15 U.S.C. § 1681a(l).) Credit card companies can:

- require that you send back an application indicating that you meet the selection criteria
- verify that you meet the criteria the company used to select the prescreening list, and
- require that you provide collateral for the offered credit (this requirement must be disclosed in the offer).

Card issuers also get around this "firm" offer requirement by preapproving very low credit limits (such as $500) and then doing a second credit check before offering any increase in credit.

What to Do With Unwanted Credit and Charge Cards

If you receive an unrequested card that you don't want—either for a new account or to replace an expiring card—don't just throw the card away. That doesn't tell the card issuer that you don't want the account or that you want to close it. Your credit file will show that you have an account with an open line of credit for whatever amount you were granted by the card issuer. Today, many creditors refuse credit to people they believe already have too much credit. Having an unused account could be grounds for denying you future accounts you do want or limiting increases on existing accounts. Instead, cut up the card and throw it away, and send a letter to the card issuer telling it to close the account and report it "closed by consumer" if it reports the closure to a credit bureau. Keep a copy of the letter. The national credit bureaus have a toll-free number (888-567-8688) that you can call to opt out of receiving offers of credit that you did not request (so-called "prescreened offers" that are based on information in your credit report).

Lost or Stolen Credit and Charge Cards

Federal law limits your liability for unauthorized charges made on your credit or charge card after it has been lost or stolen. (15 U.S.C. § 1643; 12 C.F.R. § 226.12.) If you notify the card issuer within a reasonable time after you discover the loss or theft, usually 30 days, you're not responsible for any charges made after the notification and are liable only for the first $50 for charges made before you notified the card issuer. (Some issuers won't make you pay the first $50.) If you don't notify the card issuer within a reasonable time, you could be on the hook for all charges made on your card before the time of your notification.

When you discover that a credit or charge card is lost or stolen, call the customer service department of the card issuer at once. By calling, you provide immediate notice.

Where to Call If You Lose Your Card

Your monthly billing statement or credit card disclosure lists the telephone number and address for reporting lost or stolen credit cards. If you can't find either of these (or you aren't home), call toll-free information, 800-555-1212, and ask for the number of your credit card issuer. Better yet, make a list of the customer service numbers for all of your credit cards. Keep the list in a safe place at home. Then, if a card is lost or stolen, you'll have the telephone numbers at your fingertips.

During the call, find out whom you are speaking to and get an address. Then, send a confirming letter (keep a copy for your records).

Because the credit card issuer is liable for unauthorized charges once its notified, it will act fast. The issuer will cancel your existing account, open a new one for you, issue you a new card (they often send the card by overnight mail), and remove all charges above the $50 from your statement. (Most issuers will remove all charges—even the $50 for which you're legally liable.) Also, many homeowners' insurance policies will cover the $50 if your credit card issuer doesn't waive it. If the issuer doesn't respond adequately, refuse to pay the bill and consider having a lawyer write a letter on your behalf. If that doesn't work, you may have to sue.

Below is a sample letter to use to notify a credit or charge card issuer of a lost or stolen card. Be sure to keep a copy for your file.

WARNING

Credit card "protection." Many banks or national credit or charge card issuers send letters to their cardholders urging them to buy—for about $40 per year—credit card "protection" to guard against unauthorized use of credit and charge cards. Given that your liability for unauthorized charges is $50 maximum, and then only for charges that are made prior to your notifying the card issuer, this "protection" is a waste of money.

Letter Confirming Telephone Notice of Lost or Stolen Card

Large Oil Company
Customer Service Department
1 Main Street
Enid, OK 77777
Attn: Natalie Revere

March 2, 2007

Re: Account No. 1234 5678 9012

Dear Ms. Revere:

This is to confirm my telephone call of March 1, 2007, notifying you that I lost my Large Oil Company credit card on February 26, 2007, while I was on vacation at the Grand Canyon.

I understand that under the law, my telephone call serves as timely notice to your company. I further understand that I am not liable for any unauthorized use of this card from the time of my telephone call, and the maximum I am liable for on charges made before my notification is $50.

Please contact me immediately if my understandings are not correct.

Sincerely,

Wendy Piter

Wendy Piter

Unauthorized Charges

Are you liable when your credit or charge card is not stolen, but used without your permission by someone you know? Maybe. In general, you are not liable if you didn't authorize the person to use the card and didn't benefit from its use. But if you gave your card to your 25-year-old son, anything he charges before you take the card away from him is authorized by you—and you owe the bill. This is true even if you told your son that the card was for emergency use only. If he charges beer and pizza on the card, you may have a claim against your son, but not against the credit card issuer. On the other hand, if your adult daughter took your card without your knowledge and charged a trip to Hawaii, the law limits your liability in the same way as if your card was lost or stolen.

Your biggest obstacle will be convincing your card issuer that you did not authorize your son, your daughter, or any other person to use your card. Your best bet is to send a letter explaining the situation to the card issuer. For example, emphasize that you were not at home and your daughter went to your bedroom, took your card, and charged the trip without your ever knowing it.

If the credit or charge card issuer still claims you owe the bill—that is, that you authorized the charges—you can choose not to pay. The issuer will no doubt close your account and, if the amount is high enough, sue you. If you want to fight it, you'll probably need a lawyer to help you prepare your defense of "unauthorized charges." (See Chapter 19 for tips on finding a lawyer.) You may be best off paying the bill and buying a safe into which you can put your cards—and all papers with the account numbers—to keep them from getting into the hands of people you live with who shouldn't be using them.

Blocked Credit Card

Have you ever tried using a credit card shortly after checking out of a hotel and been told by the merchant that your card was rejected? It happens because many hotels, when you check in and give the clerk your card for an imprint, put a "hold" on your credit card for the estimated amount you will spend. Hotels claim that they are merely protecting themselves in the event you go on a spending spree during your trip and don't have enough credit left on your account to cover the hotel costs. Unfortunately, they've been known to hold much more than the estimated amount you'll spend and keep the hold on for up to 45 days after you check out.

Hotels have gotten a bad rap for doing this, so the amount they hold is less than in the past. When you check in, ask if the hotel will place a hold and, if so, for how much. When you check out, insist that the hotel lift the hold. Often the hotel will, given that your charges have been put through and you are not going to incur any more expenses at the hotel.

Rental car companies, too, often put a hold on credit cards, fearing that you'll total the car and run off leaving them to pay the bill. If you rent a car, ask the company if it is placing a hold, and, if so, for how much, before you leave the agency with your rental car. When you return the car, ask that the hold be lifted. And be aware that some gasoline companies put a $50 hold on credit cards when you charge your gas purchases, in case you drive off before signing the credit slip

Billing Errors

Credit and charge card billing errors are governed by the Fair Credit Billing Act (FCBA). (15 U.S.C. §§ 1666 and following.) A "billing error" can be more than a mistake in the amount you owe. A "billing error" also includes:

- an extension of credit to someone who was not authorized to use your card
- an extension of credit for property or services that were never delivered to you
- the issuer's failure to credit your account properly, and
- an extension of credit for items that you did not accept because they were defective or different from what you ordered.

If you find an error in your credit card statement, immediately write a letter to the company that issued the card; don't just scribble a note on your bill. Send your letter to the address provided by the credit card issuer for these types of letters, not to the address where you send your payments. Give your name, your account number, an explanation of the error, and the amount involved. Also enclose copies of supporting documents, such as receipts showing the correct amount of the charge.

The credit card issuer must receive your letter within 60 days after it mailed the first bill with improper charges to you. A sample letter is below.

Sample Letter to Notify of Billing Error

Eighteenth Bank of Cincinnati
1 EBC Plaza
Cincinnati, OH 44444

May 20, 2008

Attn: Customer Service

Re: Bradley Green Account
     Number 123 456 789 0000

To Whom It May Concern:

I have found an error on my MasterCard statement dated May 15, 2008.

On March 25, 2008, I purchased with my MasterCard two roundtrip tickets on Skyway Airlines from New York to San Diego, for $1,150. My bill, however, is for $1,510. Obviously, digits were reversed.

I understand that the law requires you to acknowledge receipt of this letter within 30 days unless you correct this billing error before then. Furthermore, I understand that within two billing cycles (but in no event more than 90 days), you must correct the error or explain why you believe the amount to be correct.

I have enclosed a copy of the receipt my travel agent sent me showing the correct amount.

Sincerely,

Bradley Green
Bradley Green

WARNING

Use the right address. It is very important to write to the credit card company at the correct address, known as the *billing and error* address. If you use another address, such as the payment address, they can pretend they didn't hear from you in time. To find the billing error address, look at your monthly statement (it may be on the back, in tiny print).

Remember to keep a copy of your letter as well as any original receipts or documentation. The credit or charge card issuer must acknowledge receipt of your letter within 30 days, unless it corrects the error within that time. Furthermore, the card issuer must, within two billing cycles (but in no event more than 90 days), correct the error or explain why it believes the amount to be correct. Suppose that the credit card issuer is your bank and that you have authorized automatic payments from your deposit account. The card issuer cannot deduct the disputed amount or related finance charges from your account while the dispute is pending if it receives your billing error notice at least three business days before the automatic payment date.

During the two-billing-cycle/90-day period, the credit or charge card issuer cannot report the amount to a credit bureau or to other creditors as delinquent. Likewise, the card issuer cannot threaten or actually take any collection action against you for the disputed amount. But it can send you periodic statements. In addition, it can apply the amount in dispute to your credit limit, thereby lowering the amount available for you to charge. It can also add interest to your bill on the amount you dispute, but it must drop the interest accrued if the issuer later agrees that you were correct.

You can withhold payment of the disputed amount and related charges while you are waiting for a response from the credit or charge card issuer. If the issuer agrees that there was an error, it must correct the error and credit your account for both the disputed amount and any related charges. It also must report the resolution to all credit agencies that were notified of a delinquency.

If the credit or charge card issuer disagrees with your complaint, it must send you an explanation and, if you request it, provide you with copies of any evidence.

If you are not satisfied, you have ten days to send another letter explaining why you still refuse to pay. Then, if the issuer reports your account as delinquent, it must also report that you believe you don't owe the money. At the same time, the issuer must send you the name and address of each credit bureau and anyone else to whom it reports the delinquency. When the dispute is resolved, the issuer must send a notice to everyone to whom it has reported the delinquency.

If the card issuer doesn't comply with any of these error resolution procedures, it must credit you $50 of the disputed balance, even if you are wrong. In California, if the card issuer doesn't comply with the 90-day time limit, you don't have to pay any portion of the disputed balance. (Cal. Civil Code § 1747.50.)

Another option is to sue the company for a violation of the Fair Credit Billing Act. (15 U.S.C. § 1640.) Suing a credit card issuer can be difficult. If the amount is small, you can use small claims court. If you decide not to sue, you should still report the problem to the appropriate government agency. (See Appendix A for contact information.) You may also want to cancel the card if you don't like the way the company treated you.

Disputes Over Credit Card Purchases

The rights discussed above apply only to billing errors. Even more common than billing errors are disputes with merchants when you use your credit card to buy a product or service that is defective. Here, too, federal law gives you the right to withhold payment in certain circumstances. This is a powerful, but often underused, tool for consumers.

If you buy a defective item or service and pay for it with your credit or charge card, you can often withhold payment if the seller refuses to replace, repair, or otherwise correct the problem. (15 U.S.C. § 1666i.) Here are the rules.

You don't have to pay a particular charge on the credit card if you have a legitimate complaint about the quality of goods or services that you charged and you first make a good-faith effort to resolve the problem with the merchant directly. You must explain to the credit card issuer in writing why you are withholding payment. You can withhold only the balance on the disputed item or service that is unpaid when you first notify the seller or issuer of the problem.

There are a few other requirements:

- The goods or services you bought must have cost more than $50.
- You must have bought the goods or services in your home state or within 100 miles of your mailing address.

These last two limitations apply if you used a Visa, a MasterCard, or another card not issued by the seller. They don't apply if you used a credit card issued by the seller (such as a department store card issued by the store), if the seller controls the card issuer or vice versa, or if the seller obtained your order by mailing you an advertisement in which the card issuer participated. But, you still need to make a good-faith effort to resolve the problem with the seller in these circumstances.

> **EXAMPLE:** Nan charged a raincoat from Cliff's Department Store on her Cliff's credit card. When she got home, she discovered that the lining was torn. Cliff's refused to replace the coat or refund her money. Nan has the right to refuse to pay her bill as long as she first tries to resolve the problem with Cliff's. Had Nan charged the coat on her Visa card, she could refuse to pay only if Cliff's was located in the state where she lived or within 100 miles of her home and if the raincoat cost more than $50.

WARNING

Check your credit file following resolution of a billing error or dispute. Despite laws designed to protect consumers, a credit card issuer may negligently report an outstanding balance it removed from your account, fail to report that you dispute a charge, or fail to report that the dispute is resolved. Be sure to check your credit report and make sure that this information is correct and up to date. (See Chapter 17 for information on checking your credit report.)

Credit Cards and Merchants

Frequently, when you use a credit card in a store, the merchant takes the card, runs it through a computer, and punches in a few numbers or places a phone call. Either way, these merchants are contacting a credit card guarantee company that has a record of your credit status. That information comes directly from your card issuer. If you don't want to be denied use of your credit card, be sure you know how much you've charged and paid. The guarantee company checks for:

- **Your overall credit limit.** If you've exceeded your line of credit and attempt to make further purchases, the guarantee company probably will tell the merchant to reject your card.
- **Your daily limit.** Many credit card companies do not let cardholders use their card more than a certain number of times a day or spend more than a certain amount per day. This is meant to protect against the use of stolen

cards. If you've exceeded the daily limit, the merchant will be told to reject the card.

- **The amount of the particular purchase.** Merchants must check with the guarantee company for approval on purchases larger than a certain dollar amount (called a "floor limit"), which varies among guarantee companies and merchants.

- **Whether you are late on a payment.** If you often pay late, the guarantee company may tell the merchant to reject your card.

- **Whether the card should be taken away from you.** In some cases, the merchant receives a code on the machine to call the guarantee company directly on the telephone. If the merchant still has the card, the guarantee company will tell her to keep it. This can happen if the card was reported stolen or if you are excessively delinquent in your payments and the credit card issuer has revoked your card privileges. Some merchants receive rewards for turning in revoked cards. Most merchants, however, refuse to confiscate cards and instead simply tell you your card was not accepted.

Many merchants require a customer to charge a minimum amount on a credit card. But MasterCard and Visa claim that their agreements with merchants prohibit merchants from requiring a minimum purchase. If a merchant refuses to accept your card for a small purchase, send a letter of complaint to the bank that issued the card.

Must You Provide Personal Information When You Use a Credit Card?

When you use your credit card, can the merchant record your address and phone number on the credit card slip? If a merchant correctly processes a credit card transaction, it will be paid even if the charge exceeds the card's credit limit, so it has no reason for that information. In fact, merchants' agreements with Visa and MasterCard prohibit them from requiring a customer to furnish a phone number when paying with Visa or MasterCard. Many merchants who request telephone numbers use that information in direct marketing. Also, several states bar merchants from requiring personal information when you use a credit card. The purpose of these state laws is to make it more difficult for unauthorized persons to obtain personal and financial information about credit card users. Try to not give your address, phone number, driver's license number, or other identifying information when you use your credit card. The credit card issuer already has this information, and the merchant normally does not need it (unless, for example, you want the your purchase delivered).

If You Can't Pay Your Credit Card Bill

If you owe a credit card bill you can't afford, you have a couple of options.

Ignore the bill. You'll get a series of monthly statements and bills. After about four months, your account will be closed and your bill will be sent to a collection agency. Some issuers act sooner, especially if you exceeded your credit limit with your charges. Some issuers wait a little longer, especially if you have a good payment history. If you still don't pay after being contacted by a collection agency, you may be sued.

Ask to make lower monthly payments. You can write to the credit or charge card issuer and ask to make lower monthly payments. As explained in Chapter 6, most issuers insist that you make the minimum payment. Although the credit card industry once required that you pay at least 4% of the balance, this is no longer true. Your payments may be as low as 2% of the outstanding balance. (Some issuers, as a method to simply make a profit, charge a one-time flat fee of around $20 to permanently reduce monthly payment to 2% of the outstanding balance.) Or, the issuer might accept a half-payment, but it will freeze your credit line—that is, not let you incur any more charges—in doing so.

Your delinquent payments—or your arrangement to make reduced payments—will probably be reported to a credit bureau. See Chapter 17 to learn what it means when negative information is reported to a credit bureau.

 WARNING

Beware of the minimum payment trap. If you opt to pay only the minimum (or less) each month, you'll need years to get out of debt. California Civil Code § 1748.13(a) lists some examples: Based on an APR of 17% and a minimum payment of 2% or $10 (whichever is greater), a $1,000 balance would take over 17 years to pay off, at a total cost of over $2,500. If the balance is $5,000, it will take over 40 years and cost over $16,000 to repay. To calculate the exact length of time, use Nolo's credit card repayment calculator at www.nolo.com.

If the Card Issuer Closes Your Account or Increases the Fees or Interest Rate

If you're current on your payments, not disputing any charges, and otherwise a good customer, can the card issuer close your account anyway, tack on new fees, or increase your interest rate? Yes.

A credit card issuer might close your account or increase the cost of using the card if it decides you have become a poor credit risk. A common example is if you've gotten behind on your payments *to other creditors* or your other credit balances have gone way up. Credit card issuers do periodic checks of the credit reports of their customers, often when deciding whether or not to increase the credit line. If a card issuer sees flags in your credit report, don't be surprised if the credit card bill from the issuers you're current with comes with any of the following:

- new, higher interest rate (as high as 29%)
- reduced time before the card issuer imposes a late payment fee—if an issuer gives a few days' grace period

before slapping on a late payment fee, it might eliminate that grace period for cardholders considered high risk

- increased late payment fees (as high as $40)
- elimination of the grace period before it charges interest on new purchases, or
- return or introduction of an annual fee.

You can call the issuer and request a reversal of the charges, but as long as the terms were disclosed to you, the changes are probably legal. Although usually there is little you can do in this situation, recently some consumers have sued credit card issuers arguing that changes in terms such as increased interest rates are against the law. If the credit card issuer advertised that the initial interest rate would be permanent, a court may hold the issuer to that rate. Your success will depend on the initial solicitation and the terms of the credit card contract. A simpler route, if a credit card issuer changes the terms of your agreement and won't reinstate the old terms, is to close the account.

Cash Advances

Many people use their credit cards to obtain cash advances. Similarly, many credit card issuers send cardholders convenience checks to use—the amount of the check appears on your credit card statement as a charge. Card issuers usually treat these checks the same as cash advances.

Cash advances are generally more expensive than standard credit card charges and have fewer protections, including:

- **Transaction fees.** Most banks charge a transaction fee up to 4% to 6% for taking a cash advance. Some waive the fee on convenience checks.
- **Grace period.** Most banks charge interest from the date the cash advance is posted, even if you pay it back in full when your bill comes. A few banks give grace periods for convenience checks.
- **Interest rates.** The interest rate is often substantially higher on cash advances than it is on ordinary credit card charges.

Automated Teller Machine (ATM) and Debit Cards

ATM cards are issued by banks. In most areas, you can use an ATM card to withdraw money, make deposits, transfer money between accounts, find out your balance, get a cash advance, and even make loan payments at all hours of the day or night.

Debit cards combine the functions of ATM cards and checks. Debit cards are issued by banks but are used at stores, not just at the banks themselves. When you pay with a debit card, the money is automatically deducted from your checking account. Most banks issue debit cards that can be used wherever a merchant accepts Visa and MasterCard. In fact, most debit cards carry a credit card logo. If you don't have this kind of debit card, many merchants accept ATM cards as debit cards.

Until the early 1990s, technological incompatibility between merchants and banks meant that the use of ATM cards as debit cards was very limited. Once credit card issuers got involved, however, debit card acceptance became universal. Many consumers prefer them over checks and credit cards for two reasons:

- They don't have to carry around their checkbook and present identification but are still able to make purchases directly from their checking account.
- They are paying their bills immediately, unlike when they use credit cards and get the bill later.

Still, there are disadvantages to using debit cards. Many consumers prefer having 20–25 days to pay their credit card bills. Also, consumers using debit cards don't have the right to withhold payment (the money is immediately removed from the account) in the event of a dispute with the merchant over the goods or services. In addition, many banks and merchants charge transaction fees when you use a debit card. Finally, if your debit card number is stolen during an online purchase, the thief may drain your bank account before the bank is able to complete its investigation. For this reason, never use a debit card for online purchases.

Statement or Receipt Errors

Although ATM statements and debit receipts are not known for containing errors, mis-

takes do happen. So, always check your receipt and bank statement carefully. If you find an error, you have 60 days from the date of the statement or receipt to notify the bank (sometimes longer in extenuating circumstances). (15 U.S.C. § 1693f.) Always call first and follow up with a letter, keeping a copy for your records. If you don't notify the bank within 60 days, it has no obligation to investigate the error, and you're probably out of luck.

The financial institution has ten business days from the date of your notification to investigate the problem and tell you the result. If the bank needs more time, it can take up to 45 days, but only if it deposits the amount of money in dispute into your account. If the bank later determines that there was no error, it can take the money back, but it first must send you a written explanation.

Lost or Stolen ATM or Debit Cards

If your ATM or debit card is lost or stolen (never, never, never keep your personal identification number—PIN—on or near your card, and always take your ATM receipt after completing a transaction), call your bank immediately, and follow it up with a confirming letter. Under the Electronic Fund Transfer Act (15 U.S.C. § 1693g), your liability is:

- $0 if you report the loss or theft of the card immediately and the card has not been used
- up to $50 if you notify the bank within two business days after you realize the card is missing

- up to $500 if you fail to notify the bank within two business days after you realize the card is missing, but do notify the bank within 60 days after your bank statement is mailed to you listing the unauthorized withdrawals, and
- unlimited if you fail to notify the bank within 60 days after your bank statement is mailed to you listing the unauthorized withdrawals. You also can be liable for unlimited loss if you gave your debit card and PIN to someone else and that person drained your account. (To avoid liability in this situation, you must have instructed the card issuer not to honor that person's transactions.)

If the bank claims that you are liable for amounts over $50, it must show that the additional loss would not have occurred if you had given timely notice of the card's loss or theft. The law considers written notice to have been given when you deposit it in the mail or deliver it personally to the bank. The timelines for giving notice are extended if the delay is caused by extenuating circumstances such as extended travel or hospitalization.

If a financial institution violates any provision of the Electronic Fund Transfer Act, you can sue to recover the damages you incurred. You're entitled to your actual damages, twice the amount of any finance charge (but not less than $100 nor more than $1,000), attorneys' fees, and court costs. (15 U.S.C. § 1639m.)

In response to consumer complaints about the possibility of unlimited liability,

Visa and MasterCard voluntarily cap the loss at $50. And some debit card issuers don't charge you anything in this situation. A few states have capped the liability for unauthorized withdrawals on an ATM or debit card at $50 as well.

ATM Fees

Withdrawing money from an ATM can be expensive, especially if you use a machine not associated with the bank that issued your ATM card. You may be hit with two separate fees: one from the bank you are using, and another from your own bank for using a financial institution outside of your bank's network. If you are lucky, only one of the banks will assess a fee against you. Some banks charge flat fees, while others charge a percentage of the amount withdrawn.

Shop around when opening a bank account. Often credit unions or small banks charge the lowest ATM fees. On the other hand, larger banks often have more ATM machines—and, usually, if you use your bank's ATM machine there is no charge at all. Also, ATMs must disclose any surcharges in a prominent place at the ATM and on the ATM screen or on a printout before the customer completes the transaction.

For general information on ATM and other bank fees, check out these websites:

- www.consumersunion.org (Consumers Union)
- www.ftc.gov (Federal Trade Commission)
- www.consumer-action.org (Consumer Action).

> ⓘ **WARNING**
>
> **Avoid using private ATMs.** ATMs at gas stations, liquor stores, restaurants, and hotels are common. These ATMs are usually owned or leased by the business, not by a bank. They may be quite expensive and not secure. Your best bet is to use only ATMs that bear a bank's logo that you recognize.

■

Consumer Loans

A bank is a place where they lend you an umbrella in fair weather and ask for it back when it begins to rain.

—Robert Frost
American poet
1875-1963

If you have a loan that you are having trouble paying back, contact the lender and try to work out an arrangement. If you explain that your situation is temporary, the lender will probably grant you an extension, meaning the delinquent payments are put at the end of your loan and your account is brought up to date. Or, the lender may waive interest—that is, have you pay just principal—for a month or two. Some lenders will even rewrite loans, reducing your monthly payments by extending your time to pay. You'll probably pay more interest in the long run, however.

Before contacting your lender, carefully reread your loan agreement to try to understand all of its terms. This will help you intelligently negotiate with the lender. Below is a discussion of the federal law that covers loans: disclosures, applications, and fine-print terms. If, after reading these sections, you think that the lender may have violated the law, use the violation as leverage in negotiating with the lender. You should consult with an attorney if you believe the lender violated the law.

Negotiating With a Lender

If you're having trouble paying a loan and need to negotiate with a lender, be sure to read the appropriate sections in Chapter 6. As indicated there, the lender may waive interest, reduce your payments, or let you skip a payment but tack it on at the end. But the lender won't do something for nothing. In exchange, you might have to get a cosigner, waive the statute of limitations (see Chapter 14), pay higher interest for a longer period, or let the lender take a security interest in your house or car.

You are most vulnerable at this time. Be sure you truly understand any new loan terms and can afford to make the payments under any new agreement.

Required Loan Disclosures

The federal Truth in Lending Act (TILA) requires lenders to give you specific information about the terms of loans you are considering. (15 U.S.C. §§ 1631 and following.) The disclosures required by TILA are different for open-end loans (loans on which you continually make new charges and payments, such as credit card accounts) and closed-end loans (fixed purchases such as a home or car that you will pay off over a set period of time). Disclosures for open-end loans are discussed in Chapter 10.

Closed-End Loans

The required disclosures for closed-end loans are extensive. Among other things, the lender must provide you with information about:

- the "amount financed" (the amount of credit provided)
- an itemization of the amount financed or a disclosure of your right to get an itemization
- the "finance charge" (the amount the credit will cost you, including interest and certain fees)
- the annual percentage rate or APR (the cost of the credit on a yearly basis)—in a few situations where the loan amount is very small, this is not required
- the total of payments (the sum of the amount financed and the finance charge)
- the total number of payments needed to pay off the loan, the amount of each payment, and the payment schedule
- whether the lender is taking a security interest in the property being purchased
- the amount or percentage of any late fee
- any prepayment penalty or refund of unearned finance charge if the loan is refinanced or paid off early
- special disclosures for adjustable rate residential mortgage loans (loans where the interest rate fluctuates), including the maximum interest rate that may be charged, and

- if the creditor is also the seller, the total price of the item or service plus all other charges.

The lender must give you these disclosures before it extends credit to you. For most home mortgage transactions, the lender must give you good-faith estimates of this information within three days after the lender receives your loan application. In most cases, if the loan is not being used to finance the purchase of a house (such as second mortgages to finance home improvements), the lender must also give you notice of your right to cancel the loan within three business days after you sign the loan documents. This is called a "cooling-off period" and can be longer than three days in some circumstances. (See Chapter 4 for more information.)

Below is a sample of the form that creditors use to make these disclosures:

Extra Protections for High-Rate Loans

In an effort to stop scammers who try to steal the equity from the homes of many older and low-income homeowners, the Home Ownership Equity Protection Act (HOEPA) requires additional disclosures and places many restrictions on secured loans that are:

- closed-ended—meaning repayable over a set period of time at set amounts
- secured by your primary residence
- not used to buy or construct the property, and

ANNUAL PERCENTAGE RATE The cost of your credit as a yearly rate	FINANCE CHARGE The dollar amount the credit will cost you	Amount Financed The amount of credit provided to you on your behalf	Total of Payments The amount you will have paid after you have made all payments as scheduled	Total Sales Price The total cost of your purchase on credit, including your downpayment of $_____
%	$	$	$	$

You have the right receive at this time an itemization of the Amount Financed.

☐ I want an itemization   ☐ I do not want an itemization

Your payment schedule will be:

Number of Payments	Amount of Payments	When Payment is Due

Insurance

Credit life insurance and credit disability insurance are not required to obtain credit, and will not be provided unless you sign and agree to pay the additional cost.

Type	Premium	Signature
Credit Life		I want credit life insurance _____ Signature
Credit Disability		I want credit disability insurance _____ Signature
Credit Life and Disability		I want credit life and disability insurance _____ Signature

You must obtain property insurance from anyone you want that is acceptable to ____(creditor)____ . If you get the insurance from ____(creditor)____ , you will pay $_____

Security: You are giving a security interest in:
   ☐   the goods or property being purchased
   ☐   (brief description of other property).

Filing fees $_____   Non-filing insurance $_____

Late Charge: If a payment is late, you will be charged $_____/_____% of the payment.

Prepayment: If you pay off early, you
   ☐ may   ☐ will not   have to pay a penalty.
   ☐ may   ☐ will not   be entitled to a refund of part of the finance charge.

See your contract documents for any additional information about nonpayment, default, any required repayment in full before the scheduled date, and prepayment refunds and penalties.

_____
e means estimate

- burdened by an annual interest rate that's at least ten points (eight points for first-lien loans after October 1, 2002) above the rate on comparable government securities, or the total fees and charges are at least $547 or greater than 8% of the amount borrowed. (The government is considering changing these amounts.)

HOEPA requires lenders to provide potential borrowers with additional disclosures and the following warning three days before signing the loan papers:

> You are not required to complete this agreement merely because you have received these disclosures or have signed a loan application. If you obtain this loan, the lender will have a mortgage on your home. You could lose your home, and any money you have put into it, if you do not meet your obligations under the loan.

For a loan to refinance a mortgage made after October 1, 2002, the lenders must also describe the total amount borrowed and whether this amount includes the cost of optional insurance.

HOEPA also prohibits lenders from adding certain features to the loan, such as most prepayment penalties (charges for paying the loan back early) and balloon payments if the loan period is for less than five years. (See "Terms of Loan Agreements," below, for an explanation of balloon payments.) HOEPA provides the same three-business-day cancellation right as other loans secured by your home.

It is complicated to determine if a loan qualifies as a "HOEPA loan" and, if it does, whether the lender complied with the law. If you think your loan might qualify as a HOEPA loan, you should consult with an attorney as soon as possible. If you're already in foreclosure, you may be able to use lender violations of TILA and HOEPA as a defense to the foreclosure.

Evaluation of Credit Applications

When you apply for credit, creditors use two primary methods to evaluate your request:

- weigh your three "C"s—capacity, collateral, and character, and
- rate your "credit score," based primarily, but not exclusively, on information in your credit file.

The Three "C"s

A creditor needs information to determine the likelihood that you will repay a loan or pay charges you incur on a line of revolving credit. This is done by evaluating the three "C"s.

Capacity. This refers to the amount of debt you can realistically pay given your income. Creditors look at how long you've been on your job, your income level, and the likelihood that it will increase over time. They also look to see that you're in a stable job or at least a stable job industry. It's important when you fill out a credit application to make your job sound stable, high-level, and even "professional." Are you a "secretary," or are you an "executive secretary" or the "office manager"? Present yourself in the best possible light, but don't lie.

Finally, creditors examine your existing credit relationships, such as credit cards, bank loans, and mortgages. They want to know your credit limits (you may be denied additional credit if you already have a lot of open credit lines), your current credit balances, how long you've had each account, and your payment history—whether you pay late or on time.

Collateral. Creditors like to see that you have assets they can take from you if you don't pay your debt. Owning a home or liquid assets such as a mutual fund may offer considerable comfort to a creditor reviewing an application. This is especially true if your credit report has negative notations in it, such as late payments.

Character. Creditors develop a feeling of your financial character through objective factors that show stability. These include the length of your residency, the length of your employment, whether you rent or own your home (you're more likely to stay put if you own), and whether you have checking and savings accounts.

These days, most creditors use credit scores (see "Credit Scores," below) to evaluate applications for credit. If the creditor considers your credit score to be good, it probably will approve your application without further evaluation. If your credit score is below the creditor's threshold for routine approval, it may review your application individually and consider your "three Cs" or it may simply reject you. If you are rejected, you may be able to find

another creditor with different approval criteria. Be sure to get a copy of your credit report and credit score to see what the problem is. (Chapter 17 explains how.)

Credit Scores

Most credit files include a credit score: a single number that affects many important financial events in your life. Credit scores are numerical calculations that are supposed to indicate the risk that you will default on your payments. High credit scores indicate less risk, and lower numbers indicate potential problems. Most credit scores range from lows of 300–400 to highs of 800–900. The biggest credit scoring company, Fair Isaac and Company (FICO), estimates that 40% of Americans have scores higher than 750. Most lenders consider a score above 750 to be very good.

Creditors use credit scores to make all sorts of decisions that will positively or negatively affect your finances, such as:

- **Granting new credit.** Creditors often use credit scores to decide whether to grant you new credit, such as for buying a home or car.
- **Changing credit limits and interest rates on existing credit.** Creditors look at your credit score even after they have issued a credit card to you. If your score goes up or down, they may increase or decrease your credit limit or even increase your interest rate.
- **Renting an apartment.** Landlords may use your credit score to determine whether to rent an apartment to you.

- **Paying deposits for utilities.** Utility companies may check your credit score to decide whether to ask you to pay a deposit before providing phone or electric service.

You can obtain your credit score from credit bureaus by paying a fee of $8 to $15 (the bureau will probably try to sell you additional products, such as credit monitoring services, but you don't have to buy them). The bureau must provide your score, the range of possible scores under the scoring model used, four key factors that affected the score, the date on which the score was created, and the name of the entity that provided the score (such as Fair Isaac—see below). Be aware, however, that the score and scoring model you receive may be different from those used by your lender.

If you apply for a loan on residential property, the mortgage lender must disclose your credit score, the related information just described, and a notice with contact information for the credit bureaus that provided credit scores. Lenders that evaluate loan applications using automated systems must disclose the system's score and the key factors that affected the score.

You can buy your credit score from Fair Isaac for a fee of $15.95. To get your Fair Isaac credit score, visit www.myfico.com.

Although being able to obtain your credit score is an important right, the jury is still out on how helpful the score actually is. It is likely that you will get different scores from different companies. And consumer experts are not certain that the score you order on the Internet will be the same one that lenders use to determine whether they will extend credit to you.

How a Credit Score Is Created

According to the Federal Trade Commission, this is how companies generate your credit score:

"Information about you and your credit experiences, such as your bill-paying history, the number and type of accounts you have, late payments, collection actions, outstanding debt, and the age of your accounts, is collected from your credit application and your credit report. Using a statistical program, creditors compare this information to the credit performance of consumers with similar profiles. A credit scoring system awards points for each factor that helps predict who is most likely to repay a debt. A total number of points—a credit score—helps predict how creditworthy you are, that is, how likely it is that you will repay a loan and make the payments when due."

Credit scoring companies apparently use criteria similar to the three "C"s when creating scores. Recently, Fair Isaac and Company disclosed slightly more details about the factors that it uses in generating credit scores. Those factors include:

- Your payment history (about 35% of the score).

Mortgages for People With Poor Credit

For many years, conventional mortgage lenders wrote only "A" loans. An "A" loan was available to a person with flawless credit—someone who had paid every personal loan, student loan, credit card bill, and existing mortgage payment on time. "A" loans typically require as little as 5% to 10% down and charge the most favorable interest rate. Anyone who didn't qualify for an "A" loan had only two choices: forgo buying a home for several years (until all the negative marks came off the credit report), or borrow from a lender who required a huge down payment (35% or more) and charged near-credit card interest rates.

Many mortgage lenders now write "B" and "C" loans for people with somewhat marred credit histories. "D" loans, which require a very large down payment and charge very high interest rates, are still written for people with very bad credit histories. Here are the requirements for these loans:

- **"B" loans.** Some lenders require clean credit for the previous 12 months but allow a few missed payments before that. Others permit one or two late mortgage payments, one late personal or student loan payment, and a few late credit card payments during the previous year. Late payments cannot be more than 60 days late. "B" loans usually require 20% to 25% down; interest rates are usually one or two percentage points higher than "A" loans.
- **"C" loans.** Some lenders require clean credit for the previous 12 months but

allow a serious credit problem, such as a bankruptcy or foreclosure, several years before. Others permit three or four late mortgage payments, five or six late loan or credit card payments, or late payments more than 60 days past due during the previous year. "C" loans usually require 20% to 35% down; interest rates are usually one to three percentage points higher than "A" loans.

- **"D" loans.** "D" loans are available to people with the worst credit histories: bankruptcy or foreclosure in the past year, or habitual late payments on loans and bills. "D" loans usually require 35% to 60% down; interest rates are usually double what they are for "A" loans.

Although increased lending to people with shaky credit histories may seem like a good thing, it often isn't. A loan to anyone with less than "A minus" credit is considered a subprime loan. Subprime borrowers often pay higher fees at closing, face higher late-payment fees, are subjected to prepayment penalties, and are required to purchase credit life insurance (so the lender gets paid if the borrower dies).

How do "A," "B," "C," and "D" credit correspond to credit scores? Lenders grade differently, emphasize different criteria (such as payment history, bankruptcies, foreclosures, and loan-to-value ratio), and use different scoring models, so "A" credit at one lender may be "B" credit at another. With these disclaimers, here's how a mortgage lender might grade credit: "A plus" (a credit score of 700 and up);

Mortgages for People With Poor Credit (continued)

"A" (660 to 699); "A minus" (621 to 659); "B" (580 to 620); "C" (521 to 579); "D" (520 and below).

Many "B," "C," and "D" borrowers fall prey to predatory lenders: lenders that sell very high-rate loans that borrowers rarely can afford over time. Through tricky dealing, predatory lenders hide the exorbitant cost of the loan. How to tell if a lender is legitimate or predatory? If the lender advertises "easy credit" and low-cost loans to anyone regardless of credit history, beware. If you've already fallen prey to a predatory lender, seek legal help before you default and face foreclosure. Some states, such as New York and California, have laws against some kinds of predatory lending.

For more information on predatory lending, visit the websites of the following organizations: AARP (www.aarp.org), the National Consumer Law Center (www.nclc.org), the Community Reinvestment Association of North Carolina (www.cra-nc.org) and the Federal Trade Commission (www.ftc.gov).

Many borrowers don't have a clue whether they actually have "good" or "bad" credit. Some borrowers who think they have bad credit may actually have good (or good enough) credit to apply to an "A" lender. But they apply to a so-called subprime lender (a lender that makes "B" or lower loans) because they fear denial by an "A" lender or because only subprime lenders have a presence in their area. Mortgage industry groups have estimated that up to 50% of all subprime borrowers could have qualified for "A" credit. This means that these borrowers were overcharged for loans when they could have qualified for less-costly loans on better terms.

All of this means that you should have a realistic understanding of your credit before you apply for a mortgage. Review your credit report and credit score (see "Credit Scores," above) and understand the strengths and weaknesses of your credit. Then apply to the best lender (the one making the highest-quality loans) you can.

If the lender grants you credit terms "materially less favorable" than the most favorable terms it grants to a substantial number of consumers, and bases the credit decision on your credit report, the lender must give you a so-called risk-based pricing notice or adverse action notice. The notice explains that the credit terms granted are based on information in your credit report and that you can request a free copy of your report. The notice serves to inform you that something may be amiss in your credit report and that you received less-favorable terms than a substantial number of other customers.

If you receive a risk-based pricing or adverse action notice, it doesn't necessarily mean that the lender has acted wrongly. You should use the notice to obtain a free copy of your credit report and look for a problem that caused the lender to offer you the less-favorable terms. If you can't see a problem and want to pursue the matter, ask the lender to explain what items in your credit report caused you to receive the less-favorable terms, how your credit report differs from customers who received significantly more favorable terms, and what those terms are. (See additional discussion in Chapter 18.)

- Amounts you owe on credit accounts (about 30% of the score). Fair Isaac looks at the amount you owe on all accounts and whether there is a balance. They are looking to see whether you manage credit responsibly. It may view a large number of accounts with balances as a sign that you are overextended and count it against you.
- Length of your credit history (about 15% of the score). In general, a longer credit history increases the score.
- Your new credit (about 10% of the score). Fair Isaac likes to see that you have an established credit history and that you don't have too many new accounts. Opening several accounts in a short period of time can represent greater risk
- Types of credit (about 10% of the score). Fair Isaac is looking for a "healthy mix" of different types of credit. This factor is usually important only if there is not much other information upon which to base your score.

If you're looking for a mortgage or an auto loan, each lender you contact may request your credit report. Each request will appear in the "inquiry" section of your credit report. Consumer advocates commonly believe that this can lower your credit score or make your credit history look less attractive to lenders. Interestingly, Fair Isaac says that its credit scoring program does not penalize consumers who rate shop. In the booklet "Understanding Your FICO Score," Fair Isaac says that you can avoid lowering your FICO score by doing your rate shopping within a short period of time, such as 14 days. (See www.myfico.com.)

Credit scores are extremely important to your financial dealings, yet many credit scores are based on inaccurate information, according to a 2002 study by the Consumer Federation of America and the National Credit Reporting Association. To make sure your credit score reflects your true credit standing, review your credit report every year and take steps to correct errors in the report. (For more on obtaining your credit report, reviewing it, and correcting errors or adding missing information, see Chapter 17.)

Of course, your credit score may be low for legitimate reasons, too. If this is the case, follow the steps outlined in Chapter 17 to improve your credit.

Creditors and consumers use the term "FICO score" generically, but there are actually three FICO scoring programs used by the major credit bureaus: Equifax's BEACON, Experian's Experian/Fair Isaac Risk Model, and TransUnion's FICO Risk Score, Classic. Your score from each bureau will vary somewhat because the scoring models are different and each bureau has different data about you. Fair Isaac says that it makes the scores as consistent as possible between the three bureaus.

In 2006, the three major credit bureaus introduced VantageScore, a new credit scoring system that they developed jointly. A VantageScore consists of a number from 501 to 990 (higher numbers mean less risk) and a letter grade (A, B, C, F). The VantageScore is said to offer greater consistency because it uses a single scoring model and is said to do a better job of evaluating consumers with short credit histories (so-called "thin files"). Commentators point out that the new scoring system can be confusing to consumers because it differs from the more familiar FICO scoring. For example, a FICO score of 780 is good, but is only fair on the VantageScore scale.

Whether this new product catches on remains to be seen.

Tips for Raising Your Credit Score

Fair Isaac offers these tips for raising your credit score:

- Pay your bills on time.
- Make up missed payments and keep all your payments current.
- Maintain low balances on credit cards and other "revolving debt."
- Pay off debt rather than transferring it to a new account.
- Don't close unused credit card accounts just to raise your credit score.
- Don't get new credit cards that you don't need just to increase the credit available to you.

Other tips are included in "Understanding Your FICO Score" at the Fair Isaac website, www.myfico.com.

Terms of Loan Agreements

In looking over your loan agreement, these are the terms you may come across.

Acceleration Clause

This clause lets the lender declare the entire balance due ("accelerate" the loan) if you default—that is, miss a payment or otherwise violate a term of your loan agreement (by failing to pay taxes or maintain required insurance, for example). If you miss one or two payments, the lender will probably agree to hold off accelerating the loan if you pay what you owe and pay the remaining balance on time. If you miss additional payments, however, you can be sure you'll fall from the lender's good graces.

Once a loan is accelerated, it's very difficult to get the lender to "unaccelerate" and reinstate your old loan.

Attorneys' Fee Provision

Many creditors include a provision in a loan contract awarding them attorneys' fees if you default and they have to sue you to get paid. If your contract contains this provision but says nothing about your right to attorneys' fees, most states give you the right to attorneys' fees if you are sued—or you sue—and you win. Several states prohibit the creditor's attorneys from collecting from you a fee in excess of 15% of the amount you owed.

Balloon Payment

Many borrowers can't afford the monthly payments when they apply for a loan that requires repayment in equal monthly installments for a set period. To help them qualify, some lenders will lower the monthly payments and collect the difference at the end of the loan in one large payment called a balloon payment. Balloon payments can be dangerous. Often, borrowers with balloon payments cannot afford the large final payment when it comes due. If you don't pay, the lender may have the right to repossess or foreclose on the property pledged as collateral for the loan—often a house.

Many states prohibit balloon payments in loans for goods or services that are primarily for personal, family, or household use. Or, they give borrowers the right to refinance these loans at the lender's prevailing rate when the balloon payment comes due. In practice, many lenders let borrowers refinance balloon payments as long as the borrowers have decent credit at the time of the refinancing. Balloon payments are not allowed in high-rate loans if the loan period is less than five years.

Confession of Judgment

A "confession of judgment" is a provision that lets a lender automatically take a judgment against you if you default, without having to sue you in court. Confessions of judgment are prohibited for any consumer contract (other than for the purchase of real estate if state law allows it). (12 C.F.R. §§ 227.13, 535.2, 16 C.F.R. § 444.2.) This type of provision is very anticonsumer, and few lenders try to include one in their loans.

Cosigner or Guarantor

If you didn't qualify for a loan on your own, a lender may have let you borrow money because you had a cosigner or guarantor. This person assumed full responsibility for paying back the loan if you didn't. The cosigner or guarantor need not benefit from the loan to be liable for it.

Cosigner Notification

Federal law requires that cosigners be given the following notice:

NOTICE TO COSIGNER

You are being asked to guarantee this debt. Think carefully before you do so. If the borrower doesn't pay the debt, you will have to. Be sure you can afford to pay if you have to, and that you want to accept this responsibility.

You may have to pay up to the full amount of the debt if the borrower does not pay. You may also have to pay late fees or collection costs, which increase this amount.

The creditor can collect this debt from you without first trying to collect from the borrower. The creditor can use the same collection methods against you that can be used against the borrower, such as suing you, garnishing your wages, etc. If this debt is ever in default, that fact may become a part of your credit record.

If you file for bankruptcy and the cosigner or guarantor is a relative or personal friend, it is possible that the person could be stuck with more than just what you haven't paid on the debt. If you made payments on the loan during the year before you filed for bankruptcy, the cosigner or guarantor may be required to pay the bankruptcy court the total amount you paid during the year. This is because your payments may be considered an "illegal preference" in bankruptcy. If this is a concern for you, speak to a bankruptcy lawyer.

Many young adults with no credit history have their parents cosign or guarantee loans. Other borrowers, who may have had a serious financial setback (repossession, foreclosure, or bankruptcy) or simply don't earn enough to get a loan, ask a friend or relative to cosign or guarantee. Cosigners and guarantors should fully understand their obligations before they sign on.

Credit Insurance

Credit insurance guarantees payment of a debt if the borrower is unable to pay. It is sold by credit card companies, car dealers, finance companies, department stores, and other lenders who make loans for personal property.

Credit insurance, for the most part, is a rip-off. Consumers spend billions each year on credit insurance, often without knowing what they have bought. In most cases, it's not necessary.

There are four main types of credit insurance:

- credit property insurance (insures against damage or loss to the collateral securing the loan)

- credit life insurance (ensures that the remaining debt on a loan or credit card account will be paid off if the consumer dies during the term of the coverage)
- credit disability/accident insurance (pays a limited number of monthly payments on a loan or credit card account if the borrower becomes disabled during the term of the coverage); and
- involuntary loss of income insurance (insures against layoff or other causes of involuntary loss of income).

Many lenders will tell you that credit insurance is required as a condition of getting a loan. This is almost always wrong. For the most part, you cannot be required to buy credit insurance. The main exception is for credit property insurance: Creditors can require you to buy this type of credit insurance in certain circumstances. But even if property insurance is required, in most states, creditors cannot force you to buy the insurance from them. The creditor must allow you to shop around and buy from another company.

There are also federal and state laws that regulate credit insurance. An important federal law, applying to most mortgages obtained after July 29, 1999 requires lenders to automatically cancel private mortgage insurance once the homeowner has 22% equity in the property and allows buyers with good payment histories to request cancellation once the equity reaches 20%. (12 U.S.C. §§ 4901 and following.) In a few states, lenders cannot require credit insurance except for loans to buy real estate.

Prepayment Penalties

Lenders make money on the interest they charge for lending money. If you pay off your loan early, they don't make as much as they had anticipated. To make up some of the loss, some lenders impose "prepayment penalties"—if you repay the loan before it is due, you have to pay a penalty, usually a percentage of the balance you paid early. Anytime you have a choice, get a loan without a prepayment penalty.

Pyramiding Late Fees

If you're late on a loan payment (such as a car loan or personal loan), the lender normally imposes a late fee. These fees are generally permitted unless the lender engages in an accounting practice known as "pyramiding." Pyramiding takes place when the lender assesses a late fee that you don't pay and then applies your regular payment first to the late fee and then to partially cover the payment due. You will never fully catch up on the payments due and the lender will therefore impose a late fee every month, even when you pay on time. For the most part, pyramiding is prohibited. (12 C.F.R. §§ 227.15, 535.4, 16 C.F.R. § 444.4.)

> **EXAMPLE:** Sheila has a bank personal loan that requires her to pay $100 each month by the 5th. On May 6th, when her payment had not yet been received, her lender assessed a $5 late fee. When the lender received Sheila's $100 payment on May 17th, the lender applied the first $5 to cover the late fee and the remaining $95 toward her $100 payment. In June, Sheila was automatically assessed another late fee on the $5 balance due for May, even though her June payment was on time. With this accounting scheme, Sheila will always have a slight balance on which she will continually be assessed a late fee.

Security Interest

As described in Chapter 1, when you take out a secured loan, you give the creditor the right to take your property that secures the loan, or a portion of the property if you don't pay. This is called a security interest. The two most common security interests are mortgages, where you give the lender the right to foreclose on your home if you miss payments, and car loans, where the lender can take the car if you default.

Some consumer loans, especially for large appliances and furniture, include a security interest in the item being purchased. Also, some personal loans that are not used to purchase a specific item—and, in fact, are often used to pay off other loans—include a security interest in your home, car, or important items around your house. These personal loans can be hazardous to borrowers. The interest is usually very high, and if you default, the lender can take the item identified in the contract.

To protect borrowers, lenders are prohibited from taking a security interest in the following, unless you use the loan or credit to buy the item: your clothing,

Additional State Protections for Security Interests

If you do not find laws for your state listed here, be sure to check with your state department of consumer credit or consumer affairs to see if your state has similar protections. Note that dollar limits, although current as of the date of this chart, are subject to change. Check with your state's consumer credit department to make sure you have the latest figures.

State and statute	Restrictions on security interest for consumer loans	Restrictions on security interest in real estate for consumer credit sales[1]	Restrictions on security interest in personal property for consumer credit sales[2]
California Civil Code §§ 1747.94, 1803.2(3), 1804.3, 2984.2	Anyone offering a secured credit card must prominently disclose that it is a "secured credit card" and that the credit extended is secured; must also describe the security by item or type.	When taking a security interest in a home, the loan contract must include a 14-point boldface warning: "If you sign this contract … your home could be sold without your permission and without any court action if you miss any payment …"	Lien allowed on motor vehicle which is the subject matter of the sale, or its insurance proceeds
Colorado Colo. Rev. Stat. §§ 5-3-201, 5-3-204	To take an interest in real estate, amount financed must be over $3,000.	Amount financed must be $3,000 or more.	Amount financed must be $1,000 or more.
Indiana Ind. Code Ann. §§ 24-4.5-2-407, 24-4.5-3-510	To take an interest in real estate, amount financed must be over $3,200.	Amount financed must be $3,200 or more.	Amount financed must be $960 or more.
Iowa Iowa Code §§ 537.2307, 537.3301	To take an interest in real estate, amount financed must be over $2,000, and finance charge cannot exceed 15%.	Amount financed must be $1,000 or more.	Amount financed must be $300 or more; if security is in household goods or motor vehicle used as transportation to and from work, amount financed must be $100 or more.

[1] In a consumer credit sale, the security interest is taken in land to which the goods sold are attached or that is maintained, repaired, or improved by the goods or service.

[2] In a consumer credit sale, the security interest is taken in personal property upon which services are performed or to which goods purchased are installed or annexed.

	Additional State Protections for Security Interests (continued)		
State and statute	**Restrictions on security interest for consumer loans**	**Restrictions on security interest in real estate for consumer credit sales[1]**	**Restrictions on security interest in personal property for consumer credit sales[2]**
Kansas Kan. Stat. Ann. §§ 16a-2-307, 16a-3-301	To take an interest in real estate, amount financed must be more than $3,000, and finance charge cannot exceed 12%.	Amount financed must be $3,000 or more.	Amount financed must be $900 or more.
Maine Me. Rev. Stat. Ann. tit. 9-A, §§ 2-307, 3-301	To take an interest in real estate, amount financed must be over $2,800. May not take interest in a personal residence if APR is over 18%.	Amount financed must be $2,800 or more.	Amount financed must be $1,000 or more.
North Carolina N.C. Gen. Stat. § 25A-23		Amount financed must be $1,000 or more.	Amount financed must be $300 or more; in motor vehicle to which repairs are made, amount financed must be $100 or more.
Oklahoma Okla. Stat. Ann. tit. 14-A, § 2-407		Amount financed must be $3,800 or more.	Amount financed must be $760 or more.
South Carolina S.C. Code Ann. § 37-2-407		Amount financed must be $2,900 or more.	Amount financed must be $870 or more.
Virginia Va. Code Ann. § 6.1-281	Can't take security interest in real estate for most consumer loans.		

[1] In a consumer credit sale, the security interest is taken in land to which the goods sold are attached or that is maintained, repaired, or improved by the goods or service.

[2] In a consumer credit sale, the security interest is taken in personal property upon which services are performed or to which goods purchased are installed or annexed.

	Additional State Protections for Security Interests (continued)		
State and statute	Restrictions on security interest for consumer loans	Restrictions on security interest in real estate for consumer credit sales[1]	Restrictions on security interest in personal property for consumer credit sales[2]
West Virginia W. Va. Code § 46A-4-109	Can't take security interest in land for consumer loan of $2,000 or less, unless the loan is made by a licensed consumer lender or FDIC financial institution.		If security is in household goods not prohibited by federal law, agreement must be signed by both husband and wife, if the borrower is married.
Wisconsin Wis. Stat. Ann. § 422.417		Amount financed must be $1,000 or more.	Amount financed must be $500 or more.
Wyoming Wyo. Stat. § 40-14-241		Amount financed must be $1,000 or more.	Amount financed must be $300 or more.

[1] In a consumer credit sale, the security interest is taken in land to which the goods sold are attached or that is maintained, repaired, or improved by the goods or service.

[2] In a consumer credit sale, the security interest is taken in personal property upon which services are performed or to which goods purchased are installed or annexed.

Current as of February 2007

furniture, appliances, linens, china, crockery, kitchenware, wedding ring, one radio, one television, and personal effects. (12 C.F.R. §§ 227, 535; 16 C.F.R. § 444.) Some states provide borrowers with additional protections.

Remember: You have three business days to cancel most loans secured by your principal residence. See "You Want to Cancel a Contract," in Chapter 4, for more information.

Wage Assignment

Some lenders, especially credit unions, try to assure your repayment of a loan by suggesting that you voluntarily agree to a wage assignment. This means that each time you are paid, your employer deducts a sum of money from your paycheck and sends it to the lender. Most people feel that this method of payment is overly intrusive and prefer to pay on their own.

With the exception of real estate loans, a voluntary wage assignment is allowed only if you have the power to revoke it. (12 C.F.R. §§ 227, 535; 16 C.F.R. § 444.) If you are considering agreeing to one, keep in mind that it can help you discipline yourself if you think you won't pay on your own—and you can revoke it if you don't like it.

Wage assignments are limited in a number of states. (See "State Laws Limiting Wage Assignments in Consumer Loans," below.) In many states, if you're married, your spouse must consent before the lender can take a voluntary wage assignment.

Waivers of Exemptions

As explained in Chapter 14, if a creditor sues you and gets a court judgment, or you file for bankruptcy, some of your property is protected from your creditors—that is, it can't be taken to pay what you owe. This property is called exempt property. It usually includes your clothing and personal effects, household goods, and some of the equity in your home and car.

Some creditors try to get around the laws that let you keep exempt property by including a provision in a loan agreement whereby you waive your right to keep your exempt property. These provisions are prohibited in most non-real estate consumer contracts (12 C.F.R. §§ 227, 535; 16 C.F.R. § 444).

Mandatory Arbitration Clauses

Creditors and other businesses often include a mandatory arbitration clause in many types of consumer contracts, including contracts for employment, credit, insurance, and even nursing facility admission. These clauses require you to waive your right to go to court to resolve disputes. Instead, you must resolve any dispute by way of a private, and often costly, arbitration system usually selected by the creditor or business. Watch out for these clauses when you sign contracts. Some states will not enforce them in some circumstances.

Voluntary mediation and arbitration, on the other hand, can be helpful. These programs allow you to sue in court if you cannot resolve a dispute outside of court or if you don't like the arbitration or mediation result.

For more information about mandatory arbitration agreements, contact Public Citizen (www.citizen.org), the Trial Lawyers for Public Justice (www.tlpj.org), or the National Consumer Law Center, www.nclc.org. (NCLC argues strongly against mandatory arbitration clauses in its article, "The Small Print That's Devastating Major Consumer Rights.")

State Laws Limiting Wage Assignments in Consumer Loans

The following chart lists additional consumer protections enacted by many states. If your state is not listed here, be sure to check with the department of consumer credit or consumer affairs to see if there are similar laws or regulations in your state.

State and statute	Spouse's consent is required	Limit on the amount of wages that can be deducted	Wage assignment must be notarized
Arkansas Ark. Code Ann. § 11-4-101(b)	Yes		
California Cal. Lab. Code § 300	Yes	50%	Yes
Colorado Colo. Rev. Stat. § 8-9-104	Yes		Yes
Illinois 740 Ill. Comp. Stat. § 170/4		The lesser of 15% gross weekly salary, or the amount by which net weekly wages exceed 45 times the federal or Illinois minimum hourly wage (computed using whichever minimum wage is greater).	
Indiana Ind. Code Ann. § 22-2-7-4	Yes		Yes
Iowa Iowa Code § 539.4	Yes		
Kentucky Ky. Rev. Stat. Ann. § 286.4–570		10%	
Maryland [1] Md. Code Ann. [Com. Law] § 15-302	Yes		Yes
Massachusetts [2] Mass. Gen. Laws ch. 154, § 3	Yes	25%	Yes
Minnesota Minn. Stat. Ann. §§ 56.17, 181.07	Yes	10%	
Montana Mont. Code Ann. §§ 31-1-306, 32-5-310	Yes	10%	Yes

[1] In Maryland, a wage assignment may not remain in effect for more than six months.

[2] In Massachusetts, a wage assignment may not remain in effect for more than two years.

State Laws Limiting Wage Assignments in Consumer Loans (continued)

State and statute	Spouse's consent is required	Limit on the amount of wages that can be deducted	Wage assignment must be notarized
Nebraska Neb. Rev. Stat. §§ 36-213, 25-1558, 45-1030	Yes	25% net weekly wages (15% for the head of a family), or the amount by which net weekly earnings exceed 30 times the federal minimum hourly wage, whichever is less.	Yes
New Mexico N.M. Stat. Ann. § 14-13-11		25%	Yes
Ohio Ohio Rev. Code Ann. § 1321.31	Yes	25% if married; 50% if unmarried.	
Oklahoma Okla. Stat. Ann. tit. 14A, § 3-403	Wage assignment is not allowed on most consumer loans.		
Oregon Or. Rev. Stat. § 83.150	Wage assignment is not allowed for retail installment contracts or retail charge accounts.		
Pennsylvania 43 Pa. Cons. Stat. § 274	Yes		
Rhode Island R.I. Gen. Laws §19-14.1-7	Yes (for household furniture in the borrower's possession)		
Virginia Va. Code Ann. § 6.1-289	Yes	10%	
Washington Wash. Rev. Code Ann. § 49.48.100	Yes		
West Virginia[3] W.Va. Code §§ 46A-4-109(2), 46A-2-116		25% net weekly earnings.	
Wisconsin Wis. Stat. Ann. §§ 422.404, 241.09	Yes, plus signature of two disinterested witnesses		
Wyoming Wyo. Stat. § 27-4-111	Yes		

[3] Wage assignments are not allowed on consumer loans made by regulated lenders.

Current as of February 2007

■

Student Loans

*Education is our passport to the future, for
tomorrow belongs to the people who prepare
for it today.*

—Malcolm X

1925-1965

With the cost of education sky-rocketing, it's not surprising that student loan borrowing is on the rise. Most graduates these days face not only an uncertain economic future, but also mountains of student loan debt.

Dealing with student loan debt is often a challenge, which is compounded if you're behind in payments. Because the government guarantees most student loans, it is the government that will try to collect if you don't pay. This is significant, because the government can use far more aggressive collection tactics than private collectors. Among other things, the government can take your tax refund and garnish your wages without first getting a court judgment. To make matters worse, there's no time limit for collecting on student loans. The government can keep coming after you ten, 20, or even 30 years after you graduate.

Although you may want to throw this book across the room and try to forget that you owe thousands of dollars in student loans, denial is not the best strategy. One of the worst things you can do is pretend you're not in over your head. One of the best things you can do is learn about the types of student loans you have and the options available to you to pay them back.

Borrowing Is on the Rise

During the 1970s, 1980s, and 1990s, the government expanded student loan eligibility to help millions of people. By the late 1990s, the federal government was providing more than $65 billion in student loans each year, compared with less than $10 billion per year just a decade before. In 2003–2004, approximately 66% of students obtained federal student loans—an increase from approximately 42% in the early 1990s. In 2003–2004, the average undergraduate borrowed more than $19,000, and a quarter of undergraduates borrowed $25,000 or more. In that period, graduate students incurred additional debt ranging from $27,000 to $114,000, while law and medical school students incurred debt ranging from $81,000 to $126,000. Nearly half of the people who attended professional schools, such as law or medical school, have student loan debt in excess of their annual incomes. A 2002 survey by the State Public Interest Research Groups found that about 39% of student borrowers graduate with unmanageable levels of debt. The percentage is much higher for lower-income students and for African-American and Latino students.

There are a number of ways to deal with student loan debt. This chapter reviews the basic types of government student loans and ways to repay them. It also includes a summary of deferment, cancellation, and other options to consider if you are having trouble paying your loans.

Types of Loans

The first step to managing your student loan debt is understanding what types of loans you have. Many repayment options and other programs are available for only certain types of loans, so you need to know which type you have. This section covers the most common ones.

Federal Student Loans

Most student loans are guaranteed by the federal government, meaning that the government will reimburse your lender or the state or private guaranty agency if you don't pay what you owe. The government does this so that private lenders will have incentives to offer student loans. Other federal loans, called direct loans, are provided directly by the government to students. Through these various programs, the government provides about 70% of all student aid.

Here are the most common types of federal loans.

Stafford and Direct loans. Most federal loans are either Stafford (previously called Guaranteed Student Loans or GSLs) or Direct loans. Stafford loans are made directly by the government or by a financial institution to help pay for college or graduate school education. These loans have been around in one form or another since the 1960s. The Direct loan program is newer, beginning in

---

Student Loan Terminology

As you read this chapter, you may see unfamiliar terms or terms with meanings that may not be obvious. Here's what you need to know.

A guaranty agency is a state or private nonprofit company that insures your loans and pays the holder if you default. If that happens, the guaranty agency will receive reinsurance money from the federal Department of Education. Information about each state's guaranty agency, including how to contact it, is available at the Department of Education's website, www.ed.gov; from the alphabetical topic index, select "State Agencies and Services," then "EROD Type of Organization Lists," and finally "State Guaranty Agency." You can also get information about your state's agency by calling 800-433-3243.

The holder owns your loan or was hired by the owner to service it (that is, collect and process payments). Your loan holder may be your lender or a company that has purchased your loan from the lender. If you're in default, the holder will be a guaranty agency, the Department of Education, or a collection agency working for the Department.

The lender is the institution from which you obtained your loan. This may be a bank, a savings and loan, a credit union, your school, or the federal government.

1993. Under this program, the government makes loans directly to students, eliminating the role of banks.

Perkins loans, National Direct Student Loans, and National Defense Student Loans. A Perkins loan is a low-interest loan for undergraduate or graduate students with very low incomes. These loans were previously known as National Direct Student Loans, and before that, National Defense Student Loans. The federal government guarantees repayment of Perkins loans, but, unlike other loans, Perkins loans are made by the school with a combination of federal and school funds. This means that the school, not a bank or the government, is the lender.

PLUS loans. These loans used to be only for creditworthy parents, who could obtain PLUS loans to finance their dependent children's education. As of July 1, 2006, PLUS loans became available to creditworthy graduate and professional students as well. These loans also are federally guaranteed.

Other federal loans. There are many other types of federal loans, including loans for independent students, professionals, and nursing students. To find out more, contact your lender or the Federal Student Aid Information Center, http://studentaid.ed.gov. (800-433-3243). The Center offers a free booklet, *The Student Guide,* that explains many of the basic terms and rules governing federal loans.

Private Loans

Many students have private loans—loans made by banks and other financial institutions without being guaranteed by the federal government. Private loans are closely linked with federal loans, however. Many graduate students and some undergraduates apply for federally guaranteed loans and private loans with one application package.

Many loans are made by the Student Loan Marketing Association (Sallie Mae) or by the New England Loan Marketing Association (Nellie Mae). For more information on these loans, contact Sallie Mae at 888-272-5543 (or visit its website at www.salliemae.com) and Nellie Mae at 800-367-8848 (or visit its website at www.nelliemae.com).

State Loans

Many states have their own student loan programs. To find out about these programs, contact your state department of higher education or state guarantee agency. The Department of Education's website has contact information for each state guarantee agency, at www.ed.gov; from the alphabetical topic index, select "State Agencies and Services," then "EROD Type of Organization Lists," and finally "State Guaranty Agency."

Figuring Out Who Holds Your Student Loan

If you want to set up a repayment plan, postpone payments, consolidate your loans, cancel a loan, or apply for some other government program, you need to know both what type of loan you have, and who holds your loan. If you're in default, you've probably heard from the holder, because it's trying to collect the loan. If you're not in default, it's often more difficult to find out who holds your loan. Try these sources:

- For loans not in default, call the Department of Education at 800-433-3243 or 800-730-8913 (TTY). For loans in default, call the Department at 800-621-3115 or 877-825-9923 (TTY). Department representatives are trained to assist borrowers in default.
- The National Student Loan Database (www.nslds.ed.gov). This is the Department of Education's central database for student aid. You can get information about loan or grant amounts, outstanding balances, loan status, and disbursements. Identification information is required to access the database, including a personal identification number (PIN) that you can obtain online. You can also access the database by calling the Federal Student Aid Information Center (see below).
- Federal Student Aid Information Center (800-4-FED-AID). Center representatives can help you access the National Student Loan Database and find information about the holder of your loan.
- If you've tried all of these places and are still having trouble, consider contacting the student loan ombudsman office at 877-557-2575 or www.ombudsman.ed.gov. (See "Where to Go for Help," below, for more information on the ombudsman office.)

Repaying Student Loans

If you're struggling to repay your loans, you have good reason to feel hopeful. Many lenders, daunted by the number of students defaulting on their loans, have come up with new, flexible repayment options for student loan borrowers. Some of these plans apply only if you're not in default. Other repayment plans were created specifically to help you get out of default.

The best advice is this: Don't stick your head in the sand. If you let your loan payments slip, you'll most likely hear from the loan holders right away. If you ignore them completely, the government has all kinds of ways to come after you for collection. It's best to deal with the problem early by learning about the options available to you and taking action.

Repayment Plans

There are many flexible options for repaying federal loans. The options are more limited for private loans. This section focuses on federal loans only. If you have a private loan, you should contact your loan holder for more information about repayment plans.

Standard plan. This is the basic payment plan for federal loans. These plans carry the highest monthly payments but cost less in the long run because you pay less interest. About 90% of all borrowers either choose this plan or end up with it because they fail to choose something else. In most cases, a standard plan requires that you repay your student loans in ten years.

Graduated plan. In a graduated plan, payments start out low and increase every few years. This may be your best option if you are just starting a career or business and your income is low but likely to increase over time.

Extended repayment plan. This plan allows you to stretch your payments over a longer period of time, from 12 to 30 years, depending on the loan amount. Your monthly payments will be lower, but you'll pay more interest over the long term.

Plans for low-income borrowers. There are other plans available for low-income borrowers. You may be eligible for these plans even if your financial difficulties are only temporary. If you have a Direct loan, you can apply for an Income Contingent Repayment Plan (ICRP). Under the ICRP, your monthly payments can be as low as five dollars or even zero. The ICRP may be your only choice if you are in dire financial straits, but use it as a last resort. Because the low monthly payments often don't pay even the accruing interest, you won't make a dent in the principal balance. You must renew the plan every year, and the monthly payment amount will change if your financial circumstances change. If you make payments pursuant to an ICRP plan for 25 years, the government will cancel the remaining balance.

> ⚠ **WARNING**
>
> **You may owe taxes if the govern-ment cancels your loan.** If a government agency cancels the balance of your loan, you may owe taxes on the amount cancelled. For more on this, see Chapter 6.

If you have a federal loan other than a Direct loan, you may be eligible for an Income-Sensitive Repayment Plan (ISRP). Under this plan, you pay a monthly amount that is affordable for you, based on your annual income, family size, and total loan amount. However, unlike an ICRP, the monthly payments must at least cover accruing interest. This plan must be renewed every year, and the monthly payment changes if your financial circumstances change.

Loan Consolidation

Consolidation is a good option if you are having trouble paying your loans. You can consolidate loans even if you're already in default. In fact, consolidation is one good way to get out of default. (See "Getting Out of Default," below, for more information.)

A consolidation loan allows you to combine your federal student loans into a single loan with one monthly payment. This may be a good option if any of the following are true:

- You can't afford the monthly payments on your federal student loans under any of the options described in "Repayment Plans," above, and don't qualify for a postponement or for loan cancellation (see "Strategies When You Can't Pay," below).
- You qualify for some of the payment plans described in "Repayment Plans,"

above, but you are so deep in debt that you still can't afford your monthly payments.

- You can afford your monthly payments and intend to pay off your loans under a standard plan, but you want to refinance at a lower interest rate.
- You are in default on one or more of your student loans, and want to get out of default.

Depending on a number of factors, including the types of student loans you have and your financial situation, you may qualify for one of two types of federal consolidation loans—those offered by the Direct Loan Consolidation Program or the FFEL Loan Consolidation Program. The vast majority of federal loans are eligible for consolidation, including subsidized and unsubsidized Stafford loans, Direct loans, Supplemental Loans for Students (SLSs), Perkins loans, and PLUS Loans. All borrowers with these loans are eligible to consolidate after they graduate, leave school, or drop below half-time enrollment.

However, there are some restrictions. Private student loans cannot be included in a federal consolidation loan. In addition, spouses cannot jointly consolidate their loans into a single consolidation loan. And, borrowers who are in default must meet certain requirements before they can consolidate.

Borrowers should consider both the advantages and disadvantages of consolidation before obtaining a consolidation loan. Potential disadvantages include the possibility that, if you have old loans, consolidation will cause your interest rate to go up. More-over, consolidation will extend the repayment period, which means that you will pay more interest over the life of your loan. Consolidation will not completely clean up your credit report, either. If you were in default, your report will reflect that your previous loans were in default but are now paid in full through the new loan.

Loan consolidation offers some potential advantages, too. If you are in default on any of your government loans, consolidation may offer the opportunity to get out of default and make affordable monthly payments. With a consolidation loan, you will only make one student loan payment each month to one lender. When interest rates are low, consolidation gives you the advantage of locking in a low rate on your student loans. However, this fixed interest rate might not be as attractive if rates fall further in the future.

Direct Consolidation Loan Program

As with the Direct Loan Program, the federal government provides Direct Consolidation Loans. There are several advantages to a Direct Consolidation Loan, as opposed to an FFEL Consolidation Loan (see below), especially for low-income borrowers.

Direct Consolidation Loans come with more flexible repayment options, including a standard plan, a graduated plan, and an extended plan, and in most circumstances an Income Contingent Repayment Plan (ICRP) (see "Repayment Plans," above). The Direct Consolidation Loan program accepts eligible defaulted loans. If you are in default, a Direct Consolidation Loan is a good way to get out of default and obtain a repayment plan that you can afford. In order to get out of default through a Direct Consolidation Loan, you must make three affordable monthly payments to the loan holder first or agree to an ICRP. Borrowers are also eligible for deferments in certain circumstances.

A benefit unique to the Direct Consolidation Loan Program is that each loan consolidated under the Program keeps its interest subsidy benefit. This can be important if you return to school.

In order to qualify for a Direct Consolidation loan, borrowers must have at least one Direct loan or FFEL loan. So, if you have only a Perkins loan, for example, you can't qualify for a Direct Consolidation loan. If you have at least one FFEL loan, but no Direct loans, then you must first seek an FFEL Consolidation loan. If you can't obtain an FFEL loan, or can't obtain an FFEL loan with an Income-Sensitive Repayment Plan that you can afford, but you are eligible for an Income Contingent Repayment Plan (see "Repayment Plans," above), then you may seek a Direct Consolidation loan.

If you are confused about whether you are eligible for a Direct Consolidation loan, or are interested in applying, you should contact the Department of Education's Direct Loan Origination Center's Consolidation Department at 800-557-7392 or visit www. loanconsolidation.ed.gov. The Department also offers an online calculator that estimates your monthly payments under a Direct Consolidation loan (see www.ed.gov/DirectLoan/calc.html).

FFEL Loan Consolidation Program

FFEL Consolidation loans are made by banks, credit unions, and financial institutions other than the government. You are eligible for an FFEL Consolidation loan if you have at least one FFEL loan. The Program does not have to accept non-FFEL loans, although it has the discretion to do so.

FFEL Consolidation loans also have a number of repayment options, including a standard plan, a graduated plan, an extended plan, and an Income-Sensitive Repayment Plan (ISRP) (see "Repayment Plans," above). The FFEL Loan Consolidation Program does not have to accept defaulted student loans, although it has discretion to do so. If you are in default and wish to obtain an FFEL Consolidation loan, you must make three reasonable and affordable monthly payments to the loan holder first or agree to an ISRP. Borrowers are also eligible for deferments in certain circumstances.

Unlike the Direct Loan Consolidation Program, loans consolidated under the FFEL Loan Consolidation Program lose their interest subsidy. However, under an FFEL Consolidation loan, you can assert school-related claims against the lender. This can be important, for example, if you got a loan to attend a for-profit vocational school because it lied about the likelihood of you getting a job after graduation. If the federal lender sues you to collect the loan, you may raise the school's misrepresentation as a defense. Under the Direct Consolidation Loan Program, however, you may not be able to assert school-related claims against the lender.

If you cannot obtain an FFEL Consolidation loan, then you may obtain a Direct Consolidation loan. Even if you can obtain an FFEL Consolidation loan, you may still opt for a Direct Consolidation loan instead if you are able to certify that (1) you cannot afford an ISRP (which, at a minimum, must cover all interest on the loan as it accrues) and (2) would be eligible for an Income Contingent Repayment Plan (the monthly payment amount under an ICRP can be as low as zero). In this case, you are *not* required to first apply for and be denied an FFEL Consolidation loan.

Reconsolidation

Suppose you receive a consolidation loan and then receive another eligible student loan. You might want to reconsolidate: to combine the new loan with the consolidated loans. This is one situation when you are allowed to reconsolidate a consolidation loan. You may also be able to reconsolidate if you decide to include additional eligible loans within 180 days after receiving the consolidation loan, or if you decide to include loans received prior to the date of the first consolidation in a subsequent consolidation loan. FFEL Consolidation loan borrowers may also obtain a Direct Consolidation loan in order to obtain an Income Contingent Repayment Plan, but only if the lender has requested assistance from the guaranty agency to help the borrower avoid default.

> **WARNING**
>
> **Not all companies offering consolidation loans are legitimate.** Some will just charge their fees to your credit card before they disappear. Others will pay only a few of your creditors, or not pay your creditors on time. Check with a reputable credit or debt counseling agency (which you can find through the National Foundation for Credit Counseling website, www.nfcc.org) to see if there have been complaints about the company offering the consolidation plan you are interested in. (For more on credit counseling agencies, see Chapter 19.) If you think your debt consolidation company has lied or didn't do what it said it would do for you, contact the Federal Trade Commission at www.ftc.gov.

Strategies When You Can't Pay

If you can't make payments on your student loans, even with one of the payment plans discussed above, don't give up. You may have other options. For example, in limited circumstances, you may be able to cancel your student loans altogether. Or, if you can't cancel your loans, postponing payments by obtaining a deferment or forbearance may be an option. Eliminating your student loan debt in bankruptcy is another possibility, although remote—recent changes to the law make it very difficult to get rid of student loan debt this way.

Canceling Student Loans

You may be able to cancel your student loan under certain circumstances. If you qualify for cancellation, it is always your best option, because it completely wipes out the remaining loan balance and allows you to get reimbursement for any payments you have made or that have been taken from you through tax intercepts or wage garnishments.

Below are several ways to cancel your loan. Keep in mind that the first three—cancellation due to school closure, false certification, and unpaid refunds—apply primarily to students who attended trade schools.

School closure. Many former students were lulled into taking out student loans to attend a school (usually a trade school), only to have the school close before they could finish the program. You can cancel a Stafford, Direct, Perkins, or PLUS loan or the portion of a consolidation loan used to pay off any of these loans if (1) the loan was made after January 1, 1986, and (2) you were unable to complete the program because the school closed during one of the following time periods:

- before you began attending classes
- while you were enrolled and attending classes (and you were not able to complete your studies), or
- within 90 days after you withdrew from the school.

The Department of Education has a list of closed schools. Go to the Department's main website (www.ed.gov) and type "closed schools" in the search box. You'll find a page with links explaining how to request loan cancellation due to school closure. In most circumstances, your school must be on the list in order to qualify for a closed school cancellation, and you must meet the above timing requirements.

False certification. If the school did not make sure that you were qualified to attend the program, you may be able to cancel your loans based on "false certification." This program applies to Stafford, Direct, or PLUS loans, or the portion of a consolidation loan used to pay off one of these loans. Only loans made after January 1, 1986 qualify. The grounds for false certification are any of the following:

- You did not have a high school diploma or GED at the time of admission, and the school did not properly test your ability to benefit from the program.
- At the time of enrollment, you could not meet the licensing requirements for employment in the field for which you were to receive training (for example, you had a felony record and enrolled in a security guard course, but your state doesn't permit prior felons to work as security guards).
- Your signature was forged on the loan papers, unless the loan proceeds paid for charges you owed to the school.
- You are a victim of identity theft.

Information about cancellation for false certification is available at www.ed.gov. Type "false certification" in the search box.

Unpaid refunds. This program went into effect on July 1, 2000. It allows you to cancel all or a portion of a loan if the school failed to pay you a refund that it owed you because you never attended the school or withdrew from the school within a certain time. Loans must be Stafford, PLUS, or

Direct and must be made after January 1, 1986. In addition, some states have funds to reimburse students who didn't get refunds due them.

Permanent disability. You can cancel any federal loan if you are unable to work because of an illness or injury that is expected to continue indefinitely or result in your death. In most cases, to qualify for this cancellation, you cannot have had the injury or illness at the time you signed up for the loan. If you did have the disability at the time you got the loan, you might be able to cancel your loans if you can show substantial deterioration of your condition.

To qualify for loan cancellation due to disability, you will need to get a statement from your treating physician on a form provided by the holder of your loan. To find out who holds your loans, check the National Student Loan Database, www.nslds.ed.gov. Once you have the lender's form, get your doctor's statement, and then submit the application to the holder of your loan.

In July 2002, the Department of Education began a "conditional disability discharge" program. Even if you can prove that you are permanently and totally disabled, you will not be granted a permanent discharge right away. Instead, you will get a conditional discharge for a three-year period, starting on the date your disability began. The Department is supposed to stop collecting on your loan during this time. It will also check your earnings records to see whether you made more than 100% of the federal poverty line for a family of two. (For 2007, that number is $13,690 in the contiguous United States. To see the values for Alaska and Hawaii, and for updates to poverty line numbers, visit http://aspe.hhs.gov/poverty/poverty.shtml.) If so, you will no longer be eligible for the discharge, and the Department will start collecting on the loan again. If you are applying for a discharge more than three years after your disability began, you should be able to get the permanent discharge immediately.

Parents who took out PLUS loans together cannot both get disability cancellations unless both are disabled. If only one parent is disabled and both parents took out the loan, the nondisabled parent is still obligated to pay.

Participation in a volunteer program, teaching program, or military service. Different federal loans have different cancellation programs that apply if you are engaged in a particular type of work, such as volunteering for the Peace Corps, teaching needy populations, or serving in the military. Some programs allow you to postpone payments on your loans only while you are engaged in the service; others allow you to cancel all or a portion of the loan.

Postponing Payments

If you can't afford to make any payments right now, you may be able to postpone student loan payments for a certain period of time through either a deferment or a forbearance.

Deferments. Each type of federal loan program has different rules that allow you to postpone paying your loan in certain circumstances. These postponements are called "deferments." If you get a deferment, you will still have to pay the loan back at some point, but you can wait a while. Most important, interest will not accrue on subsidized loans during the deferment period. Deferments are available only if you are not yet in default and you meet the specific criteria for your type of loan.

The most common deferments are available if you are:

- enrolled in school at least half-time
- unemployed and seeking employment
- suffering an economic hardship (only for certain loans obtained after June 30, 1993), or
- serving in the military on active duty during a war, other military operation, or national emergency, or performing qualifying National Guard duty during a war, other military operation, or emergency (only for loans disbursed on or after July 1, 2001).

Application forms for deferments are available from the Department of Education, Federal Student Aid website at www.dlssonline.com. Click "Forms" on the menu bar.

Forbearances. If you don't qualify for a deferment but are facing hard times, your loan holder may still allow you to postpone payment on your loans or temporarily reduce your payments. An arrangement of this sort is called a forbearance. You may be able to get a forbearance even if your loans are in default.

Forbearances are less attractive than deferments, because interest continues to accrue when you are not making payments. But if you can't make your loan payments,

a forbearance will at least keep you out of default. In the long run, the cost of default is much higher than the interest that accrues during a forbearance. Even if you can't get a forbearance on all of your loans, a forbearance on some of them may give you enough breathing room to catch up financially.

Discharging Student Loans in Bankruptcy

You can discharge student loans in bankruptcy if repayment would cause you "undue hardship." This is a difficult, although not impossible, standard to meet. At one time, it was much easier to discharge *private* student loans in bankruptcy. When Congress changed the bankruptcy law in October 2005, however, it extended the "undue hardship" rule to most private student loans. If you are considering bankruptcy primarily as a way to discharge student loan debt, you should talk to an attorney to find out whether you have a chance of showing undue hardship.

In determining undue hardship, most bankruptcy courts look at the three factors discussed below. If you can show that all of the factors are present, the court is most likely to discharge your loans. If you meet only some of the factors, discharge is less likely. However, some courts might discharge a portion of your loans if doing so would help you repay the remaining portion of your loans.

In deciding whether it would be an undue hardship for you to repay your student loans, most bankruptcy courts look at the following factors:

- **Poverty.** Based on your current income and expenses, you cannot maintain a minimal living standard and repay the loans.
- **Persistence.** It is not enough that you can't currently pay your loan. You must also demonstrate to the court that your current financial condition is likely to continue for a significant portion of the repayment period.
- **Good faith.** The court will look at whether you've made a good-faith effort to repay your debt.

Some bankruptcy courts don't limit themselves to these three factors, but instead consider the totality of the circumstances, which essentially means the court will consider all of the facts it deems relevant in deciding whether undue hardship exists. Whether the court in your area uses the three-factor test or considers the totality of the circumstances, you will have a very tough time getting student loans discharged in bankruptcy. Generally, courts look for reasons to deny student loan discharges. However, if you are older (at least 50 years old), you are likely to remain poor, and you have a history of doing your best to pay off your loan, you may be able to obtain a discharge.

Even if bankruptcy is unlikely to erase your student loans, it may help you get rid of other debts, freeing up money to pay your student loans. Another option is to file for Chapter 13 bankruptcy (see Chapter 15) and pay your student loan arrears in a court-approved payment plan over three to five years.

Getting Out of Default

Getting out of default is key to dealing with student loans. Many repayment plans and most postponement options require that you not be in default. In addition, as long as you're in default, you are not eligible to get new loans or grants. You can get out of default by canceling your loan or by discharging it in bankruptcy. Here are a couple of additional ways to get out of default.

Reasonable and Affordable Payment Plans

One way to renew eligibility for new loans is to set up a "reasonable and affordable payment plan" with your loan holder. Borrowers in default have a statutory right to such a payment plan. This plan allows you to make payments in an amount that you can afford based on your financial circumstances.

If you make six consecutive and timely payments under a reasonable and affordable payment plan, you become eligible to apply for new federal student loans or grants if you want to return to school. But beware: If you default again later, you cannot enter into another reasonable and affordable payment plan; you can renew eligibility through such a payment plan only once. However, if you are unable to maintain on-time payments for six consecutive months during the first time you get a reasonable and affordable payment plan, you may try another reasonable and affordable payment plan.

In order to get out of default, you must make at least nine on-time payments in a period of ten consecutive months. At that point, the guaranty agency or Department of Education can sell your loan to a new lender. This is called loan rehabilitation. Once your loan is rehabilitated, you will be put on a standard ten-year repayment plan or you can request one of the more flexible options discussed in "Repayment Plans," above. Loan rehabilitation also wipes out the default notation on your credit report.

The option to rehabilitate, or bring current, a loan is not automatically available if the creditor has already gone to court and obtained a judgment against you for the debt. Lenders have the choice to rehabilitate these loans but are no longer required to do so.

Loan Consolidation

Loan consolidation is discussed above. Usually, consolidation is a faster way to get out of default than a reasonable and affordable payment plan. Once you go through the application process and get a Direct Consolidation Loan, you will immediately be taken out of default status. You will stay out of default as long as you keep making payments.

Consequences of Ignoring Student Loan Debt

Although student loans are not secured debt, and therefore you will not lose your home or car if you don't pay them, they are also different from most other unsecured debts. (See Chapter 1 for a discussion of secured and unsecured debts.) If you don't pay your student loans, you won't be able to get additional student loans or grants in the future. In addition, you will be subjected to a number of "special" debt collection tactics that only the government can use. These government collection tools can have very severe consequences.

First, the government can charge you hefty collection fees, often far in excess of the amount you originally borrowed. Second, unlike almost every other kind of debt, there is no statute of limitations for collection of student loans. This means that even 20 or 30 years after you went to school, the government can continue to try to collect your loans.

If you don't pay your student loans, the government can also:

- Seize your income tax refund.
- Garnish up to 15% of your disposable income.
- Attach some federal benefits that are usually exempt from collection, such as Social Security income, although the government must let you keep a certain amount of this income.

If you get notice of a wage garnishment or tax intercept, you have the right to challenge it by requesting a hearing. Sometimes just the act of requesting a hearing prompts the collector to agree to a payment plan. If you can pay a small amount, you should consider the various affordable payment plans that can get you out of default. (See "Getting Out of Default," above.)

Will the Department of Education Sue You to Collect Your Student Loans?

The Department of Education has had the power to sue defaulted borrowers for quite some time. For a long time, they rarely used this power, but those days are definitely over. Since the mid-1990s, the Department has become very aggressive in suing borrowers to collect student loans. There was a 55% increase in student loan lawsuits filed by the Justice Department from 1997 to 1998. By 1998, the government had filed over 14,000 student loan collection cases. The Department of Education expects the numbers to grow as it gets more and more aggressive in trying to collect defaulted student loans.

Where to Go for Help

Here are a few good resources for learning about and dealing with student loan debt.

The student loan ombudsman office. The Department of Education's student loan ombudsman assists borrowers with student loan problems. The ombudsman office will informally research your complaint and, if it finds that it is justified, will work with you,

the Department of Education, and your loan holder to resolve the problem. If it decides that your complaint is not justified, it will explain why. The ombudsman office is a "last resource"—usually it will help you only if you have first tried to resolve the problem on your own.

You can contact the student loan ombudsman office at 877-557-2575. Assistance is available in both English and Spanish. It also has an excellent website (www.ombudsman. ed.gov) where you can complete an online request for assistance.

The Department of Education. The Department of Education also has lots of information about student loans, as well as application forms for all of the various repayment, cancellation, postponement, and other programs discussed in this chapter. You can reach the Department at 800-621-3115 (voice) or 800-848-0983 (TDD). Or, visit its website at www.ed.gov to get information and download forms.

Legal aid. If you are having problems making your student loan payments because you have a low income or because you have been a victim of vocational school abuse, you may be able to get help from your local legal aid or legal services office. You can find a national listing of legal aid offices at www.lsc.gov/fundprog.htm.

Child Support and Alimony

The fundamental evil of the world arose from the fact that the good Lord has not created money enough.

—Heinrich Heine
German poet and critic, 1797-1856

Benjamin Franklin once said that only two things in life are certain: death and taxes. Of course, Franklin's remark was made in the 18th century. If he were alive today and a parent with a child support or alimony obligation, he would undoubtedly add that to the list.

This chapter will tell you:

- how the amount of child support and alimony is set and collected
- how you can get your child support and alimony obligation modified, and
- what happens to child support and alimony debts and obligations if you file for bankruptcy.

Whether parents live together or apart, they are legally obligated to support their children. When they live together, a court rarely involves itself with how the parents raise or support their children—unless someone claims that the children are being abused or neglected.

As soon as the parents split up, however, or one of the parents applies for welfare, the law gives the state the right to involve itself in how the children are supported. Sweeping laws enacted by Congress during the 1980s and 1990s have resulted in greatly stepped-up state child support collection efforts. These laws have changed the way child support is established, paid, and collected when past due.

Below we explain the basics about child support—how it's enforced, and strategies to deal with it. But first, a loud and clear warning: Regardless of the circumstances, pay your child support. First, your child deserves to be supported. Second, if you don't, you will be incurring the proverbial debt from hell. It never goes away. No bankruptcy judge can cancel past-due support. No state or federal judge can reduce it. It just sits there generating interest until it—and the interest—is paid in full. In the meantime, you are subject to intrusive collection techniques that can drive people nuts or into the underground economy.

It's true that many parents who don't pay child support believe they have a good reason for not doing so:

- They have a new family to support.
- Their custodial parent won't let them see their kids.
- Their custodial parent moved their kids far away.
- Their custodial parent misuses the support.
- Their custodial parent plays all day while they have to work.
- The court ordered them to pay too much.

But your reason makes no difference to the judge who's been told about your delinquency. If you owe child support and have the apparent ability to pay (even if you aren't working at the time), you will not only be subject to harsh collection techniques but may also do a stretch of jail time if a judge gets angry enough.

If You Are Owed Child Support or Alimony

This chapter addresses the concerns of debtors who pay child support or alimony, not those entitled to receive it. Many people, of course, have debt problems because they aren't receiving support to which they are entitled. While this chapter doesn't explain how to get the support to which you are entitled, reading it will nevertheless help you understand your rights and the strategies available to you.

Your first step in enforcing your right to collect child support is to contact the local child support enforcement agency in your county. That agency may be located in the courthouse, at the local prosecuting attorney's office, at the welfare department, or at some other location. These agencies help parents establish and enforce child support orders. There are also national nonprofit organizations that help custodial parents collect child support. One nonprofit group is called ACES—Association for Children for Enforcement of Support, 888-310-2237, www.childsupport-aces.

org. ACES helps custodial parents work with their local enforcement agency and provides specific advice on how to be heard and get your case processed or, if necessary, file a complaint with the agency.

Private collection agencies that try to collect child support for custodial parents have sprung up around the country. Two such collection agencies are Children's Support Services and Child Support Investigations. Be aware that a collection agency will charge an application fee (as much as $50) and will keep a percentage of what it collects—perhaps as much as 25% to 33%. Some of these agencies have been criticized for taking the application fee and then not doing anything else. If you're interested, look in your local phone book to find an office near you. Before signing up, find out exactly how much it will cost and the agency's rate of success. Then call the local Better Business Bureau and your local district attorney's office to see if any complaints have been filed.

For specific information on child support enforcement laws in your state, you can visit the Office of Child Support Enforcement website at www.acf.hhs.gov.

How Child Support Is Determined

The federal Family Support Act of 1988 requires all states to use a formula or guide-lines to calculate child support. (Each state, and the District of Columbia, sets its own formula or guidelines.) If you think your existing child support order isn't in accordance with your state's formula or guideline, you or your child's other parent can ask the court to review it. "Modifying the Amount of Child Support," below, describes how you go to court to have the judge review the support order.

RESOURCES

Child support calculators. There is fairly expensive software, as well as expensive and inexpensive websites, that can help you figure out (at least *approximately*) what you support payments should be. For links to online child support calculators for all states, see www.supportguidelines.com. Some, but not all, of these calculators will promise a result *identical* to the calculations by the court in your state.

While formulas differ from state to state, judges tend to consider many of the same criteria, including:

- the amount of time each parent spends with the child
- the type of custody granted (sole or joint)
- each parent's income
- the children's ages
- the number of children subject to the support order, and
- some hardship factors, such as having other children to support.

In addition, a court may require you to pay some of the following expenses as a part of child support:

- health and dental insurance for your children, or your child's health and dental costs if neither parent has insurance covering the children—in fact, many states mandate that a parent pay for medical insurance if the costs are reasonable
- life insurance naming your child's custodial parent as the beneficiary
- child care so that the custodial parent can work or go to school, and

- education costs for your children—sometimes including college.

Unpaid Child Support and Arrears

Unpaid child support is child support that you owe under a court order but failed to pay as it became due. This past-due support sometimes is referred to as arrears or arrearages. No matter what it's called, child support you failed to pay is a debt that cannot be reduced after the fact, nor can it be discharged in bankruptcy. Although you can ask a judge to change the amount of support you will have to pay in the future (see "Modifying the Amount of Child Support," below), no judge can change the amount of unpaid support you owe. That debt will remain until you pay it off in full, period.

Modifying the Amount of Child Support

You may realize that you owe child support you can't afford to pay, even before you fall behind on payments and the debt collector comes knocking at the door. Typically this happens when your financial situation changes for the worse, although there can be other changes in circumstance (discussed below) that might make you think the amount of child support is now set too high.

If you owe child support you can't afford, you must take the initiative to change your child support order. This requires that you go to court, request a modification, and show the judge that you have inadequate income and cannot afford the ordered support (or that some other significant change in circumstance warrants a reduction). If you don't get the order modified and your child support arrears build up, a court won't retroactively decrease it, even if you were too sick to get out of bed during the affected period. To repeat: Once child support is owed and unpaid, it (and the interest on it) remains a debt until it is paid.

Simplified Modification Procedures

Some states, including California, New Jersey, New York, and Vermont try to make it easy for parents requesting an increase or decrease in child support.

The procedure is meant to be user-friendly for parents without attorneys. But lawyers are welcome to take advantage of the procedure as well. Court clerks or case managers assist you in filling out the papers. The hearings often take place before a court magistrate or hearing examiner, not a judge. Decisions may be rendered on the spot, or within about 30 days.

To find out if your state has a simplified modification procedure, call the county court clerk, the state child support enforcement agency, or the district attorney's office.

In most states, filing a motion to modify child support requires you to fill out and file court papers, schedule a hearing, and present evidence to a judge. To do this, you'll probably need the help of a lawyer. (See Chapter 19 for advice about locating a lawyer.) The kind of evidence you need to show the court includes:

- a sworn statement from your most recent employer, if you were recently let go
- records of your job search, if you've been looking unsuccessfully, and
- sworn statements from all medical and healing professionals, if you are sick, injured, depressed, or otherwise unable to work.

Legal Reasons That Justify a Support Change

To get a judge to reduce a child support order, you must show a significant change of circumstance since the last order. What constitutes a significant change of circumstance depends on your situation. Generally, the condition must not have been considered when the original order was made and must affect the current standard of living of you, your child, or the custodial parent. Changes that qualify as significant include the following:

- **Your income has substantially decreased.** The decrease must be involuntary or due to circumstances that will ultimately improve your child's situation, like training for a better job. If you quit your job to retire or become a basket weaver, the court probably won't modify your support obligation. (In those cases, income may be "imputed" to you, based on your ability to work and your skills, even if you aren't actually working.) However, if you quit your job to attend business school, the court may temporarily decrease the amount, expecting you to earn more money and pay more child support after you graduate.

- **The custodial parent's income has substantially increased.** Not all increases in the custodial parent's income will qualify. For example, if your child's needs have increased as the custodial parent's income has risen, you probably won't get a reduction. Or, if the custodial parent's income increase is from a new spouse's earnings, few courts will consider that money, because the new spouse has no obligation to support your child.

- **Your expenses have increased.** You may be entitled to a reduction, for example, if you have a new child or have developed an expensive, ongoing medical condition.

- **Your child's needs have decreased.** You may be entitled to a reduction if, for instance, your child is no longer attending private school. Be warned, however, that as children grow older, their financial needs usually go up rather than down.

- **The children spend more time in your custody than when the court initially ordered the support.** In this situation, you may be entitled to a reduction because the other parent needs less money for the children.

As you can see, the judge won't be inclined to modify your support order if your financial condition—or the financial condition of your child or your child's other parent—hasn't changed substantially since the order was initially issued. If you just feel the court was wrong the first time, you're probably out of luck.

Child Support and Visitation

If your child's custodial parent is interfering with your visitation rights, you don't have the right to withhold support. But you can schedule a court hearing where you can present evidence to a judge that shows there has been substantial interference with your visitation right and ask the judge to rectify the situation. (Modification hearings are explained below.) You'll need to document a persistent pattern of being denied access to your children. A good way to do this is to take notes on a calendar. Missing a weekend visit or two won't be enough. If you've seen the kids once in eight months, however, a court may well hold the custodial parent in contempt of court for violating the court order allowing more frequent visitation. In addition, some judges will order your child's custodial parent to reimburse you for the expenses you incur trying to exercise your visitation rights. And a judge may suspend your obligation to pay child support if your child's custodial parent and the child have disappeared altogether, leaving no one to whom you can send the support.

Negotiate With Your Child's Other Parent

Your request to modify the amount of child support you have to pay will be either contested or uncontested. Contested means your child's other parent opposes it, files formal papers with the court in opposition, and shows up at the hearing with evidence refuting what you say. Uncontested means that your child's other parent does not file a response in court.

Child support modification hearings can be time-consuming, costly, and unpleasant. Avoid a contested hearing if at all possible. Before you file the court papers, call your child's other parent and let him or her know of your changed circumstance. He or she may voluntarily agree to reduce the amount. If you were laid off or in an accident, the other parent knows the court will probably order some change in the amount and may agree to your proposed amount ahead of time.

If you reach an agreement to reduce the amount of child support you owe, make sure to get your new agreement in writing. Then bring it to the court's attention for its approval. You may need the help of a lawyer or legal typing service to do this. (See Chapter 19 for advice on finding legal help.) Keep in mind that, once a court sets support, only a court can change it. If you make an informal modification (one that you haven't taken before a judge to approve) and your ex changes his or her mind down the line, you probably won't have any recourse.

EXAMPLE: When Mia and Zander divorced, Mia got full custody of the children, and Zander paid child support. After Zander got a larger apartment, the children began to spend every other week with him, so Mia agreed to accept half as much child support but signed no written agreement. Later on, when Zander wanted the children for the whole summer, Mia went back to court to claim arrearages of child support. Zander will be on the hook for the entire amount.

File Modification Papers If Negotiations Fail

If your child's other parent won't agree to a reduction in child support, you will have to convince a judge to grant your request. If the judge denies your request, you will have to reassess your position. If you can't come up with the necessary payments by reducing your living expenses, you may need to consider filing for bankruptcy. This will allow you to get rid of some of your debts— such as those typically owed to credit card companies and health care providers—and free up some money to meet your child support obligation.

Don't delay filing your request for child support modification (usually, by means of a motion or an Order to Show Cause). Under federal law, the effective date of a child support modification order cannot be earlier than the date that the motion or Order to Show Cause requesting modification was served on the other parties.

A special rule applies to members of the military. Parties eligible for a support modification due to military activation or out-of-state deployment may use a special "notice of activation and request" procedure. An order modifying or terminating support based on the servicemember's change in income takes effect on either the date of service of the notice on the opposing party, or the date of the member's activation, whichever is later.

WARNING

Remember: Past-due support debts will not go away. A modification of child support cannot change your obligation to pay past-due child support.

When You Are Entitled to Stop Paying Child Support

You must pay child support for as long as your child support court order says you must, unless the court changes the order. If the order does not contain an ending date, you must support your children as long as your state requires it, which can be:

- until they reach 18
- until they are 19 or finished with high school, whichever occurs first (as long as they are a full-time student and living with a parent)
- until they reach 21
- as long as they are dependent, if they are disabled, or
- until they complete college.

To find out exactly what your state law requires, you'll need to do a little legal research or talk to a lawyer. (See Chapter 19.)

RESOURCES

State laws on child support duration. For a state-by-state chart on when child support terminates, go to the website of the National Conference of State Legislatures, www.ncsl.org, and search for "child support guidelines."

In addition, your child support obligation will probably end early if: your child joins the military, gets married, or moves out of the house to live independently; a court declares your child legally emancipated; or your parental rights are terminated.

Once you are no longer liable for support, it doesn't mean that unpaid child support disappears. If the custodial parent goes to court and gets a judgment for unpaid support, that judgment can be collected for as long as your state lets a creditor enforce a judgment. This typically covers a period of at least five to 20 years, and the period is usually extended if the judgment is renewed. (Chapter 14 explains how long judgments can last.) In most states, judgments for unpaid child support can easily last your entire life.

Establishing Paternity

If you have a child for whom you're not paying child support and you never married the child's mother, you may find yourself hauled into court on a paternity and child support action—up to 18 years after the child was born. (Although a mother can also be ordered to pay child support to her child's father that she never wed, maternity is not usually disputed, for obvious reasons.) If the court declares that you are the father, you are likely to be ordered to pay support until the child turns 18. In many states, you will probably be required to pay unpaid support, covering up to three years. In other states, you aren't responsible for support until the date that the custodial parent files the support petition in court.

Most states have passed new laws making it easier and quicker to establish paternity. In many cases, the right to a hearing before a judge has been eliminated, and administrative agencies can hear cases. Although a father can volunteer for genetic testing, most commonly it is ordered by the court in response to a paternity petition filed by:

- the other parent
- a child support services agency, or
- a prosecutor.

And, in cases where the alleged father is served with notice of a paternity hearing and fails to appear, a default paternity order can be entered. To hasten the process, many states have time limits for resolving paternity issues.

In a paternity action, some or all of the following kinds of evidence may be offered against you:

- **Access.** You and the mother had an opportunity to engage in sexual intercourse during the period of conception. This can include proof of your cohabitation.
- **Potency and fertility.** You are neither impotent nor sterile.
- **Blood tests.** Blood tests can show that you might be the father or that you definitely are not the father. Initially, your blood and your child's blood will be compared for type (A, B, AB, O) and Rh factor (positive or negative). If you are not excluded by those two tests, your blood will be HLA tested. HLA tests can *disprove* paternity with nearly 98% accuracy. Unlike genetic typing (see below), a blood test cannot positively establish paternity—it can only show that someone with your blood type could have fathered the child.
- **Genetic typing.** DNA "fingerprinting" tests your genetic makeup against the child's and can prove or disprove paternity with 99.99% accuracy, when the tests are administered correctly.
- **Acknowledgment of paternity.** If you paid for the mother's hospital costs, had your name put on the birth certificate, ever acknowledged that the child is yours, voluntarily sent support, or took other steps one would expect a father to take, you'll have a large obstacle to overcome.
- **Resemblance.** If you look like the child, the mother or county attorney will probably march the kid past you while you are sitting in court, for the judge to see.

Enforcement of Child Support Obligations

This section describes the methods used to collect unpaid child support. If you owe a lot, your child's other parent may go to court and ask a judge to issue a judgment for the amount of the arrears. This is called a judgment for child support.

> **EXAMPLE:** Al was ordered to pay his ex-wife Cindy $550 per month in child support. He lost his job and hasn't made the last three payments. He is in arrears a total of $1,650 under the original child support order. Cindy can try to collect the arrears owed under the child support order, or she can go ask a judge to grant her a judgment for the amount Al owes.

In some cases, a judgment for child support may give additional remedies to the party trying to collect unpaid support. For the most part, however, a person owed child support can use the most effective and most commonly used collection methods even without a judgment.

If your child support order is at least 15 years old, it probably just requires you to send a certain amount of money each month to your child's other parent. If your order was issued more recently, however, it may be very different. Today, you will have money withheld from your paycheck, or you will be required to send money to a state agency that in turn sends a check to the custodial parent.

Parents today receive more help from the government in collecting child support payments than they did 15 years ago. Both the federal and state governments are now aggressively involved in enforcing child support orders. States are required to help parents collect child support, even if the parent that owes money has moved out of state. Extensive database and registry systems track parents who owe child support. Information is shared among states, and between the states and the federal government. For example:

- Employers must report all new hires to their state's child support enforcement agency. The agency forwards this information to the National Directory of New Hires, a centralized registry that matches employee names with the names of parents who owe child support. The National Directory sets up income-withholding orders for delinquent parents.

- States must ask for the Social Security numbers of both parents when a child is born and must pass those numbers on to the state agency that enforces child support.

- Judges sometimes order noncustodial parents to pay child support to the child support enforcement agency, which in turn pays the custodial parent. This method is often used when the noncustodial parent is without regular income (perhaps self-employed) or when parents agree to waive the automatic wage withholding (this is explained below).

WARNING

You can run but you can't hide.
You may think that, by moving frequently, you can avoid paying child support. It's possible for a while, but unlikely if the other parent is persistent. Each state and the federal government maintain a parent-locator service that searches federal, state, and local records to find missing parents. The federal parent-locator service has access to Social Security, IRS, and all other federal information records except census records. The state locator services will check welfare, unemployment, motor vehicle, and other state records.

Automatic Income Withholding

The federal Family Support Act requires all states to have an automatic income withholding program that seizes part of a parent's wages to pay child support orders that were made or modified on or after January 1, 1994. For pre-1994 child support orders, the court may order income withholding if the custodial parent goes back to court to complain that you are in arrears.

The income withholding is automatic, unless the parties agree otherwise (for example, the custodial parent agrees that she will not serve the order on your employer, as long as you pay her directly) or unless there is good cause not to require immediate withholding.

States vary on their interpretation of "good cause." For example, in some states, if the parent has a reliable history of paying child support, income withholding is not automatic. In some states, automatic income withholding is ordered regardless of payment history. It's also conceivable, although not common, that you could offer to put up a bond to guarantee payments.

Federal Child Support Enforcement

The Department of Health and Human Services (HHS) enforces federal laws having to do with child support through its Office of Child Support Enforcement in the Administration for Children and Families (ACF). For more information about these federal programs and links to state enforcement programs, visit www.acf.hhs. gov/programs/cse.

The automatic income withholding provisions also apply to orders that combine child support and alimony, but not to orders for alimony only. If income withholding is ordered in one state (for example, where your child lives), but you live in another, your own state will enforce the income withholding.

An automatic income withholding order works quite simply. After a court orders you to pay child support, the custodial parent sends a copy of the court order to your employer. Each pay period, your employer withholds a portion of your pay and sends it to the custodial parent or to the state agency that distributes child support. (If you and the custodial parent agree and the court allows it, you can avoid the income withholding and make payments directly to the custodial parent or through a third party.)

If you don't receive regular wages but do have a regular source of income, such as income from a pension, a retirement fund, an annuity, unemployment compensation, or other public benefits, the court can order the child support withheld from that income. Instead of forwarding a copy of the order and the custodial parent's name and address to an employer, the court sends the information to the retirement plan administrator or public agency from which you receive your benefits.

If your income is from Social Security or a private pension governed by either ERISA (Employee Retirement Income Security Act) or REA (Retirement Equity Act), the administrator might not honor the court order. This is because Social Security and many private pensions have "anti-alienation" clauses that prohibit the administrator from turning over the funds to anyone other than the beneficiary (you).

Intercept Your Income Tax Refunds

One of the most powerful collection methods available is the interception of your federal income tax refund. If you owe more than $500 in child support and the custodial parent has contacted the state's child support enforcement agency for help, or if you owe $150 and the custodial parent receives welfare, the child support enforcement agency in the state where the custodial parent lives will notify the U.S. Department of the Treasury. The IRS will then take the amount of arrears out of your tax refund.

If you are now married to someone other than the custodial parent to whom you owe support, the IRS will take the refund from your joint income tax return. In some states, however, your new spouse won't be liable for your child support debts. If you live in one of those states, your new spouse can request a reimbursement from the IRS by completing Form 8379, *Injured Spouse Claim and Allocation*, and filing it with Form 1040 or 1040A. You can obtain a copy of this form and directions for filling it out at the IRS's, website www.irs.gov.

States that impose income taxes also intercept tax refunds to satisfy child support debts.

Liens on Your Real and Personal Property

A custodial parent who is owed child support can place a lien on your property. A lien is a notice that tells the world that someone claims you owe some money. Usually the custodial parent files a lien with the same office where the property is registered or recorded. For example, a lien on your house would be filed with the county recorder in the county where your house is located. The lien remains until your child is no longer entitled to support and you've paid all the arrears, or until the custodial parent agrees to remove the lien. With a lien, the custodial parent can force the sale of your property or wait until the property is sold or refinanced to get the money due. Although some states require that the custodial parent obtain a judgment for the arrears before putting a lien on property, most states allow liens to be imposed on property when you miss payments under the court order for support. To check the lien requirements in your state, go to the Office of Child Support Enforcement website at www.acf.hhs.gov.

Your best defense is to schedule a hearing before a judge and claim that the lien on your property impairs your ability to pay your current support. For example, if the lien is on your house and impairs your ability to borrow money to pay the child support arrears, make that clear to the judge. You'll probably need to bring copies of loan rejection letters stating that your poor credit rating—due to the lien—was the reason for the rejection.

To help locate the assets of parents who owe child support, all states are required to maintain what is known as a "data match system." Under this system, financial institutions that do business in a state, such as banks, insurance companies, and brokers, must provide that state's child support enforcement agencies with account information on clients who have past-due support obligations. The agency can then use this information to place a lien on and seize assets of people who owe child support.

Require You to Post a Bond or Assets to Guarantee Payment

Some states allow judges to require parents with child support arrears to post a bond or assets, such as stock certificates, to guarantee payment. In some states, for example, if a self-employed parent misses a child support payment and the custodial parent requests a court hearing, the court can order the noncustodial parent to post assets (such as by putting money into an escrow account).

Most states' child support enforcement agencies have the power to require parents to post bonds or assets. But not all agencies use this measure, and others use it for extreme cases only. In practice, few bond companies will write bonds for child support debts. Most parents will find that they must put property into an escrow account, or, in some states such as Montana and Wyoming, into a trust account that is managed and invested for the child's benefit.

You must be given notice of the action to require you to post assets or a bond and an opportunity to oppose it. You may have a good defense if posting the assets or bond would impair your ability to pay your current support or to borrow money to pay the arrears.

The Arrears May Be Reported to Credit Bureaus

The law requires credit bureaus to include information about overdue child support in your credit report. Creditors and lenders may deny credit based on this information. In addition, sometimes creditors and lenders report the whereabouts of missing parents to child enforcement agencies.

Child support arrears remain on your credit report for up to seven years, unless you can make a deal with the child support enforcement agency. An agency may agree not to report negative information to the credit bureau if you pay some or all of the overdue support. But few child support enforcement agencies will agree to eliminate all negative information. Most will at least report that you were delinquent in the past. (See Chapter 17 for information on how to correct your report if information reported is wrong or obsolete).

Many states require child support enforcement agencies to notify you before reporting overdue child support information to the credit bureaus. Usually, the enforcement agency must give you a reasonable opportunity to dispute the information. Many states require agencies to report only overdue amounts exceeding $1,000. (For information on how to find your state law, see Chapter 19.)

You May Be Publicly Humiliated

Congress has encouraged states to come up with creative ways to embarrass parents into paying the child support they owe. One method used nationwide by an association of state child support enforcement agencies is the publishing of "most wanted" lists of parents who owe child support.

In some areas, for example, the family court lists the names of parents not paying child support on cable television 300 times a week and in a full-page newspaper advertisement once a month. One county using this technique claims to have located over 50% of the parents owing support. Similarly, the Iowa attorney general reports that 90% of missing fathers who owe child support have been located through the state's "most wanted" poster program.

If your name is included on a most wanted list, the only way to get your name off the list (unless you don't mind being a local "celebrity") is to turn yourself in. You'll be ordered to make monthly payments henceforth, your wages will be attached, and the court will take steps to see that you pay your back child support. But that may be better than having this kind of notoriety in your community.

You May Be Denied a State License or U.S. Passport

In most states, parents with child support arrears will be denied an original or renewed driver's or professional license (for doctors, lawyers, contractors, and the like) and, if they owe $2,500 or more, may be denied a U.S. passport. Parents who owe child support are also at risk of having their current driver's licenses suspended.

You May Be Held in Contempt of Court

Failing to obey a court order is called contempt of court. If you owe unpaid child support, the other parent of your child can ask for a hearing before a judge and ask that you be held in contempt of court. You must be served with a document ordering you to attend the hearing, and then must attend and explain why you haven't paid the support you owe. If you don't attend, the court can issue a warrant for your arrest. Many courts do issue warrants, making county jails a resting stop for fathers who don't pay child support and fail to show up in court.

If you attend the hearing, the judge can still throw you in jail for violating the order to pay the support. And the judge might do so, depending on how convincing your story is as to why you haven't paid.

To stay out of jail, go to the hearing prepared to show that you have not deliberately disobeyed the court's order to pay child support. You may have to convince the judge that you're not as irresponsible as the judge probably thinks you are. Preparing evidence is a must. Your first step is to show why you didn't pay. If you've been out of work, get a sworn statement from your most recent employer stating why you were let go. If you went job searching but had no luck, provide records of when you interviewed or filled out an application, and with whom you spoke. Remember: Disputes with the custodial parent about custody or visitation are never an acceptable excuse for not paying child support.

Next, you must explain why you didn't request a modification hearing when it became evident that you couldn't meet your support obligation. For example, if you've been in bed or otherwise immobilized—depressed, sick, or injured—get sworn statements from all medical and healing professionals who treated you. Also, get statements from friends or relatives who cared for you. Emphasize your most compelling arguments (for example, you couldn't get out of bed), but never lie.

If you spoke to lawyers about helping you file a modification request but couldn't afford their fees, be sure to bring a list of the names of lawyers you spoke to, the date you spoke to each one, and the fee the lawyer wanted to charge. If you tried to hire a legal aid lawyer to help you but you made too much money to qualify for such assistance (or the office had too many cases, or doesn't handle child support modifications), make sure you bring the name of the lawyer and the date of the conversation.

If the judge doesn't put you in jail, the judge will instead order you to make future payments and will set up a payment schedule for you to pay any unpaid support. The judge won't reduce the amount of your unpaid support—arrears cannot be modified retroactively—but may decrease your future payments. The judge may also order that your wages be withheld, that a lien be placed on your property, or that you must post a bond or other assets.

Holding a father in contempt of court and throwing him in jail used to be the primary method of enforcing child support orders. Today, the technique is still used, but sparingly, usually only if an income-withholding order and a wage garnishment won't work. Courts recognize that a jailed parent cannot take the necessary steps (like holding a job) to make child support payments.

Your Wages May Be Garnished and Other Assets Seized

Child support arrears that are made into a court judgment can be collected by the various methods described in Chapter 14. Even if the judgment was obtained in one state and you have since moved to another state, state laws allow the custodial parent to register the judgment in the second state and enforce it there.

The most common method of collecting a judgment for support is wage garnishment. A wage garnishment is similar to income withholding. A portion of your wages is removed from your paycheck and delivered to the custodial parent before you ever see any of it. In many states, the arrears need not be made into a judgment to be collected through wage garnishment.

To garnish your wages, the custodial parent obtains authorization from the court in a document usually called a writ of execution. Under this authorization, the custodial parent directs the sheriff to seize a portion of your wages. The sheriff in turn notifies you and your employer of the garnishment.

Income withholding and wage garnishments differ in one way: The amount of income withholding will be the amount of child support you have been ordered to pay each month. The amount of a wage garnishment, however, is a percentage of your paycheck. What you were once ordered to pay is irrelevant. The court simply wants to take money out of each of your paychecks—and leave you with a minimum to live on—until the unpaid support is made up.

If a court orders that your wages be garnished to satisfy any debt except child support or alimony, a maximum of roughly 25% of your net wages can be taken. For unpaid child support, however, up to 50% of your net wages can be garnished, and up to 60% if you are not currently supporting another dependent. If your check is already subject to wage withholding for your future payments or garnishment by a different creditor, the total amount taken from your paycheck cannot exceed 50% (or 65% if you are not currently supporting another dependent and are more than 12 weeks in arrears).

To put a wage garnishment order into effect, the court, custodial parent, state agency, or county attorney must notify your employer. Once your employer is told to garnish your wages, your employer tells you of the garnishment. You can request a court hearing, which will take place shortly after the garnishment has begun. At the hearing, you can make only a few objections:

- The amount the court claims you owe is wrong.
- The amount will leave you with too little to live on.
- The custodial parent actively concealed your child, as opposed to merely frustrating or denying your visitation (not all states allow this objection).
- You had custody of the child at the time the support arrears accrued.

If the wage garnishment doesn't cover the amount you owe, or you don't have wages or other income to be garnished, the custodial parent may try to get the unpaid support by going after other items of your property. Examples of the type of property that may be vulnerable include cars, motorcycles, boats, airplanes, houses, corporate stock, horses, rents payable to you, and accounts receivable. In some cases, even spendthrift trusts and your interest in a partnership may be used for payment.

The Arrears May Be Sent to the State Child Support Enforcement Agency

If the custodial parent receives welfare, the state's child support enforcement agency is required to help collect unpaid child support. For a $25 fee, the agency will also help any parent trying to collect child support. If you owe unpaid child support and move out of state, state laws require that when the custodial parent contacts the child support enforcement agency in her state, that agency must contact the agency in the state where you now live. The agency in your state then contacts you and orders you to pay the child support. If you pay that money to the state agency in your state, the agency will send it to the agency in the state where the custodial parent lives.

When the state agency is involved, you'll receive a notice requesting that you attend a conference. The purpose of the conference is to establish your income and expenses, including support for other children, and how much you should pay. The agency is likely to propose that you pay a lot. You should emphasize, truthfully, your other necessary expenses—food, shelter, clothing, other kids, and the like. Bring receipts, bills, and all other evidence of your monthly costs. If you don't show up, the agency may initiate criminal charges against you for failure to appear.

You May Be Criminally Prosecuted

In many states, it's a misdemeanor to fail to provide support for your child. While criminal prosecution isn't all that likely, the involvement of a county attorney increases the possibility. Also, if you have violated a judge's order enough times, the judge may report you to the county attorney's office.

In addition, under the federal Child Support Recovery Act of 1992 (also know as the Deadbeat Dad Law), failure to pay support for a child living in another state is a federal crime. To be prosecuted under this law, the parent must have owed more than $5,000 for more than a year, and the failure to pay must be deliberate.

Alimony

Alimony, sometimes called spousal support or maintenance, is money paid by one ex-spouse to the other for support, after a marriage is over. No federal law requires states to have guidelines for setting the amount of alimony. In some courts, however, judges have adopted informal written schedules to help them determine the appropriate level of support. Mostly, judges consider:

- the age, health, earnings, and obligations of each spouse
- whether one spouse contributed to the education, training, or career advancement of the other
- the length and standard of living of the marriage
- who will have custody of the children, if any

- the time needed for a supported spouse to become self-sufficient, and
- the tax consequences to each person.

If you cannot pay the amount of alimony you've been ordered to pay, you should file a motion for modification. You must show a material change in circumstances since the last court order. Your ex-spouse's living with someone may qualify you for a reduction in alimony in some states.

Your ex-spouse's remarriage is another change of circumstance that could affect your obligation to pay alimony. Your divorce decree probably states that alimony terminates on your ex-spouse's remarriage. Even if it doesn't, in most states, a recipient spouse's remarriage ends your obligation to pay alimony.

Other common reasons for changes in alimony include your decreased income or your ex-spouse's substantially increased income. Where you have voluntarily decreased your income, however—for example, by quitting your job, taking a lower-paying job, or becoming a perpetual student—the judge may instead consider your ability to earn, not just your actual earnings.

If child support and alimony are lumped together in one payment, the collection techniques discussed above may be used against you. If they are kept separate, however, only the following techniques can be used to collect alimony:

- interception of income tax refunds
- court hearings

- wage garnishments, and
- other judgment collection methods, such as property liens.

As with child support, alimony arrearages can be reduced to judgment and collected while the judgment is in effect.

Bankruptcy and Child Support/Alimony Debt

Bankruptcy is covered more thoroughly in Chapter 15. Bankruptcy is discussed here, however, because many debtors consider filing for bankruptcy to get rid of child support or alimony debts. As discussed already, bankruptcy won't cancel arrears or a support judgment. These debts and obligations survive bankruptcy.

The primary advantage of filing for Chapter 7 bankruptcy is that you can get rid of many of your other debts, thus freeing up money to meet your current support obligation and to pay off the arrearage.

If you file a Chapter 13 "repayment plan" bankruptcy, you also can get rid of many of your debts, but you will have to pay off the entire support arrearage over the life of your plan—between three and five years. You will also have to remain current on your support obligation during that period, and your Chapter 13 case will be dismissed if you don't. (For more information on how Chapter 7 and Chapter 13 bankruptcies work, see Chapter 15 of this book.)

How Bankruptcy Affects Marital Debts

Child support and alimony are never discharged (wiped out) in bankruptcy. However, other types of debt created in the course of a divorce or separation may be discharged—in Chapter 13 bankruptcy only, not Chapter 7—as long as they are not "in the nature of support." An example of a debt "in the nature of support" would be one spouse agreeing to pay the children's school tuition as part of a divorce settlement agreement. A debt that typically would not be considered "in the nature of support" would be an agreement by one spouse to pay off the other spouse's credit card debts as part of an overall division of the marital assets and liabilities.

These debts cannot be discharged in Chapter 7 bankruptcy; they will automatically survive and you will continue to owe them. For more on bankruptcy, see Chapter 15.

■

If You Are Sued

Lawsuits consume time and money, and rest and friends.

— George Herbert
English poet, 1593-1633

If you don't pay your debts, you'll probably be sued unless any of the following are true:

- **The creditor or collection agency can't find you.** (See Chapter 9.)
- **You're judgment proof.** As explained in Chapter 8, being judgment proof means that you have no property or income that the creditor can legally take to collect on a judgment, now or in the foreseeable future.
- **You file for bankruptcy.** One way to prevent a lawsuit is to file for bankruptcy. (See Chapter 15.) Filing for bankruptcy stops most collection efforts, including lawsuits, dead in their tracks, and you may be able to erase (discharge) many debts in your bankruptcy case.

Being sued is not the end of the world. It doesn't make you a bad person—millions of people are sued each year. Yes, it can be scary and may cause sleepless nights, but in large part that's because few people actually know what goes on in a lawsuit. Our perceptions, which typically have been shaped by television shows, movies, and famous (or infamous) trials, are usually off the mark.

As this chapter explains, if you are sued on a debt you do owe and you have no good defenses, the lawsuit usually takes very little time and money. And if you do have a good defense, depending on how complicated it is, you may be able to assert it without hiring a lawyer.

The premise of this chapter is that you owe someone money and haven't paid. Usually this is considered a breach of a contract. Therefore, this chapter explains negotiating and the types of defenses you can raise in response to being sued for breaching a contract. (Chapter 4 discusses debts that you may not owe.)

You may be sued for any number of other reasons—for example, you cause a car accident, slander someone, or infringe a copyright. These kinds of suits claim that you have injured someone's person, property, reputation, or intellectual property. This kind of injury is called a "tort." These suits are not based on a contractual obligation to pay someone money or failure to pay a pre-existing debt.

If you are sued and you have a defense to the allegations made against you, you will have to consult a source beyond this book for help. (See Chapter 19.) If the other side wins, you will owe a debt (in the form of a money judgment), and this chapter explains what you can expect.

How a Lawsuit Begins

A lawsuit starts when the creditor, or a lawyer for a creditor or collection agency, prepares a document called a complaint or petition, claiming that you owe money. The lawyer or creditor files the document with a court clerk and pays a filing fee. The lawyer or creditor then has a copy of the complaint, along with a summons, served on you. The summons is a document issued by the court, notifying you that you are being sued.

The complaint identifies:

- the plaintiff—that's the creditor or collection agency, or possibly another third party the creditor sold the debt to
- the defendant—that's you and anyone else liable for the debt, such as your spouse, a cosigner, or a guarantor
- the date the complaint was filed (this is important if you have a statute of limitations defense, as explained below)
- the court in which you are being sued
- why the creditor is suing you, and
- what the creditor wants from the lawsuit.

Where the Lawsuit Is Filed

The creditor must normally sue you in the state where you live or where the transaction took place. The creditor usually selects the state where you live if it's different from where the transaction took place, because the court requires a substantial connection between you and the state in which you are sued. For example, if you send a check from your home in South Carolina to a mail-order business in Wisconsin, and your check bounces, the creditor can sue you in South Carolina, but probably not in Wisconsin. Your connections with Wisconsin—even assuming the transaction took place there—are too insubstantial to sue you there.

After selecting the state, the creditor must select a county within the state. This is called the venue for the case. In most states, the creditor can choose the county where

you live, the county where the transaction took place, or the county where the creditor is located. If your home, the location of the transaction, and the location of the creditor's business aren't all in one county, most creditors will choose the county where they are located, simply because that is more convenient for them. If the creditor has chosen a county that is terribly inconvenient for you, you can file a motion to have the case transferred to your county. You'll almost certainly need the help of a lawyer to do this.

Once the creditor has selected the state and county, the creditor must choose the court: small claims court or civil court of general jurisdiction. You'll probably be sued in your state's civil court if any one of the following is true:

- The amount of money you owe exceeds your state's small claims limit.
- A collection agency has your debt and is prohibited from suing in small claims court.
- The creditor simply chooses not to use small claims court—no plaintiff has to use small claims court, even on a $10 debt.

The exact name of the civil court depends on your state, and possibly the amount of money involved. It may be a Circuit Court, City Court, County Court, District Court, Justice Court, Justice of the Peace Court, Magistrate's Court, Municipal Court, or Superior Court. Although the names differ, what goes on in each court is pretty much the same. You might also be sued in a federal district court if you owe money to the federal government—for example, on a federally guaranteed student loan.

Being Sued in Small Claims Court

Virtually every state has a small claims court to hear disputes involving modest amounts of money. The range is typically from $1,000 to $10,000. Small claims courts handle matters without long delays or formal rules of evidence and are intended for people to represent themselves. If you owe the creditor a few thousand dollars or less, you may be sued in your state's small claims court. Even if the amount you owe is above your state's limit, the creditor may opt to sue you in small claims court and give up (waive) the excess.

In most states, you don't need to file a written response to a lawsuit in small claims court. You simply show up on the date of the hearing. If, however, you plan to file your own claim against the creditor for money—for example, if the creditor breached a warranty (see Chapter 4)—you have to file a your own claim before the hearing so that both the creditor's claim and your claim are heard together.

Be sure you show up at the hearing. If you don't, most of the time you will lose the case by default and the court will enter a default judgment against you. At the hearing, just be yourself and tell your side of the dispute. You don't normally need to hire a lawyer, even if your state allows them in small claims court and the creditor has one. Small claims court is designed to operate without lawyers, and most small claims judges feel that people do as well or better without them. If you lose the case, the judge may let you set up a schedule to pay off the judgment in monthly payments—but don't count on it. Depending on your state's law, you may also have the right to appeal to a higher court.

The rest of this chapter assumes that you are not sued in small claims court, but in your state's civil court of general jurisdiction (often called district court, county court, court of common pleas, or a similar name).

If you're sued in small claims court, an excellent resource is *Everybody's Guide to Small Claims Court*, by Ralph Warner (Nolo). Use that book as a guide to representing yourself.

In civil court, a lawsuit can be time-consuming and expensive, although routine debt collection cases rarely are. In theory, you are required to follow formal procedural and evidentiary rules, but many judges are flexible when dealing with a person representing himself or herself. While it can be extremely difficult to represent yourself in civil court, more and more people are doing it.

RESOURCES

Resources for representing yourself in court. Californians will want to obtain a copy of *Win Your Lawsuit: A Judge's Guide to Representing Yourself in California Superior Court*, by Judge Rod Duncan (Nolo), which also contains information on defending a lawsuit. People who decide to handle their own case—in any state—will find *Represent Yourself in Court*, by Paul Bergman and Sara Berman-Barrett (Nolo), to be indispensable.

Service of Court Papers

After the creditor files papers with the court, he or she must serve them on you. In most civil courts, you must be handed the papers personally. If you can't be found, the papers can be left with someone over the age of 18 at your home or business, as long as another copy is mailed to you. The creditor cannot serve the papers on you personally, because a party to a lawsuit can't do the actual serving. Most creditors hire professionals called process servers or have a local sheriff or marshal do the job.

Sometimes, a creditor will mail you a copy of the summons and complaint with a form for you to sign and date, acknowledging that you have received the papers. If you sign and date the form, you are deemed to have been served on that date.

It's often a good idea to sign the form and send it back promptly, because you can save money. If you refuse to sign and the creditor can later prove that you declined the opportunity to do so, you may have to pay whatever costs—frequently between $35 and $150—the creditor incurred in hiring a process server or sheriff to serve the papers on you personally. That's also a reason not to hide from a process server.

Understanding the Complaint

Complaints are usually written in hyped-up legalese. You may be referred to as the "party of the second part," not simply "the defendant," and almost never just by your name. The document may include "here-tofores," "thereafters," "saids," and much

If Service Was Done Wrong

Suppose the creditor has a friend serve you, and the friend simply slides the papers under your door. Sure, you got the papers, but service was technically improper because they were not handed to you or left with a responsible person at your home or office, followed by a mailed copy. You now have two choices: You can either ignore the impropriety, or complain about it in court. Unless you complain, the court won't know that service was improper, and it will proceed as if service was proper, expecting you to respond to the suit. If you don't formally respond, a default judgment will probably be entered against you. You can ask the court to set aside the default judgment based on improper service, but you may need the advice or assistance of a lawyer to do this.

Should you complain about improper service? In most cases, no. It would probably require you to pay for a lawyer's help, and the creditor will just hire someone to serve you again. All you buy is a little time, and you might pay a lot for it.

If you have a defense to the claim, the practical course may be to file your answer and then attend the court hearing at the scheduled time. Explain to the judge why you believe the service was improper. If the judge finds that service was adequate, then present your defense and let the judge decide the case.

more. Skim through the complaint and see if you agree or disagree with the basic facts.

To find out what exactly the creditor or collects wants from you, turn to the final pages. Find the word "WHEREFORE," or a section called "Relief Requested," and start reading. You'll not only learn how much the creditor says you owe, but, most of the time, you'll also find out that the creditor is claiming you must pay interest, court costs incurred, possibly attorneys' fees, and "whatever other relief the court deems appropriate." This last phrase is a catchall added in the event the court comes up with another solution.

When Is Your Response Due?

You probably will have between 20 and 30 days to respond in writing (in a document usually called an answer) to the creditor's complaint. The summons tells you precisely how much time you have. You probably will have to pay a filing fee in order to file your answer. If you can't afford the filing fee, ask the court clerk's office if you can request a fee waiver. You may qualify for a fee waiver if you receive public benefits such as SSI or if your income is not enough to pay for the common necessaries of life and also pay court fees.

If you don't respond in time, the creditor can come into court and ask that a default judgment be entered against you. Usually the default judgment is granted for the amount the creditor requested. Some judges, however, will scrutinize the papers. If the judge feels that the creditor's claim for

interest or attorneys' fees is excessive, the judge may not allow it. Other judges will require the creditor to present evidence of actual damages before awarding any money.

FAST TRACK

When there's a judgment against you. Often the defendant has no real defense and no money to hire a lawyer to put up a fight. In fact, in most routine debt cases (80%–90%), a default judgment is taken against the defendant. If you owe money and decide to default, skip ahead to "If the Creditor Gets a Judgment Against You," below. If you are unsure as to whether you have a defense, see Chapter 4.

Negotiate

Even if you've avoided your creditor or a collection agency up to this point, it's never too late to try to negotiate. If you call and offer to settle the matter, the collector may agree to suspend, though not withdraw, the lawsuit while you are negotiating. Unless the creditor gives you an extension of time, in writing, to respond to the lawsuit, you should file an answer, even while you are negotiating. For tips on negotiating, see Chapter 6. If your efforts to negotiate with the collector are unsuccessful, consider contacting a nonprofit debt counseling agency that will work with you to set up a repayment plan by contacting your individual creditors. (See Chapter 19.)

As you decide whether to settle or fight the lawsuit, keep this in mind: If you lose, you probably will have to pay the plaintiff's attorneys' fees and court costs, and that this can be very expensive. If the plaintiff's lawyers conduct discovery or file a summary judgment motion (explained below), or have to make repeated court appearances, you could wind up having to pay more in fees and costs than the amount you owed in the first place. This does not mean you should give up if you have a good defense. You should just be realistic about the strength of your case and the amount of expenses you may face if you lose.

Lump Sum Settlement

You will be in the best position to settle with a creditor or collector (the plaintiff) if you can offer a lump sum of cash to settle the case. Usually, the plaintiff will insist that you pay between one-half and three-fourths of what you owe. The plaintiff, not wanting to start all over if you miss the payments, is unlikely to stop a lawsuit in exchange for a promise to pay in installments.

If the plaintiff agrees to take your lump sum offer, make sure it's accepted as complete settlement of what you owe. Further, make sure the plaintiff agrees to dismiss (withdraw)—and in fact *does* dismiss—the lawsuit filed against you. Ask that the plaintiff dismiss the lawsuit "with prejudice," which means that the plaintiff cannot sue you again on the same claim. (See "Sample Settlement Agreement or Release," below.) Of course, get all agreements in writing. You can check to make sure the lawsuit has been dismissed by visiting the courthouse filing office (or its

website) and looking up your case number. (The number is on the papers served on you.) The file should contain a paper called a request for dismissal or something similar.

If the plaintiff hasn't filed a request for dismissal, you may have to take some action yourself. If you can't get the plaintiff (or plaintiff's lawyer) to file the agreed-upon dismissal, prepare one yourself for the plaintiff to sign. Ask the court clerk if your state has a form to use for requesting dismissals. If it does, get a copy and fill it out, but don't sign it in the space for the plaintiff's signature. If your state doesn't have such a form, you may have to visit a law library, find a form book, and prepare a request for dismissal yourself. Once your request is completed, make a copy and send the original to whomever sued you. Ask that the form be signed and sent back to you. Once it comes back, file it with the court clerk yourself. You may have to pay a fee to file the document. Keep a file-stamped copy of the signed dismissal form.

Settlement Involving Installment Payments

Assuming the plaintiff does agree to settle the case based on your promise to make installment payments, chances are he or she will insist that you agree ("stipulate") to having a court judgment entered against you if you fail to make payments. The stipulated judgment will be for an amount that you and the plaintiff agree on to settle the case. Sign the stipulated judgment if it is acceptable to you, but make sure the collector promises

Sample Settlement Agreement or Release

This Agreement is entered into on the date below between Christopher's Contracting Company , Creditor, and Donna Markell , Debtor.

Creditor has alleged that Debtor owes him $7,745 for construction work he did on Debtor's home ;

Debtor agrees that she has not paid Creditor any money for the work done but alleges that Creditor damaged her home while doing the construction work ;

Creditor has filed Civil Action No. C49903 in the Superior Court for the County of Fairfield, State of California, seeking a money judgment ; and

Creditor and Debtor desire to settle their differences and end the above-identified litigation.

Therefore, in consideration of the undertakings set forth below, Creditor and Debtor hereby agree as follows:

1. Within 20 days of the date this Agreement is entered into, Creditor will file in the Superior Court for the County of Fairfield, State of California , a Dismissal With Prejudice in the above-identified litigation.

2. Creditor further agrees not to make any future claim or bring any future action against Debtor for the acts alleged, or which could have been alleged, in Civil Action No. C49903 , occurring up to the time of the entry of that Dismissal With Prejudice.

3. Debtor agrees not to make any future claim or bring any future action against Creditor for acts alleged, or which could have been alleged in a cross-complaint, in Civil Action No. C49903 .

4. Debtor will, at the time of executing this Agreement, pay to Creditor the sum of $5,000 as full settlement of any claim of Creditor against Debtor.

Sample Settlement Agreement or Release (cont'd)

5. Creditor agrees to remove all negative information related to this debt from the files maintained by the major credit reporting agencies.

6. *[California; other states may have similar provisions]* The releases recited in this Agreement cover all claims under California Civil Code Section 1542. Creditor and Debtor hereby waive the provisions of Section 1542 which read as follows:

> "A general release does not extend to claims which the creditor does not know or suspect to exist in his or her favor at the time of executing the release, which if known by him or her must have materially affected his or her settlement with the debtor."

7. Creditor and Debtor will bear their own costs, expenses, and attorneys' fees.

8. This Agreement embodies the entire understanding between Creditor and Debtor relating to the subject matter of this Agreement and merges all prior discussions between them.

Dated: _____ May 30, 2007 _____

Creditor's signature, address, and phone number:

Stephen Christopher

__1782 Main Street, Fairfield, CA__

__707-555-9993__

Debtor's signature, address, and phone number:

Donna Markell

__98 South Acorn Ave., Fairfield, CA__

__707-555-0081__

in writing not to file it with the court unless you fail to make the installment payments. This way, your credit file won't show that there's a judgment against you. Of course, if you stop making the agreed-on installment payments at some point, the plaintiff can file the judgment and start procedures to collect the amount you haven't paid.

If the Negotiations Hit a Sour Note

If your negotiations are going nowhere, or you're uncomfortable handling them yourself, consider hiring an attorney to negotiate for you. An attorney carries clout that might lead the collector to settle for a good deal less than you owe. But don't hire an attorney unless it's cost-effective. If an attorney charges $250 to negotiate a $700 debt down to $500, you've actually lost $50. (See Chapter 19 for information on finding an attorney.)

Alternative Dispute Resolution

Alternative dispute resolution (ADR) refers to methods used to settle a disagreement short of going to court. If you clearly owe a debt and are looking for some way to avoid court, most creditors won't agree to using ADR. If you really don't think you owe the money or have some other credible defense to the creditor's lawsuit, however, the creditor may agree to resolve the lawsuit through ADR.

ADR can be informal, fast, and inexpensive. Because of the informality of ADR, you generally don't have to follow formal procedural and evidentiary rules. You just tell your story. However, you should use ADR only if it is nonbinding (meaning both sides can still go to court if they don't like the result) or you are confident that the process will be fair. The following are the main ADR options.

Arbitration. This is the most formal type of ADR. You and the creditor or collector agree to submit your dispute to at least one neutral third person—often a lawyer or judge. If a lot of money is at stake, arbitrators usually let the parties use attorneys at arbitration hearings and impose formal rules of evidence. In other disputes, arbitration is less formal and can take place without lawyers. You often have to pay the arbitrator's fees in advance, and they can be high. If you win, however, you may be reimbursed.

If arbitration is voluntary and nonbinding (meaning you can appeal the decision in court if you don't like it), it can be a good thing. However, more and more creditors and businesses include clauses in contracts that require you to submit to binding arbitration instead of going to court. In these types of arbitration, you can rarely challenge a bad arbitration decision in court, even if the arbitrator decides not to follow the law or makes a mistake of fact.

If your contract requires that you go to arbitration, you may be able to get out of arbitration and go to court instead—but to do so is often complicated. You'll have to get help from a lawyer. If you are stuck with arbitration, find out as much as you can about the panel of arbitrators (the group from which your arbitrator will be selected). Look for any that might be sympathetic to consumers rather than creditors and businesses. For example, many arbitrators are also practicing lawyers—find out if they represent mostly creditors or mostly consumers.

Mediation or conciliation. This is the second-most common type of ADR. You and the creditor or collector work with a neutral third party to come up with a solution to your dispute. Mediation is informal, and the mediator does not have the power to impose a decision on you. An excellent resource on mediation is *Mediate, Don't Litigate*, by Peter Lovenheim and Lisa Guerin (Nolo).

Minitrial. A third option is for you and the creditor or collector to present your positions to a neutral third person who acts as a judge and issues an advisory opinion. You can agree to be bound by that opinion. A growing number of states have "rent-a-judge" programs to encourage the use of minitrials to settle disputes.

Many states encourage mediation or arbitration and encourage the court to make ADR available. These programs are usually not binding and can provide a quick way to resolve problems without battling it out in court.

If your state doesn't assign cases to mediation or another form of ADR, you can find someone to resolve your dispute yourself. Many mediators are listed in the phone book. Before hiring someone, ask for references. Call the references and find out if they were satisfied with the service. Also, the National Council of Better Business Bureaus operates a nationwide system for settling consumer disputes through arbitration and mediation. Local BBB offices handle

over two million consumer disputes each year. (To find one, go to www.bbb.org and click "Locate a Bureau.") One advantage to BBB arbitration over more formal arbitration is that it is free to consumers and is geared toward operating without lawyers.

If you would like to use ADR instead of going to court, write to the creditor and emphasize the advantages of ADR. (See "Sample Letter to Creditor Requesting ADR," below.) *Even if you send a letter requesting ADR, file a response to the complaint.* The creditor may say no, may say yes and then decide not to participate, or may say yes only after the time limit has passed for you to file an answer. As explained above, if the deadline passes and you haven't filed a response, the creditor can ask the court to have a default judgment entered against you. Protect yourself by filing your answer even while you're negotiating.

Respond in Court

If you want to respond to the lawsuit, you must do so in writing, within the time allowed. This means you must file formal legal papers, and that task can be difficult. Civil court is designed and operated by lawyers. Arcane rules dominate, and the language is often hard to understand. Clerks may be overworked and unhelpful, stonewalling even the most routine request for information with the claim that they "can't give legal advice."

This doesn't mean you can't or shouldn't represent yourself in court. You can, but you will have to educate yourself and do some legal research. You'll also need patience to

Sample Letter to Creditor Requesting ADR

Merrily Andrews, Esq.
Legal Department
Presley Hospital
900 Hollis Boulevard
Carson City, NV 88888

March 15, 2007

Re: Shawn Smith Account # 7777-SMI Civil Case # 07-0056

Dear Ms. Andrews:

I have just been served with the Summons and Complaint for the lawsuit filed by Presley Hospital against me for $7,400. I would very much like to resolve this matter and suggest that we mediate the dispute with the help of a mediator from the Nevada Consumer Council. I know that the Consumer Council has helped many people resolve their differences quickly, informally, and inexpensively.

Although I did not respond to your earlier collection efforts, it was not because I did not want to settle the matter. My wife and I were both very ill and hospitalized at Presley. My wife died, and taking care of my debts was not my highest priority.

I hope you'll agree to mediate this dispute. If so, please contact me by April 10, 2007.

Thank you,

Shawn Smith

Shawn Smith

play the game according to the lawyers' and judges' rules. For example, if you raise an argument or a defense at the wrong time, the court may refuse to consider it.

You can also hire a lawyer to represent you in court. As you know, lawyers are expensive. But you may be able to hire a lawyer and keep your expenses down by doing some of the work yourself. Some lawyers today "unbundle" their services and will assist you with specific tasks (such as preparing an answer) or in portions of the lawsuit for less than if you hired them to defend the entire lawsuit. If you have a strong claim against the creditor that could generate substantial money for you if you win, the lawyer may take your case on a contingent fee basis—which means you don't pay attorney fees unless you win.

In going to court, you want to raise any possible defenses you have, such as that the statute of limitations has expired or that the goods you received were defective.

Statute of Limitations

The creditor has a limited number of years to sue you after you fail to pay your debt. This time period is set by a state law called the statute of limitations. The time allowed varies greatly from state to state and for different kinds of debts—written contracts, oral contracts, promissory notes, or open-ended accounts like credit cards. The statute of limitations starts on the day the debt—or payment on an open-ended account—was due.

Is the Account Open- or Closed-End Credit?

The statute of limitations for open-end and closed-end credit is often different. Unfortunately, determining whether an account is open-end or closed-end is not always easy. Generally, if you can use the account repeatedly, it is open-end credit (also called "revolving credit"). Your payments vary, depending on how much credit you have used in a certain period of time. The most common example of open-end credit is a credit card. Closed-end credit usually involves a single transaction, such as the purchase of a house or car, and the payments are fixed in amount and number.

Many transactions fall somewhere in between open- and closed-end credit. Also, many creditors try to characterize a closed-end account as open-end, either to take advantage of a longer statute of limitations or to avoid providing the more extensive disclosures required for closed-end credit.

To complicate matters even more, the statute of limitations for an open-ended account is not always clear. Some states specify limits for credit card accounts only. In others, if you have a written contract with the credit card company, the statute of limitations for written contracts applies to credit card accounts. In still other states, the statute of limitations for oral contracts governs open-ended accounts. In order to find the statute of limitations for an open-ended account in your state, you'll have to do some legal research or check with a local attorney. (See Chapter 19 for help finding an attorney or for tips on doing legal research.)

If the creditor has waited too long to sue you, you must raise this as a defense in the papers you file in response to the creditor's complaint.

> **EXAMPLE:** Bart lives in Delaware, where the statute of limitations on open-end accounts is three years. Bart had a large balance on his Visa card, made a small payment in July 2004, and then paid no more. His August Big Bank Visa statement included a payment due date of August 15, 2004. Bart was sued in September 2007, three years and a few days after he first missed the payment. Bart has a statute of limitations defense. Bart must raise this defense in the papers he files opposing Big Bank's lawsuit. If Bart doesn't, he loses the defense.

Be diligent if you think the creditor has sued you when the statute of limitations has already run. It's common for credit card issuers to sell their uncollected debts to collection agencies. Those agencies then aggressively try to collect, ignoring the fact that the statute of limitations may have expired. If the collection agency sues you (or threatens to sue you) once the statute of limitations has run, the agency has probably violated the federal Fair Debt Collection Practices Act (FDCPA). (See Chapter 9.)

However, a statute of limitations does not eliminate the debt—it merely limits the judicial remedies available to the creditor or collection agency after a certain period of time. A debt collector may still seek voluntary payment of a debt so old that the law cannot force you to pay it.

In response to your claim that the statute of limitations prevents the creditor or collector from going forward with the lawsuit, the plaintiff might claim that you waived, extended, or revived the statute of limitations in your earlier dealings.

Waiving the Statute of Limitations

If you waive the statute of limitations on a debt, it means you give up your right to assert it as a defense later on. The law makes it very difficult for a consumer to waive the statute of limitations by accident. A court will uphold a waiver only if you understood what you were doing when you agreed to waive the statute of limitations for your debt. In certain circumstances, even then a waiver may be unenforceable. If you think you may have waived the statute of limitations, you should still raise it as a defense (and force the creditor to demonstrate that you waived it).

Extending or Reviving the Statute of Limitations

Extending and reviving the statute of limitations are two different things. Extending the statute is often called "tolling." Tolling or extending the statute temporarily stops the clock for a particular reason, such as the collector agreeing to extend your time to pay.

EXAMPLE: Emily owes the Farmer's Market $345. The statute of limitations for this type of debt in her state is six years. Normally the statute would begin to run when Emily stopped paying the debt, but Farmer's gave her an additional six months to pay (and therefore tolled or extended the statute of limitations for six months). After six months, Emily still cannot pay the debt. The six-year statute of limitations begins to run at this point.

Reviving a statute of limitations means that the entire time period begins again. Depending on your state, this can happen if you make a partial payment on a debt or otherwise acknowledge that you owe a debt that you haven't been paying. In some states, partial payment will only "toll" the statute rather than revive it.

EXAMPLE: Ethan owes Memorial Hospital $1,000. The statute of limitations for medical debts in his state is four years. He stopped making payments on the debt in 2002. The four-year statute began to run at this point. In 2005, Ethan made a $300 payment and then stopped making payments again. In Ethan's state, his partial payment of $300 revived the statute of limitations. The hospital now has four years from the date of the $300 payment to sue Ethan for the remainder of the debt.

A new promise to pay a debt may also revive the statute of limitations in some circumstances. In most states, an oral promise can revive a statute of limitations, although in a few states the promise must be in writing.

Statutes of Limitations

State	Written Contracts	Oral Contracts	Promissory Notes
Alabama	6 years	6 years	6 years
Alaska	3 years	3 years	3 years
Arizona	6 years	3 years	6 years
Arkansas	5 years	3 years	5 years
California	4 years	2 years	4 years
Colorado	6 years	6 years	6 years
Connecticut	6 years	3 years	6 years
Delaware	3 years	3 years	6 years
District of Columbia	3 years	3 years	3 years
Florida	5 years	4 years	5 years
Georgia	6 years	4 years	6 years
Hawaii	6 years	6 years	6 years
Idaho	5 years	4 years	5 years
Illinois	10 years	5 years	10 years
Indiana	10 years*	6 years	6 years
Iowa	10 years	5 years	10 years
Kansas	5 years	3 years	5 years
Kentucky	15 years	5 years	15 years•
Louisiana	10 years	10 years	5 years
Maine†	6 years	6 years	6 years
Maryland	3 years	3 years	3 years
Massachusetts†	6 years	6 years	6 years
Michigan	6 years	6 years	6 years
Minnesota	6 years	6 years	6 years
Mississippi	3 years	3 years	3 years

* Six years if contract is for payment of money.

• Five years if promissory note is added to a bill of sale.

† The applicable statute of limitations in Maine and in Massachusetts on a debt owed to a bank or on a promissory note signed before a witness is 20 years. Me. Rev. Stat. Ann. tit.14, § 751; Mass. Gen. Laws ch. 260, § 1.

Statutes of Limitations (continued)

State	Written Contracts	Oral Contracts	Promissory Notes
Missouri	10 years	5 years	10 years
Montana	8 years	5 years	8 years
Nebraska	5 years	4 years	5 years
Nevada	6 years	4 years	6 years
New Hampshire	3 years	3 years	3 years
New Jersey	6 years	6 years	6 years
New Mexico	6 years	4 years	6 years
New York	6 years	6 years	6 years
North Carolina	3 years	3 years	3 years
North Dakota	6 years	6 years	6 years
Ohio	15 years	6 years	15 years
Oklahoma	5 years	3 years	5 years
Oregon	6 years	6 years	6 years
Pennsylvania	4 years	4 years	4 years
Rhode Island	10 years	10 years	10 years
South Carolina	3 years	3 years	3 years
South Dakota	6 years	6 years	6 years
Tennessee	6 years	6 years	6 years
Texas	4 years	4 years	4 years
Utah	6 years	4 years	6 years
Vermont	6 years	6 years	6 years ■
Virginia	5 years	3 years	5 years
Washington	6 years	3 years	6 years
West Virginia	10 years	5 years	10 years
Wisconsin	6 years	6 years	6 years
Wyoming	10 years	8 years	10 years

■ Vermont's statute of limitations on a promissory note signed before a witness is 14 years.

Current as of February 2007

Other Defenses and Claims

If you file a response in court, you should state any reason why the creditor should not recover all or part of what the complaint asks for. You state each reason either as an affirmative defense in your answer or as a separate claim, called a counterclaim, in a complaint that you file against the creditor.

An affirmative defense goes beyond simply denying the facts and arguments in the complaint (although you must do that, too, by formally denying the facts and conclusions you disagree with). An affirmative defense sets out new facts and arguments which, if proved in court, would make the creditor lose on that part of the claim. If you prove your affirmative defense, even if what the complaint says is true, you will win or, at least, reduce the amount you owe.

Listed below are some examples of affirmative defenses you might be able to state in your answer:

- You never received the goods or services the creditor claims to have provided.
- The goods or services were defective. (See Chapter 4.)
- The creditor damaged your property when delivering the goods or services.
- The creditor threatened you or lied to you to get you to enter into the agreement. (See Chapter 4.)
- You legally canceled the contract and therefore owe nothing. (See Chapter 4.)
- You cosigned for the loan and were not told of your rights as a cosigner. (See Chapter 11.)

- The creditor was not permitted to accelerate the loan. (See Chapter 11.)
- The contract was too ambiguous to be enforced. (See Chapter 4.)
- The contract is illegal.
- The contract or the creditor has violated a consumer protection statute that makes the contract unenforceable.
- After repossessing your property, the creditor did not sell it in a "commercially reasonable manner." (See Chapter 8.)

A counterclaim is the basis of a lawsuit you have against the creditor or collector. It may be based on different issues from those in the complaint. You may even be asking for more money than the plaintiff wants from you. In many states, however, the counterclaim must arise out of the same transaction for which you are being sued.

Here are examples of some counterclaims you might want to make against the creditor or collector. To raise a counterclaim, you will usually have to serve and file your own complaint and pay a filing fee within the time you have to respond to the complaint. If you succeed on a counterclaim, you may be entitled to monetary damages from the creditor or collector, or at least to rescind (cancel) the contract with the creditor.

- The creditor breached a warranty. (See Chapter 4.)
- The creditor violated the Fair Credit Reporting Act (see Chapter 17), Truth in Lending Act (see Chapter 11), Electronic Fund Transfer Act (see Chapter 10), or Equal Credit Opportunity Act (see Chapter 17).

- A collection agency violated the Fair Debt Collections Practices Act or a state debt collection law. (See Chapter 9.)

Responding Formally

To avoid having the creditor or collector ask the court to enter a default judgment against you, you must file formal papers in response to the lawsuit. If you don't have access to a law library and can't afford a lawyer, just file a paper with the court saying why you oppose the lawsuit. In many states, as long as you file a paper resembling an answer, the court cannot enter a default judgment against you. Also, you can amend your paper after you have learned more about the process.

Once you are in court, the judge may be sympathetic to someone representing himself or herself and trying to get the right to pay in installments. On the other hand, some judges have little patience for individuals who represent themselves. For this reason, it is important to be as prepared and organized as possible.

Here's how to respond. (A sample answer is shown below.)

- Find out if your court has a standard form you should complete for your answer. If yes, get it and use it. If not, find out if your court requires any special format, such as paper with line numbers along the edge ("pleading paper").
- Unless you have to use pleading paper, get a stack of plain white, 8½" x 11" unlined paper or turn on your computer and follow the steps below.

- Have the complaint in front of you.
- On your computer screen or a sheet of paper, in the upper left corner, type your name, address, and phone number and the words "Defendant in Pro Per" (also called "Defendant in Pro Se" in some states; either way, it means that you represent yourself). Look at the way this is done on the complaint.
- Type the name of the court and the caption—the caption contains the name(s) of the plaintiff(s), the word "Plaintiff(s)," "v.," your name and any other defendants, the word "Defendant(s)," and the case number. Copy all of this information from the complaint. Place this information at approximately the same place on the page that it is on the complaint.
- On the next line in the center of the page, type the word "Answer."

Now stop typing. Go back to the complaint and read through it. Write the word "admit" near the paragraphs where you agree with *absolutely* everything said in it, such as "Plaintiff's sporting goods store is located at 74 Hollis Road, Cranston, Rhode Island."

Next, write the word "deny" near each paragraph in which you deny all or a part of what was said. For instance, if the paragraph says "Defendant bought a gym set and has refused to pay for it for no good reason," and you agree that you bought a gym set but haven't paid because it is defective and the store won't refund your money, deny the whole paragraph.

For each paragraph where you are not sure what the truth is, but you believe the

Sample Answer

Judith Morrison
355 Bryce Avenue
Hackensack, NJ 07123
201-555-7890
Defendant in Pro Per

MUNICIPAL COURT FOR THE COUNTY OF BERGEN

IN AND FOR THE STATE OF NEW JERSEY

Bergen Bank, Inc.,	)	
	)	
Plaintiff,	)	
v.	)	Case No. BC—455522
	)	
Judith Morrison,	)	
Defendant.	)	
_____	)	

ANSWER

1. Defendant admits the allegations in the following paragraphs: 1, 2, 3, 4, 7, 9, 16, 22, and 23.

2. Defendant denies the allegations in the following paragraphs: 5, 6, 8, 12, 13, 14, 15, 17, 24, and 26.

3. Defendant denies on information and belief the allegations in the following paragraphs: 10, 11, 19, 20, 21, and 25.

Sample Answer (continued)

4. Defendant denies for lack of information the allegations in the following paragraphs: 18, 27, and 28.

5. Defense: Plaintiff is not entitled to the money it claims because the applicable statute of limitations has run.

6. First Affirmative Defense: I canceled the contract as I was entitled to and therefore I owe nothing.

7. Second Affirmative Defense: Clause 14 of my loan agreement prohibits the creditor from accelerating the loan. In violation of Clause 14, the creditor has accelerated the loan and now claims the entire balance is due.

Judith Morrison   _June 17, 2008_
Judith Morrison   Date

plaintiff's statement is probably more false than true, write "deny on information and belief." An example is if the plaintiff wrote that you bought the gym set at night, but you think it was in the afternoon.

Finally, if you have no idea whether or not the allegation in a paragraph is true, for example, a paragraph saying that plaintiff is a corporation, write "deny for lack of information."

- Start typing again, this time double-spaced. Type the four lines below. Following each colon, type the corresponding paragraph numbers for the paragraphs in the complaint you just marked up:
    1. Defendant admits the allegations in the following paragraphs:
    2. Defendant denies the allegations in the following paragraphs:
    3. Defendant denies on information and belief the allegations in the following paragraphs:
    4. Defendant denies for lack of information the allegations in the following paragraphs:
- Next, type your statute of limitations defense (if applicable) and any affirmative defenses. Continue to number your paragraphs. See the discussions above for examples, and feel free to add a sentence or two if you feel further explanation is needed. List each defense and affirmative defense separately. Don't worry about how many pieces of paper you need, but number the pages.
- Type your name, sign your name, and date it at the bottom.

What to Expect While the Case Is in Court

Once you type up your answer and any counterclaim, you'll have to sign it and serve a signed copy of it on the plaintiff. You can usually serve the plaintiff by having a friend over the age of 18 send the plaintiff your papers through the mail. However, sometimes it must be done in person. Details on serving your answer and counterclaim vary considerably from state to state, but see if your court clerk provides instructions, or check a local law library for the rules. (See Chapter 19.)

After your papers are served, you must file the original papers at the court. The court will stamp the original (and one or more copies) to say that it was filed. You must also file a "proof of service," a document that shows that the plaintiff was served in the proper manner. (See the sample, below.) Keep file-stamped copies for yourself. Do not file originals of things that could be evidence, such as receipts, checks, contracts, or collection letters. Keep those for the hearing (although you should make photocopies of them for later).

After your papers are filed, you will receive written notification of all further proceedings in your case. If yours is a routine debt collection case, the next paper you will probably receive is a notice of the plaintiff's request for a trial and date. The paper after that will probably be a notice of the trial date. In some courts, however, you will be sent a notice of a settlement conference before the trial date. Be sure to attend the settlement conference or trial. If

Sample Proof of Service

Judith Morrison
355 Bryce Avenue
Hackensack, NJ 07123
201-555-7890
Defendant in Pro Per

MUNICIPAL COURT FOR THE COUNTY OF BERGEN

IN AND FOR THE STATE OF NEW JERSEY

Bergen Bank, Inc.,	)
	)
Plaintiff,	)
v.	) Case No. BC—455522
	)
Judith Morrison,	)
Defendant.	)
_____	)

PROOF OF SERVICE

I, Gordon Freed, declare that:

I am over the age of 18 years and not a party to the within action. I reside [or am employed] in the County of Bergen, State of New Jersey. My residence [or business] address is 56 Trainor Court, Englewood, New Jersey.

On June 22, 2008, I served the within ANSWER on the plaintiff by placing a true and correct copy of it in a sealed envelope with first-class postage fully prepaid in the United States mail at Englewood, New Jersey, addressed as follows:

Sample Proof of Service (continued)

Deb Miles, Esq.
Bergen Bank, Inc.
1400 Fort Lee Circle
Fort Lee, New Jersey 07333

   I declare under penalty of perjury that the foregoing is true and correct.

Executed on June 23, 2008, at Englewood, New Jersey.

   _Gordon Freed_____
Gordon Freed

you move, make sure you notify the plaintiff and court of your address change.

If yours isn't a routine debt collection case, or the creditor's lawyer wants to play the litigation game, a whole lot can go on between the time you file your answer and any counterclaim and the time you get a notice of the trial. You may want to take the offensive with some of this, especially if you filed a counterclaim. Below is a brief description of the most common of these proceedings. It's difficult for someone without a lawyer to undertake them, but it's not impossible. These descriptions are not meant to be a detailed account of how to cope with court procedures. For that, you'll want to look at *Represent Yourself in Court*, by Paul Bergman and Sara Berman-Barrett (Nolo).

Discovery

Discovery refers to the formal procedures used by parties to obtain information and documents from each other and from witnesses. The information is meant to help the party prepare for trial or settle the case. In routine debt collection cases where you don't have any defense, don't expect the plaintiff to engage in discovery. Discovery can be expensive, and, quite frankly, there is often nothing for the plaintiff to "discover." You owe the money. You haven't paid.

If you raise a strong affirmative defense or file your own counterclaim, however, the plaintiff may want to engage in discovery. Here are brief definitions of the primary discovery methods.

Deposition. A proceeding in which a witness or party is asked to answer questions orally under oath. A court reporter is present and takes down the entire proceeding.

 RESOURCES

Need more information on depositions? If you receive papers ordering you to appear at a deposition, get a copy of *Nolo's Deposition Handbook*, by Paul Bergman and Albert Moore (Nolo).

Interrogatories. Written questions sent by one party to the other to be answered in writing under oath.

Request for production of documents. A request from one party to the other to hand over certain defined documents. If you are adamant in your defense of a lawsuit that you paid the debt, the other side will most likely request that you produce for inspection (and copying) a check, money order receipt, or other document supporting your assertion.

Request for admissions. A request from one party to the other to admit or deny certain allegations in the lawsuit.

Request for inspection. A request by one party to look at tangible items (other than writings) in the possession of the other party. For instance, if you raise as an affirmative defense that the painter who sued you spilled paint on your rug and it cannot be removed, the painter may request to inspect the rug.

Request for physical examination. A request by one party that the other party be examined by a doctor if the other party's health is at issue.

Subpoena. An order telling a witness to appear at a deposition.

Subpoena duces tecum. An order telling a witness to bring certain documents to a deposition or hearing.

In some states, the trend is toward limiting discovery. For example, parties to a lawsuit can ask only a limited number of questions in their interrogatories. Also, a party or witness can be deposed only once. If the creditor sends you volumes of interrogatory questions or schedules your deposition after it's already been taken, you can ask the court to issue a "protective order" to stop the harassment.

Be sure to answer discovery requests in the time allowed, even if it's just to say you don't know the answer. Otherwise, the plaintiff may ask the court to compel you to answer and to pay costs for their trouble. Or you may be deemed to have admitted the plaintiff's assertions ("requests for admissions"). If the plaintiff agrees to let you have more time to answer, get it in writing.

Summary Judgment

The creditor may try to convince the judge that none of the facts of the case are in dispute—for example, that you signed a legal loan agreement, made no payments, and have no defense as to why you're not paying. The creditor also must convince the judge that the plaintiff is entitled to judgment as a matter of law. The creditor does this by filing a summary judgment motion. If the judge agrees with the creditor, the judge can enter a judgment against you without any trial taking place. The creditor should not win if there are any material

(important) facts in dispute (for example, if you claim you didn't sign the agreement).

You usually must file papers opposing the creditor's summary judgment motion if you want to fight it. If you don't, you'll probably lose. Because responding to a summary judgment motion can be complicated, and because the entire lawsuit is at stake, you may want to consult with an attorney. Of course, remember what we said earlier: If it costs more to hire a lawyer than what the creditor seeks in the lawsuit, it makes little sense to seek attorney assistance.

Settlement Conference

Several states and the federal court system require that the parties come together at least once before the trial to try to settle the case. To assist you in settling, you'll be scheduled to meet with a judge or attorney who has some familiarity with the area of law your case involves. You don't have to settle, but the judge or attorney will usually give you an honest indication of your chance of winning in a trial.

Trial

Once discovery is complete, any summary judgment motion is denied, and settlement efforts have gone nowhere, you will eventually find yourself at a trial. In a trial, a judge makes all the legal decisions, such as whether or not a particular item of evidence can be used. Either a judge or a jury makes the factual decisions, such as whether or not the item sold to you was defective.

Some Guidelines on Presenting Evidence

- You can testify only as to facts in your knowledge. You can't testify that "someone told you" something; this is hearsay. There are many exceptions to the general rule against hearsay evidence. To find out more, do some legal research on your own, or contact a lawyer. (See Chapter 19.)
- Bring all relevant documents—receipts, bills, letters, warranties, advertisements, and the like. Try to bring originals, but if you only have copies, bring them. Bring four extra copies of each document (one for the opposing lawyer, one for the witness, one for the court clerk, and one for the judge). Be sure that you have the original (or a copy) for your own use.
- Your witnesses can testify only to facts in their knowledge—that is, something they saw or heard. For example, if a bill collector threatened to have you jailed, a witness testifying about the truth of this statement can testify only that she heard the threat, not that you called and told her about the threat.

At the trial, you will be required to present your case according to very specific rules of procedure and evidence. As mentioned before, the book that can help you in any trial is *Represent Yourself in Court*, by Paul Bergman and Sara Berman-Barrett (Nolo). Or, you may want to consult with a lawyer before the trial to get some help.

If the Creditor Gets a Judgment Against You

Your creditor will get a judgment against you in any of the following situations:

- You don't respond to the complaint.
- You don't comply with a judge's order to respond to a discovery request.
- You lose a summary judgment motion.
- You lose a trial.

The judgment is a piece of paper issued by the court stating that the plaintiff wins the lawsuit and is entitled to a certain amount of money. The judgment must be "entered"—that is, filed with the court clerk—and this usually happens a day or two after the judge issues it. After it is filed, the court or the creditor's attorney sends you a copy.

Components of a Money Judgment

When you get a copy of the judgment, your first step is to understand the amount of money to which the plaintiff is entitled and what each portion represents. Keep in mind that the judge may have knocked off some money in response to a defense or counterclaim you raised.

A judgment usually consists of the following components:

The debt itself. This is the amount of money you borrowed from the creditor, charged on a credit card, or owe on a repossession deficiency balance.

Interest. Part of the judgment will be the interest the creditor is entitled to collect under the loan agreement or contract. If you defaulted on a $1,000 loan at 9% annual interest and the creditor obtains a judgment a year later, the court will award the creditor $90 in "prejudgment" interest ($1,000 x .09 = $90).

Interest can be added after judgment from the time the judgment is entered into the court clerk's record until you pay the judgment in full. The postjudgment interest rate is set by your state's law, generally in the 8% to 12% range (see "Postjudgment Interest Rates," below).

Court costs. Almost every state awards the winner of a lawsuit the costs incurred in bringing the case, including filing fees, service costs, discovery costs, and jury fees.

Attorneys' fees. If your original contract with the creditor includes the creditor's right to collect attorneys' fees in the event the creditor sues you and wins, these fees will be added to the judgment. They can add up to thousands of dollars. Even without an attorneys' fees provision in a contract, the creditor may be entitled to attorneys' fees if a state law allows it.

How Long Judgments Last

Depending on the state, a creditor may have from five to as many as 20 years to collect a court judgment. In addition, in most states, the judgment can be renewed indefinitely if it is not collected during the original period, thus giving the creditor an unlimited amount of time to collect a judgment.

Enforcing Judgments in Different States

Sometimes a creditor obtains a judgment against you in a state where you do not live. This can happen if you have moved since the debt was incurred or if you signed a contract in another state. Or, you may own property or have assets outside the state where the judgment was obtained. The creditor can go into court in the state where you now live or have assets and register the original out-of-state judgment. This means the creditor now has the right to use all the judgment remedies available in the state where you now live or have assets (the second state).

If the creditor goes into the second state to make the original judgment into a judgment of that state, you will be sent a notice and have an opportunity to object. If you have property in the other state, you should certainly object if the property isn't real estate, you don't reside in that state, or you didn't sign the contract that forms the basis of the lawsuit in that state. (See 15 U.S.C. § 1692i.)

How Judgments Are Enforced

Once a judgment is entered against you, the creditor is now called a judgment creditor, and you are called a judgment debtor. Judgment creditors have many more collection techniques available to them than do creditors trying to collect debts before getting a court judgment. For example, in some states, a judgment creditor can order you to come to court and answer questions

Postjudgment Interest Rates

This chart gives the interest rates set by state law for judgments where the contract or agreement does not set an interest rate. The rate is usually written in the judgment. If a contract or agreement does set a postjudgment interest rate, then that is the one that generally applies, even if it is different from the state rate. For a discussion of state usury limits on interest rates, see "Why Are Credit Card Interest Rates So High?" in Chapter 10.

State	Code Citation	Post-Judgment Interest Rates
Alabama	Ala. Code. § 8-8-10	12%
Alaska	Alaska Stat. § 09.30.070	3% above the 12th Federal Reserve discount window rate on January 2 of the year judgment is entered. If contract calls for a different rate, it must be written in the judgment. Rate posted at www.state.ak.us/courts/int.htm.
Arizona	Ariz. Rev. Stat. Ann. § 44-1201(A)	10%
Arkansas	Ark. Code Ann. § 16-65-114	Whichever is greater, 10% or contract rate
California	Cal. Civ. Proc. Code § 685.010	10%
Colorado	Colo. Rev. Stat. § 5-12-102	8%
Connecticut	Conn. Gen. Stat. Ann. § 37-3a	10% (5% for hospital debt)
Delaware	Del. Code Ann. tit. 6, § 2301(a)	5% above the Federal Reserve discount window rate at the time interest is due. Rate posted at www.federalreserve.gov/releases/h15.
District of Columbia	D.C. Code Ann. § 28-3302(c)	70% of the penalty rate for underpayment of federal taxes rounded up to the next highest full percent. (Search for the current rate for underpayment at www.irs.gov.)
Florida	Fla. Stat. Ann. § 55.03	11% for 2007. (Updated annually and posted at www.fldfs.com/aadir/interest.htm.)
Georgia	Ga. Code Ann. § 7-4-12	Prime plus 3%. Prime rate is posted at www.federalreserve.gov/releases/h15.
Hawaii	Haw. Rev. Stat. § 478-3	10%
Idaho	Idaho Code § 28-22-104(2)	5% above weekly average yield on U.S. Treasury bills for one year. Set July 1 by State Treasurer, 10.125% for July 2006 to July 2007. (Rate posted at http://sto.idaho.gov/Reports/LegalRateOfInterest.aspx.)

Postjudgment Interest Rates (continued)		
State	**Code Citation**	**Post-Judgment Interest Rates**
Illinois	735 Ill. Comp. Stat. § 5/2-1303	9%
Indiana	Ind. Code Ann. § 24-4.6-1-101	8%
Iowa	Iowa Code §§ 535.2 to 535.3, 668.13	2% above one-year treasury constant maturity rate published by the Federal Reserve immediately before judgment.
Kansas	Kan. Stat. Ann. § 16-204	4% above Federal Reserve Bank of New York average discount window rate for preceding year, 10.25% for July 2006 to July 2007. Secretary of State posts rate on July 1 at www.kssos.org/pubs/pubs_finance_rates.html.
Kentucky	Ky. Rev. Stat. Ann. § 360.040	12%
Louisiana	La. Rev. Stat. Ann. § 13:4202	3¼% above the Federal Reserve Board discount rate as of the first business day of October the previous year, 9.5% in 2007. Posted at state Office of Financial Institutions at www.ofi.state.la.us. Click on "Judicial Interest Rates."
Maine	Me. Rev. Stat. Ann. tit. 14, § 1602-C	6% above one-year T-bill rate (one year constant maturity Treasury yield for the last full week of the previous calendar year). Posted at www.federalreserve.gov/releases/h15.
Maryland	Md. Code Ann. [Cts. & Jud. Proc.] §§ 11-106, 107	10%
Massachusetts	Mass. Gen. Laws ch. 107, § 3; ch. 235, § 8	6%
Michigan	Mich. Comp. Laws §§ 600.6013(7), (8)	Judgments based on a written contract: contract rate, not to exceed 13%. All other money judgments: 1% above the average interest rate paid at auction of five-year Treasury notes for the 6 months preceding January 1 and July 1. Posted at http://courts.michigan.gov/scao/resources/other/interest.pdf.
Minnesota	Minn. Stat. Ann. § 549.09 (subd. 1(c))	Set annually in December for the following year. Based on one-year Treasury constant maturities yield for most recent month, 5% for 2007. Rate posted at www.courts.state.mn.us; search for "interest rates."
Mississippi	Miss. Code Ann. § 75-17-7	Rate stated in contract; if contract is silent, rate set by judge.

Postjudgment Interest Rates (continued)		
State	**Code Citation**	**Post-Judgment Interest Rates**
Missouri	Mo. Rev. Stat. § 408.040(1)	9%
Montana	Mont. Code Ann. § 25-9-205	10%
Nebraska	Neb. Rev. Stat. § 45-103	2% above the bond investment yield of average auction price of 26-week U.S. Treasury bills at first auction of each quarter; takes effect two weeks after price published. Posted at http://court.nol.org/community/interestrate.htm.
Nevada	Nev. Rev. Stat. Ann. § 17.130	2% above the prime rate at Nevada's largest bank on January 1 or July 1 preceding the judgment, 8¼% as of January 2007. Posted at http://fid.state.nv.us; click on "Prime Interest Rate."
New Hampshire	N.H. Rev. Stat. Ann. § 336:1(II)	2% above discount interest rate on 26-week U.S. Treasury bills at the last auction prior to September 30. Rate in effect January 1 through December 31, 6.8% for 2007. Posted at www.courts.state.nh.us/sitewidelinks/interest.htm.
New Jersey	N.J. Ct. Rule 4:42-11	For judgments of $15,000 or less: Interest equals the average rate of return of the N.J. state cash management fund for preceding fiscal year, ending June 30, 4% for 2007; if over $15,000, same rate plus 2%. Posted at www.state.nj.us/treasury/doinvest/rate1.html.
New Mexico	N.M. Stat. Ann. § 56-8-4	8.75%
New York	N.Y. C.P.L.R. Law § 5004	9%
North Carolina	N.C. Gen. Stat. § 24-1, 24-5	8%
North Dakota	N.D. Cent. Code § 28-20-34	Prime plus 3% as published in the *Wall Street Journal* on the first Monday in December of the previous year, 11.5% in 2007.
Ohio	Ohio Rev. Code Ann. §§ 1343.03(A), 5703.47	3% plus Federal short-term rate to nearest whole number as of October 15 of the previous year, 8% for 2007.
Oklahoma	Okla. Stat. Ann. tit. 12, § 727.1	Prime plus 2%. Posted at Oklahoma State Courts Network: www.oscn.net; click on "Legal Research" to find "Oklahoma Interest on Judgments."

Postjudgment Interest Rates (continued)		
State	**Code Citation**	**Post-Judgment Interest Rates**
Oregon	Or. Rev. Stat. § 82.010(2)	9%
Pennsylvania	42 Pa. Cons. Stat. Ann. § 8101; 41 Pa. Cons. Stat. Ann. § 202	6%
Rhode Island	R.I. Gen. Laws §§ 6-26-1, 9-21-8	12%
South Carolina	S.C. Code Ann. § 34-31-20(B)	Prime plus 4% as of the first edition of the *Wall Street Journal* for the calendar year, 12.25% for 2007. Posted at www.sccourts.org; click on "What's New."
South Dakota	S.D. Codified Laws Ann. §§ 54-3-5.1, 54-3-16(2)	10%
Tennessee	Tenn. Code Ann. § 47-14-121	10%
Texas	Tex. Fin. Code Ann. § 304.002	18%
Utah	Utah Code Ann. § 15-1-4	2% above federal postjudgment interest rate as of January 1, 6.99% for 2007. Posted at www.utcourts.gov/resources/intrates/interestrates.htm.
Vermont	Vt. Stat. Ann. tit. 12, § 2903; Vt. R. Civ. Proc. Rule 69	12%
Virginia	Va. Code Ann. §§ 8.01-382, 6.1-330.54	6% or the rate set in the contract, whichever is higher.
Washington	Wash. Rev. Code Ann. §§ 4.56.110, 19.52.020	Whichever is higher: 12%, or 2% above average price for 26-week (6-month) U.S. Treasury bills in month prior to judgment. Posted at www1.leg.wa.gov/documents/wsr/rates.htm.
West Virginia	W.Va. Code Ann. § 56-6-31	3% above the Fifth Federal Reserve District secondary discount rate in effect on the second day of January, but never greater than 11% or less than 7%, 9.75% in 2007. Posted at www.state.wv.us/wvsca/supreme.htm.
Wisconsin	Wis. Stat. Ann. §§ 814.04(4), 815.05(8)	12%
Wyoming	Wyo. Stat. § 1-16-102(a)	10%

Current as of February 2007

about your property and finances. Also, a judgment creditor can direct a sheriff to seize some of your property to pay the judgment.

What property the creditor can take varies from state to state. Usually, the creditor can go after a portion of your net wages (up to 25%, more if the judgment is for child support), bank and other deposit accounts, and valuable personal property, such as cars and antiques.

Not all of your property can be taken, however. Every state has certain property it declares "exempt." This means it is off limits to your creditors, even judgment creditors. Just because you owe money, you shouldn't have to lose everything. You still need to eat, keep a roof over your head, clothe yourself, and provide for your family. If you have very few possessions, you may find that most of what you own is exempt. Exempt property is covered in Chapter 16.

Debtor's Examination

Most states let a judgment creditor question you about your property and finances, in a procedure called a "debtor's examination." Basically, the judgment creditor is looking for money or property that can be legally taken to pay the debt. High on the list of property the creditor looks for are deposit accounts (such as savings, checking, certificate of deposit, and money market), tax refunds due, and other easy cash.

Written Questions

In some states, a judgment creditor sends you a form and asks you to fill it out, listing your employer's name and address, your assets, and other financial information. You

must do this under penalty of perjury. If you don't comply or the judgment creditor believes you're lying or not disclosing all relevant information, the judgment creditor can ask the court to issue an order requiring you to come to court and answer the questions.

Court Appearance

In other states, the creditor serves you with a document ordering you to show up in court and bring certain financial documents, such as bank statements or pay stubs. You may be sent the questions and given a chance to answer them in writing first. If you receive an order to appear in court and you don't show up, the court can declare you in contempt and issue a warrant for your arrest.

In a few states, if the judge issues an order for you to come to court, serving that order on you creates a lien on your personal property. The lien may make it difficult for you to sell the property without first paying the judgment. Also, if the judgment creditor believes you are about to leave the state or conceal your property to avoid paying the judgment, the creditor can ask the judge to issue a warrant for your immediate arrest. This is quite drastic, but it's been known to happen when a lot of money is owed.

If you receive an order to appear but can't take the time off from work or otherwise can't make it, call the judgment creditor or the lawyer and explain your situation. Explain that you're willing to answer questions over the phone or even in person, but at another time. If the creditor thinks you're telling the truth and hasn't already sent you a form about your finances and property, the creditor may take the information over the telephone.

If the judgment creditor agrees to change the date or to let you answer the questions over the phone, ask for a letter to you and the court verifying that you need not appear at the hearing. If the creditor won't write the letter, write your own letter confirming your conversation. Send it to the creditor and to the court.

If you can attend the hearing, or you reschedule it to a convenient time, do not take any money or expensive personal items with you. The judgment creditor can ask you to empty your pockets or purse and ask the court to order you to turn over any nonexempt money or valuable personal property in your possession, such as a college ring or leather jacket.

Wage Attachments

The first item of your property most judgment creditors will go after is your paycheck, through a wage attachment (or wage garnishment). A wage attachment is a very effective technique for a judgment creditor if you receive a regular paycheck. Your employer takes a portion of your wages each pay period and sends that money to your creditor before you ever see it.

In most states, the judgment creditor can take up to 25% of your net earnings or the amount by which your weekly net earnings exceed 30 times the federal minimum wage (currently $5.15 an hour), whichever is less. Net earnings are your gross earnings less

all mandatory deductions such as withheld income taxes and unemployment insurance.

A few states offer greater protections for judgment debtors about to lose their wages.

 WARNING

For certain debts, you have to pay more. The wage attachment laws and limitations described in this section do not apply to:

- **Child support.** Up to 50% of your wages may be taken to pay support (more if you don't currently support another dependent or are behind in your payments). Your child's other parent usually does not have to first sue you.
- **Income taxes.** If you ignore all attempts by the IRS to collect taxes you owe, the government can grab virtually all of your wages and leave you with as little as $150 a week.

To attach your wages, a judgment creditor obtains authorization from the court in a document usually called a writ. Under this authorization, the judgment creditor directs the sheriff to seize a portion of your wages. The sheriff in turn notifies your employer of the attachment, and your employer notifies you. Unless you object, your employer sends the amount withheld each pay period to the sheriff, who deducts his or her expenses and sends the balance to the judgment creditor.

You can object to the wage attachment by requesting a court hearing. In some states, the attachment can't begin until after the hearing, unless you give up your right to a hearing. In most states, however, as long as you have the opportunity to have your objection promptly considered, the attachment can take effect immediately.

Can You Be Fired for a Wage Attachment?

Your employer may consider a wage attachment a hassle and may threaten to fire you if you don't settle the debt right away. Under the law, however, an employer cannot fire you because your wages are attached to satisfy a single debt. (15 U.S.C. § 1674(a).) But, if two judgment creditors attach your wages or one judgment creditor attaches your wages to pay two different judgments, this law does not protect you from being fired. Some states protect you until you have three or more attachments; find out how to research your state's law in Chapter 19.

Most employers will work with employees who are honestly trying to clear up their debt problems. If your wages are attached, talk with your employer and explain that you are working hard to settle the matter as soon as possible. If, however, you are fired because your employer was not aware of the law or because your employer was "suddenly" unhappy with your work, consider filing a complaint. (See Chapter 19 for tips on finding a lawyer.)

Property Liens

One collection device commonly used by judgment creditors is the property lien. In about half the states, a judgment entered against you automatically creates a lien on the real property you own in the county where the judgment was obtained. In the rest of the states, the creditor must record the judgment with the county, and then the recorded judgment creates a lien on your real property. In a few states, the lien is on your real and personal property.

If a judgment creditor does not get a lien on personal property after the judgment is entered or recorded, the judgment creditor may be able to get a lien on your personal property by recording the judgment with the Secretary of State. This usually applies only to property with title papers, such as a car or a business's assets. If, for example, you tried to sell your car, the lien would appear, and you'd have to pay off the judgment creditor before selling.

Once the judgment creditor has a lien on your property, especially your real property, the creditor can safely anticipate payment. When you sell or refinance your property, title must be cleared—that is, all liens must be removed by paying the lienholder—before the deal can close.

Instead of waiting for you to sell your property, the creditor can "execute" on the lien. That means having the sheriff seize your property—typically a house—and arrange for a public sale from which the creditor is paid out of the proceeds. However, if your property is exempt, the creditor cannot do this. Even if your property is not exempt, many creditors don't want to go through the expense and hassle of a public sale. This is especially true if the creditor won't get much money through the sale.

Liens on Your Property After Judgment (In Most States Liens Can Be Extended or Renewed)				
State	**Code Section**	**Property**	**How Creditor Obtains Lien**	**How Long Lien Lasts**
Alabama	Ala. Code. §§ 6-9-210 to -211	Real & personal	Creditor registers judgment with office of probate court in any county where debtor has property now or may have property in future	10 years
Alaska	Alaska Stat. §§ 09.30.010, 09.35.020	Real	Creditor files judgment with county recorder in any county where debtor has property now or may have property in future	5 years
Arizona	Ariz. Rev. Stat. Ann. § 33-964	Real	Creditor files and records judgment with county recorder in any county where debtor has property now or may have property in future	5 years
Arkansas	Ark. Code Ann. § 16-65-117	Real	Automatic on property in county where judgment entered; otherwise creditor must file judgment with clerk of circuit court in county where property is located	10 years
California	Cal. Civ. Proc. Code §§ 697.310, 697.340	Real	Creditor records judgment with county recorder in any county where debtor has property now or may have property in future	10 years
Colorado	Colo. Rev. Stat. § 13-52-102	Real	Creditor files judgment with country recorder in any county where debtor has property now or may have property in future	6 years
Connecticut	Conn. Gen. Stat. Ann. § 52-355a	Personal	Creditor files judgment with Office of Secretary of State	5 years
	Conn. Gen. Stat. Ann. § 52-380a	Real	Creditor must attach property during lawsuit; within four months of judgment creditor must file lien certificate with town clerk where property located	20 years
Delaware	Del. Code Ann. tit. 10, §§ 4710 to 4711	Real	Automatic on property located in county of superior court where judgment rendered; for other property creditor must file judgment with superior court in county where property is located	10 years
District of Columbia	D.C. Code Ann. §§ 15-101 to -102	Real	Creditor files judgment with District of Columbia Recorder of Deeds	12 years

State	Code Section	Property	How Creditor Obtains Lien	How Long Lien Lasts
			Liens on Your Property After Judgment **(In Most States Liens Can Be Extended or Renewed) (continued)**	
Florida	Fla. Stat. Ann. §§ 55.202 to .205	Personal	Creditor files judgment with Florida Department of State	5 years
	Fla. Stat. Ann. §§ 55.081, 55.10	Real	Creditor records judgment with any county recorder where debtor has property now or may have property in future	10 years
Georgia	Ga. Code Ann. §§ 9-12-81 to -82, 9-12-60	Personal	In county of debtor's residence, creditor enters judgment in execution docket kept by clerk of superior court	7 years
	Ga. Code Ann. §§ 9-12-83, 9-12-86, 9-12-60	Real	Creditor records judgment with superior court clerk in county where debtor has property or may have property in future	7 years
Hawaii	Haw. Rev. Stat. § 636-3	Real	Creditor records judgment with Hawaii Bureau of Conveyances	as long as the underlying judgment
Idaho	Idaho Code § 11-101 to -105	Real	Creditor records judgment with county clerk in any county where debtor has property now or may have property in future	5 years
Illinois	735 Ill. Comp. Stat. §§ 5/12-101, 105, 106, 108	Real	Creditor files judgment with recorder in county where property located; to enforce against property in another county, creditor files copy with circuit court clerk	7 years
Indiana	Ind. Code Ann. § 34-55-9-2	Real & personal	Automatic on property in county where judgment handed down; for property in another county, creditor files copy with circuit court clerk	10 years
Iowa	Iowa Code Ann. §§ 624.23 to .24	Real	Automatic on property in county where judgment entered; creditor files judgment with district court clerk for property outside county where judgment is entered	10 years
Kansas	Kan. Stat. Ann. §§ 60-2202, 60-2403	Real	Automatic on property in county where judgment is entered; creditor files judgment with district court clerk for property outside county where judgment entered	5 years

	Liens on Your Property After Judgment (In Most States Liens Can Be Extended or Renewed) (continued)			
State	**Code Section**	**Property**	**How Creditor Obtains Lien**	**How Long Lien Lasts**
Kentucky	Ky. Rev. Stat. Ann. §§ 426.720, 413.090	Real	Creditor records judgment with county clerk in county where debtor has property now or may have any property in future	15 years
Louisiana*	La. Civ. Code Art. 3284 to 3303, 3355, 3359	Real	Creditor files judgment with recorder in any parish where debtor has or may have property in future	10 years
Maine	Me. Rev. Stat. Ann. tit. 14, §§ 3132, 4651-A	Real & personal	Creditor files judgment with registry of deeds in county where debtor has property	20 years
Maryland	Md. Code Ann. [Cts. & Jud. Proc.] § 11-402; Md. Ct. Rule 2-621, 2-625, 3-621, 3-622, 3-625	Real	Automatic on property in county where judgment entered; to enforce in another county creditor files certified copy with district court clerk	12 years
Massachusetts	Mass. Gen. Laws ch. 223, §§ 42, 59, 63; ch. 260, § 20	Personal	Creditor files copy with city or town clerk	30 days
		Real	Creditor files judgment with registrar of deeds in any county where debtor has property now or may have property in future	20 years
Michigan	Mich. Comp. Laws §§ 600.2809, .4035, .6004, .6017, .6018	Real & personal	Judgment must first be satisfied from personal property; if insufficient, then real property may be attached; copy of attachment must be filed with registrar of deeds in county where property located	5 years
Minnesota	Minn. Stat. Ann. § 548.09	Real	Automatic on present and future property in county where judgment entered; for property in another county, creditor records copy with that county's court administrator	10 years
Mississippi	Miss. Code Ann. §§ 11-7-189 to -197, 15-1-43	Real & personal	Automatic on property in county where judgment is enrolled; to enforce in another county, creditor files copy with circuit court clerk	7 years
Missouri	Mo. Rev. Stat. §§ 511.350 to .360; Mo. Civ. Proc. Rule 74.08, 74.13	Real	Automatic on property in county where judgment is entered; creditor files judgment with county circuit clerk for property outside county where judgment entered	10 years

* In Louisiana, a lien is known as a "judicial mortgage" and real property is known as "immovables."

			Liens on Your Property After Judgment (In Most States Liens Can Be Extended or Renewed) (continued)	
State	**Code Section**	**Property**	**How Creditor Obtains Lien**	**How Long Lien Lasts**
Missouri (continued)	Mo. Rev. Stat. §§ 511.350 to .360; Mo. Civ. Proc. Rule 74.08, 74.13	Real	Automatic on property in county where judgment is entered; creditor files judgment with county circuit clerk for property outside county where judgment entered	10 years
Montana	Mont. Code Ann. §§ 25-9-301 to -303	Real	Automatic on present and future property in county where judgment entered; for property in another county, creditor files judgment with the district court clerk where the debtor has property now or may have property in the future	10 years
Nebraska	Neb. Rev. Stat. §§ 25-1303, 25-1542	Real	Automatic on property in county where judgment is entered; creditor files judgment with district court county clerk for property outside county where judgment entered	5 years
Nevada	Nev. Rev. Stat. Ann. § 17.150	Real	Creditor files judgment with county recorder in any county where debtor has property now or may have property in future	6 years
New Hampshire	N.H. Rev. Stat. Ann. §§ 511:1, 511-A:5		Creditor may attach debtor's property during lawsuit	
		Real	Creditor files order of attachment with register of deeds in any county where debtor has property now or may have property in future	6 years
		Personal	Creditor files order with secretary of state	6 years
New Jersey	N.J. Stat. Ann. § 2A:14-5	Real	For claims brought in the Law Division, automatic on debtor's present and future property anywhere in the state; for claims in the Special Civil Part (only claims for $15,000 or less can be brought in this court), creditor must have judgment docketed in the Law Division first	20 years
New Mexico	N.M. Stat. Ann. § 39-1-6	Real	Creditor files judgment with county clerk in any county where debtor has property now or may have property in future	14 years
New York	N.Y. C.P.L.R. §§ 5201 to 5203	Real & personal	Creditor files transcript with county clerk	10 years

Liens on Your Property After Judgment (In Most States Liens Can Be Extended or Renewed) (continued)				
State	**Code Section**	**Property**	**How Creditor Obtains Lien**	**How Long Lien Lasts**
North Carolina	N.C. Gen. Stat. § 1-234	Real	Automatic on property in county where judgment is entered; creditor files judgment with county clerk for property outside county where judgment entered	10 years
North Dakota	N.D. Cent. Code § 28-20-13	Real	Automatic on property in county where judgment is entered; creditor files judgment with county clerk for property outside county where judgment entered	10 years
Ohio	Ohio Rev. Code Ann. §§ 2329.02, 2329.07	Real	Creditor files judgment with clerk of court of common pleas in any county where debtor has property now or may have property in future	5 years
Oklahoma	Okla. Stat. tit. 12, §§ 706, 735	Real	Creditor files Statement of Judgment with county clerk in any county where debtor has property now or may have property in future	5 years
Oregon	Or. Rev. Stat. §§ 18.150 to .162, 18.180	Real	Automatic on property in county where judgment entered; for property in another county, creditor records judgment in County Clerk Lien Record	10 years
Pennsylvania	42 Pa. Cons. Stat. Ann. §§ 4303, 5526(1)	Real	Creditor records judgment with clerk of the court of common pleas in county where debtor has property now or may have property in future	5 years
Rhode Island	R.I. Gen. Laws §§ 9-25-2, 9-26-14, -15, -33	Real & personal	Creditor must request execution 48 hours after entry of judgment and file execution with town clerk or recorder of deeds in town where debtor's property is located	20 years
South Carolina	S.C. Code Ann. §§ 15-35-5, 15-35-540, 15-35-810	Real	Automatic on property in county where judgment entered; for other counties creditor files transcript of judgment with clerk of the court of common pleas	10 years
South Dakota	S.D. Codified Laws Ann. § 15-16-7	Real	Automatic on debtor's present and future property in county where judgment entered; for other counties, creditor files judgment with clerk of circuit court	10 years

Liens on Your Property After Judgment
(In Most States Liens Can Be Extended or Renewed) (continued)

State	Code Section	Property	How Creditor Obtains Lien	How Long Lien Lasts
Tennessee	Tenn. Code Ann. §§ 25-5-101 to -107	Real	Creditor files certified copy of judgment with register of deeds in any county where debtor has property now or may have property in future	10 years
Texas	Tex. Prop. Code Ann. §§ 52.001 to .006	Real	Creditor files judgment with county clerk in any county where debtor has property now or may have property in future	10 years
Utah	Utah Code Ann. §§ 78-22-1 to -1.5, 78-5-119	Real	Creditor records judgment in the office of county recorder in any county where debtor has property now or may have property in future	8 years
Vermont	Vt. Stat. Ann. tit. 12, §§ 2901 to 2904	Real	Creditor records judgment with town clerk in any town where debtor has property	8 years
Virginia	Va. Code Ann §§ 8.01-251(c), 8.01-458	Real	Creditor records judgment on county recorder's lien docket in any county where debtor has property now or may have property in future	10 years
Washington	Wash. Rev. Code Ann. §§ 4.56.190, 4.56.200	Real	Automatic on property in county where judgment is entered; creditor files judgment with county clerk for property outside county where judgment is entered	10 years
West Virginia	W.Va. Code Ann. §§ 38-3-5 to -7, 38-3-18	Real	Automatic on property in county where judgment is entered; for property in other counties, creditor records abstract of judgment with clerk of county court	10 years
Wisconsin	Wis. Stat. Ann. §§ 806.14 to .15	Real	Automatic on property in county where judgment is entered; for property in other counties, creditor records copy of judgment with clerk of circuit court	10 years
Wyoming	Wyo. Stat. Ann. §§ 1-17-301 to 307, 5-9-138	Real	Automatic on property in county where judgment is entered; for property in other counties, creditor files judgment with clerk of court of same jurisdiction and records judgment with county clerk	5 years

Current as of February 2007

Any mortgage holder, government taxing authority, or other creditor who placed a lien on your property before the judgment creditor will be paid first. Then you get any homestead exemption to which you are entitled. (See Chapter 16.) Only then does the judgment creditor get his or her share.

> **EXAMPLE:** Lin lives in Wisconsin and owns a house worth $200,000. Child-Aid Medical Clinic obtained a judgment against Lin for emergency treatment of his daughter for $2,500 and, consequently, got a lien on Lin's house. Child-Aid considers seizing his house to sell it and be paid but realizes that it won't get any money because:
> - Lin owes $125,000 on his first mortgage.
> - Lin owes $23,000 on a home equity loan.
> - Lin owes the IRS $17,000.
> - Lin's homestead exemption is $40,000.
>
> These items total $205,000, more than the value of Lin's house.

Property Levies

A judgment creditor can get a "writ of execution" from the court and go after your personal property by instructing the sheriff or marshal to "levy" on it. "Levy" basically means that the officer takes the property (your baseball card collection, for example) or instructs the holder of the property (your bank, for example) to turn it over to the officer. After taking your property, the sheriff

or marshal sells it at public auction and applies the proceeds to your debt. In the case of a bank account, the amount taken from your account is applied to your debt. You must be notified any time the sheriff or marshal levies against your property. You can request a hearing to show that the property is exempt or that the seizure will cause you financial hardship.

Here is how the levying process generally works:

1. The judgment creditor gets a court order authorizing a levy on your property. This order is usually called a writ of execution.
2. The judgment creditor directs the sheriff to seize (levy on) a particular asset, such as your car.
3. The sheriff comes to your home. If you are present, the sheriff explains that he or she has an order to take a particular item of your property to sell to pay off your debt. You do not have to let the sheriff into your home, however, unless the sheriff has a special court order allowing entry.
4. If you aren't home or don't cooperate, the sheriff can use a duplicate car key or hotwire a car, as long as it is not in a locked garage. Stay calm; in most states you can be arrested for interfering with the sheriff. The sheriff can't enter your house without your authorization to take other property without a special court order allowing entry. But again, if the sheriff insists on entering anyway, don't interfere.
5. The sheriff puts the item into storage.

6. If you don't file an objection (often called a "claim exemption") within the time allowed by your state, the sheriff will put the item up for sale.

7. After the sale, the proceeds are used to pay whatever you still owe the original lender, then to pay the sheriff's costs (seizing, storage, and sale), and then to pay the judgment. If the sale doesn't cover all of what you owe, the judgment creditor can still come after you for the rest.

Assignment Orders

An assignment order lets creditors go after property you own that can't be subjected to a levy, such as an anticipated tax refund, the loan value of unmatured life insurance, or an annuity policy. Independent contractors and other self-employed people who have no regular wages to be garnished are particularly susceptible to an assignment order against their accounts receivable.

An assignment order is straightforward: The judgment creditor applies to the court for an order prohibiting you from disposing of money you have a right to receive—such as a tax refund, insurance loan, royalties, dividend payments, or commissions. You are given the date and time of the court hearing and an opportunity to oppose issuance of an assignment order. If the creditor gets the order, the creditor serves it on whomever holds your money. When payment to you comes due, the money is sent to the judgment creditor instead.

Contempt Proceedings

Sometimes, a judgment issued by the court will include a schedule for installments or periodic payments. In a few states, if a judgment doesn't include such a schedule, the judgment creditor can go back to the court and ask the judge to make an order requiring periodic payments on a debt.

Violating a court order is generally referred to as contempt of court. In a handful of states, if a judge issues an order requiring periodic payments on a debt and you miss any payments, the judge can hold you in contempt. In theory, at least, the judge could issue a warrant for your arrest and you could be jailed.

As you might hope, arresting a debtor on this kind of warrant is usually a very low priority for law enforcement agencies, and in most situations the warrants become old and moldy without anyone being arrested. But the threat of arrest and jail can be a serious incentive for many judgment debtors to send a check ASAP.

Stopping Judgment Collection Efforts

Having your property taken or your wages attached can be devastating. It's miserable enough to owe money; it's worse to have your creditors take what little property you may have left.

Fortunately, in many situations you can still take steps to try to head off collection efforts. The process of trying to grab property to pay a judgment can be quite time-consuming and burdensome for a judgment creditor. Also, the creditor might fear that you'll lose or quit your job due to a wage attachment, or that you'll file for bankruptcy. None of that would help the creditor get paid.

It's never too late to negotiate. A judgment creditor who receives a reasonable offer to pay will often stop a lien, levy, wage attachment, garnishment suit, or assignment order. (For tips on negotiating, see Chapter 6.) Or, consider contacting a debt counseling agency for help in negotiating and setting up a repayment plan. (See Chapter 19.)

Most important, just because a judgment creditor levies on your property or attaches your wages, it doesn't mean that the creditor is entitled to take the property. Every state exempts certain property from creditors. This means that creditors simply cannot have that property, no matter how much you owe. In addition, you may be able to keep property that isn't exempt if you can prove to the court that you need it to support yourself or your family.

Exempt property is described in detail in Chapter 16. In most states, your clothing, furniture, personal effects, and public benefits can't be taken to pay a debt. Nor can some of the equity in your car and house, most of your wages, and most retirement pensions. Charts for each state are in Appendix B. What follows is a discussion on how to claim that your property is exempt (or that you need nonexempt property) when the judgment creditor pursues a lien, levy, wage attachment, or assignment order.

Any time the sheriff or marshal levies against your property, you must be notified. You can request a hearing, which is usually called something like a claim of exemption hearing, to argue that it will be a financial hardship on you if the property is taken, or that your property is exempt under state law. If you lose that hearing and your wages are attached, you can request a second hearing if your circumstances have changed, causing you hardship (for example, you have sudden medical expenses or must make increased support payments).

Debts for Necessities

In most states, you cannot request a claim of exemption to protect your wages if your debt was for basic necessities, such as rent or mortgage, food, utilities, or clothing. The law says that you should pay for your necessities, even if you suffer a hardship in doing so.

Still, you can request a claim of exemption hearing if the debt (now part of the judgment) was for a basic necessity. The creditor may not challenge your claim. Or, the judge might not care whether the debt was for a basic necessity and may consider only whether or not you need the money to support your family.

Here is an overview of how a claim of exemption hearing normally works:

1. When your employer notifies you of a wage attachment request, or you are notified of a property levy (such

as a bank account attachment) or assignment order, you will be told in writing how to file a claim of exemption—that is, how to tell the judgment creditor you consider the property unavailable. The time period in which you must file your claim is usually short and strictly enforced—don't miss it.

2. Complete and send a copy of your claim of exemption to the judgment creditor. In some states, you'll also have to serve it on the levying officer, such as the sheriff. The judgment creditor will probably file a challenge to your claim. The judgment creditor may abandon the attachment, levy, or assignment order, however, if it's too expensive or time-consuming to challenge you. If the creditor does abandon it, your withheld wages or taken property will be returned to you.

3. If the judgment creditor doesn't abandon the attachment, levy, or assignment order, the creditor will schedule a hearing before a judge. If you don't attend, you'll probably lose. On the day of the hearing, come early and watch the way the judge handles other cases. If you're nervous, visit the court a day earlier to get accustomed to the surroundings.

4. At the hearing, you'll have to convince the judge that your property is exempt or that you need it to support yourself or your family. This is your opportunity to defend yourself from having your wages or other property taken. You must do all that you can to prepare for this hearing if you want to keep your property.

For example, if the creditor tries to take your "tools of trade," which are exempt to a certain value in most states, bring along someone who works in your occupation. A supervisor, union boss, or shop leader can say that you use the items in your job. You'll need to show that the items' value does not exceed the exemption amount. If you have high income one month, bring in pay stubs to show that you usually make less. Or, if your bills are higher than average, bring copies. Think carefully about your income and financial situation. There may be other creative but truthful ways to show the judge that your property is exempt or necessary to support yourself or your family.

5. The judge will listen to both you and the judgment creditor, if the judgment creditor shows up. Sometimes the judgment creditor relies on the papers already filed with the court. The judge may make a ruling or may set up an arrangement for you to pay the judgment in installments.

Bankruptcy: The Ultimate Weapon

Thou whom avenging powers obey. Cancel my debt (too great to pay). Before the sad accounting day.

—Wentworth Dillon,
English poet and translator
1633-1685

Bankruptcy might be the ultimate solution to your debt problems. For a court filing fee of $274 or $299 and the cost of a self-help law book, many people can wipe out (discharge) all—or a good portion—of their outstanding debts. But deciding whether to file for bankruptcy isn't easy. You need to understand the different types of bankruptcies and what bankruptcy can and cannot do for you.

As you may have heard, Congress enacted major changes to the laws that govern bankruptcy. These changes went into effect in October 2005. Among other things, the new law requires debtors to get credit counseling before filing for bankruptcy (and debt management counseling before they can get a bankruptcy discharge of their debts); imposes new eligibility requirements on those who want to use Chapter 7 bankruptcy; and makes it more difficult to get rid of certain types of debts. The information in this chapter includes these recent changes.

RESOURCES

Nolo's bankruptcy resources. Nolo publishes several bankruptcy aids; this chapter contains only an overview of the bankruptcy process.

- *The New Bankruptcy: Will It Work for You?*, by Stephen Elias contains all the information you need to figure out if bankruptcy is right for you, and, if so, which type of bankruptcy case you should file.
- *How to File for Chapter 7 Bankruptcy*, by Stephen Elias, Albin Renauer, and Robin Leonard, contains all the forms and instructions necessary for you to file for Chapter 7 bankruptcy.
- *Chapter 13 Bankruptcy: Repay Your Debts*, by Stephen Elias and Robin Leonard, contains all the information you need to file for Chapter 13 bankruptcy on your own.

Congress has devised two kinds of bankruptcy: liquidation and reorganization. Liquidation bankruptcy is called Chapter 7 and can be filed by either individuals or businesses. There are three different reorganization bankruptcies:

- Chapter 13 bankruptcies (for individuals)
- Chapter 11 bankruptcies (for businesses and for individuals with unusually high debts), and
- Chapter 12 bankruptcies for family farmers.

This chapter addresses only Chapter 13 bankruptcies and Chapter 7 bankruptcies for individuals.

In a Chapter 7 bankruptcy, you ask the court to erase your debts completely. In exchange, you must give up your nonexempt property or its equivalent in cash or other property.

In a Chapter 13 bankruptcy, you set up a court-approved plan to repay your debts. Under the plan, you make monthly payments to the bankruptcy court for three to five years. The court in turn pays your creditors a percentage of the money they are owed. Under the plan, you must use all of your disposable income to pay off your debts. In addition, your creditors must receive at least as much as they would have received had you filed for Chapter 7 bankruptcy—that is, the value of your nonexempt property. Some creditors, however—such as a former spouse to whom you owe alimony—are entitled to receive 100% of what you owe. In Chapter 13 bankruptcy, you usually will not be required to give up any property.

If you're deeply in debt, bankruptcy may seem like a magic wand. And it often is. But it has its drawbacks, too. First, it's intrusive. A court-appointed person, the bankruptcy trustee, must approve almost all financial transactions you make while your bankruptcy case is open. For a Chapter 7 bankruptcy, this period can last three to six months. For a Chapter 13 bankruptcy, it can be as long as five years. Second, bankruptcy can cause practical problems, especially in Chapter 7 bankruptcy, because you might have to surrender property you desperately want to keep. Finally, bankruptcy can be depressing—some people would rather struggle along under mountains of debt than be labeled bankrupt.

You may also be concerned about your credit rating. Credit bureaus can report bankruptcies on your credit record for ten years. But you can take steps to start rebuilding your credit almost immediately. (Chapter 17 explains how to do this.) And you'd be surprised at how quickly

new credit card offers will come in the mail after your bankruptcy. Some credit card companies are more than willing to extend credit to people who have recently completed a bankruptcy—they assume that given your track record, you're likely to carry a balance on the card (which means more money for them in the form of interest) and won't be able to discharge any debt for another eight years. It will take longer to qualify for other types of credit, like mortgages or car loans. But most people who pay their bills on time for two to three years after completing a bankruptcy are able to get other types of loans.

Don't Feel Guilty

Some people feel ashamed at the prospect of filing for bankruptcy. But bankruptcy has been around for a long time, with good reason: It provides a necessary safety net for people who need to regain their financial footing and get a fresh start.

More than 1.5 million individuals and couples file for bankruptcy each year. Studies show that the most common reasons for these bankruptcies are:

- job loss, followed by an inability to find work that pays nearly as well
- medical expenses that aren't reimbursed by insurance or government programs
- divorce or legal separation, and
- small business failures.

The American economy is based on consumer spending. Roughly two-thirds of the gross national product comes from consumers spending their hard-earned dollars on goods and services we deem essential to our lives. As Americans, we learn almost from birth that it's a good thing to buy all sorts of goods and services. A highly paid army of persuaders surrounds us with thousands of seductive messages each day that all say, "buy, buy, buy."

Readily available credit makes it easy to live beyond our means and difficult to resist the siren songs of the advertisers. If, because of illness, loss of work, or just plain bad planning, we can't pay for the goods or services we need, feelings of fear and guilt are often our first responses. But as we've also seen, the American economy depends on our spending—the more, the better. In short, much of American economic life is built on a contradiction.

In this age of $50-billion bailouts for poorly managed financial institutions, should you really feel guilt-ridden about the debts you've run up? That's something only you can decide, but remember that large creditors expect defaults and bankruptcies and treat them as a cost of doing business. The reason banks issue so many credit cards is that it is a very profitable business, even though some credit card debt is wiped out in bankruptcies and never repaid.

Bankruptcy is a truly worthy part of our legal system, based as it is on forgiveness rather than retribution. Certainly, it helps keep families together, frees up income and resources for children, reduces suicide rates, and keeps the ranks of the homeless from growing even larger. And, perhaps paradoxically, every successful bankruptcy returns a newly empowered person to

the ranks of the "patriotic" consumer. If you suddenly find yourself without a job; socked with huge, unexpected medical bills you can't pay; or simply snowed under by an impossible debt burden, bankruptcy provides a chance for a fresh start and a renewed, positive outlook on life.

Famous Bankruptcy Filers

Among the over one million people who file for bankruptcy each year are some familiar faces:

Samuel Clemens (aka Mark Twain), author.

Oscar Wilde, poet and author.

Milton Hershey, filed for bankruptcy for each of his first four candy companies. His fifth is now known as the Hershey Foods Corp.

Henry Ford, filed for bankruptcy for his first company. He later founded Ford Motor Co.

Mickey Rooney, actor.

Burt Reynolds, actor.

Mike Tyson, boxer.

Tom Petty, musician.

Willie Nelson, musician.

Filing for Bankruptcy Stops Your Creditors

One of the most powerful features of bankruptcy is that it stops most debt collectors dead in their tracks and keeps them at bay for the rest of your case. Once you file, all collection activity (with a few exceptions, explained below) must go through the bankruptcy court, and most creditors cannot take any further action against you directly.

TIP

You don't need bankruptcy to stop your creditors from harassing you. Many people start considering bankruptcy when their creditors start phoning them at home and at work. As explained in Chapter 9, however, federal law prohibits this activity by debt collectors once you tell them, in writing, to leave you alone.

When you file for any type of bankruptcy, something called the "automatic stay" goes into effect. The automatic stay prohibits creditors and collection agencies from taking any action to collect most kinds of debts you owe, unless the law or the bankruptcy court says they can.

Here are the collection rules for various types of debts, after you file for bankruptcy:

- **Credit card debt, medical bills, and attorney fees.** All efforts to collect these types of debts must stop when you file for bankruptcy. Creditors may not file a lawsuit or proceed with a lawsuit that's already pending, record liens against your property, seize your property or income to pay the debt, or report the debt to a credit bureau.

- **Public benefits.** Government agencies seeking to collect overpayments of public benefits, such as SSI, Medicaid, or TANF (welfare) benefits, cannot do so by reducing or terminating

your benefits while your bankruptcy is pending. If, however, you become ineligible for benefits, bankruptcy doesn't prevent the government from terminating your benefits or denying them on that basis.

- **Criminal proceedings.** If a case against you can be broken down into criminal and debt components, only the criminal part will be allowed to continue. The debt will be stayed while your bankruptcy is pending. For example, if you were convicted of writing a bad check and were ordered to do community service and pay a fine, the first obligation will continue despite the stay.

- **Foreclosures.** Foreclosure proceedings are initially stayed when you file for bankruptcy. However, the lender can ask the judge to lift the stay and allow it to proceed with the eviction—and the judge will probably do so. Also, the stay won't apply if you filed another bankruptcy within the last two years and the court, in that earlier proceeding, lifted the stay and allowed the lender to proceed with the foreclosure. In other words, you cannot prevent foreclosure by filing serial bankruptcies.

- **Evictions.** Although the automatic stay used to stop eviction proceedings, that's no longer the case. A landlord may proceed with an eviction it began before you filed, and may begin certain eviction proceedings against you during your bankruptcy. What's more, most bankruptcy judges will lift the automatic stay and allow an eviction upon the landlord's request.

- **Utilities.** Companies that provide you with utilities such as gas, heating oil, electricity, telephone service, and water, may not discontinue service because you file for bankruptcy. However, they can shut off your service 20 days after you file if you don't give them a deposit or other means to assure future payment.

- **Tax debts.** The IRS can continue certain actions, such as a tax audit, issuing a tax deficiency notice, demanding a tax return, issuing a tax assessment, or demanding payment of an assessment. The automatic stay stops the IRS from issuing a lien or seizing any of your property or income, however.

- **Domestic relations proceedings.** Almost all proceedings related to a divorce or paternity action continue as before; they are not affected by the automatic stay. These include actions to:
  - set or collect child support and alimony
  - collect unpaid child support and alimony from property that is not part of the bankruptcy estate (for example, compensation you earn after filing for bankruptcy)
  - determine child custody and visitation
  - establish paternity
  - modify child support or alimony
  - protect a spouse or child from domestic violence
  - withhold income to collect child support

  - report unpaid support to credit bureaus
  - intercept tax refunds to pay unpaid support, and
  - withhold, suspend, or restrict drivers' and professional licenses as leverage to collect child support.

Chapter 7 Bankruptcy

As explained above, there are two types of bankruptcies: liquidation and reorganization. Chapter 7 bankruptcy is the liquidation type, where your nonexempt property (if you have any) is sold—or "liquidated"—to raise money for your creditors. However, for most individual filers, there is precious little liquidation. Rather, most filers find that all their property is exempt from being sold for the benefit of the creditors. See Chapter 16 for a discussion of bankruptcy property exemptions.

How Chapter 7 Works

The Chapter 7 bankruptcy process takes about three to six months, currently costs $299 in filing and administrative fees (which may be waived or paid in installments in certain circumstances), and commonly requires only one trip to the courthouse. To begin a Chapter 7 bankruptcy case, you fill out a packet of forms and file them with the bankruptcy court in your area.

The forms ask you to describe:
- your property and income
- your debts and monthly living expenses

- the property you claim is exempt, and
- any transactions involving your property in the past year.

You must also file a form—required by the new bankruptcy law—that calculates your average income over the six months before you file, compares it to the median income for your state and household size, and, if your income exceeds the state median, determines whether you could pay off some portion of your debt over time in Chapter 13 bankruptcy. Together, these calculations are referred to as "the means test," and they are intended to prohibit people from using Chapter 7 to wipe out their debts if they could afford to pay off some of those debts in Chapter 13. (See "Who Can File for Chapter 7 Banktuptcy," below, for more information.)

In addition to these forms, you must certify that you have received credit counseling from an agency approved by the U.S. Trustee's office when you file your bankruptcy papers. This, too, is a requirement of the new bankruptcy law. Before you receive your bankruptcy discharge, you will have to get debt management counseling—and file a form proving that you did so—as well.

Until your bankruptcy case ends, the trustee assumes legal control of the nonexempt property you own as of the date you file and the debts you owe as of that date. You cannot sell or pay for anything without the trustee's consent. You have control over only your exempt property and the property you acquire and the income you receive after you file for bankruptcy.

If you are entitled to receive property when you file for bankruptcy but haven't yet received it, you must turn the property over to the trustee when you eventually get it, if it's nonexempt. Examples include proceeds of a divorce settlement, tax refunds, inheritances or life insurance from someone who has died, and personal injury recoveries.

The trustee's primary duty is to see that your unsecured creditors are paid as much as possible of what you owe them. Because the trustee is paid a percentage of the assets recovered for your creditors, the trustee is usually very interested in how you value and categorize your property.

The trustee goes through the papers you file and asks you questions at a short hearing, called the creditors' meeting, held 20–40 days after you file. For example, if your list of property is sparse, the trustee might ask you if you've forgotten anything. You must attend the creditors' meeting, though few of your creditors will. Most creditors' meetings last no more than ten minutes.

After this hearing, the trustee collects your nonexempt property, sells it, and pays your creditors. You don't have to surrender nonexempt property if you pay the trustee the property's value in cash, or if the trustee is willing to accept exempt property of roughly equal value instead. Generally, very few debtors have to give up any property in a Chapter 7 bankruptcy case.

If you file for bankruptcy and then change your mind, you can ask the court to dismiss your case. However, not all courts will allow you to do so.

At the end of your bankruptcy case, most of your debts are discharged by the court, which means you no longer owe anything to the creditor.

Are Secured Debts Dischargeable?

As explained in Chapter 1, a secured debt means that a specific item of property (called "collateral") guarantees payment of the debt. Common secured debts include personal loans from banks, car loans, and home loans. Creditors have a lien on the collateral.

Bankruptcy eliminates your personal liability for your secured debts—the creditor can't sue you for the debt itself. But bankruptcy doesn't necessarily eliminate the creditor's lien on the secured property. You will eliminate the lien if you return the secured property to the creditor or pay the creditor its current value or the debt amount, whichever is less. Or, with certain types of liens, you can file papers with the court to request that the lien be wiped out. Finally, you can agree to have the debt survive bankruptcy (called "reaffirmation"), keep the collateral, and make payments under the original loan agreement.

Who Can File for Chapter 7 Bankruptcy

Filing for Chapter 7 bankruptcy can be a powerful tool for dealing with debt, but it isn't available to everyone. Here are some situations in which you will not be allowed to file for Chapter 7.

You Can Afford a Chapter 13 Plan

Under the old bankruptcy rules, the bankruptcy judge had the power to dismiss a Chapter 7 case if he or she thought the debtor had sufficient disposable income to fund a Chapter 13 repayment plan. There were no hard and fast rules dictating when a judge should dismiss a case on these grounds—it depended on the facts of the case and the attitude of the judge.

Now that the new bankruptcy law has gone into effect, however, there are clear criteria that dictate who will be allowed to stay in Chapter 7 and who will be forced to use Chapter 13, if they choose to file for bankruptcy. Disabled veterans whose debts were incurred during active duty and people whose debts come primarily from the operation of a business get a fast pass to Chapter 7. All others must meet the requirements set out below.

How High is Your Income?

Under the new rules, the first step in figuring out whether you can file for Chapter 7 is to measure your "current monthly income" against the median income for a family of your size in your state. Your "current monthly income" is not your income at the time you file, however: It is your average income over the last six months before you file. (You don't have to include Social Security retirement and disability payments.) For many people, particularly those who are filing for bankruptcy because they recently lost a job, their "current monthly income" according to these rules will be much more than they take in each month by the time they file for bankruptcy.

Once you've calculated your income, compare it to the median income for your state. (You can find median income tables, by state and family size, at the website of the United States Trustee, www.usdoj.gov/ust; click "Means Testing Information.")

If your income is less than or equal to the median, you can file for Chapter 7. If it is more than the median, however, you must pass "the means test"—another requirement of the new law—in order to file for Chapter 7.

Can You Pass the Means Test?

The purpose of the means test is to figure out whether you have enough disposable income, after subtracting certain allowed expenses and required debt payments, to repay at least a portion of your unsecured debts over a five-year repayment period. To find out whether you pass the means test, you start with your "current monthly income," calculated as described above. From that amount, you subtract both of the following:

- certain allowed expenses, in amounts set by the IRS. Generally, you cannot subtract what you actually spend for things like transportation, food, clothing, and so on; instead, you have to use the limits the IRS imposes, which may be lower than the cost of living in your area.
- monthly payments you will have to make on secured and priority debts. Secured debts are those for which the creditor is entitled to seize property if you don't pay (such as a mortgage or car loan); priority debts are obligations that the law deems to be so important that they are entitled to jump to the head of the repayment line. Typical priority debts include child support,

alimony, tax debts, and wages owed to employees.

If your total monthly disposable income after subtracting these amounts is less than $100, you pass the means test, and will be allowed to file for Chapter 7. If your total remaining monthly disposable income is more than $166.66, you have flunked the means test, and will be prohibited from using Chapter 7, with one exception: If you can prove to the court that you're facing special circumstances that aren't reflected in the calculations above, and that effectively decrease your income or increase your expenses to bring your disposable income below the $166.66 figure, you will be allowed to use Chapter 7.

So what about those in the middle? They have to do some more math. If your remaining monthly disposable income is between $100 and $166.66, you must figure out whether what you have left over is enough to pay more than 25% of your unsecured, nonpriority debts (such as credit card bills, student loans, medical bills, and so on) over a five-year period. If so, you flunk the means test, and Chapter 7 won't be available to you. (Again, if you are facing special circumstances that alter these figures, you may be able to convince the court to allow you to use Chapter 7.) If not, you pass the means test, and Chapter 7 remains an option.

For much more information on these new requirements, including detailed worksheets that will help you figure out whether you can use Chapter 7, see *How to File for Chapter 7 Bankruptcy*, by Stephen Elias, Albin Renauer, and Robin Leonard (Nolo).

For an online calculator that will help you through the means test math, go to www.legalconsumer.com.

You Previously Received a Bankruptcy Discharge

You cannot file for Chapter 7 bankruptcy if you obtained a discharge of your debts in a Chapter 7 case filed within the last eight years, or a Chapter 13 case filed within the last six years.

A Previous Bankruptcy Was Dismissed Within the Previous 180 Days

You cannot file for Chapter 7 bankruptcy if a previous Chapter 7 or Chapter 13 case was dismissed within the past 180 days because:

- you violated a court order
- the court ruled that your filing was fraudulent or constituted an abuse of the bankruptcy system, or
- you requested the dismissal after a creditor asked for relief from the automatic stay.

You Defrauded Your Creditors

A bankruptcy court may dismiss your case if it thinks you have tried to cheat your creditors or concealed assets so you can keep them for yourself. Certain activities are red flags to the courts and trustees. If you have engaged in any of them during the past year, your bankruptcy case may be dismissed. These no-nos include:

- unloading assets to your friends or relatives to hide them from creditors or from the bankruptcy court

- running up debts for luxury items when you were clearly broke and had no way to pay them off
- concealing property or money from your spouse during a divorce proceeding, or
- lying about your income or debts on a credit application.

In addition, you must sign your bankruptcy papers under "penalty of perjury" swearing that everything in them is true. If you deliberately fail to disclose property, omit material information about your financial affairs, or use a false Social Security number (to hide your identity as a prior filer), and the court discovers your action, your case will be dismissed and you may be prosecuted for fraud.

Chapter 13 Bankruptcy

Chapter 13, like Chapter 7, immediately stops many of your creditors from taking further action against you. Currently, Chapter 13 costs $274. In a Chapter 13 bankruptcy, you keep your property whether it's exempt or not. In exchange, you pay off your creditors (sometimes in part, sometimes fully) over three to five years. Also, you cannot file for Chapter 13 bankruptcy if your unsecured debts exceed $336,900 or your secured debts exceed $1,010,650.

To begin a Chapter 13 bankruptcy, you fill out a packet of forms—much like the forms in a Chapter 7 bankruptcy—listing your income, property, expenses, and debts, and file them with the bankruptcy court.

You must also submit a repayment plan. This plan indicates how much you will pay each month and how that money will be divided among your creditors. You must devote all of your disposable income (calculated as explained in "You Can Afford a Chapter 13 Plan," above) to your plan for three years if your average monthly income over the six months before you file is less than your state's median income, and five years if your income exceeds the state median. (These figures are also explained above.)

Some creditors are entitled to 100% of what you owe, while others may receive a smaller percentage or even nothing at all, depending on how much disposable income you have. A Chapter 13 plan must pay child support in full, for example, but it doesn't have to pay off your credit card debts. You can also use a Chapter 13 repayment plan to get current on your mortgage, which is one reason why some people choose Chapter 13.

The income you use to repay creditors need not be wages. You can use benefits, pension payments, investment income, or receipts as an independent contractor. At the end of the three- or five-year period, the court will wipe out the remaining unpaid balance on your dischargeable debts.

As in Chapter 7 bankruptcy, you are required to attend a creditors' meeting. You must also attend a confirmation hearing where the judge reviews your plan and then confirms or denies it. Once your plan is confirmed, you make payments directly to the bankruptcy trustee, who in turn distributes the money to your creditors. If

your plan is denied, you can modify it, refile it, and try again.

If, for some reason, you cannot finish a Chapter 13 plan—for example, you lose your job—the trustee can modify your plan. The trustee can give you a grace period if the problem looks temporary, reduce your total monthly payments, or extend the repayment period. As long as you're acting in good faith, the trustee will try to help you through rocky periods. If it's clear that you won't be able to complete the plan because of circumstances beyond your control, the court might let you discharge the remainder of your debts on the basis of hardship.

If the bankruptcy court won't let you modify your plan or give you a hardship discharge, you can:

- convert to a Chapter 7 bankruptcy (unless you are ineligible to file), or
- dismiss your Chapter 13 case, which means you'll owe what you owed before filing for Chapter 13, less the payments you made, plus interest from the date you filed (which had stopped accruing while your case was ongoing).

Will Bankruptcy Solve Your Debt Problems?

Bankruptcy is good at wiping out unsecured debt, but you may have trouble eliminating some other kinds of debts, including child support, alimony, most tax debts, student loans, and secured debts.

What Bankruptcy Can Do

Whether you use Chapter 7 or Chapter 13, your bankruptcy discharge will wipe out your unsecured debts, including credit card debt. (For more on which debts are secured and unsecured, see Chapter 1). If you file for Chapter 13 rather than Chapter 7, you may have to pay back some portion of your unsecured debts. However, any unsecured debts that remain once your repayment plan is complete will be discharged.

What Bankruptcy Can't Do

Bankruptcy will not help you avoid paying child support or alimony, and it will offer only limited help if you are trying to get rid of tax debt or student loan debt. Here's what bankruptcy cannot do for you:

Prevent a secured creditor from repossessing property. A bankruptcy discharge eliminates debts, but it does not eliminate liens. So, if you have a secured debt, bankruptcy can eliminate the debt, but it does not prevent the creditor from repossessing the property. But after the repossession, bankruptcy does prevent the creditor from coming after you for additional money if the sale of the collateral did not generate enough cash to pay off the amount you still owed.

Eliminate child support and alimony obligations. Child support and alimony obligations survive bankruptcy—you will continue to owe these debts in full, just as if you had never filed for bankruptcy. And if you use Chapter 13, your plan will have to repay these debts in full. (See Chapter 13 of this book for more information.)

Wipe out student loans, except in very limited circumstances. Student loans can be discharged in bankruptcy only on a showing of "undue hardship"—a standard that is very tough to meet. You must be able to show not only that you cannot afford to pay your loans now, but also that you have very little likelihood of being able to pay your loans in the future. (See Chapter 12 for more information.)

Eliminate most tax debts. Eliminating tax debt in bankruptcy is not easy, but it is possible in some cases. For example, you may be able to eliminate certain older income taxes.

Eliminate other nondischargeable debts. The following debts are not dischargeable under either Chapter 7 or Chapter 13 bankruptcy. If you file for Chapter 7, these debts will remain when your case is over. If you file for Chapter 13, these debts will have to be paid in full during your repayment plan. If they are not repaid in full, the balance will remain at the end of your case.

- debts you forget to list in your bankruptcy papers, unless the creditor learns of your bankruptcy case
- debts for personal injury or death caused by your intoxicated driving
- fines and penalties imposed for violating the law, such as traffic tickets and criminal restitution, and
- recent income tax debts and all other tax debts.

In addition, some types of debts may not be discharged if the creditor convinces the judge that they should survive your bankruptcy. These include debts incurred through fraud, such as lying on a credit application or passing off borrowed property as your own to use as collateral for a loan.

What Only Chapter 13 Bankruptcy Can Do

In some situations, Chapter 13 bankruptcy offers more help than Chapter 7. You'll have to decide if this extra help is worth having to repay a portion of your debts over three to five years.

Stop a mortgage foreclosure. Though bankruptcy can delay a foreclosure, a Chapter 7 bankruptcy won't stop it for long. Chapter 13, however, was designed with foreclosure problems in mind. Filing for Chapter 13 bankruptcy will stop the foreclosure and can force the lender to accept a plan where you make up the missed payments and the loan amount through your repayment plan.

Allow you to keep nonexempt property. In Chapter 7, you must give up your valuable nonexempt property so that the trustee can sell it and use the proceeds to pay off your creditors. If you have nonexempt property that you really want to keep, and a steady source of income, Chapter 13 might make more sense. You don't have to give up any property in Chapter 13 because you use your income to fund your repayment plan. (For more on exempt and nonexempt property, see Chapter 16.)

Repay nondischargeable debt. If you have debts that are difficult or impossible to discharge in bankruptcy—such as child support or student loans—you can at least use Chapter 13 to come up with a workable plan to repay these debts over time. And, because your plan doesn't have to repay unsecured debt if you have insufficient income, you may have more money available to devote to these nondischargeable debts.

Protect a codebtor from collection efforts. If you use Chapter 7 bankruptcy to discharge a debt you owe jointly with someone else, you will no longer be liable for that debt. Your codebtor will, however, and creditors are free to come after your codebtor to try and collect. If you want to protect your codebtor, you might consider Chapter 13 bankruptcy instead. In Chapter 13, you can include the debt in your repayment plan and pay it off over time. As long as you pay off the debt in full, creditors will leave your codebtor alone.

"Cram down" secured debts that are worth more than the property that secures them. You can use Chapter 13 to reduce a debt to the replacement value of the property securing it, then pay off that debt through your plan. For example, if you owe $10,000 on a car loan and the car is worth only $6,000, you can propose a plan that pays the creditor $6,000 and have the rest of the loan discharged. However, you can't cram down a car debt if you purchased the car during the 30-month period before you filed for bankruptcy. You also can't cram down a secured debt on other personal property you purchased within one year preceding your bankruptcy filing.

 WARNING

This is a broad overview of a complicated topic. If you are seriously considering bankruptcy, you'll need to know much more about how Chapter 7 and Chapter 13 work, the advantages and disadvantages of each, which debts will be discharged, how to complete your paperwork, and much more. To get started, pick up a copy of Nolo's *The New Bankruptcy: Will It Work for You?* by Stephen Elias. If you decide that you want to file under Chapter 7 or Chapter 13, you can use one of Nolo's detailed, step-by-step guides: *How to File for Chapter 7 Bankruptcy* or *Chapter 13 Bankruptcy*.

■

Property You Do—And Don't—Get to Keep

This chapter will help you figure out what property you can protect, even though:

- a creditor has obtained a judgment against you and seeks to enforce the judgment by taking your cash, or by seizing and selling other property, or
- you decide to file for a Chapter 7 bankruptcy to wipe out some or all of your debts (see Chapter 15 for more on bankruptcy).

The good news is that you can almost certainly keep at least some of your property, no matter what. Certain types of property are "exempt," or free from seizure, by judgment creditors. For example, clothing, basic household furnishings, your house, and your car are commonly exempt, as long as they're not worth too much. However, any property you have that is *not* exempt *can* be taken to pay your debts.

If you file for bankruptcy, these same exemptions (provided by state laws) are generally used to decide which property you can keep and which items the bankruptcy trustee can sell to pay your creditors. In other words, if you file for bankruptcy, you should get to keep at least as much of your property as you would if you were simply faced with collection by a judgment creditor.

In addition, 15 states (and the District of Columbia) offer their bankruptcy filers another optional set of exemptions. These exemptions come from the federal bankruptcy code and may be more liberal than your state's regular exemptions. If you have that choice, you get to choose which set of exemptions you want to use in bankruptcy: state or federal.

But you don't get to choose which set of exemptions you use when a judgment is being collected; you can use *only* your state exemptions. That's why in this chapter we're going to walk you through a worksheet where you can list your property and compare the exemptions available in bankruptcy and the exemptions that apply if you wait for collection of a judgment. This way you can figure out what property is protected in both circumstances.

One Big Difference in Protecting Your Property

If you file for bankruptcy, only the nonexempt property you own *at the time you file* (with a few exceptions) can be taken by the bankruptcy trustee. After that, you can acquire more property, and it's almost always free from your past debts. (We say "almost always," because some debts, like past-due child support, can't be "discharged" in bankruptcy. See Chapter 15 for more on discharge of debts.)

In contrast, a creditor with a judgment can go after any of your nonexempt property—even property you acquire in the future—until the judgment is satisfied. So, the kinds of property, and the amount of property, you get to keep will definitely be different in that respect if you choose bankruptcy. Keep this difference in mind if you expect to receive a big chunk of change after filing for bankruptcy, such as a bonus or commission, an inheritance, or an insurance payout.

Certain Property Can Always Be Taken Away From You

If you are still making payments on a major purchase—typically on a home or car—your creditor most likely has a lien on the property to secure repayment. This is called a "secured" debt (see Chapter 1 for more information). In these cases, if you fall behind on your payments, you face the real possibility of foreclosure or repossession of the property that is the security for the loan. If you file for Chapter 7 bankruptcy, even if you aren't behind on the payments, the creditor can repossess the property unless you:

- agree to continue owing the underlying debt
- pay the creditor the replacement value of the property, or
- (in some states) continue making payments even though the underlying debt is wiped out.

By the time you finish this chapter you should know:

- what property you have
- what property you want to keep most
- how much of that property is exempt from collection of a judgment
- how much of that property is exempt in bankruptcy
- whether you can keep more property if you file for bankruptcy
- what you have to do to claim an exemption, whether in bankruptcy or collection

- what nonexempt property you might want to change into exempt property, and
- how to convert it legally.

Property Subject to Collection

This section discusses what property a creditor can seize when the creditor is enforcing a judgment—that is, when the creditor goes to court and gets a court order allowing it to seize your property to satisfy the debt (plus interest). Some of your property should be protected or "exempt" from "collection." (You can find your state's exemptions listed in the State and Federal Exemption Tables in Appendix B. Below, we provide a worksheet where you can list your property and figure out how much of it is exempt.)

TIP

You may be "judgment proof." You are considered "judgment proof" if your property and wages are "exempt" and cannot be taken by a creditor. You can determine whether your property is exempt by looking ahead at "Applying Exemptions." If you are judgment proof, writing a letter to a creditor explaining this may convince the creditor that it's not worth the trouble to get a judgment against you.

Property You Own and Possess

When a creditor seeks to collect a judgment against you, all your property that is not exempt under state law could be taken to satisfy the judgment. As a practical matter, few judgment creditors go after tangible personal property (furniture, clothing, heirlooms, collections) unless it's quite valuable (a boat or a plane, for example). Judgment creditors prefer to focus on real estate, deposit accounts, paychecks, stocks, and bonds.

How Do They Take My Property?

A creditor who has a judgment against you can get a writ of execution from the court and ask the sheriff to seize some of your property and put it up for auction. This is called "an attachment and execution" or a "levy of execution." (See Chapter 14.) The property doesn't have to be property that the creditor took as collateral for a loan.

The sheriff will not seize property that is protected by an exemption. (See "Applying Exemptions," below, for a discussion of exemptions.) However, the sheriff won't know what property is protected without your help. You can prevent the seizure of exempt property by filing a notice of exemption or by taking similar steps specified by your state law. In some states, you need to file papers with the sheriff or an official by a deadline. In other states, the sheriff will let you set aside exempt property at the time of seizure.

Property that belongs to someone else is not available to judgment creditors—even if you control the property—because you don't have the right to sell it or give it away.

EXAMPLE: A parent establishes a trust for her child and names you as trustee to manage the money in the trust until the child's 18th birthday. You possess and control the money, but it's solely for the child's benefit under the terms of the trust; you cannot use it for your own purposes. It can't be seized by your judgment creditor.

How Will They Find Out About My Property, Anyway?

A creditor with a judgment against you can find out what property you have, used to have, or anticipate having, at a court-ordered hearing. In some states this is called a debtor's examination. Because it is a court-ordered appearance, you can be arrested, cited for contempt, and put in jail if you fail to show up.

You will have to answer the creditor's questions under oath—and lying under oath is a crime (perjury). If the creditor learns about assets that belong to you that are not exempt, it can get a court order to make you turn over the assets. If you refuse to obey the order, you could be held in contempt of court and sent to jail.

If you have transferred property in order to defraud your creditor, the creditor may ask the court to set aside that transaction. (For more discussion of debtors' examinations, see Chapter 14.)

Property You Own but Don't Have on Hand

Any nonexempt property you own is legally available to a judgment creditor, even if you don't have physical possession of it. For instance, you may own a share of a vacation cabin in the mountains but never go there yourself. Or you may own furniture or a car that someone else is using. Other examples include a deposit held by a stockbroker or the utility company.

Property You Have Recently Given Away

People facing a judgment are often tempted to unload their property on friends and relatives or to pay favorite creditors before the other creditors show up.

If you give away your property or sell it for less than it's worth, a judgment creditor could sue you and the recipient of the property for deliberately attempting to defraud the creditor. This might result in the property being recaptured for the creditor's benefit, and you could be severely fined or prosecuted for your fraudulent activity.

You can generally choose what property to sell and which creditor to pay first. The exceptions to this rule are:

- bankruptcy (where the bankruptcy trustee gets to decide about your property)
- a security interest (where the creditor has a lien on the property)
- fraud (where you improperly dispose of property so there's less left for your

creditors—for example, by paying one creditor more than that creditor is owed).

EXAMPLE: Assume you owe two creditors $10,000 each. If you are faced with a judgment collection action by creditor A, you may safely cash out your $10,000 securities portfolio and pay that full amount to creditor B, leaving creditor A high and dry.

Property You Are Entitled to but Don't Yet Possess

A creditor with a judgment against you can go after any assets coming your way, once your right to them is firm. The most common examples are salary and commissions, earned before or after the creditor got the judgment. Other examples are refunds, vacation and severance pay, insurance payouts, royalties, inheritances, and guaranteed payments (such as from a trust or annuity). The procedure a creditor uses to seize your property in the hands of a third person is called "garnishment" or "attachment."

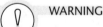 WARNING

Sometimes, the money in a trust is not protected from the beneficiary's creditors. If you are a beneficiary who gets payments from a trust, check with a lawyer regarding the terms of distribution. Trusts often make payments until the beneficiary reaches a certain age and then give the beneficiary all the principal that's left. Your creditors will probably be able to seize that money when it becomes due to you.

State law limits how much of your earnings can be taken directly from an employer—it usually depends on the kind of debt. Taking part of your earnings is called "garnishment" or "wage attachment." (For more on wage attachment, see Chapter 14.)

Future Claims

Creditors are not only interested in the property you own now—they sometimes set their sights on property or money that you'll own in the future.

For example, you might have a claim against a third party that you haven't acted on—for instance, because you haven't applied for the refund, made the insurance claim, or brought the lawsuit.

Occasionally a creditor will accept the rights to such a claim to satisfy a judgment. This is called an "assignment of rights," and it lets the creditor pursue the claim in your place. (Usually you must agree to cooperate with the creditor in pursuing the claim as part of the assignment of rights.) Typically, because the value of the claim won't be definitely settled or known when you make the assignment, you and the creditor will negotiate what you think it might be finally worth, plus interest, but minus what it will cost to pursue the claim. The claim's value might be further modified, depending on how easy or difficult it looks to successfully collect on the claim.

Stock options are another kind of future right that may have some value to a creditor. However, you won't be able to assign an option unless, at the time you make the assignment, you have a right to exercise the option. In legalese, the right must be "vested." Even if the right has vested, it is not always assignable. But be assured that, as soon as you exercise the option, your creditors will be all over your stocks or stock account.

When Is Bankruptcy Better?

Happily, most people find that in bankruptcy they can hang on to all or most of their property, including their wages and bank accounts. In contrast, when a judgment is granted, the first thing your creditors will look for and seize is part of your wages and all of your bank accounts.

In a bankruptcy, creditors generally can get their hands only on the property you have on the day you file for bankruptcy (with a few exceptions). In contrast, a creditor with a judgment hangs around, basically forever, waiting for any event that leaves you with money in your hands, whether it's a new job, sale of a major asset, or an inheritance. Creditors don't go away until the judgment is satisfied, with interest.

These are the main reasons that people decide to file for bankruptcy rather than struggling to pay a judgment—to protect their future money from seizure, and to get creditors off their backs so they can make a fresh start.

Property That Is Only Partially Exempt

State and federal laws protect certain kinds of property from seizure by creditors (and bankruptcy trustees). This protection is called an "exemption." Sometimes, property is protected only up to a certain value. Property is partially exempt if its value is greater than the amount protected by the exemption. A creditor can seize and sell an asset that is only partially exempt, if the creditor pays you the value of your exemption.

A creditor can also wait for your fully exempt property to increase to a value greater than the amount protected under your state's exemption law; this would also make your property partially exempt. However, for practical purposes, the creditor will not bother to seize the property until it appreciates sufficiently that the creditor will net enough money after the sale to make it worth the trouble.

> **EXAMPLE:** You bought your house for $90,000 in cash, just before a creditor gets a judgment against you. In your state, a primary residence with a value of up to $100,000 is exempt from seizure. After a number of years, a similar house in your neighborhood sells for $150,000. The creditor still has a valid judgment and forces the sale of your house. It fetches $150,000. You get the first $100,000 from the proceeds. The costs of sale and the creditor's judgment get paid next. You get any money left over.

> **EXAMPLE:** You bought your house for $90,000 with $10,000 in cash and a mortgage for $80,000, just before a creditor gets a judgment against you. Your state's exemption protects a primary residence up to $100,000. After a number of years the mortgage has been paid down to $75,000 and the house is worth $150,000, so your equity in the house is now $75,000. The creditor won't bother to force the sale at this time, because after the sale the mortgage holder would be paid the first $75,000 of the sale proceeds, then you would be paid $75,000 (up to $100,000 of your equity is exempt). There would be nothing left over for the creditor.

Selling a noncash asset may be expensive and not very productive for the creditor. Creditors frequently choose to wait, either for the property to appreciate more, or for you to die or sell the property yourself. This is one reason why a judgment lien may sit on a house for years after the owner's equity has exceeded the exemption cap.

Your Share of Marital Property

When you are (or have been) married, the property that is subject to collection depends partly on:

- whether you live in a "community property" state or a "common law" state
- whether the property being seized was a gift or inheritance

- when the debt was incurred (before, during, or after the marriage), and
- why the debt was incurred.

The community property states are Alaska (if the spouses agree in writing), Arizona, California, Idaho, Louisiana, Nevada, New Mexico, Texas, Washington, and Wisconsin. Otherwise, your property ownership is decided under "common law" rules.

The next question is, when was the debt incurred, relative to the marriage? In all states, debts incurred before marriage or after divorce are owed only by the person who incurred them. In deciding who owes a debt during marriage, states divide "marriage" into two time periods: before and after permanent separation.

 CROSS-REFERENCE

Domestic partnership and marital property. As explained in Chapter 3, couples who register as domestic partners in California or join in a civil union in Connecticut, New Jersey, or Vermont, are also subject to these rules about marital property and debts.

Community Property States

In community property states, debts incurred during marriage (and before permanent separation) are joint debts for which both spouses are liable, unless the creditor didn't know about the marriage and was looking for payment only from the spouse who incurred the debt.

In a community property state, both spouses are liable for any debts incurred after a permanent separation but before divorce, as long as the debt was incurred for necessities for both husband and wife or their children—such as paying for the upkeep of the family home—but each is individually responsible for his or her own debts incurred solely for his or her benefit.

> **EXAMPLE:** Mary and John are married and living together. They buy a house. Both of them are liable for the house payments.

> **EXAMPLE:** Mary is married but buys a car in her own name, using her own credit and an inheritance from her uncle. Mary will be liable for the car payments.

> **EXAMPLE:** Mary and John are married but John has moved out. John buys a motorcycle. Mary and John are both responsible for property taxes on their home. John is liable for payments on the motorcycle.

Common Law States

In common law states, all debts incurred by the spouses jointly during marriage (and before permanent separation) are joint debts. Debts incurred by only one spouse during marriage are separate debts unless any of the following are true:

- The creditor looked to both spouses for repayment or considered both spouses' credit information.

- The debt was incurred for family necessities such as food, clothing, and shelter.
- The debt was incurred for medical purposes (in about half of the common law states).

In common law states, both spouses are liable for debts incurred after a permanent separation but before divorce, if the debts pay for "family necessities." Otherwise each is individually liable for his or her own debts.

If you live in a common law property state, there is a special, technical way to keep the property that you own *together* from being seized to satisfy one spouse's separate debt: You can usually make the property exempt by holding title to the property as "tenants by the entirety"—as opposed to, for example, "joint tenants." However, a creditor may still be able to take the property if both spouses are liable on the debt. So, if you live in a state that recognizes this form of ownership, you should certainly do some research or talk to a lawyer to find out whether and how it applies to you. (See Chapter 19 for more information on research and lawyers.)

Property Subject to Bankruptcy Court's Authority

When you file for Chapter 7 bankruptcy, everything you own when you file becomes subject to the bankruptcy court's authority. This property is collectively called your "bankruptcy estate." With a few exceptions

(discussed below), property you acquire after you file for Chapter 7 bankruptcy isn't included in your bankruptcy estate. If you originally filed for Chapter 13 bankruptcy and now want to convert your case to a Chapter 7 bankruptcy, everything you owned on the date you filed your Chapter 13 petition is the property of your Chapter 7 bankruptcy estate. (11 U.S.C. § 348(f)(1)(A).)

Property You Own and Possess

Property that you own and possess—for example, clothing, books, computers, cameras, TV, stereo system, furniture, tools, car, real estate, boat, artworks, and stock certificates—is included in your bankruptcy estate.

Property that belongs to someone else is not part of your bankruptcy estate—even if you control the property—because you don't have the right to sell it or give it away. Here are some examples.

EXAMPLE: Your sister has gone to Zimbabwe for an indefinite period and has loaned you her computer system while she's gone. Although you might have use of the equipment for years to come, you don't own it. It isn't part of your bankruptcy estate.

EXAMPLE: You are making monthly payments on a leased car. You are entitled to possess the car as long as you make the monthly payments, but you don't own it. It is not part of your bankruptcy estate (but the lease itself is).

Property You Own but Don't Possess

Any property you own is part of your bankruptcy estate, even if you don't have physical possession of it. For instance, you may own a share of a vacation cabin in the mountains but never go there yourself. Or you may own furniture or a car that someone else is using. Other examples include a deposit held by a stockbroker, contractual rights to a royalty or commission, or a security deposit held by your landlord or the utility company.

Property You Have Recently Given Away

People contemplating bankruptcy are often tempted to unload their property on friends and relatives or pay favorite creditors before the bankruptcy filing. Don't bother. Property given away or paid out shortly before you file for bankruptcy is still part of your bankruptcy estate—and the trustee has the legal authority to take it back.

Giving Away Property

You might be thinking about signing over the title certificate to an item of property to a relative or the person you live with, then not listing it in your bankruptcy papers. This is both dishonest and foolhardy. On your bankruptcy forms, which you must sign under penalty of perjury, you must list all property transactions made within the previous year. Knowingly failing to report a transaction is perjury—a felony. And, if the

unreported transfer is discovered, the trustee can seize the item from whoever has it and sell it to pay your creditors if:

- you didn't receive a reasonable amount for the item (selling an item for less than it's worth is the same as giving a gift for bankruptcy purposes), or
- the transfer either left you insolvent or gave you a big push in that direction.

And prosecution for perjury might not be the only disaster that befalls you if you transfer property with the intent to defraud your creditors. The court may refuse to discharge *any* of your debts. (11 U.S.C. § 727(a)(2).)

Paying Off a Favorite Creditor

You can't pay a favorite creditor, such as a relative or friend, before you file for bankruptcy, then leave your other creditors with less than they would have otherwise received. Payments and repossessions made shortly before filing for bankruptcy are called "preferences." The trustee can sue the creditor for the amount of the preference and make it a part of the bankruptcy estate, so it can be distributed among all of your creditors. In general, a preference exists when you pay or transfer property worth more than $600 to a creditor:

- within 90 days before filing for bankruptcy, or
- within one year before filing, if the creditor was someone close to you (such as a relative or business partner). (11 U.S.C. § 547.)

Are Stock Options Part of Your Bankruptcy Estate?

Whether stock options are part of your bankruptcy estate depends on when you received them and when they vest.

If you own stock options, you have the right to purchase stock at a specific price that is assigned at the time the stock options are granted. Making such a purchase is called "exercising your stock options." As a general rule, stock options that you own when you file for bankruptcy are part of your bankruptcy estate. In addition, any stock you purchase by exercising your stock options is also part of the estate, even if you exercise those options after you file for bankruptcy. Courts treat these stock purchases as proceeds earned on property of the estate.

Sometimes, your stock options do not vest (that is, they cannot be exercised) until you have been with your company for a certain period of time. In that case, only those stock options that have already vested on the date you file for bankruptcy will be included in your bankruptcy estate.

To calculate the value of your stock options, multiply the number of vested stock options you own by the difference between your option price and the fair market value of the stock. Even if the potential value of your options is very uncertain, they are still part of your bankruptcy estate, and the trustee will take them if they are marketable.

Property You Are Entitled to Receive but Don't Yet Possess

Property to which you are legally entitled at the time you file for bankruptcy is included in your bankruptcy estate, even if you haven't actually received it yet. The most common examples are wages you have earned but have not yet been paid and tax refunds that are legally owed to you. Here are some other examples:

- Vacation or severance pay earned before you filed for bankruptcy.
- Property you've inherited, but not yet received, from someone who has died. By contrast, if you're a beneficiary in the will or revocable living trust of someone who is alive, you don't have to list that on your bankruptcy papers—he or she could change the will or trust before dying. If he or she has already died, however, you have a legal right to receive the property, and you must list it.
- Property you will receive from a trust. If you receive periodic payments from a trust but aren't entitled to the full amount of the trust yet, the full amount of the trust is considered property of your bankruptcy estate anyway. List it on the Worksheet and your bankruptcy papers. Although the bankruptcy trustee may not be able to get the money (depending on the type of trust), you don't want to be accused of hiding it.
- Proceeds of an insurance policy, if the death, injury, or other event that triggers payment has occurred. For

example, if you were the beneficiary of your father's life insurance policy, and your father has died but you haven't received your money yet, that amount is part of your bankruptcy estate.

- A legal claim to monetary compensation (sometimes called a legal "cause of action"), even if the value of the claim hasn't yet been determined. For example, if you have a claim against someone for injuring you in a car accident, you must include this potential source of money in your bankruptcy papers, even if the amount has not yet been determined in a lawsuit, settlement agreement, or insurance claim.

- Accounts receivable (money owed you for goods or services you've provided). Even if you don't think you'll be paid, that money is considered part of your bankruptcy estate. It's the trustee's job to go after the money; leaving it off the bankruptcy forms can get you into trouble.

- Money earned (but not yet received) from property in your bankruptcy estate. This includes, for example, rent from commercial or residential real estate, dividends earned on stocks, and royalties from copyrights or patents.

Proceeds From Property of the Bankruptcy Estate

If property in your bankruptcy estate earns income or otherwise produces money after you file for bankruptcy, this money is also part of your bankruptcy estate. For example, suppose a contract to receive royalties for a book you have written is part of your bankruptcy estate. Any royalties you earn under this contract after you file for bankruptcy are also property of the estate.

One exception to this rule is money you earn from work you do after filing for bankruptcy. This money isn't part of your bankruptcy estate. The royalties you earn for working on a new edition of a book after filing for bankruptcy would not be part of your bankruptcy estate.

Certain Property Acquired Within 180 Days After You File for Bankruptcy

Most property you acquire—or become entitled to acquire—after you file for bankruptcy isn't included in your bankruptcy estate. But there are exceptions. If you acquire (or become entitled to acquire) certain items within 180 days after you file, you must report them to the bankruptcy court—and the bankruptcy trustee may take them unless you can claim them as exempt. (11 U.S.C. § 541(a)(5).)

The 180-day rule applies to:

- property you inherit during the 180-day period
- property from a marital settlement agreement or divorce decree, and
- death benefits or life insurance policy proceeds that become owed to you during the 180-day period.

You must report these items on a supplemental form, even if your bankruptcy case is over.

Your Share of Marital Property

Marital property is the property you and your spouse own together. The amount of marital property that will be included in your bankruptcy estate depends on two factors: (1) whether you file for bankruptcy jointly or alone, and (2) the laws of your state regarding marital property. (Chapter 3 explains marital property in detail.)

Community Property States

The community property states are Alaska (if the spouses sign an agreement), Arizona, California, Idaho, Louisiana, Nevada, New Mexico, Texas, Washington, and Wisconsin. In those states, in general, all the property you acquire before marriage or after divorce is separate property, while all property acquired during marriage (except inheritances or gifts to one of you) is community property.

If you are married, live in a community property state, and file for bankruptcy, all the community property you and your spouse own is considered part of your bankruptcy estate, even if your spouse doesn't file. This is true even if the community property might not be divided 50–50 if you were to divorce. (See Chapter 3 for information on what constitutes community and separate property.)

EXAMPLE: Paul and Sonya live in California, a community property state. Sonya contributed $20,000 of her separate property toward the purchase of their house. All the rest of the money used to pay for the house is from community funds, and the house is considered community property. If Paul and Sonya were to divorce and split the house proceeds, Sonya would be entitled to $20,000 more than Paul as reimbursement for her down payment. But they aren't divorced, and Paul files for bankruptcy without Sonya. Their house is worth $250,000. Paul must list that entire value on his bankruptcy papers—that is, he can't subtract the $20,000 Sonya would be entitled to if they divorced.

The separate property of the spouse filing for bankruptcy is also part of the bankruptcy estate. But the separate property of the spouse *not* filing for bankruptcy is not part of the bankruptcy estate.

EXAMPLE: Paul owns a twin-engine Cessna as his separate property (he owned it before he married Sonya). Sonya came to the marriage owning a grand piano. Because only Paul is filing for bankruptcy, Paul's aircraft will be part of his bankruptcy estate, but Sonya's piano won't be.

Common Law Property States

If your state is not a community property state, it is a common law property state.

When only one spouse files for bankruptcy in a common law property state, all of that spouse's separate property plus half of the couple's jointly owned property go into the filing spouse's bankruptcy estate.

Before you can figure out which property goes into the bankruptcy estate, you'll need to know the general rules of property ownership in common law states. They are:

- Property that has only one spouse's name on a title certificate (such as a car, house, or stocks), even if bought with joint funds, is that spouse's separate property.

- Property that was purchased or received as a gift or inheritance by both for the use of both spouses is jointly owned, unless title is held in only one spouse's name (which means it belongs to that spouse separately, even if both spouses use it).

- Property that one spouse buys with separate funds or receives as a gift or inheritance for that spouse's separate use is that spouse's separate property (unless, again, a title certificate shows differently).

See Chapter 3 for more information on property ownership and responsibility for debts in common law states.

Tenancy by the Entirety

In some common law states, married people can hold title to property as "tenants by the entirety." This form of ownership has special consequences when one or both of the owners files for bankruptcy.

Usually, property that spouses own as "tenants by the entirety" is part of the bankruptcy estate when the spouses file for bankruptcy together (subject to the usual exemptions that apply to that type of property: land, house, car, and so on). However, if one spouse owes most of the debts and files for bankruptcy *alone*, property held as "tenancy by the entirety" cannot be taken by the trustee or any creditor to pay debts. Because the property belongs to the marriage (rather than to one spouse or the other), neither spouse can give it away or encumber it with debts on his or her own.

There are many variations on this general rule. For example, some states recognize tenancy by the entirety as a form of ownership that applies only to real estate. Some states presume that spouses who own property together own it as tenants by the entirety, while others require spouses to specify how they hold the property.

This tenancy by the entirety exemption is potentially a very powerful tool for debtors who declare bankruptcy: If your property falls within this rule, you may be able to keep it, regardless of its value. This means that you might be able to keep your house, for example, even if your equity well exceeds your state's homestead exemption.

If you live in a state that recognizes this form of ownership, you should certainly talk to a lawyer to find out whether and how it applies to you. (See Chapter 19 for more information on legal research and lawyers.)

Applying Exemptions

As you know by now, when a creditor gets a judgment (court order) against you, the creditor wants to seize your property to satisfy the judgment. And if you file for bankruptcy, the bankruptcy trustee is also looking for property with which to pay your secured creditors. Fortunately, a judgment creditor or bankruptcy trustee can't seize your property if an "exemption" is available to protect it. Exemptions are protections that are provided by state and federal laws. For a list of your state's exemptions and the federal exemptions, see Appendix B.

Understanding the Property Exemption System

Exempt property is the property you can keep in spite of a collection judgment or bankruptcy. Nonexempt property is the property that the creditors or bankruptcy trustee are entitled to take away from you. Therefore, the more property you can claim as exempt, the better off you are.

Figuring out exactly what property you're legally entitled to keep takes some work, but it's very important. It's your responsibility—and to your benefit—to claim all exemptions to which you're entitled. If you don't claim property as exempt, you could lose it to your creditors.

Each state has a set of exemptions for use by people who face collection of a judgment or who file for bankruptcy in that state. In addition, some states allow debtors who file bankruptcy to choose between their state's exemptions and federal bankruptcy exemptions. Debtors have this choice in Arkansas, Connecticut, the District of Columbia, Hawaii, Massachusetts, Michigan, Minnesota, New Hampshire, New Jersey, New Mexico, Pennsylvania, Rhode Island, Texas, Vermont, Washington, and Wisconsin.

California has adopted its own unique exemption system. Although California doesn't allow debtors to use the federal exemptions, California offers two sets of state exemptions for people filing bankruptcy. As in the states that let people choose the federal bankruptcy exemptions, people filing bankruptcy in California must choose one or the other set of California's state exemptions. If you are trying to find an exemption to protect property against collection of a judgment, you must use California's System 1.

> **TIP**
> **You might be able to negotiate to keep certain nonexempt property.** You don't have to surrender a specific item of nonexempt property to the bankruptcy trustee or creditors if you can pay them the property's value in cash, or if they are willing to accept exempt property of roughly equal value instead. Also, the bankruptcy trustee or creditor might reject or "abandon" the item if it would be too costly or cumbersome to sell. In that case, you also get to keep it. So remember, even when we say that you have to "give up property," you still might be able to barter with the trustee or creditor about which property they take.

Types of Exemptions

Exemptions come in several basic flavors:

- exemptions of a type of property, up to a specified value
- exemptions of a type of property, regardless of value
- "wildcard" exemptions that can be applied to any property.

Specific Property, Up to Specified Value

The first kind of exemption protects the value of your ownership in a particular item or type of property, but only up to a set dollar limit.

> **EXAMPLE:** The New Mexico state exemptions allow you to keep $4,000 of equity in a motor vehicle. If you were subject to collection, or if you were filing Chapter 7 bankruptcy in that state and using the state exemption list, you could keep your car if it was worth $4,000 or less.

Even if the property is worth more than the dollar limit of the exemption amount, you can keep the property if selling it would not raise enough money both to pay what you still owe on it and to give you the full value of your exemption.

> **EXAMPLE:** You own a car worth $20,000 but still owe $16,000 on it. Selling it would raise $16,000 for the lender and $4,000 for you, thanks to your New Mexico exemption. Since there would be nothing left over to pay your creditors, the creditor or trustee wouldn't take the car. Instead, you would be allowed to keep it as long as you are—and remain—current on your payments.

However, if your equity in the property exceeds the dollar amount of the exemption, the creditor or trustee may sell the property to raise money. A creditor would return your exemption amount to you, plus any money left over from the sale after costs are deducted and the judgment is paid. The bankruptcy trustee would return your exemption amount but use any extra money to pay your unsecured creditors.

> **EXAMPLE:** You own a car worth $20,000, and your state says $4,000 of your equity in it is exempt. Let's say you only owe $10,000 on that car. Selling the car for $20,000 would pay off the lender in full, pay your $4,000 exemption, and leave a portion of the remaining $6,000 (after the costs of sale are deducted) to be distributed to your other creditors. In this scenario, you are entitled to the full value of your exemption—$4,000—but not to the car itself.

Specified Property, Regardless of Value

Another type of exemption allows you to keep specified property, regardless of its value. For instance, the Utah state exemptions allow you to keep a refrigerator, freezer, microwave, stove, sewing machine, and carpets with no limit on their value.

Wildcard Exemption

Some states (and the federal exemption list that applies only in bankruptcy) provide a general-purpose exemption called a "wildcard" exemption. This exemption gives you a dollar amount that you can apply to any type of property. This is like the wildcard in poker, which you can use as any card you want. The same principle applies here. You can apply the wildcard exemption to property that would not otherwise be exempt.

> **EXAMPLE:** Suppose you own a $3,000 boat in a state that doesn't exempt boats but does have a wildcard of $5,000. You can take $3,000 of the wildcard and apply it to the boat, which means the boat will now be considered exempt. And, if you have other nonexempt property, you can apply the remaining $2,000 to that property.

Or, you can use a wildcard exemption to increase an existing exemption.

> **EXAMPLE:** If you have $5,000 worth of equity in your car but your state only allows you to exempt $1,500 of its value, you will likely lose the car. However, if your state has a $5,000 wildcard exemption, you could use the $1,500 motor vehicle exemption and $3,500 of the wildcard exemption to exempt your car entirely. And you'd still have $1,500 of the wildcard exemption to use on other nonexempt property.

Why State Exemptions Vary So Much

Each state's exemptions are unique. The property you can keep varies considerably from state to state. Why the differences? The exemptions reflect the attitudes of state legislators about how much property, and which property, a debtor should be forced to part with when a judgment is being collected. These attitudes are rooted in local values and concerns.

But, in many cases, there is another reason why state exemptions differ. Some state legislatures have raised exemption levels in recent times, while other states last looked at their exemptions many decades ago. In the states that don't reconsider exemption amounts very often, you can expect to find lower exemption amounts.

Doubling Exemptions If You Are Married

If the federal bankruptcy exemptions are available in your state and you decide to use them, you may double all of the exemptions if you are married and filing bankruptcy jointly. This means that you and your spouse can each claim the full amount of each exemption.

If you are using your state's exemptions—whether in bankruptcy or against collection of a judgment—you may be able to double some exemptions but not others. For instance, in the California exemption System 1 list, the exemption motor vehicles may not be doubled, but the exemption for tools of the trade may be doubled in some circumstances. Also, you can double for a single piece of property only if title to the property is held in both of your names.

The exemption chart in Appendix B notes whether a court or state legislature has expressly allowed or prohibited doubling. If the chart doesn't say one way or the other, it is probably safe to double. However, keep in mind that this area of the law changes rapidly—legislation or court decisions issued after the publication date of this book will not be reflected in the chart. (See Chapter 19 for information on doing your own legal research.)

Claiming Your Exemptions

In a few states, to take advantage of the state exemptions, you must file an exemption declaration with the court clerk, county recorder, county clerk, or similar official. The declaration is a simple form in which you describe (or list) your property and give its location. In the states where you must file a declaration, you can sometimes file it even after you've been sued or you've filed for bankruptcy.

Call the court clerk, county recorder, or county clerk, and ask whether the office has an exemption declaration form. If it does, fill it out and file it. If the clerk's office doesn't have a form, ask whether people file exemption declarations there anyway. If they don't, you probably don't have to, either.

In most states, any real estate or personal property in which you reside, such as a mobile home or boat, will qualify for the homestead exemption. To take advantage of the homestead protection, you usually must be living in the homestead when you claim it as exempt in your declaration.

This puts your creditors on notice that they shouldn't bother to go after that particular property. If they do, you need only point out your filed declaration for protection.

If you don't have to file an exemption declaration, you still must act to take advantage of your state's exemptions. If you file for bankruptcy, you must list all of the exemptions you claim on your bankruptcy forms. And, as pointed out in Chapter 14, if a judgment creditor goes after your exempt property, you must file a claim of exemption.

Is Your Property Exempt?

List Your Property

Go through Worksheet 3: Property Checklist, below, and check off everything that you have. Then enter the things you have into Column 1 of Worksheet 4: Property Exemptions.

When you complete Column 1 of Worksheet 4, you will have a complete inventory of your property. List everything you own that could bring in more than $50 at a garage sale. Lump together low-valued items, such as kitchen utensils. Keep in mind that many items you originally paid hundreds of dollars for are now worth much, much less.

Worksheet 3: Property Checklist

1. **Real estate**
   - ☐ Residence
   - ☐ Condominium or co-op apartment
   - ☐ Mobile home
   - ☐ Mobile home park space
   - ☐ Rental property
   - ☐ Vacation home or cabin
   - ☐ Business property
   - ☐ Undeveloped land
   - ☐ Farm land
   - ☐ Boat/marina dock space
   - ☐ Burial site
   - ☐ Airplane hangar
   - ☐ Time-share

2. **Cash on hand**
   - ☐ In your home
   - ☐ In your wallet
   - ☐ Under your mattress

3. **Deposits of money**
   - ☐ Bank deposit
   - ☐ Brokerage account (with stockbroker)
   - ☐ Certificates of deposit (CDs)
   - ☐ Credit union deposit
   - ☐ Escrow account
   - ☐ Money market account
   - ☐ Money in a safe deposit box
   - ☐ Savings and loan deposit

4. **Security deposits**
   - ☐ Electric
   - ☐ Gas
   - ☐ Heating oil
   - ☐ Prepaid rent
   - ☐ Security deposit on a rental unit
   - ☐ Rented furniture or equipment
   - ☐ Telephone
   - ☐ Vehicle lease
   - ☐ Water

5. **Household goods, supplies, and furnishings**
   - ☐ Antiques
   - ☐ Appliances
   - ☐ Barbecue
   - ☐ Carpentry tools
   - ☐ Cell phones, PDAs
   - ☐ China and crystal
   - ☐ Clocks
   - ☐ Dishes
   - ☐ Electronic entertainment devices and equipment
   - ☐ Food (total value)
   - ☐ Furniture
   - ☐ Gardening tools
   - ☐ Home computer (for personal use)
   - ☐ Home printer, fax, or copier
   - ☐ Lamps
   - ☐ Lawn mower or tractor
   - ☐ Microwave oven
   - ☐ Patio or outdoor furniture
   - ☐ Radios
   - ☐ Rugs
   - ☐ Sewing machine
   - ☐ Silverware and utensils
   - ☐ Small appliances
   - ☐ Snow blower
   - ☐ Sound system
   - ☐ Telephones and answering machines
   - ☐ Televisions
   - ☐ Tools
   - ☐ Vacuum cleaner
   - ☐ Video equipment (VCR, DVD player, camcorder, digital camera)

Worksheet 3: Property Checklist (continued)

6. **Books, pictures, art objects; stamps, coin, and other collections**

   ☐ Art prints

   ☐ Bibles

   ☐ Books

   ☐ Coins

   ☐ Collectibles (such as political buttons, baseball cards)

   ☐ Compact discs, records, and tapes

   ☐ Family portraits

   ☐ Figurines

   ☐ Original artworks

   ☐ Photographs

   ☐ Sculpture

   ☐ Stamps

   ☐ Videotapes, DVDs

7. **Apparel**

   ☐ Clothing

   ☐ Furs

   ☐ Sports clothes

8. **Jewelry**

   ☐ Bracelets, necklaces, and earrings

   ☐ Engagement and wedding ring

   ☐ Gems

☐ Precious metals

☐ Watches

9. **Firearms, sports equipment, and other hobby equipment**

   ☐ Bicycles

   ☐ Board games

   ☐ Camera equipment

   ☐ Electronic musical equipment

   ☐ Exercise machine

   ☐ Fishing gear

   ☐ Guns (rifles, pistols, shotguns, muskets)

   ☐ Hang gliding/parasailing equipment

   ☐ Model or remote cars or planes

   ☐ Musical instruments

   ☐ Scuba diving equipment

   ☐ Ski or snowboard equipment

   ☐ Surfboard

   ☐ Other sports equipment

   ☐ Other weapons (swords and knives)

10. **Interests in insurance policies**

    ☐ Credit insurance

    ☐ Disability insurance

☐ Health insurance

☐ Homeowners' or renters' insurance

☐ Term life insurance

☐ Whole or universal life insurance

11. **Annuities**

12. **Pension or profit-sharing plans**

    ☐ IRA

    ☐ Keogh

    ☐ Pension or retirement plan

    ☐ 401(k) account

    ☐ 457 account

13. **Stocks and interests in incorporated and unincorporated companies**

14. **Interests in partnerships**

    ☐ General partnership interest

    ☐ Limited partnership interest

15. **Government and corporate bonds and other investment instruments**

    ☐ Corporate bonds

    ☐ Deeds of trust

    ☐ Mortgages you own

Worksheet 3: Property Checklist (continued)

☐ Municipal bonds

☐ Promissory notes

☐ U.S. savings bonds

16. Accounts receivable

☐ Accounts receivable from business

☐ Commissions already earned

17. Family support

☐ Alimony (spousal support, maintenance) due under court order

☐ Child support payments due under court order

☐ Payments due under divorce property settlement

18. Other debts owed you where the amount owed is known and definite

☐ Disability benefits due

☐ Disability insurance due

☐ Judgments obtained against third parties but not yet collected

☐ Sick pay earned

☐ Social Security benefits due

☐ Tax refund due for returns already filed

☐ Vacation pay earned

☐ Wages due

☐ Workers' compensation due

19. Powers exercisable for your benefit other than those listed under real estate

☐ Right to receive, at some future time, cash, stock, or other personal property placed in an irrevocable trust

☐ Current payments of interest or principal from a trust

☐ General power of appointment over personal property

20. Interests you have because of another person's death

☐ Expected proceeds from a life insurance policy, if the insured has died

☐ Inheritance from an existing estate in probate (the owner has died and the court is overseeing the distribution of the property), even if the final amount is not yet known

☐ Inheritance under a will that is contingent upon one or more events occurring, but only if the will writer has died

☐ Property you are entitled to receive as a beneficiary of a living trust, if the trustor has died

21. All other contingent claims and claims where the amount owed you is not known, including tax refunds, counterclaims, and rights to setoff claims (claims you think you have against a person, government, or corporation but haven't yet sued on)

☐ Claims against a corporation, government entity, or individual

☐ Potential tax refund but return not yet filed

22. Patents, copyrights, and other intellectual property

☐ Copyrights

☐ Patents

☐ Trade secrets

☐ Trademarks

☐ Tradenames

23. Licenses, franchises, and other general intangibles

☐ Building permits

☐ Cooperative association holdings

☐ Exclusive licenses

Worksheet 3: Property Checklist (continued)

☐ Liquor licenses

☐ Nonexclusive licenses

☐ Patent licenses

☐ Professional licenses

24. Automobiles and other vehicles (not leased)

☐ Car

☐ Minibike or motorscooter

☐ Mobile or motor home if on wheels

☐ Motorcycle

☐ Off-road or all terrain vehicle

☐ Recreational vehicle (RV)

☐ Trailer

☐ Truck

☐ Van

25. Boats, motors, and accessories

☐ Boat (canoe, kayak, pontoon, rowboat, sailboat, shell, yacht, etc.)

☐ Boat radar, radio, or telephone

☐ Jet ski

☐ Navigation/GPS equipment

☐ Outboard motor

26. Aircraft and accessories

☐ Aircraft

☐ Aircraft radar, radio, GPS, and other accessories

27. Office equipment, furnishings, and supplies

☐ Artwork in your office

☐ Cell phones, PDAs

☐ Computers, software, modems, printers (for business use)

☐ Copier

☐ Fax machine

☐ Furniture

☐ Rugs

☐ Scanner

☐ Supplies

☐ Telephones

☐ Typewriters

28. Machinery, fixtures, equipment, and supplies used in business

☐ Military uniforms and accoutrements

☐ Tools of your trade

29. Business inventory

30. Livestock, poultry, and other animals

☐ Birds

☐ Cats

☐ Dogs

☐ Fish and aquarium equipment

☐ Horses

☐ Livestock and poultry

☐ Other pets

31. Crops—growing or harvested

32. Farming equipment and implements

33. Farm supplies, chemicals, and feed

34. Other personal property of any kind not already listed

☐ Church pew

☐ Country club or golf club membership

☐ Health aids (for example, wheelchair, crutches)

☐ Portable spa or hot tub

☐ Season tickets

	1	2	3	4	5	6
Worksheet 4: Property Exemptions						
Your property	**Value of property**	**Your ownership share (%, $)**	**Amount of liens**	**Amount of your equity**	**Exempt? If not, enter nonexempt amount**	
1. Real estate						
2. Cash on hand (state source of money)						
3. Deposits of money (indicate sources of money)						
4. Security deposits						
5. Household goods, supplies, and furnishings						

		Worksheet 4: Property Exemptions			
1	2	3	4	5	6
Your property	Value of property	Your ownership share (%, $)	Amount of liens	Amount of your equity	Exempt? If not, enter nonexempt amount
6. Books, pictures, art objects; stamp, coin, and other collections					
7. Apparel					
8. Jewelry					
9. Firearms, sports equipment, and other hobby equipment					
10. Interests in insurance policies					
11. Annuities					

Worksheet 4: Property Exemptions

1	2	3	4	5	6
Your property	Value of property	Your ownership share (%, $)	Amount of liens	Amount of your equity	Exempt? If not, enter nonexempt amount
12. Pension or profit-sharing plans					
13. Stocks and interests in incorporated and unincorporated companies					
14. Interests in partnerships					
15. Government and corporate bonds and other investment instruments					
16. Accounts receivable					

Worksheet 4: Property Exemptions					
1	2	3	4	5	6
Your property	Value of property	Your ownership share (%, $)	Amount of liens	Amount of your equity	Exempt? If not, enter nonexempt amount
17. Family support					
18. Other debts owed you where the amount owed is known and definite					
19. Powers exercisable for your benefit, other than those listed under real estate					
20. Interests you have because of another person's death					
21. All other contingent claims and claims where the amount owed you is not known					
22. Patents, copyrights, and other intellectual property					
23. Licenses, franchises, and other general intangibles					
24. Automobiles and other vehicles					

Worksheet 4: Property Exemptions					
1	**2**	**3**	**4**	**5**	**6**
Your property	**Value of property**	**Your ownership share (%, $)**	**Amount of liens**	**Amount of your equity**	**Exempt? If not, enter nonexempt amount**
25. Boats, motors, and accessories					
26. Aircraft and accessories					
27. Office equipment, furnishings, and supplies					
28. Machinery, fixtures, equipment, and supplies used in business					
29. Business inventory					

Worksheet 4: Property Exemptions

1	2	3	4	5	6
Your property	Value of property	Your ownership share (%, $)	Amount of liens	Amount of your equity	Exempt? If not, enter nonexempt amount
30. Livestock, poultry, and other animals					
31. Crops—growing or harvested					
32. Farming equipment and implements					
33. Farm supplies, chemicals, and feed					
34. Other personal property					
	Subtotal (column 6):				
	Wildcard Exemption			−	
	Total Value of NONEXEMPT Property				

Value Your Property

In Column 2 (again in Worksheet 4), enter a value for each item of property listed in Column 1. For your cash, deposits, publicly traded stock holdings, bonds, mutual funds, and annuities, enter the cash amount. For shares of stock in small business corporations, any ownership share in a partnership, business equipment, copyrights, patents, or other assets that may seem hard to sell, do your best to assign a reasonable dollar amount.

If you own an item jointly, put its entire value here. In Column 3, you'll enter your share.

Here are some suggestions for valuing specific items.

Real estate. If your interest is ownership of a house, get an estimate of its market value from a local real estate agent or appraiser. If you own another type of real estate—such as land used to grow crops—put the amount it would sell for.

If you don't know how to arrive at a value, or if you have an unusual asset such as a life estate (a current right to live in a house until you die) or a lease, leave this column blank.

Older goods. A local thrift store, used goods store, newspapers, want ads, and eBay are good places to look for prices.

Jewelry, antiques, and other collectibles. Any valuable jewelry or collection should be appraised.

Life insurance. Put the current net cash surrender value; call your insurance agent to find out that amount. Term life insurance has a cash surrender value of zero. Don't put the amount of benefits the policy will pay, unless you're the beneficiary of an insurance policy and the insured person has died.

Stocks, bonds, and so on. You can check the stock's current value by looking it up in a newspaper business section. If you can't find the listing, or the stock isn't traded publicly, call your broker and ask. If you have a brokerage account, use the value from your latest statement.

Cars. Start with the *Kelley Blue Book.* You can find this book at the public library or online at www.kbb.com. You can also find price information at www.nada.com. If the car needs substantial repairs, reduce the value by the amount it would cost you to fix the car.

Total Column 2 and enter the figure in the space provided.

Calculate Your Ownership Share

In Column 3, enter two amounts: the percentage of your separate ownership interest in the property and the dollar value of your ownership interest in the property.

If you own an item alone, your percentage is 100%. If you are married and own an item together, your ownership share depends on several factors, including the form of title (for example, joint tenancy or tenancy by the entirety) and the laws in the state where you live or where the property is located. Whether a collector or creditor can get property held by your spouse depends on the type of debt. For example, usually a creditor cannot take the separately owned property of one spouse to pay the separate debts of the other spouse. (See Chapter 3 for more on property rights and debt liability of married, divorced, or separated people.)

> **EXAMPLE:** Audrey and her brother jointly bought a music synthesizer currently worth $10,000. They still owe the music store $3,000, but that is not subtracted in this column. Audrey's ownership share is one-half, or $5,000.

List Liens

In Column 4, put the value of any legal claim (lien) against the property. For example, if you owe money on your house or car, the creditor probably has a security interest in that property. The property is collateral for the debt. Even if you own only part of the property, for example, and your spouse or partner owns a share, enter the full value of the lien. If you didn't sign a security agreement or the creditor has not put a lien on your property, there is no lien, even if you still owe money.

> **EXAMPLE:** Marian owns a house and owes her mortgage lender $135,000. Last winter Marian had a new roof put on her house. She was not satisfied with the roofer's work and therefore didn't pay him all of his bill. He recorded a mechanic's lien on her house for $5,000. Marian also owes the IRS $25,000, and so the IRS recorded a lien on her house. In Column 4, Marian enters the total of all her liens: $135,000 + $5,000 + $25,000 = $165,000.

Liens must be paid off before property can be transferred to a new owner—such as a creditor with a judgment against you or the bankruptcy trustee. If the value of the lien exceeds the property's value, you're probably in luck. The creditor or trustee won't want the property; once the lienholders are paid, there won't be anything for the creditor or trustee.

Include all of the following in Column 4:

- mortgages and home equity loans
- personal loans for which you pledged items of property that you already own as security for your repayment
- security agreements with a department store that specifically takes a security interest in items purchased
- motor vehicle loans
- liens held by contractors who worked on your house without getting paid what they claim you owe (mechanic's liens)
- liens placed by the IRS after you fail to pay a bill for past taxes, and
- judgment liens recorded against you by someone who won a lawsuit.

 TIP

If you plan to file for bankruptcy, ignore liens against your personal property when computing the property's value. If you owe money to a major consumer lender, or bought a large appliance with payments over time, the lender or seller may have taken a lien on some of your personal property. You can sometimes remove this lien if you choose to file bankruptcy. Similarly, you may have a lien against your personal property if a creditor has obtained a court judgment against you. These liens too can frequently be removed in bankruptcy.

Calculate Your Equity

Your equity is the amount you would get to keep if you sold the property. If you own the property alone, calculate your equity by subtracting the amount in Column 4 from the property's total value (in Column 2). Put the amount in Column 5. If you get a negative number, enter "0."

If you own the property with your spouse and the two of you are considering filing for bankruptcy, or you together owe a creditor, calculate your equity by subtracting the amount in Column 4 from the property's total value in Column 2. If you co-own the property with someone other than a spouse, use the following formula:

1. If the liens in Column 4 are from debts jointly incurred by you and the other owner of the property, figure the total equity (Column 2 less Column 4). Then multiply that number by your ownership share (the percentage you figured in Column 3). Enter this figure in Column 5.

EXAMPLE: Bill and Lee, brother and sister, inherited their parents' $150,000 house in equal proportions. Bill and Lee owe $100,000 on the house's mortgage. Bill owes money to several creditors and wants to figure out his equity in the house. It's $25,000—the total value of the house ($150,000) less what he and Lee owe on the mortgage ($100,000), multiplied by Bill's percentage share (50%). ($150,000 − $100,000 = $50,000; $50,000 x 50% = $25,000.)

2. If the liens in Column 4 are from debts incurred solely by you, then deduct the total amount of the lien from the figure in Column 2. Only your assets—not a co-owner's—will go to pay your secured creditors.

EXAMPLE: Now assume that Bill and Lee inherited the $150,000 house free and clear of any mortgage. Bill owes the IRS $30,000, however, and the IRS placed a lien for that amount on the property. Now Bill's equity is $45,000—the total value of the house ($150,000), multiplied by Bill's percentage share (50%), less the lien ($30,000). ($150,000 x 50% = $75,000; $75,000 − $30,000 = $45,000.)

Determine What Property Is Exempt

As explained above, each state has exemption laws that determine which items of property can't be taken away from people with debt problems and what amounts are protected.

The exemption list for each state is in Appendix B. Mark the page for your state's list in Appendix B, because you will be referring to that list as you fill out the worksheet.

TIP

Focus on the property you really want to keep. If you have a lot of property and get bogged down in exemption jargon and dollar signs, start with the property you would feel really bad about losing. Focus on finding exemptions for that. Later, if you like, you can search for exemptions that would let you keep property that is less important to you.

TIP

Err on the side of exemption. If you can think of a reason why a particular property item might be exempt, list it even if you aren't sure that the exemption applies. If you later decide to file for Chapter 7 bankruptcy, you will only be expected to do your best to fit the exemptions to your property. Of course, if you do misapply an exemption and the bankruptcy trustee files a formal objection within the required time, you may have to scramble to keep the property that you mistakenly thought was exempt.

Step 1: Figure Out Which Exemptions You Can Use

If you are looking at your exemptions only to figure out which property you can keep safe from judgment creditors, turn to the exemption list for the state where you live in Appendix B. (In California, use the System 1 exemptions.) Skip ahead to Step 2.

If you want to figure out which property you can keep if you file for bankruptcy, however, things are a bit more complicated. First, you will you will have to figure out which state's exemptions are available to you

under the new bankruptcy law. Then, if that state offers you a choice between the state's exemption list and the federal bankruptcy exemptions, you must decide which to use.

Domicile Requirements for Claiming Exemptions
Prior to the new bankruptcy law, filers used the exemptions of the state where they lived when they filed for bankruptcy. Under the new rules, however, some filers have to use the exemptions of the state where they *used* to live. Congress was concerned about people gaming the system by moving to states with generous exemptions just to file for bankruptcy. As a result, it passed "domicile" requirements that filers must meet before they can use a state's exemption system.

Where's Your Domicile?

To figure out which exemptions you can use, you need to know where your domicile is. As Congress defines it, your domicile is where you make your permanent home: the state where you vote, send your children to school, pay taxes, apply for your driver's license, register your car, receive your mail, and so on. This means something more than your residence, which generally means wherever you are living at any given time. Even if you reside in one state, your domicile may be elsewhere if you consider another state to be your true home. This might be the case if you must move temporarily for military service or to take a temporary position in another state: The state where you are staying temporarily is your residence, while the state to which you will return home is your domicile.

There are different domicile rules for personal property and for your home. If you own a home, these rules apply:

- If you bought your home at least 40 months before filing, use the exemptions of the state where your home is.
- If you bought your home at least two years before filing, use the exemptions of the state where your home is. However, if you bought your home within the last 40 months, your homestead exemption is capped at $136,875, unless you bought the home using the proceeds from the sale of another home in the state. (Of course, this cap won't affect you unless your state has quite a generous homestead exemption.)
- If you bought your home within the last two years, then you must use the exemptions of the state where you were domiciled for the better part of the 180-day period ending two years before your filing date—and you are still subject to the $136,875 cap.

EXAMPLE 1: Eighteen months ago, Sarah moved from Seattle to Boston, where she bought an apartment. Her apartment is now worth $300,000; Sarah owes $200,000 on her mortgage and there's a mechanic's lien against the apartment for $10,000, so her equity is $90,000. If Sarah files for bankruptcy, she cannot use the Massachusetts exemptions because she hasn't lived there for two years. And that's a shame: Massachusetts allows homeowners to exempt a whopping $500,000 worth of equity.

Because Sarah lived in Seattle for years before making the move, she will have to use the exemptions for Washington, which allow homeowners to exempt only $40,000 worth of equity.

EXAMPLE 2: Now let's assume that Sarah waited another year to file for bankruptcy. Her apartment is now worth $340,000, her mortgage is now $195,000, and the lien remains. Her equity is now $135,000. She has been domiciled in Massachusetts long enough to use its exemptions, but now she has to watch out for the cap: Because she didn't buy her apartment at least 40 months ago, her exemption—that would otherwise easily cover all of her equity—will be limited to $136,875.

These are the rules that apply to everything but a home:

- If you have been domiciled in your current state for at least two years, use that state's exemptions.
- If you have been domiciled in your current state for less than two years, you must use the exemptions of the state where you were domiciled for the better part of the 180-day period ending two years before your filing date.
- If the state where you will file for bankruptcy offers you a choice between the state and federal bankruptcy exemptions, you can choose the federal exemptions no matter how long you've been domiciled there. (You may

file for bankruptcy in a state only if you've lived there for at least 91 days).

- If these rules deprive you of the right to use any state's exemptions, you can use the federal exemptions. For example, some states allow their exemptions to be used only by current state residents, which might leave former residents who haven't lived in their new home state for at least two years without any available state exemptions.

Are the Federal Exemptions Available to You?

Now that you know which state's exemptions you can use, you'll need to figure out whether you have a choice between those exemptions and the federal bankruptcy exemptions. The states that offer this choice are Arizona, Connecticut, the District of Columbia, Hawaii, Massachusetts, Michigan, Minnesota, New Hampshire, New Jersey, New Mexico, Pennsylvania, Rhode Island, Texas, Vermont, Washington, and Wisconsin. You must choose either your state exemptions or the federal bankruptcy exemptions. You have to choose one set of exemptions or the other—you can't mix and match some state exemptions with some federal exemptions.

Locate these exemption lists from Appendix B:

- the federal bankruptcy exemptions (this list appears after all the states), and
- your state's exemptions plus the federal *nonbankruptcy* exemptions (also after all of the states).

If you live in California, compare the System 1 exemptions with the System 2

exemptions, and remember to apply the federal *nonbankruptcy* exemptions as well. (You don't have the option to use the federal bankruptcy exemptions in California.)

Compare the federal bankruptcy exemptions to your state exemptions (or compare the two California exemption systems) for large items, such as your home and car.

- **Your home.** If the equity in your home is your major asset, your choice may be dictated by the homestead exemption alone. Compare your state's homestead exemption to the federal $20,200 exemption (or $40,400 for married couples). In some states, the homestead exemption is more than $20,000, so you'll get greater protection in bankruptcy by using your state exemption. In other states, the homestead exemption is less than $10,000, and so the federal exemptions may offer greater protections in bankruptcy.

   In California, the homestead exemption in System 1 protects up to $150,000 in equity, while the System 2 list protects only $20,725. Most homeowners in California end up choosing System 1, for obvious reasons.

 WARNING

In many states, you must file a homestead declaration to claim the homestead in a bankruptcy. If the notes under "homestead" in your state's exemption list in Appendix B say you have to file a declaration with your county recorder to claim the homestead in bankruptcy, it can't hurt to file a homestead declaration for your (nonbankruptcy) judgment collection action.

- **Your valuable property.** If you don't own a home or the equity amount in your home isn't a factor in your decision, identify the most valuable items you own. Look at the federal bankruptcy exemptions and your state and the federal nonbankruptcy exemptions. Which lets you keep the most in bankruptcy?

- **Small items.** If you're still having trouble choosing, look for small differences. For example, federal bankruptcy exemptions limit most personal property exemptions to $475 per item, $9,850 total. Some states have no such limit. On the other hand, if you don't have a house, the federal bankruptcy system has a wildcard exemption of up to $10,225 allowing you to claim anything you want. If you do have a house and use the homestead exemption, the $10,225 is reduced by the amount of exemption that you use

Step 2: Figure Out Which Property Is Exempt

Go though each item on Worksheet 4 and see whether it fits in an exemption category. If an exemption has no dollar limit, apply it to all items that fit the description.

EXAMPLE: The exemption system you're using exempts "furnishings and house-

hold goods." You could argue that all of your household furniture, fixtures, appliances, kitchenware, and electronic equipment are exempt.

In evaluating whether or not your cash on hand and deposits of money are exempt, look to the source of the money, such as welfare benefits, disability benefits, insurance proceeds, or wages.

If you use your state exemptions—this includes all Californians—you may also select from a list of federal nonbankruptcy exemptions, listed at the end of Appendix B. These exemptions are mostly survivors' benefits and pensions for federal employees. Despite their name, you can use them both in bankruptcy and against judgment creditors. You can use both your state's and the federal nonbankruptcy exemptions, unless they're duplicative. If both your state and the federal nonbankruptcy exemptions allow you to exempt a certain amount in one category, such as 75% of unpaid wages, you cannot add them together; 75% is all you can claim.

Step 3: Double Your Exemptions If You're Married and State Law Allows It

If you are married and filing jointly, you can double all exemptions unless your state expressly prohibits it. Look in your state's listing in Appendix B to see whether or not doubling is allowed. If you're using the federal bankruptcy exemptions, you may double all exemptions. If your state's chart doesn't say doubling is prohibited, go ahead and double.

Step 4: Apply Any Available Wildcard Exemption

If the exemption system you are using has a wildcard exemption, apply it to property you couldn't otherwise exempt, such as property worth more than the exemption limit or an item that isn't exempt at all.

Step 5: Determine the Value of Nonexempt Property

If an item (or group of items) is exempt to an unlimited amount, put "0" in Column 6.

If an item (or group of items) is exempt to a certain amount (for example, household goods to $4,000), total up the value of all items that fall into the category using the values in Column 5. Subtract from the total the amount of the exemption. What is left is the nonexempt value. Enter that in Column 6.

> **EXAMPLE:** Jeremiah lives in Vermont, where the exemption amount for house-hold goods is $2,500. Jeremiah adds up the value of all his household goods listed in Column 5 of the Worksheet. The total is $4,000. To find the non-exempt amount, Jeremiah subtracts the exemption amount from the total value: $4,000 – $2,500 = $1,500. The nonexempt amount in this example is $1,500. Jeremiah enters this amount in Column 6 of the Worksheet on the line for Household goods.

If an item (or group of items) is not exempt at all, copy the amount from Column 5 to Column 6.

When you're done, total up Column 6. This is the value of your nonexempt property.

Step 6: Do It Again

Unless your choice of exemption lists is dictated by your home equity, you'll be best served by going through the Worksheet twice if another set of exemptions is available to you. The first time through, use your state's exemption (or System 1 in California). The second time, use the federal bankruptcy exemptions (or System 2 in California).

After you apply both exemption lists to your property, compare the results and decide which exemption list will do you the most good. You may find federal exemptions that don't exist in your state's exemption list or that are more generous than your state's exemptions. Or vice versa. You may be sorely tempted to pluck some exemptions out of one list and add them to the other list, but this isn't allowed. You'll have to use either your state's exemption list or the federal bankruptcy exemptions—you can't mix and match them.

> **EXAMPLE:** Paula rents a condo in Albuquerque, New Mexico. Other than clothing, household furniture, and personal effects, the only property Paula owns is a vintage 1967 Chevy Camaro Rally Sport. Paula often checks out local car magazines and knows that the model she owns typically sells for about $10,000, although this price varies by several thousand dollars based on the car's condition. Paula wants to know

what will happen to her car if she files for Chapter 7 bankruptcy.

Because Paula has lived in New Mexico for more than two years, she will use that state's exemption laws. Her first step is to locate the exemptions for New Mexico in Appendix B. At the bottom of the New Mexico exemption listings for personal property, Paula finds an entry for motor vehicles and sees that the exemption is $4,000. Paula begins to worry that she may lose her car, since it is worth more than double the exemption limit.

Paula's next step is to search the New Mexico state exemptions for a wildcard exemption. Paula discovers (at the bottom of the list) that she has a $2,500 wildcard exemption that she can apply to any property, including the Camaro. Add that to the $4,000 regular motor vehicle exemption, and Paula can now exempt $6,500. This amount still doesn't cover the Camaro's fair market value, which means the trustee would probably sell it, give Paula her $6,500 exemption, and distribute the rest of the sales proceeds ($3,500) to Paula's unsecured creditors.

Paula's next step is to see whether New Mexico allows debtors to use the federal bankruptcy exemptions. She looks at the top of the exemption page and sees a note that the federal bankruptcy exemptions are available in her state. She turns to the end of Appendix B (right after Wyoming) and finds the federal bankruptcy exemption

list. Under personal property she sees a listing for motor vehicles in the amount of $2,950. Oops. That's going in the wrong direction.

Paula next examines the federal bankruptcy exemptions to see whether they provide a wildcard exemption. She discovers that the federal bankruptcy exemptions let her use one half of the $18,450 homestead exemption as a wildcard. Because Paula has no home equity to protect, she can apply $9,225 worth of wildcard to the Camaro, in addition to the federal exemption for motor vehicles of $2,950. Paula also sees that she can get an additional wildcard exemption of $975 under the federal exemption system, just in case she has other nonexempt property.

Because Paula is most concerned about keeping her car, and because the federal bankruptcy exemptions let her keep her car while the state exemptions don't, Paula decides to use the federal bankruptcy exemption list.

Turning Nonexempt Property Into Exempt Property

If you have an asset that is not exempt, you may want to sell it before you file for bankruptcy or before a judgment creditor has a chance to grab it. But be careful: If you file for bankruptcy, and the court believes you converted your property to cheat your creditors, you could get in big trouble.

If a Creditor Has a Judgment Against You

Unless you file for bankruptcy, you remain indebted to your judgment creditors. This doesn't mean, however, that you must willingly turn over your property to your creditors, unless a court orders you to. Thus, you can convert your nonexempt property into exempt property, even if the judgment creditor is on your tail.

> **EXAMPLE:** Charlie, a carpenter, lives in Alaska. He has a savings account of $1,500. He also owes a judgment creditor $1,300. Charlie's bank account isn't exempt. But Alaska's tools of trade exemption is $3,360. Charlie closes his account and buys new carpenter's tools, fully protecting his $1,500 from his judgment creditor.

There is one big caveat to converting property. If you give away nonexempt property or sell it for less than it is worth, a creditor may claim that you were fraudulently trying to hide assets. Selling property to close friends and relatives is especially suspicious. The creditor can sue the recipient of the property and ask the court to order the recipient to turn the property over to the creditor. If this happens, you could be fined. And, to add insult to injury, your relative who bought the item from you could sue you for compensation.

If you plan on unloading—or have already unloaded—some nonexempt property, you probably should see a lawyer. (See Chapter 19.)

If You Plan to File for Bankruptcy

Converting nonexempt property into exempt property in contemplation of bankruptcy is more difficult, because bankruptcy rules prohibit some types of conversions, which are assumed to be fraud on your creditors. And, if the bankruptcy judge believes you acted fraudulently, you may be denied a bankruptcy discharge.

There are two ways to reduce your nonexempt property: You can replace nonexempt property with exempt property, or use your nonexempt property to pay debts.

Replace Nonexempt Property With Exempt Property

There are several ways to replace your nonexempt property holdings with exempt property. You can:

- Sell a nonexempt asset and use the proceeds to buy an asset that is completely exempt. For example, you can sell a nonexempt coin collection and purchase clothing, which in most states is exempt without regard to its value.
- Sell a nonexempt asset and use the proceeds to buy an asset that is exempt up to the amount received in the sale. For example, you can sell a nonexempt coin collection worth $1,200 and purchase a car that is exempt up to $1,200 in value.
- Sell an asset that is only partially exempt and use the proceeds to replace it with a similar asset of lesser

value. For example, if jewelry items are only exempt up to a value of $200 each, you could sell your $500 watch and buy one for $200, putting the remaining cash into other exempt assets such as clothing or appliances.

- Use cash (which isn't exempt in most states) to buy an exempt item, such as furniture or tools.

Pay Debts

If you choose to reduce your nonexempt property by using the money from the sale of your nonexempt property to pay debts, keep the following points in mind.

Don't pay off a debt that could be discharged in bankruptcy. Dischargeable debts such as credit card bills can almost always be completely discharged in bankruptcy. The main reasons to pay a dischargeable debt would be to:

- keep good relations with a valued creditor, such as a store that you rely on for necessities, or
- pay a debt for which a relative or friend is a cosigner, because the friend or relative will be stuck with paying the whole debt if you get it discharged.

In either case, if the payment is more than $600, you must wait at least 90 days—one year if the creditor is a friend, relative, or close business associate—after you pay that creditor before filing for bankruptcy. Otherwise, the payment is considered a "preference," and the trustee can set it aside and take back the money to give to your other creditors.

You can, however, pay regular monthly bills right up until bankruptcy. So keep paying monthly phone bills, utilities, rent, and mortgage payments.

Fraudulent Transactions in Anticipation of Bankruptcy

There's one major limitation on selling nonexempt property and using it to purchase exempt property before filing for bankruptcy. You can't do it to defraud your creditors. There are two main factors a judge looks at:

Your motive. The bankruptcy court may go along with your conversion if your primary motive is to buy property that will help you make a fresh start after bankruptcy. You probably can sell a second car and buy some tools needed in your business or clothing for your kids. But if you sell your second car and buy a diamond ring or new stereo system, a court might consider it a greedy attempt to cheat your creditors, even if the item is legally exempt. If the court thinks that you're trying to preserve the value of your nonexempt property for use after bankruptcy rather than acquiring property you really need, your efforts will probably fail.

The amount of property involved. If the amount of nonexempt property you get rid of before you file is enough to pay off a healthy portion of your debts, the court may dismiss your bankruptcy case.

If you make prebankruptcy conversions that the bankruptcy court questions, the burden will be on you to justify your actions. Here are important guidelines to keep in mind in making prebankruptcy conversions and then dealing with the court:

- **Be honest.** Accurately report all transactions in your bankruptcy forms. If the subject comes up with the trustee, freely admit that you arranged your property holdings so that you could get a better fresh start. If you attempt to cover up your actions, the court may consider it evidence of fraudulent intent.
- **Sell and buy for equivalent value.** If you sell a $500 nonexempt item and purchase an exempt item worth $100, the court will want to know where the other $400 went.
- **Sell property at reasonable prices.** When you sell nonexempt property to purchase exempt property, make the price as close to the item's market value as possible.

- **Don't make last-minute transfers or purchases.** The longer you can wait to file for bankruptcy after making these kinds of property transfers, the less likely the court will disapprove.
- **Don't merely change the way you hold title to property.** Merely changing the way property is held from a nonexempt form to an exempt form usually arouses suspicion. For example, if tenancy by the entirety property is exempt in your state, but you and your spouse hold your house in joint tenancy (not exempt), don't just change the title from joint tenancy to tenancy by the entirety.

Before engaging in any prebankruptcy transactions of this kind, you should consult with a bankruptcy lawyer.

■

Rebuilding Your Credit

Credit is like a looking-glass, which, once sullied by a breath, may be wiped clear again.

—Sir Walter Scott, Scottish poet and novelist, 1771-1832

If you've gone through a financial crisis—bankruptcy, repossession, fore-closure, history of late payments, or something similar—you may think that you'll never get credit again. Not true. Although a bankruptcy filing can be reported on your credit record for ten years, and other negative information can be reported for seven, in about two years you can probably rebuild your credit to the point that you won't be turned down for a major credit card or loan (assuming your financial troubles are behind you). Even in the limited situations in which negative information can be reported indefinitely, creditors will give less weight to old, negative information if you successfully rebuild your credit.

When reviewing a credit application from someone with poor credit, most creditors look for steady employment, a recent history of making and reliably paying for purchases on credit, and maintaining a checking and savings account since the financial setback. And many creditors disregard or downplay a bankruptcy discharge (often thought of as the most devastating of all financial setbacks) after about five years.

RESOURCES

Want more information on re-building your credit? This chapter provides a thorough overview of cleaning up your credit. For more detailed information, including 30 sample forms, see *Credit Repair,* by Robin Leonard and John Lamb (Nolo).

Avoid Overspending

Before you can start to rebuild your credit, you must understand where your money goes. With that information in hand, you can make intelligent choices about how to spend your money. If you'd rather not create a budget yourself, you can contact a nonprofit debt counseling agency. These organizations primarily help debtors negotiate with creditors, but they can also help you set up a budget for free or a nominal fee. (See Chapter 19 for more information on finding a reliable debt counselor.)

Figure Out Where Your Money Goes

Before you put yourself on a budget that limits how much you spend, take some time to figure out exactly how much money you spend now. To do this, make at least four copies of Worksheet 5: Daily Expenses, below, and fill them out for a month. Write down every cent you spend—50¢ for the paper, $5 for your morning coffee and muffin, $10 for lunch, $5 for the bridge or tunnel toll, and so on. Be sure to include the money you lay out maybe only once a month, such as $50 for your child's swim class, $10 for an office party gift, or a $20 donation to a local charity.

Be sure to also include monthly payments such as your rent or mortgage; educational

Worksheet 5
Daily Expenses for the Week of

Sunday's Expenses	Cost	Monday's Expenses	Cost
Daily Total		**Daily Total**	

Tuesday's Expenses	Cost	Wednesday's Expenses	Cost
Daily Total		**Daily Total**	

Worksheet 5 (continued)
Daily Expenses for the Week of [   ]

Thursday's Expenses	Cost	Friday's Expenses	Cost
Daily Total		**Daily Total**	

Saturday's Expenses	Cost	Other Expenses	Cost
Daily Total		**Daily Total**	

loans; credit card payments; car payments; insurance payments; utility; telephone and cell phones; Internet; and cable bills; and other similar expenses.

Be tough-minded—if you omit any money, your picture of how much you spend, and your budget, will be inaccurate.

At the end of the 30 days, review Worksheet 5. Are you surprised at the dollar total or at the number of items you purchased? Are you impulsively spending your money, or do you tend to consistently spend it on the same types of things?

Make a Spending Plan

After you've kept track of your expenses for a month, you're ready to create a spending plan, or budget. Your twin goals in making a spending plan are to control your impulses to overspend and to help you start saving money—an essential part of rebuilding your credit.

To make and use a monthly budget, follow these steps:

1. Make several copies of Worksheet 6: Monthly Budget. Making a budget you can live with is a process of trial and error, and you may have to draft a few plans before you get it right.

2. Get out Worksheet 1: Monthly Income (from Chapter 2) and Worksheet 5: Daily Expenses.

3. Review the expenses listed on Worksheet 6. As you'll see, they are divided into common categories, such as home expenses, food, and transportation. If you don't have any expenses in a

particular category, you can cross it out, delete it on your computer, or simply leave it blank. If you have a type of expense that isn't listed on the form, add that category to a blank line.

4. In the first column (labeled "Projected"), list your average actual monthly expenses in each category. Calculate these amounts by adding together your actual expenses for the month you tracked. If you have seasonal, annual, or quarterly expenses, include a monthly amount for those as well. For example, if you pay $3,600 in property taxes each year, you should list a projected expense of $300 a month ($3,600 divided by 12) in this category.

5. Add up all of your projected monthly expenses and enter the total on the line marked "Total Expenses" at the bottom of the "Projected" column.

6. Enter your projected monthly income (from Worksheet 2) below your projected total expenses.

7. Compare your projected income to your projected expenses. If you are spending more than you earn, you'll either have to earn more or spend less to make ends meet. Unless you're anticipating a big raise, planning to take on a second job, or selling valuable assets, you'll probably have to lower your expenses. Review each category to look for ways to cut costs. Rather than trying to cut out an entire expense, look for expenses you can reduce slightly without depriving yourself of items or services you really need. For example, you might be

Worksheet 6: Monthly Budget

Expense Category	Projected				
Home					
Rent/Mortgage					
Property Tax					
Insurance					
Homeowners' Assn. Dues					
Telephone					
Gas & Electric					
Water & Sewer					
Cable					
Garbage & Recycling					
Household Supplies					
Housewares					
Furniture & Appliances					
Cleaning					
Yard/Pool Care					
Repairs & Maintenance					
Food					
Groceries					
Breakfast Out					
Lunch Out					
Dinner Out					
Coffee & Tea					
Snacks					
Clothing					
Clothes, Shoes, & Accessories					
Laundry, Dry Cleaning					
Mending					
Self Care					
Toiletries/Cosmetics					
Haircuts					
Massage					
Gym Membership					
Total Expenses Page 1					

Expense Category	Projected				
Worksheet 6: Monthly Budget (continued)					
Donations					
Health Care					
Insurance					
Medications					
Vitamins					
Doctor					
Dentist					
Eye Care					
Therapy					
Transportation					
Car Payments (buy or lease)					
Insurance					
Registration					
Gas					
Maintenance & Repairs					
Parking					
Tolls					
Public Transit					
Parking Tickets					
Road Service (such as AAA)					
Entertainment					
Music					
Movies & Rentals					
Concerts, Theater, Ballet, etc.					
Museums					
Sporting Events					
Hobbies & Lessons					
Club Dues or Membership					
Film & Developing Costs					
Books, Magazines, & Newspapers					
Software & Games					
Total Expenses Page 2					

Worksheet 6: Monthly Budget (continued)

Expense Category	Projected				
Dependent Care					
Child Care					
Clothing					
Allowance					
School Expenses					
Toys & Entertainment					
Pets					
Food & Supplies					
Veterinarian					
Grooming					
Education					
Tuition					
Loan Payments					
Books & Supplies					
Travel					
Gifts & Cards					
Personal Business					
Supplies					
Copying					
Postage					
Bank & Credit Card Fees					
Legal Fees					
Accountant					
Taxes					
Insurance					
Savings & Investments					
Other					
Total Expenses Page 3					
Total Expenses Page 1					
Total Expenses Page 2					
Total Expenses					

willing to forgo one trip to a restaurant per month, subscribe to a less expensive cable package, or spend less on clothing.

8. Return to your budget and enter the adjustments you came up with. When you're finished, add up these new figures and come up with a new total expense amount. If it's less than your income, your budget is complete. If not, go back and try to find other places to cut back.

9. Label the remaining columns with the months of the year. Unless you wrote your budget on the first of the month, start with next month. During the course of the month, use a pencil (or computer) to write down and update your expenses in each category.

10. At the end of the month, total up how much you spent. How did you do? Are you close to your projected figures? If not, go back and try to make some changes to keep the numbers in balance.

Check your figures periodically to help you keep track of how you're doing. Don't think of your budget as etched in stone. If you do, and you spend more on an item than you've budgeted, you'll only find yourself frustrated. Use your budget as a guide. If you constantly overspend in one area, don't berate yourself: Instead, change the projected amount for that category and find another place to cut. Keep in mind that a budget is just a tool to help you recognize what you can afford and where your money is going.

Prevent Future Financial Problems

There are no magic rules that will solve everyone's financial troubles. But the following suggestions should help you stay out of financial hot water. If you have a family, everyone will have to participate—no one person can do all the work alone. So make sure your spouse or partner and children understand that the family is having financial difficulties and agree together to take the steps that will lead to recovery.

- **Create a realistic budget and stick to it.** This means periodically checking it and readjusting your figures and spending habits.

- **Eat at home.** It is much cheaper and often healthier to cook using fresh or dried ingredients like potatoes, beans and rice, pasta, fruits, and vegetables. To save time, cook enough at one time for two meals.

- **Don't impulse buy.** When you see something you hadn't planned to buy, don't purchase it on the spot. Go home and think it over. It's unlikely you'll return to the store and buy it.

- **Avoid sales.** Buying a $500 item on sale for $400 isn't a $100 savings if you didn't need the item to begin with. It's spending $400 unnecessarily.

- **Get medical insurance if at all possible.** Even a stopgap policy with a large deductible can help if a medical crisis comes up. You can't avoid medical emergencies, but living without medical insurance is an invitation to financial ruin.

- **Charge items only if you can afford to pay for them now.** If you don't currently have the cash, don't charge based on future income—sometimes future income doesn't materialize. If you must charge, a good rule of thumb is not to charge anything that won't exist when the statement arrives (such as meals, groceries, or movie tickets).
- **Commit to living without credit for a while.** Studies by Visa show that on average credit customers spend 20% to 30% more than cash customers at quick service restaurants—and that doesn't include the cost of the cards. Using cash only can be a relatively painless way to cut spending. (See Chapter 10 for information on which credit card accounts to close and how to properly close them.)
- **Avoid large rent or house payments.** Obligate yourself only for what you can now afford, and increase your mortgage payments only as your income increases. If you are married and both working, keep the payments low enough that you can handle them even if one of you loses your job. Consider refinancing your house if your payments are unwieldy. (See Chapter 6 for information on avoiding rip-offs when refinancing.)
- **Avoid cosigning or guaranteeing a loan for someone.** Your signature obligates you as if you were the primary borrower. You can't be sure that the other person will pay.

- **Avoid joint obligations with people who have questionable spending habits**— even a spouse or partner. If you incur a joint debt, you're probably liable for it all if the other person defaults.
- **Don't make high-risk investments.** Opt for certificates of deposit, money market funds, and government bonds over speculative real estate, penny stocks, and junk bonds.

For more suggestions on cutting expenses, see Chapter 7.

Are You a Compulsive Spender?

Habitual overspending can be just as hard to overcome as excessive gambling or drinking. If you think you may be a compulsive spender, one of the worst things you can do is rebuild your credit. Instead, you need to get a handle on your spending habits.

Debtors Anonymous, a 12-step support program similar to Alcoholics Anonymous, has programs nationwide. If a Debtors Anonymous group or a therapist recommends that you stay out of the credit system for a while, follow that advice. Even if you don't feel you're a compulsive spender, paying as you spend may still be the way to go—because of finance charges, transaction fees, and other charges, buying on credit costs between 15% and 20% more than paying with cash.

Debtors Anonymous groups meet all over the country. For local meetings and other information visit www.debtorsanonymous.org, or call them at 781-453-2743.

Clean Up Your Credit Report

If you have serious debt problems, you are probably concerned about what's in your credit report. There's no question that your credit rating will suffer if you don't pay your bills. Bankruptcies, repossessions, foreclosures, lawsuits to collect debt, and even missed or late payments get into credit reports. Potential creditors see the negative information and often use it to deny you a loan or credit card or to charge you a higher rate of interest if they do grant you credit.

To understand the credit world and how to rebuild your credit, you need to know how credit is established and how credit information is used.

Establishing credit involves taking steps to make sure that when you apply for a loan or credit card, or even for an apartment or job, the lender, landlord, or employer will find favorable information on you when he or she runs a credit check. A credit check is a search of information found in a computer file assembled and maintained by a credit bureau. If the information indicates that you are a good risk—that you'll probably pay the loan (or your rent) on time or will be a reliable employee—you have "good credit." If it shows that you have a history of paying bills late or not at all, you have "bad credit."

Today, your credit score often determines whether a creditor thinks you have "good" or "bad" credit. A credit score is a numerical summary of a person's credit worthiness based on information from credit bureaus. Credit scores may range from 300 to 850, with higher numbers meaning that a person

is a better "credit risk." (For more on credit scores see Chapter 11.)

If the prospective lender, landlord, or employer finds no credit report, he or she cannot assess your creditworthiness one way or the other. A lender may hesitate to lend you money or to let you open up a credit card account. Similarly, without a credit history, a landlord may decide against renting to you. An employer, too, may conclude that a 35-year-old applicant doesn't have a stable life if the employer finds no credit report.

Many of us first established credit in our late teens or early twenties when we accepted a gasoline or local department store preapproved credit card after high school graduation. Or, perhaps we were lured by the credit card companies that set up shop on our college's campus and offered all kinds of perks for signing up. With many of these first credit cards, our parents were guarantors—meaning if we missed the payments, they would foot the bill.

Others may have waited until buying a first car or getting a first job. And anyone who financed a college education with student loans established a credit history the day he or she made (or missed) the first loan payment.

A few of us believe we've never taken steps to establish credit. We have no credit cards and pay cash for everything. But, as stated above, we don't establish credit just by taking out a loan or buying items with a credit card. Often, by applying for a job, apartment, or insurance policy, we start down the road to establishing credit. Employers, landlords, and insurance companies often request copies of credit information from credit bureaus. For this reason, nearly every adult in the United States has a credit report.

Credit Bureaus and Credit Reports

Credit bureaus are private, for-profit companies that gather and sell information about a person's credit history. Credit bureaus sell credit information about consumers to banks, mortgage lenders, credit unions, credit card companies, department stores, insurance companies, landlords, and employers. They in turn use the credit information to supplement applications for credit, insurance, housing, and employment.

If the bureau has no information on you, it has nothing to sell. Thus, credit bureaus are always searching for more information.

There are three major credit bureaus: Equifax (www.equifax.com), Experian (www.experian.com), and TransUnion (www.transunion.com). Recently a fourth, Inovis, joined the scene (www.inovis.com). The major bureaus have credit files on more than 150 million Americans and generate more than a billion credit reports each year.

Credit bureaus get most of their data from creditors such as department stores, mortgage lenders, banks, and credit card issuers. Credit bureaus also search court records, looking for lawsuits, judgments, and bankruptcy filings. And they go through county records offices to find recorded tax, judgment, or mechanic's liens or other liens (legal claims).

Data gathered in a credit file usually includes your name (and any former names), past and present addresses, Social Security number, employment history, lawsuits to which you are a party, outstanding child support payments, and liens (legal claims on your property). If you've been through bankruptcy, it will show up in your credit report.

The bulk of information in a credit report is your credit history—positive and negative. Each entry typically contains the name of the creditor, the type of account (such as revolving credit line, student loan, mortgage), your account number (or partial account number), when the account was opened, your credit limit or the original amount of the loan, whether anyone else is obligated on the account, your current balance, and your payment pattern for the previous 24–36 months (whether you pay on time or have been 30, 60, 90, or 120 days past due). The report will show if any accounts have been turned over to a collection agency, if you are disputing a charge, or if you've wiped out the debt in bankruptcy.

> **EXAMPLE:** Martin visits Cars for Less and finds a used Porsche for $20,000. Martin plans to put one-third down and to use the dealer's financing for the rest. Although Martin brought $6,000 cash, Cars for Less wants to be sure that he can make payments of about $300 per month on the balance.
>
> The finance manager at Cars for Less checks Martin's credit with the

credit bureau it uses. She submits his name, address, and Social Security number using the dealer's computer link. Martin's credit report shows that he makes his credit card and mortgage payments on time but owes $250 in back property taxes. The computer reports that Martin's credit score is 680. The finance manger decides that this score and Martin's 33% down payment qualify him for a low-interest-rate loan on the Porsche.

Laws Regulating Credit Bureaus

Credit bureaus are regulated by the Federal Trade Commission under the provisions of the federal Fair Credit Reporting Act (FCRA) (15 U.S.C. §§ 1681 and following) and by state law.

The Fair Credit Reporting Act

The FCRA was passed in 1970 to address consumers' concerns about the proliferation of credit bureaus and the accuracy of information in credit reports. The law is designed to bar inaccurate or obsolete information from credit reports. Amendments to the FCRA have addressed the accuracy of information in credit reports and problems caused by identity theft. The Act requires credit bureaus to adopt reasonable procedures for gathering, maintaining, and distributing information and sets accuracy standards for creditors that provide information to bureaus.

The FCRA also regulates who can look at your credit report and how long negative information can be reported. In general, only people or businesses with a "permissible purpose" can access your credit report. The most common are:

- **Creditors.** Creditors can look at your report whenever you apply for credit or for a loan.
- **Employers.** Employers can look at your report, but only under certain circumstances and only if you give them written authorization.
- **Government agencies.** Government agencies can request your report to determine whether you are eligible for a license or public assistance. State and local government officials can also get reports to help determine whether you can make child support payments.
- **Insurance companies.** Insurance companies can review your credit report in connection with underwriting insurance.
- **Judgment creditors.** Judgment creditors are allowed to look at credit reports in order to decide whether to begin collection efforts.
- **Landlords and mortgage lenders.** These people and businesses are also allowed to review your report.
- **Utility companies.** Utilities can request your credit report. However, in many circumstances, utility companies cannot deny you service due to bad credit.

The FCRA also regulates the type of information that can be reported, how consumers can get copies of their reports, and how long information can appear on your credit report. (These rules are explained below.)

RESOURCES

More on credit repair and credit bureaus. *Credit Repair*, by Robin Leonard and John Lamb (Nolo), is a complete guide to rebuilding your credit. Among other things, it discusses in detail the credit reporting system, how to read your credit report, and the laws regulating credit bureaus. In addition, it provides all the plain-English instructions and forms you need to clean up your credit report and build good credit.

State Credit Bureau Laws

All states have laws governing credit reporting agencies. The FCRA preempts a great many state law requirements and prohibitions. To find out if your state's law provides more protections to consumers than the federal law does, contact your state's consumer protection office. (See Appendix A for contact information for state consumer protection offices.)

Get a Free Copy of Your Credit Report

The FCRA requires each major credit bureau—Equifax, Experian, and Trans Union—to provide a free copy of your credit report once every 12 months.

There are three routes for requesting your free credit report:

- Internet—www.annualcreditreport.com
- Telephone—877-322-8228
- Mail—Annual Credit Report Service, P.O. Box 105281, Atlanta, GA 30348-5281 (you can find a request form at www.ftc.gov/bcp/conline/include/requestformfinal.pdf).

Beware of Imposter Sites

The three major credit bureaus have set up one central website, toll-free number, and mailing address for ordering free credit reports (listed above). The only authorized website is www.annualcreditreport.com.

Other websites have similar names and advertise that they offer free credit reports, but beware. The free report often comes with strings attached, such as a service that you have to pay for when the introductory period ends, and some sites collect personal information. Don't respond to an email or click on a pop-up ad claiming it's from annualcreditreport.com: The official annualcreditreport.com website will never send you an email solicitation for your free report, use pop-up ads, or call you to ask for personal information.

Some imposter sites have names confusingly similar to annualcreditreport.com. The best way to get to the authorized website is through the Federal Trade Commission's website, www.ftc.gov.

Once you have provided the required information to annualcreditreport.com, you will be directed to the three major credit bureaus' individual websites. They may offer to sell you additional services (credit monitoring products, for example) but you are not required to purchase them to receive your free report.

Three at Once or One at a Time?

The FCRA allows you to get a free credit report from each agency every 12 months. You can choose to check all three at once, or to request one at a time during the course of a year. There are arguments in favor of either approach. By reviewing all of three reports at once, you'll have a complete picture of your credit at that point; different creditors report to different credit bureaus, so the information in each of your reports may differ. On the other hand, ordering one at a time gives you an opportunity to monitor your credit over the course of the year. To use that system, every four months you can ask the Annual Credit Report Service (www.annualcreditreport.com) for a different company's report.

You must provide your name, address, Social Security number, and date of birth when you order. If you moved in the last two years, you may also have to provide your previous address. To confirm your identity, you may also be required to provide information that only you would know. So, be prepared to answer questions about your previous address or the amount of your monthly mortgage payment. As a security measure, you can instruct the bureaus not to show your entire Social Security number on the copy of the report they send you.

Online results can be immediate; reports requested by phone or mail can take up to 15 days to process. The credit bureaus are allowed to take longer if they need more information to confirm your identity.

You are also entitled to a free copy of your credit report if any of the following is true:

- You've been denied credit because of information in your credit report. You are entitled to a free copy of your report from the bureau that reported the information, but even if you request it from a different bureau, that bureau will probably provide you with a copy. A creditor that denies you credit in this situation will tell you the name and address of the credit bureau reporting the information that led to the denial. You must request your copy within 60 days of being denied credit.

- You are unemployed and planning to apply for a job within 60 days following your request for your credit report. You must enclose a statement swearing that this is true. It might also help to include a copy of a recent unemployment check, layoff notice, or similar document verifying your unemployment. You are entitled to one free report in any 12-month period.

- You receive public assistance. Enclose a statement swearing that this is true and a copy of your most recent public assistance check as verification. You are entitled to one free report in any 12-month period.

- You are a victim of identity theft or fraud or think that you may be. The FCRA gives consumers the right to request free credit reports in connection with fraud alerts.

- If you suspect in good faith that you are, or may be, a victim of identity theft or another fraud, you can instruct the major bureaus to add a "fraud alert" to your file. You can request a free copy of your report from each bureau once it places the fraud alert in your file.
- If you *are* a victim of identity theft, you can send the major bureaus an identity theft report and instruct them to add an extended fraud alert to your file. You can request two free copies of your credit report from each bureau during the next 12 months once it places the extended fraud alert in your file. (See "If Someone Steals a Credit Card or Your Identity," below.)

To request your credit report based on any of these circumstances, contact one or more of the credit bureaus.

If you've been denied credit, it's important to check your credit report to see what the problem is. For example, you may find inaccurate information that you should dispute or forgotten debts that you can take care of. It's also important to check your credit report if you're worried about identity theft.

If you don't qualify for a free report, you'll have to pay a fee of $10, unless you're in a state that has lowered the fee. Expect to receive your report in a week to ten days.

TIP

Don't buy the hype. The credit bureaus will attempt to sell you things that you do not need and attempt to charge you for things you can get for free. For example, you can probably do without the "credit monitoring" service. And they'll offer credit reports from all three bureaus (a "three-bureau" or "3-in-1" report for "only" $30 or $40). This is a bad deal: You can get a free copy from each bureau every 12 months.

Credit Scores for a Fee

You can obtain your credit score from credit bureaus that develop or distribute them, by paying $8–$15 (they'll probably try to sell you additional products also, such as credit monitoring services, but you don't have to buy them). The bureau must provide your score, the range of possible scores under the scoring model used, four key factors that affected the score, the date on which the score was created, and the name of the entity that provided the score (such as Fair, Isaac Corporation). Be aware, however, that the score and scoring model that you receive may be different from those used by your lender. (See Chapter 11 for more on credit scores.)

If you apply for a loan on residential property, the mortgage lender must disclose your credit score, the related information just described, and a notice with contact information for the credit bureaus that provided credit scores. Lenders that evaluate loan applications using automated systems must disclose the system's score and the key factors that affected the score.

In California, if you apply to an auto dealer for a loan or lease on a vehicle and the dealer obtains your credit score, the dealer must give you your score, a notice containing the range of possible scores, and contact information for the credit bureau that provided the score.

You can buy your credit score from Fair, Isaac for a fee of $15.95. To get your Fair, Isaac credit score, visit www.myfico.com.

Credit Bureaus' Contact Information

Equifax
P.O. Box 740241
Atlanta, GA 30374
800-685-1111
www.equifax.com

Experian
www.experian.com

TransUnion
877-322-8228
www.transunion.com

Review the Contents of Your Credit Report

A credit bureau will give you the data in your report, the sources of the data, and the names of people who requested copies of your report—called inquiries—within the last two years.

Review your report carefully. One of the biggest problems with credit reports is that they contain incorrect or out-of-date information. According to a recent investigation by the U.S. Public Interest Research Group, more than 70% of the credit reports examined contained an error.

Sometimes credit bureaus confuse names, addresses, Social Security numbers, or employers. If you have a common name, say John Brown, your report may contain information on other John Browns, John Brownes, or Jon Browns. Or it may erroneously contain information on family members with similar names.

Ironically, concern over identity theft (see "If Someone Steals a Credit Card or Your Identity," below) contributes to mistakes in credit reports. Businesses now ask consumers for the minimum of identifying information when they open accounts. The unintended consequence of not putting a full Social Security number or a date of birth next to a reported consumer transaction or delinquency is that it's easier than ever for a credit bureau to confuse one consumer for another. It's also common for bureaus to fail to note accounts in which delinquencies have been remedied.

Because consumers are generally not told when information is placed in their reports, they usually discover errors only when they are denied credit and then request a copy of their credit report. The consequences of such errors can be serious. Each year, people are wrongfully denied mortgages, student loans, car loans, insurance policies, employment, or a place to live because of credit bureau mistakes. Or, if they are granted credit, it may be at a higher interest rate than if the information in their report were accurate. It can be a bureaucratic nightmare to try to clear up the report—extending by months, or even years, the time it takes to get a loan. Cautious consumers can avoid some of these problems by checking their credit reports annually, or at least before applying for credit.

As you read through your credit report, make a list of everything that is incomplete, inaccurate, too old, or improperly included in your report. In particular, look for the following:

- incorrect or incomplete name, address, phone number, Social Security number, marital status, or birthdate
- incorrect, missing, or outdated employment information
- bankruptcies that are more than ten years old or not identified by the specific chapter of the bankruptcy code
- credit inquiries that are more than two years old
- credit inquiries by automobile dealers when you simply test drove a car or from other businesses when you were only comparison shopping (these creditors cannot lawfully pull your credit report without your permission until you indicate a desire to enter into a sale or lease)
- credit accounts that are not yours
- lawsuits you were not involved in
- incorrect account histories—look especially for late payments when you've paid on time
- a missing notation when you disputed a charge on a credit card bill (some agencies require you to file a written statement of dispute)
- a collection agency listed separately from the original creditor, making it

appear that you are delinquent on more than one debt
- closed accounts incorrectly listed as open—it may look as if you have too much open credit, and
- any account you closed that doesn't have a "closed by consumer" notation; if it's not there, you'll want it added, otherwise it looks like the creditor closed the account.

Other common snafus include:

- commingled accounts—credit histories for someone with a similar or the same name
- premarital debts of your current spouse attributed to you
- voluntary surrender of your vehicle listed as a repossession
- paid tax, judgment, mechanic's, or other liens listed as unpaid
- accounts that incorrectly list you as a cosigner, and
- paid accounts listed as unpaid.

If credit bureaus report information about medical providers, it must not identify the provider or disclose your medical condition.

You should also review your credit report for out-of-date information. Credit bureaus are prohibited from reporting certain kinds of negative information after certain periods of time. Here are the basic rules:

- Bankruptcies can be reported for no more than ten years from the date of the last activity. The date of the last activity for most bankruptcies is the date you receive your discharge or the date your case is dismissed.
- Lawsuits and judgments may be reported from the date of the entry of

judgment against you for up to seven years or until the governing statute of limitations has expired, whichever is longer.

- Paid tax liens may be reported from the date of the last payment activity for up to seven years.
- Most criminal records, such as information about indictments or arrests, may be reported for only seven years. But records of criminal convictions may be reported indefinitely. (Experian's website states that it does not collect or report criminal record information. The same appears to be true for Equifax and TransUnion, but their websites don't say so specifically.)
- Accounts sent for collection, accounts charged off, or any other similar action may be reported from the date of the last activity on the account for up to seven years. The date of last activity is no later than 180 days from the last delinquency. Creditors must include the date of the delinquency when they report past due accounts to credit bureaus. The clock does not start ticking again if the account is sold to another collection agency.
- Overdue child support may be reported for seven years.
- Some adverse information regarding U.S. government-insured or -guaranteed student loans, or national direct student loans, may be reported for more than seven years.
- Bankruptcies, lawsuits, paid tax liens, accounts sent out for collection,

criminal records, overdue child support, and any other adverse information may be reported beyond the usual time limits if you apply for $150,000 or more of credit or life insurance, or if you apply for a job with an annual income of at least $75,000. However, as a practical matter, credit bureaus usually delete all items after seven or ten years.

- Positive information may be reported indefinitely.

Obtaining Medical Information

The Medical Insurance Bureau (MIB) is a nationwide "specialty" consumer reporting agency that maintains records on medical conditions of approximately 20% of consumers. Members of MIB send it information on significant medical conditions as part of their underwriting process for life, health, disability, or long-term care insurance. Members may check the information in a consumer's application for insurance against information provided by MIB.

You can get a free copy of your MIB record once each year by calling 866-692-6901 (TTY 866-346-3642). You will be required to provide identification information, which MIB may validate. You may dispute inaccurate information in your record by writing MIB, Inc., P.O. Box 105, Essex Station, Boston, MA 02112. General information on MIB is available at www.mib.com.

If Someone Steals a Credit Card or Your Identity

If you discover that someone has stolen a credit card or, worse, your identity, you should take immediate action. Identity theft is a growing national epidemic. The Federal Trade Commission calls identity theft the fastest-growing crime in the nation, with nearly ten million victims each year, costing businesses $52 billion, and costing consumers nearly $5 billion. The FTC has some helpful information on identity theft at www.ftc.gov; click "Fighting Back Against Identity Theft."

If you believe that someone has stolen your identity, file a police report immediately with your local police department or the police department where the theft occurred. Get plenty of copies of the report; you will need to send copies to credit bureaus, creditors, collectors, banks, and the like.

Report the theft to any of the three nation-wide credit bureaus. The one you contact will automatically share the fraud alert with the other credit bureaus. All three should send you free copies of your credit report, so you can check for inaccurate information due to fraud. Check each report carefully when you receive it. Look for accounts that you didn't apply for or open, inquiries that you didn't initiate, and defaults and delinquencies that you didn't cause. Also, check your identifying information carefully, especially your Social Security number, address(es), name or initials, and employers.

Request that each credit bureau block the reporting of identity theft-related fraudulent information in your report. You must send the bureau proof of your identity and an identity theft report (an official report you have filed with a federal, state, or local law enforcement agency, and additional information the bureau may require). You must identify the fraudulent information and include a statement that the information does not relate to any transaction by you. The bureau normally must block reporting of the information and must inform the creditor that provided the information that it has been blocked. The creditor cannot then sell, transfer, or place the debt for collection. (This is one practical reason to check your credit report and request the blocking of identity-theft-related information as soon as you learn that you may be the victim of identity theft.)

Request that one of the fraud alerts described here be placed in your file.

Initial alert. You can request an initial alert if you are a victim of identity theft or other fraud or think that you may become a victim. You must submit appropriate proof of identity, which may include your Social Security number. The credit bureau receiving the alert must notify the other nationwide bureaus, and each must place an alert in your file for 90 days. The alert states that you do not authorize an additional card on an existing account, an increase in the credit limit of an existing account, or new credit (other than an extension of credit on an existing credit card account). The alert may delay your ability to get credit. Each bureau also must provide the alert each time it generates your credit score. You can get one free copy of your credit report from each bureau when you place an alert.

Extended alert. If you *are* a victim of identity theft, you can send the credit bureau an identity theft report and request that it place an extended alert in your file. An identity theft report is an official report you have filed with a federal, state, or local law enforcement agency, and additional information the bureau may require. You must include appropriate proof of identity, which may include your Social Security number.

The extended alert is similar to the initial alert, but it remains in place for seven years and you can get two free copies of your credit report from each bureau during the next 12 months. In addition, for five years, each bureau must exclude you from lists that it prepares for creditors or insurers with offers of credit or insurance that you did not request (so-called "prescreened offers").

Active duty alert. If you are on active military duty, you can add an active duty alert to your file at a nationwide credit bureau. You must submit appropriate proof of identity, which may include your Social Security number. The active duty alert is similar to the other alerts, but it remains in place for 12 months, the exclusion from prescreened lists lasts for two years, and you are not entitled to a free credit report.

Creditor's duty when alert is in place. A creditor or other user of a credit report containing one of these alerts must take extra steps to verify the identity of the person requesting credit before it proceeds with the transaction. In the case of an extended alert, you may include a telephone number that the creditor must call to confirm that the request for credit is not the result of identity theft.

If someone steals your identity, you should take additional steps to clean up the mess. For example, contact the Social Security Administration to see if your Social Security number has been used fraudulently. If someone got a job using your number, you'd notice earnings for jobs you've never held listed on your Social Security Earnings and Benefit Statement. You should receive your earnings statement automatically each year if you have worked and are 25 or older. Or, you can get a copy of your earnings report by calling 800-772-1213 (or by visiting the SSA's website at www.ssa.gov).

Credit Bureau Fraud Departments

Call the toll-free fraud number of any of the three credit bureaus to place a fraud alert in your credit report. The bureau you call is required to contact the other two bureaus, which will also place alerts in their versions of your report. If you do not receive a confirmation from a bureau, contact it directly to place a fraud alert.

- **Experian:** 888-EXPERIAN (397-3742); www.experian.com; P.O. Box 9532, Allen, TX 75013
- **Equifax:** 800-525-6285; www.equifax.com; P.O. Box 740241, Atlanta, GA 30374-0241
- **TransUnion:** 800-680-7289; www.transunion.com; Fraud Victim Assistance Division, P.O. Box 6790, Fullerton, CA 92834-6790.

You should also contact any creditors that have reported the fraudulent information on your credit report. Ask to speak with someone in the security or fraud department. Ask them to close any accounts you did not open, and to remove any charges you did not incur. Ask them to provide corrected information to the credit bureaus. You may have to send them a copy of your police report or the FTC's identity theft affidavit (below), or fill out the company's own fraud report. Send a confirming letter and ask that the company send you a letter stating that the accounts have been closed, the fraudulent charges removed, and the corrected information sent to the credit bureaus.

Notify your bank if checks were stolen, and close your account. Immediately close any accounts that have been tampered with, and open new ones with new personal identification (PIN) numbers and passwords. When choosing a password, don't use one based on easily available information such as your mother's maiden name or your birth date.

To find out more about identity theft, call the Federal Trade Commission's Identity Theft Hotline at 877-438-4338 or 866-653-4261 (TTY), or go to www.ftc. gov and click the "Avoid ID Theft" button. The FTC has useful information on identity theft, especially "About Identity Theft" and "Take Charge: Fighting Back Against Identity Theft." The FTC also has developed an identity theft affidavit, which some creditors accept when you claim that you aren't responsible for a new account or for transactions on an existing account.

The State of California's Office of Privacy Protection (www.privacy.ca.gov) has good general information on identity theft, plus California-specific information. You can also get information from www.identitytheft.org or www.privacyrights.org.

Dispute Incomplete and Inaccurate Information in Your Credit Report

Once you've compiled a list of all incomplete, inaccurate, or out-of-date information you want changed or removed, fill in the form provided to dispute items in your report. That form either came with your report or is available online. You can submit the form electronically but, if you will submit documents, it's a better idea to submit it by mail.

List each incorrect item and explain exactly what is wrong. Also, enclose copies of documents that support your claim. You should also send a copy to the creditor who furnished the incorrect or incomplete information to the credit bureau. These "furnishing" creditors have a duty to correct and update the information they send to credit bureaus, if they determine it is incomplete or inaccurate. Be sure to keep a photocopy of your request for reinvestigation and letter to the furnishing creditor. Requesting a reinvestigation won't cost you anything.

Once the credit bureau receives your letter, it must reinvestigate the matter and get back in touch with you within 30 days (45 days if you send the bureau additional relevant information during the 30-day period). These requirements are not hard for a credit bureau to meet. Credit bureaus and 6,000 of the nation's creditors are linked by computer, which speeds up the verification process. Furthermore, if you let a credit bureau know that you're trying to obtain a mortgage or car loan, they can often do a "rush" verification.

The bureau is not required to investigate any dispute that it determines is frivolous or irrelevant because, for example, you don't provide enough information to allow the bureau to investigate the dispute. The bureau must notify you of its decision, including the reasons behind it, within five business days after making it.

You might be concerned that if information is incomplete or incorrect with one credit bureau, it will be wrong with the others. That may be the case, which is one reason you should get copies of your files from all three bureaus if you find errors in one credit report.

If you don't hear from the bureau by the 30- or 45-day deadline, send a follow-up letter, and send a copy to the Federal Trade Commission, the agency that oversees credit bureaus. Again, keep a copy for your records.

If the credit bureau cannot verify the information, or agrees that the information is inaccurate or incomplete, the bureau must modify the information or remove it from your file. The bureau also must inform the furnishing creditor that the information has been modified or deleted. Credit bureaus will sometimes remove an item on request without an investigation if rechecking the item is more bother than it's worth.

Security Freezes

In some states, you can instruct the credit bureau to place a "security freeze" or "file freeze" in your credit file. A security freeze is a notice in your file that prohibits the credit bureau from releasing your credit report or information in it without your consent. You can "unfreeze" your file for a period of time or to allow a specific creditor to access your file.

Security freezes currently are available in California, Colorado, Connecticut, Delaware, Florida, Hawaii, Illinois, Kansas, Kentucky, Louisiana, Maine, Minnesota, Nevada, New Hampshire, New Jersey, New York, North Carolina, Oklahoma, Rhode Island, South Dakota, Texas, Utah, Vermont, Washington, and Wisconsin. Security freezes are different than the initial, extended, and military alerts that the Fair Credit Reporting Act now makes available (see "If Someone Steals a Credit Card or Your Identity," below).

You should carefully consider the pros and cons of a security freeze. Consumer advocates favor them if you are worried about identity theft, while the credit bureaus favor their own credit monitoring services. As a practical matter, having a security freeze can delay your own applications for credit, and removing a freeze can be cumbersome.

EXAMPLE: Jim's credit file with Credit Gatherers reporting agency shows that he has not paid a $275 bill from Acrelong Drug Store. But Jim has never done business with Acrelong.

Credit Gatherers contacts Acrelong for verification. Acrelong has no information showing that Jim owes $275 and cannot verify the debt. Credit Gatherers removes the information from Jim's file.

Credit bureaus must do much more than simply contact the creditor reporting the information to verify its accuracy. A credit bureau must:

- complete its investigation within 30 days of receiving your complaint (45 days if you send the bureau additional relevant information during the 30-day period)
- contact the creditor reporting the incorrect information within five business days of receiving your complaint
- review all relevant information supplied by you
- remove all inaccurate, incomplete, or unverifiable information; or modify it, as appropriate, based on the results of the reinvestigation
- promptly notify the creditor that furnished the information that it has been modified or deleted
- adopt procedures to keep the information from reappearing
- reinsert removed information only if the provider of the information certifies its accuracy and the credit bureau notifies you in writing within five business days of the reinsertion, and
- provide you with the results of its reinvestigation, including a new credit report, within five business days of completion.

If you receive favorable action from a credit bureau, you should take the following steps:

- find out whether other credit bureaus' files contain the same error and, if so, send the results of the investigation to those agencies as well, and
- get a copy of your report three to six months later to make sure that the credit bureau has not reinserted the information.

You can ask the bureau to notify past users of your report that inaccurate or unverifiable information has been deleted from it. The bureau must notify users whom you specify who received your report for employment purposes within the past two years, and other users who received your report within the past six months.

If the credit bureau responds that the information you dispute is accurate and will remain in your report, you will have to take more aggressive action. Start by contacting the creditor that is reporting the information and demand that it be removed. Write to the customer service department, vice president of marketing, and president or CEO. If the information was reported by a collection agency, send the agency a copy of your letter, too. Under the Fair Credit Reporting Act, the creditor must do the following:

- not ignore information they know contradicts what they have on file
- not report incorrect information when they learn that the information is incorrect

- provide credit bureaus with correct information when they learn that they are reporting incorrect information.
- notify credit bureaus when you dispute information
- note when accounts are "closed by the consumer"
- provide credit bureaus with the month and year of the delinquency of all accounts placed for collection, charged off, or similarly treated, and
- finish their investigation of your dispute within the 30-day or 45-day periods the credit bureau has to complete its investigation.

If the creditor cannot or will not assist you in removing the incorrect or incomplete information from your file, you will have to contact the credit bureau for additional help.

If all else fails, consider calling your congressional representative or senator. That person can call an official at the Federal Trade Commission, the federal agency that regulates credit bureaus, and demand action. (See Appendix A.)

Consider Adding a Brief Statement to Your Credit File

If the credit bureau's investigation doesn't resolve the dispute to your satisfaction, you have the right to file a brief statement describing the nature of the dispute. The bureau must include your statement, or a summary or codification of it, in any report that includes the disputed information. If the reporting agency helps you write the summary, it will be limited to 100 words.

Otherwise, there is no word limit, but it is a good idea to keep the statement very brief.

The credit bureau is only required to provide a summary or coded version of your statement (not your actual statement) to anyone who requests your file. If your statement is short, the credit bureau is more likely to pass on your statement, unedited. If your statement is long, the credit bureau will probably condense your explanation to just a few sentences or codes. To avoid this problem, keep your statement clear and as short as possible.

If you request it, the bureau must also give the statement or summary to anyone who received a copy of your file within the past six months—or two years if your file was given out for employment purposes. This service is free if you request it within 30 days after the bureau has notified you of the results of the investigation. Otherwise, you will have to pay the same amount as the bureau would normally charge for a credit report (up to $10).

Credit bureaus are only required to include a statement in your file if you are disputing the completeness or accuracy of a particular item. The bureau does not have to include a statement if you are only explaining extenuating circumstances or other reasons why you haven't been able to pay your debts. If the bureau does allow you to add such a statement, it can charge you a fee.

Don't assume that adding a brief statement is the best approach. It's often wiser to simply explain the negative mark to subsequent creditors in person than to try to explain it in such a short statement.

Many statements or summaries are simply ineffective. Few creditors who receive credit reports read them, and credit scoring programs may ignore your statement. In any David (consumer) vs. Goliath (credit bureau) dispute, creditors tend to believe Goliath.

Sample Statements

Here are a few examples of statements describing disputes:

- A credit report includes a lawsuit filed by a roofing company for failure to pay for its work. The information is accurate, but the consumer didn't pay because the work was done incorrectly. The consumer might add a statement to the file reading, "Defective workmanship, refuse to pay until fixed."
- A credit report indicates that a consumer is unemployed, but the consumer has in fact worked as an independent contractor during that time. The consumer might send a statement reading, "I work as a freelance technical writer, averaging $50,000 annually."
- A credit report states that the consumer owes a debt to an electronics store. The consumer bought a CD player that doesn't work, and the store refused to take it back or provide a refund. The consumer might submit this statement, "Merchandise is defective, and the store refuses to provide a refund or replacement."

Complaints About a Credit Bureau

If a credit bureau employee violates the law, you can complain to the Federal Trade Commission. (See Appendix A.) For the best result, complain using the complaint form at www.ftc.gov. Include the name of the credit bureau, its address and phone number, the name of the employee you dealt with, the nature of the problem, and the dates of your contact with the credit bureau. Identify documents that support your position. Be sure to print a copy for yourself and send another copy to the credit bureau.

In many states, you should also complain to the state agency that regulates illegal or unethical conduct by businesses (such as your state Attorney General or consumer protection agency). If the credit bureau is associated with a collection agency, complain to the FTC and your state agency that regulates collection agencies. For addresses of state consumer protection agencies, see Appendix A.

If you were seriously harmed by the credit bureau—for example, it continued to give out false information after you requested corrections—you may be able to sue. The FCRA lets you sue a credit bureau for negligent or willful noncompliance with the law within two years after you discover the violation (but no more than five years after the violation occurred). You can sue for actual damages, for example, lost wages, and if you win, you can recover attorneys' fees and court costs. In the case of truly outrageous behavior, you can recover punitive damages—damages meant to punish for malicious or willful conduct.

You will need to use (or at least consult) a lawyer if you want to pursue this type of lawsuit (See Chapter 19.)

Add Positive Account Histories to Your Credit Report

Often, credit reports don't include accounts that you might expect to find. Some creditors don't report the status of accounts to credit bureaus. Others report only infrequently. If your credit file is missing credit histories for accounts you pay on time, send the credit bureaus a copy of a recent account statement and copies of canceled checks (never originals) showing your payment history. Ask the credit bureaus to add the information to your file. Although credit bureaus aren't required to do so, they often will, although they may charge a fee.

Add Information Showing Stability to Your Credit Report

Your credit history isn't the only thing lenders consider in deciding whether to extend credit. They also want to see stability in your life. If any of the items listed below are missing from your file, consider sending a letter to the credit bureaus asking that the information be added.

- **Your current employment**—employer's name and address, and your job title. You may wisely decide not to add this if you think a creditor may sue you or a creditor has a judgment against you. Current employment information

may be a green light for a wage garnishment.

- **Your previous employment,** especially if you've had your current job less than two years. Include your former employer's name and address and your job title.
- **Your current residence,** and if you own it, say so. Not all mortgage lenders report their accounts to credit bureaus. Again, don't do this if you've been sued or you think a creditor may sue you. Real estate is an excellent collection source.
- **Your previous residence,** especially if you've lived at your current address less than two years.
- **Your telephone number,** especially if it's unlisted. If you haven't yet given the credit bureaus your phone number, consider doing so now. A creditor who cannot verify a telephone number is often reluctant to grant credit.
- **Your date of birth.** A creditor will probably not grant you credit if it does not know your age. However, creditors cannot discriminate based on age. (See Chapter 18.)
- **Your Social Security number.** The credit bureaus use this number to help distinguish between people with similar names.

Credit bureaus aren't required to add any of this information, but they often do. They are most likely to add information on jobs and residences, as that information is used by creditors in evaluating applications for credit. They will also add your telephone number, date of birth, and Social Security number, because those items help identify you and lessen the chances of "mixed" credit files—that is, getting other people's credit histories in your file.

Enclose photocopies (never originals) of any documentation that verifies information you're providing, such as your driver's license, a canceled check, a bill addressed to you, a pay stub showing your employer's name and address, or anything else similar. Remember to keep photocopies of all letters you send.

 CROSS-REFERENCE

Advice about credit, from the folks who keep score. Refer to "Tips for Raising Your Credit Score," in Chapter 11.

Build Credit in Your Own Name

If you are married, separated, or divorced, and most of the credit you have is in your spouse's or ex-spouse's name only, you should start to get credit in your name, too.

Getting credit in your own name is also an excellent strategy for repairing your credit if:

- all or more of your financial problems can be attributed to your spouse, or
- you and your spouse have gone through financial difficulties together, but most of your credit was in your spouse's name only.

To understand how this works, you first must learn about which of your spouse's accounts can appear on your report. Here are the rules:

- Credit bureaus must include information about your spouse's account on your credit report in two situations: (1) you and your spouse have a joint account (that is, you both can use it), or (2) you are obligated (responsible for paying) on an account belonging to your spouse, even if your spouse is the primary signor or obligor on the account.
- Credit bureaus cannot include information about your spouse's account on your credit report if the account is not joint or you are not responsible for paying the account.

This is usually good news if you are worried that your spouse's negative credit history may reflect badly on you—delinquent accounts in your spouse's name only should not appear on your credit report. However, if you are not divorced or separated and most loans and credit cards were in your spouse's name only, you won't have a lengthy history of good credit in your report. You now need to start building good credit in your own name. If you are still married, you can start by making sure that all joint accounts and accounts that you are obligated to pay appear on your credit report, too. Then, follow the steps outlined in the rest of this chapter to improve your credit.

Ask Creditors to Consider Your Spouse's Credit History

A credit bureau can include information about your spouse's positive credit accounts on your credit report only if the account meets one of the following two criteria listed above. If you are applying for a loan, credit card, or other type of credit, however, you can always ask the creditor to consider any of your spouse's accounts that reflect favorably on your creditworthiness, too. For example, if you and your spouse make payments on your spouse's account with joint checks, bring this to the creditor's attention. A creditor doesn't have to consider this information, but it may.

Use Existing or New Credit Cards

If your financial problems are behind you and you managed to hold onto one of your credit or charge cards, use it and pay your bills on time. Your credit history will improve quickly. Most credit reports show payment histories for 24–36 months. If you charge something every month, no matter how small, and pay every month, your credit report will show steady and proper use of revolving credit.

> ### WARNING
>
> **Charge only a small amount each month and pay it in full.** By paying in full, you will avoid interest charges (assuming your card has a grace period). To emphasize the cost of paying only the minimum required, here's an example from California Civil Code § 1748.13(a): At 17% interest, if you just pay the 2% minimum on a $1,000 balance, it will take you over 17 years and over $2,500 to pay off the debt.

Applying for Credit Cards

The best way to develop a positive credit history is to obtain credit and make timely payments. But, don't try to do this while you are steeped in financial trouble. You'll be more likely to get credit from a subprime predatory lender (see "Mortgages for People With Poor Credit" in Chapter 11) and be in danger of getting into deeper debt. Getting a new credit card before you're on your feet may send you down the same path that got you into trouble in the first place.

However, if you are ready to start using credit again, go ahead and apply for a credit card. It's often easiest to obtain a card from a department store or gasoline company. They'll usually open your account with a very low credit line. If you start with one credit card, charge items, and pay the bill on time, other companies will issue you cards. When you use department store and gasoline cards, try not to carry a balance from one month to the next. The interest rate on these cards is very high.

Next, apply for a regular bank credit card, such as a Visa card, MasterCard, American Express card, or Discover card. Competition for new customers is fierce among card issuers, and you may be able to find a card with relatively low initial rates. Depending on how bad your credit history is, however, you may qualify only for a low credit line or a card with a high interest rate and high annual fee. If you use the card and make your payments, however, after a year or so you can apply for an increase in your line of credit and possibly a reduction in your interest rate or annual fee.

The following tips will help you when you apply for credit cards or an increased credit limit.

Be consistent with the name you use. Either use your middle initial always or never. Always use your generation (Jr., Sr., II, III, and so on).

Take advantage of preapproved gasoline, department store, and bank credit cards. If your credit is shot, you may not have the luxury of shopping around.

Be honest, but appear sympathetic. On applications, paint a picture of yourself in the best light. Lenders are especially apt to give less weight to past credit problems that were out of your control, such as a job layoff, illness or death in the family, recent divorce, or new child support obligation. Don't emphasize that you forgot to write checks because you were too busy or on an extended vacation.

Apply for credit when you are most likely to get it. For example, apply when you are working, when you've lived at the same address for at least a year, and when you haven't had an unusually high number of inquiries on your credit report in the last two years. A lot of inquiries is a sign that you are either desperate for credit or preparing to commit fraud.

Apply for credit from creditors with whom you've done business. For example, your phone company or insurance company may offer Visa or MasterCards to their customers. If you have a good relation with your bank, it may offer you a Visa or MasterCard.

Don't get swept up by credit card gimmicks. Before applying for a credit card that gives you rebates, credit for future purchases, or other "benefits," make sure you will benefit by the offer. Some are good deals, especially if you like to travel and can get a card that helps you build up frequent flyer miles. But in general, a card with no annual fee and low interest usually beats the cards with deals.

Look carefully at preapproval solicitations for nonbank cards. A gold or platinum card with a high credit limit (as much as $10,000) may be nothing more than a card that lets you purchase items through catalogues provided by the company itself. No other merchant accepts these cards, and the company won't report your charges and payments to the credit bureaus. You usually have to pay a fee for the card and then another one for the catalogue. And the items in the catalogues are usually high-priced and of poor quality.

Once you receive a credit card, protect yourself and your efforts to repair your credit by following these suggestions.

Send your creditors a change of address when you move. Many creditors provide change of address boxes on their monthly bills. For your other creditors, you can send a letter, call the customer service phone number, or use a post office change of address postcard. Don't let your monthly statements go to your old address. You may miss making payments on time, or someone may steal your statement and use your identifying information to gain access to your account or obtain credit in your name.

If you need an increase in your credit limit, ask for it. Many creditors will close accounts or charge late fees on customers who exceed their credit limits. Pay close attention; if you're charging to the limit on your credit card, you may be heading for financial trouble.

Take steps to protect your cards. Sign your cards as soon as they arrive. If you have a personal identification number (PIN) that allows you to take cash advances, keep the number in your head; never write it down near your credit card. Make a list of your credit card issuers, the account numbers, and the issuer's phone numbers so you can quickly call if you need to report a lost or stolen card. Keep this list in a safe place at home.

Don't give your credit card or checking account number to anyone over the phone, unless you placed the call and are certain of the company's reputation. Never, never, never give your credit card or checking account number to someone who calls you and tries to sell you something or claims to need your account number to send you a "prize." Never give your credit card number, checking account number, or personal information to a caller who claims to represent a company you do business with and wants to "confirm" or "update" your account information. The same is true for Internet inquiries like this. *These are all scams.*

For more on credit cards, see Chapter 10.

Cosigners and Guarantors

A cosigner is someone who promises to repay a loan or credit card charges if the primary debtor defaults. Similarly, a guarantor promises to pay if the primary debtor does not. Usually, neither the cosigner's nor the guarantor's name appears on the credit account.

Must a Cosigner Live Nearby?

If you apply for credit with a cosigner from out of state, the lender may balk. There is no law to prohibit out-of-state cosigners, but lenders have their own policies about whom they'll accept to cosign a loan.

The lender is concerned that if the primary borrower defaults, the lender will have to run all over the country to collect from the cosigner. To address that concern, you can promise to inform the lender of any changes in the cosigner's address. If the lender is still reluctant, consider asking your cosigner to offer to submit to the jurisdiction of the lender's state. This means that—if you later default on the loan and the lender wants to go after your cosigner—the lender can sue locally instead of wherever the cosigner lives. If the lender won't accept that offer, look for a different lender or a local cosigner. Again, be sure that the cosigner understands the obligation he or she is taking on. (See "Notice to Cosigner" in Chapter 11.) This is especially important if the cosigner is consenting to jurisdiction in another state, where it will be difficult (and quite inconvenient) to defend a collection lawsuit if you default

---

Although getting a cosigner or guarantor will help you get credit, it may not help you build credit in all situations. On some cosigned accounts, the creditor will report the information on the cosigner's credit report only. For this reason, ask the creditor if you can use a guarantor instead of a cosigner. It should make no difference to the creditor.

Cosigners and guarantors must understand their obligations before signing on. If you don't pay the debt, or you erase it in bankruptcy, the cosigner or guarantor remains fully liable. See Chapter 11 for more information.

Secured Credit Cards

Many people with poor credit histories are denied regular credit cards. If your application is rejected, consider whether you truly need a credit card. Millions of people get along just fine without them. If you decide that you really need a card—for example, to reserve hotel rooms and rent cars—then you can apply for a secured credit card. With a secured credit card, you deposit money into a savings account. The bank freezes the account while you have the card. If you fail to pay your credit card debts, the bank can use the money in your account to cover your charges. Usually the secured card issue will give you a credit limit equal to 100% of your deposit. But some will give you less. Depending on the bank, you'll be required to deposit as little as $100 or as much as a few thousand.

Unfortunately, secured credit cards can be expensive. Many banks charge hefty application and processing fees in addition to an annual fee. Also, the interest rate on secured credit cards is often between 20% and 30%, while you earn only 2% or 3% (or less) on the money you deposit. And some banks have eliminated the grace period— that is, interest on your balance begins to

accrue on the date you charge, not 25 days later. (If you find a card with a grace period and pay your bill in full each month, you can avoid the interest charges.) Another problem with secured credit cards is that some creditors don't accept or give much weight to credit history established with a secured credit card.

Before you sign up for a card, ask the card issuer if it reports to the three major credit bureaus. If the issuer doesn't, you've lost an important benefit of having a secured card. Some smaller issuers don't report to the credit bureaus, but most major banks do.

Try to get a secured credit card with a conversion option. This lets you convert the card into a regular credit card after several months or a year, if you use the secured card responsibly. And a regular credit card typically has a lower interest rate and annual fees than a secured card.

Use the secured credit card to make smallish purchases that you can pay off each month. Always pay on time. This will help you build your credit. After you pay on time for a year, you may be able to qualify for an unsecured credit card with a lower interest rate.

Avoid 900-number advertisements for "instant credit" or other come-ons. Obtaining a secured credit card through one of these programs will probably cost you a lot—in application fees, processing fees, and phone charges. Sometimes you call one 900 number and are told you must call a second or third number. These ads also frequently mislead consumers into thinking their line of credit will be higher than it is. If you have to deposit $5,000 to get a card, your credit line may only be $2,500 to $4,000 (50% to 80%). Also, be aware of secured credit cards that can be used only to purchase merchandise from the card issuer's catalogue. The merchandise often is shoddy and high-priced, and the issuer probably won't report your charges and payments to the credit bureaus. Credit cards like that cannot help you.

Don't Carry Too Many Credit Cards

Once you succeed in getting a credit card, you might be hungry to apply for many more cards. Not so fast. Having too much credit may have contributed to your debt problems in the first place. Ideally, you should carry one bank credit card, maybe one department store card, and one gasoline card. Your inclination may be to charge everything on your bank card and not bother using a department store or gasoline card. When creditors look in your credit file, however, they want to see that you can handle more than one credit account at a time. You don't need to build up interest charges on these cards, but use them and pay the bill in full each month.

Creditors frown on applicants who have a lot of open credit. So keeping many cards may mean that you'll be turned down for other credit—perhaps credit you really need. And if your credit applications are turned down, your file will contain inquiries from the companies that rejected you. Your credit file will look like you were desperately trying to get credit—something creditors never like to see.

Shop around before getting a secured card. You may be able to get a less-expensive, unsecured card just as easily. Even if you've had credit problems or filed for bankruptcy, you may still get lots of offers for unsecured cards in the mail, often with much better terms than secured cards.

WARNING

Don't get a card secured by your home. Some secured credit cards require that you put your home up as collateral. If you default, your home is in jeopardy. Don't get one of these cards.

RESOURCES

To find a secured credit card. For lists of banks issuing secured credit cards, including their rates and terms, do some research on the Internet. Websites such as www.bankrate.com and www.cardweb.com provide a wealth of information about available secured credit cards.

Open Deposit Accounts

Creditors look for bank accounts as a sign of stability. Quite frankly, they also look for bank accounts as a source of how you will pay your bills. If you fill out a credit application and cannot provide a checking account number, you probably won't be given credit.

A savings or money market account, too, will improve your standing with creditors. Even if you never deposit additional money into the account, creditors assume that people who have savings or money market accounts use them. Having an account reassures creditors of two things: You are making an effort to build up savings, and if you don't pay your bill and the creditor must sue you to collect, it has a source from which to collect its judgment.

Just because you've had poor credit history, you shouldn't be denied an account. You might be denied an account, however, if you have a bad check-writing history. Check verification companies (such as ChexSystems) keep track of banks' experiences with their customers, much as credit bureaus do for creditors. Most banks will check your check-writing history with a check verification company before they will open an account for you. If you are denied a bank account because of information provided by a check verification company, call the company to discuss the problem and try to provide information that resolves it. If there is incomplete or inaccurate information in the company's files, you can dispute it, just as you can with a credit bureau.

If you open a checking account, be very careful not to bounce the checks you write. A federal law called "Check 21" allows banks to process electronic images of checks instead of the paper originals. One result is that checks clear much faster than most of us are used to, increasing the risk that they will bounce. It's therefore more important than ever not to write a check unless the funds are already in the account to cover it. (For more information on Check 21, go to www.consumersunion.org/finance/ckclear1002.htm.)

If you bounce a check to a creditor, it most likely will report a late or missed

payment to a credit bureau, jeopardizing your hard work repairing your credit. A history of bounced checks also may make it harder to open bank accounts in the future.

Shop around and compare fees, such as check-writing fees, ATM fees, teller transaction fees, monthly service charges, the minimum balance to waive the monthly charge (many banks waive the minimum if you have your paycheck or other income directly deposited into the account), and the interest rates on savings. To learn more about ATM and other bank fees, visit the following websites: www.uspirg.org (U.S. Public Interest Research Group), www.consumersunion.org (Consumers Union), www.consumer-action.org (Consumer Action), and www.ftc.gov (Federal Trade Commission).

Work With Local Merchants

Another way to rebuild your credit is to approach a local merchant (such as a jewelry or furniture store) and arrange to purchase an item on credit. Many local stores will work with you in setting up a payment schedule, but be prepared to put down a deposit of up to 30% or to pay a high rate of interest. If you still don't qualify, the merchant might agree to give you credit if you get someone to cosign or guarantee the loan (see "Cosigners and Guarantors," above). Or, you may be able to get credit at the store later, by first buying an item on layaway.

When you purchase an item on layaway, the seller keeps the merchandise until you fully pay for it. Only then are you entitled to pick it up. One advantage of layaway is that you don't pay interest. One disadvantage is that it may be months before you actually get the item. This might be fine if you're buying a dress for your cousin's wedding that is eight months away. It isn't so fine if your mattress is so shot that you wake up with a backache every morning.

Layaway purchases are not reported to credit bureaus. If you purchase an item on layaway and make all the payments on time, however, the store may be willing to issue you a store credit card or store credit privileges.

Obtain a Bank Loan

One way to rebuild your credit is to take some money you've saved and open a savings account. Then, ask the bank to give you a loan against the money in your account. In exchange, you have no access to your money—you give your passbook to the bank and the bank won't give you an ATM card for the account—so there's no risk to the bank if you fail to make the payments. If the bank doesn't offer these loans, called passbook loans, apply for a personal loan and offer either to get a cosigner or to secure it against some collateral you own (*not your house*).

No matter what type of loan you get, be sure you know the following:

- **Does the bank report these loan payments to credit bureaus?** This is key; the whole reason you take out the loan is to rebuild your credit. If the bank doesn't report your payments to a credit bureau, there's no reason to take out a loan.

- **What is the minimum deposit amount for a passbook loan?** Some banks won't give you a loan unless you have $3,000 in an account; others will lend you money on $50. Find a bank that fits your budget.

- **What is the interest rate?** The interest rate on the loan is usually much higher than what people with good credit pay. Yes, this means you'll lose a little money on the transaction, but it can be worth it if you're determined to rebuild your credit.

- **What is the maximum amount you can borrow?** On passbook loans, banks won't lend you 100% of what's in your account; most will lend you between 80% and 90%.

- **What is the repayment schedule?** Banks usually give you one to three years to repay the loan. Some banks have no minimum monthly repayment amount on passbook loans; you could pay nothing for nearly the entire loan period and then pay the entire balance in the last month.

 TIP

Take some time to repay the loan. Even if you could pay back the loan in only one or two payments, don't. Pay it off over at least 12 months so that monthly installment payments appear in your credit file. Also, it's extremely important not to miss a loan payment. If you do, the bank will report the late or missed payment to a credit bureau, and you will have set back your efforts to repair your credit.

Avoid Credit Repair Clinics

You've probably seen ads for companies that claim they can fix your credit, qualify you for a loan, or get you a credit card. Their pitches are tempting, especially if your credit is bad and you desperately want to buy a car or house.

Don't be tempted by the ads. Many of these companies' practices are fraudulent, deceptive, and even illegal. Some have been caught stealing the credit files or Social Security numbers of people who are under 18, have died, or live in out-of-the-way places like Guam or the U.S. Virgin Islands, and substituting these for the files of people with poor credit histories.

Other credit clinics hack into computers in an attempt to change or erase bad credit reports. Still others suggest that you create a new credit identity by applying for a nine-digit employer identification number and using it in place of your Social Security number. These schemes are just the beginning. Credit repair clinics devise new illegal methods just as soon as consumer protection agencies catch onto their old ones.

Even assuming that a credit repair company is legitimate, don't listen to its come-ons. These companies can't do anything for you that you can't do yourself or with the help of a nonprofit debt counselor (see Chapter 19). What they will do, however, is charge you between $250 and $5,000 for their unnecessary services.

Here's what credit repair clinics claim to be able to do for you.

Remove incorrect information from your credit file. You can do that yourself under the Fair Credit Reporting Act.

Remove correct, but negative, information from your credit file. Negative items in your credit report can legally stay there for seven or ten years, as long as they are correct. No one can wave a wand and make them go away. One tactic of credit repair services is to try to take advantage of the law requiring credit bureaus to verify information if the customer disputes it. Credit repair clinics do this by challenging every item in a credit report—negative, positive, or neutral—with the hope of overwhelming the credit bureau into removing information without verifying it. Credit bureaus are aware of this tactic and often dismiss these challenges on the ground that they are frivolous, a right credit bureaus have under the Fair Credit Reporting Act. You are better off reviewing your report and selectively challenging the outdated, incorrect, or incomplete items.

Even if a credit bureau removes information that it had the right to include in your file, it's only a temporary removal. Most correct information reappears after 30–60 days when the creditor that first reported the information to the credit bureaus reports it again.

Get outstanding debt balances and court judgments removed from your credit file. Credit repair clinics often advise debtors to pay outstanding debts if the creditor agrees to remove the negative information from your credit file. This is certainly a negotiation tactic you want to consider, but you don't need a credit repair clinic for this advice.

Get a major credit card. Credit repair clinics can give you a list of banks that offer secured credit cards. While this information is helpful in rebuilding credit, it's not worth hundreds or thousands of dollars—you can find it yourself online.

Federal law regulates for-profit credit repair clinics under the Credit Repair Organizations Act (CROA). (15 U.S.C. §§ 1679 and following.) Some dubious credit repair clinics have tried to get around these regulations by setting themselves up as nonprofits but still taking your money and providing poor results. Before using any organization that claims to be a nonprofit, carefully check the company's fees, claims of what it can do, and reputation. Call the Better Business Bureau or ask to contact satisfied customers.

Under the federal law, a credit repair clinic must:

- inform you, in a separate written document, of your rights under the Fair Credit Reporting Act
- accurately represent what it can and cannot do
- not collect any money until all promised services are performed
- provide a written contract containing complete payment information and a list of services to be performed, and
- let you cancel the contract without penalty within three business days of signing.

You cannot waive your rights under the CROA, even if you sign an agreement that claims to do so. A contract that doesn't comply with the CROA's requirements is void.

Any lawsuit you bring against a credit repair clinic for violation of federal law must be filed within five years of the violation. A court may award actual damages, punitive (meant to punish) damages, and attorneys' fees. Your state's law may have different time limits and limits on damages.

Almost all states provide additional protections to consumers who use credit repair clinics. For example, some states give you five days to cancel the credit repair contract, require the credit repair clinic to perform the promised services within a specific amount of time, and require that the credit repair clinic inform you about available nonprofit credit counseling services.

Most states also have strict licensing or registration requirements for credit repair businesses and require them to post bonds or maintain a security or trust account. This way, a customer injured by the company can be recompensed for any damage done, at least up to the amount of the bond or account. In those states, the credit repair company must tell you how to make a claim against the bond or account and give you the address of the bonding agency or the financial institution where the account is kept.

The chart below lists the state laws that provide consumer protections stronger than the federal law. To find out the details of the additional protections in your state, look up the code sections listed in the chart. For information on how to do this, see Chapter 19.

Additional State Protections Concerning Credit Repair Clinics

Arizona

Ariz. Rev. Stat. Ann. §§ 44-1701 to 44-1712

Credit repair service may not charge or collect a fee for referring consumer to a retail seller who will or may extend credit that is on substantially the same terms as those available to the general public.

Arkansas

Ark. Code Ann. §§ 4-91-101 to 4-91-109

Credit repair service may not charge or collect a fee for referring consumer to a retail seller who will or may extend credit that is on substantially the same terms as those available to the general public.

Cancellation rights. May cancel contract within 5 days of signing. Any payment must be returned within 10 days of receipt of cancellation notice.

California

Cal. Civ. Code §§ 1789.10 to 1789.22

Credit repair service may not charge or collect a fee for referring consumer to a retail seller who will or may extend credit that is on substantially the same terms as those available to the general public or on the same terms that would have been extended without the assistance of the credit repair organization; submit a debtor's dispute to a consumer credit reporting agency without the debtor's knowledge; or use a consumer credit reporting agency's telephone system or toll-free number to represent the caller as the debtor without the debtor's authorization.

Cancellation rights. May cancel contract within 5 working days of signing.

Time limit for performing services. 6 months.

Colorado

Colo. Rev. Stat. §§ 12-14.5-101 to 12-14.5-113

Cancellation rights. May cancel contract within 5 working days of signing.

Connecticut

Conn. Gen. Stat. Ann. § 36a-700

State protections do not exceed federal laws.

Delaware

Del. Code Ann. tit. 6, §§ 2401 to 2414

Credit repair service may not charge or collect a fee for referring consumer to a retail seller who will or may extend credit that is on substantially the same terms as those available to the general public.

Credit repair service must disclose a complete and accurate statement of the availability of nonprofit credit counseling services.

Time limit for performing services. 180 days.

District of Columbia

D.C. Code Ann. §§ 28-4601 to 28-4608

Credit repair service may not charge or collect a fee for referring consumer to a retail seller who will or may extend credit that is on substantially the same terms as those available to the general public.

Cancellation rights. May cancel contract within 5 calendar days of signing. Must be reimbursed within 10 days of receipt of cancellation notice.

Additional State Protections Concerning Credit Repair Clinics (continued)

Florida

Fla. Stat. Ann. §§ 817.701 to 817.706

Cancellation rights. May cancel contract within 5 days of signing. Any payment must be returned within 10 days of receipt of cancellation notice.

Georgia

Ga. Code Ann. §§ 16-9-59, 18-5-1 to 18-5-3

Credit repair service may not charge more than 7.5% of the amount the debtor provides each month for distribution to creditors.

Who may provide service. Only nonprofit organizations or federally regulated banks may offer credit repair services; attorneys and real estate brokers may provide credit repair services incidental to their regular business practice.

Hawaii

Haw. Rev. Stat. § 481B-12

State protections do not exceed federal laws.

Idaho

Idaho Code §§ 26-2222, 26-2223

Who may provide service. Only nonprofit organizations may provide credit counseling or other debt management services.

Illinois

815 Ill. Comp. Stat. §§ 605/1 to 605/16

Credit repair service may not charge or collect a fee for referring consumer to a retail seller who will or may extend credit that is on substantially the same terms as those available to the general public.

Cancellation rights. Any payment must be returned within 10 days of receipt of cancellation notice.

Indiana

Ind. Code Ann. §§ 24-5-15-1 to 24-5-15-11

Credit repair service may not charge or collect a fee for referring consumer to a retail seller who will or may extend credit that is on substantially the same terms as those available to the general public.

Credit repair service must disclose a complete and accurate statement of the availability of nonprofit credit counseling services.

Cancellation rights. Any payment must be returned within 10 days of receipt of cancellation notice or any other written notice.

Iowa

Iowa Code §§ 538A.1 to 538A.14

Credit repair service may not charge or collect a fee for referring consumer to a retail seller who will or may extend credit that is on substantially the same terms as those available to the general public.

Cancellation rights. Any payment must be returned within 10 days of receipt of cancellation notice.

Kansas

Kan. Stat.Ann §§ 50-1116 to 520-1135

Credit repair service must comply with an extensive list of requirements, including educating debtors, specifying the scope of an

Additional State Protections Concerning Credit Repair Clinics (continued)

agreement, itemizing fees, and disclosing the consumer's rights.

Credit repair service may not delay payments, make false promises or deceptive statements, give or receive compensation for referrals, or collect fees above $20 per month from the customer (after a $50 initial consultation fee).

For more information contact your state's consumer protection agency, listed in Appendix A.

Kentucky

Ky. Rev. Stat. Ann. §§ 380.010 to 390.990

Who may provide service. Debt adjustment services may be provided only by a nonprofit organization, attorney, debtor's regular full-time employee, creditor providing service at no cost, or lender who, at the debtor's request, adjusts debts at no additional cost as part of disbursing the loan funds.

Louisiana

La. Rev. Stat. Ann. §§ 9:3573.1 to 9:3573.17

Credit repair service must disclose a complete and accurate statement of the availability of nonprofit credit counseling services, disclose all payments expected from the consumer, give estimated completion date, and wait for payment until services are complete.

Cancellation rights. May cancel contract within 5 days of signing. Any payment must be returned within 10 days of receipt of cancellation notice.

Maine

Me. Rev. Stat. Ann. tit. 9-A, §§ 10-101 to 10-401

Credit repair service is required to keep consumer fees in an escrow account separate from any operating accounts of the business, pending completion of services offered.

Maryland

Md. Code Ann. [Com. Law] §§ 14-1901 to 14-1916

Credit repair service may not charge or collect a fee for referring consumer to a retail seller who will or may extend credit that is on substantially the same terms as those available to the general public or assist a consumer to obtain credit at a rate of interest which is in violation of federal or state maximum rate.

Cancellation rights. Any payment must be returned within 10 days of receipt of cancellation notice.

Massachusetts

Mass. Gen. Laws ch. 93, §§ 68A to 68E

Credit repair service may not charge or collect a fee for referring consumer to a retail seller who will or may extend credit that is on substantially the same terms as those available to the general public.

Cancellation rights. Any payment must be returned within 10 days of receipt of cancellation notice.

Michigan

Mich. Comp. Laws §§ 445.1821 to 445.1825

Credit repair service may not charge or collect a fee for referring consumer to a retail seller who will or may extend credit that is on

Additional State Protections Concerning Credit Repair Clinics (continued)

substantially the same terms as those available to the general public, submit a debtor's dispute to a consumer credit reporting agency without the debtor's knowledge, or provide a service that is not pursuant to a written contract.

Time limit for performing services. 90 days.

Minnesota

Minn. Stat. Ann. §§ 332.52 to 332.60

Credit repair service may not charge or collect a fee for referring consumer to a retail seller who will or may extend credit that is on substantially the same terms as those available to the general public.

Credit repair service must disclose the name and address of any person who directly or indirectly owns or controls a 10% or greater interest in the credit services organization; any litigation or unresolved complaint filed within the preceding 5 years with the state, any other state, or the U.S., or a notarized statement that there has been no such litigation or complaint; and the percentage of customers during the past year for whom the credit services organization fully and completely performed the services it agreed to provide.

Cancellation rights. May cancel contract within 5 days of signing. Any payment must be returned within 10 days of receipt of cancellation notice.

Mississippi

Mississippi Nonprofit Debt Management Services Act, Miss. Code Ann. §§ 81-22-1 to 81-22-29

Who may provide service. Only a nonprofit organization may operate as a licensed Debt Management Service.

Credit repair service may not purchase any debt, lend money or provide credit, operate as a debt collector, or structure a negative amortization agreement for the consumer.

Credit repair service is required to maintain separate account records for each consumer. May not commingle trust accounts with any business operating accounts

Fees. May not charge more than a one-time fee of $75 for setting up a debt management plan, $30 per month to maintain plan, $15 for obtaining an individual credit report, or $25 for a joint report. Educational courses and products may be offered for a fee, but consumer must be informed that purchasing them is not mandatory for receiving debt management services.

Missouri

Mo. Rev. Stat. §§ 407.635 to 407.644

Credit repair service may not charge or collect a fee for referring consumer to a retail seller who will or may extend credit that is on substantially the same terms as those available to the general public.

Credit repair service must disclose a complete and accurate statement of the availability of nonprofit credit counseling services.

Cancellation rights. Any payment must be returned within 10 days of receipt of cancellation notice.

Time limit for performing services. 180 days.

Nebraska

Neb. Rev. Stat. §§ 45-801 to 45-815

Credit repair service may not charge or collect a fee for referring consumer to a retail

Additional State Protections Concerning Credit Repair Clinics (continued)

seller who will or may extend credit that is on substantially the same terms as those available to the general public.

Cancellation rights. Any payment must be returned within 10 days of receipt of cancellation notice.

Nevada

Nev. Rev. Stat. Ann. §§ 598.741 to 598.787

Credit repair service may not charge or collect a fee for referring consumer to a retail seller who will or may extend credit that is on substantially the same terms as those available to the general public, submit a debtor's dispute to a consumer credit reporting agency without the debtor's knowledge, or call a consumer credit reporting agency and represent the caller as the debtor.

Credit repair service must disclose a complete and accurate statement of the availability of nonprofit credit counseling services, including toll-free numbers if available.

Cancellation rights. May cancel contract within 5 days of signing.

New Hampshire

N.H. Rev. Stat. Ann. §§ 359-D:1 to 359-D:11

Credit repair service may not charge or collect a fee for referring consumer to a retail seller who will or may extend credit that is on substantially the same terms as those available to the general public.

Cancellation rights. May cancel contract within 5 days of signing. Any payment must be returned within 5 days of receipt of cancellation notice.

New Jersey

N.J. Stat. Ann. §§ 17:16G-1 to 17:16G-6; N.J. Admin. Code tit. 3, § 25-1.2

Who may provide service. Only nonprofit organizations may provide credit counseling or debt adjustment services. No more than 40% of the board of directors can be employed by a corporation or institution which offers credit to the general public.

Fees. Monthly debt adjustment fee cannot exceed 1% of the debtor's gross monthly income or $25, whichever is less. Credit counseling services fee cannot exceed $60 per month.

New Mexico

N.M. Stat. Ann. §§ 56-2-1 to 56-2-4

Who may provide service. Nonprofit corporations organized as a community effort to assist debtors may provide debt adjustment services. Exceptions: attorney; regular, full-time employee of a debtor who does it as part of job; person authorized by court or state or federal law; creditor who provides debt adjustment without cost; and lender who, at the debtor's request, adjusts debts at no additional cost as part of disbursing the loan funds.

New York

N.Y. Gen. Bus. Law §§ 458-a to 458-k

Credit repair service is required to annex a copy of the consumer's current credit report to the contract and clearly mark the adverse entries proposed to be modified.

Additional State Protections Concerning Credit Repair Clinics (continued)

North Carolina

N.C. Gen. Stat. §§ 66-220 to 66-226

Credit repair service may not charge or collect a fee for referring consumer to a retail seller who will or may extend credit that is on substantially the same terms as those available to the general public.

Cancellation rights. Any payment must be returned within 10 days of receipt of cancellation notice.

North Dakota

N.D. Cent. Code §§ 13-06-01 to 13-06-03, 13-07-01 to 13-07-07

Credit repair service may not enter into an agreement with a debtor unless a thorough written budget analysis indicates that the debtor can reasonably meet the requirements of the financial adjustment plan and will benefit from it.

Credit repair service is required to credit any interest accrued as a result of payments deposited in a trust account to debt management education programs.

Fees. May charge an origination fee of up to $50; may take up to 15% of any sum deposited by the debtor for distribution as partial payment of the service's total fee.

Ohio

Ohio Rev. Code Ann. §§ 4712.01 to 4712.99

Credit repair service may not charge or collect a fee for referring consumer to a person that extends credit, except when credit has actually been extended as a result of the referral; submit the debtor's disputes to a consumer reporting agency without

the debtor's signed, written authorization and positive identification; or contact a consumer reporting agency to submit or obtain information about a debtor, stating or implying to be the debtor or debtor's attorney, guardian, or other legal representative.

Credit repair service must disclose a complete and accurate statement of the availability of nonprofit budget and debt counseling services; the percentage of customers during the past year for whom the credit services organization fully and completely performed the services it agreed to provide.

Time limit for performing service. 60 days.

Oklahoma

Okla. Stat. Ann. tit. 24, §§ 131 to 139

Credit repair service may not charge or collect a fee for referring consumer to a retail seller who will or may extend credit that is on substantially the same terms as those available to the general public.

Cancellation rights. May cancel contract within 5 days of signing. Any payment must be returned within 10 days of receipt of cancellation notice.

Oregon

Or. Rev. Stat. §§ 646.380 to 646.396

Credit repair service may not charge or collect a fee for referring consumer to a retail seller who will or may extend credit that is on substantially the same terms as those available to the general public.

Credit repair service is required to print all contracts in at least 10-point type.

Additional State Protections Concerning Credit Repair Clinics (continued)

Pennsylvania

73 Pa. Cons. Stat. Ann. §§ 2181 to 2192

Credit repair service may not charge or collect a fee for referring consumer to a retail seller who will or may extend credit that is on substantially the same terms as those available to the general public.

Cancellation rights. May cancel contract within 5 days of signing. Any payment must be returned within 15 days of receipt of cancellation notice.

Tennessee

Tenn. Code Ann. §§ 47-18-1001 to 47-18-1011

Credit repair service may not charge or collect a fee for referring consumer to a retail seller who will or may extend credit that is on substantially the same terms as those available to the general public; use a program or plan which charges installment payments directly to a credit card prior to full and complete performance of the services it has agreed to perform.

Credit repair service must disclose a complete and accurate statement of the availability of nonprofit budget and debt counseling services.

Cancellation rights. May cancel contract within 5 business days of signing. Any payment must be returned within 10 days of receipt of cancellation notice.

Texas

Tex. Fin. Code Ann. §§ 393.001 to 393.505

Credit repair service may not charge or collect a fee for referring consumer to a retail seller who will or may extend credit that is on

substantially the same terms as those available to the general public.

Credit repair service must disclose a complete and accurate statement of the availability of nonprofit budget and debt counseling services.

Cancellation rights. Any payment must be returned within 10 days of receipt of cancellation notice.

Time limit for performing service. 180 days.

Utah

Utah Code Ann. §§ 13-21-1 to 13-21-7

Credit repair service may not charge or collect a fee for referring consumer to a retail seller who will or may extend credit that is on substantially the same terms as those available to the general public.

Cancellation rights. May cancel contract within 5 days of signing. Any payment must be returned within 10 days of receipt of cancellation notice.

Vermont

Vt. Stat. Ann. tit. 8, §§ 4861 to 4876

Credit repair service must state in writing all services it will perform and all fees consumers will pay; state that debt adjustment plans are not suitable for all debtors; disclose if creditors may compensate the licensee; disclose the right to cancel within 3 days, without penalty; and make these disclosures in the language used to negotiate the agreement.

Credit repair service may not engage in false or deceptive advertising or communications, threaten to disclose information about debt, or charge more than a $50 initial fee plus 10%

Additional State Protections Concerning Credit Repair Clinics (continued)

of payments received from the debtor for distribution to creditors.

For more information contact your state's consumer protection agency, listed in Appendix A.

Virginia

Va. Code Ann. §§ 59.1-335.1 to 59.1-335.12

Credit repair service may not charge or collect a fee for referring consumer to a retail seller who will or may extend credit that is on substantially the same terms as those available to the general public.

Credit repair service must disclose: Information statement must include the following notice in at least 10-point bold type: "You have no obligation to pay any fees or charges until all services have been performed completely for you." The notice must also be conspicuously posted on a sign in the repair service's place of business, so that it is noticeable and readable when consumers are being interviewed.

Cancellation rights. Any payment must be returned within 10 days of receipt of cancellation notice.

Washington

Wash. Rev. Code Ann. §§ 19.134.010 to 19.134.900

Credit repair service may not charge or collect a fee for referring consumer to a retail seller who will or may extend credit that is on substantially the same terms as those available to the general public.

Cancellation rights. May cancel contract within 5 days of signing. Any payment must

be returned within 10 days of receipt of cancellation notice.

West Virginia

W.Va. Code §§ 46A-6C-1 to 46A-6C-12

Credit repair service may not charge or collect a fee for referring consumer to a retail seller who will or may extend credit that is on substantially the same terms as those available to the general public.

Credit repair service must disclose a complete and accurate statement of the availability of nonprofit budget and debt counseling services.

Cancellation rights. Any payment must be returned within 10 days of receipt of cancellation notice.

Time limit for performing service. 180 days.

Wisconsin

Wis. Stat. Ann. §§ 422.501 to 422.506

Credit repair service may not charge or collect a fee for referring consumer to a retail seller who will or may extend credit that is on substantially the same terms as those available to the general public.

Cancellation rights. May cancel contract within 5 days of signing. Any payment must be returned within 15 days of receipt of cancellation notice.

Wyoming

Who may provide service. Only nonprofits and attorneys may offer debt adjustment services.

Current as of January 2007

Don't Fall for the "File Segregation" Scam

Some credit repair organizations advertise "Credit File Segregation" or "File Segregation" in classified ads, and on TV, the radio, and the Internet. For a fee paid in advance, they promise to tell you how to create a new identity by obtaining an Employer Identification Number (EIN) from the IRS and using it instead of your Social Security number. An EIN is a nine-digit number that resembles a Social Security number.

The organization will instruct you to use your new EIN when you apply for credit. Doing this is illegal. It's a federal crime to make false statements on an application for a loan or credit. It's also a federal crime to misrepresent your Social Security number and to obtain an EIN from the IRS under false pretenses. If that's not bad enough, using an EIN instead of your Social Security number to repair your credit doesn't work. Further, if you use an EIN at work instead of your Social Security number, you won't earn Social Security benefits on your earnings.

Credit Discrimination

... prejudice marks a mental land mine.

—Gloria Steinem
Feminist and author, 1934–

Several powerful federal laws prohibit discrimination in credit transactions. Two of those laws, the Equal Credit Opportunity Act (ECOA) and the Fair Housing Act (FHA), cover most situations in the credit area. Others, such as the Community Reinvestment Act, are useful as well. State antidiscrimination laws often provide even more protection than do federal laws.

The ECOA and the FHA

The ECOA (15 U.S.C. §§ 1691 and following) is quite broad in scope. It prohibits discrimination in any part of a credit transaction, including:

- applications for credit
- credit evaluation
- restrictions in granting credit such as requiring collateral or security deposits
- credit terms
- loan servicing
- treatment upon default, and
- collection procedures.

The ECOA requires a creditor to give you notice when it denies your credit application revokes credit, changes the terms of an existing credit arrangement, or refuses to grant credit or terms substantially as requested. If the creditor denies you credit, it must give you a written notice that tells you either the specific reasons for rejecting you or that you can request them within 60

days. An acceptable reason might be "Your income is too low"; an unacceptable reason would be "You don't meet our minimum standards."

The ECOA prohibits a creditor from refusing to grant credit because of your:

- sex
- marital status
- race or color
- religion
- national origin
- age, or
- public assistance status.

The federal Fair Housing Act (FHA) (42 U.S.C. §§ 3601–3631) prohibits discrimination in residential real estate transactions. It covers loans for purchasing, improving, or maintaining your house, and loans in which your home is used as collateral. Other provisions of the FHA prohibit discrimination in the rental housing market. Like the ECOA, the FHA prohibits discrimination based on race, color, religion, national origin, and sex. In addition, the FHA prohibits discrimination based on:

- familial status and
- disability.

State antidiscrimination laws often provide even more protection than the federal laws (for example, some states prohibit arbitrary discrimination on the basis of occupation, personal characteristics, or sexual orientation).

Sex Discrimination

The ECOA, the FHA, and many state laws prohibit credit discrimination based on sex. This category often overlaps with the "marital status" category.

Specific examples of prohibited sex discrimination include:

- rating female-specific jobs (such as waitress) lower than male-specific jobs (such as waiter) for the purpose of obtaining credit
- denying credit because an applicant's income comes from sources historically associated with women—for example, part-time jobs, alimony, or child support (however, a creditor may ask you to prove that you have received alimony, child support, or separate maintenance consistently)
- requiring married women who apply for credit alone to provide information about their husbands while not requiring married men to provide information about their wives, and
- denying credit to a pregnant woman who anticipates taking a maternity leave.

However, a creditor is allowed to ask your sex when you apply for a real estate loan. The federal government collects this information for statistical purposes. Other creditors may ask for this information as well, although provision of the information is optional, and the creditor can use the information only to check its own practices for discrimination.

Marital Status Discrimination

The ECOA and many state laws prohibit discrimination based on marital status. The FHA has a similar provision which prohibits discrimination based on familial status.

These laws prohibit a creditor from requiring an applicant's spouse to cosign on an individual account as long as no jointly held or community property is involved and the applicant meets the creditor's standards on his or her own.

These laws also prohibit a creditor from asking about your spouse or former spouse when you apply for your own credit, unless any of the following is true:

- Your spouse will be permitted to use the account.
- Your spouse will be liable for the account.
- You are relying on your spouse's income to pay the account.
- You live in a community property state (Arizona, California, Idaho, Louisiana, Nevada, New Mexico, Texas, Washington, or Wisconsin) or you are relying on property located in a community property state to establish your creditworthiness.
- You are relying on alimony, child support, or other maintenance payments from a spouse to repay the creditor. (You are not required to reveal this income if you don't want the creditor to consider it in evaluating your application.) A creditor may ask whether you have to pay alimony, child support, or separate maintenance.

The prohibition against marital status discrimination also means that a creditor must consider the combined incomes of an unmarried couple applying for a joint obligation if it considers the combined income of married coapplicants.

No federal law specifically prohibits credit discrimination based on sexual orientation. However, a few states prohibit this type of discrimination.

Race Discrimination

In general, lenders are prohibited from asking a person's race on a credit application or ascertaining it from any means (such as a credit file) other than the personal observation of a loan officer. There is one important exception to this law: A mortgage lender may ask someone to voluntarily disclose his or her race for the sole purpose of monitoring home mortgage applications. Other creditors may ask for this information, although provision of the information is optional, and the creditor can use the information only to check its own practices for discrimination.

Unfortunately, race discrimination has not disappeared. In fact, lenders are accused of getting around race discrimination prohibitions by redlining—that is, denying credit to residents of predominantly non-white neighborhoods.

In one attempt to stop redlining, Congress enacted the Home Mortgage Disclosure Act. (12 U.S.C. §§ 2801 and following.) Under that law, mortgage lenders must maintain and disclose their lending practices for certain areas. Critics complain, however, that the data lenders must disclose is inadequate to analyze discrimination.

Congress also enacted the Community Reinvestment Act to address redlining and other types of discrimination. (12 U.S.C. §§ 2901–2908.) The CRA requires that bank mortgage lenders demonstrate that they serve the needs of the communities which they are chartered to serve. If the bank fails to do so, bank regulators can deny the bank the right to establish branches or to do other activity requiring regulatory approval.

More recently, credit discrimination laws have been used to challenge what is known as "reverse redlining." In "reverse redlining," instead of avoiding certain neighborhoods, creditors target low-income, often nonwhite, neighborhoods to sell loan products with extremely high interest rates and other costly terms.

National Origin Discrimination

Discrimination based on national origin is prohibited under the ECOA, the FHA, and most state credit discrimination laws. The exact definition of "national origin" is often unclear, but it generally refers to an individual's ancestry. A creditor might be discriminating based on national origin by treating people with Latino or Asian surnames differently from people with European names. This category extends to discrimination against non-English speakers, but it does not necessarily include noncitizens. A creditor is allowed to consider an applicant's residency status in the United States in certain circumstances.

Age Discrimination

The ECOA and many state laws prohibit credit discrimination based on age. This is mostly meant to protect the elderly (defined in the ECOA as people aged 62 or over). Creditors are allowed to consider age in order to give more favorable treatment to an older person (for example, considering an older person's long payment history, which a younger person hasn't had time to build yet). However, age cannot be used to an older person's detriment. For example, a creditor cannot automatically refuse to consider income often associated with the elderly, such as part-time employment or retirement benefits.

Other Discrimination Prohibited by State Law

A few states have enacted laws barring credit discrimination on grounds other than those covered by the federal laws (such as sexual orientation, mental disability, or political affiliation). Check with your state consumer protection office (see Appendix A) or do some research on your own (see Chapter 19) to see if there are additional protections in your state. If you feel that a creditor has discriminated against you on one of these grounds, complain to the federal agency that regulates the particular creditor. (See Appendix A.) Also, register your complaint with your state consumer protection office.

Postbankruptcy Discrimination

If you're considering filing for bankruptcy or you've been through bankruptcy, you may be worried that you'll suffer discrimination. Bankruptcy laws prohibit discrimination by the government. All federal, state, and local governmental entities are prohibited from denying, revoking, suspending, or refusing to renew a license, permit, charter, franchise, or other similar grant solely because you filed for bankruptcy. Nor may they deny or terminate employment, or discriminate in employment. (11 U.S.C. § 525(a).) In interpreting this law, judges have ruled that the government cannot, based solely on your bankruptcy filing:

- deny you a job or fire you
- deny or terminate your public benefits
- deny or evict you from public housing
- deny or refuse to renew your state liquor license
- withhold your college transcript
- deny you a driver's license, or
- deny you a contract, such as a contract for a construction project.

In general, once any government-related debt has been canceled in bankruptcy, all acts against you that arise out of that debt also must end. For example, if a state university has withheld your transcript because you haven't paid back your student loan, once the loan is discharged, you must be given your transcript.

Remember, though, that the law only protects you from government denials that are based solely on your bankruptcy. You could still be denied a government loan, job, or apartment, based on reasons apart

Risk-Based Pricing Notice

Some auto finance companies and auto manufacturers charge minority customers greater finance charges or higher interest rates than they charge nonminority customers with similar credit ratings, without any legitimate reasons for these markups. A new notice required by the federal Fair Credit Reporting Act may help expose and prevent this kind of credit discrimination.

Whenever a creditor extends credit on terms "materially less favorable" than the most favorable terms it grants to a substantial number of consumers, and bases the credit decision on the consumer's credit report, the creditor must give the consumer a so-called risk-based pricing notice or adverse action notice. The notice explains that the credit terms granted are based on information in the consumer's credit report and explains how the consumer can obtain a free copy of that credit report.

In a modern-day credit transaction, consumers usually apply for the best credit terms for which they can qualify, rather than for

specific terms. Creditors may offer consumers credit terms tailored to their risk profile, so that the consumers pay a higher price or receive less-favorable terms than they would have received but for their credit report. The notice informs consumers that something may be amiss in their credit reports and that they received less-favorable terms than a substantial number of other customers.

If you receive a risk-based pricing or adverse action notice, it doesn't necessarily mean that the creditor has discriminated against you. You should use the notice to obtain a free copy of your credit report and look for a problem that caused the creditor to offer you the less-favorable terms. If you can't see a problem and want to pursue the matter, ask the creditor to explain what items in your credit report caused you to receive the less-favorable terms, how your credit report differs from customers who received significantly more favorable terms, and what those terms are.

from the bankruptcy—and that includes a conclusion that your future creditworthiness is poor.

In addition, private employers may not fire you or otherwise discriminate against you solely because you filed for bankruptcy. (11 U.S.C. § 525(b).) It is unclear, however, whether or not the act prohibits employers from not hiring you because you went through bankruptcy.

Unfortunately, other forms of discrimination in the private sector aren't necessarily illegal. If you seek to rent an apartment and the landlord does a credit check and refuses to rent to you because you filed for bankruptcy, there's not much you can do other than try to show that you'll pay your rent and be a responsible tenant. If a bank refuses to give you a loan because it perceives you as a poor credit risk, you may have little recourse.

If you suffer illegal discrimination because of your bankruptcy, you can sue in state court or in the bankruptcy court. You'll probably need the assistance of an attorney.

What to Do If a Creditor Discriminates Against You

Although this chapter provides an overview of your rights, you may want to learn more. Chapter 19 explains how to do legal research. Also, the following websites provide information about credit discrimination:

- www.nclc.org (National Consumer Law Center)

- www.innercitypress.org
- www.usdoj.gov (U.S. Department of Justice), and
- www.communitychange.org (Nonprofit Center for Community Change).

If you think that a creditor has discriminated against you on a prohibited basis, you should complain to the Federal Trade Commission and the federal agency that regulates the particular creditor. (See Appendix A for contact information.) If the discrimination is related to housing, contact the Department of Housing and Urban Development (www.hud.gov). You may also want to contact an attorney for help.

■

Help Beyond the Book

It takes nearly as much ability to know how to profit by good advice as to know how to act for one's self.

— François de La Rochefoucauld
French writer and moralist, 1613-1680

This book gives you strategies for coping with your debts. But the suggestions outlined here may not be enough—bill collectors might continue to harass you even after you tell them to stop, you might want help in negotiating with your creditors, you might be sued, you may want to sue a creditor, or you may decide to file for bankruptcy.

This chapter suggests some ways to get more information or advice than this book provides. Before discussing the methods in more detail, here's a general piece of advice: Get information, then make decisions for yourself. By reading this book, you've shown that you're willing to take responsibility for doing research and making informed decisions about your legal and financial affairs. If you decide to get help from others, apply this same self-empowerment principle—shop around until you find an adviser who values your competence and intelligence and recognizes your right to make your own decisions.

Do Your Own Legal Research

Often, you can handle a legal problem yourself if you're willing to do some research. The trick is to know where to turn for the type of information you need. One obvious source is a lawyer. But lawyers aren't the only source for legal help. There's a lot you can do on your own. Both the Internet and law libraries are full of valuable information, such as state and federal statutes. For example, you could read the Fair Debt Collection Practices Act, find out that harassment by collection agencies is illegal, and then read court cases that have decided what types of behavior constitute harassment by a bill collector.

If you decide to take the library route, you must first find a law library that's open to the public. You might find such a library in your county courthouse or at your state capitol. Publicly funded law schools generally permit the public to use their libraries, and some private law schools grant access to their libraries—sometimes for a modest fee.

Don't overlook the reference department of the public library if you're in a large city. Many large public libraries have a fairly decent legal research collection. Also, ask about using the law library in your own lawyer's office. Some lawyers, on request, will share their books with their clients.

The Internet has also become a tremendous legal research tool. (See "Online Legal Research" below.)

 RESOURCES

Want detailed advice on legal research? We don't have space here to show you how to do your own legal research in anything approaching a comprehensive fashion. To go further, get a copy of *Legal Research: How to Find*

& *Understand the Law,* by Stephen Elias and Susan Levinkind (Nolo). This nontechnical book gives easy-to-use, step-by-step instructions on how to find legal information.

State and Federal Laws

Debt collection and credit reporting are governed by state and federal law. Generally, when laws overlap, the stricter laws will apply. In practical terms, this usually means that the laws that give debtors the most protection will prevail over less-protective laws.

State Statutes

We refer to many of the state laws affecting debtors throughout this book and include citations so that you can do additional research. State laws or codes are collected in volumes and are available in many public libraries and in most law libraries. Depending on the state, statutes may be organized by subject matter or by title number ("chapter"), with each title covering a particular subject matter, or simply numbered sequentially, without regard to subject matter.

"Annotated codes" contain not only all the text of the laws (as do the regular codes) but also a brief summary of some of the court decisions interpreting each law and often references to treatises and articles that discuss the law. Annotated codes have comprehensive indexes by topic and are kept up to date with paperback supplements ("pocket parts") stuck in a pocket inside the back cover of each volume.

TIP

Try your state consumer protection agency. Your state consumer protection agency or attorney general's office may provide publications at little or no cost explaining state laws on debt, credit, and general consumer matters. A list of state consumer protection offices appears in Appendix A. Consumer Action posts an excellent list at www.consumeraction.gov/state.shtml.

Federal Statutes and Regulations

Congress has enacted laws, and federal agencies such as the Federal Trade Commission have adopted regulations, covering most of the topics in this book. We refer to many federal agencies and include citations for many of the federal laws affecting debtors throughout this book. The U.S. Code is the starting place for research on most federal laws. It consists of 50 separate numbered titles. Each title covers a specific subject matter. For example, Title 15 contains the Consumer Credit Act; Title 11 contains the Bankruptcy Act. Two versions of the U.S. Code are published in annotated form: the United States Code Annotated (West Publishing Co.) and the United States Code Service (Bancroft-Whitney/Lawyer's Co-op). Most law libraries carry both.

Most federal regulations are published in the Code of Federal Regulations (C.F.R.), organized by subject into 50 separate titles.

Court Decisions

Sometimes the answer to a legal question cannot be found in a statute. This happens when:

- court cases and opinions have explained the statute, taking it beyond its obvious or literal meaning, or
- the law that applies to your question has been made by judges, not legislators.

Court Decisions That Explain Statutes

Statutes and ordinances do not explain themselves. For example, the Fair Debt Collection Practices Act prohibits collection agencies from using the telephone to harass you, but that statute doesn't define harassment. Chances are, however, that others before you have had the same questions, and they may have come up in the context of a lawsuit. If a judge interpreted the statute and wrote an opinion on the matter, that written opinion, once published, will become part of "the law" as much as the statute itself. If a higher court (an appellate court) has also examined the question, then its opinion will rule.

To find out if there are written court decisions that interpret a particular statute or ordinance, look in an "annotated code." At the end of each section, you'll find summaries of cases that have interpreted it. If you find a case that seems to answer your question, it's crucial to make sure that the decision you're reading is still "good law"— that a more recent opinion from a higher court has not reached a different conclusion. To make sure that you are relying on the latest and highest judicial pronouncement, you must use the library research tool known as *Shepard's*, which sends you to later cases that have said something about

the case you found. *Legal Research: How to Find & Understand the Law*, by Stephen Elias and Susan Levinkind (Nolo), has a good, easy-to-follow explanation of how to use the *Shepard's* system to expand and update your research.

Court Decisions That Make Law

Many laws that govern the way creditors must conduct their business do not have an initial starting point in a statute. These laws are entirely court-made and are known as "common" law. For example, in many states, creditors collecting their own debts are not allowed to harass debtors. (Remember, the federal Fair Debt Collection Practices Act applies only to collection agencies.)

Researching common law is more difficult than statutory law, because you do not have the launching pad of a statute. With a little perseverance, however, you can certainly find your way to the cases that have developed and explained the legal concept you wish to understand. A good beginning is to ask the librarian for any "practice guides" in the field of debtor-creditor relations. These are outlines of the law, written for lawyers, that are kept up to date and are designed to get you quickly to key information. Because they are so popular and easy to use, they are usually kept behind the reference counter and cannot be checked out. More sophisticated research techniques, such as using a set of books called "Words and Phrases" (which sends you to cases based on key words), are explained in the book *Legal Research*, mentioned above.

How to Read a Case Citation

If you find a citation to a case that looks important, you should read the opinion. You'll need the title of the case and its citation, which is like an address for the set of books, volume, and page where the case can be found. Ask the law librarian for help.

Although it may look about as decipherable as hieroglyphics, once understood, a case citation gives lots of useful information in a small space. It tells you the names of the people or companies involved, the volume of the reporter (series of books) in which the case is published, the page number on which it begins, and the year in which the case was decided.

Use Background Resources

If you want to research a legal question but don't know where to begin, several resources are available on consumers' and debtors' rights issues. The best all-around sources are the publications of the National Consumer Law Center (www.consumerlaw. org). Their very thorough and annually updated volumes include the following titles:

- Consumer Bankruptcy Law and Practice
- Consumer Class Actions
- Student Loan Law
- Consumer Arbitration Agreements
- Consumer Banking and Payments Law
- Credit Discrimination
- Fair Credit Reporting Act
- Fair Debt Collection
- Repossessions and Foreclosures
- Consumer Warranty Law

- Truth in Lending
- Unfair and Deceptive Acts and Practices
- The Cost of Credit
- Auto Fraud, and
- Access to Utility Service.

Unfortunately, not all law libraries have these volumes. You may need to call several law and public libraries until you find a library that does carry them. For more information, call the National Consumer Law Center (617-542-9595), or contact them at nclc@consumerlaw.org.

Online Legal Research

If you have access to the Internet, you can accomplish a good deal of legal research using your computer. But you can't do it all—not every court decision is available online. Furthermore, unless you know what you are looking for—the case name and citation or the code section—you may have difficulty finding it.

Finding Debt, Credit, and Consumer Information Online

Often, the best place to start your quest is with websites that contain information about debt, credit, finance, consumer protection, and bankruptcy. Here are a few good ones:

- **www.nolo.com**
  Nolo's site includes a vast amount of legal information for consumers. Under the heading "Property & Money," you'll find articles on credit repair, debt, bankruptcy, and more.

- **www.nclc.org**

  This is the website of the National Consumer Law Center.

- **www.myvesta.org**

  Myvesta.org (formerly Debt Counselors of America) is a nonprofit online resource dedicated to helping people get out of debt. Their advice covers budgeting, financial recovery, debt management, and debt payoff. The site is updated daily and is free. It lists software, publications, and information; contains special programs to help you get out of debt; and has a debt forum where you can post your specific questions for its counselors.

- **www.bbb.org**

  The Better Business Bureau allows you to file consumer complaints online (and also to check the reputation of many businesses before you do business with them); click "Locate a Bureau" from the home page.

- **www.pueblo.gsa.gov**

  The Federal Citizen Information Center provides the latest in consumer news as well as many publications of interest to consumers, including the Consumer Information Catalog and a free consumer handbook.

- **www.fdic.gov**

- **www.ftc.gov**

- **www.federalreserve.gov**

  The Federal Deposit Insurance Corporation, Federal Trade Commission, and Federal Reserve Board offer consumer protection rules, guides, and publications.

- **www.irs.gov**

  The Internal Revenue Service provides tax information, forms, and publications. Another feature lets you post your individual question to the IRS; you'll get an email response in a few days. (The information is fairly generic but will help you get started researching a question.)

Finding Statutes and Regulations Online

You can find federal statutes, the entire Code of Federal Regulations, and most state statutes by visiting Nolo's website at www.nolo.com/statute. Your best bet for state regulations is FindLaw, at www.findlaw.com. FindLaw also offers federal statutes, federal regulations, and state statutes.

There is often a delay between the time a statute is passed and the time it is included in the overall compilation of laws. Almost every state maintains its own website for pending and recently enacted legislation. These sites contain not only the most current version of a bill, but also its history. To find your state's website, see "Finding Court and Government Agency Websites," below. Finally, the United States Congress maintains a website at http://thomas.loc.gov that contains all pending federal bills and a link to the U.S. Code.

 **RESOURCES**

Information for Californians. You can get the text of appellate court decisions at www.courtinfo.ca.gov, and the text of all California statutes and pending legislation at www.leginfo. ca.gov. For a catalogue of University of California libraries, the California State Library, and law school libraries, check out www.cdlib.org. Use the "Melvyl Catalog" button to search the entire U.S. Library system by author, title, subject, or keywords

Finding Court and Government Agency Websites

Many courts and government agencies have websites that provide statutes and case law, plus other useful information such as forms, answers to frequently asked questions, and downloadable pamphlets on various legal topics. To find to your state's website, open your browser and type in www.state.<your state's postalcode>.us. (Your state's postal code is the two-letter abbreviation you use for mailing addresses. For example, for New York, you would type www.state.ny.us. If your state has a more creative Web address, you can find it under "State Government" at www.usa.gov.

Once you find your state's website, look for links to state statutes, state courts, and state court decisions. Also, look for websites of university libraries and your State Library.

Local, state, and federal court websites are also available at the National Center for State Courts' website, www.ncsconline.org. The federal judiciary's website is www.uscourts. gov. And, of course, Nolo's website, www. nolo.com, provides all kinds of useful links.

Finding Cases on the Web

If you are looking for a case and know the case name or citation, you may be able to find it online.

State cases. If the case is recent (within the last few years), you may be able to find it free on the Internet. A good place to start is FindLaw at www.findlaw.com or LexisNexis at www.lexisone.com. Also, many state websites now publish recent cases. See "Finding Court and Government Agency Websites," above, for information on how to find your state's website.

If the case is older, you can still find it on the Internet, but you will probably have to pay a private company for access to its database. VersusLaw at www.versuslaw.com maintains an excellent library of older state court cases. You can do unlimited research on VersusLaw for a small monthly fee. You can also get state cases online through the Lexis and Westlaw databases. (For more information, see "Using Westlaw and Lexis to Do Legal Research on the Web," below.)

U.S. Supreme Court cases. Nolo's Legal Research Center, available at www.nolo.com, provides U.S. Supreme Court cases decided within the last hundred years.

Other federal cases. FindLaw, at www. findlaw.com, contains cases decided by the federal Circuit Courts of Appeal within the last ten or so years, some bankruptcy opinions, and very recent tax court cases. The Cornell Law School Legal Information Institute at www.law.cornell.edu provides access to all federal appellate court cases, some District Court cases, and some bankruptcy opinions. VersusLaw (explained above) also has some U.S. District Court cases, and some bankruptcy opinions. If you can't find the case you're looking for on one of these websites, your best bet is to use Westlaw or Lexis, or hit the books at the library.

Using Lexis and Westlaw to Do Legal Research on the Web

Lexis and Westlaw are the chief electronic legal databases that contain the full text of many of the legal resources found in law libraries, including almost all reported cases from state and federal courts, all federal statutes, the statutes of most states, federal regulations, law review articles, commonly used treatises, and practice manuals.

Although Westlaw and Lexis databases are available over the Internet, subscriptions are pricey. However, both offer some free and some fee-based services to nonsubscribers that are both helpful and reasonably priced (between $9 and $10 per document). To find out more about these services, visit Westlaw at www.westlaw.com or Lexis at www. lexis.com. Also, some county and state law libraries now offer free or affordable access to Lexis and Westlaw

Lexis does offer a free online service that gives access to state cases and higher-level federal cases from the past five years, at www.lexisone.com.

Lawyers

As a general rule, you should get an attorney involved in your situation if the dispute is of high enough value to justify the attorney's fees. For example, if a you owe a creditor $1,200, but the goods were defective and you feel you shouldn't have to pay, and an attorney will cost $800, you're probably better off handling the matter yourself, even though this increases the risk that the creditor will win. If, however, you owe $10,000 and the attorney will cost $1,000, hiring the attorney may make sense. You also may want to consult an attorney if the stakes are high—for example, you are facing foreclosure.

What Lawyers Can Do for You

There are four basic ways a lawyer can help you.

Consultation and advice. A lawyer can analyze your situation and advise you on your best plan of action. Ideally, the lawyer will describe all your alternatives so you can make your own choices. Lawyers have a fiduciary duty to their clients, and they're not supposed to put their own economic interests above yours. Still, beware that some lawyers might steer you in a direction that will net them the largest fee.

Negotiation. A lawyer can help you negotiate with your creditors, particularly if the lawyer has experience settling disputes through negotiation. If the creditor has an attorney, that attorney may be more apt to settle with your lawyer than with you. And an attorney's letterhead itself lets a creditor know you are serious about settling.

Representation. If you are sued or want to sue, especially if you have a good defense or a claim against the creditor, you may want to hire a lawyer to represent you. This, however, could get expensive, so be sure you want to be represented by a lawyer before you hire one. You also may consider hiring a lawyer to assist you if you decide to file for bankruptcy. While many bankruptcies are routine and debtors can often represent themselves when armed with a good self-help book, some cases get complex and need the involvement of a bankruptcy lawyer.

Unbundled services. Some lawyers today "unbundle" their services. This means that they will assist you with a certain task (such as preparing a response to a lawsuit filed against you) or a certain portion of a lawsuit (such as discovery) for a fee that is less than if you hired them to handle the entire lawsuit.

How to Find a Lawyer

Here are several ways to find a lawyer.

Legal Aid. Legal Aid offices offer legal assistance in many areas, especially for people with debt problems. To qualify for Legal Aid, you must be low-income. Usually that means your household income cannot exceed 135% of the federal poverty level, although some offices have different guidelines. To find a Legal Aid office, go to the federal Legal Services Corporation's website at www.lsc.gov. You can look in

your local phone book, too, but be careful. Some unscrupulous nonlawyers have been known to pose as legal aid organizations, even using "legal aid" in their names. These groups may take your money and not do anything or may take actions that you haven't authorized.

Legal clinic. Many law schools sponsor legal clinics and provide free legal advice to consumers. Some legal clinics have the same income requirements as Legal Aid offices—others offer free services to low- to moderate-income people.

Personal referrals. This is the most common approach. If you know someone who was pleased with the services of a lawyer, call that lawyer first. If that lawyer doesn't handle debtor's rights matters or can't take your case, ask for a recommendation to someone else. Be careful, however, when selecting a lawyer from a personal referral. Just because a lawyer performed satisfactorily in one situation doesn't guarantee the same performance in your case.

Group legal plans. Some unions, employers, and consumer action organizations offer group plans to their members or employees, who can obtain comprehensive legal assistance free or for low rates. If you're a member of such a plan, check with it first for a lawyer.

Prepaid legal insurance. Prepaid legal insurance plans offer some services for a low monthly fee and charge more for additional or different work. Participating lawyers may use the plan as a way to get clients who are attracted by the low-cost, basic services, and then sell them more expensive services. If the lawyer recommends an expensive course of action, get a second opinion before you agree.

But if a plan offers extensive free advice, or you can use the lawyer to write several letters to your hounding creditors, the consultation or service you receive may be worth the cost of membership.

There's no guarantee that the lawyers available through these plans are of the best caliber. Check out the plan carefully before signing up. Ask about the plan's complaint system, whether you get to choose your lawyer, and whether or not the lawyer will represent you in court.

Consumer organizations. Many national or local consumer organizations can recommend an attorney who handles debtors' rights cases. One place to start is the National Association of Consumer Advocates (www.naca.net). In some large urban areas, consumer advocates publish guides of consumer-oriented legal organizations and lawyers. Check the library to see if it has such a guide.

Lawyer referral panels. Most county bar associations will refer you to attorneys who practice in your area and who have at least some knowledge of the subject you need help with. But bar associations don't always provide meaningful screening for the attorneys listed, which means those who participate may not be the most experienced or competent.

What to Look for in a Lawyer

No matter what approach you take to finding a lawyer, here are three suggestions on how to make sure you have the best possible working relationship.

First, fight any urge to surrender your will and be intimidated by a lawyer. You should be the one who decides what you feel comfortable doing about your legal and financial affairs. Keep in mind that you're hiring the lawyer to perform a service for you; shop around if the price or personality isn't right.

Second, you must be as comfortable as possible with any lawyer you hire. When making an appointment, ask to talk directly to the lawyer. If you can't, this may give you a hint about the lawyer's accessibility.

If you do talk directly to the lawyer, ask some specific questions. Do you get clear, concise answers? If not, try someone else. If the lawyer says little except "I can take care of it"—with a substantial fee—watch out. Don't be a passive client or hire a lawyer who wants you to be one. If the lawyer admits to not knowing an answer, that isn't necessarily bad. In most cases, the lawyer must do some research.

Also, pay attention to how the lawyer responds to your having considerable information. If you've read this book, you're already better informed about debtors' rights laws than most clients are. Some lawyers are threatened when the client knows too much—and you'll want to avoid them.

When you've narrowed your search to several lawyers, check their disciplinary history on your state bar's website. This website also may say where the lawyers went to school, how long they've been in practice, and whether they're certified as specialists in any areas of practice.

Once you find a lawyer you like, make an appointment to discuss your situation fully. Your goal at the initial conference is to find out what the lawyer recommends and how much it will cost. Go home and think about the lawyer's suggestions. If they don't make sense or if you have other reservations, call someone else.

Third, keep in mind that the lawyer works for you. Once you hire a lawyer, you have the absolute right to switch to another—or to fire the lawyer and handle the matter yourself—at any time, for any reason.

How Much Lawyers Charge

If all you want is a consultation with an attorney to find out where you stand and what options you have, be sure to find out the hourly fee ahead of time. Some charge as little as $75 an hour, while others charge $500 or more per hour.

A letter doesn't take that long to write, however, and as long as you are clear about what you want the lawyer to do and not do, you can keep the bill low. If you want the lawyer to do some negotiating, the fee could add up.

If you're sued by a creditor and hire a lawyer to represent you, the lawyer's fee will probably add up fast. A few lawyers might represent you for a flat fee, for example, $500, but most charge by the hour. If you have a claim against a creditor and might win damages—for example, if a bill collector posted your name throughout the town as a "deadbeat"—the lawyer might take your case on a contingency fee basis. That means

the lawyer gets paid only if you win your case. If you don't win, the lawyer doesn't get paid a cent, but will probably expect you to reimburse costs. Most lawyers tend to take only those cases they think they have a good chance of winning on contingency.

If you plan to hire a lawyer to help you file for bankruptcy, expect to pay $1,000 to $2,000, or more if your bankruptcy case is not simple. Many bankruptcy attorneys let you pay in installments. Also, the attorney must report the fee to the bankruptcy court for approval. The court can make the attorney justify the fee if it's high. This rarely happens, however, because attorneys know what local bankruptcy judges will allow and set their fees accordingly.

One final word: No matter why you hire a lawyer, and for whatever fee, be sure the lawyer puts the fee arrangement in a written contract for both you and the lawyer to sign. If the lawyer doesn't mention a written fee agreement, ask about one. If you hire a lawyer to help you with your debt problems, you don't want lawyer's fee to become another debt you can't or won't pay.

Debt and Credit Counseling Agencies

Credit and debt counseling agencies are organizations funded primarily by major creditors, such as department stores, credit card companies, and banks, who can work with you to help you repay your debts and improve your financial picture.

To use a credit or debt counseling agency to help you pay your debts, you must have some disposable income. A counselor contacts your creditors to let them know that you've sought assistance and need more time to pay. Based on your income and debts, the counselor, with your creditors, decides on how much you will pay to your creditors each month. You then make one payment each month to the counseling agency, which in turn pays your creditors. The agency asks the creditors to return a small percentage of the money to fund its work. This arrangement is generally referred to as a debt management program. It generally takes 36 to 60 months to repay debts through a debt management program.

Some creditors will make concessions to help you when you're on a debt management program. But few creditors will make interest concessions, such as waiving a portion of the accumulated interest to help you repay the principal. More likely, you'll get late fees dropped and the opportunity to reinstate your credit if you successfully complete a debt management program.

The combination of high consumer debt and easy access to information (the Internet) has led to an explosion in the number of credit and debt counseling agencies ready to offer you help. Some provide limited services, such as budgeting and debt repayment, while others offer a range of services, from debt counseling to financial planning and education. Shop carefully. Some of these agencies were established primarily to sell you products and services and don't provide good-quality counseling.

Critics of credit and debt counseling agencies point out that they get most of their funding from creditors. (Some offices

also receive grants from private and federal agencies.) These critics claim that counselors cannot be objective in counseling debtors to file for bankruptcy because they know the agency won't receive funds from its supporters. Critics also say that agencies tend to focus on unsecured creditors (who pay the agencies' bills) and neglect secured creditors.

In response to these and other consumer concerns, credit and debt counseling agencies accredited by the National Foundation for Consumer Credit (the majority are) reached an agreement with the Federal Trade Commission to disclose the following to consumers:

- that creditors fund a large portion of the cost of their operations
- that the agency must balance the ability of the debtor to make payments with the requirements of the creditors that fund the office, and
- a reliable estimate of how long it will take a debtor to repay his or her debts under a debt management program.

When choosing a credit or debt counseling agency, look for a company that is truly a nonprofit. Many for-profit outfits use names that sound like a nonprofit, such as "foundation," to confuse you. And, your inquiry shouldn't stop there. Many unscrupulous credit and debt counseling companies have nonprofit status. These companies often try get you to pay "voluntary contributions" up front or pay other fees. At a minimum, always ask about fees and get a quote in writing before agreeing to give your business to a particular counselor. And

Questions to Ask a Credit or Debt Counseling Agency

Myvesta.org (formerly Debt Counselors of America) suggests that you ask the following questions before using any counseling agency (the explanations below are paraphrased from Myvesta's website):

1. **Will you send me information about your organization and programs?** An agency should be willing to give you information about its services—and you shouldn't have to provide account numbers, debts amounts, or other information to get it. If an agency won't give you information up front about its programs, consider it a warning sign.

2. **Is there a minimum amount of debt I have to have in order to work with you?** An agency should not turn you away because you have less than a certain amount of debt.

3. **Will you help me with all my debts?** Most credit counseling agencies work only with credit card debt because secured lenders (those that offer mortgages and car loans, for example) won't make automatic reductions in rates and terms. Some agencies will make payments on secured debts as a convenience to you, however. If this is important to you, ask about it.

4. **Can you still help me if I cannot afford the minimum payment in a debt management program?** Avoid agencies that turn you away or tell you to file for bankruptcy because you can't meet their requirements. A good agency should be able to guide you to other resources that can help.

5. **How high are the fees?** Look for a group with low or no fees. Some agencies charge steep up-front fees just to participate in their program. Ask for information about set-up fees, monthly fees, and other charges, and make sure the agency doesn't charge a fee to close your account.

6. **What kind of security measures do you have to protect my information?** Make sure the agency you use has sufficient security in place to protect your Social Security number and other confidential information.

7. **Can I get up-to-date, regular reports of the status of my account?** You want to be able to check your account status at any time. Look for secure, encrypted Web access to your account. If access is by phone only, find out whether someone will be available to answer your questions when you call.

8. **Will you sell my name or address to outside parties?** Get a copy of the agency's privacy policy and read it. Make sure that the agency doesn't disclose your confidential information to inappropriate third parties. Ask whether your name and address will be included on mailing lists sold to outside organizations.

9. **Does counseling affect my report?** Although credit counseling agencies don't report your participation to the

Questions to Ask a Credit or Debt Counseling Agency (continued)

credit bureaus, many creditors do. Ask the agency to explain what effect this might have on your credit report.

10. **How often do you send payments to creditors?** Look for an agency that sends payments out at least weekly. If an agency pays only once a month and your payment is late, it might sit at the agency for weeks before the creditor receives it.

11. **What are my payment options?** Find an agency that gives you some convenient payment choices.

12. **Does your organization have accreditation?** Look for an agency that has been

accredited by an independent organization, such as BSI Management Systems.

13. **What kind of training do your counselors have?** A good counseling agency provides both internal training and training with outside experts.

14. **Are you comfortable?** You might be in this program for years, so make sure you feel comfortable with the people you'll be dealing with. Look for friendly, courteous staff who are willing to answer your questions.

review "Questions to Ask a Credit or Debt Counseling Agency," above.

Consumer Credit Counseling Service (CCCS) is the oldest credit or debt counseling agency in the country. Actually, CCCS isn't one agency. CCCS is the primary operating name of many credit and debt counseling agencies affiliated with the National Foundation for Consumer Credit (NFCC). CCCS may charge you a start-up fee (around $20) and a small monthly fee (an average of about $14) for setting up a repayment plan. CCCS also helps people make monthly budgets. CCCS has more than 1,100 offices, located in every state. Look in the phone book to find the one nearest you or visit www.nfcc.org.

With a few exceptions, all bankruptcy filers are now required to get credit and

debt management counseling. Filers must get this counseling from a nonprofit agency that meets a number of requirements and has been approved by the Office of the U.S. Trustee. If you decide to get help with debt management, you would do well to choose one of these agencies—the U.S. Trustee's office oversees their operation, which gives you some protection against fraudulent practices. You can find a list of approved agencies at the U.S. Trustee's website, at www.usdoj.gov/ust.

Before you sign up with a credit and debt counseling agency, check with the Better Business Bureau (www.bbb.org) to see what its reputation is and whether it has unresolved complaints. Make similar inquiries to your state's Attorney General's and consumer protection offices. Finally, ask the agency if there are people who are currently in the debt management program and who have finished the program who are willing to speak to you regarding their experiences with it.

WARNING

Make sure your bills get paid. If you sign up for a debt management plan, keep paying your bills directly until you know that your creditors have approved the plan. Make sure the agency's schedule will allow it to pay your debts before they are due each month. Call each of your creditors the first month to make sure the agency paid them on time.

■

Glossary

This glossary defines certain terms that appear frequently in this book.

Acceleration clause. A provision in a contract requiring the debtor to pay the entire balance of the contract immediately because of a failure to meet some condition, such as a failure to make payments on time.

Arrears. A general term used to describe any loan payment or debt that is past due. It's most often used to describe back-owed child support or alimony. Some people use the term "arrearages," which means the same thing.

Balloon payment. A final lump sum payment on an installment contract, such as a mortgage or car loan, which is larger than the earlier payments.

Bankruptcy. A legal proceeding in which you are relieved from paying your debts. There are two kinds of bankruptcies for individuals: Chapter 7 and Chapter 13. In Chapter 7 bankruptcy, you may be required to give up some property in exchange for the erasure of your debts. In Chapter 13 bankruptcy, you don't have to give up any property, but you must pay off a portion of your debts over three to five years. At the end of the three-to-five-year period, the balance of what you owe is wiped out.

Closed-end credit: Credit that usually involves one transaction, such as a car loan or a mortgage, with a fixed amount borrowed and a fixed repayment plan. (Compare *Open-end credit*, below.)

Collateral. Property pledged as security for repayment of a secured debt.

Cosigner. A person who signs a loan agreement or credit application along with the primary debtor. If the primary debtor does not pay, the cosigner is fully responsible for the loan or debt. Many people use cosigners to qualify for a loan or credit card.

Credit repair. As we use this term, the legitimate steps that a person takes to rebuild their credit. It also refers to getting outdated, incorrect, or incomplete information removed from one's credit report.

Credit repair organization. A business that charges substantial money and claims to be able to remove negative information from someone's credit report.

Credit score. A numerical rating that predicts how creditworthy a consumer is—that is, how likely the consumer is to repay a loan and make payments when due. A credit score is created, using a statistical program, from information about a consumer and his or her credit experiences, such as bill-paying history, the number and type of accounts, late payments, collection actions, outstanding debt, and the age of accounts, collected from the consumer's credit application and credit report.

Default judgment. If you are sued and you do not file papers in response to the lawsuit within the time allowed, the plaintiff (the person who sued you) can ask the court to enter a default judgment against you. When a default judgment is entered, you have lost the case. You can try to get the default judgment set aside, but it can be difficult to do so.

Deficiency balance. The difference between the amount you owe a creditor who has foreclosed on your house or repossessed an item of personal property and the amount that the sale of the property brings in.

Discharge. When a bankruptcy court erases your debts.

Exempt property or exemption. Items of property you are allowed to keep if a creditor gets a judgment against you or you file for bankruptcy.

Foreclosure. The forced sale of a house by the mortgage lender or another creditor with a lien on the house (such as the IRS or an unpaid contractor) to recover what the homeowner owes.

Guarantor. A person who pledges to repay a loan or debt in the event the primary debtor does not pay. Many people use guarantors to qualify for a loan or credit card.

Installment contract. A written agreement to pay for purchased goods or services by making regularly scheduled payments of principal and interest.

Judgment. The decision issued by a court at the end of a lawsuit.

Judgment creditor. A creditor who has sued you and obtained a court judgment.

Judgment debtor. Once a creditor sues you and gets a court judgment, you may be referred to as a judgment debtor.

Judgment proof. Having little or no property or income that a creditor can legally take to collect on a judgment, now or in the foreseeable future.

Lien. A notice a creditor attaches to property telling the world that the property owner owes the creditor money.

Necessities. Articles needed to sustain life, such as food, clothing, medical care, and shelter.

Nonexempt property. The property at debtor is at risk of losing if a creditor gets a judgment against the debtor or the debtor files for bankruptcy.

Open-end credit. A credit plan that involves repeated transactions, a fluctuating balance, and no fixed repayment period. The creditor sets a credit limit and allows the consumer to charge up to that limit as long as he or she makes required payments. Open-end credit plans are often called "revolving credit," and include retail installment accounts and bank credit cards.

Postjudgment interest. Interest on a court judgment that a creditor may add from the time the judgment is entered in the court clerk's record until it is paid.

Prejudgment attachment. A legal procedure that lets an unsecured creditor tie up property before obtaining a court judgment. The attachment freezes the property—it can't be sold, spent (in the case of money), or given away.

Prejudgment interest. The interest a creditor is entitled to collect under a loan agreement or by operation of law before obtaining a court judgment.

Prepayment penalty. A fee imposed by some lenders if a loan is paid off early and the lender doesn't earn all the interest it had anticipated.

Secured credit card. A credit card obtained by depositing some money into a savings account while the consumer has no access to that account. The money deposited is security for paying the charges on the card.

Secured creditor. A creditor owed a secured debt—that is, a debt for which payment is guaranteed by a specific item of property (collateral). If the debt isn't paid, the secured creditor can take the collateral.

Secured debt. A debt for which a specific item of property (called "collateral") guarantees payment of the debt. If the debt isn't paid, the creditor can take the collateral.

Security agreement. A contract a consumer must sign when taking out a secured loan.

The agreement specifies precisely what property (collateral) can be taken by the creditor in case of default.

Security interest. The right of a secured creditor to take property in the event of default.

Statute of limitations. The time limit to file a lawsuit, as determined by state law.

Unsecured creditor. A creditor who is owed an unsecured debt. If the debtor doesn't pay, an unsecured creditor's primary recourse is to sue, obtain a court judgment, and then attach wages or seize property.

Unsecured debt. A debt for which no specific item of property guarantees repayment.

Wage assignment. A method of voluntarily paying a debt through deductions from the debtor's paycheck.

Wage attachment. A method of involuntarily paying a debt through deductions from the debtor's paycheck, commonly used to collect court judgments and back-owed child support.

Wage withholding. A method of collecting child support through withholding a portion of the debtor's paycheck.

■

State and Federal Agencies

Where to Complain About Credit Discrimination

If you believe you have been a victim of credit discrimination, here are the appropriate government agencies to contact:

Consumer Response Center
Federal Trade Commission
Washington, DC 20580

Contact the FTC if you have been discriminated against by a store, mortgage company, small loan and finance company, oil company, public utility, state credit union, government lending program, or travel and expense credit card company. Although the FTC doesn't intervene in individual disputes, the information you provide may show a pattern of violations on which it can act.

Comptroller of the Currency
Compliance Management
Mail Stop 7-5
Washington, DC 20219

Use this address if your complaint is about a nationally chartered bank ("National" or "N.A." will be in its name).

Federal Deposit Insurance Corporation
Consumer Affairs Division
Washington, DC 20429

Contact the FDIC if your complaint is about a state-chartered bank that is insured by the FDIC but is not a member of the Federal Reserve System.

Office of Thrift Supervision
Consumer Affairs Program
Washington, DC 20552

Use this address to complain about a federally chartered or federally insured savings and loan association.

National Credit Union Administration
Consumer Affairs Division
Washington, DC 20456

Use this address if your complaint is about a federally chartered credit union.

Department of Justice
Civil Rights Division
Washington, DC 20530

You can complain to the Justice Department about any type of creditor.

State Consumer Protection Agencies

Alabama

Consumer Affairs Division
Office of Attorney General
Alabama State House
11 South Union Street, Third Floor
Montgomery, AL 36130
334-242-7300
800-392-5658
www.ago.state.al.us

Alaska

Consumer Protection Unit
Fair Business Practices Section
Office of the Attorney General
1031 West 4th Avenue, Suite 200
Anchorage AK 99501-5903
907-269-5100
www.law.state.ak.us/consumer

Arizona

Consumer Information and Complaints
Office of Attorney General
1275 West Washington Street
Phoenix, AZ 85007-2926
602-542-5763
800-352-8431
602-542-5002 (TTY)
www.ag.state.az.us

Arkansas

Consumer Protection Division
Office of the Attorney General
323 Center Street, Suite 200
Little Rock, AR 72201
501-682-2341
800-482-8982
501-682-6073 (TTY)
www.ag.state.ar.us/consumer/home.htm

California

Public Inquiry Unit
Office of the Attorney General
Department of Justice
P.O. Box 944255
Sacramento, CA 94244-2550
916-322-3360
800-952-5225
916-324-5564 (TDY)
http://caag.stateca.us/consumers

Colorado

Consumer Protection Section
Office of Attorney General
1525 Sherman Street, Fifth Floor
Denver, CO 80203-1768
303-866-5189
800-222-4444
www.ago.state.co.us/consprot.stm

Connecticut

Department of Consumer Protection
165 Capitol Avenue
Hartford, CT 06106-1630
860-713-6300
800-831-7225
860-713-7240 (TDD)
www.ct.gov/dcp

Delaware

Consumer Protection Unit
Office of the Attorney General
820 North French Street
Carvel State Building
Wilmington, DE 19801
302-577-8600
800-220-5424
www.state.de.us/attgen/fraud/
    consumerprotection/consumerprotection.
    htm

District of Columbia

Department of Consumer and Regulatory
  Affairs
941 North Capitol Street, NE
Washington, DC 20002
202-442-4400
202-442-9480 (TDD-TTY)
www.dcra.dc.gov/dcra

Florida

Division of Consumer Services
Department of Agriculture and Consumer
  Services
2005 Apalachee Parkway
Tallahassee, FL 32399-6500
850-488-2221
800-435-7352
www.doacs.state.fl.us or www.800helpfla.com

Georgia

Governor's Office of Consumer Affairs
2 Martin Luther King, Jr. Drive, Suite 356
Atlanta, GA 30334
404-651-8600
800-869-1123
www2.state.ga.us/gaoca

Hawaii

Office of Consumer Protection
235 S. Beretonia Street
Suite 801
Leiopapa A Kamehameha Building
Honolulu, HI 96813
808-587-3222
808-586-2630
www.state.hi.us/dcca/areas/ocp

Idaho

Consumer Protection Unit
Office of Attorney General
700 W. Jefferson Street
P.O. Box 83720
Boise, ID 83720-0010
208-334-2400
800-432-3545
www.state.id.us/ag/consumer

Illinois

Consumer Protection Division
Office of Attorney General
100 W. Randolph Street
Chicago, IL 60601
312-814-3000
800-386-5438
800-964-3013 (TTY)
www.ag.state.il.us/consumer/consumer.htm

Indiana

Consumer Credit Division
Department of Financial Institutions
30 South Meridian Street
Suite 300
Indianapolis, IN 46204
317-232-3955
800-382-4880
www.in.gov/dfi

Iowa

Consumer Protection Division
Office of Attorney General
1305 E. Walnut Street
Des Moines, IA 50319
515-281-5926
www.state.ia.us/government/ag/
  consumer.html

Kansas

Consumer Protection and Antitrust Division
Office of Attorney General
120 S.W. Tenth Avenue
Topeka, KS 66612-1597
785-296-3751
800-432-2310
785-291-3767 (TTY)
www.accesskansas.org/ksag/Divisions/
    consumer

Kentucky

Consumer Protection Division
Office of the Attorney General
1024 Capitol Center Drive
Suite 200
Frankfort, KY 40601
502-696-5389
888-423-9257
www.ag.ky.gov/cp

Louisiana

Consumer Protection Section
Office of the Attorney General
P.O. Box 94095
Baton Rouge, LA 70804-9095
225-326-6465
800-351-4889
www.ag.state.la.us/consumers.aspx

Maine

Consumer Information and Mediation Service
Public Protection Division
Office of the Attorney General
6 State House Station
Augusta, ME 04333-0006
207-626-8800
207-626-8865 (TTY)
www.maine.gov/ag/?r=protection

Maryland

Consumer Protection Division
Office of Attorney General
200 St. Paul Place
Baltimore, MD 21202-2022
410-576-6550
888-743-0023
www.oag.state.md.us/consumer

Massachusetts

Office of Consumer Affairs and Business
    Regulation
10 Park Plaza, Suite 5170
Boston, MA 02116
617-973-8787 (hotline)
617-973-8700
888-283-3757
www.mass.gov/consumer

Michigan

Consumer Protection Division
Office of Attorney General
P.O. Box 30213
Lansing, MI 48909
517-373-1140
877-765-8388
www.ag.state.mi.us/cp

Minnesota

Consumer Protection Division
Office of Attorney General
1400 NCL Tower
445 Minnesota Street
St. Paul, MN 55101-2130
651-296-3353
800-657-3787
651-297-7206 (TTY)
800-366-4812 (TTY)
www.ag.state.mn.us/consumer

Mississippi

Consumer Protection Division
Office of the Attorney General
P.O. Box 22947
Jackson, MS 39225-2947
601-359-4230
800-281-4418
www.ago.state.ms.us/divisions/consumer

Missouri

Consumer Protection Division
Attorney General's Office
P.O. Box 899
Jefferson City, MO 65102
573-751-3321
800-392-8222
www.ago.state.mo.us/fraud.htm

Montana

Consumer Protection Office
1219 Eighth Avenue
P.O. Box 200151
Helena, MT 59620-0151
406-444-4500
www.discoveringmontana.com/doa/
    consumerprotection

Nebraska

Consumer Protection Division
Office of Attorney General
2115 State Capitol Building
Lincoln, NE 68509-8920
402-471-2682
800-727-6432
www.ago.state.ne.us

Nevada

Consumer Affairs Division
Department of Business and Industry
1850 E. Sahara Avenue, Suite 101
Las Vegas, NV 89104

702-486-7355
[or]
4600 Kietzke Lane
Building B, Suite 113
Reno, NV 89502
775-688-1800
www.fyiconsumer.org

New Hampshire

Consumer Protection and Antitrust Bureau
Department of Justice
33 Capitol Street
Concord, NH 03301-6397
603-271-3658
www.nh.gov/nhdoj/consumer

New Jersey

Division of Consumer Affairs
Department of Law and Public Safety
124 Halsey Street
Newark, NJ 07102
973-504-6200
800-242-5846
973-504-6588 (TDD)
www.njconsumeraffairs.gov

New Mexico

Consumer Protection Division
Office of Attorney General
P.O. Drawer 1508
Santa Fe, NM 87504-1508
505-827-6000
800-678-1508
www.ago.state.nm.us/divs/cons/cons.htm

New York

Consumer Protection Board
5 Empire State Plaza, Suite 2101
Albany, NY 12223-1556
518-474-3514
518-474-8583 (Complaint Unit)

434 | SOLVE YOUR MONEY TROUBLES

800-697-1220
800-788-9898 (TTY)
www.consumer.state.ny.us

North Carolina

Consumer Protection Division
Department of Justice, Attorney General's
Office
9001 Mail Service Center
Raleigh, NC 27699-9001
919-716-6000
877-566-7226
www.ncdoj.com/consumer protection/cp_
about.jsp

North Dakota

Consumer Protection Division
Office of Attorney General
600 East Boulevard Avenue
Dept. 125
Bismarck, ND 58505-0040
701-328-3404
800-472-2600
www.ag.state.nd.us/CPAT/CPAT.htm

Ohio

Consumer Protection Division
Office of Attorney General
State Office Tower
30 East Broad Street, 17th Floor
Columbus, OH 43215-3428
614-466-4320
800-282-0515
www.ag.state.oh.us/sections/consumer_
protection

Oklahoma

Consumer Protection Unit
Office of the Attorney General
4545 N. Lincoln Boulevard, Suite 112

Oklahoma City, OK 73105-3498
405-521-3921
www.oag.state.ok.us/oagweb.nsf/consumer

Oregon

Financial Fraud/Consumer Protection Section
1162 Court Street, NE
Salem, OR 97301-4096
503-378-4320
503-229-5576 (Portland toll-free)
877-877-9392
www.doj.state.or.us/FinFraud/welcome3.htm

Pennsylvania

Bureau of Consumer Protection
Office of Attorney General
Strawberry Square, 14th Floor
Harrisburg, PA 17120
717-787-9707
800-441-2555
www.attorneygeneral.gov/ppd/bcp

Rhode Island

Consumer Protection Unit
Department of Attorney General
150 S. Main Street
Providence, RI 02903
401-274-4400
800-852-7776
401-453-0410 (TTY)
www.riag.state.ri.us/civil/consumer.php

South Carolina

Department of Consumer Affairs
P.O. Box 5757
3600 Forest Drive, 3rd Floor
Columbia, SC 29250
803-734-4200
800-922-1594
www.state.sc.us/consumer

South Dakota

Division of Consumer Protection
Office of the Attorney General
500 East Capitol Avenue
Pierre, SD 57501-5070
605-773-4400
800-300-1986
www.state.sd.us/attorney/office/divisions/
consumer

Tennessee

Division of Consumer Affairs
Department of Commerce and Insurance
500 James Robertson Parkway
Nashville, TN 37243-0600
615-741-4737
800-342-8385
www.state.tn.us/consumer

Texas

Consumer Protection Division
Office of the Attorney General
P.O. Box 12548
Austin, TX 78711-2548
512-463-2185
800-621-0508
www.oag.state.tx.us/consumer/consumer.shtml

Utah

Division of Consumer Protection
Department of Commerce
160 E. 300 South
SM Box 146704
Salt Lake City, UT 84114-6704
801-530-6601
800-721-7233
www.commerce.utah.gov/dcp

Vermont

Consumer Assistance Program
Office of Attorney General
104 Morrill Hall, UVM
Burlington, VT 05405-0106
802-656-3183
800-649-2424
www.atg.state.vt.us/disply.php?smod=8

Virginia

Office of Consumer Affairs
Department of Agriculture and Consumer
  Services
1100 Bank Street
Suite 100
Richmond, VA 23219
804-786-2042
800-552-9963
www.vdacs.state.va.us/consumers

Washington

Consumer Resource Center
Office of the Attorney General
P.O. Box 40100
1125 Washington Street SE
Olympia, WA 98504-0100
360-753-6200
800-551-4636
800-276-9883 (TDD)
www.wa.gov/ago/consumer

West Virginia

Consumer Protection Division
Office of the Attorney General
1900 Kanawha Boulevard
Room 26E
Charleston, WV 25305-9924
304-558-8986
800-368-8808
www.state.wv.us/wvag

Wisconsin

Bureau of Consumer Protection

Department of Agriculture, Trade, and
   Consumer Protection

P.O. Box 8911

Madison, WI 53708-8911

608-224-4960

800-422-7128

608-224-5058 (TTY)

www.datcp.state.wi.us/core/consumerinfo

Wyoming

Consumer Protection Unit

Attorney General's Office

123 Capitol

200 W. 24th Street

Cheyenne, WY 82002

307-777-7874

800-438-5799

www.attorneygeneral.state.wy.us/consumer.htm

■

State and Federal Exemption Tables

Alabama

Federal bankruptcy exemptions not available. All law references are to Alabama Code unless otherwise noted.

ASSET	EXEMPTION	LAW
homestead	Real property or mobile home to $5,000; property cannot exceed 160 acres	6-10-2
	Must record homestead declaration before attempted sale of home	6-10-20
insurance	Annuity proceeds or avails to $250 per month	27-14-32
	Disability proceeds or avails to an average of $250 per month	27-14-31
	Fraternal benefit society benefits	27-34-27
	Life insurance proceeds or avails	6-10-8; 27-14-29
	Life insurance proceeds or avails if clause prohibits proceeds from being used to pay beneficiary's creditors	27-15-26
	Mutual aid association benefits	27-30-25
pensions	Tax-exempt retirement accounts, including 401(k)s, 403(b)s, profit-sharing and money purchase plans, SEP and SIMPLE IRAs, and defined-benefit plans	11 U.S.C. § 522(b)(3)(C)
	Traditional and Roth IRAs to $1,095,000 per person	11 U.S.C. § 522(b)(3)(C); (n)
	IRAs & other retirement accounts	19-3-1
	Judges (only payments being received)	12-18-10(a),(b)
	Law enforcement officers	36-21-77
	State employees	36-27-28
	Teachers	16-25-23
personal property	Books of debtor & family	6-10-6
	Burial place for self & family	6-10-5
	Church pew for self & family	6-10-5
	Clothing of debtor & family	6-10-6
	Family portraits or pictures	6-10-6
public benefits	Aid to blind, aged, disabled; & other public assistance	38-4-8
	Crime victims' compensation	15-23-15(e)
	Southeast Asian War POWs' benefits	31-7-2
	Unemployment compensation	25-4-140
	Workers' compensation	25-5-86(b)
tools of trade	Arms, uniforms, equipment that state military personnel are required to keep	31-2-78
wages	With respect to consumer loans, consumer credit sales, & consumer leases, 75% of weekly net earnings or 30 times the federal minimum hourly wage; all other cases, 75% of earned but unpaid wages; bankruptcy judge may authorize more for low-income debtors	5-19-15; 6-10-7
wildcard	$3,000 of any personal property, except wages	6-10-6

Alaska

Alaska law states that only the items found in Alaska Statutes §§ 9.38.010, 9.38.015(a), 9.38.017, 9.38.020, 9.38.025, and 9.38.030 may be exempted in bankruptcy. In *In re McNutt*, 87 B.R. 84 (9th Cir. 1988), however, an Alaskan debtor used the federal bankruptcy exemptions. All law references are to Alaska Statutes unless otherwise noted.

Alaska exemption amounts are adjusted regularly by administrative order. Current amounts are found at 8 Alaska Admin. Code tit. 8, § 95.030.

ASSET	EXEMPTION	LAW
homestead	$67,500 (joint owners may each claim a portion, but total can't exceed $67,500)	09.38.010(a)
insurance	Disability benefits	09.38.015(b); 09.38.030(e)(1),(5)
	Fraternal benefit society benefits	21.84.240
	Life insurance or annuity contracts, total avails to $12,500	09.38.025
	Medical, surgical, or hospital benefits	09.38.015(a)(3)
miscellaneous	Alimony, to extent wages exempt	09.38.030(e)(2)
	Child support payments made by collection agency	09.38.015(b)
	Liquor licenses	09.38.015(a)(7)
	Property of business partnership	09.38.100(b)
pensions	Tax-exempt retirement accounts, including 401(k)s, 403(b)s, profit-sharing and money purchase plans, SEP and SIMPLE IRAs, and defined-benefit plans	11 U.S.C. § 522(b)(3)(C)
	Traditional and Roth IRAs to $1,095,000 per person	11 U.S.C. § 522(b)(3)(C); (n)
	Elected public officers (only benefits building up)	09.38.015(b)
	ERISA-qualified benefits deposited more than 120 days before filing bankruptcy	09.38.017
	Judicial employees (only benefits building up)	09.38.015(b)
	Public employees (only benefits building up)	09.38.015(b); 39.35.505
	Roth & traditional IRAs, medical savings accounts	09.38.017(e)(3)
	Teachers (only benefits building up)	09.38.015(b)
	Other pensions, to extent wages exempt (only payments being received)	09.38.030(e)(5)
personal property	Books, musical instruments, clothing, family portraits, household goods, & heirlooms to $3,750 total	09.38.020(a)
	Building materials	34.35.105
	Burial plot	09.38.015(a)(1)
	Cash or other liquid assets to $1,750; for sole wage earner in household, $2,750 (restrictions apply—see *wages*)	09.38.030(b)
	Deposit in apartment or condo owners' association	09.38.010(e)
	Health aids needed	09.38.015(a)(2)
	Jewelry to $1,250	09.38.020(b)
	Motor vehicle to $3,750; vehicle's market value can't exceed $25,000	09.38.020(e)
	Personal injury recoveries, to extent wages exempt	09.38.030(e)(3)

personal property (continued)	Pets to $1,250	09.38.020(d)
	Proceeds for lost, damaged, or destroyed exempt property	09.38.060
	Tuition credits under an advance college tuition payment contract	09.38.015(a)(8)
	Wrongful death recoveries, to extent wages exempt	09.38.030(e)(3)
public benefits	Adult assistance to elderly, blind, disabled	47.25.550
	Alaska longevity bonus	09.38.015(a)(5)
	Crime victims' compensation	09.38.015(a)(4)
	Federally exempt public benefits paid or due	09.38.015(a)(6)
	General relief assistance	47.25.210
	Senior care (prescription drug) benefits	09.38.015(a)(10)
	20% of permanent fund dividends	43.23.065
	Unemployment compensation	09.38.015(b); 23.20.405
	Workers' compensation	23.30.160
tools of trade	Implements, books, & tools of trade to $3,500	09.38.020(c)
wages	Weekly net earnings to $438; for sole wage earner in a household, $688; if you don't receive weekly or semimonthly pay, can claim $1,750 in cash or liquid assets paid any month; for sole wage earner in household, $2,750	9.38.030(a),(b); 9.38.050(b)
wildcard	None	

Arizona

Federal bankruptcy exemptions not available. All law references are to Arizona Revised Statutes unless otherwise noted.

ASSET	EXEMPTION	LAW
homestead	Real property, an apartment, or mobile home you occupy to $150,000; sale proceeds exempt 18 months after sale or until new home purchased, whichever occurs first (husband & wife may not double)	33-1101(A)
	May record homestead declaration to clarify which one of multiple eligible parcels is being claimed as homestead	33-1102
insurance	Fraternal benefit society benefits	20-877
	Group life insurance policy or proceeds	20-1132
	Health, accident, or disability benefits	33-1126(A)(4)
	Life insurance cash value or proceeds, or annuity contract if owned at least two years and beneficiary is dependent family member	33-1126(A)(6); 20-1131(D)
	Life insurance proceeds to $20,000 if beneficiary is spouse or child	33-1126(A)(1)
miscellaneous	Alimony, child support needed for support	33-1126(A)(3)
	Minor child's earnings, unless debt is for child	33-1126(A)(2)
pensions see also wages	Tax-exempt retirement accounts, including 401(k)s, 403(b)s, profit-sharing and money purchase plans, SEP and SIMPLE IRAs, and defined-benefit plans	11 U.S.C. § 522(b)(3)(C)
	Traditional and Roth IRAs to $1,095,000 per person	11 U.S.C. § 522(b)(3)(C); (n)

pensions (continued)	Board of regents members, faculty & administrative officers under board's jurisdiction	15-1628(I)
	District employees	48-227
	ERISA-qualified benefits deposited over 120 days before filing	33-1126(B)
	IRAs & Roth IRAs	33-1126(B); *In re Herrscher*, 121 B.R. 29 (D. Ariz. 1989)
	Firefighters	9-968
	Police officers	9-931
	Rangers	41-955
	State employees retirement & disability	38-792; 38-797.11
personal property *husband & wife may double all personal property*	2 beds & bedding; 1 living room chair per person; 1 dresser, table, lamp; kitchen table; dining room table & 4 chairs (1 more per person); living room carpet or rug; couch; 3 lamps; 3 coffee or end tables; pictures, paintings, personal drawings, family portraits; refrigerator, stove, washer, dryer, vacuum cleaner; TV, radio, stereo, alarm clock to $4,000 total	33-1123
	Bank deposit to $150 in one account	33-1126(A)(9)
	Bible; bicycle; sewing machine; typewriter; burial plot; rifle, pistol, or shotgun to $500 total	33-1125
	Books to $250; clothing to $500; wedding & engagement rings to $1,000; watch to $100; pets, horses, milk cows, & poultry to $500; musical instruments to $250	33-1125
	Food & fuel to last 6 months	33-1124
	Funeral deposits to $5,000	32-1391.05(4)
	Health aids	33-1125(9)
	Motor vehicle to $5,000 ($10,000, if disabled)	33-1125(8)
	Prepaid rent or security deposit to $1,000 or 1-1/2 times your rent, whichever is less, in lieu of homestead	33-1126(C)
	Proceeds for sold or damaged exempt property	33-1126(A)(5),(8)
	Wrongful death awards	12-592
public benefits	Unemployment compensation	23-783(A)
	Welfare benefits	46-208
	Workers' compensation	23-1068(B)
tools of trade *husband & wife may double*	Arms, uniforms, & accoutrements of profession or office required by law	33-1130(3)
	Farm machinery, utensils, seed, instruments of husbandry, feed, grain, & animals to $2,500 total	33-1130(2)
	Library & teaching aids of teacher	33-1127
	Tools, equipment, instruments, & books to $2,500	33-1130(1)
wages	75% of earned but unpaid weekly net earnings or 30 times the federal minimum hourly wage; 50% of wages for support orders; bankruptcy judge may authorize more for low-income debtors	33-1131
wildcard	None	

Arkansas

Federal bankruptcy exemptions available. All law references are to Arkansas Code Annotated unless otherwise noted.

Note: *In re Holt*, 894 F.2d 1005 (8th Cir. 1990) held that Arkansas residents are limited to exemptions in the Arkansas Constitution. Statutory exemptions can still be used within Arkansas for nonbankruptcy purposes, but they cannot be claimed in bankruptcy

ASSET	EXEMPTION	LAW
homestead *choose Option 1 or 2*	1. For married person or head of family: unlimited exemption on real or personal property used as residence to 1/4 acre in city, town, or village, or 80 acres elsewhere; if property is between 1/4–1 acre in city, town, or village, or 80-160 acres elsewhere, additional limit is $2,500; homestead may not exceed 1 acre in city, town, or village, or 160 acres elsewhere (husband & wife may not double)	Constitution 9-3; 9-4, 9-5; 16-66-210; 16-66-218(b)(3), (4) *In re Stevens*, 829 F.2d 693 (8th Cir. 1987)
	2. Real or personal property used as residence to $800 if single; $1,250 if married	16-66-218(a)(1)
insurance	Annuity contract	23-79-134
	Disability benefits	23-79-133
	Fraternal benefit society benefits	23-74-403
	Group life insurance	23-79-132
	Life, health, accident, or disability cash value or proceeds paid or due to $500	16-66-209; Constitution 9-1, 9-2; *In re Holt*, 894 F. 2d 1005 (8th Cir. 1990)
	Life insurance proceeds if clause prohibits proceeds from being used to pay beneficiary's creditors	23-79-131
	Life insurance proceeds or avails if beneficiary isn't the insured	23-79-131
	Mutual assessment life or disability benefits to $1,000	23-72-114
	Stipulated insurance premiums	23-71-112
pensions	Tax-exempt retirement accounts, including 401(k)s, 403(b)s, profit-sharing and money purchase plans, SEP and SIMPLE IRAs, and defined-benefit plans	11 U.S.C. § 522(b)(3)(C)
	Traditional and Roth IRAs to $1,095,000 per person	11 U.S.C. § 522(b)(3)(C); (n)
	Disabled firefighters	24-11-814
	Disabled police officers	24-11-417
	Firefighters	24-10-616
	IRA deposits to $20,000 if deposited over 1 year before filing for bankruptcy	16-66-218(b)(16)
	Police officers	24-10-616
	School employees	24-7-715
	State police officers	24-6-205; 24-6-223
personal property	Burial plot to 5 acres, if choosing federal homestead exemption (Option 2)	16-66-207; 16-66-218(a)(1)
	Clothing	Constitution 9-1, 9-2
	Motor vehicle to $1,200	16-66-218(a)(2)
	Prepaid funeral trusts	23-40-117
	Wedding rings	16-66-219

public benefits	Crime victims' compensation	16-90-716(e)
	Unemployment compensation	11-10-109
	Workers' compensation	11-9-110
tools of trade	Implements, books, & tools of trade to $750	16-66-218(a)(4)
wages	Earned but unpaid wages due for 60 days; in no event less than $25 per week	16-66-208; 16-66-218(b)(6)
wildcard	$500 of any personal property if married or head of family; $200 if not married	Constitution 9-1, 9-2; 16-66-218(b)(1),(2)

California—System 1

Federal bankruptcy exemptions not available. California has two systems; you must select one or the other. All law references are to California Code of Civil Procedure unless otherwise noted. Many exemptions do not apply to claims for child support.

Note: California's exemption amounts are no longer updated in the statutes themselves. California Code of Civil Procedure section 740.150 deputized the California Judicial Council to update the exemption amounts every three years. (The next revision will be in 2010.) As a result, the amounts listed in this chart will not match the amounts that appear in the cited statutes. The current exemption amounts can be found on the California Judicial Council website, www.courtinfo.ca.gov/forms/exemptions.htm.

ASSET	EXEMPTION	LAW
homestead	Real or personal property you occupy including mobile home, boat, stock cooperative, community apartment, planned development, or condo to $50,000 if single & not disabled; $75,000 for families if no other member has a homestead (if only one spouse files, may exempt one-half of amount if home held as community property & all of amount if home held as tenants in common); $150,000 if 65 or older, or physically or mentally disabled; $150,000 if 55 or older, single, & earn under $15,000 or married & earn under $20,000 & creditors seek to force the sale of your home; forced sale proceeds received exempt for 6 months after (husband & wife may not double)	704.710; 704.720; 704.730 *In re McFall*, 112 B.R. 336 (9th Cir. B.A.P. 1990)
	May file homestead declaration to protect exemption amount from attachment of judicial liens and to protect proceeds of voluntary sale for 6 months	704.920
insurance	Disability or health benefits	704.130
	Fidelity bonds	Labor 404
	Fraternal benefit society benefits	704.170
	Fraternal unemployment benefits	704.120
	Homeowners' insurance proceeds for 6 months after received, to homestead exemption amount	704.720(b)
	Life insurance proceeds if clause prohibits proceeds from being used to pay beneficiary's creditors	Ins. 10132; Ins. 10170; Ins. 10171
	Matured life insurance benefits needed for support	704.100(c)
	Unmatured life insurance policy cash surrender value completely exempt. Loan value exempt to $10,775	704.100(b)
miscellaneous	Business or professional licenses	695.060

miscellaneous (continued)	Inmates' trust funds to $1,350 (husband & wife may not double)	704.090
	Property of business partnership	Corp. 16501-04
pensions	Tax-exempt retirement accounts, including 401(k)s, 403(b)s, profit-sharing and money purchase plans, SEP and SIMPLE IRAs, and defined-benefit plans	11 U.S.C. § 522(b)(3)(C)
	Traditional and Roth IRAs to $1,095,000 per person	11 U.S.C. § 522(b)(3)(C); (n)
	County employees	Gov't 31452
	County firefighters	Gov't 32210
	County peace officers	Gov't 31913
	Private retirement benefits, including IRAs & Keoghs	704.115
	Public employees	Gov't 21255
	Public retirement benefits	704.110
personal property	Appliances, furnishings, clothing, & food	704.020
	Bank deposits from Social Security Administration to $2,700 ($4,050 for husband & wife); unlimited if SS funds are not commingled with other funds	704.080
	Bank deposits of other public benefits to $1,350 ($2,025 for husband & wife)	
	Building materials to repair or improve home to $2,700 (husband & wife may not double)	704.030
	Burial plot	704.200
	Funds held in escrow	Fin. 17410
	Health aids	704.050
	Jewelry, heirlooms, & art to $6,750 total (husband & wife may not double)	704.040
	Motor vehicles to $2,550, or $2,550 in auto insurance for loss or damages (husband & wife may not double)	704.010
	Personal injury & wrongful death causes of action	704.140(a); 704.150(a)
	Personal injury & wrongful death recoveries needed for support; if receiving installments, at least 75%	704.140(b),(c),(d); 704.150(b),(c)
public benefits	Aid to blind, aged, disabled; public assistance	704.170
	Financial aid to students	704.190
	Relocation benefits	704.180
	Unemployment benefits	704.120
	Union benefits due to labor dispute	704.120(b)(5)
	Workers' compensation	704.160
tools of trade	Tools, implements, materials, instruments, uniforms, books, furnishings, & equipment to $6,750 total ($13,475 total if used by both spouses in same occupation)	704.060
	Commercial vehicle (Vehicle Code § 260) to $4,850 ($9,700 total if used by both spouses in same occupation)	704.060
wages	Minimum 75% of wages paid within 30 days prior to filing	704.070
	Public employees' vacation credits; if receiving installments, at least 75%	704.113
wildcard	None	

California—System 2

Refer to the notes for California—System 1, above.

Note: Married couples may not double any exemptions. (*In re Talmadge*, 832 F.2d 1120 (9th Cir. 1987); *In re Baldwin*, 70 B.R. 612 (9th Cir. B.A.P. 1987).)

ASSET	EXEMPTION	LAW
homestead	Real or personal property, including co-op, used as residence to $20,725; unused portion of homestead may be applied to any property	703.140(b)(1)
insurance	Disability benefits	703.140(b)(10)(C)
	Life insurance proceeds needed for support of family	703.140(b)(11)(C)
	Unmatured life insurance contract accrued avails to $11,075	703.140(b)(8)
	Unmatured life insurance policy other than credit	703.140(b)(7)
miscellaneous	Alimony, child support needed for support	703.140(b)(10)(D)
pensions	Tax-exempt retirement accounts, including 401(k)s, 403(b)s, profit-sharing and money purchase plans, SEP and SIMPLE IRAs, and defined-benefit plans	11 U.S.C. § 522(b)(3)(C)
	Traditional and Roth IRAs to $1,095,000 per person	11 U.S.C. § 522(b)(3)(C); (n)
	ERISA-qualified benefits needed for support	703.140(b)(10)(E)
personal property	Animals, crops, appliances, furnishings, household goods, books, musical instruments, & clothing to $525 per item	703.140(b)(3)
	Burial plot to $20,725, in lieu of homestead	703.140(b)(1)
	Health aids	703.140(b)(9)
	Jewelry to $1,350	703.140(b)(4)
	Motor vehicle to $3,300	703.140(b)(2)
	Personal injury recoveries to $20,725 (not to include pain & suffering; pecuniary loss)	703.140(b)(11)(D),(E)
	Wrongful death recoveries needed for support	703.140(b)(11)(B)
public benefits	Crime victims' compensation	703.140(b)(11)(A)
	Public assistance	703.140(b)(10)(A)
	Social Security	703.140(b)(10)(A)
	Unemployment compensation	703.140(b)(10)(A)
	Veterans' benefits	703.140(b)(10)(B)
tools of trade	Implements, books, & tools of trade to $2,075	703.140(b)(6)
wages	None (use federal nonbankruptcy wage exemption)	
wildcard	$1,100 of any property	703.140(b)(5)
	Unused portion of homestead or burial exemption of any property	703.140(b)(5)

Colorado

Federal bankruptcy exemptions not available. All law references are to Colorado Revised Statutes unless otherwise noted.

ASSET	EXEMPTION	LAW
homestead	Real property, mobile home, manufactured home, or house trailer you occupy to $45,000; sale proceeds exempt 1 year after received	38-41-201; 38-41-201.6; 38-41-203; 38-41-207; *In re Pastrana*, 216 B.R. 948 (Colo., 1998)

homestead (continued)	Spouse or child of deceased owner may claim homestead exemption	38-41-204
insurance	Disability benefits to $200 per month; if receive lump sum, entire amount exempt	10-16-212
	Fraternal benefit society benefits	10-14-403
	Group life insurance policy or proceeds	10-7-205
	Homeowners' insurance proceeds for 1 year after received, to homestead exemption amount	38-41-209
	Life insurance cash surrender value to $50,000, except contributions to policy within past 48 months	13-54-102(1)(l)
	Life insurance proceeds if clause prohibits proceeds from being used to pay beneficiary's creditors	10-7-106
miscellaneous	Child support	13-54-102.5
	Property of business partnership	7-60-125
pensions *see also wages*	Tax-exempt retirement accounts, including 401(k)s, 403(b)s, profit-sharing and money purchase plans, SEP and SIMPLE IRAs, and defined-benefit plans	11 U.S.C. § 522(b)(3)(C)
	Traditional and Roth IRAs to $1,095,000 per person	11 U.S.C. § 522(b)(3)(C); (n)
	ERISA-qualified benefits, including IRAs & Roth IRAs	13-54-102(1)(s)
	Firefighters & police officers	31-30.5-208; 31-31-203
	Public employees' pensions & defined contribution plans as of 2006	24-51-212
	Public employees' deferred compensation	24-52-105
	Teachers	22-64-120
	Veteran's pension for veteran, spouse, or dependents if veteran served in war or armed conflict	13-54-102(1)(h); 13-54-104
personal property	1 burial plot per family member	13-54-102(1)(d)
	Clothing to $1,500	13-54-102(1)(a)
	Food & fuel to $600	13-54-102(1)(f)
	Health aids	13-54-102(1)(p)
	Household goods to $3,000	13-54-102(1)(e)
	Jewelry & articles of adornment to $1,000	13-54-102(1)(b)
	Motor vehicles or bicycles used for work to $3,000; to $6,000 if used by a debtor or by a dependent who is disabled or 65 or over	13-54-102(j)(I), (II)
	Personal injury recoveries	13-54-102(1)(n)
	Family pictures & books to $1,500	13-54-102(1)(c)
	Proceeds for damaged exempt property	13-54-102(1)(m)
	Security deposits	13-54-102(1)(r)
public benefits	Aid to blind, aged, disabled; public assistance	26-2-131
	Crime victims' compensation	13-54-102(1)(q); 24-4.1-114
	Earned income tax credit	13-54-102(1)(o)
	Unemployment compensation	8-80-103
	Veteran's benefits for veteran, spouse, or child if veteran served in war or armed conflict	13-54-102(1)(h)
	Workers' compensation	8-42-124

tools of trade	Livestock or other animals, machinery, tools, equipment, & seed of person engaged in agriculture, to $25,000 total	13-54-102(1)(g)
	Professional's library to $3,000 (if not claimed under other tools of trade exemption)	13-54-102(1)(k)
	Stock in trade, supplies, fixtures, tools, machines, electronics, equipment, books, & other business materials, to $10,000 total	13-54-102(1)(i)
	Military equipment personally owned by members of the National Guard	13-54-102(1)(h.5)
wages	Minimum 75% of weekly net earnings or 30 times the federal minimum wage, whichever is greater, including pension & insurance payments	13-54-104
wildcard	None	

Connecticut

Federal bankruptcy exemptions available. All law references are to Connecticut General Statutes Annotated unless otherwise noted.

ASSET	EXEMPTION	LAW
homestead	Real property, including mobile or manufactured home, to $75,000; applies only to claims arising after 1993, but to $125,000 in the case of a money judgment arising out of services provided at a hospital.	52-352a(e); 52-352b(t)
insurance	Disability benefits paid by association for its members	52-352b(p)
	Fraternal benefit society benefits	38a-637
	Health or disability benefits	52-352b(e)
	Life insurance proceeds if clause prohibits proceeds from being used to pay beneficiary's creditors	38a-454
	Life insurance proceeds or avails	38a-453
	Unmatured life insurance policy avails to $4,000 if beneficiary is dependent	52-352b(s)
miscellaneous	Alimony, to extent wages exempt	52-352b(n)
	Child support	52-352b(h)
	Farm partnership animals & livestock feed reasonably required to run farm where at least 50% of partners are members of same family	52-352d
pensions	Tax-exempt retirement accounts, including 401(k)s, 403(b)s, profit-sharing and money purchase plans, SEP and SIMPLE IRAs, and defined-benefit plans	11 U.S.C. § 522(b)(3)(C)
	Traditional and Roth IRAs to $1,095,000 per person	11 U.S.C. § 522(b)(3)(C); (n)
	ERISA-qualified benefits, including IRAs, Roth IRAs, & Keoghs, to extent wages exempt	52-321a; 52-352b(m)
	Medical savings account	52-321a
	Municipal employees	7-446
	State employees	5-171; 5-192w
	Teachers	10-183q
personal property	Appliances, food, clothing, furniture, bedding	52-352b(a)
	Burial plot	52-352b(c)
	Health aids needed	52-352b(f)
	Motor vehicle to $1,500	52-352b(j)

personal property (continued)	Proceeds for damaged exempt property	52-352b(q)
	Residential utility & security deposits for 1 residence	52-3252b(l)
	Spendthrift trust funds required for support of debtor & family	52-321(d)
	Transfers to a nonprofit debt adjuster	52-352b(u)
	Wedding & engagement rings	52-352b(k)
public benefits	Crime victims' compensation	52-352b(o); 54-213
	Public assistance	52-352b(d)
	Social Security	52-352b(g)
	Unemployment compensation	31-272(c); 52-352b(g)
	Veterans' benefits	52-352b(g)
	Workers' compensation	52-352b(g)
tools of trade	Arms, military equipment, uniforms, musical instruments of military personnel	52-352b(i)
	Tools, books, instruments, & farm animals needed	52-352b(b)
wages	Minimum 75% of earned but unpaid weekly disposable earnings, or 40 times the state or federal hourly minimum wage, whichever is greater	52-361a(f)
wildcard	$1,000 of any property	52-352b(r)

Delaware

Federal bankruptcy exemptions not available. All law references are to Delaware Code Annotated (in the form title number-section number) unless otherwise noted.

Note: A single person may exempt no more than $25,000 total in all exemptions (not including retirement plans); a husband & wife may exempt no more than $50,000 total (10-4914).

ASSET	EXEMPTION	LAW
homestead	Real property or manufactured home used as principal residence to $50,000 (spouses may not double)	10-4914(c)
	Property held as tenancy by the entirety may be exempt against debts owed by only one spouse	*In re Kelley,* 289 B.R. 38 (Bankr. D. Del. 2003)
insurance	Annuity contract proceeds to $350 per month	18-2728
	Fraternal benefit society benefits	18-6218
	Group life insurance policy or proceeds	18-2727
	Health or disability benefits	18-2726
	Life insurance proceeds if clause prohibits proceeds from being used to pay beneficiary's creditors	18-2729
	Life insurance proceeds or avails	18-2725
pensions	Tax-exempt retirement accounts, including 401(k)s, 403(b)s, profit-sharing and money purchase plans, SEP and SIMPLE IRAs, and defined-benefit plans	11 U.S.C. § 522(b)(3)(C)
	Traditional and Roth IRAs to $1,095,000 per person	11 U.S.C. § 522(b)(3)(C); (n)
	IRAs, Roth IRAs, & any other retirement plans	*In re Yuhas,* 104 F.3d 612 (3rd Cir. 1997)
	Kent County employees	9-4316
	Police officers	11-8803
	State employees	29-5503
	Volunteer firefighters	16-6653

personal property	Bible, books, & family pictures	10-4902(a)
	Burial plot	10-4902(a)
	Church pew or any seat in public place of worship	10-4902(a)
	Clothing, includes jewelry	10-4902(a)
	College investment plan account (limit for year before filing is $5,000 or average of past two years' contribution, whichever is more)	10-4916
	Principal and income from spendthrift trusts	12-3536
	Pianos & leased organs	10-4902(d)
	Sewing machines	10-4902(c)
public benefits	Aid to blind	31-2309
	Aid to aged, disabled, general assistance	31-513
	Crime victims' compensation	11-9011
	Unemployment compensation	19-3374
	Workers' compensation	19-2355
tools of trade	Tools of trade and/or vehicle necessary for employment to $15,000 each	10-4914(c)
	Tools, implements, & fixtures to $75 in New Castle & Sussex Counties; to $50 in Kent County	10-4902(b)
wages	85% of earned but unpaid wages	10-4913
wildcard	$500 of any personal property, except tools of trade, if head of family	10-4903

District of Columbia

Federal bankruptcy exemptions available. All law references are to District of Columbia Code unless otherwise noted.

ASSET	EXEMPTION	LAW
homestead	Any property used as a residence or co-op that debtor or debtor's dependent uses as a residence	15-501(a)(14)
	Property held as tenancy by the entirety may be exempt against debts owed by only one spouse	*Estate of Wall*, 440 F.2d 215 (D.C. Cir. 1971)
insurance	Disability benefits	15-501(a)(7); 31-4716.01
	Fraternal benefit society benefits	31-5315
	Group life insurance policy or proceeds	31-4717
	Life insurance payments	15-501(a)(11)
	Life insurance proceeds if clause prohibits proceeds from being used to pay beneficiary's creditors	31-4719
	Life insurance proceeds or avails	31-4716
	Other insurance proceeds to $200 per month, maximum 2 months, for head of family; else $60 per month	15-503
	Unmatured life insurance contract other than credit life insurance	15-501(a)(5)
miscellaneous	Alimony or child support	15-501(a)(7)
pensions *see also wages*	Tax-exempt retirement accounts, including 401(k)s, 403(b)s, profit-sharing and money purchase plans, SEP and SIMPLE IRAs, and defined-benefit plans	11 U.S.C. § 522(b)(3)(C)
	Traditional and Roth IRAs to $1,095,000 per person	11 U.S.C. § 522(b)(3)(C); (n)
	ERISA-qualified benefits, IRAs, Keoghs, etc. to maximum deductible contribution	15-501(b)(9)

pensions (continued)	Any stock bonus, annuity, pension, or profit-sharing plan	15-501(a)(7)
	Judges	11-1570(f)
	Public school teachers	38-2001.17; 38-2021.17
personal property	Appliances, books, clothing, household furnishings, goods, musical instruments, pets to $425 per item or $8,625 total	15-501(a)(2)
	Cemetery & burial funds	43-111
	Cooperative association holdings to $50	29-928
	Food for 3 months	15-501(a)(12)
	Health aids	15-501(a)(6)
	Higher education tuition savings account	47-4510
	Residential condominium deposit	42-1904.09
	All family pictures; & all the family library, to $400	15-501(a)(8)
	Motor vehicle to $2,575	15-501(a)(1)
	Payment including pain & suffering for loss of debtor or person depended on	15-501(a)(11)
	Uninsured motorist benefits	31-2408.01(h)
	Wrongful death damages	15-501(a)(11); 16-2703
public benefits	Aid to blind, aged, disabled; general assistance	4-215.01
	Crime victims' compensation	4-507(e); 15-501(a)(11)
	Social Security	15-501(a)(7)
	Unemployment compensation	51-118
	Veterans' benefits	15-501(a)(7)
	Workers' compensation	32-1517
tools of trade	Library, furniture, tools of professional or artist to $300	15-501(a)(13)
	Tools of trade or business to $1,625	15-501(a)(5)
	Mechanic's tools to $200	15-503(b)
	Seal & documents of notary public	1-1206
wages	Minimum 75% of earned but unpaid wages, pension payments; bankruptcy judge may authorize more for low-income debtors	16-572
	Nonwage (including pension & retirement) earnings to $200/mo for head of family; else $60/mo for a maximum of two months	15-503
	Payment for loss of future earnings	15-501(e)(11)
wildcard	Up to $850 in any property, plus up to $8,075 of unused homestead exemption	15-501(a)(3)

Florida

Federal bankruptcy exemptions not available. All law references are to Florida Statutes Annotated unless otherwise noted.

ASSET	EXEMPTION	LAW
homestead	Real or personal property including mobile or modular home to unlimited value; cannot exceed half acre in municipality or 160 acres elsewhere; spouse or child of deceased owner may claim homestead exemption	222.01; 222.02; 222.03; 222.05; Constitution 10-4 *In re Colwell*, 196 F.3d 1225 (11th Cir. 1999)
	May file homestead declaration	222.01

homestead (continued)	Property held as tenancy by the entirety may be exempt against debts owed by only one spouse	*Havoco of America, Ltd. v. Hill*, 197 F.3d 1135 (11th Cir. Fla.,1999)
insurance	Annuity contract proceeds; does not include lottery winnings	222.14; *In re Pizzi*, 153 B.R. 357 (S.D. Fla. 1993)
	Death benefits payable to a specific beneficiary, not the deceased's estate	222.13
	Disability or illness benefits	222.18
	Fraternal benefit society benefits	632.619
	Life insurance cash surrender value	222.14
miscellaneous	Alimony, child support needed for support	222.201
	Damages to employees for injuries in hazardous occupations	769.05
pensions *see also wages*	Tax-exempt retirement accounts, including 401(k)s, 403(b)s, profit-sharing and money purchase plans, SEP and SIMPLE IRAs, and defined-benefit plans	11 U.S.C. § 522(b)(3)(C)
	Traditional and Roth IRAs to $1,095,000 per person	11 U.S.C. § 522(b)(3)(C); (n)
	County officers, employees	122.15
	ERISA-qualified benefits, including IRAs & Roth IRAs	222.21(2)
	Firefighters	175.241
	Police officers	185.25
	State officers, employees	121.131
	Teachers	238.15
personal property	Any personal property to $1,000 (husband & wife may double)	Constitution 10-4 *In re Hawkins*, 51 B.R. 348 (S.D. Fla. 1985)
	Federal income tax refund or credit	222.25
	Health aids	222.25
	Motor vehicle to $1,000	222.25
	Pre-need funeral contract deposits	497.56(8)
	Prepaid college education trust deposits	222.22(1)
	Prepaid hurricane savings accounts	222.22(4)
	Prepaid medical savings account deposits	222.22(2)
public benefits	Crime victims' compensation, unless seeking to discharge debt for treatment of injury incurred during the crime	960.14
	Public assistance	222.201
	Social Security	222.201
	Unemployment compensation	222.201; 443.051(2),(3)
	Veterans' benefits	222.201; 744.626
	Workers' compensation	440.22
tools of trade	None	
wages	100% of wages for heads of family up to $500 per week either unpaid or paid & deposited into bank account for up to 6 months	222.11
	Federal government employees' pension payments needed for support & received 3 months prior	222.21
wildcard	*See personal property*	

Georgia

Federal bankruptcy exemptions not available. All law references are to the Official Code of Georgia Annotated unless otherwise noted.

ASSET	EXEMPTION	LAW
homestead	Real or personal property, including co-op, used as residence to $10,000 (to $20,000 if married, whether or not spouse is filing); up to $5,000 of unused portion of homestead may be applied to any property	44-13-100(a)(1); 44-13-100(a)(6); *In re Burnett*, 303 B.R. 684 (M.D. Ga. 2003)
insurance	Annuity & endowment contract benefits	33-28-7
	Disability or health benefits to $250 per month	33-29-15
	Fraternal benefit society benefits	33-15-62
	Group insurance	33-30-10
	Proceeds & avails of life insurance	33-26-5; 33-25-11
	Life insurance proceeds if policy owned by someone you depended on, needed for support	44-13-100(a)(11)(C)
	Unmatured life insurance contract	44-13-100(a)(8)
	Unmatured life insurance dividends, interest, loan value, or cash value to $2,000 if beneficiary is you or someone you depend on	44-13-100(a)(9)
miscellaneous	Alimony, child support needed for support	44-13-100(a)(2)(D)
pensions	Tax-exempt retirement accounts, including 401(k)s, 403(b)s, profit-sharing and money purchase plans, SEP and SIMPLE IRAs, and defined-benefit plans	11 U.S.C. § 522(b)(3)(C)
	Traditional and Roth IRAs to $1,095,000 per person	11 U.S.C. § 522(b)(3)(C); (n)
	Employees of nonprofit corporations	44-13-100(a)(2.1)(B)
	ERISA-qualified benefits & IRAs	18-4-22
	Public employees	44-13-100(a)(2.1)(A); 47-2-332
	Payments from IRA necessary for support	44-13-100(a)(2)(F)
	Other pensions needed for support	18-4-22; 44-13-100(a)(2)(E); 44-13-100(a)(2.1)(C)
personal property	Animals, crops, clothing, appliances, books, furnishings, household goods, musical instruments to $300 per item, $5,000 total	44-13-100(a)(4)
	Burial plot, in lieu of homestead	44-13-100(a)(1)
	Compensation for lost future earnings needed for support to $7,500	44-13-100(a)(11)(E)
	Health aids	44-13-100(a)(10)
	Jewelry to $500	44-13-100(a)(5)
	Motor vehicles to $3,500	44-13-100(a)(3)
	Personal injury recoveries to $10,000	44-13-100(a)(11)(D)
	Wrongful death recoveries needed for support	44-13-100(a)(11)(B)
public benefits	Aid to blind	49-4-58
	Aid to disabled	49-4-84
	Crime victims' compensation	44-13-100(a)(11)(A)
	Local public assistance	44-13-100(a)(2)(A)
	Old age assistance	49-4-35
	Social Security	44-13-100(a)(2)(A)

public benefits (continued)	Unemployment compensation	44-13-100(a)(2)(A)
	Veterans' benefits	44-13-100(a)(2)(B)
	Workers' compensation	34-9-84
tools of trade	Implements, books, & tools of trade to $1,500	44-13-100(a)(7)
wages	Minimum 75% of earned but unpaid weekly disposable earnings, or 40 times the state or federal hourly minimum wage, whichever is greater, for private & federal workers; bankruptcy judge may authorize more for low-income debtors	18-4-20; 18-4-21
wildcard	$600 of any property	44-13-100(a)(6)
	Unused portion of homestead exemption to $5,000	44-13-100(a)(6)

Hawaii

Federal bankruptcy exemptions available. All law references are to Hawaii Revised Statutes unless otherwise noted.

ASSET	EXEMPTION	LAW
homestead	Head of family or over 65 to $30,000; all others to $20,000; property cannot exceed 1 acre; sale proceeds exempt for 6 months after sale (husband & wife may not double)	651-91; 651-92; 651-96
	Property held as tenancy by the entirety may be exempt against debts owed by only one spouse	*Security Pacific Bank v. Chang*, 818 F.Supp. 1343 (D. Haw. 1993)
insurance	Annuity contract or endowment policy proceeds if beneficiary is insured's spouse, child, or parent	431:10-232(b)
	Accident, health, or sickness benefits	431:10-231
	Fraternal benefit society benefits	432:2-403
	Group life insurance policy or proceeds	431:10-233
	Life insurance proceeds if clause prohibits proceeds from being used to pay beneficiary's creditors	431:10D-112
	Life or health insurance policy for spouse or child	431:10-234
miscellaneous	Property of business partnership	425-125
pensions	Tax-exempt retirement accounts, including 401(k)s, 403(b)s, profit-sharing and money purchase plans, SEP and SIMPLE IRAs, and defined-benefit plans	11 U.S.C. § 522(b)(3)(C)
	Traditional and Roth IRAs to $1,095,000 per person	11 U.S.C. § 522(b)(3)(C); (n)
	IRAs, Roth IRAs, and ERISA-qualified benefits deposited over 3 years before filing bankruptcy	651-124
	Firefighters	88-169
	Police officers	88-169
	Public officers & employees	88-91; 653-3
personal property	Appliances & furnishings	651-121(1)
	Books	651-121(1)
	Burial plot to 250 sq. ft. plus tombstones, monuments, & fencing	651-121(4)
	Clothing	651-121(1)
	Jewelry, watches, & articles of adornment to $1,000	651-121(1)
	Motor vehicle to wholesale value of $2,575	651-121(2)
	Proceeds for sold or damaged exempt property; sale proceeds exempt for 6 months after sale	651-121(5)

public benefits	Crime victims' compensation & special accounts created to limit commercial exploitation of crimes	351-66; 351-86
	Public assistance paid by Dept. of Health Services for work done in home or workshop	346-33
	Temporary disability benefits	392-29
	Unemployment compensation	383-163
	Unemployment work relief funds to $60 per month	653-4
	Workers' compensation	386-57
tools of trade	Tools, implements, books, instruments, uniforms, furnishings, fishing boat, nets, motor vehicle, & other property needed for livelihood	651-121(3)
wages	Prisoner's wages held by Dept. of Public Safety (except for restitution, child support, & other claims)	353-22.5
	Unpaid wages due for services of past 31 days	651-121(6)
wildcard	None	

Idaho

Federal bankruptcy exemptions not available. All law references are to Idaho Code unless otherwise noted.

ASSET	EXEMPTION	LAW
homestead	Real property or mobile home to $50,000; sale proceeds exempt for 6 months (husband & wife may not double)	55-1003; 55-1113
	Must record homestead exemption for property that is not yet occupied	55-1004
insurance	Annuity contract proceeds to $1,250 per month	41-1836
	Death or disability benefits	11-604(1)(a); 41-1834
	Fraternal benefit society benefits	41-3218
	Group life insurance benefits	41-1835
	Homeowners' insurance proceeds to amount of homestead exemption	55-1008
	Life insurance proceeds if clause prohibits proceeds from being used to pay beneficiary's creditors	41-1930
	Life insurance proceeds or avails for beneficiary other than the insured	11-604(d); 41-1833
	Medical, surgical, or hospital care benefits	11-603(5)
	Unmatured life insurance contract, other than credit life insurance, owned by debtor	11-605(8)
	Unmatured life insurance contract interest or dividends to $5,000 owned by debtor or person debtor depends on	11-605(9)
miscellaneous	Alimony, child support	11-604(1)(b)
	Liquor licenses	23-514
pension see also wages	Tax-exempt retirement accounts, including 401(k)s, 403(b)s, profit-sharing and money purchase plans, SEP and SIMPLE IRAs, and defined-benefit plans	11 U.S.C. § 522(b)(3)(C)
	Traditional and Roth IRAs to $1,095,000 per person	11 U.S.C. § 522(b)(3)(C); (n)
	ERISA-qualified benefits	55-1011
	Firefighters	72-1422
	Government & private pensions, retirement plans, IRAs, Roth IRAs, Keoghs, etc.	11-604A
	Police officers	50-1517

pensions (continued)	Public employees	59-1317
personal property	Appliances, furnishings, books, clothing, pets, musical instruments, 1 firearm, family portraits, & sentimental heirlooms to $500 per item, $5,000 total	11-605(1)
	Building materials	45-514
	Burial plot	11-603(1)
	College savings program account	11-604A(4)(b)
	Crops cultivated on maximum of 50 acres, to $1,000; water rights to 160 inches	11-605(6)
	Health aids	11-603(2)
	Jewelry to $1,000	11-605(2)
	Motor vehicle to $3,000	11-605(3)
	Personal injury recoveries	11-604(1)(c)
	Proceeds for damaged exempt property for 3 months after proceeds received	11-606
	Wrongful death recoveries	11-604(1)(c)
public benefits	Aid to blind, aged, disabled	56-223
	Federal, state, & local public assistance	11-603(4)
	General assistance	56-223
	Social Security	11-603(3)
	Unemployment compensation	11-603(6)
	Veterans' benefits	11-603(3)
	Workers' compensation	72-802
tools of trade	Arms, uniforms, & accoutrements that peace officer, National Guard, or military personnel is required to keep	11-605(5)
	Implements, books, & tools of trade to $1,500	11-605(3)
wages	Minimum 75% of earned but unpaid weekly disposable earnings, or 30 times the federal hourly minimum wage, whichever is greater; pension payments; bankruptcy judge may authorize more for low-income debtors	11-207
wildcard	$800 in any tangible personal property	11-605(10)

Illinois

Federal bankruptcy exemptions not available. All law references are to Illinois Compiled Statutes Annotated unless otherwise noted.

ASSET	EXEMPTION	LAW
homestead	Real or personal property including a farm, lot, & buildings, condo, co-op, or mobile home to $15,000; sale proceeds exempt for 1 year	735-5/12-901; 735-5/12-906
	Spouse or child of deceased owner may claim homestead exemption	735-5/12-902
	Illinois recognizes tenancy by the entirety, with limitations	750-65/22; 765-1005/1c; *In re Gillissie*, 215 B.R. 370 (Bankr. N.D. Ill. 1998); *Great Southern Co. v. Allard*, 202 B.R. 938 (N.D. Ill. 1996)
insurance	Fraternal benefit society benefits	215-5/299.1a

insurance (continued)	Health or disability benefits	735-5/12-1001(g)(3)
	Homeowners' proceeds if home destroyed, to $15,000	735-5/12-907
	Life insurance, annuity proceeds, or cash value if beneficiary is insured's child, parent, spouse, or other dependent	215-5/238; 735-5/12-1001(f)
	Life insurance proceeds to a spouse or dependent of debtor to extent needed for support	735-5/12-1001(f),(g)(3)
miscellaneous	Alimony, child support	735-5/12-1001(g)(4)
	Property of business partnership	805-205/25
pensions	Tax-exempt retirement accounts, including 401(k)s, 403(b)s, profit-sharing and money purchase plans, SEP and SIMPLE IRAs, and defined-benefit plans	11 U.S.C. § 522(b)(3)(C)
	Traditional and Roth IRAs to $1,095,000 per person	11 U.S.C. § 522(b)(3)(C); (n)
	Civil service employees	40-5/11-223
	County employees	40-5/9-228
	Disabled firefighters; widows & children of firefighters	40-5/22-230
	IRAs and ERISA-qualified benefits	735-5/12-1006
	Firefighters	40-5/4-135; 40-5/6-213
	General assembly members	40-5/2-154
	House of correction employees	40-5/19-117
	Judges	40-5/18-161
	Municipal employees	40-5/7-217(a); 40-5/8-244
	Park employees	40-5/12-190
	Police officers	40-5/3-144.1; 40-5/5-218
	Public employees	735-5/12-1006
	Public library employees	40-5/19-218
	Sanitation district employees	40-5/13-805
	State employees	40-5/14-147
	State university employees	40-5/15-185
	Teachers	40-5/16-190; 40-5/17-151
personal property	Bible, family pictures, schoolbooks, & clothing	735-5/12-1001(a)
	Health aids	735-5/12-1001(e)
	Motor vehicle to $2,400	735-5/12-1001(c)
	Personal injury recoveries to $15,000	735-5/12-1001(h)(4)
	Pre-need cemetery sales funds, care funds, & trust funds	235-5/6-1; 760-100/4; 815-390/16
	Prepaid tuition trust fund	110-979/45(g)
	Proceeds of sold exempt property	735-5/12-1001
	Wrongful death recoveries	735-5/12-1001(h)(2)
public benefits	Aid to aged, blind, disabled; public assistance	305-5/11-3
	Crime victims' compensation	735-5/12-1001(h)(1)
	Restitution payments on account of WWII relocation of Aleuts & Japanese Americans	735-5/12-1001(12)(h)(5)
	Social Security	735-5/12-1001(g)(1)
	Unemployment compensation	735-5/12-1001(g)(1),(3)
	Veterans' benefits	735-5/12-1001(g)(2)

public benefits (continued)	Workers' compensation	820-305/21
	Workers' occupational disease compensation	820-310/21
tools of trade	Implements, books, & tools of trade to $1,500	735-5/12-1001(d)
wages	Minimum 85% of earned but unpaid weekly wages or 45 times the federal minimum hourly wage (or state minimum hourly wage, if higher); bankruptcy judge may authorize more for low-income debtors	740-170/4
wildcard	$4,000 of any personal property (does not include wages)	735-5/12-1001(b)

Indiana

Federal bankruptcy exemptions not available. All law references are to Indiana Statutes Annotated unless otherwise noted.

ASSET	EXEMPTION	LAW
homestead see also wildcard	Real or personal property used as residence to $15,000	34-55-10-2(c)(1)
	Property held as tenancy by the entirety may be exempt against debts incurred by only one spouse	34-55-10-2(c)(5); 32-17-3-1
insurance	Employer's life insurance policy on employee	27-1-12-17.1
	Fraternal benefit society benefits	27-11-6-3
	Group life insurance policy	27-1-12-29
	Life insurance policy, proceeds, cash value, or avails if beneficiary is insured's spouse or dependent	27-1-12-14
	Life insurance proceeds if clause prohibits proceeds to be used to pay beneficiary's creditors	27-2-5-1
	Mutual life or accident proceeds needed for support	27-8-3-23; In re Stinnet, 321 B.R. 477 (S.D. Ind. 2005)
miscellaneous	Property of business partnership	23-4-1-25
pensions	Tax-exempt retirement accounts, including 401(k)s, 403(b)s, profit-sharing and money purchase plans, SEP and SIMPLE IRAs, and defined-benefit plans	11 U.S.C. § 522(b)(3)(C)
	Traditional and Roth IRAs to $1,095,000 per person	11 U.S.C. § 522(b)(3)(C); (n)
	Firefighters	36-8-7-22 36-8-8-17
	Police officers	36-8-8-17; 10-12-2-10
	Public employees	5-10.3-8-9
	Public or private retirement benefits & contributions	34-55-10-2(c)(6)
	Sheriffs	36-8-10-19
	State teachers	5-10.4-5-14
personal property	Health aids	34-55-10-2(c)(4)
	Money in medical care savings account	34-55-10-2(c)(7)
	Spendthrift trusts	30-4-3-2
	$300 of any intangible personal property, except money owed to you	34-55-10-2(c)(3)
public benefits	Crime victims' compensation, unless seeking to discharge the debts for which the victim was compensated	5-2-6.1-38
	Unemployment compensation	22-4-33-3
	Workers' compensation	22-3-2-17

tools of trade	National Guard uniforms, arms, & equipment	10-16-10-3
wages	Minimum 75% of earned but unpaid weekly disposable earnings, or 30 times the federal hourly minimum wage; bankruptcy judge may authorize more for low-income debtors	24-4.5-5-105
wildcard	$8,000 of any real estate or tangible personal property	34-55-10-2(c)(2)

Iowa

Federal bankruptcy exemptions not available. All law references are to Iowa Code Annotated unless otherwise noted.

ASSET	EXEMPTION	LAW
homestead	May record homestead declaration	561.4
	Real property or an apartment to an unlimited value; property cannot exceed 1/2 acre in town or city, 40 acres elsewhere (husband & wife may not double)	499A.18; 561.2; 561.16
insurance	Accident, disability, health, illness, or life proceeds or avails	627.6(6)
	Disability or illness benefit	627.6(8)(c)
	Employee group insurance policy or proceeds	509.12
	Fraternal benefit society benefits	512B.18
	Life insurance proceeds if clause prohibits proceeds from being used to pay beneficiary's creditors	508.32
	Life insurance proceeds paid to spouse, child, or other dependent (limited to $10,000 if acquired within 2 years of filing for bankruptcy)	627.6(6)
	Upon death of insured, up to $15,000 total proceeds from all matured life, accident, health, or disability policies exempt from beneficiary's debts contracted before insured's death	627.6(6)
miscellaneous	Alimony, child support needed for support	627.6(8)(d)
	Liquor licenses	123.38
pensions *see also wages*	Tax-exempt retirement accounts, including 401(k)s, 403(b)s, profit-sharing and money purchase plans, SEP and SIMPLE IRAs, and defined-benefit plans	11 U.S.C. § 522(b)(3)(C)
	Traditional and Roth IRAs to $1,095,000 per person	11 U.S.C. § 522(b)(3)(C); (n)
	Disabled firefighters, police officers (only payments being received)	410.11
	Federal government pension	627.8
	Firefighters	411.13
	Other pensions, annuities, & contracts fully exempt; however, contributions made within 1 year prior to filing for bankruptcy not exempt to the extent they exceed normal & customary amounts	627.6(8)(e)
	Peace officers	97A.12
	Police officers	411.13
	Public employees	97B.39
	Retirement plans, Keoghs, IRAs, Roth IRAs, ERISA-qualified benefits	627.6(8)(f)
personal property	Bibles, books, portraits, pictures, & paintings to $1,000 total	627.6(3)
	Burial plot to 1 acre	627.6(4)
	Clothing & its storage containers, household furnishings, appliances, musical instruments, and other personal property to $7,000	627.6(5)
	Health aids	627.6(7)

personal property (continued)	Jewelry to $2,000	627.6(1)(b)
	One motor vehicle to $7,000	627.6(9)
	Residential security or utility deposit, or advance of rent, to $500	627.6(14)
	Rifle or musket; shotgun	627.6(2)
	Wedding or engagement rings, limited to $7,000 if purchase after marriage and within two years before filing	627.6(1)(a)
	Wrongful death proceeds and awards needed for support of debtor & dependents	627.6(15)
public benefits	Adopted child assistance	627.19
	Aid to dependent children	239B.6
	Any public assistance benefit	627.6(8)(a)
	Social Security	627.6(8)(a)
	Unemployment compensation	627.6(8)(a)
	Veterans' benefits	627.6(8)(b)
	Workers' compensation	627.13
tools of trade	Farming equipment; includes livestock, feed to $10,000	627.6(11)
	Nonfarming equipment to $10,000	627.6(10)
wages	Expected annual earnings / Amount NOT exempt per year $0 to $12,000 $250 $12,000 to $16,000 $400 $16,000 to $24,000 $800 $24,000 to $35,000 $1,000 $35,000 to $50,000 $2,000 More than $50,000 10% Not exempt from spousal or child support	642.21
	Wages or salary of a prisoner	356.29
wildcard	$1,000 of any personal property, including cash	627.6(13)

Kansas

Federal bankruptcy exemptions not available. All law references are to Kansas Statutes Annotated unless otherwise noted.

ASSET	EXEMPTION	LAW
homestead	Real property or mobile home you occupy or intend to occupy to unlimited value; property cannot exceed 1 acre in town or city, 160 acres on farm	60-2301; Constitution 15-9
insurance	Cash value of life insurance; not exempt if obtained within 1 year prior to bankruptcy with fraudulent intent.	60-2313(a)(7); 40-414(b)
	Disability & illness benefits	60-2313(a)(1)
	Fraternal life insurance benefits	60-2313(a)(8)
	Life insurance proceeds	40-414(a)
miscellaneous	Alimony, maintenance, & support	60-2312(b)
	Liquor licenses	60-2313(a)(6); 41-326
pensions	Tax-exempt retirement accounts, including 401(k)s, 403(b)s, profit-sharing and money purchase plans, SEP and SIMPLE IRAs, and defined-benefit plans	11 U.S.C. § 522(b)(3)(C)
	Traditional and Roth IRAs to $1,095,000 per person	11 U.S.C. § 522(b)(3)(C); (n)

pensions (continued)	Elected & appointed officials in cities with populations between 120,000 & 200,000	13-14a10
	ERISA-qualified benefits	60-2308(b)
	Federal government pension needed for support & paid within 3 months of filing for bankruptcy (only payments being received)	60-2308(a)
	Firefighters	12-5005(e); 14-10a10
	Judges	20-2618
	Police officers	12-5005(e); 13-14a10
	Public employees	74-4923; 74-49,105
	State highway patrol officers	74-4978g
	State school employees	72-5526
	Payment under a stock bonus, pension, profit-sharing, annuity, or similar plan or contract on account of illness, disability, death, age, or length of service, to the extent reasonably necessary for support	60-2312(b)
personal property	Burial plot or crypt	60-2304(d)
	Clothing to last 1 year	60-2304(a)
	Food & fuel to last 1 year	60-2304(a)
	Funeral plan prepayments	60-2313(a)(10); 16-310(d)
	Furnishings & household equipment	60-2304(a)
	Jewelry & articles of adornment to $1,000	60-2304(b)
	Motor vehicle to $20,000; if designed or equipped for disabled person, no limit	60-2304(c)
public benefits	Crime victims' compensation	60-2313(a)(7); 74-7313(d)
	General assistance	39-717(c)
	Social Security	60-2312(b)
	Unemployment compensation	60-2313(a)(4); 44-718(c)
	Veterans' benefits	60-2312(b)
	Workers' compensation	60-2313(a)(3); 44-514
tools of trade	Books, documents, furniture, instruments, equipment, breeding stock, seed, grain, & stock to $7,500 total	60-2304(e)
	National Guard uniforms, arms, & equipment	48-245
wages	Minimum 75% of disposable weekly wages or 30 times the federal minimum hourly wage per week, whichever is greater; bankruptcy judge may authorize more for low-income debtors	60-2310
wildcard	None	

Kentucky

Federal bankruptcy exemptions not available. All law references are to Kentucky Revised Statutes unless otherwise noted.

ASSET	EXEMPTION	LAW
homestead	Real or personal property used as residence to $5,000; sale proceeds exempt	427.060; 427.090

insurance	Annuity contract proceeds to $350 per month	304.14-330
	Cooperative life or casualty insurance benefits	427.110(1)
	Fraternal benefit society benefits	427.110(2)
	Group life insurance proceeds	304.14-320
	Health or disability benefits	304.14-310
	Life insurance policy if beneficiary is a married woman	304.14-340
	Life insurance proceeds if clause prohibits proceeds from being used to pay beneficiary's creditors	304.14-350
	Life insurance proceeds or cash value if beneficiary is someone other than insured	304.14-300
miscellaneous	Alimony, child support needed for support	427.150(1)
	Property of business partnership	362.270
pensions	Tax-exempt retirement accounts, including 401(k)s, 403(b)s, profit-sharing and money purchase plans, SEP and SIMPLE IRAs, and defined-benefit plans	11 U.S.C. § 522(b)(3)(C)
	Traditional and Roth IRAs to $1,095,000 per person	11 U.S.C. § 522(b)(3)(C); (n)
	ERISA-qualified benefits, including IRAs, SEPs, & Keoghs deposited more than 120 days before filing	427.150
	Firefighters	67A.620; 95.878
	Police officers	427.120; 427.125
	State employees	61.690
	Teachers	161.700
	Urban county government employees	67A.350
personal property	Burial plot to $5,000, in lieu of homestead	427.060
	Clothing, jewelry, articles of adornment, & furnishings to $3,000 total	427.010(1)
	Health aids	427.010(1)
	Lost earnings payments needed for support	427.150(2)(d)
	Medical expenses paid & reparation benefits received under motor vehicle reparation law	304.39-260
	Motor vehicle to $2,500	427.010(1)
	Personal injury recoveries to $7,500 (not to include pain & suffering or pecuniary loss)	427.150(2)(c)
	Prepaid tuition payment fund account	164A.707(3)
	Wrongful death recoveries for person you depended on, needed for support	427.150(2)(b)
public benefits	Aid to blind, aged, disabled; public assistance	205.220(c)
	Crime victims' compensation	427.150(2)(a)
	Unemployment compensation	341.470(4)
	Workers' compensation	342.180
tools of trade	Library, office equipment, instruments, & furnishings of minister, attorney, physician, surgeon, chiropractor, veterinarian, or dentist to $1,000	427.040
	Motor vehicle of auto mechanic, mechanical, or electrical equipment servicer, minister, attorney, physician, surgeon, chiropractor, veterinarian, or dentist to $2,500	427.030
	Tools, equipment, livestock, & poultry of farmer to $3,000	427.010(1)
	Tools of nonfarmer to $300	427.030

wages	Minimum 75% of disposable weekly earnings or 30 times the federal minimum hourly wage per week, whichever is greater; bankruptcy judge may authorize more for low-income debtors	427.010(2),(3)
wildcard	$1,000 of any property	427.160

Louisiana

Federal bankruptcy exemptions not available. All law references are to Louisiana Revised Statutes Annotated unless otherwise noted.

ASSET	EXEMPTION	LAW
homestead	Property you occupy to $25,000 (if debt is result of catastrophic or terminal illness or injury, limit is full value of property as of 1 year before filing); cannot exceed 5 acres in city or town, 200 acres elsewhere (husband & wife may not double)	20:1(A)(1),(2),(3)
	Spouse or child of deceased owner may claim homestead exemption; spouse given home in divorce gets homestead	20:1(B)
insurance	Annuity contract proceeds & avails	22:647
	Fraternal benefit society benefits	22:558
	Group insurance policies or proceeds	22:649
	Health, accident, or disability proceeds or avails	22:646
	Life insurance proceeds or avails; if policy issued within 9 months of filing, exempt only to $35,000	22:647
miscellaneous	Property of minor child	13:3881(A)(3); Civil Code Art. 223
pensions	Tax-exempt retirement accounts, including 401(k)s, 403(b)s, profit-sharing and money purchase plans, SEP and SIMPLE IRAs, and defined-benefit plans	11 U.S.C. § 522(b)(3)(C)
	Traditional and Roth IRAs to $1,095,000 per person	11 U.S.C. § 522(b)(3)(C); (n)
	Assessors	11:1403
	Court clerks	11:1526
	District attorneys	11:1583
	ERISA-qualified benefits, including IRAs, Roth IRAs, & Keoghs, if contributions made over 1 year before filing for bankruptcy	13:3881(D)(1); 20:33(1)
	Firefighters	11:2263
	Gift or bonus payments from employer to employee or heirs whenever paid	20:33(2)
	Judges	11:1378
	Louisiana University employees	11:952.3
	Municipal employees	11:1735
	Parochial employees	11:1905
	Police officers	11:3513
	School employees	11:1003
	Sheriffs	11:2182
	State employees	11:405
	Teachers	11:704
	Voting registrars	11:2033

personal property	Arms, military accoutrements; bedding; dishes, glassware, utensils, silverware (nonsterling); clothing, family portraits, musical instruments; bedroom, living room, & dining room furniture; poultry, 1 cow, household pets; heating & cooling equipment, refrigerator, freezer, stove, washer & dryer, iron, sewing machine	13:3881(A)(4)
	Cemetery plot, monuments	8:313
	Engagement & wedding rings to $5,000	13:3881(A)(5)
	Spendthrift trusts	9:2004
public benefits	Aid to blind, aged, disabled; public assistance	46:111
	Crime victims' compensation	46:1811
	Earned Income tax credit	13:3881 (A)(6)
	Unemployment compensation	23:1693
	Workers' compensation	23:1205
tools of trade	Tools, instruments, books, $7,500 of equity in a motor vehicle, one firearm to $500, needed to work	13:3881(A)(2)
wages	Minimum 75% of disposable weekly earnings or 30 times the federal minimum hourly wage per week, whichever is greater; bankruptcy judge may authorize more for low-income debtors	13:3881(A)(1)
wildcard	None	

Maine

Federal bankruptcy exemptions not available. All law references are to Maine Revised Statutes Annotated, in the form title number-section number, unless otherwise noted.

ASSET	EXEMPTION	LAW
homestead	Real or personal property (including cooperative) used as residence to $35,000; if debtor has minor dependents in residence, to $70,000; if debtor over age 60 or physically or mentally disabled, $70,000; proceeds of sale exempt for six months	14-4422(1)
insurance	Annuity proceeds to $450 per month	24-A-2431
	Death benefit for police, fire, or emergency medical personnel who die in the line of duty	25-1612
	Disability or health proceeds, benefits, or avails	14-4422(13)(A),(C); 24-A-2429
	Fraternal benefit society benefits	24-A-4118
	Group health or life policy or proceeds	24-A-2430
	Life, endowment, annuity, or accident policy, proceeds or avails	14-4422(14)(C); 24-A-2428
	Life insurance policy, interest, loan value, or accrued dividends for policy from person you depended on, to $4,000	14-4422(11)
	Unmatured life insurance policy, except credit insurance policy	14-4422(10)
miscellaneous	Alimony & child support needed for support	14-4422(13)(D)
	Property of business partnership	31-305
pensions	Tax-exempt retirement accounts, including 401(k)s, 403(b)s, profit-sharing and money purchase plans, SEP and SIMPLE IRAs, and defined-benefit plans	11 U.S.C. § 522(b)(3)(C)
	Traditional and Roth IRAs to $1,095,000 per person	11 U.S.C. § 522(b)(3)(C); (n)

pensions	ERISA-qualified benefits	14-4422(13)(E)
(continued)	Judges	4-1203
	Legislators	3-703
	State employees	5-17054
personal property	Animals, crops, musical instruments, books, clothing, furnishings, household goods, appliances to $200 per item	14-4422(3)
	Balance due on repossessed goods; total amount financed can't exceed $2,000	9-A-5-103
	Burial plot in lieu of homestead exemption	14-4422(1)
	Cooking stove; furnaces & stoves for heat	14-4422(6)(A),(B)
	Food to last 6 months	14-4422(7)(A)
	Fuel not to exceed 10 cords of wood, 5 tons of coal, or 1,000 gal. of heating oil	14-4422(6)(C)
	Health aids	14-4422(12)
	Jewelry to $750; no limit for one wedding & one engagement ring	14-4422(4)
	Lost earnings payments needed for support	14-4422(14)(E)
	Military clothes, arms, & equipment	37-B-262
	Motor vehicle to $5,000	14-4422(2)
	Personal injury recoveries to $12,500	14-4422(14)(D)
	Seeds, fertilizers, & feed to raise & harvest food for 1 season	14-4422(7)(B)
	Tools & equipment to raise & harvest food	14-4422(7)(C)
	Wrongful death recoveries needed for support	14-4422(14)(B)
public benefits	Maintenance under the Rehabilitation Act	26-1411-H
	Crime victims' compensation	14-4422(14)(A)
	Public assistance	22-3180, 22-3766
	Social Security	14-4422(13)(A)
	Unemployment compensation	14-4422(13)(A),(C)
	Veterans' benefits	14-4422(13)(B)
	Workers' compensation	39-A-106
tools of trade	Books, materials, & stock to $5,000	14-4422(5)
	Commercial fishing boat, 5-ton limit	14-4422(9)
	One of each farm implement (& its maintenance equipment needed to harvest & raise crops)	14-4422(8)
wages	None (use federal nonbankruptcy wage exemption)	
wildcard	Unused portion of exemption in homestead to $6,000; or unused exemption in animals, crops, musical instruments, books, clothing, furnishings, household goods, appliances, tools of the trade, & personal injury recoveries	14-4422(15)
	$400 of any property	14-4422(15)

Maryland

Federal bankruptcy exemptions not available. All law references are to Maryland Code of Courts & Judicial Proceedings unless otherwise noted.

ASSET	EXEMPTION	LAW
homestead	None; however, property held as tenancy by the entirety is exempt against debts owed by only one spouse	*In re Birney*, 200 F.3d 225 (4th Cir. 1999)

insurance	Disability or health benefits, including court awards, arbitrations, & settlements	11-504(b)(2)
	Fraternal benefit society benefits	Ins. 8-431; Estates & Trusts 8-115
	Life insurance or annuity contract proceeds or avails if beneficiary is insured's dependent, child, or spouse	Ins. 16-111(a); Estates & Trusts 8-115
	Medical insurance benefits deducted from wages plus medical insurance payments to $145 per week or 75% of disposable wages	Commercial Law 15-601.1(3)
pensions	Tax-exempt retirement accounts, including 401(k)s, 403(b)s, profit-sharing and money purchase plans, SEP and SIMPLE IRAs, and defined-benefit plans	11 U.S.C. § 522(b)(3)(C)
	Traditional and Roth IRAs to $1,095,000 per person	11 U.S.C. § 522(b)(3)(C); (n)
	ERISA-qualified benefits, including IRAs, Roth IRAs, & Keoghs	11-504(h)(1), (4)
	State employees	State Pers. & Pen. 21-502
personal property	Appliances, furnishings, household goods, books, pets, & clothing to $1,000 total	11-504(b)(4)
	Burial plot	Bus. Reg. 5-503
	Health aids	11-504(b)(3)
	Perpetual care trust funds	Bus. Reg. 5-602
	Prepaid college trust funds	Educ. 18-1913
	Lost future earnings recoveries	11-504(b)(2)
public benefits	Baltimore Police death benefits	Code of 1957 art. 24, 16-103
	Crime victims' compensation	Crim. Proc. 11-816(b)
	General assistance	Code of 1957 88A-73
	Unemployment compensation	Labor & Employment 8-106
	Workers' compensation	Labor & Employment 9-732
tools of trade	Clothing, books, tools, instruments, & appliances to $5,000	11-504(b)(1)
wages	Earned but unpaid wages, the greater of 75% or $145 per week; in Kent, Caroline, & Queen Anne's of Worcester Counties, the greater of 75% or 30 times federal minimum hourly wage	Commercial Law 15-601.1
wildcard	$6,000 in cash or any property, if claimed within 30 days of attachment or levy	11-504(b)(5)
	An additional $5,000 in real or personal property	11-504(f)

Massachusetts

Federal bankruptcy exemptions available. All law references are to Massachusetts General Laws Annotated, in the form title number-section number, unless otherwise noted.

ASSET	EXEMPTION	LAW
homestead	If statement of homestead is not in title to property, must record homestead declaration before filing bankruptcy	188-2
	Property held as tenancy by the entirety may be exempt against debt for nonnecessity owed by only one spouse.	209-1
	Property you occupy or intend to occupy (including mobile home) to $500,000 (special rules if over 65 or disabled)	188-1; 188-1A
	Spouse or children of deceased owner may claim homestead exemption	188-4

insurance	Disability benefits to $400 per week	175-110A
	Fraternal benefit society benefits	176-22
	Group annuity policy or proceeds	175-132C
	Group life insurance policy	175-135
	Life insurance or annuity contract proceeds if clause prohibits proceeds from being used to pay beneficiary's creditors	175-119A
	Life insurance policy if beneficiary is married woman	175-126
	Life or endowment policy, proceeds, or cash value	175-125
	Medical malpractice self-insurance	175F-15
miscellaneous	Property of business partnership	108A-25
pensions *see also wages*	Tax-exempt retirement accounts, including 401(k)s, 403(b)s, profit-sharing and money purchase plans, SEP and SIMPLE IRAs, and defined-benefit plans	11 U.S.C. § 522(b)(3)(C)
	Traditional and Roth IRAs to $1,095,000 per person	11 U.S.C. § 522(b)(3)(C); (n)
	Credit union employees	171-84
	ERISA-qualified benefits, including IRAs & Keoghs to specified limits	235-34A; 246-28
	Private retirement benefits	32-41
	Public employees	32-19
	Savings bank employees	168-41; 168-44
personal property	Bank deposits to $125	235-34
	Beds & bedding; heating unit; clothing	235-34
	Bibles & books to $200 total; sewing machine to $200	235-34
	Burial plots, tombs, & church pew	235-34
	Cash for fuel, heat, water, or light to $75 per month	235-34
	Cash to $200/month for rent, in lieu of homestead	235-34
	Cooperative association shares to $100	235-34
	Food or cash for food to $300	235-34
	Furniture to $3,000; motor vehicle to $700	235-34
	Moving expenses for eminent domain	79-6A
	Trust company, bank, or credit union deposits to $500	246-28A
	2 cows, 12 sheep, 2 swine, 4 tons of hay	235-34
public benefits	Aid to families with dependent children	118-10
	Public assistance	235-34
	Unemployment compensation	151A-36
	Veterans' benefits	115-5
	Workers' compensation	152-47
tools of trade	Arms, accoutrements, & uniforms required	235-34
	Fishing boats, tackle, & nets to $500	235-34
	Materials you designed & procured to $500	235-34
	Tools, implements, & fixtures to $500 total	235-34
wages	Earned but unpaid wages to $125 per week	246-28
wildcard	None	

Michigan

Federal bankruptcy exemptions available. All law references are to Michigan Compiled Laws Annotated unless otherwise noted.

Under Michigan law, bankruptcy exemption amounts are adjusted for inflation every three years (first adjustments were made in 2005). These amounts have already been adjusted, so the amounts listed in the statutes are not current. Find the current amounts at www.michigan.gov/documents/BankruptcyExemptions2005_141050_7.pdf or by going to www.michigan.gov/treasury and typing "bankruptcy exemptions" in the search box.

ASSET	EXEMPTION	LAW
homestead	Property held as tenancy by the entirety may be exempt against debts owed by only one spouse	600.5451(1)(o)
	Real property including condo to $31,900 ($47,825 if over 65 or disabled; spouses or co-owners may not double); property cannot exceed 1 lot in town, village, city, or 40 acres elsewhere; spouse or children of deceased owner may claim homestead exemption	600.5451(1)(n); (5)(d); *In re Lindstrom*, 331 B.R. 267 (E.D.Mich. 2005; *Vinson v. Dakmak*, 347 B.R. 620 (E.D.Mich. 2006)
insurance	Disability, mutual life, or health benefits	600.5451(1)(j)
	Employer-sponsored life insurance policy or trust fund	500.2210
	Fraternal benefit society benefits	500.8181
	Life, endowment, or annuity proceeds if clause prohibits proceeds from being used to pay beneficiary's creditors	500.4054
	Life insurance	500.2207
miscellaneous	Property of business partnership	449.25
pensions	Tax-exempt retirement accounts, including 401(k)s, 403(b)s, profit-sharing and money purchase plans, SEP and SIMPLE IRAs, and defined-benefit plans	11 U.S.C. § 522(b)(3)(C)
	Traditional and Roth IRAs to $1,095,000 per person	11 U.S.C. § 522(b)(3)(C); (n)
	ERISA-qualified benefits, except contributions within last 120 days	600.5451(1)(m)
	Firefighters, police officers	38.559(6); 38.1683
	IRAs & Roth IRAs, except contributions within last 120 days	600.5451(1)(l)
	Judges	38.2308; 38.1683
	Legislators	38.1057; 38.1683
	Probate judges	38.2308; 38.1683
	Public school employees	38.1346; 38.1683
	State employees	38.40; 38.1683
personal property	Appliances, utensils, books, furniture, & household goods to $475 each, $3,200 total	600.5451(1)(c)
	Building & loan association shares to $1,075 par value, in lieu of homestead	600.5451(1)(k)
	Burial plots, cemeteries	600.5451(1)(a)
	Church pew, slip, seat for entire family to $525	600.5451(1)(d)
	Clothing; family pictures	600.5451(1)(a)
	Food & fuel to last family for 6 months	600.5451(1)(b)
	Crops, animals, and feed to $2,125	600.5451(1)(d)
	1 motor vehicle to $2,950	600.5451(1)(g)
	Computer & accessories to $525	600.5451(1)(h)
	Household pets to $525	600.5451(1)(f)
	Professionally prescribed health aids	600.5451(a)

public benefits	Crime victims' compensation	18.362
	Social welfare benefits	400.63
	Unemployment compensation	421.30
	Veterans' benefits for Korean War veterans	35.977
	Veterans' benefits for Vietnam veterans	35.1027
	Veterans' benefits for WWII veterans	35.926
	Workers' compensation	418.821
tools of trade	Arms & accoutrements required	600.6023(1)(a)
	Tools, implements, materials, stock, apparatus, team, motor vehicle, horse, & harness to $1,000 total	600.6023(1)(e)
wages	Head of household may keep 60% of earned but unpaid wages (no less than $15/week), plus $2/week per nonspouse dependent; if not head of household may keep 40% (no less than $10/week)	600.5311
wildcard	None	

Minnesota

Federal bankruptcy exemptions available. All law references are to Minnesota Statutes Annotated, unless otherwise noted.

NOTE: Section 550.37(4)(a) requires certain exemptions to be adjusted for inflation on July 1 of even-numbered years; this table includes all changes made through July 1, 2004. Exemptions are published in the May 1 issue of the Minnesota State Register, www.comm.media.state.mn.us/bookstore/stateregister.asp, or call the Minnesota Dept. of Commerce at 651-296-7977.

ASSET	EXEMPTION	LAW
homestead	Home & land on which it is situated to $200,000; if homestead is used for agricultural purposes, $500,000; cannot exceed 1/2 acre in city, 160 acres elsewhere (husband & wife may not double)	510.01; 510.02
	Manufactured home to an unlimited value	550.37 subd. 12
insurance	Accident or disability proceeds	550.39
	Fraternal benefit society benefits	64B.18
	Life insurance proceeds to $38,000, if beneficiary is spouse or child of insured, plus $9,500 per dependent	550.37 subd. 10
	Police, fire, or beneficiary association benefits	550.37 subd. 11
	Unmatured life insurance contract dividends, interest, or loan value to $7,600 if insured is debtor or person debtor depends on	550.37 subd. 23
miscellaneous	Earnings of minor child	550.37 subd. 15
pensions	Tax-exempt retirement accounts, including 401(k)s, 403(b)s, profit-sharing and money purchase plans, SEP and SIMPLE IRAs, and defined-benefit plans	11 U.S.C. § 522(b)(3)(C)
	Traditional and Roth IRAs to $1,095,000 per person	11 U.S.C. § 522(b)(3)(C); (n)
	ERISA-qualified benefits needed for support, up to $57,000 in present value	550.37 subd. 24
	IRAs or Roth IRAs needed for support, up to $57,000 in present value	550.37 subd. 24
	Public employees	353.15; 356.401
	State employees	352.96 subd. 6; 356.401
	State troopers	352B.071; 356.401

personal property	Appliances, furniture, jewelry, radio, phonographs, & TV to $8,550 total	550.37 subd. 4(b)
	Bible & books	550.37 subd. 2
	Burial plot; church pew or seat	550.37 subd. 3
	Clothing, one watch, food, & utensils for family	550.37 subd. 4(a)
	Motor vehicle to $3,800 (up to $38,000 if vehicle has been modified for disability)	550.37 subd. 12(a)
	Personal injury recoveries	550.37 subd. 22
	Proceeds for damaged exempt property	550.37 subds. 9, 16
	Wedding rings to $1,225	550.37 subd. 4(c)
	Wrongful death recoveries	550.37 subd. 22
public benefits	Crime victims' compensation	611A.60
	Public benefits	550.37 subd. 14
	Unemployment compensation	268.192 subd. 2
	Veterans' benefits	550.38
	Workers' compensation	176.175
tools of trade *total (except teaching materials) can't exceed $13,000*	Farm machines, implements, livestock, produce, & crops	550.37 subd. 5
	Teaching materials of college, university, public school, or public institution teacher	550.37 subd. 8
	Tools, machines, instruments, stock in trade, furniture, & library to $9,500 total	550.37 subd. 6
wages	Minimum 75% of weekly disposable earnings or 40 times federal minimum hourly wage, whichever is greater	571.922
	Wages deposited into bank accounts for 20 days after depositing	550.37 subd. 13
	Wages, paid within 6 mos. of returning to work, after receiving welfare or after incarceration; includes earnings deposited in a financial institution in the last 60 days	550.37 subd. 14
wildcard	None	

NOTE: In cases of suspected fraud, the Minnesota constitution permits courts to cap exemptions that would otherwise be unlimited. *In re Tveten*, 402 N.W.2d 551 (Minn. 1987); *In re Medill*, 119 B.R. 685 (Bankr. D. Minn. 1990); *In re Sholdan*, 217 F.3d 1006 (8th Cir. 2000).

Mississippi

Federal bankruptcy exemptions not available. All law references are to Mississippi Code unless otherwise noted.

ASSET	EXEMPTION	LAW
homestead	May file homestead declaration	85-3-27; 85-3-31
	Mobile home does not qualify as homestead unless you own land on which it is located (*see personal property*)	*In re Cobbins*, 234 B.R. 882 (S.D. Miss. 1999)
	Property you own & occupy to $75,000; if over 60 & married or widowed may claim a former residence; property cannot exceed 160 acres; sale proceeds exempt	85-3-1(b)(i); 85-3-21; 85-3-23
insurance	Disability benefits	85-3-1(b)(ii)
	Fraternal benefit society benefits	83-29-39
	Homeowners' insurance proceeds to $75,000	85-3-23
	Life insurance proceeds if clause prohibits proceeds from being used to pay beneficiary's creditors	83-7-5; 85-3-11

miscellaneous	Property of business partnership	79-12-49
pensions	Tax-exempt retirement accounts, including 401(k)s, 403(b)s, profit-sharing and money purchase plans, SEP and SIMPLE IRAs, and defined-benefit plans	11 U.S.C. § 522(b)(3)(C)
	Traditional and Roth IRAs to $1,095,000 per person	11 U.S.C. § 522(b)(3)(C); (n)
	ERISA-qualified benefits, IRAs, Keoghs deposited over 1 yr. before filing bankruptcy	85-3-1(f)
	Firefighters (includes death benefits)	21-29-257; 45-2-1
	Highway patrol officers	25-13-31
	Law enforcement officers' death benefits	45-2-1
	Police officers (includes death benefits)	21-29-257; 45-2-1
	Private retirement benefits to extent tax-deferred	71-1-43
	Public employees retirement & disability benefits	25-11-129
	State employees	25-14-5
	Teachers	25-11-201(1)(d)
	Volunteer firefighters' death benefits	45-2-1
personal property	Mobile home to $20,000	85-3-1(e)
	Personal injury judgments to $10,000	85-3-17
	Sale or insurance proceeds for exempt property	85-3-1(b)(i)
	Tangible personal property to $10,000: any item worth less than $200; furniture, dishes, kitchenware, household goods, appliances, 1 radio & 1 TV, 1 firearm, 1 lawnmower, clothing, wedding rings, motor vehicles, tools of the trade, books, crops, health aids, domestic animals (does not include works of art, antiques, jewelry, or electronic entertainment equipment)	85-3-1(a)
public benefits	Assistance to aged	43-9-19
	Assistance to blind	43-3-71
	Assistance to disabled	43-29-15
	Crime victims' compensation	99-41-23(7)
	Social Security	25-11-129
	Unemployment compensation	71-5-539
	Workers' compensation	71-3-43
tools of trade	*See personal property*	
wages	Earned but unpaid wages owed for 30 days; after 30 days, minimum 75% of earned but unpaid weekly disposable earnings, or 30 times the federal hourly minimum wage, whichever is greater (bankruptcy judge may authorize more for low-income debtors)	85-3-4
wildcard	*See personal property*	

Missouri

Federal bankruptcy exemptions not available. All law references are to Annotated Missouri Statutes unless otherwise noted.

ASSET	EXEMPTION	LAW
homestead	Property held as tenancy by the entirety may be exempt against debts owed by only one spouse	*In re Eads*, 271 B.R. 371 (Bankr. W.D. Mo. 2002).

homestead (continued)	Real property to $15,000 or mobile home to $5,000 (joint owners may not double)	513.430(6); 513.475 *In re Smith*, 254 B.R. 751 (Bank. W.D. Mo. 2000)
insurance	Assessment plan or life insurance proceeds	377.090
	Disability or illness benefits	513.430(10)(c)
	Fraternal benefit society benefits to $5,000, bought over 6 months before filing	513.430(8)
	Life insurance dividends, loan value, or interest to $150,000, bought over 6 months before filing	513.430(8)
	Life insurance proceeds if policy owned by a woman & insures her husband	376.530
	Life insurance proceeds if policy owned by unmarried woman & insures her father or brother	376.550
	Stipulated insurance premiums	377.330
	Unmatured life insurance policy	513.430(7)
miscellaneous	Alimony, child support to $750 per month	513.430(10)(d)
	Property of business partnership	358.250
pensions	Tax-exempt retirement accounts, including 401(k)s, 403(b)s, profit-sharing and money purchase plans, SEP and SIMPLE IRAs, and defined-benefit plans	11 U.S.C. § 522(b)(3)(C)
	Traditional and Roth IRAs to $1,095,000 per person	11 U.S.C. § 522(b)(3)(C); (n)
	Employee benefit spendthrift trust	456.014
	Employees of cities with 100,000 or more people	71.207
	ERISA-qualified benefits, IRAs, Roth IRAs, & other retirement accounts needed for support	513.430(10)(e), (f)
	Firefighters	87.090; 87.365; 87.485
	Highway & transportation employees	104.250
	Police department employees	86.190; 86.353; 86.1430
	Public officers & employees	70.695; 70.755
	State employees	104.540
	Teachers	169.090
personal property	Appliances, household goods, furnishings, clothing, books, crops, animals, & musical instruments to $3,000 total	513.430(1)
	Burial grounds to 1 acre or $100	214.190
	Health aids	513.430(9)
	Motor vehicle to $3,000	513.430(5)
	Personal injury causes of action	*In re Mitchell*, 73 B.R. 93 (Bankr. E.D. Mo. 1987)
	Wedding ring to $1,500, & other jewelry to $500	513.430(2)
	Wrongful death recoveries for person you depended on	513.430(11)
public benefits	Crime victim's compensation	595.025
	Public assistance	513.430(10)(a)
	Social Security	513.430(10)(a)
	Unemployment compensation	288.380(10)(l); 513.430(10)(c)
	Veterans' benefits	513.430(10)b)
	Workers' compensation	287.260

tools of trade	Implements, books, & tools of trade to $3,000	513.430(4)
wages	Minimum 75% of weekly earnings (90% of weekly earnings for head of family), or 30 times the federal minimum hourly wage, whichever is more; bankruptcy judge may authorize more for low-income debtors	525.030
	Wages of servant or common laborer to $90	513.470
wildcard	$1,250 of any property if head of family, else $600; head of family may claim additional $350 per child	513.430(3); 513.440

Montana

Federal bankruptcy exemptions not available. All law references are to Montana Code Annotated unless otherwise noted.

ASSET	EXEMPTION	LAW
homestead	Must record homestead declaration before filing for bankruptcy	70-32-105
	Real property or mobile home you occupy to $100,000; sale, condemnation, or insurance proceeds exempt for 18 months	70-32-104; 70-32-201; 70-32-213
insurance	Annuity contract proceeds to $350 per month	33-15-514
	Disability or illness proceeds, avails, or benefits	25-13-608(1)(d); 33-15-513
	Fraternal benefit society benefits	33-7-522
	Group life insurance policy or proceeds	33-15-512
	Hail insurance benefits	80-2-245
	Life insurance proceeds if clause prohibits proceeds from being used to pay beneficiary's creditors	33-20-120
	Medical, surgical, or hospital care benefits	25-13-608(1)(f)
	Unmatured life insurance contracts to $4,000	25-13-609(4)
miscellaneous	Alimony, child support	25-13-608(1)(g)
pensions	Tax-exempt retirement accounts, including 401(k)s, 403(b)s, profit-sharing and money purchase plans, SEP and SIMPLE IRAs, and defined-benefit plans	11 U.S.C. § 522(b)(3)(C)
	Traditional and Roth IRAs to $1,095,000 per person	11 U.S.C. § 522(b)(3)(C); (n)
	ERISA-qualified benefits deposited over 1 year before filing bankruptcy or up to 15% of debtor's gross annual income	31-2-106
	Firefighters	19-18-612(1)
	IRA & Roth IRA contributions & earnings made before judgment filed	25-13-608(1)(e)
	Police officers	19-19-504(1)
	Public employees	19-2-1004; 25-13-608(i)
	Teachers	19-20-706(2); 25-13-608(j)
	University system employees	19-21-212
personal property	Appliances, household furnishings, goods, animals with feed, crops, musical instruments, books, firearms, sporting goods, clothing, & jewelry to $600 per item, $4,500 total	25-13-609(1)
	Burial plot	25-13-608(1)(h)
	Cooperative association shares to $500 value	35-15-404
	Health aids	25-13-608(1)(a)
	Motor vehicle to $2,500	25-13-609(2)
	Proceeds from sale or for damage or loss of exempt property for 6 mos. after received	25-13-610

public benefits	Aid to aged, disabled needy persons	53-2-607
	Crime victims' compensation	53-9-129
	Local public assistance	25-13-608(1)(b)
	Silicosis benefits	39-73-110
	Social Security	25-13-608(1)(b)
	Subsidized adoption payments to needy persons	53-2-607
	Unemployment compensation	31-2-106(2); 39-51-3105
	Veterans' benefits	25-13-608(1)(c)
	Vocational rehabilitation to blind needy persons	53-2-607
	Workers' compensation	39-71-743
tools of trade	Implements, books, & tools of trade to $3,000	25-13-609(3)
	Uniforms, arms, accoutrements needed to carry out government functions	25-13-613(b)
wages	Minimum 75% of earned but unpaid weekly disposable earnings, or 30 times the federal hourly minimum wage, whichever is greater; bankruptcy judge may authorize more for low-income debtors	25-13-614
wildcard	None	

Nebraska

Federal bankruptcy exemptions not available. All law references are to Revised Statutes of Nebraska unless otherwise noted.

ASSET	EXEMPTION	LAW
homestead	$12,500 for married debtor or head of household; cannot exceed 2 lots in city or village, 160 acres elsewhere; sale proceeds exempt 6 months after sale (husband & wife may not double)	40-101; 40-111; 40-113
	May record homestead declaration	40-105
insurance	Fraternal benefit society benefits to $100,000 loan value unless beneficiary convicted of a crime related to benefits	44-1089
	Life insurance proceeds and avails to $100,000	44-371
pensions *see also wages*	Tax-exempt retirement accounts, including 401(k)s, 403(b)s, profit-sharing and money purchase plans, SEP and SIMPLE IRAs, and defined-benefit plans	11 U.S.C. § 522(b)(3)(C)
	Traditional and Roth IRAs to $1,095,000 per person	11 U.S.C. § 522(b)(3)(C); (n)
	County employees	23-2322
	Deferred compensation of public employees	48-1401
	ERISA-qualified benefits including IRAs & Roth IRAs needed for support	25-1563.01
	Military disability benefits	25-1559
	School employees	79-948
	State employees	84-1324
personal property	Burial plot	12-517
	Clothing	25-1556(2)
	Crypts, lots, tombs, niches, vaults	12-605
	Furniture, household goods & appliances, household electronics, personal computers, books, & musical instruments to $1,500	25-1556(3)

personal property (continued)	Health aids	25-1556(5)
	Medical or health savings accounts to $25,000	8-1, 131(2)(b)
	Perpetual care funds	12-511
	Personal injury recoveries	25-1563.02
	Personal possessions	25-1556
public benefits	Aid to disabled, blind, aged; public assistance	68-1013
	General assistance to poor persons	68-148
	Unemployment compensation	48-647
	Workers' compensation	48-149
tools of trade	Equipment or tools including a vehicle used in/or for commuting to principal place of business to $2,400 (husband & wife may double)	25-1556(4); *In re Keller*, 50 B.R. 23 (D. Neb. 1985)
wages	Minimum 85% of earned but unpaid weekly disposable earnings or pension payments for head of family; minimum 75% of earned but unpaid weekly disposable earnings, or 30 times the federal hourly minimum wage, whichever is greater, for all others; bankruptcy judge may authorize more for low-income debtors	25-1558
wildcard	$2,500 of any personal property, except wages, in lieu of homestead	25-1552

Nevada

Federal bankruptcy exemptions not available. All law references are to Nevada Revised Statutes Annotated unless otherwise noted.

ASSET	EXEMPTION	LAW
homestead	Must record homestead declaration before filing for bankruptcy	115.020
	Real property or mobile home to $350,000	115.010; 21.090(1)(m)
insurance	Annuity contract proceeds to $350 per month	687B.290
	Fraternal benefit society benefits	695A.220
	Group life or health policy or proceeds	687B.280
	Health proceeds or avails	687B.270
	Life insurance policy or proceeds if annual premiums not over $1,000	21.090(1)(k); *In re Bower*, 234 B.R. 109 (Nev. 1999)
	Life insurance proceeds if you're not the insured	687B.260
miscellaneous	Alimony & child support	21.090(1)(r)
	Property of business partnership	87.250
pensions	Tax-exempt retirement accounts, including 401(k)s, 403(b)s, profit-sharing and money purchase plans, SEP and SIMPLE IRAs, and defined-benefit plans	11 U.S.C. § 522(b)(3)(C)
	Traditional and Roth IRAs to $1,095,000 per person	11 U.S.C. § 522(b)(3)(C); (n)
	ERISA-qualified benefits, deferred compensation, SEP IRA, Roth IRA, or IRA to $500,000	21.090(1)(q)
	Public employees	286.670
personal property	Appliances, household goods, furniture, home & yard equipment to $12,000 total	21.090(1)(b)
	Books, works of art, musical instruments, & jewelry to $5,000	21.090(1)(a)

personal property (continued)	Burial plot purchase money held in trust	689.700
	Funeral service contract money held in trust	689.700
	Health aids	21.090(1)(p)
	Keepsakes & pictures	21.090(1)(a)
	Metal-bearing ores, geological specimens, art curiosities, or paleontological remains; must be arranged, classified, catalogued, & numbered in reference books	21.100
	Mortgage impound accounts	645B.180
	Motor vehicle to $15,000; no limit on vehicle equipped for disabled person	21.090(1)(f),(o)
	One gun	21.090(1)(i)
	Personal injury compensation to $16,500	21.090(t)
	Restitution received for criminal act	21.090(w)
	Wrongful death awards to survivors	21.090(u)
public benefits	Aid to blind, aged, disabled; public assistance	422.291
	Crime victim's compensation	21.090
	Industrial insurance (workers' compensation)	616C.205
	Public assistance for children	432.036
	Unemployment compensation	612.710
	Vocational rehabilitation benefits	615.270
tools of trade	Arms, uniforms, & accoutrements you're required to keep	21.090(1)(j)
	Cabin or dwelling of miner or prospector; mining claim, cars, implements, & appliances to $4,500 total (for working claim only)	21.090(1)(e)
	Farm trucks, stock, tools, equipment, & seed to $4,500	21.090(1)(c)
	Library, equipment, supplies, tools, inventory, & materials to $10,000	21.090(1)(d)
wages	Minimum 75% of disposable weekly earnings or 30 times the federal minimum hourly wage per week, whichever is more; bankruptcy judge may authorize more for low-income debtors	21.090(1)(g)
wildcard	None	

New Hampshire

Federal bankruptcy exemptions available. All law references are to New Hampshire Revised Statutes Annotated unless otherwise noted.

ASSET	EXEMPTION	LAW
homestead	Real property or manufactured housing (& the land it's on if you own it) to $100,000	480:1
insurance	Firefighters' aid insurance	402:69
	Fraternal benefit society benefits	418:17
	Homeowners' insurance proceeds to $5,000	512:21(VIII)
miscellaneous	Jury, witness fees	512:21(VI)
	Property of business partnership	304-A:25
	Wages of minor child	512:21(III)

pensions	Tax-exempt retirement accounts, including 401(k)s, 403(b)s, profit-sharing and money purchase plans, SEP and SIMPLE IRAs, and defined-benefit plans	11 U.S.C. § 522(b)(3)(C)
	Traditional and Roth IRAs to $1,095,000 per person	11 U.S.C. § 522(b)(3)(C); (n)
	ERISA-qualified retirement accounts including IRAs & Roth IRAs	512:2 (XIX)
	Federally created pension (only benefits building up)	512:21(IV)
	Firefighters	102:23
	Police officers	103:18
	Public employees	100-A:26
personal property	Beds, bedding, & cooking utensils	511:2(II)
	Bibles & books to $800	511:2(VIII)
	Burial plot, lot	511:2(XIV)
	Church pew	511:2(XV)
	Clothing	511:2(I)
	Cooking & heating stoves, refrigerator	511:2(IV)
	Domestic fowl to $300	511:2(XIII)
	Food & fuel to $400	511:2(VI)
	Furniture to $3,500	511:2(III)
	Jewelry to $500	511:2(XVII)
	Motor vehicle to $4,000	511:2(XVI)
	Proceeds for lost or destroyed exempt property	512:21(VIII)
	Sewing machine	511:2(V)
	1 cow, 6 sheep & their fleece, 4 tons of hay	511:2(XI); (XII)
	1 hog or pig or its meat (if slaughtered)	511:2(X)
public benefits	Aid to blind, aged, disabled; public assistance	167:25
	Unemployment compensation	282-A:159
	Workers' compensation	281-A:52
tools of trade	Tools of your occupation to $5,000	511:2(IX)
	Uniforms, arms, & equipment of military member	511:2(VII)
	Yoke of oxen or horse needed for farming or teaming	511:2(XII)
wages	50 times the federal minimum hourly wage per week	512:21(II)
	Deposits in any account designated a payroll account	512:21(XI)
	Earned but unpaid wages of spouse	512:21(III)
wildcard	$1,000 of any property	511:2(XVIII)
	Unused portion of bibles & books, food & fuel, furniture, jewelry, motor vehicle, & tools of trade exemptions to $7,000	511:2(XVIII)

New Jersey

Federal bankruptcy exemptions available. All law references are to New Jersey Statutes Annotated unless otherwise noted.

ASSET	EXEMPTION	LAW
homestead	None, but survivorship interest of a spouse in property held as tenancy by the entirety is exempt from creditors of a single spouse	*Freda v. Commercial Trust Co. of New Jersey,* 570 A.2d 409 (N.J.,1990)

insurance	Annuity contract proceeds to $500 per month	17B:24-7
	Disability benefits	17:18-12
	Disability, death, medical, or hospital benefits for civil defense workers	App. A:9-57.6
	Disability or death benefits for military member	38A:4-8
	Group life or health policy or proceeds	17B:24-9
	Health or disability benefits	17:18-12; 17B:24-8
	Life insurance proceeds if clause prohibits proceeds from being used to pay beneficiary's creditors	17B:24-10
	Life insurance proceeds or avails if you're not the insured	17B:24-6b
pensions	Tax-exempt retirement accounts, including 401(k)s, 403(b)s, profit-sharing and money purchase plans, SEP and SIMPLE IRAs, and defined-benefit plans	11 U.S.C. § 522(b)(3)(C)
	Traditional and Roth IRAs to $1,095,000 per person	11 U.S.C. § 522(b)(3)(C); (n)
	Alcohol beverage control officers	43:8A-20
	City boards of health employees	43:18-12
	Civil defense workers	App. A:9-57.6
	County employees	43:10-57; 43:10-105
	ERISA-qualified benefits for city employees	43:13-9
	Firefighters, police officers, traffic officers	43:16-7; 43:16A-17
	IRAs	*In re Yuhas*, 104 F.3d 612 (3rd Cir. 1997)
	Judges	43:6A-41
	Municipal employees	43:13-44
	Prison employees	43:7-13
	Public employees	43:15A-53
	School district employees	18A:66-116
	State police	53:5A-45
	Street & water department employees	43:19-17
	Teachers	18A:66-51
	Trust containing personal property created pursuant to federal tax law, including 401(k) plans, IRAs, Roth IRAs, & higher education (529) savings plans	25:2-1; *In re Yuhas*, 104 F.3d 612 (3d Cir. 1997)
personal property	Burial plots	45:27-21
	Clothing	2A:17-19
	Furniture & household goods to $1,000	2A:26-4
	Personal property & possessions of any kind, stock or interest in corporations to $1,000 total	2A:17-19
public benefits	Old age, permanent disability assistance	44:7-35
	Unemployment compensation	43:21-53
	Workers' compensation	34:15-29
tools of trade	None	
wages	90% of earned but unpaid wages if annual income is less than 250% of federal poverty level; 75% if annual income is higher	2A:17-56
	Wages or allowances received by military personnel	38A:4-8
wildcard	None	

New Mexico

Federal bankruptcy exemptions available. All law references are to New Mexico Statutes Annotated unless otherwise noted.

ASSET	EXEMPTION	LAW
homestead	$30,000	42-10-9
insurance	Benevolent association benefits to $5,000	42-10-4
	Fraternal benefit society benefits	59A-44-18
	Life, accident, health, or annuity benefits, withdrawal or cash value, if beneficiary is a New Mexico resident	42-10-3
	Life insurance proceeds	42-10-5
miscellaneous	Ownership interest in unincorporated association	53-10-2
	Property of business partnership	54-1A-501
pensions	Tax-exempt retirement accounts, including 401(k)s, 403(b)s, profit-sharing and money purchase plans, SEP and SIMPLE IRAs, and defined-benefit plans	11 U.S.C. § 522(b)(3)(C)
	Traditional and Roth IRAs to $1,095,000 per person	11 U.S.C. § 522(b)(3)(C); (n)
	Pension or retirement benefits	42-10-1; 42-10-2
	Public school employees	22-11-42A
personal property	Books & furniture	42-10-1; 42-10-2
	Building materials	48-2-15
	Clothing	42-10-1; 42-10-2
	Cooperative association shares, minimum amount needed to be member	53-4-28
	Health aids	42-10-1; 42-10-2
	Jewelry to $2,500	42-10-1; 42-10-2
	Materials, tools, & machinery to dig, drill, complete, operate, or repair oil line, gas well, or pipeline	70-4-12
	Motor vehicle to $4,000	42-10-1; 42-10-2
public benefits	Crime victims' compensation	31-22-15
	General assistance	27-2-21
	Occupational disease disablement benefits	52-3-37
	Unemployment compensation	51-1-37
	Workers' compensation	52-1-52
tools of trade	$1,500	42-10-1; 42-10-2
wages	Minimum 75% of disposable earnings or 40 times the federal hourly minimum wage, whichever is more; bankruptcy judge may authorize more for low-income debtors	35-12-7
wildcard	$500 of any personal property	42-10-1
	$2,000 of any real or personal property, in lieu of homestead	42-10-10

New York

Federal bankruptcy exemptions not available. All references are to Consolidated Laws of New York unless otherwise noted; Civil Practice Law & Rules are abbreviated C.P.L.R.

ASSET	EXEMPTION	LAW
homestead	Real property including co-op, condo, or mobile home, to $50,000	C.P.L.R. 5206(a); *In re Pearl*, 723 F.2d 193 (2nd Cir. 1983)
insurance	Annuity contract benefits due the debtor, if debtor paid for the contract; $5,000 limit if purchased within 6 mos. prior to filing & not tax-deferred	Ins. 3212(d); Debt. & Cred. 283(1)
	Disability or illness benefits to $400/month	Ins. 3212(c)
	Life insurance proceeds & avails if the beneficiary is not the debtor, or if debtor's spouse has taken out policy	Ins. 3212(b)
	Life insurance proceeds left at death with the insurance company, if clause prohibits proceeds from being used to pay beneficiary's creditors	Est. Powers & Trusts 7-1.5(a)(2)
miscellaneous	Alimony, child support	C.P.L.R. 5205 (d)(3); Debt. & Cred. 282(2)(d)
	Property of business partnership	Partnership 51
pensions	Tax-exempt retirement accounts, including 401(k)s, 403(b)s, profit-sharing and money purchase plans, SEP and SIMPLE IRAs, and defined-benefit plans	11 U.S.C. § 522(b)(3)(C)
	Traditional and Roth IRAs to $1,095,000 per person	11 U.S.C. § 522(b)(3)(C); (n)
	ERISA-qualified benefits, IRAs, Roth IRAs, & Keoghs, & income needed for support	C.P.L.R. 5205(c); Debt. & Cred. 282(2)(e)
	Public retirement benefits	Ins. 4607
	State employees	Ret. & Soc. Sec. 10
	Teachers	Educ. 524
	Village police officers	Unconsolidated 5711-o
	Volunteer ambulance workers' benefits	Vol. Amb. Wkr. Ben. 23
	Volunteer firefighters' benefits	Vol. Firefighter Ben. 23
personal property	Bible, schoolbooks, other books to $50; pictures; clothing; church pew or seat; sewing machine, refrigerator, TV, radio; furniture, cooking utensils & tableware, dishes; food to last 60 days; stoves with fuel to last 60 days; domestic animal with food to last 60 days, to $450; wedding ring; watch to $35; exemptions may not exceed $5,000 total (including tools of trade & limited annuity)	C.P.L.R. 5205(a)(1)-(6); Debt. & Cred. 283(1)
	Burial plot without structure to 1/4 acre	C.P.L.R. 5206(f)
	Cash (including savings bonds, tax refunds, bank & credit union deposits) to $2,500, or to $5,000 after exemptions for personal property taken, whichever amount is less (for debtors who do not claim homestead)	Debt. & Cred. 283(2)
	College tuition savings program trust fund	C.P.L.R. 5205(j)
	Health aids, including service animals with food	C.P.L.R. 5205(h)
	Lost future earnings recoveries needed for support	Debt. & Cred. 282(3)(iv)

personal property (continued)	Motor vehicle to $2,400	Debt. & Cred. 282(1); *In re Miller*, 167 B.R. 782 (S.D. N.Y. 1994)
	Personal injury recoveries up to 1 year after receiving	Debt. & Cred. 282(3)(iii)
	Recovery for injury to exempt property up to 1 year after receiving	C.P.L.R. 5205(b)
	Savings & loan savings to $600	Banking 407
	Security deposit to landlord, utility company	C.P.L.R. 5205(g)
	Spendthrift trust fund principal, 90% of income if not created by debtor	C.P.L.R. 5205(c),(d)
	Wrongful death recoveries for person you depended on	Debt. & Cred. 282(3)(ii)
public benefits	Aid to blind, aged, disabled	Debt. & Cred. 282(2)(c)
	Crime victims' compensation	Debt. & Cred. 282(3)(i)
	Home relief, local public assistance	Debt. & Cred. 282(2)(a)
	Public assistance	Soc. Serv. 137
	Social Security	Debt. & Cred. 282(2)(a)
	Unemployment compensation	Debt. & Cred. 282(2)(a)
	Veterans' benefits	Debt. & Cred. 282(2)(b)
	Workers' compensation	Debt. & Cred. 282(2)(c); Work. Comp. 33, 218
tools of trade	Farm machinery, team, & food for 60 days; professional furniture, books, & instruments to $600 total	C.P.L.R. 5205(a),(b)
	Uniforms, medal, emblem, equipment, horse, arms, & sword of member of military	C.P.L.R. 5205(e)
wages	90% of earned but unpaid wages received within 60 days before & anytime after filing	C.P.L.R. 5205(d)
	90% of earnings from dairy farmer's sales to milk dealers	C.P.L.R. 5205(f)
	100% of pay of noncommissioned officer, private, or musician in U.S. or N.Y. state armed forces	C.P.L.R. 5205(e)
wildcard	None	

North Carolina

Federal bankruptcy exemptions not available. All law references are to General Statutes of North Carolina unless otherwise noted.

ASSET	EXEMPTION	LAW
homestead	Property held as tenancy by the entirety may be exempt against debts owed by only one spouse	*In re Chandler*, 148 B.R. 13 (E.D. N.C., 1992)
	Real or personal property, including co-op, used as residence to $18,500; up to $5,000 of unused portion of homestead may be applied to any property	1C-1601(a)(1),(2)
insurance	Employee group life policy or proceeds	58-58-165
	Fraternal benefit society benefits	58-24-85
	Life insurance on spouse or children	1C-1601(a)(6); Const. Art. X § 5

miscellaneous	Alimony, support, separate maintenance, and child support necessary for support of debtor and dependents	1C-1601(a)(12)
	Property of business partnership	59-55
	Support received by a surviving spouse for 1 year, up to $10,000	30-15
pensions	Tax-exempt retirement accounts, including 401(k)s, 403(b)s, profit-sharing and money purchase plans, SEP and SIMPLE IRAs, and defined-benefit plans	11 U.S.C. § 522(b)(3)(C)
	Traditional and Roth IRAs to $1,095,000 per person	11 U.S.C. § 522(b)(3)(C); (n)
	Firefighters & rescue squad workers	58-86-90
	IRAs & Roth IRAs	1C-1601(a)(9)
	Law enforcement officers	143-166.30(g)
	Legislators	120-4.29
	Municipal, city, & county employees	128-31
	Retirement benefits from another state to extent exempt in that state	1C-1601(a)(11)
	Teachers & state employees	135-9; 135-95
personal property	Animals, crops, musical instruments, books, clothing, appliances, household goods & furnishings to $5,000 total; may add $1,000 per dependent, up to $4,000 total additional (all property must have been purchased at least 90 days before filing)	1C-1601(a)(4),(d)
	Burial plot to $18,500, in lieu of homestead	1C-1601(a)(1)
	College savings account established under 26 U.S.C. § 529 to $25,000, excluding certain contributions within prior year	1C-1601(a)(10)
	Health aids	1C-1601(a)(7)
	Motor vehicle to $3,500	1C-1601(a)(3)
	Personal injury & wrongful death recoveries for person you depended on	1C-1601(a)(8)
public benefits	Aid to blind	111-18
	Crime victims' compensation	15B-17
	Public adult assistance under work first program	108A-36
	Unemployment compensation	96-17
	Workers' compensation	97-21
tools of trade	Implements, books, & tools of trade to $2,000	1C-1601(a)(5)
wages	Earned but unpaid wages received 60 days before filing for bankruptcy, needed for support	1-362
wildcard	$5,000 of unused homestead or burial exemption	1C-1601(a)(2)
	$500 of any personal property	Constitution Art. X § 1

North Dakota

Federal bankruptcy exemptions not available. All law references are to North Dakota Century Code unless otherwise noted.

ASSET	EXEMPTION	LAW
homestead	Real property, house trailer, or mobile home to $80,000 (husband & wife may not double)	28-22-02(10); 47-18-01
insurance	Fraternal benefit society benefits	26.1-15.1-18; 26.1-33-40
	Life insurance proceeds payable to deceased's estate, not to a specific beneficiary	26.1-33-40

insurance (continued)	Life insurance surrender value to $100,000 per policy, if beneficiary is insured's dependent & policy was owned over 1 year before filing for bankruptcy; limit does not apply if more needed for support	28-22-03.1(3)
miscellaneous	Child support payments	14-09-09.31
pensions	Tax-exempt retirement accounts, including 401(k)s, 403(b)s, profit-sharing and money purchase plans, SEP and SIMPLE IRAs, and defined-benefit plans	11 U.S.C. § 522(b)(3)(C)
	Traditional and Roth IRAs to $1,095,000 per person	11 U.S.C. § 522(b)(3)(C); (n)
	Disabled veterans' benefits, except military retirement pay	28-22-03.1(4)(d)
	ERISA-qualified benefits, IRAs, Roth IRAs, & Keoghs to $100,000 per plan; no limit if more needed for support; total exemption (with life insurance surrender value) cannot exceed $200,000	28-22-03.1(3)
	Public employees deferred compensation	54-52.2-06
	Public employees pensions	28-22-19(1)
personal property	1. All debtors may exempt:	
	Bible, schoolbooks; other books to $100	28-22-02(4)
	Burial plots, church pew	28-22-02(2),(3)
	Clothing & family pictures	28-22-02(1),(5)
	Crops or grain raised by debtor on 160 acres where debtor resides	28-22-02(8)
	Food & fuel to last 1 year	28-22-02(6)
	Insurance proceeds for exempt property	28-22-02(9)
	Motor vehicle to $1,200 (or $32,000 for vehicle that has been modified to accommodate owner's disability)	28-22-03.1(2)
	Personal injury recoveries to $7,500	28-22-03.1(4)(b)
	Wrongful death recoveries to $7,500	28-22-03.1(4)(a)
	2. Head of household not claiming crops or grain may claim $5,000 of any personal property or:	28-22-03
	Books & musical instruments to $1,500	28-22-04(1)
	Household & kitchen furniture, beds & bedding, to $1,000	28-22-04(2)
	Library & tools of professional, tools of mechanic, & stock in trade, to $1,000	28-22-04(4)
	Livestock & farm implements to $4,500	28-22-04(3)
	3. Non-head of household not claiming crops or grain may claim $2,500 of any personal property	28-22-05
public benefits	Crime victims' compensation	28-22-19(2)
	Old age & survivor insurance program benefits	52-09-22
	Public assistance	28-22-19(3)
	Social Security	28-22-03.1(4)(c)
	Unemployment compensation	52-06-30
	Workers' compensation	65-05-29
tools of trade	*See personal property, Option 2*	
wages	Minimum 75% of disposable weekly earnings or 40 times the federal minimum wage, whichever is more; bankruptcy judge may authorize more for low-income debtors	32-09.1-03
wildcard	$7,500 of any property in lieu of homestead	28-22-03.1(1)

Ohio

Federal bankruptcy exemptions not available. All law references are to Ohio Revised Code unless otherwise noted.

ASSET	EXEMPTION	LAW
homestead	Property held as tenancy by the entirety may be exempt against debts owed by only one spouse	*In re Pernus,* 143 B.R. 856 (N.D. Ohio, 1992)
	Real or personal property used as residence to $5,000	2329.66(A)(1)(b)
insurance	Benevolent society benefits to $5,000	2329.63; 2329.66(A)(6)(a)
	Disability benefits to $600 per month	2329.66(A)(6)(e); 3923.19
	Fraternal benefit society benefits	2329.66(A)(6)(d); 3921.18
	Group life insurance policy or proceeds	2329.66(A)(6)(c); 3917.05
	Life, endowment, or annuity contract avails for your spouse, child, or dependent	2329.66(A)(6)(b); 3911.10
	Life insurance proceeds for a spouse	3911.12
	Life insurance proceeds if clause prohibits proceeds from being used to pay beneficiary's creditors	3911.14
miscellaneous	Alimony, child support needed for support	2329.66(A)(11)
	Property of business partnership	1775.24; 2329.66(A)(14)
pensions	Tax-exempt retirement accounts, including 401(k)s, 403(b)s, profit-sharing and money purchase plans, SEP and SIMPLE IRAs, and defined-benefit plans	11 U.S.C. § 522(b)(3)(C)
	Traditional and Roth IRAs to $1,095,000 per person	11 U.S.C. § 522(b)(3)(C); (n)
	ERISA-qualified benefits needed for support	2329.66(A)(10)(b)
	Firefighters, police officers	742.47
	IRAs, Roth IRAs, & Keoghs needed for support	2329.66(A)(10)(c), (a)
	Public employees	145.56
	Public safety officers' death benefit	2329.66(A)(10)(a)
	Public school employees	3309.66
	State highway patrol employees	5505.22
	Volunteer firefighters' dependents	146.13
personal property	Animals, crops, books, musical instruments, appliances, household goods, furnishings, firearms, hunting & fishing equipment to $200 per item; jewelry to $400 for 1 item, $200 for all others; $1,500 total ($2,000 if no homestead exemption claimed)	2329.66(A)(4)(b),(c),(d); *In re Szydlowski,* 186 B.R. 907 (N.D. Ohio 1995)
	Beds, bedding, clothing to $200 per item	2329.66(A)(3)
	Burial plot	517.09; 2329.66(A)(8)
	Cash, money due within 90 days, tax refund, bank, security, & utility deposits to $400 total	2329.66(A)(4)(a); *In re Szydlowski,* 186 B.R. 907 (N.D. Ohio 1995)
	Compensation for lost future earnings needed for support, received during 12 months before filing	2329.66(A)(12)(d)
	Cooking unit & refrigerator to $300 each	2329.66(A)(3)
	Health aids (professionally prescribed)	2329.66(A)(7)
	Motor vehicle to $1,000	2329.66(A)(2)(b)

personal property (continued)	Personal injury recoveries to $5,000, received during 12 months before filing	2329.66(A)(12)(c)
	Tuition credit or payment	2329.66(A)(16)
	Wrongful death recoveries for person debtor depended on, needed for support, received during 12 months before filing	2329.66(A)(12)(b)
public benefits	Crime victim's compensation, received during 12 months before filing	2329.66(A)(12)(a); 2743.66(D)
	Disability assistance payments	2329.66(A)(9)(f); 5115.07
	Public assistance	2329.66(A)(9)(d); 5107.12, 5108.08
	Unemployment compensation	2329.66(A)(9)(c); 4141.32
	Vocational rehabilitation benefits	2329.66(A)(9)(a); 3304.19
	Workers' compensation	2329.66(A)(9)(b); 4123.67
tools of trade	Implements, books, & tools of trade to $750	2329.66(A)(5)
wages	Minimum 75% of disposable weekly earnings or 30 times the federal hourly minimum wage, whichever is higher; bankruptcy judge may authorize more for low-income debtors	2329.66(A)(13)
wildcard	$400 of any property	2329.66(A)(18)

Oklahoma

Federal bankruptcy exemptions not available. All law references are to Oklahoma Statutes Annotated (in the form title number-section number), unless otherwise noted.

ASSET	EXEMPTION	LAW
homestead	Real property or manufactured home to unlimited value; property cannot exceed 1 acre in city, town, or village, or 160 acres elsewhere; $5,000 limit if more than 25% of total sq. ft. area used for business purposes; okay to rent homestead as long as no other residence is acquired	31-1(A)(1); 31-1(A)(2); 31-2
insurance	Annuity benefits & cash value	36-3631.1
	Assessment or mutual benefits	36-2410
	Fraternal benefit society benefits	36-2718.1
	Funeral benefits prepaid & placed in trust	36-6125
	Group life policy or proceeds	36-3632
	Life, health, accident, & mutual benefit insurance proceeds & cash value, if clause prohibits proceeds from being used to pay beneficiary's creditors	36-3631.1
	Limited stock insurance benefits	36-2510
miscellaneous	Alimony, child support	31-1(A)(19)
	Beneficiary's interest in a statutory support trust	6-3010
	Liquor license	37-532
	Property of business partnership	54-1-504
pensions	Tax-exempt retirement accounts, including 401(k)s, 403(b)s, profit-sharing and money purchase plans, SEP and SIMPLE IRAs, and defined-benefit plans	11 U.S.C. § 522(b)(3)(C)

pensions (continued)	Traditional and Roth IRAs to $1,095,000 per person	11 U.S.C. § 522(b)(3)(C); (n)
	County employees	19-959
	Disabled veterans	31-7
	ERISA-qualified benefits, IRAs, Roth IRAs, Education IRAs, & Keoghs	31-1(A)(20),(23),(24)
	Firefighters	11-49-126
	Judges	20-1111
	Law enforcement employees	47-2-303.3
	Police officers	11-50-124
	Public employees	74-923
	Tax-exempt benefits	60-328
	Teachers	70-17-109
personal property	Books, portraits, & pictures	31-1(A)-7
	Burial plots	31-1(A)(4); 8-7
	Clothing to $4,000	31-1(A)(8)
	College savings plan interest	31-1(24)
	Deposits in an IDA (Individual Development Account)	31-1(22)
	Federal earned income tax credit	31-1(A)(25)
	Food & seed for growing to last 1 year	31-1(A)(17)
	Health aids (professionally prescribed)	31-1(A)(9)
	Household & kitchen furniture	31-1(A)(3)
	Livestock for personal or family use: 5 dairy cows & calves under 6 months; 100 chickens; 20 sheep; 10 hogs; 2 horses, bridles, & saddles; forage & feed to last 1 year	31-1(A)(10),(11),(12),(15),(16),(17)
	Motor vehicle to $3,000	31-1(A)(13)
	Personal injury & wrongful death recoveries to $50,000	31-1(A)(21)
	Prepaid funeral benefits	36-6125(H)
	War bond payroll savings account	51-42
	1 gun	31-1(A)(14)
public benefits	Crime victims' compensation	21-142.13
	Public assistance	56-173
	Social Security	56-173
	Unemployment compensation	40-2-303
	Workers' compensation	85-48
tools of trade	Implements needed to farm homestead, tools, books, & apparatus to $5,000 total	31-1(A)(5),(6); 31-1(C)
wages	75% of wages earned in 90 days before filing bankruptcy; bankruptcy judge may allow more if you show hardship	12-1171.1; 31-1(A)(18); 31-1.1
wildcard	None	

Oregon

Federal bankruptcy exemptions not available. All law references are to Oregon Revised Statutes unless otherwise noted.

ASSET	EXEMPTION	LAW
homestead	Prepaid rent & security deposit for renter's dwelling	*In re Casserino*, 379 F.3d 1069 (9th cir. 2004)
	Real property of a soldier or sailor during time of war	408.440
	Real property you occupy or intend to occupy to $30,000 ($39,600 for joint owners); mobile home on property you own or houseboat to $23,000 ($30,000 for joint owners); mobile home not on your land to $20,000 ($27,000 for joint owners); property cannot exceed 1 block in town or city or 160 acres elsewhere; sale proceeds exempt 1 year from sale, if you intend to purchase another home	18.428; 18.395; 18.402
	Tenancy by entirety not exempt, but subject to survivorship rights of nondebtor spouse	*In re Pletz*, 225 B.R. 206 (D. Or., 1997)
insurance	Annuity contract benefits to $500 per month	743.049
	Fraternal benefit society benefits to $7,500	748.207; 18.348
	Group life policy or proceeds not payable to insured	743.047
	Health or disability proceeds or avails	743.050
	Life insurance proceeds or cash value if you are not the insured	743.046, 743.047
miscellaneous	Alimony, child support needed for support	18.345(1)(i)
	Liquor licenses	471.292 (1)
pensions	Tax-exempt retirement accounts, including 401(k)s, 403(b)s, profit-sharing and money purchase plans, SEP and SIMPLE IRAs, and defined-benefit plans	11 U.S.C. § 522(b)(3)(C)
	Traditional and Roth IRAs to $1,095,000 per person	11 U.S.C. § 522(b)(3)(C); (n)
	ERISA-qualified benefits, including IRAs & SEPs; & payments to $7,500	18.358; 18.348
	Public officers, employees pension payments to $7,500	237.980; 238.445; 18.348 (2)
personal property	Bank deposits to $7,500; cash for sold exempt property	18.348; 18.345(2)
	Books, pictures, & musical instruments to $600 total	18.345(1)(a)
	Building materials for construction of an improvement	87.075
	Burial plot	65.870
	Clothing, jewelry, & other personal items to $1,800 total	18.345(1)(b)
	Compensation for lost earnings payments for debtor or someone debtor depended on, to extent needed	18.345(1)(L),(3)
	Domestic animals, poultry, & pets to $1,000 plus food to last 60 days	18.345(1)(e)
	Federal earned income tax credit	18.345(1)(n)
	Food & fuel to last 60 days if debtor is householder	18.345(1)(f)
	Furniture, household items, utensils, radios, & TVs to $3,000 total	18.345(1)(f)
	Health aids	18.345(1)(h)
	Higher education savings account to $7,500	348.863; 18.348(1)
	Motor vehicle to $2,150	18.345(1)(d),(3)
	Personal injury recoveries to $10,000	18.345(1)(k),(3)
	Pistol; rifle or shotgun (owned by person over 16) to $1,000	18.362

public benefits	Aid to blind to $7,500	411.706; 411.760; 18.348
	Aid to disabled to $7,500	411.706; 411.760; 18.348
	Civil defense & disaster relief to $7,500	401.405; 18.348
	Crime victims' compensation	18.345(1)(j)(A),(3); 147.325
	General assistance to $7,500	411.760; 18.348
	Injured inmates' benefits to $7,500	655.530; 18.348
	Medical assistance to $7,500	414.095; 18.348
	Old-age assistance to $7,500	411.706; 411.760; 18.348
	Unemployment compensation to $7,500	657.855; 18.348
	Veterans' benefits & proceeds of Veterans loans	407.125; 407.595; 18.348(m)
	Vocational rehabilitation to $7,500	344.580; 18.348
	Workers' compensation to $7,500	656.234; 18.348
tools of trade	Tools, library, team with food to last 60 days, to $3,000	18.345(1)(c),(3)
wages	75% of disposable wages or $170 per week, whichever is greater; bankruptcy judge may authorize more for low-income debtors	18.385
	Wages withheld in state employee's bond savings accounts	292.070
wildcard	$400 of any personal property not already covered by existing exemption	18.348(1)(o)

Pennsylvania

Federal bankruptcy exemptions available. All law references are to Pennsylvania Consolidated Statutes Annotated unless otherwise noted.

ASSET	EXEMPTION	LAW
homestead	None; however, property held as tenancy by the entirety may be exempt against debts owed by only one spouse	*In re Martin*, 269 B.R. 119 (M.D. Pa. 2001)
insurance	Accident or disability benefits	42-8124(c)(7)
	Fraternal benefit society benefits	42-8124(c)(1),(8)
	Group life policy or proceeds	42-8124(c)(5)
	Insurance policy or annuity contract payments, where insured is the beneficiary, cash value or proceeds to $100 per month	42-8124(c)(3)
	Life insurance & annuity proceeds if clause prohibits proceeds from being used to pay beneficiary's creditors	42-8214(c)(4)
	Life insurance annuity policy cash value or proceeds if beneficiary is insured's dependent, child, or spouse	42-8124(c)(6)
	No-fault automobile insurance proceeds	42-8124(c)(9)
miscellaneous	Property of business partnership	15-8342
pensions	Tax-exempt retirement accounts, including 401(k)s, 403(b)s, profit-sharing and money purchase plans, SEP and SIMPLE IRAs, and defined-benefit plans	11 U.S.C. § 522(b)(3)(C)
	Traditional and Roth IRAs to $1,095,000 per person	11 U.S.C. § 522(b)(3)(C); (n)
	City employees	53-13445; 53-23572; 53-39383; 42-8124(b)(1)(iv)
	County employees	16-4716
	Municipal employees	53-881.115; 42-8124(b)(1)(vi)

pensions (continued)	Police officers	53-764; 53-776; 53-23666; 42-8124(b)(1)(iii)
	Private retirement benefits to extent tax-deferred, if clause prohibits proceeds from being used to pay beneficiary's creditors; exemption limited to deposits of $15,000 per year made at least 1 year before filing (limit does not apply to rollovers from other exempt funds or accounts)	42-8124(b)(1)(vii), (viii),(ix)
	Public school employees	24-8533; 42-8124(b)(1)(i)
	State employees	71-5953; 42-8124(b)(1)(ii)
personal property	Bibles & schoolbooks	42-8124(a)(2)
	Clothing	42-8124(a)(1)
	Military uniforms & accoutrements	42-8124(a)(4); 51-4103
	Sewing machines	42-8124(a)(3)
public benefits	Crime victims' compensation	18-11.708
	Korean conflict veterans' benefits	51-20098
	Unemployment compensation	42-8124(a)(10); 43-863
	Veterans' benefits	51-20012; 20048; 20098; 20127
	Workers' compensation	42-8124(c)(2)
tools of trade	Seamstress's sewing machine	42-8124(a)(3)
wages	Earned but unpaid wages	42-8127
	Prison inmates wages	61-1054
	Wages of victims of abuse	42-8127(f)
wildcard	$300 of any property, including cash, real property, securities, or proceeds from sale of exempt property	42-8123

Rhode Island

Federal bankruptcy exemptions available. All law references are to General Laws of Rhode Island unless otherwise noted.

ASSET	EXEMPTION	LAW
homestead	$300,000 in land & buildings you occupy or intend to occupy as a principal residence (husband & wife may not double)	9-26-4.1
insurance	Accident or sickness proceeds, avails, or benefits	27-18-24
	Fraternal benefit society benefits	27-25-18
	Life insurance proceeds if clause prohibits proceeds from being used to pay beneficiary's creditors	27-4-12
	Temporary disability insurance	28-41-32
miscellaneous	Earnings of a minor child	9-26-4(9)
	Property of business partnership	7-12-36
pensions	Tax-exempt retirement accounts, including 401(k)s, 403(b)s, profit-sharing and money purchase plans, SEP and SIMPLE IRAs, and defined-benefit plans	11 U.S.C. § 522(b)(3)(C)
	Traditional and Roth IRAs to $1,095,000 per person	11 U.S.C. § 522(b)(3)(C); (n)
	ERISA-qualified benefits	9-26-4(12)
	Firefighters	9-26-5

pensions (continued)	IRAs & Roth IRAs	9-26-4(11)
	Police officers	9-26-5
	Private employees	28-17-4
	State & municipal employees	36-10-34
personal property	Beds, bedding, furniture, household goods, & supplies, to $8,600 total (husband & wife may not double)	9-26-4(3); *In re Petrozella*, 247 B.R. 591 (R.I. 2000)
	Bibles & books to $300	9-26-4(4)
	Burial plot	9-26-4(5)
	Clothing	9-26-4(1)
	Consumer cooperative association holdings to $50	7-8-25
	Debt secured by promissory note or bill of exchange	9-26-4(7)
	Jewelry to $1,000	9-26-4 (14)
	Motor vehicles to $10,000	9-26-4 (13)
	Prepaid tuition program or tuition savings account	9-26-4 (15)
public benefits	Aid to blind, aged, disabled; general assistance	40-6-14
	Crime victims' compensation	12-25.1-3(b)(2)
	Family assistance benefits	40-5.1-15
	State disability benefits	28-41-32
	Unemployment compensation	28-44-58
	Veterans' disability or survivors' death benefits	30-7-9
	Workers' compensation	28-33-27
tools of trade	Library of practicing professional	9-26-4(2)
	Working tools to $1,200	9-26-4(2)
wages	Earned but unpaid wages due military member on active duty	30-7-9
	Earned but unpaid wages due seaman	9-26-4(6)
	Earned but unpaid wages to $50	9-26-4(8)(iii)
	Wages of any person who had been receiving public assistance are exempt for 1 year after going off of relief	9-26-4(8)(ii)
	Wages of spouse & minor children	9-26-4(9)
	Wages paid by charitable organization or fund providing relief to the poor	9-26-4(8)(i)
wildcard	None	

South Carolina

Federal bankruptcy exemptions not available. All law references are to Code of Laws of South Carolina unless otherwise noted.

ASSET	EXEMPTION	LAW
homestead	Real property, including co-op, to $5,000	15-41-30(1)
insurance	Accident & disability benefits	38-63-40(D)
	Benefits accruing under life insurance policy after death of insured, where proceeds left with insurance company pursuant to agreement; benefits not exempt from action to recover necessaries if parties agree	38-63-50
	Disability or illness benefits	15-41-30(10)(C)

insurance	Fraternal benefit society benefits	38-38-330
(continued)	Group life insurance proceeds; cash value to $50,000	38-63-40(C); 38-65-90
	Life insurance avails from policy for person you depended on to $4,000	15-41-30(8)
	Life insurance proceeds from policy for person you depended on, needed for support	15-41-30(11)(C)
	Proceeds & cash surrender value of life insurance payable to beneficiary other than insured's estate & for the express benefit of insured's spouse, children, or dependents (must be purchased 2 years before filing)	38-63-40(A)
	Proceeds of life insurance or annuity contract	38-63-40(B)
	Unmatured life insurance contract, except credit insurance policy	15-41-30(7)
miscellaneous	Alimony, child support	15-41-30(10)(D)
	Property of business partnership	33-41-720
pensions	Tax-exempt retirement accounts, including 401(k)s, 403(b)s, profit-sharing and money purchase plans, SEP and SIMPLE IRAs, and defined-benefit plans	11 U.S.C. § 522(b)(3)(C)
	Traditional and Roth IRAs to $1,095,000 per person	11 U.S.C. § 522(b)(3)(C); (n)
	ERISA-qualified benefits; your share of the pension plan fund	15-41-30(10)(E),(13)
	Firefighters	9-13-230
	General assembly members	9-9-180
	IRAs & Roth IRAs needed for support	15-41-30(12)
	Judges, solicitors	9-8-190
	Police officers	9-11-270
	Public employees	9-1-1680
personal property	Animals, crops, appliances, books, clothing, household goods, furnishings, musical instruments to $2,500 total	15-41-30(3)
	Burial plot to $5,000, in lieu of homestead	15-41-30(1)
	Cash & other liquid assets to $1,000, in lieu of burial or homestead exemption	15-41-30(5)
	College investment program trust fund	59-2-140
	Health aids	15-41-30(9)
	Jewelry to $500	15-41-30(4)
	Motor vehicle to $1,200	15-41-30(2)
	Personal injury & wrongful death recoveries for person you depended on for support	15-41-30(11)(B)
public benefits	Crime victims' compensation	15-41-30(11)(A); 16-3-1300
	General relief; aid to aged, blind, disabled	43-5-190
	Local public assistance	15-41-30(10)(A)
	Social Security	15-41-30(10)(A)
	Unemployment compensation	15-41-30(10)(A)
	Veterans' benefits	15-41-30(10)(B)
	Workers' compensation	42-9-360
tools of trade	Implements, books, & tools of trade to $750	15-41-30(6)
wages	None (use federal nonbankruptcy wage exemption)	
wildcard	None	

South Dakota

Federal bankruptcy exemptions not available. All law references are to South Dakota Codified Law unless otherwise noted.

ASSET	EXEMPTION	LAW
homestead	Gold or silver mine, mill, or smelter not exempt	43-31-5
	May file homestead declaration	43-31-6
	Real property to unlimited value or mobile home (larger than 240 sq. ft. at its base & registered in state at least 6 months before filing) to unlimited value; property cannot exceed 1 acre in town or 160 acres elsewhere; sale proceeds to $30,000 ($170,000 if over age 70 or widow or widower who hasn't remarried) exempt for 1 year after sale (husband & wife may not double)	43-31-1; 43-31-2; 43-31-3; 43-31-443-45-3
	Spouse or child of deceased owner may claim homestead exemption	43-31-13
insurance	Annuity contract proceeds to $250 per month	58-12-6; 58-12-8
	Endowment, life insurance, policy proceeds to $20,000; if policy issued by mutual aid or benevolent society, cash value to $20,000	58-12-4
	Fraternal benefit society benefits	58-37A-18
	Health benefits to $20,000	58-12-4
	Life insurance proceeds, if clause prohibits proceeds from being used to pay beneficiary's creditors	58-15-70
	Life insurance proceeds to $10,000, if beneficiary is surviving spouse or child	43-45-6
pensions	Tax-exempt retirement accounts, including 401(k)s, 403(b)s, profit-sharing and money purchase plans, SEP and SIMPLE IRAs, and defined-benefit plans	11 U.S.C. § 522(b)(3)(C)
	Traditional and Roth IRAs to $1,095,000 per person	11 U.S.C. § 522(b)(3)(C); (n)
	City employees	9-16-47
	ERISA-qualified benefits, limited to income & distribution on $250,000	43-45-16
	Public employees	3-12-115
personal property	Bible, schoolbooks; other books to $200	43-45-2(4)
	Burial plots, church pew	43-45-2(2),(3)
	Cemetery association property	47-29-25
	Clothing	43-45-2(5)
	Family pictures	43-45-2(1)
	Food & fuel to last 1 year	43-45-2(6)
public benefits	Crime victim's compensation	23A-28B-24
	Public assistance	28-7A-18
	Unemployment compensation	61-6-28
	Workers' compensation	62-4-42
tools of trade	None	
wages	Earned wages owed 60 days before filing bankruptcy, needed for support of family	15-20-12
	Wages of prisoners in work programs	24-8-10
wildcard	Head of family may claim $6,000, or non-head of family may claim $4,000 of any personal property	43-45-4

Tennessee

Federal bankruptcy exemptions not available. All law references are to Tennessee Code Annotated unless otherwise noted.

ASSET	EXEMPTION	LAW
homestead	$5,000; $7,500 for joint owners (if 62 or older, $12,500 if single; $20,000 if married; $25,000 if spouse is also 62 or older)	26-2-301
	2–15 year lease	26-2-303
	Life estate	26-2-302
	Property held as tenancy by the entirety may be exempt against debts owed by only one spouse, but survivorship right is not exempt	*In re Arango*, 136 B.R. 740 aff'd, 992 F.2d 611 (6th Cir. 1993); *In re Arwood*, 289 B.R. 889 (Bankr. E.D. Ten. 2003)
	Spouse or child of deceased owner may claim homestead exemption	26-2-301
insurance	Accident, health, or disability benefits for resident & citizen of Tennessee	26-2-110
	Disability or illness benefits	26-2-111(1)(C)
	Fraternal benefit society benefits	56-25-1403
	Life insurance or annuity	56-7-203
miscellaneous	Alimony, child support owed for 30 days before filing for bankruptcy	26-2-111(1)(E)
	Educational scholarship trust funds & prepayment plans	49-4-108; 49-7-822
pensions	Tax-exempt retirement accounts, including 401(k)s, 403(b)s, profit-sharing and money purchase plans, SEP and SIMPLE IRAs, and defined-benefit plans	11 U.S.C. § 522(b)(3)(C)
	Traditional and Roth IRAs to $1,095,000 per person	11 U.S.C. § 522(b)(3)(C); (n)
	ERISA-qualified benefits, IRAs, & Roth IRAs	26-2-111(1)(D)
	Public employees	8-36-111
	State & local government employees	26-2-105
	Teachers	49-5-909
personal property	Bible, schoolbooks, family pictures, & portraits	26-2-104
	Burial plot to 1 acre	26-2-305; 46-2-102
	Clothing & storage containers	26-2-104
	Health aids	26-2-111(5)
	Lost future earnings payments for you or person you depended on	26-2-111(3)
	Personal injury recoveries to $7,500; wrongful death recoveries to $10,000 ($15,000 total for personal injury, wrongful death, & crime victims' compensation)	26-2-111(2)(B),(C)
	Wages of debtor deserting family, in hands of family	26-2-109
public benefits	Aid to blind	71-4-117
	Aid to disabled	71-4-1112
	Crime victims' compensation to $5,000 (*see personal property*)	26-2-111(2)(A); 29-13-111
	Local public assistance	26-2-111(1)(A)
	Old-age assistance	71-2-216

public benefits (continued)	Relocation assistance payments	13-11-115
	Social Security	26-2-111(1)(A)
	Unemployment compensation	26-2-111(1)(A)
	Veterans' benefits	26-2-111(1)(B)
	Workers' compensation	50-6-223
tools of trade	Implements, books, & tools of trade to $1,900	26-2-111(4)
wages	Minimum 75% of disposable weekly earnings or 30 times the federal minimum hourly wage, whichever is more, plus $2.50 per week per child; bankruptcy judge may authorize more for low-income debtors	26-2-106,107
wildcard	$4,000 of any personal property including deposits on account with any bank or financial institution	26-2-103

Texas

Federal bankruptcy exemptions available. All law references are to Texas Revised Civil Statutes Annotated unless otherwise noted.

ASSET	EXEMPTION	LAW
homestead	Unlimited; property cannot exceed 10 acres in town, village, city or 100 acres (200 for families) elsewhere; sale proceeds exempt for 6 months after sale (renting okay if another home not acquired, Prop. 41.003)	Prop. 41.001; 41.002; Const. Art. 16 §§ 50, 51
	Must file homestead declaration, or court will file it for you & charge you for doing so	Prop. 41.005(f); 41.021 to 41.023
insurance	Church benefit plan benefits	1407a (6)
	Fraternal benefit society benefits	Ins. 885.316
	Life, health, accident, or annuity benefits, monies, policy proceeds, & cash values due or paid to beneficiary or insured	Ins. 1108.051
	Texas employee uniform group insurance	Ins. 1551.011
	Texas public school employees group insurance	Ins. 1575.006
	Texas state college or university employee benefits	Ins. 1601.008
miscellaneous	Alimony & child support	Prop. 42.001(b)(3)
	Higher education savings plan trust account	Educ. 54.709(e)
	Liquor licenses & permits	Alco.Bev.Code 11.03
	Prepaid tuition plans	Educ. 54.639
	Property of business partnership	6132b-5.01
pensions	Tax-exempt retirement accounts, including 401(k)s, 403(b)s, profit-sharing and money purchase plans, SEP and SIMPLE IRAs, and defined-benefit plans	11 U.S.C. § 522(b)(3)(C)
	Traditional and Roth IRAs to $1,095,000 per person	11 U.S.C. § 522(b)(3)(C); (n)
	County & district employees	Gov't. 811.006
	ERISA-qualified government or church benefits, including Keoghs & IRAs	Prop. 42.0021
	Firefighters	6243e(5); 6243a-1(8.03); 6243b(15); 6243e(5); 6243e.1(1.04)
	Judges	Gov't. 831.004

pensions (continued)	Law enforcement officers, firefighters, emergency medical personnel survivors	Gov't. 615.005
	Municipal employees & elected officials, state employees	6243h(22); Gov't. 811.005
	Police officers	6243d-1(17); 6243j(20); 6243a-1(8.03); 6243b(15); 6243d-1(17)
	Retirement benefits to extent tax-deferred	Prop. 42.0021
	Teachers	Gov't. 821.005
personal property *to $60,000 total for family, $30,000 for single adult (see also tools of trade)*	Athletic & sporting equipment, including bicycles	Prop. 42.002(a)(8)
	Burial plots (exempt from total)	Prop. 41.001
	Clothing & food	Prop. 42.002(a)(2),(5)
	Health aids (exempt from total)	Prop. 42.001(b)(2)
	Health savings accounts	Prop. 42.0021
	Home furnishings including family heirlooms	Prop. 42.002(a)(1)
	Jewelry (limited to 25% of total exemption)	Prop. 42.002(a)(6)
	Pets & domestic animals plus their food: 2 horses, mules, or donkeys, & tack; 12 head of cattle; 60 head of other livestock; 120 fowl	Prop. 42.002(a)(10),(11)
	1 two-, three- or four-wheeled motor vehicle per family member or per single adult who holds a driver's license; or, if not licensed, who relies on someone else to operate vehicle	Prop. 42.002(a)(9)
	2 firearms	Prop. 42.002(a)(7)
public benefits	Crime victims' compensation	Crim. Proc. 56.49
	Medical assistance	Hum. Res. 32.036
	Public assistance	Hum. Res. 31.040
	Unemployment compensation	Labor 207.075
	Workers' compensation	Labor 408.201
tools of trade *included in aggregate dollar limits for personal property*	Farming or ranching vehicles & implements	Prop. 42.002(a)(3)
	Tools, equipment (includes boat & motor vehicles used in trade), & books	Prop. 42.002(a)(4)
wages	Earned but unpaid wages	Prop. 42.001(b)(1)
	Unpaid commissions not to exceed 25% of total personal property exemptions	Prop. 42.001(d)
wildcard	None	

Utah

Federal bankruptcy exemptions not available. All law references are to Utah Code unless otherwise noted.

ASSET	EXEMPTION	LAW
homestead	Must file homestead declaration before attempted sale of home	78-23-4
	Real property, mobile home, or water rights to $20,000 if primary residence; $5,000 if not primary residence	78-23-3(1),(2),(4)
	Sale proceeds exempt for 1 year	78-23-3(5)(b)
insurance	Disability, illness, medical, or hospital benefits	78-23-5(1)(a)(iii)
	Fraternal benefit society benefits	31A-9-603

insurance (continued)	Life insurance policy cash surrender value, excluding payments made on the contract within the prior year	78-23-5(a)(xiii)
	Life insurance proceeds if beneficiary is insured's spouse or dependent, as needed for support	78-23-5(a)(xi)
	Medical, surgical, & hospital benefits	78-23-5(1)(a)(iv)
miscellaneous	Alimony needed for support	78-23-5(1)(a)(vi)
	Child support	78-23-5(1)(a)(vi), (f),(k)
	Property of business partnership	48-1-22
pensions	Tax-exempt retirement accounts, including 401(k)s, 403(b)s, profit-sharing and money purchase plans, SEP and SIMPLE IRAs, and defined-benefit plans	11 U.S.C. § 522(b)(3)(C)
	Traditional and Roth IRAs to $1,095,000 per person	11 U.S.C. § 522(b)(3)(C); (n)
	ERISA-qualified benefits, IRAs, Roth IRAs, & Keoghs (benefits that have accrued & contributions that have been made at least 1 year prior to filing)	78-23-5(1)(a)(xiv)
	Other pensions & annuities needed for support	78-23-6(3)
	Public employees	49-11-612
personal property	Animals, books, & musical instruments to $500	78-23-8(1)(c)
	Artwork depicting, or done by, a family member	78-23-5(1)(a)(ix)
	Bed, bedding, carpets	78-23-5(1)(a)(viii)
	Burial plot	78-23-5(1)(a)(i)
	Clothing (cannot claim furs or jewelry)	78-23-5(1)(a)(viii)
	Dining & kitchen tables & chairs to $500	78-23-8(1)(b)
	Food to last 12 months	78-23-5(1)(a)(viii)
	Health aids	78-23-5(1)(a)(ii)
	Heirlooms to $500	78-23-8(1)(d)
	Motor vehicle to $2,500	78-23-8(3)
	Personal injury, wrongful death recoveries for you or person you depended on	78-23-5(1)(a)(x)
	Proceeds for sold, lost, or damaged exempt property	78-23-9
	Refrigerator, freezer, microwave, stove, sewing machine, washer & dryer	78-23-5(1)(a)(viii)
	Sofas, chairs, & related furnishings to $500	78-23-8(1)(a)
public benefits	Crime victims' compensation	63-25a-421(4)
	General assistance	35A-3-112
	Occupational disease disability benefits	34A-3-107
	Unemployment compensation	35A-4-103(4)(b)
	Veterans' benefits	78-23-5(1)(a)(v)
	Workers' compensation	34A-2-422
tools of trade	Implements, books, & tools of trade to $3,500	78-23-8(2)
	Military property of National Guard member	39-1-47
wages	Minimum 75% of disposable weekly earnings or 30 times the federal hourly minimum wage, whichever is more; bankruptcy judge may authorize more for low-income debtors	70C-7-103
wildcard	None	

Vermont

Federal bankruptcy exemptions available. All law references are to Vermont Statutes Annotated unless otherwise noted.

ASSET	EXEMPTION	LAW
homestead	Property held as tenancy by the entirety may be exempt against debts owed by only one spouse	*In re McQueen,* 21 B.R. 736 (D. Ver. 1982)
	Real property or mobile home to $75,000; may also claim rents, issues, profits, & outbuildings	27-101
	Spouse of deceased owner may claim homestead exemption	27-105
insurance	Annuity contract benefits to $350 per month	8-3709
	Disability benefits that supplement life insurance or annuity contract	8-3707
	Disability or illness benefits needed for support	12-2740(19)(C)
	Fraternal benefit society benefits	8-4478
	Group life or health benefits	8-3708
	Health benefits to $200 per month	8-4086
	Life insurance proceeds for person you depended on	12-2740(19)(H)
	Life insurance proceeds if clause prohibits proceeds from being used to pay beneficiary's creditors	8-3705
	Life insurance proceeds if beneficiary is not the insured	8-3706
	Unmatured life insurance contract other than credit	12-2740(18)
miscellaneous	Alimony, child support	12-2740(19)(D)
pensions	Tax-exempt retirement accounts, including 401(k)s, 403(b)s, profit-sharing and money purchase plans, SEP and SIMPLE IRAs, and defined-benefit plans	11 U.S.C. § 522(b)(3)(C)
	Traditional and Roth IRAs to $1,095,000 per person	11 U.S.C. § 522(b)(3)(C); (n)
	Municipal employees	24-5066
	Other pensions	12-2740(19)(J)
	Self-directed accounts (IRAs, Roth IRAs, Keoghs); contributions must be made 1 year before filing	12-2740(16)
	State employees	3-476
	Teachers	16-1946
personal property	Appliances, furnishings, goods, clothing, books, crops, animals, musical instruments to $2,500 total	12-2740(5)
	Bank deposits to $700	12-2740(15)
	Cow, 2 goats, 10 sheep, 10 chickens, & feed to last 1 winter; 3 swarms of bees plus honey; 5 tons coal or 500 gal. heating oil, 10 cords of firewood; 500 gal. bottled gas; growing crops to $5,000; yoke of oxen or steers, plow & ox yoke; 2 horses with harnesses, halters, & chains	12-2740(6),(9)-(14)
	Health aids	12-2740(17)
	Jewelry to $500; wedding ring unlimited	12-2740(3),(4)
	Motor vehicles to $2,500	12-2740(1)
	Personal injury, lost future earnings, wrongful death recoveries for you or person you depended on	12-2740(19)(F),(G),(I)
	Stove, heating unit, refrigerator, freezer, water heater, & sewing machines	12-2740(8)

public benefits	Aid to blind, aged, disabled; general assistance	33-124
	Crime victims' compensation needed for support	12-2740(19)(E)
	Social Security needed for support	12-2740(19)(A)
	Unemployment compensation	21-1367
	Veterans' benefits needed for support	12-2740(19)(B)
	Workers' compensation	21-681
tools of trade	Books & tools of trade to $5,000	12-2740(2)
wages	Entire wages, if you received welfare during 2 months before filing	12-3170
	Minimum 75% of weekly disposable earnings or 30 times the federal minimum hourly wage, whichever is greater; bankruptcy judge may authorize more for low-income debtors	12-3170
wildcard	Unused exemptions for motor vehicle, tools of trade, jewelry, household furniture, appliances, clothing, & crops to $7,000	12-2740(7)
	$400 of any property	12-2740(7)

Virginia

Federal bankruptcy exemptions not available. All law references are to Code of Virginia unless otherwise noted.

ASSET	EXEMPTION	LAW
homestead	$5,000 plus $500 per dependent; rents & profits; sale proceeds exempt to $5,000 (unused portion of homestead may be applied to any personal property)	*Cheeseman v. Nachman,* 656 F.2d 60 (4th Cir. 1981); 34-4; 34-18; 34-20
	May include mobile home	*In re Goad,* 161 B.R. 161 (W.D. Va. 1993)
	Must file homestead declaration before filing for bankruptcy	34-6
	Property held as tenancy by the entirety may be exempt against debts owed by only one spouse	*In re Bunker,* 312 F.3d 145 (4th Cir., 2002)
	Surviving spouse may claim $15,000; if no surviving spouse, minor children may claim exemption	64.1-151.3
insurance	Accident or sickness benefits	38.2-3406
	Burial society benefits	38.2-4021
	Cooperative life insurance benefits	38.2-3811
	Fraternal benefit society benefits	38.2-4118
	Group life or accident insurance for government officials	51.1-510
	Group life insurance policy or proceeds	38.2-3339
	Industrial sick benefits	38.2-3549
	Life insurance proceeds	38.2-3122
miscellaneous	Property of business partnership	50-73.108
pensions *see also wages*	Tax-exempt retirement accounts, including 401(k)s, 403(b)s, profit-sharing and money purchase plans, SEP and SIMPLE IRAs, and defined-benefit plans	11 U.S.C. § 522(b)(3)(C)
	Traditional and Roth IRAs to $1,095,000 per person	11 U.S.C. § 522(b)(3)(C); (n)
	City, town, & county employees	51.1-802
	ERISA-qualified benefits to $25,000	34-34
	Judges	51.1-300
	State employees	51.1-124.4(A)
	State police officers	51.1-200

personal property	Bible	34-26(1)
	Burial plot	34-26(3)
	Clothing to $1,000	34-26(4)
	Family portraits & heirlooms to $5,000 total	34-26(2)
	Health aids	34-26(6)
	Household furnishings to $5,000	34-26(4a)
	Motor vehicle to $2,000	34-26(8)
	Personal injury causes of action & recoveries	34-28.1
	Pets	34-26(5)
	Prepaid tuition contracts	23-38.81(E)
	Wedding & engagement rings	34-26(1a)
public benefits	Aid to blind, aged, disabled; general relief	63.2-506
	Crime victims' compensation unless seeking to discharge debt for treatment of injury incurred during crime	19.2-368.12
	Payments to tobacco farmers	3.1-1111.1
	Unemployment compensation	60.2-600
	Workers' compensation	65.2-531
tools of trade	For farmer, pair of horses, or mules with gear; one wagon or cart, one tractor to $3,000; 2 plows & wedges; one drag, harvest cradle, pitchfork, rake; fertilizer to $1,000	34-27
	Tools, books, & instruments of trade, including motor vehicles, to $10,000, needed in your occupation or education	34-26(7)
	Uniforms, arms, equipment of military member	44-96
wages	Minimum 75% of weekly disposable earnings or 40 times the federal minimum hourly wage, whichever is greater; bankruptcy judge may authorize more for low-income debtors	34-29
wildcard	Unused portion of homestead or personal property exemption	34-13
	$2,000 of any property for disabled veterans	34-4.1

Washington

Federal bankruptcy exemptions available. All law references are to Revised Code of Washington Annotated unless otherwise noted.

ASSET	EXEMPTION	LAW
homestead	Must record homestead declaration before sale of home if property unimproved or home unoccupied	6.15.040
	Real property or mobile home to $40,000; unimproved property intended for residence to $15,000 (husband & wife may not double)	6.13.010; 6.13.030
insurance	Annuity contract proceeds to $2,500 per month	48.18.430
	Disability proceeds, avails, or benefits	48.36A.180
	Fraternal benefit society benefits	48.18.400
	Group life insurance policy or proceeds	48.18.420
	Life insurance proceeds or avails if beneficiary is not the insured	48.18.410
miscellaneous	Child support payments	6.15.010(3)(d)

pensions	Tax-exempt retirement accounts, including 401(k)s, 403(b)s, profit-sharing and money purchase plans, SEP and SIMPLE IRAs, and defined-benefit plans	11 U.S.C. § 522(b)(3)(C)
	Traditional and Roth IRAs to $1,095,000 per person	11 U.S.C. § 522(b)(3)(C); (n)
	City employees	41.28.200; 41.44.240
	ERISA-qualified benefits, IRAs, Roth IRAs, & Keoghs	6.15.020
	Judges	2.10.180; 2.12.090
	Law enforcement officials & firefighters	41.26.053
	Police officers	41.20.180
	Public & state employees	41.40.052
	State patrol officers	43.43.310
	Teachers	41.32.052
	Volunteer firefighters	41.24.240
personal property	Appliances, furniture, household goods, home & yard equipment to $2,700 total for individual ($5,400 for community)	6.15.010(3)(a)
	Books to $1,500	6.15.010(2)
	Burial ground	68.24.220
	Burial plots sold by nonprofit cemetery association	68.20.120
	Clothing, no more than $1,000 in furs, jewelry, ornaments	6.15.010(1)
	Fire insurance proceeds for lost, stolen, or destroyed exempt property	6.15.030
	Food & fuel for comfortable maintenance	6.15.010(3)(a)
	Health aids prescribed	6.15.010(3)(e)
	Keepsakes & family pictures	6.15.010(2)
	Motor vehicle to $2,500 total for individual (two vehicles to $5,000 for community)	6.15.010(3)(c)
	Personal injury recoveries to $16,150	6.15.010(3)(f)
public benefits	Child welfare	74.13.070
	Crime victims' compensation	7.68.070(10)
	General assistance	74.04.280
	Industrial insurance (workers' compensation)	51.32.040
	Old-age assistance	74.08.210
	Unemployment compensation	50.40.020
tools of trade	Farmer's trucks, stock, tools, seed, equipment, & supplies to $5,000 total	6.15.010(4)(a)
	Library, office furniture, office equipment, & supplies of physician, surgeon, attorney, clergy, or other professional to $5,000 total	6.15.010(4)(b)
	Tools & materials used in any other trade to $5,000	6.15.010(4)(c)
wages	Minimum 75% of weekly disposable earnings or 30 times the federal minimum hourly wage, whichever is greater; bankruptcy judge may authorize more for low-income debtors	6.27.150
wildcard	$2,000 of any personal property (no more than $200 in cash, bank deposits, bonds, stocks, & securities)	6.15.010(3)(b)

West Virginia

Federal bankruptcy exemptions not available. All law references are to West Virginia Code unless otherwise noted.

ASSET	EXEMPTION	LAW
homestead	Real or personal property used as residence to $25,000; unused portion of homestead may be applied to any property	38-10-4(a)
insurance	Fraternal benefit society benefits	33-23-21
	Group life insurance policy or proceeds	33-6-28
	Health or disability benefits	38-10-4(j)(3)
	Life insurance payments from policy for person you depended on, needed for support	38-10-4(k)(3)
	Unmatured life insurance contract, except credit insurance policy	38-10-4(g)
	Unmatured life insurance contract's accrued dividend, interest, or loan value to $8,000, if debtor owns contract & insured is either debtor or a person on whom debtor is dependent	38-10-4(h)
miscellaneous	Alimony, child support needed for support	38-10-4(j)(4)
pensions	Tax-exempt retirement accounts, including 401(k)s, 403(b)s, profit-sharing and money purchase plans, SEP and SIMPLE IRAs, and defined-benefit plans	11 U.S.C. § 522(b)(3)(C)
	Traditional and Roth IRAs to $1,095,000 per person	11 U.S.C. § 522(b)(3)(C); (n)
	ERISA-qualified benefits, IRAs needed for support	38-10-4(j)(5)
	Public employees	5-10-46
	Teachers	18-7A-30
personal property	Animals, crops, clothing, appliances, books, household goods, furnishings, musical instruments to $400 per item, $8,000 total	38-10-4(c)
	Burial plot to $25,000, in lieu of homestead	38-10-4(a)
	Health aids	38-10-4(i)
	Jewelry to $1,000	38-10-4(d)
	Lost earnings payments needed for support	38-10-4(k)(5)
	Motor vehicle to $2,400	38-10-4(b)
	Personal injury recoveries to $15,000	38-10-4(k)(4)
	Prepaid higher education tuition trust fund & savings plan payments	38-10-4(k)(6)
	Wrongful death recoveries for person you depended on, needed for support	38-10-4(k)(2)
public benefits	Aid to blind, aged, disabled; general assistance	9-5-1
	Crime victims' compensation	38-10-4(k)(1)
	Social Security	38-10-4(j)(1)
	Unemployment compensation	38-10-4(j)(1)
	Veterans' benefits	38-10-4(j)(2)
	Workers' compensation	23-4-18
tools of trade	Implements, books, & tools of trade to $1,500	38-10-4(f)
wages	Minimum 30 times the federal minimum hourly wage per week; bankruptcy judge may authorize more for low-income debtors	38-5A-3
wildcard	$800 plus unused portion of homestead or burial exemption, of any property	38-10-4(e)

Wisconsin

Federal bankruptcy exemptions available. All law references are to Wisconsin Statutes Annotated unless otherwise noted.

ASSET	EXEMPTION	LAW
homestead	Property you occupy or intend to occupy to $40,000; sale proceeds exempt for 2 years if you intend to purchase another home (husband & wife may not double)	815.20
insurance	Federal disability insurance benefits	815.18(3)(ds)
	Fraternal benefit society benefits	614.96
	Life insurance proceeds for someone debtor depended on, needed for support	815.18(3)(i)(a)
	Life insurance proceeds held in trust by insurer, if clause prohibits proceeds from being used to pay beneficiary's creditors	632.42
	Unmatured life insurance contract (except credit insurance contract) if debtor owns contract & insured is debtor or dependents, or someone debtor is dependent on	815.18(3)(f)
	Unmatured life insurance contract's accrued dividends, interest, or loan value to $4,000 total, if debtor owns contract & insured is debtor or dependents, or someone debtor is dependent on	815.18(3)(f)
miscellaneous	Alimony, child support needed for support	815.18(3)(c)
	Property of business partnership	178.21(3)(c)
pensions	Tax-exempt retirement accounts, including 401(k)s, 403(b)s, profit-sharing and money purchase plans, SEP and SIMPLE IRAs, and defined-benefit plans	11 U.S.C. § 522(b)(3)(C)
	Traditional and Roth IRAs to $1,095,000 per person	11 U.S.C. § 522(b)(3)(C); (n)
	Certain municipal employees	62.63(4)
	Firefighters, police officers who worked in city with population over 100,000	815.18(3)(ef)
	Military pensions	815.18(3)(n)
	Private or public retirement benefits	815.18(3)(j)
	Public employees	40.08(1)
personal property	Burial plot, tombstone, coffin	815.18(3)(a)
	College savings account or tuition trust fund	14.64(7); 14.63(8)
	Deposit accounts to $1,000	815.18(3)(k)
	Fire & casualty proceeds for destroyed exempt property for 2 years from receiving	815.18(3)(e)
	Household goods & furnishings, clothing, keepsakes, jewelry, appliances, books, musical instruments, firearms, sporting goods, animals, & other tangible personal property to $5,000 total	815.18(3)(d)
	Lost future earnings recoveries, needed for support	815.18(3)(i)(d)
	Motor vehicles to $1,200; unused portion of $5,000 personal property exemption may be added	815.18(3)(g)
	Personal injury recoveries to $25,000	815.18(3)(i)(c)
	Tenant's lease or stock interest in housing co-op, to homestead amount	182.004(6)
	Wages used to purchase savings bonds	20.921(1)(e)
	Wrongful death recoveries, needed for support	815.18(3)(i)(b)

public benefits	Crime victims' compensation	949.07
	Social services payments	49.96
	Unemployment compensation	108.13
	Veterans' benefits	45.03(8)(b)
	Workers' compensation	102.27
tools of trade	Equipment, inventory, farm products, books, & tools of trade to $7,500 total	815.18(3)(b)
wages	75% of weekly net income or 30 times the greater of the federal or state minimum hourly wage; bankruptcy judge may authorize more for low-income debtors	815.18(3)(h)
	Wages of county jail prisoners	303.08(3)
	Wages of county work camp prisoners	303.10(7)
	Wages of inmates under work-release plan	303.065(4)(b)
wildcard	None	

Wyoming

Federal bankruptcy exemptions not available. All law references are to Wyoming Statutes Annotated unless otherwise noted.

ASSET	EXEMPTION	LAW
homestead	Property held as tenancy by the entirety may be exempt against debts owed by only one spouse	*In re Anselmi*, 52 B.R. 479 (D. Wy. 1985)
	Real property you occupy to $10,000 or house trailer you occupy to $6,000	1-20-101; 102; 104
	Spouse or child of deceased owner may claim homestead exemption	1-20-103
insurance	Annuity contract proceeds to $350 per month	26-15-132
	Disability benefits if clause prohibits proceeds from being used to pay beneficiary's creditors	26-15-130
	Fraternal benefit society benefits	26-29-218
	Group life or disability policy or proceeds, cash surrender & loan values, premiums waived, & dividends	26-15-131
	Individual life insurance policy proceeds, cash surrender & loan values, premiums waived, & dividends	26-15-129
	Life insurance proceeds held by insurer, if clause prohibits proceeds from being used to pay beneficiary's creditors	26-15-133
miscellaneous	Liquor licenses & malt beverage permits	12-4-604
pensions	Tax-exempt retirement accounts, including 401(k)s, 403(b)s, profit-sharing and money purchase plans, SEP and SIMPLE IRAs, and defined-benefit plans	11 U.S.C. § 522(b)(3)(C)
	Traditional and Roth IRAs to $1,095,000 per person	11 U.S.C. § 522(b)(3)(C); (n)
	Criminal investigators, highway officers	9-3-620
	Firefighters' death benefits	15-5-209
	Game & fish wardens	9-3-620
	Police officers	15-5-313(c)
	Private or public retirement funds & accounts	1-20-110
	Public employees	9-3-426

personal property	Bedding, furniture, household articles, & food to $2,000 per person in the home	1-20-106(a)(iii)
	Bible, schoolbooks, & pictures	1-20-106(a)(i)
	Burial plot	1-20-106(a)(ii)
	Clothing & wedding rings to $1,000	1-20-105
	Medical savings account contributions	1-20-111
	Motor vehicle to $2,400	1-20-106(a)(iv)
	Prepaid funeral contracts	26-32-102
public benefits	Crime victims' compensation	1-40-113
	General assistance	42-2-113(b)
	Unemployment compensation	27-3-319
	Workers' compensation	27-14-702
tools of trade	Library & implements of profession to $2,000 or tools, motor vehicle, implements, team, & stock in trade to $2,000	1-20-106(b)
wages	Earnings of National Guard members	19-9-401
	Minimum 75% of disposable weekly earnings or 30 times the federal hourly minimum wage, whichever is more	1-15-511
	Wages of inmates in adult community corrections program	7-18-114
	Wages of inmates in correctional industries program	25-13-107
	Wages of inmates on work release	7-16-308
wildcard	None	

Federal Bankruptcy Exemptions

Married couples filing jointly may double all exemptions. All references are to 11 U.S.C. § 522. These exemptions were last adjusted in 2007. Every three years ending on April 1, these amounts will be adjusted to reflect changes in the Consumer Price Index. Debtors in the following states may select the federal bankruptcy exemptions:

Arkansas	Massachusetts	New Hampshire	Pennsylvania	Vermont	Wisconsin
Connecticut	Michigan	New Jersey	Rhode Island	Washington	Hawaii
District of Columbia	Minnesota	New Mexico	Texas		

ASSET	EXEMPTION	SUBSECTION
homestead	Real property, including co-op or mobile home, or burial plot to $20,200; unused portion of homestead to $10,125 may be applied to any property	(d)(1); (d)(5)
insurance	Disability, illness, or unemployment benefits	(d)(10)(C)
	Life insurance payments from policy for person you depended on, needed for support	(d)(11)(C)
	Life insurance policy with loan value, in accrued dividends or interest, to $10,775	(d)(8)
	Unmatured life insurance contract, except credit insurance policy	(d)(7)
miscellaneous	Alimony, child support needed for support	(d)(10)(D)
pensions	Tax exempt retirement accounts (including 401(k)s, 403(b)s, profit-sharing and money purchase plans, SEP and SIMPLE IRAs, and defined-benefit plans	(b)(3)(C)
	IRAs and Roth IRAs to $1,095,000 per person	(b)(3)(C)
personal property	Animals, crops, clothing, appliances, books, furnishings, household goods, musical instruments to $525 per item, $10,775 total	(d)(3)
	Health aids	(d)(9)

personal property	Jewelry to $1,350	(d)(4)
	Lost earnings payments	(d)(11)(E)
	Motor vehicle to $3,225	(d)(2)
	Personal injury recoveries to $20,200 (not to include pain & suffering or pecuniary loss)	(d)(11)(D)
	Wrongful death recoveries for person you depended on	(d)(11)(B)
public benefits	Crime victims' compensation	(d)(11)(A)
	Public assistance	(d)(10)(A)
	Social Security	(d)(10)(A)
	Unemployment compensation	(d)(10)(A)
	Veterans' benefits	(d)(10)(A)
tools of trade	Implements, books, & tools of trade to $2,025	(d)(6)
wages	None	
wildcard	$1,075 of any property	(d)(5)
	Up to $10,125 of unused homestead exemption amount, for any property	(d)(5)

Federal Nonbankruptcy Exemptions

These exemptions are available only if you select your state exemptions. You may use them for any exemptions in addition to those allowed by your state, but they cannot be claimed if you file using federal bankruptcy exemptions. All law references are to the United States Code.

ASSET	EXEMPTION	LAW
death & disability benefits	Government employees	5 § 8130
	Longshoremen & harbor workers	33 § 916
	War risk, hazard, death, or injury compensation	42 § 1717
retirement	Civil service employees	5 § 8346
	Foreign Service employees	22 § 4060
	Military Medal of Honor roll pensions	38 § 1562(c)
	Military service employees	10 § 1440
	Railroad workers	45 § 231m
	Social Security	42 § 407
	Veterans' benefits	38 § 5301
survivor's benefits	Judges, U.S. court & judicial center directors, administrative assistants to U.S. Supreme Court Chief Justice	28 § 376
	Lighthouse workers	33 § 775
	Military service	10 § 1450
miscellaneous	Indian lands or homestead sales or lease proceeds	25 § 410
	Klamath Indians tribe benefits for Indians residing in Oregon	25 §§ 543; 545
	Military deposits in savings accounts while on permanent duty outside U.S.	10 § 1035
	Military group life insurance	38 § 1970(g)
	Railroad workers' unemployment insurance	45 § 352(e)
	Seamen's clothing	46 § 11110
	Seamen's wages (while on a voyage) pursuant to a written contract	46 § 11109
	Minimum 75% of disposable weekly earnings or 30 times the federal minimum hourly wage, whichever is more; bankruptcy judge may authorize more for low-income debtors	15 § 1673

Worksheets and Forms

Worksheet 1: Monthly Income

(Combine for you and your spouse, partner, or other joint debtor)

You need to compute your monthly net income. Net income is your gross income less deductions, such as federal, state, and local taxes; FICA; union dues; and money your employer takes out of your paycheck for your retirement plan, health insurance, child support, or loan repayment.

To figure out your monthly net income, do the following calculations (unless you are paid once a month):

- If you're paid weekly, multiply your net income by 52 and divide by 12.
- If you're paid every two weeks, multiply your net income by 26 and divide by 12.
- If you're paid twice a month, multiply your net income by 2.
- If you're paid irregularly, divide your annual net income by 12.

Net Wages or Salary	You		Spouse, Partner, or Joint Debtor		Total Monthly Income
Job 1	$	+	$	=	$
Job 2		+		=	
Other Monthly Income					
Bonuses		+		=	
Commissions		+		=	
Tips		+		=	
Dividends or interest		+		=	
Rent, lease, or license payments		+		=	
Royalties		+		=	
Note or trust payments		+		=	
Alimony or child support		+		=	
Pension or retirement pay		+		=	
Social Security		+		=	
Disability pay		+		=	
Unemployment insurance		+		=	
Public assistance		+		=	
Help from relatives or friends		+		=	
Other		+		=	
Total Income	$	+	$	=	$

Worksheet 2: Your Debts

(Combine for you and your spouse, partner, or other joint debtor)

1	2	3	4	5
Debts and other monthly living expenses	**Outstanding balance**	**Monthly payment**	**Total you are behind**	**Is the debt secured? (If yes, list collateral)**
Home loans—mortgages, home equity loans				
Homeowners' Association Dues				
Motor vehicle loans/leases				
Personal and other secured loans				
Department store charges with security agreements				
Judgment liens recorded against you				
Statutory liens recorded against you				
Total this page	$	$	$	

Debts and other monthly living expenses	Outstanding balance	Monthly payment	Total you are behind	Is the debt secured? (If yes, list collateral)
Tax debts (lien recorded)				
Student loans				
Unsecured personal loans				
Medical bills				
Lawyers' and accountants' bills				
Credit card bills				
Total this page	$	$	$	

Debts and other monthly living expenses	Outstanding balance	Monthly payment	Total you are behind	Is the debt secured? (If yes, list collateral)
Department store (unsecured) and gasoline company bills				
Alimony and child support				
Back rent				
Tax debts (no lien recorded)				
Unpaid utility bills				
Other				
Total this page	$	$	$	
Total page 1				
Total page 2				
Total all pages				
Total Monthly Income (from Worksheet 1)				

Worksheet 3: Property Checklist

1. Real estate

- ☐ Residence
- ☐ Condominium or co-op apartment
- ☐ Mobile home
- ☐ Mobile home park space
- ☐ Rental property
- ☐ Vacation home or cabin
- ☐ Business property
- ☐ Undeveloped land
- ☐ Farm land
- ☐ Boat/marina dock space
- ☐ Burial site
- ☐ Airplane hangar
- ☐ Time share

2. Cash on hand

- ☐ In your home
- ☐ In your wallet
- ☐ Under your mattress

3. Deposits of money

- ☐ Bank deposit
- ☐ Brokerage account (with stockbroker)
- ☐ Certificates of deposit (CDs)
- ☐ Credit union deposit
- ☐ Escrow account
- ☐ Money market account
- ☐ Money in a safe deposit box
- ☐ Savings and loan deposit

4. Security deposits

- ☐ Electric
- ☐ Gas
- ☐ Heating oil
- ☐ Prepaid rent
- ☐ Security deposit on a rental unit
- ☐ Rented furniture or equipment
- ☐ Telephone
- ☐ Vehicle lease
- ☐ Water

5. Household goods, supplies, and furnishings

- ☐ Antiques
- ☐ Appliances
- ☐ Barbecue
- ☐ Carpentry tools
- ☐ Cell phones, PDAs
- ☐ China and crystal
- ☐ Clocks
- ☐ Dishes
- ☐ Electronic entertainment devices and equipment
- ☐ Food (total value)
- ☐ Furniture
- ☐ Gardening tools
- ☐ Home computer (for personal use)
- ☐ Home printer, fax, or copier
- ☐ Lamps
- ☐ Lawn mower or tractor
- ☐ Microwave oven
- ☐ Patio or outdoor furniture
- ☐ Radios
- ☐ Rugs
- ☐ Sewing machine
- ☐ Silverware and utensils
- ☐ Small appliances
- ☐ Snow blower
- ☐ Sound system
- ☐ Telephones and answering machines
- ☐ Televisions
- ☐ Tools
- ☐ Vacuum cleaner
- ☐ Video equipment (VCR, DVD player, camcorder, digital camera)

Worksheet 3: Property Checklist (continued)

6. **Books, pictures, art objects; stamps, coin, and other collections**

   ☐ Art prints

   ☐ Bibles

   ☐ Books

   ☐ Coins

   ☐ Collectibles (such as political buttons, baseball cards)

   ☐ Compact discs, records, and tapes

   ☐ Family portraits

   ☐ Figurines

   ☐ Original artworks

   ☐ Photographs

   ☐ Sculpture

   ☐ Stamps

   ☐ Videotapes, DVDs

7. **Apparel**

   ☐ Clothing

   ☐ Furs

   ☐ Sports clothes

8. **Jewelry**

   ☐ Bracelets, necklaces, and earrings

   ☐ Engagement and wedding ring

   ☐ Gems

☐ Precious metals

☐ Watches

9. **Firearms, sports equipment, and other hobby equipment**

   ☐ Bicycles

   ☐ Board games

   ☐ Camera equipment

   ☐ Electronic musical equipment

   ☐ Exercise machine

   ☐ Fishing gear

   ☐ Guns (rifles, pistols, shotguns, muskets)

   ☐ Hang gliding/parasailing equipment

   ☐ Model or remote cars or planes

   ☐ Musical instruments

   ☐ Scuba diving equipment

   ☐ Ski or snowboard equipment

   ☐ Surfboard

   ☐ Other sports equipment

   ☐ Other weapons (swords and knives)

10. **Interests in insurance policies**

    ☐ Credit insurance

    ☐ Disability insurance

☐ Health insurance

☐ Homeowners' or renters' insurance

☐ Term life insurance

☐ Whole or universal life insurance

11. **Annuities**

12. **Pension or profit-sharing plans**

    ☐ IRA

    ☐ Keogh

    ☐ Pension or retirement plan

    ☐ 401(k) account

    ☐ 457 account

13. **Stocks and interests in incorporated and unincorporated companies**

14. **Interests in partnerships**

    ☐ General partnership interest

    ☐ Limited partnership interest

15. **Government and corporate bonds and other investment instruments**

    ☐ Corporate bonds

    ☐ Deeds of trust

    ☐ Mortgages you own

Worksheet 3: Property Checklist (continued)

☐ Municipal bonds

☐ Promissory notes

☐ U.S. savings bonds

16. Accounts receivable

☐ Accounts receivable from business

☐ Commissions already earned

17. Family support

☐ Alimony (spousal support, maintenance) due under court order

☐ Child support payments due under court order

☐ Payments due under divorce property settlement

18. Other debts owed you where the amount owed is known and definite

☐ Disability benefits due

☐ Disability insurance due

☐ Judgments obtained against third parties but not yet collected

☐ Sick pay earned

☐ Social Security benefits due

☐ Tax refund due for returns already filed

☐ Vacation pay earned

☐ Wages due

☐ Workers' compensation due

19. Powers exercisable for your benefit other than those listed under real estate

☐ Right to receive, at some future time, cash, stock, or other personal property placed in an irrevocable trust

☐ Current payments of interest or principal from a trust

☐ General power of appointment over personal property

20. Interests you have because of another person's death

☐ Expected proceeds from a life insurance policy, if the insured has died

☐ Inheritance from an existing estate in probate (the owner has died and the court is overseeing the distribution of the property), even if the final amount is not yet known

☐ Inheritance under a will that is contingent upon one or more events occurring, but only if the will writer has died

☐ Property you are entitled to receive as a beneficiary of a living trust, if the trustor has died

21. All other contingent claims and claims where the amount owed you is not known, including tax refunds, counterclaims, and rights to setoff claims (claims you think you have against a person, government, or corporation but haven't yet sued on)

☐ Claims against a corporation, government entity, or individual

☐ Potential tax refund but return not yet filed

22. Patents, copyrights, and other intellectual property

☐ Copyrights

☐ Patents

☐ Trade secrets

☐ Trademarks

☐ Tradenames

23. Licenses, franchises, and other general intangibles

☐ Building permits

☐ Cooperative association holdings

☐ Exclusive licenses

Worksheet 3: Property Checklist (continued)

☐ Liquor licenses

☐ Nonexclusive licenses

☐ Patent licenses

☐ Professional licenses

24. Automobiles and other vehicles (not leased)

☐ Car

☐ Minibike or motorscooter

☐ Mobile or motor home if on wheels

☐ Motorcycle

☐ Off-road or all terrain vehicle

☐ Recreational vehicle (RV)

☐ Trailer

☐ Truck

☐ Van

25. Boats, motors, and accessories

☐ Boat (canoe, kayak, pontoon, rowboat, sailboat, shell, yacht, etc.)

☐ Boat radar, radio, or telephone

☐ Jet ski

☐ Navigation/GPS equipment

☐ Outboard motor

26. Aircraft and accessories

☐ Aircraft

☐ Aircraft radar, radio, GPS, and other accessories

27. Office equipment, furnishings, and supplies

☐ Artwork in your office

☐ Cell phones, PDAs

☐ Computers, software, modems, printers (for business use)

☐ Copier

☐ Fax machine

☐ Furniture

☐ Rugs

☐ Scanner

☐ Supplies

☐ Telephones

☐ Typewriters

28. Machinery, fixtures, equipment, and supplies used in business

☐ Military uniforms and accoutrements

☐ Tools of your trade

29. Business inventory

30. Livestock, poultry, and other animals

☐ Birds

☐ Cats

☐ Dogs

☐ Fish and aquarium equipment

☐ Horses

☐ Livestock and poultry

☐ Other pets

31. Crops—growing or harvested

32. Farming equipment and implements

33. Farm supplies, chemicals, and feed

34. Other personal property of any kind not already listed

☐ Church pew

☐ Country club or golf club membership

☐ Health aids (for example, wheelchair, crutches)

☐ Portable spa or hot tub

☐ Season tickets

Worksheet 4: Property Exemptions

1 Your property	2 Value of property	3 Your ownership share (%, $)	4 Amount of liens	5 Amount of your equity	6 Exempt? If not, enter nonexempt amount
1. Real estate					
2. Cash on hand (state source of money)					
3. Deposits of money (indicate sources of money)					
4. Security deposits					
5. Household goods, supplies, and furnishings					

Worksheet 4: Property Exemptions (continued)

1	2	3	4	5	6
Your property	Value of property	Your ownership share (%, $)	Amount of liens	Amount of your equity	Exempt? If not, enter nonexempt amount
6. Books, pictures, art objects; stamp, coin, and other collections					
7. Apparel					
8. Jewelry					
9. Firearms, sports equipment, and other hobby equipment					
10. Interests in insurance policies					
11. Annuities					

Worksheet 4: Property Exemptions (continued)					
1	2	3	4	5	6
Your property	Value of property	Your ownership share (%, $)	Amount of liens	Amount of your equity	Exempt? If not, enter nonexempt amount
12. Pension or profit-sharing plans					
13. Stocks and interests in incorporated and unincorporated companies					
14. Interests in partnerships					
15. Government and corporate bonds and other investment instruments					
16. Accounts receivable					

Worksheet 4: Property Exemptions (continued)					
1	2	3	4	5	6
Your property	Value of property	Your ownership share (%, $)	Amount of liens	Amount of your equity	Exempt? If not, enter nonexempt amount
17. Family support					
18. Other debts owed you where the amount owed is known and definite					
19. Powers exercisable for your benefit, other than those listed under real estate					
20. Interests you have because of another person's death					
21. All other contingent claims and claims where the amount owed you is not known					
22. Patents, copyrights, and other intellectual property					
23. Licenses, franchises, and other general intangibles					
24. Automobiles and other vehicles					

Worksheet 4: Property Exemptions (continued)					
1	2	3	4	5	6
Your property	Value of property	Your ownership share (%, $)	Amount of liens	Amount of your equity	Exempt? If not, enter nonexempt amount
25. Boats, motors, and accessories					
26. Aircraft and accessories					
27. Office equipment, furnishings, and supplies					
28. Machinery, fixtures, equipment, and supplies used in business					
29. Business inventory					

Worksheet 4: Property Exemptions (continued)

1 Your property	2 Value of property	3 Your ownership share (%, $)	4 Amount of liens	5 Amount of your equity	6 Exempt? If not, enter nonexempt amount
30. Livestock, poultry, and other animals					
31. Crops—growing or harvested					
32. Farming equipment and implements					
33. Farm supplies, chemicals, and feed					
34. Other personal property					
	Subtotal (column 6):				
	Wildcard Exemption			–	
	Total Value of NONEXEMPT Property				

Worksheet 5:
Daily Expenses for the Week of _____

Sunday's Expenses	Cost	Monday's Expenses	Cost
Daily Total		**Daily Total**	

Tuesday's Expenses	Cost	Wednesday's Expenses	Cost
Daily Total		**Daily Total**	

Worksheet 5 (continued)
Daily Expenses for the Week of

Thursday's Expenses	Cost	Friday's Expenses	Cost
Daily Total		**Daily Total**	

Saturday's Expenses	Cost	Other Expenses	Cost
Daily Total		**Daily Total**	

Worksheet 6: Monthly Budget

Expense Category	Projected				
Home					
Rent/Mortgage					
Property Tax					
Insurance					
Homeowners' Assn. Dues					
Telephone					
Gas & Electric					
Water & Sewer					
Cable					
Garbage & Recycling					
Household Supplies					
Housewares					
Furniture & Appliances					
Cleaning					
Yard/Pool Care					
Repairs & Maintenance					
Food					
Groceries					
Breakfast Out					
Lunch Out					
Dinner Out					
Coffee & Tea					
Snacks					
Clothing					
Clothes, Shoes, & Accessories					
Laundry, Dry Cleaning					
Mending					
Self Care					
Toiletries/Cosmetics					
Haircuts					
Massage					
Gym Membership					
Total Expenses Page 1					

Worksheet 6: Monthly Budget (continued)					
Expense Category	**Projected**				
Donations					
Health Care					
Insurance					
Medications					
Vitamins					
Doctor					
Dentist					
Eye Care					
Therapy					
Transportation					
Car Payments (buy or lease)					
Insurance					
Registration					
Gas					
Maintenance & Repairs					
Parking					
Tolls					
Public Transit					
Parking Tickets					
Road Service (such as AAA)					
Entertainment					
Music					
Movies & Rentals					
Concerts, Theater, Ballet, etc.					
Museums					
Sporting Events					
Hobbies & Lessons					
Club Dues or Membership					
Film & Developing Costs					
Books, Magazines, & Newspapers					
Software & Games					
Total Expenses Page 2					

Worksheet 6: Monthly Budget (continued)					
Expense Category	**Projected**				
Dependent Care					
Child Care					
Clothing					
Allowance					
School Expenses					
Toys & Entertainment					
Pets					
Food & Supplies					
Veterinarian					
Grooming					
Education					
Tuition					
Loan Payments					
Books & Supplies					
Travel					
Gifts & Cards					
Personal Business					
Supplies					
Copying					
Postage					
Bank & Credit Card Fees					
Legal Fees					
Accountant					
Taxes					
Insurance					
Savings & Investments					
Other					
Total Expenses Page 3					
Total Expenses Page 1					
Total Expenses Page 2					
Total Expenses					

Form 1: Letter to Collector or Creditor to Make Payment If Negative Information Removed/Account Re-aged

Use this letter to create a written record of an agreement you reach with a creditor or collector to resolve a debt. Even if you believe you've reached a perfectly clear agreement by phone, it's very important to put the terms of the agreement in writing. This way, you'll have proof of the agreement. You can also use the written agreement to make sure that the creditor or collector removes negative information about the debt from your credit report.

To use this letter, complete the top lines with the creditor's name and address, then fill in the remaining information requested (the date, your account number, and so on).

Fill in the amounts you have agreed to pay, whether all at once or in installments. Check the first box if you propose to make a lump sum payment and you don't dispute the amount of the debt. Check the second box if you propose to make a lump sum payment and you do dispute the amount of the debt. Check the third box if you propose to make installment payments. Sign and print your name at the bottom, and give your address and phone. The letter instructs the creditor or collector to sign and return the letter to indicate its acceptance of the terms you propose, so be sure to include a stamped, self-addressed envelope when you mail it.

_____

_____

_____

Attn: _____

Date: _____

Name(s) on account: _____

Account number: _____

Dear _____ :

As we have discussed, I am prepared to resolve your claim with respect to the above account.

I can pay a lump sum amount of $ _____ [or, I can pay installments in the amount of $ _____ per month for _____ months] if you will agree to do the following:

☐ If I make a lump sum payment of $ _____ by _____ , 20 _____ , you will release all claims against me arising from this account and will submit a Universal Data Form to Experian, Equifax, and TransUnion deleting the account/trade line.

☐ I dispute the amount of the debt. If I make a lump sum payment of $ _____ by _____ , 20 _____ , you will acknowledge that the balance owed on the account is $[the amount of the lump sum payment], you will release all claims against me arising from this account, and you will submit a Universal Data Form to Experian, Equifax, and TransUnion deleting the account/trade line.

☐ If I agree to pay off the debt in installments, you agree to re-age my account—that is, make the current month the first repayment month and show no late payments as long as I make the agreed-upon monthly payments.

If my offer is acceptable to you, please initial the accepted proposal, sign the acceptance below, and return this letter to me in the enclosed envelope.

Sincerely,

_____

Name: _____

Address: _____

_____

Home phone: _____

Agreed to and accepted this _____ day of _____ , 2 _____

By: _____

Name (print): _____

Signature: _____

Title: _____

Index

■

Get the Latest in the Law

Nolo's Legal Updater
We'll send you an email whenever a new edition of your book is published!
Sign up at **www.nolo.com/legalupdater**.

Updates at Nolo.com
Check **www.nolo.com/update** to find recent changes in the law that
affect the current edition of your book.

Nolo Customer Service
To make sure that this edition of the book is the most recent one, call us at
800-728-3555 and ask one of our friendly customer service representatives
(7:00 am to 6:00 pm PST, weekdays only). Or find out at **www.nolo.com**.

Complete the Registration & Comment Card ...
... and we'll do the work for you! Just indicate your preferences below:

Registration & Comment Card

NAME _____ DATE _____

ADDRESS _____

CITY _____ STATE _____ ZIP _____

PHONE _____ EMAIL _____

COMMENTS _____

WAS THIS BOOK EASY TO USE?   (VERY EASY)   5   4   3   2   1   (VERY DIFFICULT)

☐ Yes, you can quote me in future Nolo promotional materials. *Please include phone number above.*

☐ Yes, send me **Nolo's Legal Updater** via email when a new edition of this book is available.

Yes, I want to sign up for the following email newsletters:

   ☐ **NoloBriefs** (monthly)
   ☐ **Nolo's Special Offer** (monthly)
   ☐ **Nolo's BizBriefs** (monthly)
   ☐ **Every Landlord's Quarterly** (four times a year)

☐ Yes, you can give my contact info to carefully selected
partners whose products may be of interest to me.

NOLO

MT 11.0

Nolo
950 Parker Street
Berkeley, CA 94710-9867
www.nolo.com